THE FAMILY HANDYMAN®
HELPFUL HINTS

READER'S DIGEST

THE FAMILY HANDYMAN®
HELPFUL HINTS

QUICK AND EASY SOLUTIONS

TIMESAVING TIPS

TRICKS OF THE TRADE

THE READER'S DIGEST ASSOCIATION (CANADA) LTD.

THE FAMILY HANDYMAN® HELPFUL HINTS

STAFF

Project Editors
Joseph Gonzalez
Robert V. Huber
Alice Philomena Rutherford

Project Art Editor
Carol Nehring
Andrée Payette

Editor
Don Earnest

Research Editor
Wadad Bashour

Senior Associate Editors
Carolyn Chubet
Theresa Lane

Copy Editor
Joseph Marchetti

Editorial Assistant
Elizabeth Eastman
Joanne Wosahla

Co-ordinator
Susan Wong

Production Manager
Holger Lorenzen

CONTRIBUTORS

Designers
Virginia Wells Blaker
Joan Gramatte
Marta Strait

Art Production Coordinator
Jessica Mitchell

Copy Editor
Katherine G. Ness

Associate Editor
Tracy O'Shea

Indexer
Sidney Wolfe Cohen

Writers
Thomas Christopher
Mark Feirer
Wade A. Hoyt
Laura Tringali

Researcher
Willard Lubka

Artists
Sylvia Bokor
Ron Chamberlain
Mario Ferro
Don Mannes
Robert Steimle

Consultants
Charles Avoles
Roy Barnhart
Steven Beatty
Bob Buteyn
Phil Englander
Dora Galitzki
Allan R. Hildenbrand
Thor Johanneson
Jim McCann
Tim McCreight
Americo Napolitano
Robert A. Nelson
Kathleen Poer
Evan Powell
Meryl Prichard-O'Rourke
Dee Quigley
Mark Russo
Stanley H. Smith, Ph.D.
Jay Stein
Paul Weissler
Tom Zera

THE FAMILY HANDYMAN REVIEW TEAM

Chief Liaison
Mark Thompson, *Managing Editor*

Reviewers
Gary Havens, *Editor*
Art Rooze, *Senior Editor*
Ken Collier, *Associate Editor*
Donna Wyttenbach, *Copy Editor*

Canadian Cataloging in Publication Data

Main entry under title:

The Family handyman® helpful hints : quick and easy solutions, timesaving tips, tricks of the trade.

At head of title: Reader's Digest.
Includes index.
ISBN 0-88850-320-2

1. Do-it-yourself work. 2. Dwellings—Maintenance and repair—Amateurs' manuals.
I. Reader's Digest Association (Canada).

TX323.F35 1995   643'.7   C94-900835-4

Warning
All do-it-yourself activities involve a degree of risk. Skills, materials, tools, and site conditions vary widely. Although the editors have made every effort to ensure accuracy, the reader remains responsible for the selection and use of tools, materials, and methods. Always obey local codes and laws, follow manufacturers' operating instructions, and observe safety precautions.

ABOUT THIS BOOK

This is a do-it-yourself guide with a difference. Unlike most how-to manuals, it doesn't set out to show you how to carry out complex projects. Rather, it has something different to offer. Within its pages are thousands of nuggets of information that make up a treasure trove of hints, tips, and tricks of the trade. These priceless tidbits will make your do-it-yourself jobs easier and faster and will save you time, money, effort, and grief. And what's more, they'll help you not just once but over and over again.

The inspiration for this book was the Handy Hints® column that appears each month in *The Family Handyman,* North America's leading how-to magazine and a member of the Reader's Digest family of publications. For more than a dozen years, *The Family Handyman* has promoted a spirited competition among its do-it-yourself readers, inviting them to submit their solutions to whatever vexing problems they have encountered in carrying out projects around the house and in the workshop, yard, and garage. More than half of the 2,000 lively hints and tips on the following pages are based on suggestions that readers sent in and that were published by the magazine. As readers' letters poured in each month—often accompanied by diagrams or photographs—*The Family Handyman* editors sorted through them, weighing each suggestion. They were on the lookout for ideas that are truly ingenious and practical, ideas that save time and work, ideas that are likely to cause you to exclaim, "Why didn't I think of that!" And in rounding out those hints with tips from other sources, we, the editors of this book, have applied the same standards in assembling a genuinely helpful combination of quick and easy solutions, tricks of the trade, and timesaving tips.

THE FAMILY HANDYMAN® HELPFUL HINTS contains 11 chapters. The first three cover the fundamentals: Basic Tools and Equipment, Workshop Organization, and Shop Skills. The next five chapters concentrate on tips that help you upgrade your home and make it a better place to live in: Household Storage, Home Improvements, Paint and Wallcoverings, Home Systems (electricity, plumbing, heating and cooling), and Household Repairs. Then there's a chapter on Yard and Garden and one on Car and Garage. The final chapter, More Hints, is a miscellany of tips and tricks on a variety of subjects, a bonanza of solid suggestions that are just too good to leave out.

In addition to the hints and tips, you'll find dozens of special boxes that will help you work more safely, keep your home healthy, and select the best tools for a job. Longer features show you step by step the best way to perform basic do-it-yourself tasks, such as changing a window screen or repairing a fence. The Recycling Directory at the back of the book is especially helpful in these days of environmental awareness. It lists alphabetically the items that we often toss out or tuck away, and it leads you to the hints that show you how to reuse these items instead of just consigning them to a landfill.

We hope you will enjoy reading and using this book as much as we enjoyed gathering this collection of remarkable hints and tips for you.

—The Editors

CONTENTS

CHAPTER 1

BASIC TOOLS AND EQUIPMENT

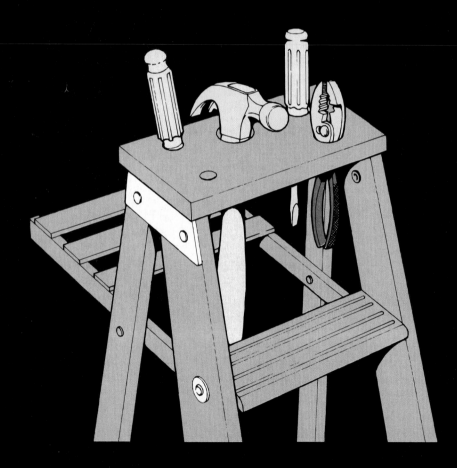

DRILLS AND DRILL BITS

Drilling basics

Hold it right ▲

To drill a straighter hole and avoid breaking a bit, hold the drill so that the force you exert helps push the bit straight into the wall. Place the palm of your hand in line with the chuck, extending your index finger along the drill body. Pull the trigger with your second finger.

Keep it level

Newer power drills often have one or two built-in levels to help you drill straight perpendicular holes. To upgrade an older drill, cut the hooks off a mason's line level and attach it to the top of the drill with duct tape. ▼

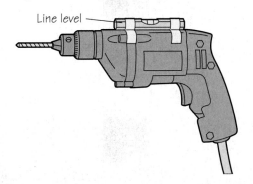

Line level

Hole starters

To keep the bit from skating around when you are starting a hole in wood and most materials (except masonry and tile), draw cross marks where you want to drill. Then use a center punch to dimple the cross marks. Use a star drill for masonry. For ceramic tile, scratch an X with a carbide masonry bit. ▼

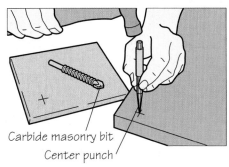

Carbide masonry bit

Center punch

How deep?

When drilling to a precise depth, mark the depth on the bit with a piece of masking tape. Cut the piece a little long and stick the overlapping ends together to make a flag. When the right depth is reached, the flag will brush away the debris.

The right-size bit

Suppose you need to drill a clearance hole for a bolt or screw, but you don't have a drill gauge at hand. Use the fastener itself and the drill's chuck to gauge the right bit diameter. Chuck the fastener lightly into the drill; then remove it without changing the chuck setting. Try shanks of various bits until one fits snugly.

Replacing a drill chuck

If you find that the chuck jaws of your trusty old electric drill don't hold bits tightly enough, replace the old chuck with a new one. You can buy one that requires a key or one that needs no key. In either case, you'll have to remove the old chuck first. Apply some penetrating oil inside the chuck, place the drill on your workbench, and insert the key so that it is parallel with the bench top. Next, follow the steps shown below. To mount a keyless chuck, follow the directions on the package. Finally, lightly lubricate the new chuck's jaws and work it back and forth until it operates smoothly. ▼

Use a ball-peen hammer to strike the key with a solid blow so that the key will turn in a counterclockwise direction.

Next, unscrew the old chuck, using pliers (locking or slip-joint) if necessary. Screw the new chuck on.

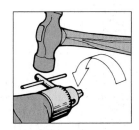

To lock a new keyed chuck in place, insert the chuck key and tap the key lightly in a clockwise direction.

DRILLS AND DRILL BITS

More basics

Straight bits

A bent bit is likely to break and damage your work. Because bits bend easily (especially the thinner ones), test them for straightness before use and discard any bent ones. To test a bit, roll it slowly with your fingertips on a flat surface. If the bit wobbles, it's bent. Or place the bit against a straightedge and look for gaps between the two surfaces. ▼

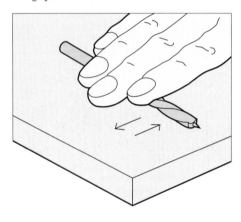

Pointed bits

Brad point

When drilling wood, use a brad-point bit instead of a common twist bit. The little spur on the tip of a brad-point bit cuts cleanly into the wood and keeps the bit from skating around when you start the hole or from drifting if the bit hits a knot.

Spade bit

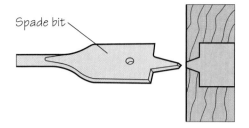

Splinter-free drilling ▲

Drilling a hole completely through stock leaves a rough, splintery edge where it exits. To make a clean hole, look (don't feel) for the point of the bit as it pierces the back side of the work. Pull out the bit, and using the little hole as a centering guide, drill from the back. This method works with spade, auger, Forstner, and brad-point bits.

Metal tips

Use a high-speed steel (HSS) bit for drilling metal. To protect the bit and keep the drill and the bit from overheating, lubricate the surface with plenty of light machine oil. If you need to drill a large-diameter hole ($\frac{1}{2}$ inch or larger) in thick metal, work up to the desired diameter in stages: first $\frac{1}{4}$ inch, then $\frac{3}{8}$ inch, and so on.

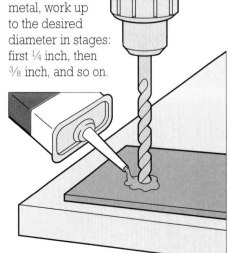

The hard stuff

For drilling tile, concrete, and masonry, use a masonry bit with a carbide tip. When drilling into concrete, start with a small hole, then enlarge it. If you have to drill many holes in concrete, rent or buy a hammer drill and drill bits specially designed for it. By actually pounding the spinning bit into the surface, a hammer drill makes your work much easier.

Wall hang-ups

Drilling into a plastered wall often damages the wall's surface and leaves a mess on the floor. To avoid both problems, tape an open paper bag or coffee filter under the location of the new hole, with the tape covering the spot you intend to drill into. When you've finished drilling, peel off the tape and empty and reuse the dust catcher.

Another dust catcher

Here's how to keep the dust from falling all over the floor or into your eyes when you drill into a ceiling. Simply drill through the center of a plastic coffee can lid, leave the lid on the drill bit, and drill the hole. Any size lid will do; clear plastic ones allow you to see the bit as you drill.

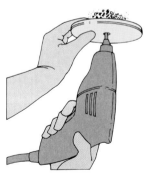

Neat and clean

Here's the pitch

Used on resinous wood, a bit becomes coated with wood pitch. If allowed to build up, the pitch dulls the bit. To clean a bit, lay it on newspaper and spray it with oven cleaner. (Or to contain the fumes, you can put the bit inside a plastic bag and then spray.) Let the bit soak for about 20 minutes, and then wipe it clean with a rag.

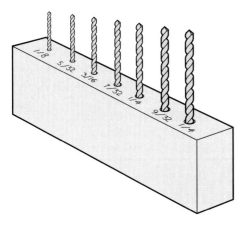

Bit holder ▲

To keep drill bits from bumping against other tools or against each other, and thereby losing their cutting edge, don't store them loose. You can either a buy bit holder for a few dollars at a hardware store or improvise your own with a compartment or niche for each bit. To make the holder shown here, drill different-size holes in a block of wood and label each hole with the size of the bit it will hold. If you always keep the bits in their proper places in the holder, they will stay sharp and be easy to find.

Put a cork on it

Protect the business end of expensive bits such as brad-point, spade, and Forstner bits by screwing a piece of cork onto the end of each bit. The cork, which should have a diameter slightly larger than the bit, will protect the bit's lead-in point and the cutting spurs.

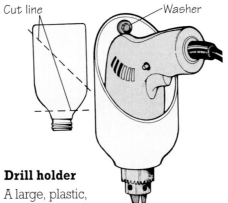

Cut line — Washer

Drill holder

A large, plastic, pop bottle makes a handy holder for your drill. Cut off the bottom and the top of the bottle as shown, and attach it to the wall with drywall screws and washers. You can also make a power tool holder out of an 8-inch length of 4-inch-diameter PVC pipe. Cut a notch into the top rim to accommodate the tool's handle.

Another hang-up

To hang your drill on a perf-board hook, insert a screw eye into the chuck and tighten it.

BUYING A DRILL

A good basic electric drill has a ⅜-inch chuck and a variable-speed reversing (VSR) capability. Such a drill accepts bits with shanks up to ⅜ inch and lets you control how fast you drill. Buy the best, most powerful model you can afford. Be sure that the drill fits comfortably in your hand. A built-in level is a handy feature.

Cordless drills are very convenient, but they are usually slower and less powerful than the plug-in type and of course require recharging (from 15 minutes to several hours). As a result, you may opt to use a plug-in drill and a cordless one as a team.

Cordless drills come in three categories: screwdrivers, light drills, and full-size drill/drivers. The first type lives up to its name, and not much more. The second kind is more powerful and is easy to handle overhead. However, a charge powers only about 10 minutes of drilling time and the built-in recharger is slow. Full-size drill/drivers have more features than the light drills, usually have a detachable battery, and are powerful enough to handle most drilling jobs yet are good at driving screws. If you buy a second battery pack, you can use one while the other is recharging, and drill as long as you wish.

SCREWS AND SCREWDRIVERS

Treat it right

By using a screwdriver for a job it was not designed for, you risk damaging the tool and injuring yourself. Try not to use a screwdriver as a pry bar, chisel, hole punch, scraper, or paint stirrer. If you must use a screwdriver for one of these tasks, choose an old one that's already damaged.

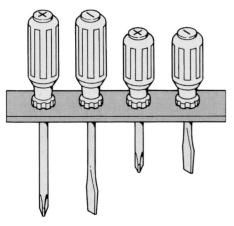

This end up ▲

To protect your screwdrivers and make it easy to find the size you're looking for, store them with their handles up. If your screwdrivers are not color-coded, you can make identification even easier by marking the tops of the handles with a minus sign for slot screwdrivers or with a plus sign for Phillips screwdrivers. Either write the sign with indelible ink on a piece of tape and attach it to the top of the handle, or burn the sign into the handle with a soldering gun.

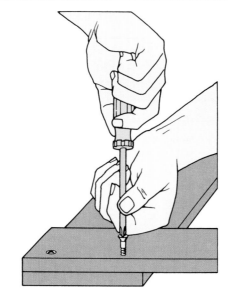

Avoiding slips ▲

▷ When driving a screw, always hold the screwdriver blade in the screw slot. If you hold the work as you drive the screw, the blade can easily slip out of the slot and injure your hand.
▷ In selecting a screwdriver, be sure that the tip fits the slot perfectly. If the tip is too big or too small, the blade will slip out of the slot.
▷ A screwdriver with a damaged (rounded) tip or edges can slip and injure you or damage the work. Similarly, a screwdriver that has a split or broken handle can cause injury.
▷ Keep screwdriver handles clean. A greasy handle can easily slip out of your hand.
▷ Never use a screwdriver near live wires or for electrical testing.
▷ Don't use pliers to increase the torque (turning power) of a screwdriver. Use a wrench for this purpose, and only with square-shank screwdrivers.

Smoother driving

Holding power

Before driving a screw, dip the tip of the screwdriver blade into a small mound of scouring powder or dig it into a cone of carpenter's chalk. The coating of chalk or cleanser will help the tool stay in the screw slot.

Magnetic tip

To start screws in tight places, use a magnetized screwdriver. You can either buy a factory-magnetized screwdriver or magnetize one yourself by dragging its blade over a magnet several times in one direction. To prevent the charge from draining out of a magnetized screwdriver, keep it away from other metal objects. A home-magnetized screwdriver should hold its charge for about a week. To demagnetize the tool, just drag the blade over the magnet in the opposite direction.

Lube job

You'll have an easier time driving a screw if you first pull its threads across a bar of soap, beeswax, paste wax, or lip balm. Dipping a screw in linseed oil before driving not only eases the job, it also protects the screw from rust.

Getting a grip

Another way to start screws in difficult places is to push the screw through the sticky side of a piece of adhesive tape, insert the screwdriver into the slot, and wrap the tape around the blade of the screwdriver. Or try dabbing a little rubber cement on the screwhead.

Sticky side

Hammer time

Despite the rule that says you should never hit a screw with a hammer, a few light taps when a screw is almost in place causes the wood fibers to compress and slant downward against the screw threads. As the screw is given its final tightening, it will get a better bite.

Brass screws

Brass screws make attractive but fragile fasteners. Because the metal is soft, a screwdriver can damage the slot or break the screw. To avoid this problem, drill a pilot hole, pick a steel screw the same size as the brass one, and drive it in the hole. Then remove the steel screw, lubricate the threads of the brass one with soap, and drive it into place.

Set in shellac

To keep a screw from being loosened by vibrations, dab shellac underneath the screwhead. If it's necessary to remove the screw later on, you can break the shellac film by pressing firmly on the screwdriver as you turn it. (When working with shellac, follow the maker's safety instructions.)

SCREWDRIVERS

Having the right screwdriver in hand makes most jobs a lot easier. A basic screwdriver set includes four standard slot-tip and four cross-tip (Phillips) drivers in various shaft lengths and blade sizes. Larger sets may also include a few star-shaped Torx screwdrivers, handy when repairing household appliances, cars, and yard and garden equipment. Square-drive (Robertson) screwdrivers can be bought individually for recessed screws in furniture, boats, and recreational vehicles. If you plan to work with many different screw types and sizes, consider buying a set of tips that fit just one handle.

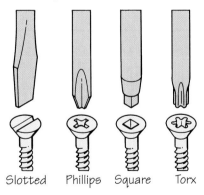

Slotted   Phillips   Square   Torx

Buyer's guide. Buy only the best screwdrivers, never the cheap kind. The best tools have handles made of butyrate or other strong plastic and strong steel blades that are rough-finished or ridged to resist slippage. Cheap screwdrivers are likely to be made of steel that is softer than many fasteners. Choose screwdrivers that feel comfortable in your hand. You may find that a triangular handle or one that has deep ridges is easiest to grip and turn. As you shop, keep in mind that the larger the handle, the more torque (turning power) you can bring to bear on the screw.

Power drivers. The proliferation of power screwdrivers coincides with the widespread use of hardened drywall screws instead of wood screws. (The drywall screw has a deeply cut Phillips head that is ideal for power driving.) The most basic type of power driver is the pocket-size cordless screwdriver, which although slow, is convenient for driving any type of small screw. A drill/driver is essentially a drill, typically cordless, that has a variable-speed trigger to adjust the drill's torque or a low-speed setting for screwdriving.

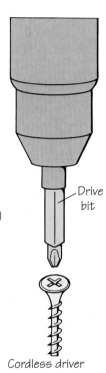

Drive bit

Cordless driver and drywall screw

SCREWS AND SCREWDRIVERS

Reusing and adapting

Renew-a-screw

Removing and reseating a slotted or Phillips-head screw often results in a damaged slot, especially if the blade of your screwdriver didn't fit the slot in the first place. If you don't have a replacement screw on hand, try restoring the old screw by running a hacksaw along the slot (or slots in the case of a Phillips-head screw) to deepen it. If you're repairing a screw out of its hole, don't hold the screw in your fingers. Put it in a vise between two wood scraps. This way you'll avoid injury and protect the threads. ▼

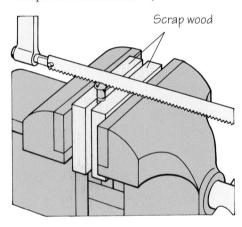

Scrap wood

Converting Phillips-head screws

Suppose you need to seat or remove a Phillips-head screw and you have only a slotted screwdriver on hand. Use a hacksaw to extend one of the slots in the screwhead so that it goes all the way across the screw. Again, if the screw is out of its hole, make sure to hold it in a vise, not in your fingers.

Unclog it

To remove a screw whose slot is clogged with paint, first use a scratch awl to dig out the paint from the slot.

Keeping track

When disassembling a piece that needs to be repaired or moved, thread the screws into the edge of a strip of corrugated cardboard. Then tape the strip to one of the larger parts. To make reassembly easier, write notes about the screws' positions on the strip of cardboard.

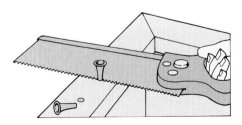

Golf tee trick

To restore a worn or stripped screw hole, plug it with several glue-covered toothpicks, a piece of dowel, or a wooden golf tee. Fill the hole with glue and insert the plug. When the glue has set, cut off the excess plug. You'll then be ready to drill the pilot hole and drive the screw. ▼

Stuck screws

Break it up

Winning the war against stuck screws usually depends on breaking up the layer of corrosion (grime and rust) that develops around the head. Before you try to force the offending screw, spray it with a lubricant, such as WD 40 or SuperLube. If you don't have a lubricant on hand, try using a little vinegar, lemon juice, or cola drink (the carbonate fizz does the work). Allow some time for the lubricant to do its job; then help break the bond by tapping a hammer on the area surrounding the screw.

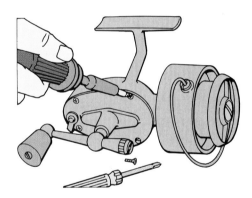

Hot metal ▲

If you still can't get that screw out of a metal object, lubricate the screw as described above and then heat it with a soldering iron or a propane torch. (An iron works well on the thin metal of home appliances; you'll need a propane torch if the screws are large and the metal thicker.) The heat makes the lubricant thinner, so it can seep into the threads. While the screw is still hot, tap the area around the screw with a hammer.

HAMMERS AND NAILS

Basic tips

Swing time

Everyone bends a nail now and then. To reduce your chances of doing so, try to drive a nail home with the fewest possible hammer blows—no more than three or four. Hold the hammer at its end, not in the middle, and swing your arm like a clock pendulum, keeping your wrist stiff during the swing. Always wear eye protection.

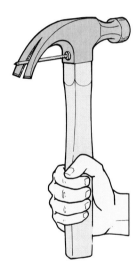

One-handed start ▲

Starting a nail with one hand allows you to hold on to the work or to the side of a ladder with your free hand; it also makes it much easier to drive a nail in a hard-to-reach place. One way to do this is to wedge the nail tightly in the claw of your hammer, with the nailhead against the base of the hammerhead. Swing the hammer, claw side first, to start the nail; then lift the hammer off the nail and drive it in the usual way.

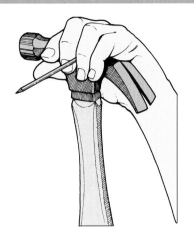

Another nail starter ▲

Grasp the hammerhead in your fist as shown, and hold the nail firmly between your fingers and against the side, or *cheek,* of the hammer. To start the nail, rap the nail point against the work.

No more smashed fingers

Holding a small nail or a brad when you start it often results in pain. To keep your fingertips out of harm's way, stick the nail through one end of a folded sheet of stiff paper. Using the paper as a holder, drive in the nail. Before finally seating the nail, tear the paper away. The teeth of a comb, tweezers, or needle-nose pliers can also serve as nail holders. ▼

Protective cover

Here's a way to shield a work surface from an accidental hammer blow when you're driving finishing nails. Simply drive the nail through a hole in a scrap of perf board with ¼-inch holes. As you near the surface, lift off the perf board and use a nail set to sink the nail. ▼

Cushion the blow

Need to tap a joint together without marring the wood? Convert your hammer into a mallet by slipping a rubber furniture leg tip over the hammer's striking face. Or cut an X in an old tennis ball and slip the ball over the hammer's face.

Directory assistance

When hammering indoors, use a pair of thick city telephone books as a work surface. The books will not only protect the surface but also deaden the sound. (And if you're working on a messy project, you can tear out the pages of the book and use them to catch spills.)

HAMMERS AND NAILS

Easy driving

Pilot holes

Driving a nail into hardwood is easier if you drill a pilot hole first, just as you would for a screw. If you don't have the right drill bit, nip off the head of a nail that is the same size as the nail you are going to drive, and chuck it tightly in the drill. ▼

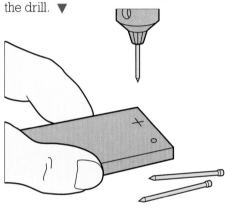

Fast driver

Another strategy for easing nails into hardwood is to lubricate the nails. Beeswax, lubricating (household) oil, even lip balm, all work well. If your hammer has a wood handle, you can drill a hole in the handle end and fill it with beeswax or lip balm. ▼

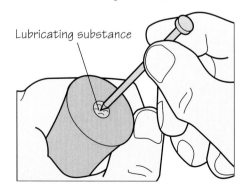

Lubricating substance

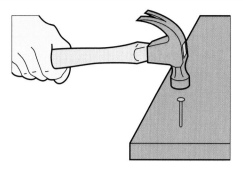

No more split wood ▲

To keep wood from splitting when you drive a nail into it, blunt the point of the nail slightly: Turn the nail so that the point faces up, and tap it with a hammer. Then try to drive the nail into the soft lighter areas of the wood, not the darker grain lines.

Nail attractor

Glue a small magnet to the end of your hammer handle. When you want to pick up a few nails, just stick the handle into your nail container or apron pocket.

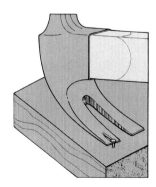

Mini-claw ▲

To pull nails too small for the claw of your hammer to grip, create a miniature nail puller by filing a V-shaped notch into one claw tip. A triangular-shaped needle file will do the job nicely.

Versatile nail-pulling wedge

To get just the right leverage under the hammerhead when you're pulling a nail, make a nail-puller block like the one shown below from a scrap piece of 4 x 4. Cutting the piece at about a 35° angle will give you a great deal of flexibility. ▼

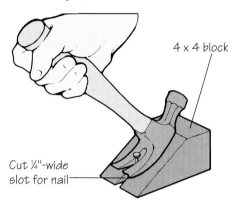

4 x 4 block

Cut ¼"-wide slot for nail

Care and handling

Put on a smooth face

A good-quality hammer will perform well for years. But with use—and abuse—its face will become nicked and gouged. When that happens, you can restore the hammer's face by lightly filing it smooth. Make sure the outer edge of the face remains beveled so that it is less likely to leave hammer marks on the work.

Sharp claws

The claw, that handy nail puller and sometime pry bar, may need restoration too. When the claw becomes damaged, restore the ends and the inside edges of the V with a flat metal file. Deepen the point of the V with a triangular file.

Clean face

When you are fastening a project with cement-coated nails, you may find that you are bending more than your share of nails. That's a signal that the hammerhead has become coated with cement. To clean the head, rub it with a scrap of sandpaper or a bit of steel wool.

Handle remedies

If your wood hammer handle is loose, put it in a jar of linseed oil for an hour. The wood fibers swell in the oil, making for a snugger fit. If a handle cracks or breaks, replace it or discard the hammer. To attach a new handle, first shape it to fit. Then coat the handle tip with 5-minute epoxy, insert it in the hammerhead, drive in the end wedges, and let the epoxy cure for 24 hours.

Hammer hold

Make your nail apron do double duty as a convenient holder for your hammer. Just drill two holes in a 1½-inch PVC pipe coupling and thread one of the apron strings through the holes. ▼

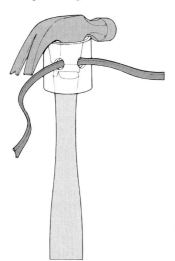

HAMMERS

Most types of hammers come in a variety of head weights and handle lengths. Handles made of ash, hickory, tubular steel (with a rubber grip), or fiberglass absorb shock well, are comfortable to hold, and provide a good grip. The head should be cleanly forged (not cast) of quality steel. The face of a hammer intended for general use should be smooth and have slightly beveled edges. A textured face clings to nails and is best for long nailing sessions. However, a textured face will mar the work surface. A smooth face, found on peen hammers, mallets, and sledges, is designed to strike either a work surface or other tools, such as a cold chisel or a punch.

Curved-claw hammer

Ball-peen hammer   Cross-peen hammer

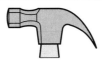

Bricklayer's hammer

Carpenter's mallet

Rubber mallet

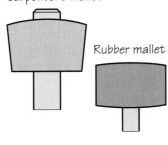

Claw hammers. The basic household hammer is a 16-ounce curved-claw hammer. For rough construction work, choose a 22-ounce straight claw, called a *ripping* hammer; for finish carpentry, use a light 12-ounce hammer.

Peen hammers. Instead of a claw, these hammers have a second striking surface, called a peen. The rounded ball peen is used to bend and shape soft metal. The hammer used by cabinetmakers has a long, thin cross peen to start a brad and a flat face to drive a nail. A bricklayer's hammer has a flat end to settle masonry into place and a long chisel-like face to score bricks before they're cut.

Mallets and sledges. To strike woodworking chisels and assemble wood parts, use a carpenter's mallet. Assemble other projects and pound out dents in metal with a rubber mallet. Sledgehammers (not shown) have solid steel heads weighing from 2 to 28 pounds. Long-handled heavy sledges are used for demolition work, such as breaking up concrete. The lighter, short-handled type is used to drive stakes and spikes into place.

STAPLERS

Staple gun operation

Quick screen fix

A staple gun makes short work of small household repairs. For example, to repair a screen that has pulled out of its wood frame, staple the screen to the frame, folding a hem as you go. Doubling over the screen makes the fastening stronger and reduces the chance that the wires will unravel and work loose again. ▼

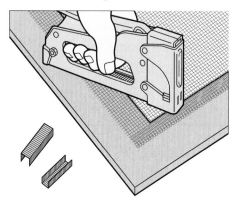

A better angle

When stapling fabric or screen mesh to a surface, place the staples at an angle to the weave or mesh. This way the staple has more material to grip, making the attachment more secure. ▼

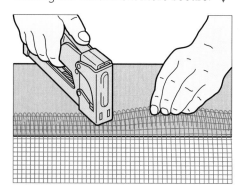

Temporary stapling ▲

Some fastening jobs, such as stapling plastic sheets over a window, are meant to be temporary. Here's a way to make staple removal hassle-free. Slip a heavy-duty rubber band around the staple gun as shown. The rubber band acts as a spacer, leaving the staples sticking up slightly so that they are easy to remove with a staple remover. This method also keeps the staples from cutting through very thin materials.

Specialized staplers

For stereo and phone wire

A quick, neat way to run phone and stereo wire is to staple it in place with a special (but not very expensive) wiring tacker. This tool shoots staples that bridge the wire without damaging it. Wire tackers shoot various-size staples, so measure the wire you are running to determine which tacker to buy. You can also buy a general-purpose stapler that has a wire tacker attachment.

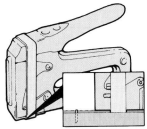

Hammer tacker

This handy tool is great for attaching a vapor barrier, insulation, and roofing and builder's felt. A hammer tacker is useful for any job that does not require great accuracy of placement. The tacker also makes it easier to work overhead and is kinder to arm muscles and hands than a regular stapler. To set a staple, just strike the tacker. If you do a lot of stapling, a power stapler is a worthwhile investment. ▼

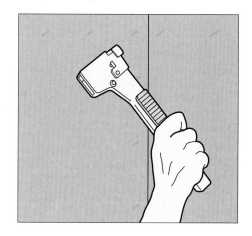

COMMON STAPLES

SIZE	USE
¼-in. leg	Light upholstering, such as valances and shades
5⁄16-in. leg	Heavy upholstering, draperies, thin insulation
⅜-in. leg	Light insulation, weather-stripping, roofing papers, wire mesh, electrical wire
½-in. leg	Carpet underlayment, canvas, felt stripping
9⁄16-in. leg	Insulation board, roofing felt

WRENCHES AND PLIERS

Wrenching techniques

Pliers or wrench?

Always turn a nut with a wrench. Using pliers for this purpose will round the edges of the nut and make it even harder to remove later on. If necessary hold the bolt with pliers, but turn the nut with a wrench.

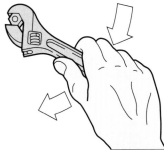

Turn it right ▲

When using an adjustable wrench, pull on the handle so that the stronger fixed side of the jaw is applying pressure rather than the weaker adjustable side. Before you turn the wrench, be sure that the jaws are holding the nut tightly.

Padded jaws

If you're using a pair of pliers on an easily scratched surface, such as chrome, brass, or plastic, be sure to pad the jaws. Either wrap them with adhesive tape, or snip the fingers off an old leather glove and slip these "sleeves" over the jaws.

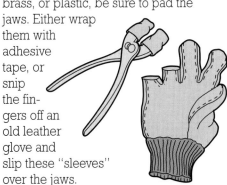

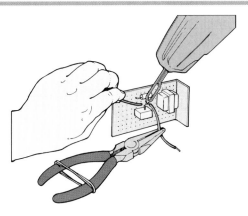

A third hand ▲

Long-nose locking pliers act as a third hand that can grip small objects while you assemble, solder, or clamp them. You can convert ordinary pliers into a mini-vise by slipping a rubber band over the handle. The rubber band will keep the pliers' jaws clamped closed while you work.

Working with bolts

Small nut

Positioning a small nut in a tight place often involves a certain amount of fumbling. To facilitate matters, wrap a strip of double-faced carpet tape around the end of your finger. Use the tape to pick up the nut and hold it in place on the end of the bolt. Then turn the bolt to secure the nut.

Hard to reach, easy to fit ▲

Threading a washer and nut onto a bolt in a blind spot can be awkward. The job will be much easier if you glue the washer and nut together. Apply a drop of glue from a hot-glue gun where the washer and nut meet (be sure to keep the glue off the threads). When the glue has set, thread the nut.

Another nut trick

Say you need to remove a nut with an open-end wrench that's too large for it. Simply insert a nickel, dime, penny, or washer between the wrench and the nut. The coin or washer (you'll have to experiment to determine which one best fills the gap) will serve as a wedge, making it possible to turn the nut. ▼

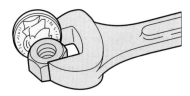

Homemade lock washer

If you don't have a lock washer to secure a nut, wrap a rubber band or a layer of plastic film around the threaded end of the bolt and tighten the nut. As the nut tightens, the material will run into the threads, locking the nut in place.

CUTTING AND SHAPING TOOLS

Files and rasps

Get into shaping

Single-cut

Double-cut

Rasp

A *single-cut* file has parallel rows of ridged teeth that smooth and sharpen metal. A *double-cut* file has a second, crossing, set of parallel ridges; it removes metal and wood stock rapidly. A *rasp* has individual teeth rather than ridges and gives a rough cut on wood and soft metals; the bigger the teeth, the coarser the finish. You can use a *bastard* file for a coarse finish, a *second-cut* file for a medium to coarse finish, and a *smooth* file for a fine finish. Generally the bigger the job, the longer the file. A large file removes a lot of stock quickly; a small file removes less stock but gives you more control. Most jobs require only an all-purpose flat file. But if you are enlarging a round or contoured shape, use a round or half-round file. If you're working on rectangular holes or corners, use a square file, and for acute internal angles, a taper (triangular) file. ▼

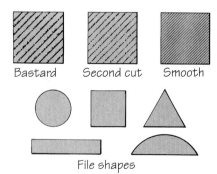

Bastard   Second cut   Smooth

File shapes

Get a handle on it

For safety and better control, make sure a file has a handle on its tang before you use it. Some handles screw onto the tang. Others are held by friction. In the latter case, insert the tang into the handle, hold it vertically, and rap the handle on a firm surface to seat the file. Don't strike the file or the handle with a hammer.

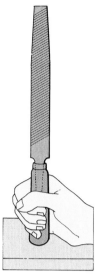

One-way stroke

Files cut only on the push stroke, never on the return. To avoid dulling the teeth, lift the tool off the work surface at the end of the push stroke.

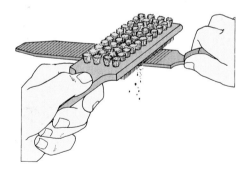

Card sharp ▲

If your file glides over the work without cutting the surface, clean the file teeth with a special wire brush called a file card. To use the card, run the wire bristles over the file, parallel to the grooves of the file teeth.

Chisels and planes

Easy glider

To make a plane glide across a surface, rub the soleplate with paste wax or a bit of candle. Buff well to spread a thin, even coating. Warming the sole with a hair dryer first will make the job easier.

Tray organizer

Nothing dulls chisel blades faster than bumping into other tools. Either store them individually in a kitchen utensil tray, or if you wish to put more than one chisel in a compartment, add a layer of cotton or bubble packing between tools.

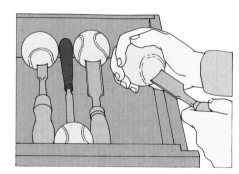

Guard duty ▲

Another way to keep chisels away from other tools is to protect the ends with inexpensive plastic chisel covers. You can also make your own chisel protectors out of slit tennis balls or hollowed-out pieces of cork.

Plane rest

To protect the cutting edge of a plane when it is not in use, set it down on its side or rest it on a block of polystyrene, such as Styrofoam. To store the plane, secure a block of polystyrene to the tool with a couple of sturdy rubber bands.

HANDSAWS

Sharp ideas

The right way to hold a saw

Instead of gripping the handle with all four fingers around it, extend your index finger and place it against the handle as though you were pointing along the saw blade. You'll have better control and cut a straighter, truer line. ▼

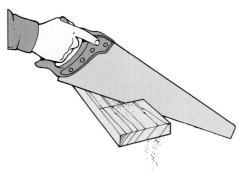

Don't gum it up

Sawing resinous softwoods such as pine clogs saw teeth with a gummy buildup that soon makes the saw seem dull. To remove the resin, apply oven cleaner (see p.27). To keep the sticky stuff from adhering in the first place, spray silicone on the teeth. Or try polishing them often with hard paste wax or running a bar of soap across them. *Note:* Saws treated this way should be used only for construction work, not for finished pieces.

Keeping your (hacksaw) teeth clean

If you cut soft metals with a hacksaw, the saw's teeth will soon clog. You can avoid this problem by using a blade with bigger teeth, slowing down your strokes (so the metal doesn't melt), and pushing down more gently on the saw.

THE RIGHT SAW

For most "around-the-house" jobs you can probably get away with owning just two handsaws: a hacksaw for metal and a general-purpose, or combination, saw that will make cross-grain and ripping (with the grain) cuts in wood. For home improvement jobs that require cutting holes in wallboard, choose a wallboard (drywall) saw. If you plan to make joints in wood, you'll want a backsaw and, for complicated joints, a smaller dovetail saw. These saws make finer cuts because they have more teeth per inch (tpi) than a combination saw, ripsaw, or crosscut saw. (The more teeth, the smoother—and slower—the saw cuts.) In addition, the teeth of a backsaw and dovetail saw are set to make a narrow kerf and so are useful in making tightly fitting joints in cabinetry.

Japanese saws. Unlike Western saws, which cut on the push stroke, Japanese saws cut on the pull stroke. General-purpose standard saws are made of heavy steel to keep them from bowing as they cut. But because the pulling action doesn't bow the blade, Japanese blades can be extremely thin. These saws cut a very fine kerf that allows work to be very precise. The most common one, the ryoba saw, has teeth on both sides of the blade: one for ripping (7 tpi) and one for crosscutting (14 to 20 tpi).

How dull

How can you tell if a saw is dull *before* you use it? Check the teeth closely to see if the points are rounded and the cutting edges show wear. (Use a magnifying glass to inspect fine-tooth saws.) If the saw appears dull, take it to a pro for resharpening. ▼

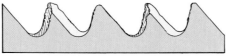

Dull saw blade

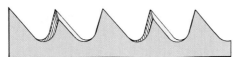

Sharp saw blade

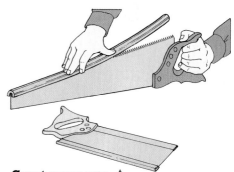

Great cover-ups ▲

When you store handsaws, be sure to cover the cutting teeth. In lieu of a store-bought saw case, cover the teeth with a section of old garden hose that has been slit along its length. You can also use a section of rigid foam or a couple of slip-on spines from a plastic report cover.

KEEPING TOOLS SHARP

DIY sharpening

On edge

Dull tools are dangerous and inefficient. Save time and money by learning how to sharpen the blades of simple hand tools like chisels, planes, knives, and shears (see facing page; for tips on sharpening large garden tools, see p.281). However, let a professional sharpen tools that have complex or contoured cutting edges, such as router and drill bits, handsaws, and circular saw blades. Similarly, leave tools with hardened (carbide-tip and diamond-coated) surfaces to the pros.

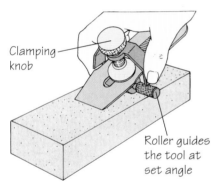

Clamping knob

Roller guides the tool at set angle

Honing guide ▲

This handy device holds the tool you are sharpening at the correct angle. Insert the tool into the guide, squaring the blade to the stone; then adjust the angle setting (the method varies from guide to guide) and tighten the clamp.

Homemade strop

Need a honing strop to give a fine finish to the edges of newly sharpened tools? You can recycle an old leather belt. Just cut off a 6-inch length of leather and glue it to a board. If necessary, add a little oil.

Substitute bench grinder ▲

You can use a belt sander, fitted with a worn 100-grit aluminum oxide belt, to rough-grind a tool. Have a helper hold the sander on its side on a mat of foam carpet padding, angling it if necessary so the belt will turn freely. Put on safety goggles. Hold the tool against the belt, pointing it in the direction of the belt's movement. Otherwise, the tool will catch dangerously on the belt.

Abrasive block

You can make a honing tool by gluing a piece of silicon carbide paper to a wood block. Clamp the block in a vise, and draw the blade along it a few times to give the final touch to a sharpened tool or to touch up a cutting edge. ▼

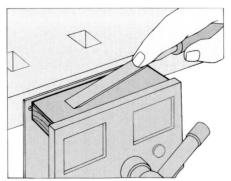

HOW TO SHARPEN

To restore the original bevel, or angle, of a tool, a flat stone or a honing rod (for long blades) will suffice. To remove a nick and to do rough grinding, you'll need a bench grinder. To detect nicks—and to check your progress in restoring the edge—examine both sides of the tool under a magnifying glass.

Chisel and plane angles range between 15° and 30°. Some tools have a narrow secondary bevel at the tip that is 5 degrees greater than the primary one. This secondary bevel slows the dulling of the blade. (Its width varies from $1/16$ inch to a micro bevel.)

Using a bench grinder. Before mounting a wheel, test it for cracks: Insert an old screwdriver into the wheel's center hole. Hold the wheel in the air and tap it in several places with the handle of another screwdriver. If it rings, the wheel is intact; if it thuds or rattles, discard it.

The grinding technique shown at right is for rough sharpening or removing nicks. In either case, be sure that the tool doesn't overheat and lose its temper.

Caution: Wear safety goggles and use the wheel guard and eye shield. Never grind on the side of a wheel unless it is designed to be used that way. Keep the tool rest $1/16$ inch from the wheel. For more on power tool safety, see p.24.

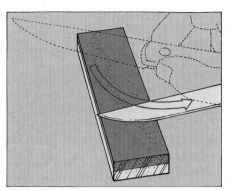

Sharpen a dull knife on a coarse stone first; then finish on a fine stone. Move the blade to the right as you pivot and pull it. Repeat on the other side of the blade, pushing it away as you pivot. Stroke alternate faces the same number of times. Keep the angle and pressure consistent.

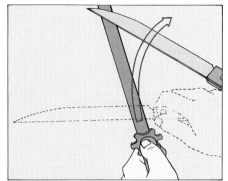

Use a honing rod for long-bladed knives. Holding the rod motionless, begin with the heel of the blade near the rod handle. Move the length of the blade along the rod in an arcing motion. Stroke each side equally. Keep the blade angle and the pressure constant.

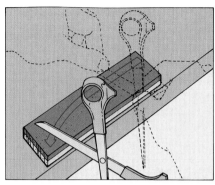

Scissor blades have a secondary bevel that can be sharpened. Place the bevel on the stone, and pull the blade toward you and slightly to the right. Use a pulling motion only.

When sharpening a chisel or a plane iron, use the stone's coarse side first. Rub the primary bevel back and forth a few times. Move the tool across the stone so the stone will wear evenly. To create a secondary bevel, raise the tool slightly and rub again on the fine side. To remove the raised burr, turn the tool over and gently rub the flat side.

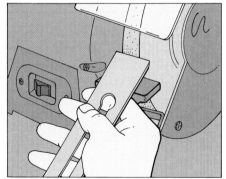

To sharpen a chisel or a plane iron on a bench grinder, set the tool rest so it supports the tool at the correct angle. Hold the tool, bevel side down and square to the wheel, with your forefinger against the tool rest. Keep the metal cool by repeatedly dipping it in water. Use a medium-grit wheel; then finish on a stone.

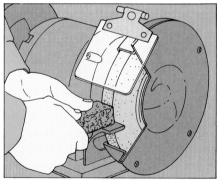

When the wheel of a bench grinder becomes clogged with foreign material or gouged from use, it needs to be cleaned, or dressed. One way to do this is to run a silicon carbide stick over the face of the wheel; the stick will clean and flatten the face, exposing new grit.

POWER TOOL SAFETY

Plugging in

Join the pros

Some of the major power tool manufacturers sell two lines of tools: one that is for professional use and another for the do-it-yourselfer. Professional tools are usually more powerful, heavier, and more costly. But they are also safer for an experienced do-it-yourselfer—and are usually worth the money, especially if they will be used a lot.

Amps of power

When you are comparison shopping for a power tool, don't rely on the boldly promoted horsepower rating as an indicator of the tool's power. Such ratings are less than accurate. Instead, compare how many amperes each tool's motor draws—the more amperes, the more powerful the tool. If the amperage isn't listed on the tool's packaging, check the nameplate on the tool itself. For more on power tools and ampere measures, see p.43.

Go ahead and blow it

Sawdust is the enemy of all power tool motors. It accumulates inside the motor, around the motor housing, and in the motor vents. Vacuum the stuff from the housing and from the vents every month or so. Or blow it out with compressed air, using either an air compressor or canned air, available at photography supply stores. (Be sure to wear eye protection.) If you fail to keep the vents open and the housing free of sawdust, your tools will likely overheat.

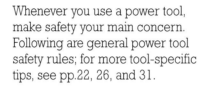

AVOIDING ACCIDENTS

Whenever you use a power tool, make safety your main concern. Following are general power tool safety rules; for more tool-specific tips, see pp.22, 26, and 31.

Read, understand, and follow the directions in the owner's manual. Use a tool only for the jobs for which it was designed. Don't force a tool or otherwise cause its motor to overheat.

Analyze the job environment. Never operate a tool in a damp, wet, or fume-filled atmosphere. Keep your workspace well lit, well ventilated, and free of clutter.

Dress safely. Don't wear jewelry or loose clothing. Keep long hair tied back. Wear the appropriate safety gear (p.65).

Evaluate your mood. If you are out of sorts, ill, or taking a medication that could affect your alertness or judgment, postpone the job.

Think before you act. Know the consequences of every move you make. This will slow you down at first, but after a while knowing what's safe—and what's not—will become second nature to you.

Concentrate on the job. Don't talk to anyone while you work, and keep children and pets away. Focus on what you are doing at the moment, not on the next step.

Take your time. Hurrying and taking shortcuts are major causes of workshop accidents.

Maintain your balance. Wear nonslip footwear, and make sure your footing is secure. Grip a portable tool firmly. Don't reach too far with a tool or work with it held over your head; stand on a sturdy stepladder instead.

Listen to the sound of the motor. If a tool makes an unfamiliar noise or vibration, turn it off and unplug it.

A plug for safety ▶

You should unplug a power tool whenever you're adjusting or cleaning it or not using it. To keep a young child from plugging in a power tool, insert an ordinary key ring through the hole in a plug prong. (Older children will be able to figure out how to unthread the key ring.)

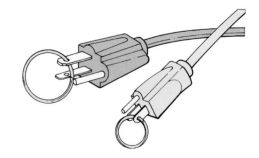

POWER SANDERS

Sanding alternatives

Make a stand

Sanding small pieces with a portable sander is awkward, if not impossible. The stand shown here is designed to hold a sander upside down so that you can press a workpiece against it. To create the cutout for the sander, make a wire template that fits around the sander body, outline it on the board, and cut the hole with a saber saw. Go over the edges with a rasp until the sander fits snugly. Make the frame deep enough so that the sander doesn't touch the workbench. To reduce vibration, attach strips of foam insulation on the bottom of the frame and the edges of the opening. ▼

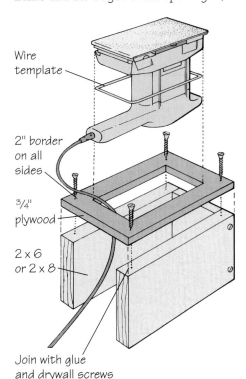

Wire template

2" border on all sides

3/4" plywood

2 x 6 or 2 x 8

Join with glue and drywall screws

Random orbiter

Next time you're in the market for a power sander, take a look at a random-orbit sander. Like its cousin the orbital sander, the random orbiter moves the abrasive in tight little circles—but the circles in this case are random, moving first one way, then another, then another. As a result, the sander removes stock faster and doesn't leave those telltale little circles on your finished piece.

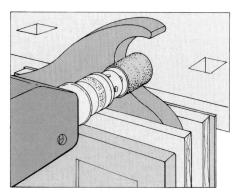

Sanding drill ▲

Tired of hand-sanding curved edges and other tight or hard-to-reach spots? Try a sanding drum attachment on your drill. Some models take special self-stick abrasive paper, others a custom cylindrical sanding sleeve. As you sand, hold the drill so that the drum smooths the surface uniformly.

Abrasive advice

Put it on tape

To strengthen sandpaper and sanding belts and keep them from tearing, apply duct or masking tape to the back. Write the grit on the tape; on a sanding belt, mark the direction of rotation as well.

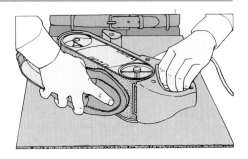

Prolonged life ▲

Sanding belts are expensive and quickly clog up. To remove buildup, place the sander on its side, angling it slightly if necessary so the belt turns freely. Hold the bottom of an old crepe-soled shoe or a belt-cleaning stick against the moving belt near the rear wheel. You can use a wire suede brush instead, but only on aluminum oxide belts (the brush would tear garnet or other natural crystalline belts). To use the brush, run it from side to side over the moving belt. Place the sander on a piece of foam carpet padding to help hold the tool.

Put it away

To store sheet abrasives, stick them on a clipboard and hang it on a hook. To help a sanding belt keep its shape and prevent unwanted creases, hang it on a perf-board hook covered with an old paint roller or a length of PVC pipe.

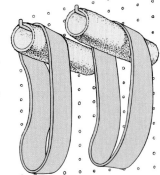

ROUTERS AND ROUTER BITS

Setting up

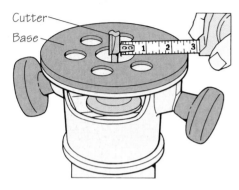

Cutter
Base

Measure for straightedge guide ▲

A straightedge clamped in place on the work serves as a guide for cutting dadoes or grooves and for trimming or squaring imperfect edges. The trick to setting the guide accurately is to measure from the edge of the cutter to the outside edge of the router base. Measure the same distance on your workpiece; clamp the straightedge tightly in place.

Get a grip

When you insert a bit into the collet, push it in all the way. Then before you tighten the collet, withdraw the bit slightly, about ⅛ inch. This enables the collet to get a good grip on the bit and makes it easier to remove the bit.

Plan a path

Before turning on the router, make sure its path is clear, with no small fasteners or nails lying around. To avoid tripping when working on a large piece, check that the area where you will walk is unobstructed.

Router tables

Table talk

A router becomes more versatile and easier to use when installed on a router table. Look for a bench-top model that will accept nearly all routers, has a smooth-working adjustable fence, and has a see-through blade guard.

Router table switch

Even though a router table is very useful, reaching the switch under the table can be awkward. If you are handy with things electrical, you can solve the problem by installing a foot-control switch from a sewing machine on your router. That way both hands are free to handle the workpiece.

Homemade mount

Instead of buying a router table, you can make one from a piece of ¾-inch plywood and clamp it to your workbench.

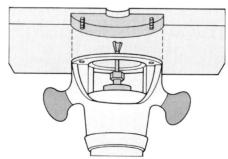

1. Rout a ½-in.-deep recess in one side of the plywood, using the router baseplate as a template. Then cut a hole for the bit in the middle of the recess. Next, unscrew the baseplate, place the router in the recess, and attach it to the plywood base with several countersunk screws.

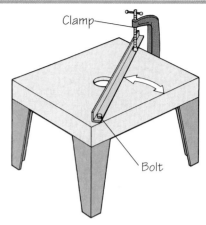

Clamp

Bolt

Quick guide ▲

Here's an easy-to-adjust fence for all routing jobs (except edge routing). Loosely bolt an aluminum angle to one corner of the table. Clamp the other end to the table at the desired position. To adjust the fence, pivot it and reclamp.

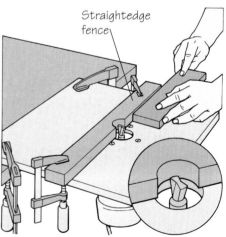

Straightedge fence

2. Clamp the plywood firmly to the workbench. Make a straightedge fence for the table, cutting an opening to accept the bit (inset). On narrow work, use a push stick to move the work safely past the bit. To make workpieces slide more smoothly, glue a piece of hardboard on top of the plywood.

Putting things away

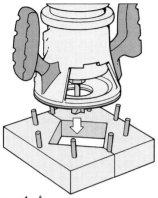

Router rest ▲

After you switch off a router, it takes a while for the bit to stop turning. If placed on its side, a router can roll around. A better idea is to build this simple stand so you can rest the router upright. Cut V-shapes into two pieces of 2 x 4 to make an opening for the spinning bit; then glue the pieces together. Draw the outline of the baseplate on the stand and insert 2-inch-long dowels at an angle around the circumference line.

Toothbrush tip ▲

To remove resin buildup on a bit, spray it with oven cleaner, scrub it as needed with a toothbrush, and rinse it in water. Wear gloves and safety goggles.

BUYER'S GUIDE

A router with a 1½-horsepower motor can do most jobs and will last a lifetime. Try handling some models in the store. Look for one that can be switched on and off while both hands hold the tool. Check for balance and weight by running it along the edge of a surface.

Router bits. Consider investing in the more expensive carbide-tipped bits. Carbide-tipped bits can rout hard- and softwoods, plastic, and manufactured woods; they stay sharp for hundreds of uses. Less expensive machined-steel bits can't be used on manufactured wood and require frequent resharpening.

Basic shapers. Shown here are the most commonly used router bits. A rabbeting or other edge-shaping bit usually comes with a guide, called a *pilot*. The pilot of a machined-steel bit spins as fast as the bit and tends to burn the work. A carbide-tipped bit has a ball-bearing pilot that rotates much more slowly and will not harm the work. Bits that make an inner groove (straight, V-shaped, core-box, and dovetail) have no pilots.

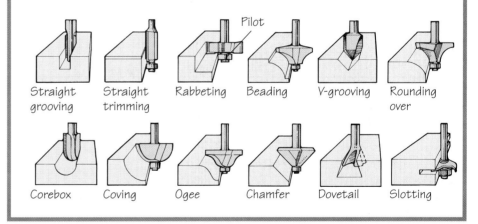

Straight grooving — Straight trimming — Rabbeting — Beading — V-grooving — Rounding over

Corebox — Coving — Ogee — Chamfer — Dovetail — Slotting

Protect those bits ▶

To protect router bits from bumping into other tools and each other—and to store them so they are easy to find—line a small cardboard box or workbench drawer with rigid foam or foam rubber. Cut out recesses in the liner to create a resting place for each bit.

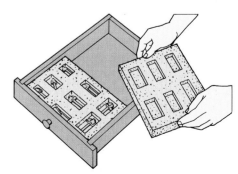

PORTABLE SAWS

Circular saws

The right blade

Two kinds of circular saw blades will see you through just about any job. The first should be a general-purpose combination blade with 20 to 24 teeth; the other should be a fine cutting blade with about 40 teeth. Both blades should be carbide-tipped.

Cutting metal

If you plan to cut metal, use a special metal-cutting blade—and brace yourself for a shower of sparks. To ensure safety, wear hearing protectors and goggles or a full face mask and work far away—say 50 feet—from sawdust, flammable liquids, and anything else that is likely to catch fire. Don't try to saw metal unless your saw has a metal blade guard; a plastic guard will melt.

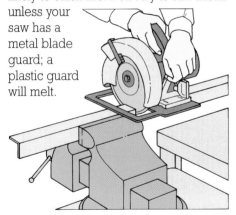

Permanent marker

The cuts you make with a circular saw will be more accurate if you mark the cutting line on the front of the saw's baseplate. Do it with paint or an indelible felt-tip marker.

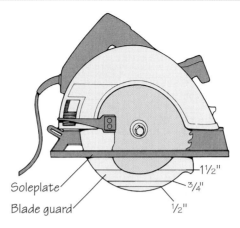

Soleplate
Blade guard
1½"
¾"
½"

Measuring circular saw cuts ▲

Here's an easy way to measure and set your circular saw's cutting depth without having to pull out a measuring tape every time. Mark ½-inch, ¾-inch, and 1½-inch blade depth measurements on the saw's blade guard with a fine-point permanent marker. Then just line up the bottom of the saw's soleplate with the appropriate mark.

Cord drape

To keep the saw cord out of your way—especially on long cuts—drape it like a cape across your shoulders. It will then move with you and be less likely to snag on something.

Wax works

Want your saw to glide as it cuts? Rub a block of paraffin wax on the underside of the saw's baseplate. If you first heat the surface slightly with a hair dryer, the wax will coat the area more completely.

Saber saws

Cutting curves

Need to cut a curve with a small radius? Choose a ³⁄₁₆-inch-wide blade over a ³⁄₈-inch blade. But be careful—the skinnier the blade, the easier it is to break.

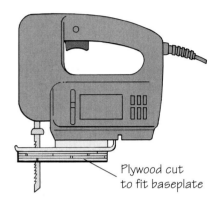

Plywood cut to fit baseplate

Put more teeth into it ▲

As a saber saw blade makes its "sewing machine" up-and-down motion, only a few of the teeth do the actual cutting. With use, these teeth become dull and the blade useless. You can extend the life of a blade by adding a piece of plywood to the baseplate. This auxiliary baseplate should be at least as thick as the length of the saw stroke. Use your saber saw to cut a notch in the plywood to accept the blade. Then outline and cut the plywood to fit the metal baseplate. Sand, finish, and wax the plywood to make it as smooth as the original metal plate. (It will also guide the blade and keep it from wandering as much.) Mount the plywood base with double-faced tape or hot glue. When the blade wears in the new spot, remove the base and change the blade.

Cleaning and storing

Oven cleaner

Sawing a lot of pine causes pitch and resin to build up on saw blades, making even sharp teeth seem dull. To clean a blade, spray it with oven cleaner. For easy application, suspend a circular blade on a dowel and hang it inside a cardboard box. Because oven cleaner fumes are toxic, close the flaps of the box for the 10 to 20 minutes it takes to loosen the gunk. Then wash the blade off with soap and warm water, dry it, and spray it with a lubricant to protect it from corrosion.

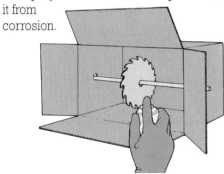

Soaking pan

To clean saw blades by soaking in acetone or turpentine, you'll need a shallow pan with a lid to contain the fumes, rubber gloves, and a stick or other lever for handling the blade. You can recycle an old pizza pan and cover it with aluminum foil. Or cut off the bottom of a plastic 5-gallon pail with a utility knife and use it as your soaking tray (the pail's lid can serve as a cover).

Capping saw teeth

When you are finished for the day, store your unmounted circular saw blades (and table and radial arm saw blades) so that the teeth stay sharp and won't injure anyone. You can buy a carrier made for the purpose or make your own saw cover by slitting a length of garden hose or the inside of an old inner tube. Other possibilities include stacking saw blades in a round plastic pie or cake container (put cardboard spacers between the blades). Or slip them into old record album covers (one blade in each sleeve). If you use album covers, be sure to reinforce the covers' edges with strong tape, because the teeth will cut the cardboard.

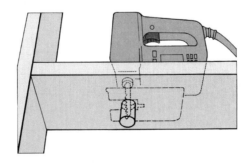

Shelf insert ▲

To store a saber saw upright on a shelf, cut a hole through the shelf to accept the blade. Cover the blade by gluing a length of tubing to the underside of the shelf. Then just rest the saw on the shelf.

SABER SAWS

If you would like to have a great saber saw, try one with orbital action rather than one with only a simple up-and-down movement. The orbital action, which pushes the teeth into the work on the cutting stroke and away from it on the return stroke, cuts amazingly fast and cleanly.

To make the most of a saber saw, you need to buy the right blades. Here's a sample of what's available: (a) a hollow-ground blade for fine cuts; (b) a double-sided blade that can back out of tight spots; (c) a flush-cutting blade that makes straight cuts flush to a wall or other obstruction (it's too wide to cut a curve); (d) a knife-edge for leather and carpeting; (e) a carbide-grit abrasive blade to cut hard materials such as ceramic tile; and (f) a metal-cutting blade that will work on aluminum, steel, and pipe with ⅛-inch-thick walls.

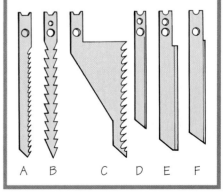

A   B   C   D   E   F

TABLE SAWS

Tips and tricks

Room to work

Setting up your table saw? If you'll be working with 4 x 8 sheets of plywood, allow enough free room for them around the saw. For ripping, you'll need at least 10 feet at the front of the saw and 8 feet at the rear. For crosscutting, leave 8 feet on each side of the blade.

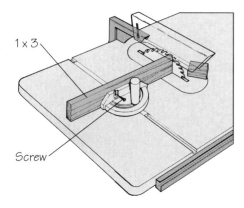

1 x 3

Screw

Miter gauge guide ▲

When you're crosscutting, a miter gauge places the work at the proper angle to the blade. However, the gauge doesn't show you exactly where the blade is going to cut, nor does it provide enough support to cut long pieces. To make a cut-off guide that will provide added support, attach a 1 x 3 permanently to your miter gauge so that it extends from the edge of the saw to just beyond the path of the blade. Make a pass to cut off the excess. The cut end will mark the exact cut-off point of your saw. To keep the work from shifting as it comes in contact with the blade, glue a piece of sandpaper to the face of the 1 x 3.

Parallel and square ▶

To ensure a proper rip cut and avoid kickback, align your table saw blade so it is parallel to the fence and square to the table. Here's a way to check that the blade is aligned properly: Measure the distance between the blade and the fence at both the front and the back. The measurements should be the same. Adjust the fence if necessary. Set the blade and the miter gauge to 0° and test-cut a piece of scrap 2 x 4. Turn one piece upside down and place the cut ends together. If the pieces match perfectly, the blade is aligned correctly.

Make a height gauge

Here's a jig that will help you adjust the height of your saw blade quickly and precisely. Take a scrap piece of plywood and cut accurate notches in ⅛-inch steps, alternating sides as you cut (this way, each notch is ¼ inch higher than the one below it). Mark the fractions on the jig. To set the blade, place the gauge over it and raise it until it just touches the appropriate notch in the gauge. **Caution:** Don't forget to unplug the saw when you're adjusting the blade.

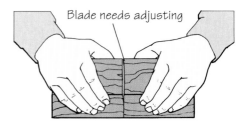

Cut is correct

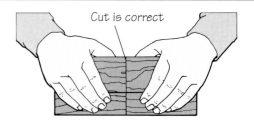

Blade needs adjusting

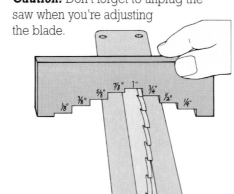

Improvements

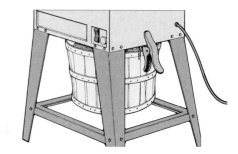

Collecting dust ▲

Ripping wood on a table saw generates a great deal of sawdust. Here are two ways to collect most of the larger sawdust particles as they fall: Attach a heavy-duty, jumbo garbage bag to the underside of the table saw with clothespins or duct tape. Or mount a large basket inside the saw apron, holding it in place with two spring clamps through the handles. These dust catchers are easy to empty and remount, but for safety reasons, unplug the saw firsts.

Wax your table

To keep the metal surface of your table saw free from rust—and help the work move smoothly as you cut—rub the surface with paste floor wax.

Bumpers for fence guides

Don't leave those metal fence guides that protrude beyond the saw base unprotected. Slit a pair of tennis balls and fit them over the ends. You'll save yourself many a bruise and avoid causing a head or eye injury to a child. ▼

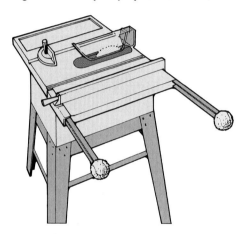

Seeing red ▲

As a graphic reminder to keep your fingers and hands away from the blade of your table saw (and any other stationary power saw, for that matter), paint the area around the blade a bright red. First make a new table insert and paint it red. Then spray paint 4 inches in front of and behind the blade. Be sure to mask the fence and any other areas you don't want painted.

Hang the accessories

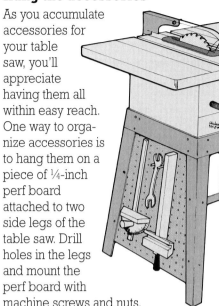

As you accumulate accessories for your table saw, you'll appreciate having them all within easy reach. One way to organize accessories is to hang them on a piece of ¼-inch perf board attached to two side legs of the table saw. Drill holes in the legs and mount the perf board with machine screws and nuts.

Push sticks and feather boards

When you're ripping stock, you need to guide the board accurately while keeping your fingers from coming too close to the blade. Using a push stick on small pieces keeps fingers at a safe distance (at least 3 inches away). To brace the work, clamp a feather board to the saw table so that it is in front of the blade (side pressure next to the blade would cause it to bind in the cut). Adjust the splitter to keep the cut open.

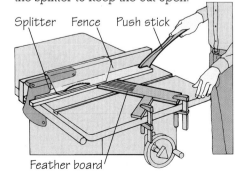

Splitter   Fence   Push stick

Feather board

POWER SAWS

▷ Always let the saw reach its full speed before you do any cutting.
▷ Keep all levers and clamps tight.
▷ Support both the work and the waste when cutting.
▷ Keep your fingers away from the saw blade.
▷ Always wear protective gear for your eyes and ears.
▷ Feed the work against the rotation of a stationary saw's blade.

Table saws

▷ Never remove the blade guard.
▷ Never reach behind a moving saw blade.
▷ Set the blade so that it protrudes just ⅛ to ¼ inch above the work.
▷ Use push sticks, as shown at left.
▷ Hold the widest portion of the board you are ripping against the fence. Feed the work until it is completely clear of the blade.
▷ Never cut freehand.
▷ Use either the fence or the miter gauge—never both at once.

Radial arm saws

▷ Stay out of the path of the blade.
▷ When ripping, use a push stick and the antikickback mechanism.

Band saws

▷ Follow the manual's guidelines on the proper speed, rate of feed, and turning radius for each blade.
▷ Keep the blade guide ⅛ to ¼ inch above the work.

For more on power tool safety,
see p.24.

MEASURING TOOLS

Home rules

Go for the money

Who says our dollars are shrinking? If you are ever at a loss for a ruler, check your wallet. Laid out flat, a $2 bill is 6 inches long. Folded in half, the bill is 3 inches; folded in half again, it measures 1½ inches. Folded lengthwise, the 2¾-inch-wide bill gives you a measurement that is very close to 1⅝ inches.

Painted numbers

Have you noticed that the numbers and graduation marks etched in metal measuring tools become hard to read after a while? You don't need to replace the tools when that happens. Instead, paint them white and wipe off the excess paint while it is wet. The numbers and marks will be easy to read again. On aluminum tools, use black paint.

For good measure

Rather than discard an old tape measure, snip off a 6-inch section and keep it in your wallet. This portable ruler is especially handy for checking the size of small items in hardware stores.

Oversize ruler ▶

Cutting lumber to size is much easier if you have an oversize ruler painted on your workshop floor. To make such a ruler, begin at one wall and scribe lines every 6 inches. Number every other line to indicate the distance in feet from the wall. When you're ready to measure, butt the lumber against the wall. If you need to find intermediate lengths, use a 12-inch ruler. To protect the marks from foot traffic, coat them with a varnish or a clear sealer.

BE YOUR OWN RULER

If you need a tape measure or a ruler and there's none to be had, take a cue from our ancestors and use your body to estimate distances from less than an inch to as much as 7 feet. The illustrations below give some approximate measurements and their traditional names. To achieve more exact guidelines, measure your own fingers, hands, limbs, etc. (Be sure you are fully extended when you do so.) Memorize the results and you're ready to go.

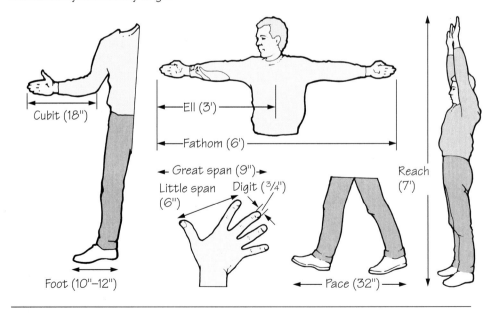

Cubit (18")

Ell (3')

Fathom (6')

Great span (9")

Little span (6")

Digit (¾")

Foot (10"–12")

Pace (32")

Reach (7')

Mounted yardstick

For quick and easy measuring, tack a yardstick or glue a metal rule to your workbench. If you glue a smaller rule to your toolbox, you'll find that measuring on the run is a snap.

Make a transfer

Because an incorrect measurement can ruin a project, transferring it accurately is critical. If you don't have the right measuring tool handy, slip a thin rubber band around a straight stick. This way, you'll have a sliding marker that will preserve your last measurement. For best results, don't use a rubber band that is so large you have to double it over to make it snug.

Magnetic measurer

You can also use a scrap piece of metal to transfer a measurement. Mark the place with a small rectangular or square magnet. It will clamp onto the metal and stay there as long as needed.

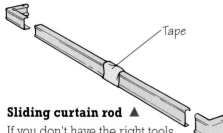

Tape

Sliding curtain rod ▲

If you don't have the right tools to measure an inside dimension, press a sliding curtain rod into service. Cut off the elbows of the rod, stretch it to fit the space, wrap tape around the point where the sections of the rod overlap to keep them from sliding out of position, then remove the rod and measure it. To measure smaller inside dimensions, cut the rod down.

Dip straw

Would you like a simple, accurate, and spill-proof way to measure out a small amount of stain or other liquids? Dip one end of a plastic straw in the liquid just deep enough to get the amount needed. Then place a finger on the other end to hold the liquid in the straw. Keep your finger on the straw while you take it to its new destination. For greater accuracy, mark often-used measures on the straw.

Hammer gauge

If one hand holds the hammer and the second hand holds the nail, how do you gauge the distance between nails without using a third hand to measure? Let your hammer be a measuring tool. Framing hammers are longer than 16 inches, the usual distance between studs. Wrap tape of one color 16 inches from the head of the hammer; use different colors to mark off a foot and other often-used lengths.

12"

16"

Wax tape

Pros use a steel tape because it gives an accurate measurement and retracts at the touch of a button. To protect the numbers and keep the action smooth, coat the tape with a little paste wax; then buff it thoroughly with a cloth. ▼

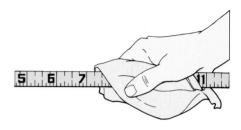

Taking notes

You'll always have a place to jot down measurements if you stick a self-adhesive label to the side of your tape measure. Either replace the label when you're done or erase the marks and reuse it.

Inch rule

The hook of a metal tape—so handy when measuring from one edge—gets in the way of a measurement that starts in the middle of a surface. To obtain an accurate measurement in this case, begin your measurement at the 1-inch mark. Just remember to subtract the inch later on.

MARKING TOOLS

Sandpaper sharpener

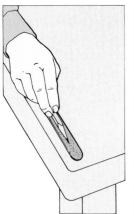

A sharp pencil is indispensable for making precise layouts. One way to keep your pencils sharp at all times is to tape or hot-glue a strip of medium-grit sandpaper or an emery board to your workbench or a nearby wall. To sharpen a pencil, just rub the pencil point back and forth a few times against the abrasive surface. To achieve the chisel-shaped point that's best for marking wood, rub only the opposite sides of the point.

Another one-handed sharpener

You can also hot-glue a small plastic pencil sharpener to the underside of your workbench. To catch the shavings, position the sharpener over a trash can.

Chalk talk

The colored chalk used for snapping lines is highly visible, but it can be hard to remove from porous surfaces such as brick and unfinished wood. To make cleanup easier in such cases, carry in your tool kit an extra chalk box filled with baby or talcum powder. The white stuff is almost as visible as the traditional chalks on dark-colored surfaces and is easy to remove. On lighter surfaces, however, the white can be hard to see.

Snap line holder

When snapping a chalk line, both ends of the line must be anchored while the line is snapped. On wood, tie the line around a nail driven in one end of the stock or panel. Or cut a saw kerf and hook the string in the kerf.

Mechanical compass

To avoid having to resharpen and reposition the little pencil in a compass over and over again, substitute a mechanical pencil for the wood one. You'll have a durable marking tool that needs no sharpening and little adjusting. All you have to do to get a fresh point is push down on (or twist) the end.

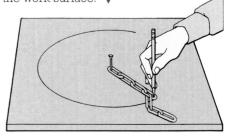

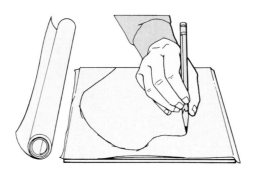

Draw anywhere ▲

Ceramic tiles, glass, and metal are hard to mark. One solution is to cover the area to be marked with a tape that's easy to peel off, such as artist's tape, or with a sheet of contact adhesive paper. This way you'll be able to draw (and see) your pencil marks. Leave the tape or contact paper in place until you've finished cutting.

Circle chain

Use a length of flat-link chain to draw various-size circles. Drive the tip of a nail through one of the links and into the center of your circle. Use this nail as a pivot point, and insert the point of a pencil at the desired radius. To make your circle accurate, keep the chain taut and the pencil perpendicular to the work surface. ▼

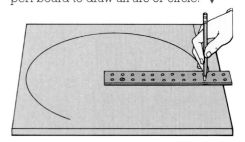

Perf-board circle

A 2-inch-wide strip of perf board makes a great substitute trammel—a tool used to mark large circles—because the perf board's holes offer a variety of radii. To use your perf-board trammel, first locate the pivot point by fastening one end of the perf board to the workpiece with a screw. Use a screw that fits the hole, but leave it a little loose so that the perf board can pivot freely. Place a pencil in the appropriate hole and rotate the perf board to draw an arc or circle. ▼

LAYOUT TOOLS

Improvisations

Marble-ous level

If you don't have a level, you can still check your work. Place a marble at the midpoint of the work and at various positions along the work surface. If it doesn't roll in any direction, your work is level.

Here's the pitch

If you want an easy way to align your work to a specific angle or pitch, try this: Place the level at the desired angle; then mark the positions of the bubbles by placing tape on the glass vial at the ends of each bubble. To duplicate this pitch, angle the level in a new location, centering the bubbles between the pieces of tape. When the job is done, remove the tape.

Plumb bob imposter

If you don't have a plumb bob handy, try using a chalk line box as a substitute. Secure the hook end of the chalk line and extend the string; then mark the spot, using the tapered bottom end of the chalk box as a reference. ▼

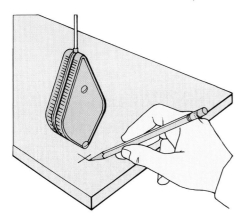

Checking up

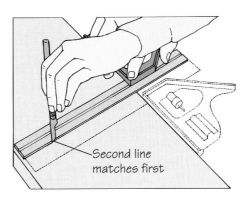

Second line matches first

Test for square ▲

Every so often, it's a good idea to test your combination square to see if it is true. Place the tool on a straight board and draw a line along the square's blade. Then turn the square over, place the blade at the line, and draw a line; if the lines match, the square is true.

Protect your tools

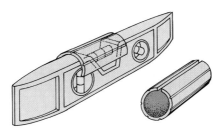

Bubble cover ▲

It's easy to break one of those little glass vials in a level inadvertently. To protect the glass, cut 3-inch lengths of garden hose and slit them lengthwise. Between jobs slip the covers over the vials.

On the level

Always check a level before you buy it, and test it periodically afterward. To make the test, place the level on the floor or on a table, mark where you've placed it, and note the bubble positions on the vials. Then rotate the level, end for end, align it on the same spot, and note the reading. Finally, turn the level over top to bottom, and make a final reading. All three readings should be the same. If your level has tiny screws, you can adjust them to true the level. If there are no screws and the level isn't true, you'll have to buy another level. ▼

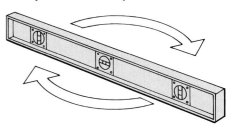

Hanging square

The best way to ensure the accuracy of a square year after year is to take good care of the tool. Try not to drop it accidentally, and always hang it on the wall when you're not using it. To hang your square, take a piece of 1 x 3 and either bevel one edge at a 45° angle or cut a thin groove to accept the square. Nail the strip securely to the wall. ▼

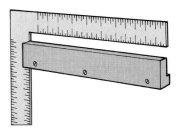

CLAMPS AND VISES

Clamp improvements

Recycled film caps

A tight C-clamp can mar a work surface. To protect your projects, hot-glue caps from plastic 35mm film containers to the C-clamp jaws. When you no longer need the caps, just pop them off.

Magnetic pads

Ever wish you had a third hand when fitting protective wood blocks between a workpiece and steel pipe-clamp jaws? Magnets fitted into the blocks can make the job easier. Cut recesses in the blocks so the magnets will be flush with the surface; then glue the magnets in place with epoxy.

Red flag

The ends of long bar and pipe clamps often stick out during a clamping job. To avoid bumping into them, drape a brightly colored rag over the end of each clamp. That way you won't hurt yourself or tear your clothing. ▼

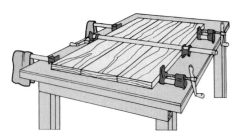

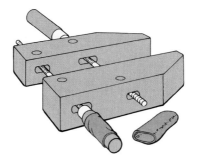

Turning point ▲

If you have trouble getting enough torque (turning pressure) on the smooth handles of a hand-screw clamp, stretch a length of a bicycle tube over the handle. The tube will go on easily if you dust the inside with talcum powder.

Squeeze-out protection

To keep your clamps free from rust and dried glue, rub them with paraffin or paste wax. The coating adds moisture resistance and allows you to easily chip off any accidental gobs of glue. ▼

Vise advice

Vise cushions

To keep a vise from marring wood or other soft material, make two wood cushions the same size as the jaws of the vise. To hold the cushions in place on the vise, attach magnetic strips to them with construction adhesive.

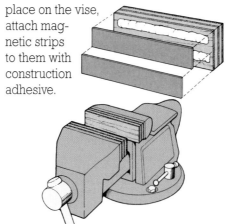

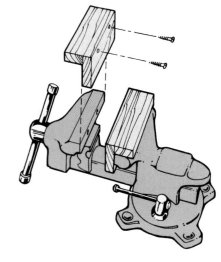

Shield a vise ▲

Another way to protect a work surface from the jaws of a bench vise is with a pair of wood shields. The ones shown here are easy to make out of four pieces of scrap wood glued and screwed together to form L-joints.

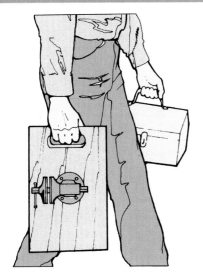

You *can* take it with you ▲

Have you ever been away from your workshop and needed a vise? Here are two ways to take the vise to the job. Bolt a 3-inch vise to a 15-inch-long 2 x 12 board with a cut-out handle. This size board is heavy enough to keep things steady. Or bolt a 2 x 2 block of wood to the end of your toolbox. Then when you need to support a workpiece on a small job, clamp a 3-inch vise onto the wood block. ▼

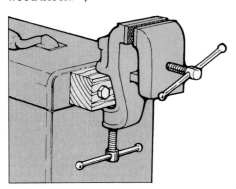

USER-FRIENDLY CLAMPS

Clamps make great shop assistants. Many home shops are stocked with C-clamps, spring clamps, pipe clamps, and hand screws, but there are other types to meet just about any job. Some of the handiest are shown below.

Bar clamps

Quick-Grip bar clamp

Trigger

A *Quick-Grip bar clamp* can be set one-handed. To slide the jaw into place, pull the trigger. To add pressure, squeeze the grip. Removable rubber pads protect the work.

Aluminum bar clamp

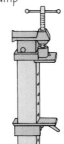

Lightweight aluminum bar clamps work as well as, or even better than, steel bar clamps. The lighter weight makes a large glue-up easier to move, and the aluminum won't leave glue stains.

Cam-action bar clamp

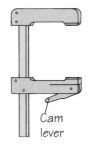

Cam lever

Try a *cam-action bar clamp* for light-duty jobs. To set one, slide the movable jaw to the work; lock it in place by turning the cam lever so that it is perpendicular to the bar of the clamp.

Specialty clamps

Band clamp

Choose a *band clamp* when you need to hold irregularly shaped pieces together, and when you are working with interlocking joints (such as those in a chair).

Deep-throat C-clamp

Use *deep-throat C-clamps* to apply pressure to the center of wide pieces. These clamps come in a variety of sizes, and they are fairly inexpensive.

Edge clamp

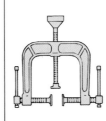

When you need to hold an edging, such as trim, molding, or laminate, in place, use an *edge clamp*. As you set it, make sure that all the screws are applying equal pressure.

SUPPLIES AND EQUIPMENT

Glues

Economical refills

If you use a lot of carpenter's or other glue, buy it in large quantities. You'll save money and avoid the hassle of running out of glue in the middle of a job. To dispense the glue, use old ketchup or mustard squeeze bottles with twist-seal nozzles or flip-top caps. Be sure to remove the labels and clearly mark the bottle with its new contents.

Slick tip

Have you ever struggled to get a stuck cap off a tube of glue? If so, here's an easy fix. Dab a little petroleum jelly on the tip before replacing the cap; the jelly will keep the glue from sticking.

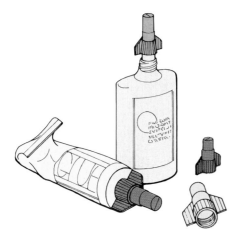

Top substitute ▲

Wire connectors, sold at hardware and electrical supply stores, make good substitute caps for glue bottles or tubes. Keep several sizes of wire connectors on hand and you won't have to waste time searching for misplaced caps.

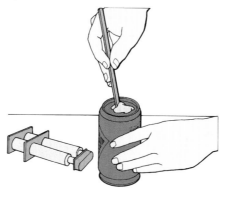

Cool it ▲

To keep epoxy from setting up too quickly in warm weather or in a heated workshop, turn over a cold unopened can of soda and mix the ingredients in the recessed bottom of the can. The cold aluminum will slow the setting-up process, and the recess in the can makes a fine mixing bowl.

Other adhesives

Cement can collar

When applying contact cement, keep the rim of the cement can clean by covering it with an aluminum foil collar. The foil will catch the drips and prevent gummy buildup. Once the job is done, discard the foil; the lid will sit tightly in place. ▼

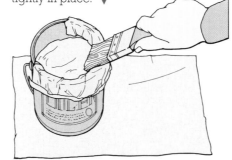

Removable adhesive

Inexpensive wall adhesive, also known as white glue, has many uses around the workshop. Use it to secure a screw on the tip of a screwdriver, to hold nuts and washers together, and to post assembly instructions and notes to yourself. In many situations it's a good substitute for tape or staples.

Carpet scrap applicator

Cleaning brushes that have been used to apply contact cement is an impossible job. Instead of throwing away brush after brush, make a reusable applicator out of scrap wood; then just staple a fresh scrap of carpet to the block for each new job.

Storing adhesives

An upside-down trick

Storing glue bottles and tubes upside down keeps the contents ready to pour. To make a holder for your glue bottles, drill holes through an existing shelf in your workshop. Another option is to drill holes into a scrap 1 x 4 and attach it to the wall.

Hang tubing

Here's a clever solution to a common workshop storage problem. Since plastic squeeze tubes of contact cement and caulk don't lie flat and can't be stacked, try hanging them up. Cut a piece of duct tape about 2 inches long and trim it to fit the width of the tube. Stick one end of the tape on the bottom of the tube; then fold the tape in half over the tube, pinching the sticky sides together. Punch a hole through the tape and hang it on a nail or on a perf-board hook.

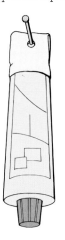

Glue gun holder

The hot dripping tip of a glue gun can be a safety hazard. To keep it out of harm's way, park it in this handy holder made by mounting a spring-metal broom clip on a small piece of scrap lumber. To catch the drips, screw a small jar lid to the holder. ▼

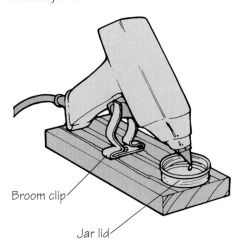

Broom clip

Jar lid

DISPOSING OF HAZARDOUS WASTE

Products containing solvents or other ingredients that carry cautionary warning labels (such as *flammable, explosive,* and *corrosive*) are likely to be classified as hazardous waste. Before you buy such a product, try to find a safer (water-base) substitute. If none is available, buy only as much as you can use. If you are unsure of how to dispose of a material, contact your municipality or the provincial ministry responsible for environmental protection or health. The table below outlines some general guidelines for shop materials. See p.301 for disposal of automotive waste.

TYPE OF WASTE	●	◆	▼	▲
Contact cement, solvent-base*		◆		▲
Contact cement, water-base		◆		
Degreasing chemicals				▲
Glue, adhesive, and sealants, solvent-base				▲
Glue, adhesive, and sealants, water-base		◆		
Kerosene			▼	
Paint, latex		◆		
Paint and varnish stripper (lye)	●			
Paintbrush cleaner, phosphate	●			
Paintbrush cleaner, solvent				▲
Paint remover or thinner (residue)				▲
Paints, oil (alkyd) and rust-inhibiting				▲
Polish, furniture (solvent-base)				▲
Rust remover, phosphoric acid	●			
Wood finishes (polyurethane, oil, varnish)				▲
Wood preservative				▲

● Dilute *small* amount with plenty of water and pour down the drain. For *large* amount or if you have a septic tank, recycle or treat as hazardous waste.

◆ Let evaporate away from people and pets, or solidify with absorbent material, such as cat litter. Double-wrap in plastic; discard with garbage going to landfill or incinerator.

▼ Recycle at special center set up for the purpose, or treat as hazardous waste.

▲ Do not discard this hazardous waste. Save for special collection day or contact your municipality or provincial environmental department for instructions.

*Wrap and discard applicators when dry. Any unused cement is hazardous waste.

SUPPLIES AND EQUIPMENT

Putty and filler

Airless container ▲

Filler and putty dry out quickly when exposed to the air. To slow the drying, use a putty knife to transfer the material to a small self-seal plastic bag. Seal the bag, then cut a small hole in one corner. To dispense the material, just squeeze the bag as if you were decorating a cake. When the job is done, twist the corner closed and secure it with a twist tie. Store the closed bag in the original container.

Reviving Plastic Wood

Acetone-base cellulose fiber filler, known as Plastic Wood, also dries out quickly. To restore Plastic Wood that has begun to harden, mix in a little acetone-base fingernail polish remover. As long as you don't add too much remover, the Plastic Wood will be as good as new. If, however, the material has dried out thoroughly, there's no rescuing it.

Steel wool and brushes

Magnetic attraction

Small particles of steel wool can collect on a workpiece and even become airborne as metal dust. To contain metal particles and avoid breathing metal dust, wrap a small or medium-size magnet in the wad of steel wool. As you work, periodically wipe off the magnet. When the job is done, run the magnet over the work to remove any remaining metal particles. Always wear a dust mask when working with steel wool.

Magnet

For tight spots

How can you rub steel wool effectively in a tight corner or a groove? Cut off the end of a plastic or rubber bicycle handlebar grip. Then stuff a piece of steel wool tightly into the opening, leaving a knot of the stuff protruding. The handle lets you apply pressure—and protects your hands. ▼

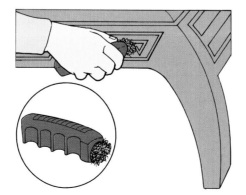

Adjust a brush

Here's a way to convert an ordinary paintbrush into a light-duty scrub brush: Simply wrap the bristles securely with masking tape. The closer the tape is to the tips of the bristles, the stiffer the brush will be.

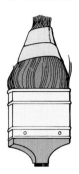

Wire brush renewal

The front section of a wire brush always wears out before the rest. To rejuvenate a worn brush, clamp it upside down in a vise and saw about 1 inch off the brush along with the worn bristles. Another option is to snip off bent or damaged edges with a wire cutter. Cut them diagonally so the ends will be sharp. Wear eye protection when cutting.

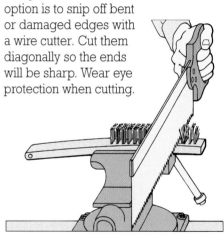

Oil

About spouts

To reduce the flow of oil from a spout, you need to make the opening smaller. One way to do this is to dab a little fingernail polish over the tip. When the polish is dry, reopen the spout by poking it with a pin.

Straw applicator

You can extend the reach of an oil can by holding a straw from a broom next to the spout. Or if holding the straw is awkward, you can tape it to the spout. In either case, the drops of oil will follow the broom straw to its end.

Knives in the workshop

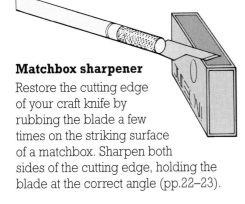

Matchbox sharpener

Restore the cutting edge of your craft knife by rubbing the blade a few times on the striking surface of a matchbox. Sharpen both sides of the cutting edge, holding the blade at the correct angle (pp.22–23).

Quick-change artist

Ever wished there was an easier way to change the blade in your utility knife? Take a look in hardware stores and home centers for knives that will do so with the push of a button and a twist of the wrist. No more messing around with a screwdriver and then trying to line up the halves of the knife so that it works properly again.

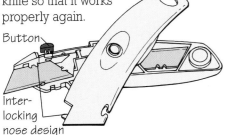

Button

Inter-
locking
nose design

Sharp storage ideas

If you need to take a razor blade to a job, tear the matches out of a matchbook, insert the blade, and close the cover. Back in your workshop, you can store your razor blades in slots cut into a small scrap piece of rigid foam packing material.

Plans and instructions

Write your own

If you are tackling a job that doesn't come with its own instructions, take a few minutes to write your own *before* you begin. It also helps to make your notes on an oversize pad of paper, such as the flip charts you see in conference and meeting rooms. Available at office supply stores, flip charts provide all the room you need to write down instructions and to draw plans and diagrams. For easy viewing, mount the pad on a nail in a workshop wall.

Blow it up

Ever strained to see the fine print and small details of assembly instructions? A trip to a photocopier that can enlarge your original is in order. By enlarging hard-to-read instructions, you can work without reading glasses or eyestrain.

Sheer protection

Protect plans, drawings, and instructions with a piece of clear self-sticking plastic. The papers stay clean and dry, won't tear with use, and are easy to roll up. If needed, you can make notes on the plastic with a grease pencil. To erase the marks, just rub them with a cloth.

Hang 'em high

Instead of leaving instruction sheets on your workbench, where they can get lost, torn, or badly soiled, separate the pages and tape them at eye level to the wall just above your work area.

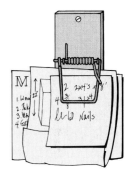

Mousetrapping ▲

Mount a spring-type mousetrap to your workshop wall with screws and you'll have a sturdy holder for your plans. Before you mount the trap, however, pry the bait holder off with a screwdriver.

Handy manuals

Can't find your owner's manual when you need it? Keep the manuals for all your power tools in one place. Punch holes in them and store them in a three-ring binder, or keep them in a magazine storage file. Or make your own file by cutting off one end of a large detergent box as shown. Make it a habit to put the manual for a new tool in your special storage place as soon as you finish reading it.

SUPPLIES AND EQUIPMENT

Pails and buckets

Recycled plastic pails

Large plastic pails have a multitude of uses, from storing extension cords (far right), to mixing plaster, to serving as scrub pails. Because some building supplies come in pails, construction sites can be a good source of free or cheap pails. If you have small children, empty a pail after each use and store it where a child can't get at it. It's not unheard of for a child to crawl into a pail, become stuck, and drown or suffocate.

Heavy load

When you are carrying a heavy load in a bucket, the container's thin handle can cut painfully into your hand. Make the task easier by fitting an open-ended wrench around the handle as shown. The wrench is kinder to your hand and stabilizes the load.

Leaky buckets

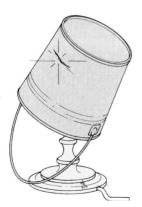

To find the exact location of a bucket leak, turn on a small table lamp, remove the shade, and place the bucket upside down over it. The light will shine through the hole.

Hole repairs

To make a temporary patch over a small hole in a plastic pail, fill the hole from both sides with pure silicone caulk. (The caulk layers adhere to each other better than to plastic.) Or drip candle wax over the hole. The wax plug will stay intact, however, only if the bucket is filled with cold water—hot water will melt the wax.

Ropes

Rope saver

To keep a rope from fraying where it rubs against something, slip a length of rubber hose over the rope at the stressed spot. Hold the hose in place with knots tied on either side of it.

No more unraveling

The ends of a length of rope will not unravel if you dab them with either silicone sealant, liquid (air-dry) rubber, or vinyl coating.

Untangle that mess

Don't struggle with a snarled string, rope, or cord. Begin untangling by gently pulling outward all around the edges of the snarl. As the tangled mass becomes bigger and looser, the loops will eventually untangle themselves, and you'll be left with fewer knots to undo.

Extension cords

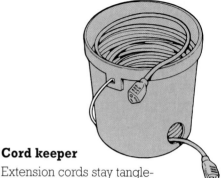

Cord keeper

Extension cords stay tangle-free when kept in a 5-gallon pail. Near the bottom of the pail, cut or drill a hole large enough so that the cord's pronged end can pass through it. Then coil the rest of the cord into the bucket. The cord will come out easily when pulled. Plug the ends of the cord together when it's not in use. You can use the space in the center of the coil to carry tools to a work site.

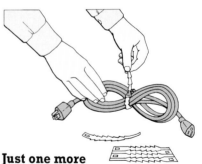

Just one more

If you want to store your cords flat—and keep them organized—coil or loop the cord as shown above. Then cinch the center of the cord tightly with one of the plastic "key lock" ties that come with large polyethylene garbage bags. To hold very long cords, join two or more plastic ties together.

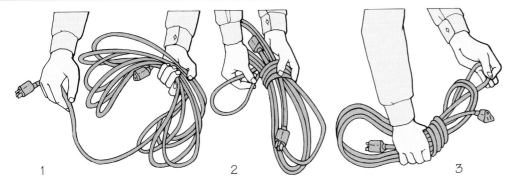

1   2   3

Coil and hang ▲

Here are three quick steps to coiling and hanging a long extension cord. Hold the end of the cord in one hand. With the other hand, loop it back and forth in figure 8's (1). When the cord is coiled, take a single loop and wrap it twice around one end of the coil (2). Finally, insert that same loop through the center of the smaller coil opening and pull it tight (3). To store the cord, hang this loop on a large nail or peg.

Preventing a sudden disconnect ▶

Does the plug of your power tool tend to pull out of the extension cord when you are working overhead or are moving around a lot? To keep this from happening with any portable power tool, tie the ends of the two cords together in a simple knot.

THE RIGHT EXTENSION CORD FOR THE TOOL

The wire gauge of an extension cord determines how much current it can safely carry. (The smaller the wire gauge number, the larger the wire and the greater its current-carrying capacity.) Other measures of current are *amperage* and *wattage*. Look for these ratings on the cord and on the tool's specifications plate; the cord ratings should be equal to or greater than those of the tool. *Note:* If a cord seems hot, or is over 50 feet long, choose the next larger wire gauge (lower number).

WIRE GAUGE	AMP RATING	WATT RATING	TYPICAL TOOL TO USE
#16	5–8	960	Small drill, belt sander, reciprocating saw
#14	8–12	1,440	Router, circular saw
#12	12–15	1,800	Small table saw
#10	15–20	2,400	Large table saw, radial arm saw, band saw

In tight places

To drive a screw in a dark corner, attach a little pen-light to the shaft of your screwdriver. You'll be able to see the screw-head easily.

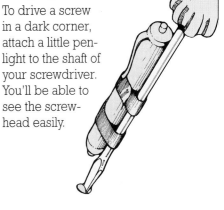

A point of light

Create a mini light for small jobs in tight places by plugging a night-light into a household extension cord. You'll be able to move this little light as far as the cord will reach. When finished, you can disassemble the pieces in a flash.

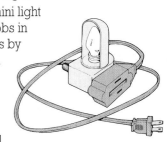

Prop it up

Turn a pair of pliers into a flashlight stand. Prop the flashlight at the needed angle in the jaws of the pliers. To hold the jaws tightly around the flashlight, place a rubber band around the handles of the pliers.

LADDERS

Hand over hand

To raise an extension ladder, place its feet at the base of the wall. Starting at the top, walk the ladder up, hand over hand, until it is vertical. Then pull its feet out from the wall, extend the ladder to the height you want it, lock the extension, and set the 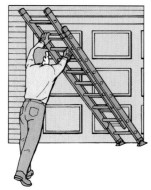 feet of the ladder at a 75° angle—you should be able to stand with your toes against the feet of the ladder, your arms and back straight, and your hands on the rungs at shoulder height (below). To move a ladder, lower it, hand over hand, and carry it parallel to the ground. ▼

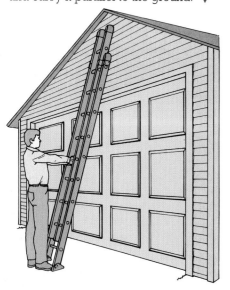

Ground support

If you've ever tried to use a ladder on soft ground, you know that the ladder's feet will sink as soon as you start to climb. To keep the legs from sinking, set them on a piece of ¾-inch plywood that is at least 6 to 8 inches deeper and wider than the ladder. The board acts like a snowshoe, distributing the load over a greater area.

Padded ends

The best ladders have padded ends that protect the surfaces they lean against. If your ladder lacks pads, buy rubber ones or make your own by wrapping rags around the ends and tying them with elastic cord. Still another option is to cover the ends with thick socks or heavy-duty work gloves.

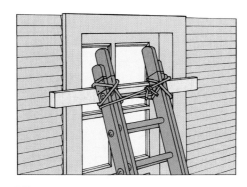

Window treatment ▲

When a job calls for you to rest the top of your ladder in the center of a window opening, you run the risk of damaging the sill or breaking the glass. One way to avoid problems is to attach a store-bought stabilizer bar, which widens the top of the ladder. Or tie a 2 x 4 securely to the top rung so that the board spans the opening and rests on the window frame or the siding on both sides.

Tie one on

When using a ladder as a way to get up and down from the roof, tie the ladder to the gutter with an elastic cord or rope. (Never rest the ladder on the gutter.) A gust of wind can knock over an unsecured ladder, damaging whatever is in its path and leaving you stranded.

Customizing ladders

Tools at hand ▲

Tired of climbing up and down a step-ladder to retrieve fallen tools? Just drill some holes in the top step of the ladder to hold your most-used tools.

Basket case

To turn your ladder's shelf into a handy tool and equipment holder, use an elastic cord to fasten a plastic household basket to the shelf.

Shoe cleaner

Clean shoes mean surer footing on a ladder. Staple or glue a strip of scrap carpet to the bottom rung of your ladder, and use it to wipe the soles of your shoes each time you climb the ladder.

More on treads

To improve traction on ladder steps, glue strips of asphalt shingle or sandpaper to the treads. Another way to slip-proof the treads is to paint them and then sprinkle a layer of sand into the wet paint. When the coating dries, you'll have a nice gritty surface to step on.

Keep it closed

A simple hook-and-eye fastener will keep a wooden stepladder closed while you're carrying or storing it. Screw the hook into one leg and the eye in the other leg, directly across from the hook. If you have a metal stepladder, cinch the legs with a belt or a Velcro strap.

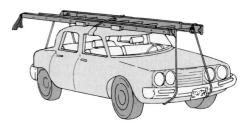

Car carrier ▲

How do you get a rented extension ladder home if you don't have a roof rack? One solution is a low-cost kit sold to haul canoes. Consisting of notched foam pads and nylon straps or rope ties, the kit makes easy work of hauling long ladders. Tie on a couple of red caution flags and be sure the ladder is secure before you drive away.

Bucket holder ▲

Keep a paint can or small bucket within easy reach on an extension ladder by hanging it on a length of broom handle or plastic water pipe extending from one of the ladder's hollow rungs. The pole should be about 2 feet longer than the width of the ladder; notch it at both ends to keep the bucket in place.

Storage

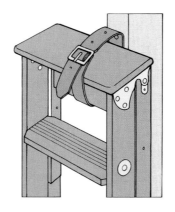

Buckle up ▲

When it's time to store a ladder, don't just lean it against the wall—it can easily fall over. A better way is to attach an old leather belt to the wall and wrap it around the ladder's top step. Or mount a stepladder vertically on a pair of pegs securely fastened to the wall. Hang an extension ladder horizontally on pegs spaced no more than 6 feet apart.

Theft protection

Never store a ladder outside or in an unlocked garage. A burglar may use it to reach a window that would otherwise be out of reach. If you have to leave a ladder out, chain it securely to a tree.

Compact ladder

If you don't have room to store an extension ladder, consider buying a multipurpose articulated ladder, which unfolds to make a 10-foot extension ladder. An articulated ladder is fairly expensive, but it can double as a stepladder and as a support for plank scaffolding.

Rack steady ▲

Keeping your balance while standing on a ladder is of utmost importance. A metal towel rack fastened to the top step of the ladder makes a convenient handrail for steadying yourself.

TOOL CARE AND STORAGE

Better boxes

Toolbox organizer

Use magnets to hold your favorite flat tools, such as wrenches and pliers, against the inside lid of your toolbox. Purchase magnets of various sizes and of sufficient strength to hold the tools, and hot-glue the magnets to the inside lid of the box.

Handy storage

A bread box or old lunch box will comfortably hold all the tools you need for small jobs around the house. Such containers are also good for keeping a duplicate set of your favorite and most-used hand tools in a place other than your workshop. Having the right tools close at hand may keep you from putting off needed repairs.

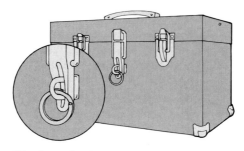

Keyless lockup ▲

To keep curious small children out of your toolbox, secure its lock hasp with a spring-steel key ring rather than with a lock. This way, you can childproof the toolbox (little hands are not strong enough to remove the key ring) without having to carry around another key.

Tool cushion

Line the bottom of your toolbox with felt, scrap carpeting, or bubble wrap. The padding will protect the tools and help reduce noise when you handle them.

Tool toting tips

Pick some pockets

A jacket or vest with lots of pockets, like those worn by professional photographers and sport fishermen, can help you organize and hold small tools, fasteners, and other items you need on a job.

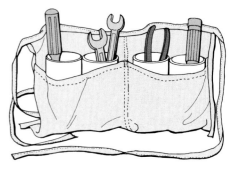

Pockets for tools ▲

Use empty tin cans, frozen juice cans, or short lengths of 2-inch plastic pipe to transform the deep, wide pockets of a nail pouch into a convenient tote for wrenches, pliers, and screwdrivers. If you use cans, remove their tops and bottoms. Glue or tape the cylinders together to keep them from shifting around, and slip them into the pouches to create dividers.

Tool roll-up

A handy way to store drill bits, chisels, and files is to roll them up in one of those segmented silverware pouches. If you don't have one, make your own by sewing parallel seams in a nail pouch.

Multipurpose box ▶

This simple plywood toolbox doubles as a step for reaching high places or as a portable mini workbench/sawhorse. Make the box 15 inches high, 26 to 30 inches wide, and just deep enough to accommodate a sturdy plastic cutlery tray. (Use the tray for storing small tools, bits, and fasteners.) Using a saber saw, make cutouts for carrying the unit.

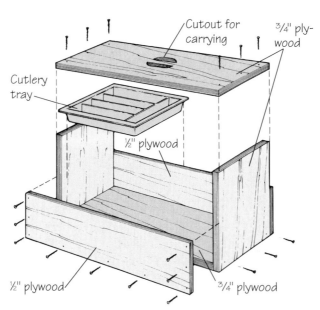

Cutout for carrying

3/4" plywood

Cutlery tray

1/2" plywood

1/2" plywood

3/4" plywood

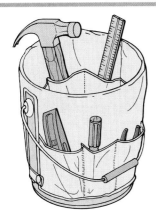

Bucket belts ▲

Turn an empty 5-gallon plastic pail into a handy tool hauler by fitting it with a sturdy tool, or carpenter's, belt. Some hardware stores and home centers may even carry "belts" specially designed for buckets, such as the 14-pocket fold-over style shown here. Even when filled, either version will leave plenty of room in the bucket for storing larger tools, such as saws, levels, extension cords, and small power tools.

Keeping track

Tag time

Before lending a tool, write your name on a stick-on label and affix it to the handle. The label will serve as a reminder to the borrower to return the tool when the job is done.

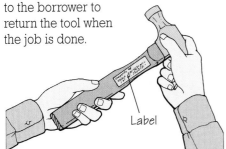

Label

Permanent ID

Another way to identify your tools permanently (and discourage thieves in the process) is to engrave your name on them with an electric etcher.

Show your colors

If you are working with a partner on a job and are using similar tools, code them with colored tape so there'll be no mix-ups at the end of the day. Using reflective tape provides an added advantage: A mislaid tool is easier to spot by day and, with a flashlight, by night.

Rust busting

An ounce of prevention

Moisture in the air invites rust, and if moist air gets into a toolbox, it corrodes the tools. One way to keep the air in your toolbox dry is to drop in some packets of silica gel, sold at hardware stores and craft shops or available free in the packing of new products. Once the silica gel becomes saturated, renew the packets by placing them near a lit 60-watt light bulb for 15 minutes.

Two more ounces of prevention

Other effective moisture absorbers that will keep the contents of your toolbox rust-free are a handful of mothballs and a 1-ounce cube of camphor (sold at local pharmacies). Because camphor loses its effectiveness after about 6 months, you'll have to replace the cube twice a year.

The brush-off

If your tools do become corroded, you'll find that a wire brush is useful for scrubbing off the rust. To make your own sturdy brush, all you need is a strip of window screening and a screw cap from a bottle of laundry detergent. First, make a fringe of wire "bristles" at one edge of the screening by cutting two or three rows of horizontal wire strands. Then roll up the screening tightly, secure it with wire, and wedge it firmly in the cap.

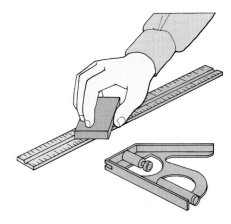

Wonderful bar ▲

A molded rubber and silicon carbide bar works like an eraser to clean and polish metal that's become dirty and corroded. To clean a tool, just rub the bar over the surface and wipe off the dust. You can use it dry or wet (with water, oil, or detergent). These lightweight flexible bars are sold through major tool and woodworking catalogs.

WORKSHOP ORGANIZATION

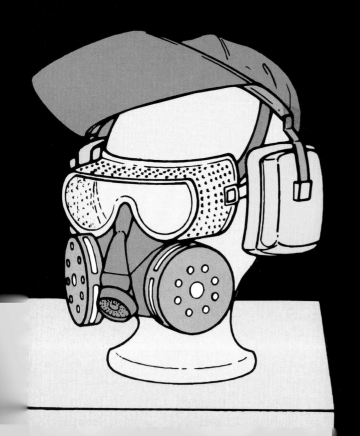

SHOP BASICS

Creature comforts

Foot ease

Here's relief from tired feet and legs: Cover the floor in front of your workbench with a scrap of low-pile carpet. Besides providing cushioning, it prevents a major cause of leg discomfort— the transfer of body heat from legs and feet to cold concrete. And it cleans easily with a shop vacuum. You can also reduce strain on leg and back muscles by standing on a rubber antifatigue mat, available from home centers and floor covering stores.

Trailer clearance light

Home alone ▲

Can't hear the doorbell in your shop? Buy a 12-volt trailer clearance light at an auto parts store and connect it to the doorbell wiring at the point where the wires run closest to your shop. Install it at eye level so that it will catch your attention whenever someone rings the bell. For your shop phone, telephone stores carry a simple device that turns a light on and off when the phone rings.

Attention getter

Family members can also call you to come to dinner or to the phone by "ringing" a trailer clearance light. Just hook it to a separate doorbell transformer and to a doorbell button inside the house. It's a lot safer than getting an unexpected tap on your shoulder while you're running a machine.

It's not the heat

If your workshop is damp, install a dehumidifier. In addition to making life less muggy for you, it will keep tools from rusting, prevent lumber from swelling, and speed the drying of glue, paint, and other finishes.

Clearing the air

To rid your shop of fine dust particles and noxious fumes, it's essential to have good cross-ventilation. If your shop has two facing windows, open one and place a fan in the other so that it blows out. If there is only one window, consider installing an exhaust fan in the wall opposite it.

Chilly workshop?

Give it a quick warm-up by installing an infrared heat lamp over your workbench. It will warm your hands and tools so that you can work on cool days. Use a heat lamp that screws into a regular light bulb socket (make sure the socket is ceramic). Heat lamps typically draw 250 watts, so check that the wiring can handle the lamp plus whatever other equipment you use on that circuit.

Extended work season

Is your shop in an unfinished, unheated garage? For the cost of insulation, you can use the space for a greater part of the year and increase your comfort in both hot and cold weather. Give priority to the roof, where most heat is lost or gained. Staple fiberglass batts, vapor barrier down, between the joists or rafters, or install a ceiling of wallboard and lay insulation between the joists. ▼

Save steps

Take a cue from kitchen designers. Arrange your shop in an efficient triangle that puts the workbench, tool storage, and assembly areas all within easy reach of one another. Set up your lumber storage and wood-cutting and wood-shaping tools in similar fashion. ▼

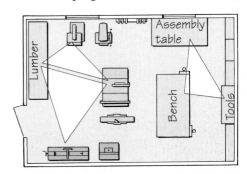

Assembly table

Lumber

Bench

Tools

SHOP BASICS

Noise control

Shop door sealants

Keep both noise and dirt out of the rest of the house by sealing the gaps around your shop door. Tack spring metal or tubular gasket weatherstripping along the edges of the frame and mount a sweep along the door bottom. If yours is a lightweight hollow-core door, glue or staple acoustical tiles on its shop side or replace it with a solid lumber door.

Sound barrier

Contain workshop noises by sound-proofing the walls between your shop and living areas. If a wall is unfinished, install batts of fiberglass insulation between the studs and cover them with wallboard. Cover a finished wall (or ceiling) with acoustical tiles, or even better, apply sound-deadening board, such as corkboard or beaverboard, and a second layer of wallboard.

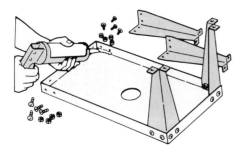

Glue rattling parts together ▲

To silence a freestanding piece of shop equipment, take apart its base, stand, or cabinet. As you reassemble the piece, apply a bead of silicone sealant wherever metal parts join. This will bond the parts and keep them from vibrating against one another.

Clamp down on vibes

Reduce the noisy vibrations of a bench-top power tool by putting a rubber pad or carpet scrap under each tool leg and clamping the tool to the bench.

Shedding light

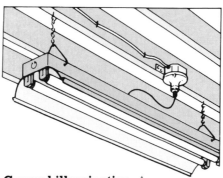

General illumination ▲

Replace overhead incandescent bulbs with fluorescent fixtures, which are cheaper to operate, last longer, and give an even diffused light. Suspend two-tube units over major work areas. Choose 48-inch units or, for a large shop, 96-inch ones. Plug each unit directly into a ceiling light outlet. If that's not possible, have an electrician install permanently wired units. Fluorescents sometimes give less light below 10°C (50°F). If your shop is unheated, get units with low-temperature ballasts or buy enclosed fixtures that hold the heat.

Reflected glory

To improve visibility in your shop, paint wall and ceiling areas white or a light color (the lighter the color, the better it will reflect both natural and artificial light). In a basement, paint the window wells white for better daylight reflection.

Workbench lighting

A folding-arm lamp is perfect for close work. But having it clamped on the workbench edge can limit its usefulness.

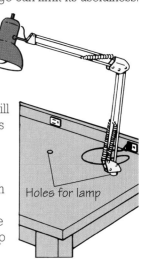

Holes for lamp

To put the lamp wherever you need it, remove the lamp bracket and drill holes at various points in the bench top for the lamp to fit into. Make each hole the same diameter as the hole in the lamp bracket.

Mobile light

Clip-on lamps with reflectors also provide a flexible source of light for close work. If you don't have a shelf that you can attach them to, mount a 1 x 2 on the wall a foot or two above your workbench. This arrangement will let you light your work from many different angles or from two angles at once. ▼

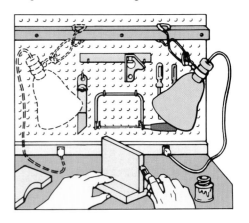

Prevent popping lights

Flying debris produced by power tools can shatter a hot light bulb. Use shatter-proof bulbs or tape window screening over the front of the lamp reflector.

Power supply

Dust off

Keep your shop's electrical outlets from becoming sawdust-clogged fire hazards. Cap unused receptacles with plug-in "childproof" plastic covers. Or install outdoor weatherproof covers that snap shut when a receptacle is not in use.

Cord hangers

Use clip-on clothespins to keep power cords out of your way. Screw or glue them to overhead joists or other strategic spots. Or, for a hanger that lets a cord move without chafing it, slit a short length of old garden hose diagonally. Open the slit to tack the hanger in place and to insert or remove the cord. ▼

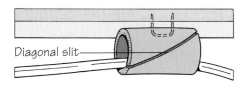

Diagonal slit

Convenient outlets

A multi-outlet power strip installed under the front edge of your workbench provides a handy place to plug in power tools while keeping cords out of your way. Use a CSA-approved, grounded (or GFCI-protected) power strip with a fuse or circuit breaker to prevent overloads. Make sure it is rated to handle the maximum amperage that you will use on it.

Power from above

For easy access to electricity, hang a retractable (reel-type) extension cord from a hook screwed into an overhead joist. Or mount a multi-outlet power strip on a drop-down board bolted to a joist, as shown. Plug your new overhead power source into a ceiling light outlet. If you have to run an extension cord to it, secure the cord loosely with slit-hose hangers, like the one shown below, left. Permanently attaching an extension cord violates most electrical codes. ▼

Turn button

Board swings up when not in use

Rewiring?

Make sure you have enough circuits and well-located GFCI-protected outlets for future needs. Have your electrician install a subpanel near the shop to control all shop circuits. This way, you can easily turn off all power to the shop and lock the subpanel to prevent unapproved use of your power tools. By placing the subpanel near the shop, you also won't have far to go when a breaker trips or if an emergency requires you to turn off the power as quickly as possible.

SAFETY FIRST

AVOID SHOCK

Here are some simple ways to cut electrical risks in your shop:

GFCI's. Equip your shop with ground-fault circuit interrupters (GFCI's). If there is a power leakage, a GFCI stops the power almost instantly, fast enough to save you from a life-threatening shock. Use plug-in GFCI outlets, or have permanently wired GFCI receptacles or circuit breakers installed. GFCI-protected receptacles are widely required by code on new basement and garage wiring. (See GFCI's on p.205.)

Cords and plugs. Replace frayed or cracked cords and plugs. Damaged cords are extremely dangerous and should be replaced immediately. Never try to fix a cord with electrical tape. Keep cords from underfoot and away from the work area as much as possible. Always use heavy-duty cords rated to handle more current than your tools will draw (see chart, p.43). Avoid octopus outlets and spaghetti tangles.

Grounding. If you have a metal workbench, have it grounded to reduce the chances of a shock from shorted equipment. An electrician can ground it by running a wire from the bench to an electrical subpanel or other metallic electrical conduit.

THE WORKBENCH

AN ALL-PURPOSE BENCH

No workbench is ideal for everyone, but this sturdy, easily assembled design will fit many needs. It has two shelves for power tools and room for a shop vacuum underneath. It measures 66 inches long, 24 inches deep, and 36 inches high. Feel free to modify it to fit your needs.

Materials: You'll need five 12-foot 2 x 4's, two 4 x 8-foot sheets of ½-inch sanded G1S-grade plywood, 2¾-inch and 1¾-inch drywall screws, wood glue, and 6d nails.

Assembly: First, screw together the frames for the top and the two shelves, and screw the legs to them. Then screw on the side and back bottom frame pieces, the shelf ends and shelves, and the side and back panels. Tack one top piece to the frame, spread wood glue on it, and screw the other sheet to it and the frame. Predrill holes for all screws.

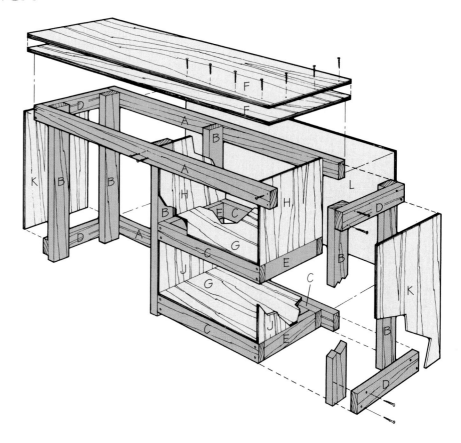

Cutting guides

Plywood (48" x 96" sheets)

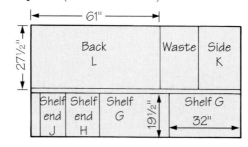

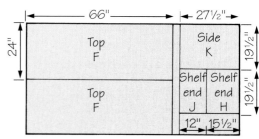

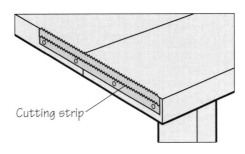

Side view

24"

22½"

1½"

21"

Front view

66"

1½"

32"

33"

1½"

63"

2 x 4's (72" lengths)

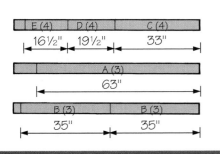

E (4)	D (4)	C (4)

16½"   19½"   33"

A (3)

63"

B (3)	B (3)

35"   35"

Bench amenities

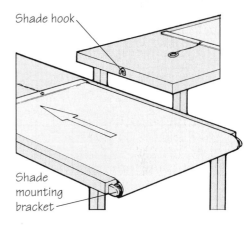

Cutting strip

Handy cutter ▲

Tack a cutting strip from a foil or plastic wrap box to your workbench and use it to cut tape and cords. An old hacksaw blade will also work. Mount the cutter on an edge that's easily accessible but where you're unlikely to brush against it.

Hooked in place

If your bench tends to move when you are working on it, attach each end to a wall stud with a hook and eye.

Sprout a leaf

½" steel rod

Add extra inches to your workbench when you need them with a removable extension leaf. Cut a 2 x 10 or 2 x 12 to fit along the edge. Drill matching ½-inch holes, 6 inches deep, in the leaf and the bench edge. Then fit ½-inch steel rods, 12 inches long, in the holes.

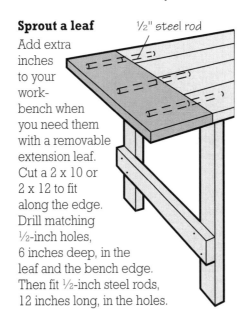

Solid bench top

Want a bench top with the durability of hardwood butcher block without the cost? Get a birch solid-core flush door from your lumberyard.

Bench top savers

Roll-on protection

To avoid staining your bench with paint, mount an old window shade on one end. When painting, pull out the shade and hook it to the other end. Let the painted object dry before rerolling the shade. ▼

Shade hook

Shade mounting bracket

Cheap resurfacing

For a smooth surface that can take a lot of punishment, tack ¼-inch hardboard over your bench top and seal it with pure tung oil. When it becomes pitted, just flip it over or replace it. Also use a scrap of 2 x 12 as a cutting board to absorb drill holes and saw and knife cuts.

Mat top

Don't mar your project on a rough, battered bench top. Cover the work area with a rubber bath mat or carpet scrap.

OTHER SHOP FURNITURE

Sawhorse savvy

Soft saddle

The scraggy saw-chewed top rails of most sawhorses can scratch finished wood or furniture. To provide a non-marring surface, cover a foot or two at one end of the rails with scrap carpeting. Even better, make a cap for each sawhorse from two 1 x 3's and a 1 x 4 as shown, and cover its top with carpet. Then you can slip the caps on the sawhorses whenever you need them. ▼

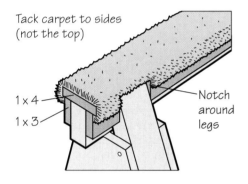

Tack carpet to sides (not the top)

1 x 4
1 x 3

Notch around legs

Tools at your fingertips

Add a tool tray between the legs of your sawhorse. Make a shallow box—a 1 x 4 frame with a plywood bottom—and attach it to cross braces running between each pair of legs. Put the tray on just one sawhorse so the pair will still stack.

Instant measure

Nail, screw, or glue an old steel tape measure blade to the side of your sawhorse's top rail. You'll find it invaluable every time you need to make a cut. Don't use a wooden yardstick because most yardsticks aren't accurate enough.

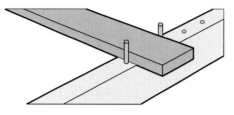

Sawhorse dogs ▲

To hold your work in place on saw-horses, drill a series of holes along each top rail, then put nails or pegs in the holes. Measuring from a hole near the rail's center, make the distance to each hole correspond to a standard lumber dimension—$1\frac{1}{2}$, $2\frac{1}{2}$, $3\frac{1}{2}$, $4\frac{1}{2}$, $5\frac{1}{2}$, $7\frac{1}{4}$, $9\frac{1}{4}$, and $11\frac{1}{4}$ inches (see chart, p.67). At most, you'll need to apply light hand pressure to steady a piece.

Build your own ▶

Here is a design for a strong sawhorse with the load bearing directly on the legs. There are no nails in the top rails to dam-age your saw blade, and the slot between the rails serves as a built-in handle for easy carrying. The sawhorse is made entirely from 2 x 4's, and all ends are cut square or at a $17\frac{1}{2}°$ angle.

Knock-down horses

Here's a way to quickly set up and take apart sawhorses made with standard metal sawhorse brackets and 2 x 4's. Screw the brackets to the legs, but not to the top rail. On each pair of legs, hinge a brace on one leg and cut a slot for it on the other leg. When you force the brace between the legs, the bracket bites into the top rail and forms a sturdy sawhorse. When you release the brace, the rail lifts out and the legs fold.

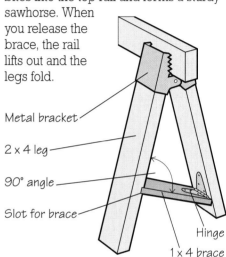

Metal bracket
2 x 4 leg
90° angle
Slot for brace
Hinge
1 x 4 brace

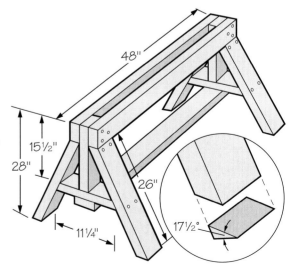

48"
15½"
28"
11¼"
26"
17½°

Sawhorse substitute

No sawhorse? Your stepladder can often provide instant support for sawing, sanding, planing, or painting lumber. Simply lay the ladder on its side, open its legs, and support the lumber as shown.

Relieve your aching back

When oversize projects force you out onto the driveway or patio, don't keep stooping to retrieve drills, saws, rulers, pencils, and other items from the ground. Instead, take along this fold-up tool table. Made of ¾-inch plywood, the table is bench height when set up but only 5 inches deep when collapsed. ▼

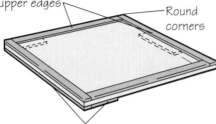

24" square top with ½" molding around upper edges

Round corners

Nail molding under top to position base

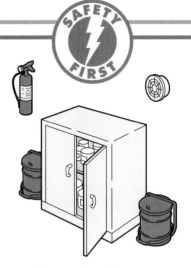

FIGHTING FIRE

In a home workshop, a fire extinguisher is more essential than any piece of furniture. Get one rated ABC, indicating that it can handle most common types of fires: wood and paper, flammable liquid, and electrical. Locate it in a highly visible, easily accessible place away from volatile substances, preferably near an exit. Check periodically to make sure it's fully charged. Install a smoke alarm as well. Keep flammable paints and solvents in sealed containers in a locked metal cabinet. Don't store them near any flame source or in a living area, basement, or confined space with little airflow. Also get two self-sealing metal garbage cans—one for sawdust and wood chips and the other for oily and solvent-soiled rags. Empty both cans frequently. (For more on the proper disposal of hazardous workshop waste materials, see p.39.)

Versatile pieces

Extra reach

Need to hold a wider piece in your portable workbench? Make four extension pieces from 1 x 2's. At one end of each piece, drill a hole and glue in a dowel that fits in the bench dog hole on the bench. At the other end of each piece, drill a hole that will accept the bench dog.

Bench dog

1 x 2 extension

Dowel

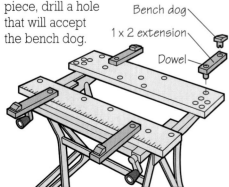

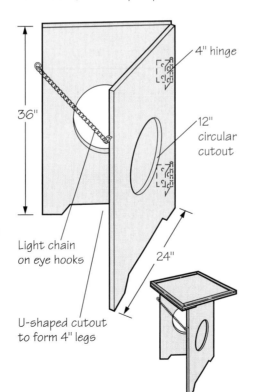

36"

4" hinge

12" circular cutout

Light chain on eye hooks

24"

U-shaped cutout to form 4" legs

SHOP STORAGE

Free organizers

Instant order

Get your shop shipshape fast by storing everything you can in same-size cardboard boxes. Cut off the tops, label the boxes by general categories, such as "plumbing" or "sandpaper," and arrange them alphabetically on shelves. Identical boxes measuring about 1 foot in height, width, and depth work well. Storage-shipping firms and office supply stores are good box sources.

Recycled dish rack

Turn that old vinyl-coated wire dish rack into storage racks. Use bolt cutters and pliers to cut and bend the rack into the sizes and shapes you need. The long sides of a dish rack make convenient wall racks for hanging tools and supplies. Turn the bottom and ends into a portable table rack by bending the cut wire ends at the bottom and fitting them into holes in wood dowels as shown. ▼

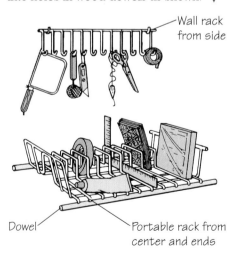

Wall rack from side

Dowel

Portable rack from center and ends

Serving up hardware

Turn discarded muffin pans (or other items with a projecting top lip such as baking pans, cookie sheets, or cafeteria trays) into pullout shelves for tools or fasteners. Mount the trays in a box made of plywood with grooves routed in the sides so that the trays can slide in and out of the box. ▼

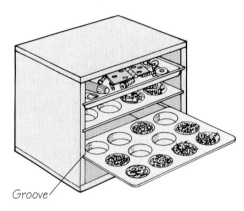

Groove

Perf-board lore

Put it everywhere

Don't limit your use of perforated hardboard, such as Peg-Board, to shop walls. Mount it on the inside of cabinet doors and on the sides of your workbench and cabinets. Lightweight $1/8$-inch perf board is fine for hand tools; use $1/4$-inch perf board for heavier items. (To install perf board, see p.127.)

Hook security

Keep a perf-board hook from coming loose by putting a dab of hot glue on the ends that hook into the board. If you need to move the hook, a light tug will usually free it. If necessary, you can soften the glue with a heat gun.

Outline reminder

You'll always return tools to their proper places on perf board if you outline each tool with a wide felt-tip marker. Or put up tool silhouettes cut out of a colored adhesive plastic such as Con-Tact.

Drawer magic

Protect your toes

To avoid pulling a heavy drawer out too far and spilling its contents, paint lines on the drawer edges to indicate how far it can be safely pulled out. Also attach a wood block on the back that will catch on the frame. Pivot the block and make one end longer than the other. That way it will hang vertically but you can turn it aside to take out the drawer. ▼

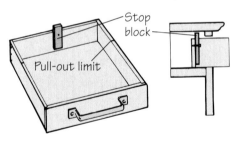

Stop block

Pull-out limit

Stronger pull

Does the handle on a tool-laden drawer keep pulling off? Replace it with a garage door handle secured with bolts going through the drawer front. Put a flat washer, then a lock washer, on each bolt before screwing on the nut. ▼

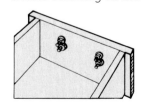

Garage shop shelves

Open stud wall?

Narrow 1 x 4 shelves installed between open studs in a garage workshop are ideal for storing quart cans of paint, jars of fasteners, and auto supplies. Secure the shelves with 2½-inch drywall screws going through predrilled holes in the studs into the shelf ends; stagger the shelves in adjacent spaces. ▼

Deeper shelves on studs ▲

To store larger items in the space between studs, install ¾-inch plywood shelves supported by 2 x 4 brackets. When making a bracket, cut the diagonal support's ends at a 45° angle; attach both pieces to the stud and to each other with 2½-inch drywall screws. Mount a bracket on every other stud for a moderate load, on every stud for heavier loads. Notch the shelves to fit around the studs, and attach them to the brackets with 1½-inch drywall screws.

UTILITY SHELVING

Great for basement workshops with no exposed studs to hold shelves, this freestanding four-shelf, 11½-inch-deep storage unit can be up to 98 inches high and up to 36 inches wide. To make it, you need five 8-foot 2 x 2's, two 6-foot 1 x 12's, one 8-foot 1 x 4, and two 8-foot 1 x 2's; use construction-grade lumber. Multiple units can be screwed together.

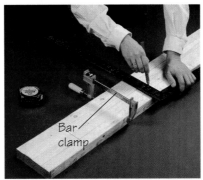

Bar clamp

1 Clamp four of the 2 x 2's together. With a carpenter's square and pencil, mark across all four pieces the overall length you want the legs and the position of each cleat. Cut the legs to size.

2 From the remaining 2 x 2, cut cleats that are the same length as the shelves' depth. Then align each cleat on a marked line and attach it to the legs with 2½-in. drywall screws.

3 Cut the shelves to the length you want. With the end frames on edge, secure the shelves to the cleats with 1½-in. drywall screws. Stand the unit up and check that it's level and square.

4 Mark and cut a 1 x 4 brace to run diagonally across the back from the top shelf to the bottom shelf. Attach it with 1½-in. drywall screws. Add 1 x 2 braces to both sides the same way.

SHOP STORAGE

Handy hand tools

Easy-reach holder

Make a tool holder out of scrap wire mesh (also called hardware cloth). Form the mesh into the shape shown below by bending it over the edge of a board, and attach it to the wall with screws and washers. A ½-inch square mesh holds a variety of tools. ▼

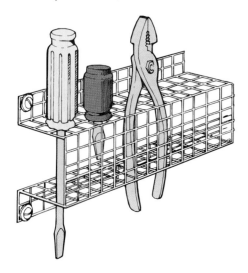

Holding power

For a convenient spot to park screwdrivers, scissors, punches, and other small hand tools, screw a magnetic knife-holder strip to the underside of a shelf over your workbench. Available in kitchenware stores, these powerful magnetic strips can hold hardware items, tool wrenches, and chuck keys, too; they work equally well when mounted on the sides of the stands for table saws and other large stationary tools.

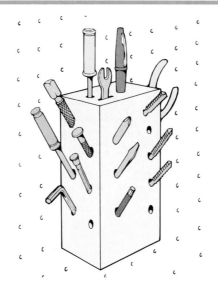

Small tool organizer ▲

Mount a block of polystyrene foam, such as Styrofoam, above your workbench and press punches, bits, knives, screwdrivers, and other such tools into it to keep them handy. Buy the foam plastic from a home center or craft store, or recycle foam used as packing material.

Tool belt

Tack an old leather or strong canvas belt along the edge of a shelf to hold tools. As you nail it, leave small loops in the belt for tools to slip into. ▼

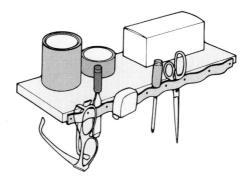

Handle holder

Chest handles—standard hardware store items—are great for hanging large tools, such as hammers and hand axes. Mount the handles on a plywood backing, putting them upside-down so that the handles stick out from the wall. You can recycle the drop handles from the sides of an old metal garbage can the same way.

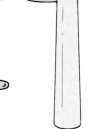

Orderly power tools

Power tower

To keep power tools handy, build a tall, narrow box out of 1 x 12's or plywood. Then staple carpet scraps between the sides to form soft cradles for your tools.

Concentrated power

Put your most frequently used power tools on a solidly mounted shelf over your workbench. Cut slots along the back for your circular and saber saws, and bore 1-inch holes along the front for your drill, power driver, and router. ▼

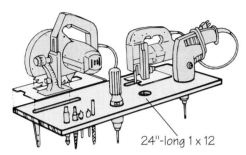

24"-long 1 x 12

In the wall

Another way to keep tools close at hand yet out of the way is to store them on shelves built between exposed studs. Make the shelves out of 1 x 4's, and cut notches into them so that the tools seat firmly. Nail 1 x 2 cleats to the studs, angling them slightly downward toward the wall to keep the tools from falling. Then glue the shelves to the cleats with construction adhesive. ▼

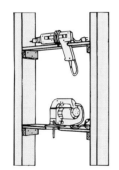

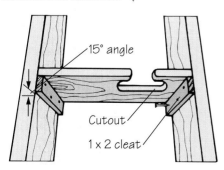

15° angle

Cutout

1 x 2 cleat

String out

Make a dispenser for string by cutting off the bottom half of a 2-liter plastic bottle. Then mount the top half upside-down on the wall with the string coming out of the bottle neck.

All-in-one tape dispenser

A toilet paper holder mounted on a shop wall or on a workbench makes a great dispenser for as many as five or six rolls of masking, friction, duct, and other types of tape. For easy cutting, tie scissors to the dispenser with a length of string.

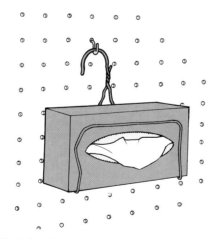

Quick wipes ▲

Facial tissues are great for quickly cleaning up water, oil, and glue and for wiping your hands when the phone rings. To make a holder for a box of tissues, bend a wire coat hanger as shown and hang it on a hook or a nail.

FIRST-AID KITS

An inexpensive and essential safety item for any shop is a well-stocked first-aid kit. Buy one at a local drugstore, and mount it where it is easy to see and reach. A standard kit will include antiseptic, bandages, gauze, elastic and adhesive tape, cotton swabs, eye drops, tweezers, and scissors. Latex gloves and an instant cold pack are also useful. Make sure the container closes tightly to keep out dirt and dust.

When working with paint, solvents, strippers, or any chemical with an eye hazard warning, keep a squeeze bottle of eyewash solution handy. If any chemical gets into your eyes, use the solution immediately. If a chemical irritates your skin, wash it off with water. *A first-aid kit is for minor injuries only. Get prompt medical attention for a serious injury such as a deep cut or puncture or a head blow. Also see a doctor if eye irritation persists after washing.*

SHOP STORAGE

Nuts 'n' nails

Self-identification

Here's an easy way to label boxes of nails, screws, and other fasteners: Just attach a sample of each item to the outside of its box with a hot-glue gun. You'll be able to see in a glance what you have in stock and where it is.

Recycled labels

If you store screws or other fasteners in small glass jars, cut the label from the package the item was purchased in and push the label inside the jar before filling it. Hold the label face out against the inside of the jar as you pour in the fasteners. The label will remain visible through the glass.

Great cheap parts bins

Use clean plastic oil containers to make bins for screws, bolts, nuts, and other small items. Cut each container as shown with scissors or a utility knife; make a simple wooden frame to hold the bins. ▼

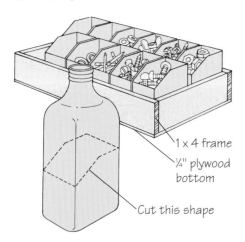

1 x 4 frame
¼" plywood bottom
Cut this shape

Spill preventer

Put a magnet in a container of small items such as screws or brads. This way, the metal pieces will bind together in a ball around the magnet and won't spill out if you accidentally knock over the container. If a few items do scatter, use the magnet to pick them up. For inexpensive magnets, buy a roll of magnetic edging at a hardware store and cut it into whatever lengths you need.

Nut rings

Store nuts and washers on metal shower curtain rings hung from perf-board hooks. (The ring's pear shape and latching action allow for secure storage.) Hang nuts and washers of similar size on their own ring, so that you can find the right size quickly. ▼

Ready-made storage modules

Plastic electrical boxes, either single or double size, are just right for storing small items like fasteners. The boxes are inexpensive, and they stack or fit neatly side by side. Just make sure to remove any flanges or "wings" meant for attaching the boxes to studs.

Neat nail organizers ▲

Large plastic bottles with a section of their tops cut out make great nail bins. When the bottles are stored on their sides, the weight of the nails keeps them from rolling. Off the shelves, the bottles can stand upright, and their handles make for easy carrying to a job site.

Workbench catchall

Don't let nuts, bolts, and other leftovers clutter your workbench. Bolt a cake or muffin pan under a shelf. Swing it out and drop your odds and ends into it as you work. Occasionally pick over the pan's contents to separate the useful from the useless. ▼

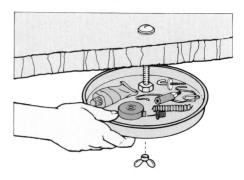

Under-shelf storage

Make the most of your workshop shelf space by storing nails, nuts, and other fasteners in jars attached to the underside of a shelf. To mount the jars, simply screw their lids to the bottom of the shelf (place a washer under each screwhead for better security). ▼

Lumber and long goods

Gutter shelving

Inexpensive vinyl rain gutters provide convenient, surprisingly strong storage for molding, lightweight lumber, pipes, and other long thin items. To install them, just screw the mounting brackets to studs and snap in the gutters. Use the brackets alone as hooks for garden hoses, extension cords, and wire coils. ▼

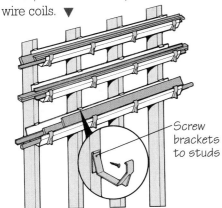

Screw brackets to studs

Stand-up storage

Fill a sturdy cardboard box with sawed-off shipping tubes (or scraps of large-diameter PVC pipe) and use it to organize all those short pieces of molding, pipe, and dowels.

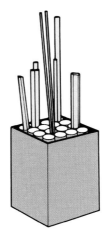

Retreads

Tie a series of old auto tires to overhead joists and use them to hold long pieces of lumber and pipe. You can also lay old tires flat on the floor or ground to provide a pallet that will keep lumber and plywood sheets high and dry.

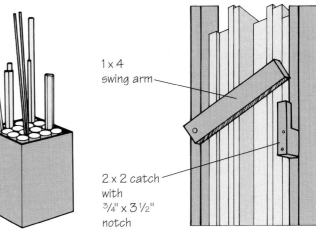

1 x 4 swing arm

2 x 2 catch with ³⁄₄" x 3 ¹⁄₂" notch

Easy-reach lumber ▲

Store lumber vertically between open studs. Hold it in place with a 1 x 4 swing arm, fastened to one stud with a 2-inch drywall screw. Make a catch on the other stud with a piece of 2 x 2, notched and attached with 3-inch drywall screws.

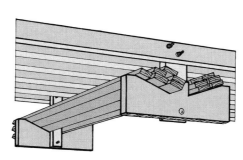

Timber overhead ▲

Keep lumber out of the way yet handy with these "inverted T" racks. Bolt two to the bottom of your garage roof trusses; space them about 5 ¹⁄₂ feet apart to support 8-foot lengths of lumber. To avoid straining the trusses, limit stored pieces to the equivalent of twenty 2 x 4's and distribute the load evenly.

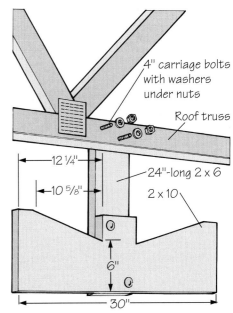

4" carriage bolts with washers under nuts

Roof truss

12 ¹⁄₄"

10 ⁵⁄₈"

24"-long 2 x 6

2 x 10

6"

30"

SHOP CLEANUP

Picking up small items

Nuts and bolts scoop

Get small fasteners back into their containers quickly with a scoop made from a plastic juice jug or fabric softener container that has a handle. Use kitchen shears to cut off the bottom half of the jug at an angle as shown. ▼

Magnetic bagger

Here's an easy way to pick up spilled washers, nuts, or nails: Drop a bar magnet into a plastic sandwich bag. The spilled items will stick to the magnet through the plastic. Then turn the bag inside out and pour the items back into their container. Similarly, to clean up small metallic filings, put plastic wrap around a magnet, sweep it over the work area, then fold the wrap over the filings and discard it.

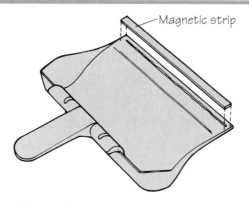
Magnetic strip

Magnetic sweep ▲

Separate out screws, nails, and other potentially reusable small metal items while sweeping up. Use contact cement to glue a flexible magnetic strip onto the edge of a dustpan. The items will cling to the strip when you empty the pan.

Dust busting

Brush it off

No vacuum readily at hand? Trim the frayed bristles from an old paintbrush and use it to sweep fine sawdust or filings from your bench top or to clean out blind corners on a drill press or lathe. Also, keep a child's broom handy for sweeping around stationary tools, workbench legs, and other tight spots you can't reach with a regular broom.

Blow it away

If you have a spare hair dryer, use it to blow away dust, dirt, and shavings in the shop; to dry sweaty hands before handling new lumber; and to speed the drying of paint touch-ups.

Enclose it

Before undertaking a large messy sanding or sawing job, tape or staple plastic sheets around the work area to contain the dust. If your home's heating or cooling ducts serve your shop, turn off the system while doing heavy sanding; otherwise it will spread fine particles all over the house.

Trap it

To capture fine airborne dust when sawing or sanding, mount a furnace filter on the air-intake side of a box fan, using duct tape, wire, or an elastic stretch cord. Put the fan next to your work area, blowing away from you. Vacuum the filter when it becomes filled with dust. ▼

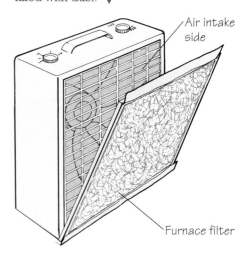
Air intake side

Furnace filter

Recycle it

Save the sawdust from your shop projects. It will come in handy for soaking up grease, oil, paint, or other spills. You can also use it to rub glue off your hands or mix it with carpenter's glue to make a wood filler.

Vacuuming

Thrifty timesaver

Extend the life of your shop vacuum filter and avoid having to clean it frequently. Cut off the legs of an old pair of panty hose, tie the cut ends as shown, and then stretch the waistband top over the filter. The suction won't be affected, and you can clean the panty hose by just rinsing it.

Easy-empty vacuum

To avoid the mess of emptying a shop vacuum, line the vacuum canister with a large plastic trash bag (fold the bag over the canister rim so the top holds the bag in place). To empty the vacuum, all you need to do is take the bag out.

Long reach

If the crevice tool on your vacuum isn't long enough to reach the accumulated sawdust behind your shop cabinets, make your own extra-long crevice vacuum attachment using the cardboard tube from a roll of gift-wrap paper. Fit one tube end in the hose nozzle and secure it with duct tape. Then flatten the tube along the rest of its length.

BUYING A SHOP VACUUM

A wet/dry shop vacuum is an invaluable aid that quickly gobbles up sawdust, large chips, and nails as well as large and small spills. You can also hook one to a sander or other tool to remove dust as you work (but a vacuum is no substitute for a proper dust collector if you do a lot of sawing and sanding).

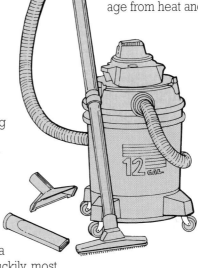

Power and performance. Determining a shop vacuum's power is not an easy matter. Neither a high "peak horsepower" nor a gee-whiz demonstration of lifting power is a reliable indicator of a unit's capabilities. Luckily, most brand-name units sold in home centers and department stores are adequate for a home workshop. If you do want to compare units, multiply the vacuum's "sealed pressure" (also called sealed suction, water lift, static pressure, or just SP) by its "airflow" (given in cfm, cubic feet per minute). The resulting figure should be at least 5,000; the higher the number, the better. If the information is not available at the store, most manufacturers will send product fact sheets on request.

Tank body. Plastic is the most common material and is fine for most workshops. It has the advantages of being lightweight, rust-proof, and dent-resistant. Steel, used on some higher-end models, is durable and less prone to damage from heat and solvents. A 10- to 16-gallon capacity is adequate for most home shops.

Filter type. If you vacuum mostly dry debris, a pleated paper cartridge filter provides more surface area for dust, reducing the number of filter cleanings. But the pleats are hard to clean when the dust is wet or caked on. If you do a lot of wet pickup, a flat paper (or foam) filter is better. Some units accept both filter types.

Attachments. Large- and small-diameter hoses (typically $2\frac{1}{2}$ and $1\frac{1}{4}$ inches) are available. A large-diameter hose is handy for picking up sawdust and chips, a small one for picking up nails and heavy particles. Many large-hose units have adaptors to accept small hoses. Extension wands, a floor nozzle, and a crevice tool are essential.

WORK GEAR AND PERSONAL CLEANUP

Work clothes

Take it off

Never wear a watch, ring, neck chain, or other piece of jewelry when working with a power tool. Mount a bright-colored hook over your workbench to hold these items. The hook will remind you to take them off when you come into the shop, and you'll always know where you put them.

Extended life

Reinforce knees, elbows, pocket bottoms, and other heavy-wear areas on work clothes by putting iron-on patches on their undersides. Coat the edges of pockets with clear fingernail polish to prevent fraying.

Rubber gloves hanger

Can't ever find your rubber (or work) gloves when you need them? Use a binder clip (available from office supply stores) to hang them on a perf-board hook in full view. ▼

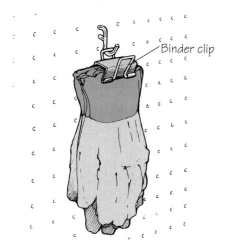

Binder clip

Coming to grips

Rub clear silicone sealant onto the palms of your work gloves. Once the sealant cures you'll be able to get a much firmer grip with the gloves.

Safety gloves

Fine sawdust can make your fingers slip when you are working with a power tool. To avoid this, wear household latex gloves with nonslip palms. Put talcum powder inside the gloves to ensure easy removal. To cut down on the likelihood of your slipping on a dust-strewn floor, wear rubber-soled shoes.

Trim off bottom

Instant aprons ▲

Keep a box of plastic garbage bags in your shop to use as aprons for messy chores; buy the type with built-in handles. Trim off an inch or so along the bottom of a bag, then pull it over your head, slipping your arms through the handles.

Easy-on, easy-off apron

Tired of fumbling to tie your shop apron behind your back? Replace the strings with a single piece of ½-inch twill tape (a standard sewing item). Sew the tape to one side of the apron; then attach it snugly and neatly to the other side of the apron with Velcro fasteners.

Eyewear

No more broken glasses

Do your reading glasses keep falling out of your shirt pocket when you bend over? Attach a removable metal clip from a ballpoint pen to one of your glasses' stems. Position the clip so that it catches comfortably in your pocket, and use pliers to gently squeeze it on. ▼

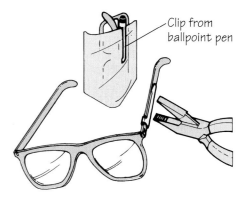

Clip from ballpoint pen

A clearer view

Fine sawdust tends to stick to safety glasses because of the static electricity that builds up in dry shop air. To cut static and remove dust, wipe the surface of your safety eyewear with a sheet of fabric softener—one already used in the dryer so that it won't scratch or smear the surface of the glasses.

Face-shield wrap

To keep your plastic face shield clean and scratch-free, cover the front with clear plastic wrap. It won't affect your vision, and when it gets dirty, you can just peel it off and replace it. ▼

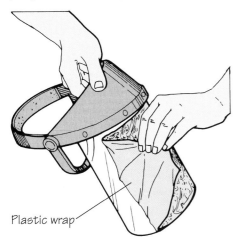

Plastic wrap

Quick spray and wipe

Keeping your safety goggles crystal clear takes only a matter of seconds if you just equip your workbench with a bottle of window cleaner and a roll of paper towels.

Keeping clean

Skin protection

Before beginning a messy job, give your exposed skin a light coat of petroleum jelly. It keeps paint or grease from getting into pores and washes off with soap. Rubbing undiluted liquid soap on your hands and letting it dry will also repel grease. To keep dirt from collecting under your fingernails, scrape your nails over a bar of soap first.

PROTECTIVE GEAR

Store your safety goggles, ear protectors, and respirator on a foam head made for displaying hats and wigs (a store that sells hats or wigs may be willing to give you an old foam head or at least the name of a supplier). Put the head in a prominent place in your shop, and it will serve as a constant reminder to use your safety gear. Here are some tips on selecting safety gear.

Eye protectors. Don't rely on ordinary eyeglasses to guard your eyes. Wear special protective safety glasses with side shields or safety goggles, which can be worn over your regular eyeglasses. For full face protection, wear a face shield.

Ear protectors. Earmuffs are easier to take off and put on than earplugs and harder to misplace. Your choice may depend on other equipment worn, eyeglasses, for example. A secure fit is vital.

Respiratory protectors. Choose a respirator for the specific hazard. There are models to protect against solvents, hazardous chemicals, sandblasting, and so on. For ordinary dust, use disposable dust masks. The Canadian Standards Association recommends products certified by agencies such as the National Institute for Occupational Safety and Health or the Mine Safety and Health Administration.

Safe and effective cleaner ▶

Clean your greasy or paint-stained hands with vegetable oil. It's inexpensive and works well. More important, it won't irritate your skin or be absorbed through it like solvents. Put the vegetable oil into a plastic spray bottle; that way, you can just spray it on your hands and it won't spill. Laundry prewash and shampoo for oily hair are also good grease busters.

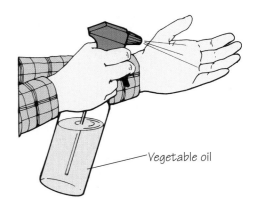

Vegetable oil

SHOP SKILLS

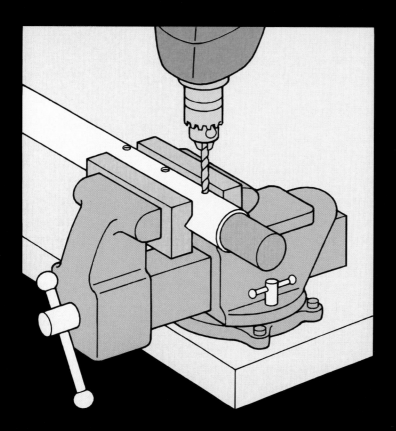

WOOD BASICS

Buying wood

Numbers game

When buying a board, you'll find that its actual dimensions are smaller than those specified. That's because lumber is sold by "nominal size"—the size it is when it's cut at the mill. After planing and shrinkage, the actual size is a bit smaller. To remind you of lumber's real dimensions, make a chart and tack it to a shop wall.

Nominal size	Actual size
1 x 6	¾" x 5½"
1 x 8	¾" x 7¼"
1 x 10	¾" x 9¼"
1 x 12	¾" x 11¼"
2 x 2	1½" x 1½"
2 x 4	1½" x 3½"
2 x 8	1½" x 7¼"
2 x 12	1½" x 11¼"
4 x 4	3½" x 3½"

Board feet

Hardwood is sold by the board foot, which is determined by multiplying the nominal thickness by the nominal width (both in inches) by the actual length (in feet), then dividing by 12. A board that measures 1 inch x 12 inches x 1 foot and one that measures 2 inches x 6 inches x 1 foot both equal 1 board foot. Lumber is sold in lengths of 1-foot and (more commonly) 2-foot increments.

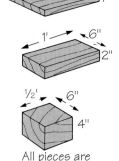

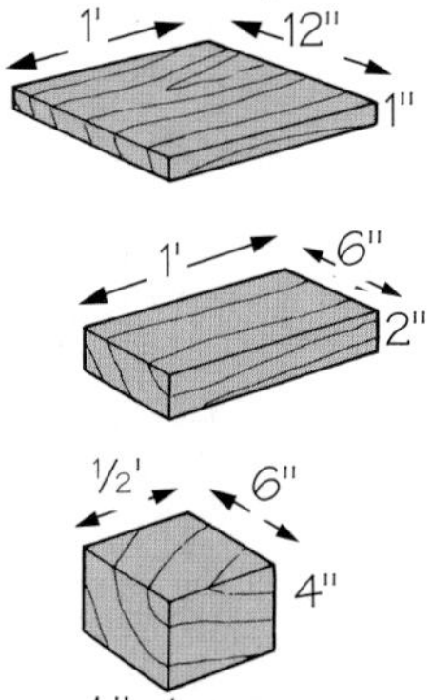

All pieces are 1 board foot

Resuscitating old lumber

Before chucking old lumber into the garbage, consider reusing it. Remove any nails (a magnetic stud finder will find nails covered by plugs). Fill the nail holes with wooden toothpicks or matchsticks dipped in wood glue. If a knot falls out, glue it back in with wood glue.

Warped

Is it straight?

If one side of a piece of lumber dries faster than another, the wetter side may develop a hump, or crown. To detect warpage, sight along the length of the board. A slight crown is to be expected, but reject any board that has a very pronounced one. Also check boards for cracks, stains, and other damage.

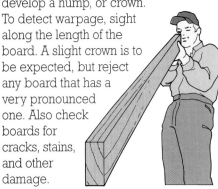

Stacking it up

To ensure air circulation and minimize warping, store boards off the ground and separate the layers with small dry strips of 1 x 1's. Position the strips at each end of the stack and at about 16-inch intervals along the length of the boards.

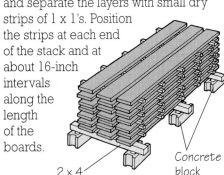

2 x 4   Concrete block

Get rid of that warpage

Place a warped board, concave side down, on wet grass on a sunny day. The ground moisture on the concave side of the board and the sun's heat on the convex side may straighten the board in 4 hours to 4 days. If one end is more warped than the other, weight it down with a heavy rock.

Getting a handle on it

Hammer carrier

Carrying a full sheet of plywood (or wallboard or paneling) can be awkward at best. A claw hammer can help. Hook the claws under the bottom edge of the plywood, near the center of the sheet. The hammer handle makes a convenient carrying grip. Use your free hand to steady the load.

All tied up ▲

Another way to carry a sheet of plywood is with an 18-foot-long rope tied into a loop. Slip the loop over the two bottom corners of the plywood sheet. Grasp the middle sections of the loop with one hand; steady the board with the other.

MEASURING

Boxed in

If you don't have a folding rule with a metal extension bar, you can still accurately measure inside a drawer or similar workpiece by using a retractable tape measure and a combination square. Place the square against one corner. Starting at the opposite corner, measure the remaining distance with the tape measure. Add the two measurements for the total width. ▼

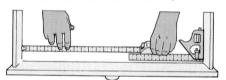

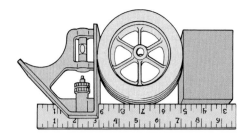

Too round for rules? ▲

Finding the exact diameter of a round object isn't that tricky. Place the object against a straightedge rule and between two blocks or other items with true straight edges. Then just read the diameter on the rule (the distance between the blocks). You can create variations of this gauge with a mix of try squares, framing squares, and combination squares.

Blind hole

Improvise a depth gauge for blind holes or recesses with a bolt and two nuts. With the nuts on the bolt, place the bolt in the hole. Twist the nuts down to the surface of the work. To hold the measure in place, tighten the top nut to the bottom one.

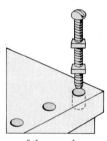

Rubber gauge

An auto mechanic's gauge for measuring tire treads is also a handy gadget for the woodworker. Use the gauge (which measures in increments down to $1/32$ inch) to check the depth of blind holes and shallow recesses.

Deep down

Use a combination square to determine the depth of a recess. Making sure the blade is free to slide, rest the square on a flat edge of the work. Adjust the blade to the depth of the recess, then lock the blade in place using the thumbscrew. Besides measuring the recess, you can use the square to transfer the depth dimension to other workpieces. ▼

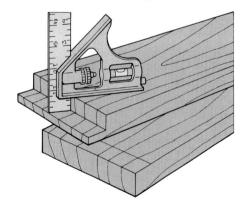

Bright idea

If you're not sure that an edge is straight, place it against a known straightedge and hold the two pieces up to a light. If the light shines through, the edge isn't straight. To straighten it, shave off the high spots with a file, sander, or plane.

Get it square

When making a rectangular object, such as a drawer, check that it is actually square. Here's how: First measure across the workpiece diagonally from corner to corner. Then measure the opposite diagonal. If the two measurements match, the workpiece is square.

Another angle

To make sure that a right angle is true, use the 3:4:5 method of triangulation. For example, to check a corner for squareness, measure 3 feet along one wall and 4 feet

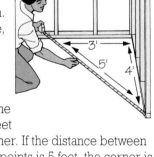

along the other. If the distance between the two end points is 5 feet, the corner is square. To create a right angle, tack two strings where you want the right angle to be. Measure out two legs of a triangle so that one is 3 feet and the other is 4 feet. Position the two legs so that the distance between their end points is 5 feet. You can also figure in inches or in multiples of 3, 4, and 5 if you use the same multiple for all three figures.

MARKING

Chalk it up

Back to school

To identify parts when assembling a project, use white or yellow blackboard chalk. It's easy to sand off, and chalk doesn't leave a hard-to-remove impression the way a pen or pencil can.

Snappy line

When marking building material with a chalk line, first remove excess chalk from the line by snapping it on the ground or subfloor or against studs or joists. Then you'll be ready to stretch the line over the material and snap it as usual. The result will be a crisp line.

Dividing rules

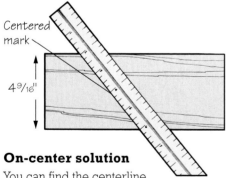

Centered mark

4⁹/₁₆"

On-center solution

You can find the centerline of an odd-size board without having to divide unwieldy fractions. Place a rule or measuring tape diagonally across the board with an even-numbered inch mark on each of the board's two edges. The inch mark halfway between these two numbers accurately locates the center of the board.

Plumb bobbing

A windy day can make it difficult to use a plumb bob. To keep the bob from bobbing around, sink the weighted end in a bucket of water. (The bob shouldn't touch the side or the bottom of the bucket.) Since you can't align the work

directly against the plumb bob cord, measure the distance between the work and the cord at the top and bottom. If they are aligned, the measurements will be the same.

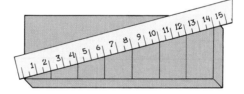

Equal time ▲

To mark equal segments, angle a ruler across the work. Place the beginning of the ruler on one edge of the work, and adjust the angle so that an inch mark divisible by the number of segments needed lies at the other end of the work. For example, to divide the work into 7 segments, let the ruler measure 14 inches; then mark every 2 inches.

Walk this way

Another way to mark equal segments is with dividers or a compass. Set the points at the desired distance; then walk the dividers along a straightedge by swinging one point in front of the other.

In the round

Center finder

To find the center of a circle, clamp a combination square to a framing or try square. The combination square should be set against the framing square so that its rule intersects the inside corner of the framing square at 45°. Slide the contraption over the work until both sides of the framing square rest against it. Using the rule

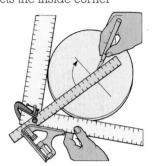

of the combination square as a guide, draw a pencil line on the work; rotate the work and draw a second line. The intersection of the lines marks the center. You can also make a plywood jig. Cut out a right angle in the plywood; then attach a straightedge to it with screws, creating a 45° angle. Use the jig in the same way as the one above.

Cylindrical trick

To mark equal distances around a cylinder, measure the circumference with a strip of paper; then lay the paper flat and mark off equal segments with a compass (see left). Wrap the paper around the cylinder, tape down the end, and transfer the marks.

LAYING OUT

Let your finger do the work ▲

When scribing a straight line near the edge of a board, use your finger as a guide (but only if the edge of the board is straight). Hold the pencil between your thumb and first finger, and rest the tip of your middle finger on the edge of the board. Slide your hand along the board by adjusting your arm at the elbow and shoulder and keeping the wrist steady. With just a little practice your finger will soon be gauging straight lines.

Clothespin on the line

Here's how to turn a wooden clothespin into a handy gauge. Cut off one prong at a right angle. Then drill a series of holes at measured intervals along the length of the intact prong; make the holes large enough to accommodate a pencil point. Butt the head of the pin against the work, and slide it along to mark the line.

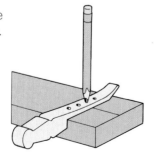

That versatile square

A combination square is an accurate aid for marking straight lines. Adjust the blade to the desired length, and position the square along the edge of the wood. Set the pencil at the end of the blade and pull the two toward you in a smooth motion. If you have problems keeping the pencil steady, you can file a notch into the end of the blade; the notch should be just wide enough to accommodate the pencil point. ▼

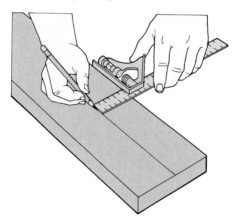

No more bumpy lines ▲

When you're using a marking gauge, it's not unusual for the scribe to be a little wavy near the edge of the wood. (The reason is that as the body of the gauge passes the edge of the wood, the pin may jump.) Instead of pulling or pushing the gauge all the way to the end of the work, stop just short of it—about ½ inch. Reposition the gauge so that the pin is at the end of the wood; then push or pull it until the two scribed lines meet.

Down the center

Use this jig to mark the center of your work without first measuring. You'll need four ¼-inch dowels and a block of wood at least 2 inches wide and 8 inches long (longer if you're working with material more than 6 inches wide). Mark centerlines (p.69) down the length and across the width of the block on both faces. Drill a hole wide enough for a pencil through the center of the block. On one face drill two dowel holes on the longer centerline, 1 inch in from each end; on the other face drill two holes on the same line, centered 1 inch on either side of the pencil hole. Glue dowels into the holes. To use the jig, insert a pencil and place the jig over the work, with the dowels pressed tightly against the edges of the work.

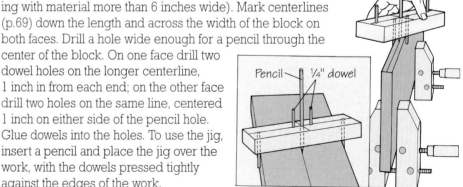

Pencil   ¼" dowel

Going round in circles

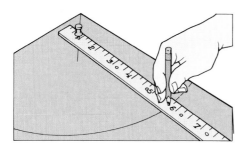

Double-duty yardstick ▲

If your compass isn't large enough to make the circle or arc you need, try using a yardstick. Drill a hole large enough for a pushpin at the 1-inch mark. Then drill holes for a pencil point at the distances you need along the yardstick. When you're ready to use this homemade compass, insert a pushpin through the hole at the 1-inch mark and into the work. The yardstick will pivot at the pushpin. (Because the pivot is set at the 1-inch mark, make sure you add 1 inch to your measurements.)

Adjustable rod

A standard curtain rod is ideal for creating a large adjustable compass. Tape a 16d nail securely to one end of the rod as a pivot; then tape a pencil to the opposite end. Slide the curtain rod sections to the desired radius, and clamp them together with a small C-clamp. You're ready to scribe a circle.

Irregularities

For the perfect fit

To fit together two objects, one of which is irregularly shaped (for instance, a lipped cabinet against a wall with molding), use a compass. Set the compass point on the wall and the pencil point on the cabinet. With a slow, steady motion and without varying the distance between the compass legs, follow the original contour with the point. The pencil will trace the shape onto the work.

The two points should always be at the same height

Lipped edge

Chair rail

Shape it with solder

Bendable wire solder can become the perfect contour gauge, especially when you're making duplicates of odd shapes. Place the solder against the irregular object and push it in to fit the contour. Then position the bent solder on the workpiece and trace the contour onto it.

Dressmaker's trick

To transfer patterns—especially curved ones—to wood, slip a sheet of dressmaker's tracing paper between the work and the pattern. Then use a tracing wheel to copy the pattern onto the work. The radiating points on the wheel will pierce the pattern and press against the tracing paper, leaving a dotted ink line on the work.

Save your pattern

Often-used woodworking patterns soon become frayed and worn. To preserve your patterns, use the originals to make longer-lasting templates. Suitable materials include cardboard, which is easy to cut with a utility knife, thin plywood, hardboard, and acrylic plastic sheet, which is easy to shape with most woodworking tools. An extra advantage to the clear acrylic template is that you'll be able to see the work under the template and know exactly where the pattern will fall—which means you can avoid knots and select sections that have better-looking grain.

Make it larger (or smaller)

A three-sided drafter's rule, available at art supply stores, is the tool you need to reduce or enlarge objects or patterns. To make your own version of a drafter's rule, make several photocopies of a 12-inch ruler, scaled at various ratios such as 25, 50, 75, 100, 125, 150 and 175 percent. Cut out the rules and glue them to two four-sided sticks—one with decreasing ratios, the other with increasing ratios. Use the 100-percent rule to measure the object or pattern that you wish to copy; then look for the measurement on the rule with the desired ratio.

DRILLING

Bull's eye

Making the curve

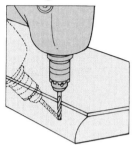

Drilling a hole on a curved surface, such as molding, can be tricky because the bit has a tendency to wander. To keep the bit centered, first use an awl to punch a hole where you plan to drill. Then start drilling the hole with the bit perpendicular to the surface; once the bit takes, swing it gradually to the proper angle.

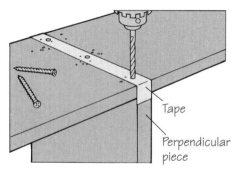

Tape

Perpendicular piece

At the joint ▲

Masking tape is an ideal guide for drilling into dado and butt joints. The tape should be the same width as the end of the workpiece (for example, a shelf or a partition in a stereo cabinet) that butts against the face of the other workpiece. Lay the tape across the work with the ends overhanging and lining up with the perpendicular piece. Mark the hole locations on the tape and begin drilling. When you remove the masking tape, you'll find that the wood will be less chipped than usual.

Groovy jig ▶

Here's how to make a handy two-in-one jig for guiding drill bits. Cut a V-groove in each end of a scrap block of wood. One groove should be at a 90° angle for drilling perpendicular holes; the other one at another commonly used angle, such as 45°. Use the jig to start the drill bit at the desired angle; then remove it to continue drilling.

Shelf help

Drilling holes for shelf pins is a snap with this handy hole-spacing template. Cut a strip of perf board three to five holes wide and long enough to cover the height of the work. To avoid drilling too many holes, cover every other row of holes with tape. Because the lowest shelf normally starts 8 inches from the bottom, you can also cover the bottom 8 inches of holes with tape. Label the top end of the template so you don't accidentally position it the wrong way around. Secure the template flush to the edge of the work with spring clamps. Then start drilling through the center strip of holes.

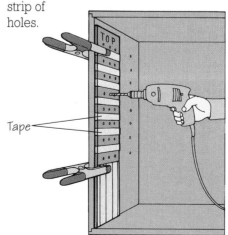

Tape

Groovy jig (illustration)

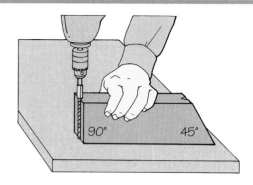

90°   45°

Hole truth

A bit of a trick

When drilling through some woods and all plywood, the bit may chew up the exit hole unless you drill the hole partway from both sides. A faster and neater method is to back up the work with a piece of sacrificial scrap wood. The bit will chew up the scrap, not the work.

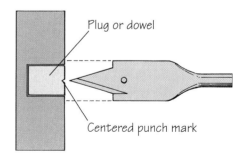

Plug or dowel

Centered punch mark

Hole in a hole ▲

Centering a drill bit can be difficult when you're enlarging an existing hole. The solution is to first fill the hole with a same-size dowel or plug (which you can make with a hole saw). Punch the center of the dowel or plug with an awl; then use the punch mark to center the spade bit for the larger hole.

CHISELING AND PLANING

Chisel it away

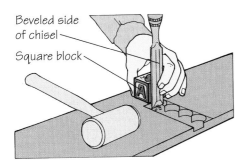

Beveled side of chisel

Square block

Hold it straight ▲

To create a neat cut when making a dado, mortise, or dovetail, the chisel must be held perpendicular to the wood. One way to guide the chisel is to hold a square block against the blade (with the chisel's bevel toward the waste). Or try clamping a board with a straight edge along the chisel line.

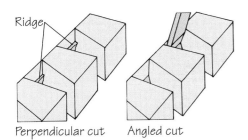

Ridge

Perpendicular cut   Angled cut

Another angle ▲

Perpendicular chisel cuts to remove waste in dovetail joints rarely line up at the halfway point where the cuts meet from the two opposite sides. Ridges that jut out at the halfway point require a separate removal step. To avoid this extra step, after making the first initial cuts along the marking lines with the chisel perpendicular to the work, continue the remaining cuts with the blade angled away from the waste slightly.

Plane sense

It's just scribble

It's hard to know if you've missed a spot after planing a large surface. Here's one way to be sure. Before you start planing, scribble on the surface with a pencil. As you plane, the scribbling will disappear. Repeat this step for additional passes.

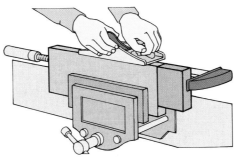

No more splinters ▲

To keep the end of a workpiece from splintering as it's being planed, clamp a block of scrap wood to the end. The height of the scrap should be the same as the height of the work.

Knotty solution

If there's a knot close to an edge that you want to plane, try holding the plane at an angle. The slicing action you get from an angled blade yields a better cut than a standard pass.

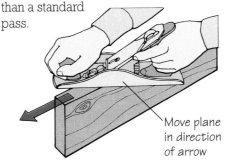

Move plane in direction of arrow

Holding block

When planing a long board, you may find that the clamps interfere with the plane. To avoid having to reposition the clamps, make two V-shaped holding blocks, and clamp the blocks rather than the workpiece. With the clamps out of the way, you can plane the work without encountering any interference.

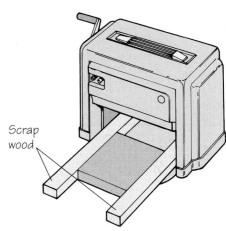

Scrap wood

Too small for a planer? ▲

Here's how to plane short pieces of lumber in a thickness planer. Hot-glue scrap wood to each side of the work, with the bottom faces of all three pieces flush. After planing, tap the pieces of scrap wood to break them off the work. To plane stock under ½ inch thick, use cloth-backed double-sided carpet tape to attach the stock to a scrap board wider and at least 1 inch longer than the work. (The scrap must be of a uniform thickness and free of warps.)

SAWING

Avoiding splinters

Here's the bad side

Cutting plywood across the grain can create a splintered edge on one side of the board. This won't matter as long as you have a good side and a bad side on the workpiece. The trick is to cut on the correct side. Here are the rules: good side facing up for a handsaw, table saw, and radial arm saw; good side facing down for a circular saw and saber saw.

Haven't got a bad side?

If both faces of the plywood are intended as good sides, you have two options. One is to first make a deep score line with a sharp knife on both faces of the wood. This will ensure a cleaner saw cut and prevent the saw from leaving a ragged edge. The other option (which doesn't always work) is to apply masking tape on both faces of the board where you intend to cut. Mark your cut line on the tape. After you make the cut, peel off the two strips of tape.

Handsaw

Guidance ▶

To ensure a straight cut, use a guide to keep the saw vertically straight, and make frequent visual checks of the blade. A block of 2 x 2 wood cut straight and square will suffice as a guide for short cuts. For a guide for long cuts in thin plywood, clamp a length of 2 x 2 wood alongside the cutting line.

Deep thoughts

This depth gauge will help you cut saw kerfs to a specific depth. First measure the desired depth from the tips of the saw teeth up on both sides of the saw blade; then draw lines parallel to the teeth, again on both sides of the blade. Position strips of wood with a straight edge along the guidelines, straight edges facing down. Secure the strips to the blade with a pair of spring clamps or tape. Make the cut until the edges of the depth gauge meet the work surface.

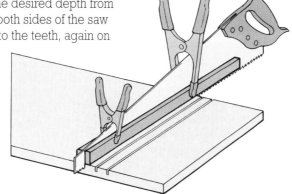

Circular saw

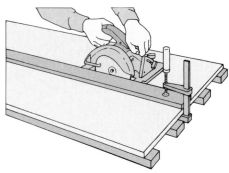

Ground level ▲

Forget about struggling with sheets of plywood on sawhorses. Here are three ways to cut plywood on the floor:
▷ Support the plywood on two or more long 2 x 4's.
▷ Put another piece of plywood under the one you're cutting, and set your saw depth so that the blade just barely grazes the lower sheet.
▷ Set your saw so that the blade doesn't go all the way through; then break apart the two pieces and clean up the cut edges with a bit of sandpaper.

Binding kerf

A circular saw blade tends to catch the work when the kerf behind it closes up. Keep the kerf from binding the blade by inserting a wood shim or other small object into the kerf. When making longer cuts, slide the shim closer (but not too close) to the blade as you progress.

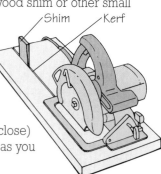

Shim   Kerf

Easy measuring

For those of you who have to cut several boards to the same length, here's a way to speed up the job. Cut one end of each board square; butt those ends against a straightedge nailed to your bench. On one board, measure and mark the desired length minus the distance between the saw blade and the end of the shoe; clamp a straightedge at this mark, extending it across all the boards. Now you can make one pass. ▼

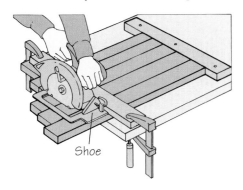

Shoe

Kerf bender

Bending wood is as easy as making a series of straight kerfs with your circular saw, using a square to guide the cuts. There's no rule of thumb about how far apart or how deep to cut the kerfs. Practice on scrap first. For tighter bends, space the kerfs more closely, but don't make them too deep or they will be visible from the opposite side. Before bending the wood, briefly soak it in hot water.

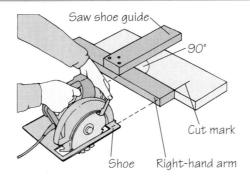

Saw shoe guide

90°

Cut mark

Shoe   Right-hand arm

Seeking guidance ▲

If you plan to cut a lot of wood to the same length, give this jig a try. Use any scrap pieces of wood with straight and squared edges. Attach the two pieces with glue and screws, making sure they are set at an exact right angle. Make the right-hand arm of the guide slightly longer than the distance from the circular saw blade to the left edge of the saw's shoe. Your first pass with the guide will cut off the arm's extra length. When you're ready to use the guide, line up the right end of the guide with the cut mark on the wood.

Saber saw

Take an iron to it

It takes more than a penciled line and good intentions to cut a straight line with a saber saw. For long cuts, use a length of 1-inch angle iron as a straightedge guide. Clamped along the measured mark, the angle iron will guide the blade along the cut line and will keep the blade perpendicular to the work.

Supporting role

To support the work while using a saber saw, clamp it to your workbench so that the area you are cutting juts past the edge of the bench. Or support the work on blocks made from scrap wood that is thicker than the length of your blade. As you reach the end of a cut, the work can collapse toward the cut and bind the blade. To prevent this from happening, slide additional blocks under the work after you cut halfway through it. Make sure the path for the saw blade avoids the bench and blocks.

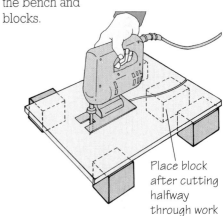

Place block after cutting halfway through work

Taking the plunge

To start a cut in the center of the wood —not at an edge—without drilling a hole first, tilt the saw, resting the front of its shoe on the work; then, with the saw on medium speed, slowly and firmly lower the blade into the wood.

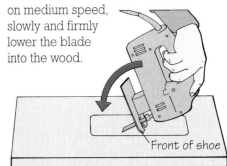

Front of shoe

SAWING

Miter saw

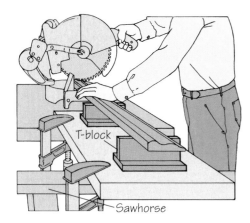
T-block
Sawhorse

Supporting role ▲

If you don't have a helper around to support long pieces of wood, make a couple of T-blocks. They'll support the work whether you're working on a table or on the floor. If your miter saw is set up in a permanent area, you can nail or screw the T-blocks in place.

Ending repetition

If you have to cut a series of workpieces to the same length, try avoiding repetitive measuring and marking by using a stop block. To raise the stop block to the correct height, nail it to another block of the same thickness as the bed of the miter saw. Clamp the block in place.

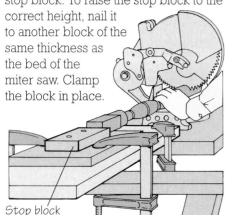
Stop block

On the wide side

Here's how to trick your miter saw into making a wider cut: Slide a piece of ¾-inch scrap wood under the workpiece. This raises the work so that a wider part of the blade will reach it.

Table saw

Ripping fun

To rip an uneven board straight when neither edge is true, nail a straight board on top of it. Use the straight board as a guide to run against the rip fence; the newly cut edge of the uneven board will then be true.

Straightedge

Double-headed nail is easy to remove

Narrow escape

To safely cut a narrow board, fasten a wider board to its edge with hot-melt glue. After the cut is complete, break the boards apart; there'll be no damage.

Tall order ▶

To create a raised panel for a door, make a tenon, or cut a slot into the end of a board, use this jig to make a smoother, more controlled cut. The jig is designed to straddle the rip fence of a table saw. Make the jig out of scrap wood and plywood, and size it to fit your needs—the jig's face can be smaller or larger, depending on the project. The jig should slide snugly and smoothly on the fence. Secure the work to the jig with C-clamps or other small clamps.

Mighty miter jig

With this jig on your table saw, you'll cut perfect miter angles every time. To guide the jig, fit two strips of hardwood into the miter gauge grooves in the saw's table; then glue a ⅝- or ¾-inch plywood base to the top of the strips and square the base to the table. Cut a slot for the blade partway through the base. Mark a 45° angle from both sides of the blade slot; screw two wood blocks with straight edges along these lines. Glue sandpaper strips to the outside edges of the wood blocks to keep the work from slipping. ▼

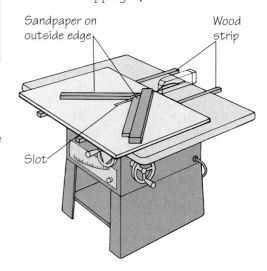
Sandpaper on outside edge
Wood strip
Slot

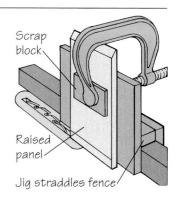
Scrap block
Raised panel
Jig straddles fence

Radial arm saw

Stop action

Controlling the depth of the blade cut is easy with this depth stop. Lower the blade to the desired height, measure the distance between the column castings, and cut a piece of scrap wood to that measurement. Place the wood between the castings and hold it in place with a hose clamp. ▼

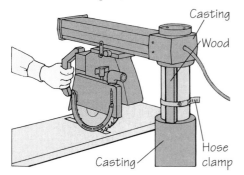

Casting
Wood
Hose clamp
Casting

Narrow rip

To rip a thin strip of wood or avoid getting your fingers too close to the blade, clamp a straightedge guide to the wood. The guide should slide along the front edge of the saw's table. With this setup the blade won't hang far out on the arm, which reduces cutting accuracy. ▼

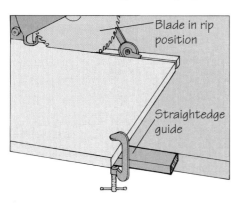

Blade in rip position

Straightedge guide

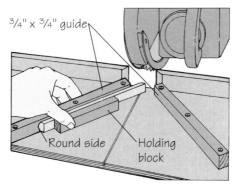

³/₄" x ³/₄" guide
Round side
Holding block

Mind over miter ▲

This jig allows you to cut accurate miters on rounded stock or molding. Screw two guides to a plywood base at opposite 45° angles to the saw blade. Place the rounded stock against the guide that will give you the desired miter angle. Press a square holding block against the stock, and make the cut. The holding block will keep the piece upright and will also prevent it from creeping out of place while it's being cut.

Band and scroll saws

Blade aid

If the band saw blade slips off the wheel when you try to replace it, use masking tape to hold it in place temporarily. Tape the blade to the top wheel; then slip the blade around the lower wheel and tighten it in place. Remove the tape.

Super duping

When cutting duplicate parts on a band or scroll saw, stack the parts together, using double-faced tape between the pieces to hold them in place. The whole stack can then be cut without any worry about the pieces moving.

Veneer

To make clean band or scroll saw cuts in thin sheets of veneer or metal, layer the work between two pieces of plywood. To indicate the position of the work, set the work on the bottom layer; then mark and drill holes through the plywood at each corner of the work. Dab hot-melt glue along each edge of the work, and place the second piece of plywood on top. (Or tape the plywood layers together.) Flip over the assembly; using the holes as a guide to the corners of the work, mark the cutting lines or glue a cutting pattern to the plywood.

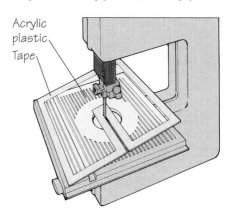

Acrylic plastic
Tape

Work jam ▲

Small pieces can drop into the band saw table slot and jam against the blade. To keep this from happening, cut a sheet of ⅛-inch acrylic plastic the same dimensions as the saw table. Drill a ¼-inch hole in the plastic where the blade will be located; then cut a slot from the back edge of the plastic to the hole. Anchor the plastic to the saw's table with strips of double-faced tape down the center and around all four edges. Besides reducing the clearance around the blade, it also provides a smooth work surface. For a larger blade, drill a larger hole.

ROUTING

Router rules

Which way to go?

When it comes to moving a router, the basic rule is: left to right as you face the cut. When making an interior cut, move the router clockwise. For perimeters, move it counterclockwise. If you're using a router table (in which case the router is mounted upside down), move the work from right to left. ▼

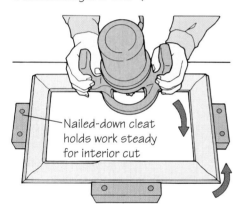

Nailed-down cleat holds work steady for interior cut

Four easy solutions

Here are simple solutions to common router problems:
▷ Burned edges: Move the router faster; check for a dull bit.
▷ Chatter marks: Move the router slower over the wood; check for a dull bit.
▷ Corner tearouts: Rout the end grain first, then remove splinters by routing the sides; instead of one pass, make your cut in two or three passes.
▷ Uneven depth of cut: Tighten the router's depth adjustment and collet; replace the collet if it is worn.

Shaping the work

Look! No clamps

This friction board may solve the problem of clamps in your router's path. Attach a block of wood to one end of a length of plywood. Spread white glue on the plywood, lay medium-grit sandpaper on it, and set the board upside down until the glue dries. Then hook the block over the edge of the worktable or hold it in a vise. The friction from the sandpaper will hold your work in place.

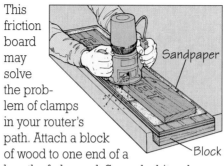

Sandpaper

Block

Dado jig

Make a T-square by screwing together two pieces of straight wood at a perfect right angle. Clamp the jig to a piece of scrap, and rout with the bit you plan to use. The jig will then have a dado in it. To use the jig, mark the work where you want a dado, and clamp the jig in place so that the dado in the jig is lined up with the mark. Use this jig only with the same router and the same size bit.

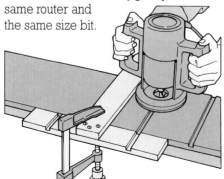

Tipping over the edge

When routing along a narrow edge, the router base can tip and create an uneven profile. For more control, clamp or hot-glue a straight board along the edge of the work.

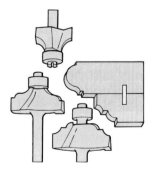

Straight board

Again and again

If you are making a number of duplicate shapes with a router, you can simplify the job by using the original pattern to make a template out of 1/4-inch-thick Masonite. Cut the workpiece to about 1/32 inch outside the layout line. Then nail the template to the bottom side of the workpiece, and rout off the excess with a ball-bearing bit designed for trimming plastic laminate.

Combining bits ▲

Even if you own a complete set of bits, you don't have to settle for predesigned shapes. To increase the variety and style of the edges you make, try combining two or more bits.

JOINING WOOD

Edge, miter, and tenon

An edgy solution

The table saw is the best tool for cutting straight gluing edges. If a table saw isn't available, first glue together the sections to be joined. When the glue has completely dried, cut the pieces apart with a circular saw, making sure the blade runs down the center of the glued seam. The blade will remove a bit of the wood from each edge; even if the cut wavers, the edges will vary the same amount and will butt together perfectly.

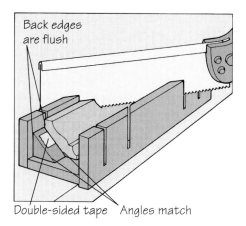

Back edges are flush

Double-sided tape   Angles match

Mitering molding ▲

Here's an aid to prevent crown molding from slipping in a miter box. Cut one edge of a 2 x 4 scrap block at an angle that matches that of the molding. Apply double-sided tape along the cut edge, or glue a strip of sandpaper to it. Trim the block so that its back edge is flush with the back edge of the molding. Set the molding on the angled edge of the block. Hold the molding and the block against the miter box as you saw. The tape or sandpaper will grip the molding. To clamp the molding, see p.84.

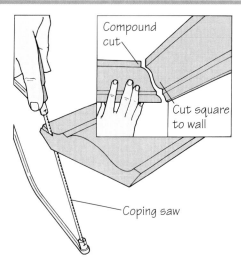

Compound cut

Cut square to wall

Coping saw

Coping a joint ▲

To install crown molding at an inside corner, you will have to make a compound cut. First cut one piece to fit butt to the wall. Then make a 45° inside miter cut on the end of the other piece. With a coping saw, cut along this profile at the face of the trim, undercutting the edge about 30°. With practice, you'll get it to fit, creating a neat coped joint.

Binding tenon

To find out where a tenon is binding in a mortise, tape a piece of carbon paper over the tenon and drive it into the mortise until it binds. When you remove the tenon, you'll find a smudge on it that indicates where the joint is binding.

Joining with dowels

To the point

Mount an old pencil sharpener on your workshop wall and use it not only to sharpen pencils but also to chamfer dowels for joining wood workpieces.

Just a flute

A fluted dowel holds better in wood because it allows more glue to surround it. Make your own flutes on cheaper plain dowels by crimping the dowels with the serrated jaws of your pliers.

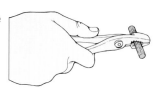

It goes in but won't come out

When test-fitting a dowel joint, the fit may be so snug that you can't pull the joint apart. To prevent this, use test dowels. Make them by cutting a slot into each end at right angles (use a dovetail or small backsaw). After the test fit, use regular dowels to assemble the joint.

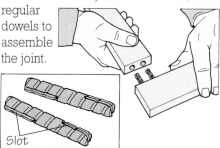

Slot

A better butt

Increase the holding power at a butt joint by driving the screw through a dowel. Drill a hole for a ½-inch dowel so that it cuts across the path of the screw that will be driven into the end grain of one of the workpieces. Put carpenter's glue in the hole and insert the dowel.

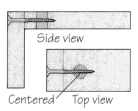

Side view

Centered   Top view

When the glue has dried, drive in the screw and sand or cut the dowel flush to the surface.

SANDING

Handling the paper

Curling clues

Sandpaper will curl up and crack if it's left lying around. To keep the paper from curling, place a weight on it. Or store the paper in the freezer so that heat and humidity won't affect the adhesive holding the abrasive to the paper.

Flexing paper

Sandpaper is usually stiff and brittle, making it tough to fold and likely to leave scuff marks on the work surface. To make the paper more flexible, pull it, with the grit side up, back and forth over the edge of a table or workbench.

Hack it up

If you cut a lot of sandpaper, here's one way to save time and effort. Screw a hacksaw blade to the edge of a piece of plywood; the teeth should point up and jut above the plywood. For a fence, glue or screw a straightedge or ruler along one side of the plywood. Draw lines at often-used intervals for easy measuring.

▼

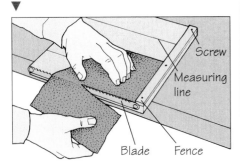

Screw

Measuring line

Blade   Fence

TYPES OF SANDPAPER

Sandpaper (more properly, abrasive paper) is available in a bewildering number of types. Here are the main choices and the jobs that they're best suited for.

SANDPAPER	CHARACTERISTICS	USES
Aluminum oxide	Familiar light brown paper with tough, durable synthetic grains.	Best general-purpose sandpaper for the money.
Flint	Inexpensive but cuts slowly and dulls quickly. Grit described in words ("fine"), not numbers (see below).	Small jobs and sticky surfaces that clog any paper quickly. Otherwise best to avoid.
Garnet	Reddish in color. Garnet grains fracture during use, exposing fresh, sharp cutting edges; cuts quickly but wears quickly too.	Good all-purpose abrasive, particularly for hand-sanding.
Silicon carbide	Black wet-or-dry paper; has hardest grit and removes material very quickly. Can be wet with water or oil to keep it from gumming up. Available only in fine grits.	Ideal for very fine sanding, such as between coats of varnish and other finishes. Hard enough to sand metal.
Stearated	Called "no-fill"; a carbide or aluminum oxide paper coated with a zinc compound to prevent clogging. Fast-cutting and long-lasting but expensive.	Extremely good for woodworking, especially on softwoods, which can gum up ordinary papers.

GRADES OF SANDPAPER

Sandpaper is classified by a number reflecting the size of the grit particles on it. Higher numbers indicate smaller grains for finer sanding. Here are the common grades of sandpaper with their grit numbers and uses.

GRIT	TEXTURE	USE
50–60	Coarse	Rough sanding and shaping; removing paint.
80–100	Medium	Intermediate sanding after rough sanding; sanding on previously painted surfaces.
120–150	Fine	Final sanding before applying finish.
160–240	Very fine	Smoothing primer and paint.
280–320	Extra-fine	Smoothing between undercoats.
360–400	Superfine	Wet-sanding varnish or lacquer for ultrasmooth finish.

HAND-SANDING

Sanding can make or break a wood project's appearance. Even perfect-looking factory-planed wood needs hand-sanding to open the grain and promote even staining. A final hand-sanding is also essential to remove the tiny swirl marks left by oscillating power sanders. For professional-looking results, follow these tips:

Use the right grit size. Depending on the smoothness of the surface, start with 60-grit paper (for example, on work that has been cut on a table saw or run through a jointer or planer). Progress through finer grits, such as 80, 100, and 120, without skipping any steps. Your first, coarsest sanding should flatten high spots. Subsequent sandings should replace larger scratches with finer ones. Where to stop depends on the work. In general, sand surfaces to be painted to 120 grit, fine objects to be stained and varnished to about 150. An ultrasmooth oiled finish may require even finer grits and a longer progression, such as 120, 150, 180, and 220, then polishing with 400 wet-or-dry paper and oil.

Sand with the grain. Sanding at an angle to the grain leaves scratches that are difficult to remove. Overlap sanding strokes and apply equal pressure on both forward and backward strokes. Sand across the grain only when you want to remove a large amount of wood; then follow up by thoroughly sanding with the grain.

Use a sanding block. With a flat backing, sandpaper can remove bumps and span low spots. Buy a sanding block or fit a half sheet of paper around a ¾- x 4½- x 4½-inch wood block. Don't use your fingers on flat surfaces—the sandpaper will follow any irregularities in the wood, leaving a wavy surface.

Don't sand out gouges and dents. You'll get wide, shallow, very noticeable craters. Instead, fill any deep scratches with wood putty; try raising dents with a steam iron (p.239).

Use a sanding block to ensure flat sanding, but take care not to let the block go more than halfway off the end of the workpiece, or it'll round the edge.

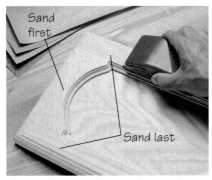

Avoid cross-grain scratches on pieces that butt at an angle by first sanding the piece with its ends set to the adjacent pieces, then the pieces with free ends.

A sanding sponge is a good alternative for sanding rounded or irregularly shaped pieces. You can also use a sponge for sanding wet surfaces.

Wet-sand between coats of varnish to produce an ultrasmooth satin finish. Use 400- or 600-grit wet-or-dry silicon carbide paper on a block with water or oil.

SANDING

Odd shapes and sizes

Mopping about

For sanding walls and ceilings before painting or for smoothing wallboard joints, you can buy a pole sander—or you can make one from your sponge mop. Remove the sponge, wrap a sheet of sandpaper around a block of wood the same size as the sponge, and screw or clamp the block to the mop. The frame will hold the paper to the block.

▼

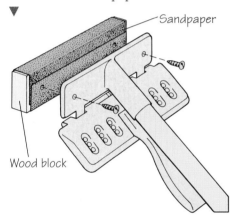

Sandpaper

Wood block

Shapely paper

When sanding a flat surface, you need to use sandpaper with a supportive backing. The same is not true, however, when you're sanding curved shapes. You can shape sandpaper with your fingers or the palm of your hand to match the contour of a rounded or irregularly shaped surface. To sand a long turning, such as a chair leg, wrap the sandpaper around the wood (making sure the ends overlap) and slide the paper up and down. For shorter sections on a turning, hold a strip of sandpaper at both ends and run it back and forth over the area as if you were shining a shoe.

A crooked deck

If a sanding sponge isn't handy when you need to smooth a curved surface, improvise one with a deck of playing cards. Wrap sandpaper around the deck, hold it on edge, and press it firmly against the surface. The cards will conform to the shape of the work and sand it evenly.

Deck of cards

Matching curves

To smooth curved indentations, cut a short piece of old garden hose and make a slit down the length of it. Wrap sandpaper, grit side out, around the hose and tuck the ends into the slit. (You can also glue or tape the paper in place.) For smaller grooves, wrap the sandpaper around a wooden dowel. Or fold the sandpaper and fit the crease into the groove; apply pressure alternately on each side of the groove. For larger surfaces, wrap sandpaper around a cylindrical plastic container.

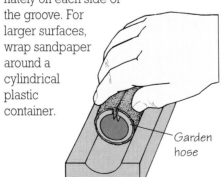

Garden hose

Not just a nail file ▲

Intricate cuts and small, hard-to-reach places can be easy to sand if you use emery boards; these filelike sanders are easy to handle and provide two sanding grits. For a greater range of grits, glue different grades of sandpaper onto ice cream or frozen pop sticks.

Sticky fingers

Another way to sand hard-to-reach areas is to attach self-adhesive sandpaper to your fingertip. You'll have a good feel for the surface you're sanding and greater control over the work. To sand into a corner, apply the sandpaper to the blade of a stiff putty knife. As the paper wears, pull it off the blade, move it up, and tear off the used portion.

Holding the work

Padded workbench

To keep the bottom of a workpiece from being scratched while you're sanding the top, use a rubber-backed carpet scrap as a pad for your workbench. When you've finished sanding, clean the carpet with your shop vacuum cleaner.

Against the grit

When sanding small parts, it's easier to rub the part against the sandpaper than to rub the paper against the part. To make the job even easier, set the sandpaper on plywood or sturdy cardboard and hold it in place with spring clips.

Spring clip

Against the grit II

To rub pieces against sandpaper, you can cover a block of wood with sandpaper, securing the edges with a rubber band; then hold the block in a vise.

On a stick

Another way to sand small work is to dab hot glue on the back of the piece and stick it on the end of a dowel. Hold the work by the dowel while sanding. To unstick the piece, pop the assembly into the freezer for a few minutes. The cold will quickly free the workpiece.

Power-sanding

Snagging stockings

A problem with power sanders is they don't tell you when the job is done. To test for smoothness, slip an old stocking over your hand and pass it lightly over the work in the direction of the grain. Rough spots will snag the stocking.

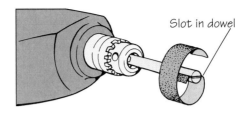

Slot in dowel

Creating a flap ▲

To sand the inside of a hole that is too small for a drum sander, make a flap sander with a 6-inch length of ⅜-inch dowel. Using a thin blade in a saw, cut a slot in one end of the dowel. Chuck the opposite end of the dowel into a drill, and slip a strip cut from a sanding belt into the slot. With the slotted end of the dowel facing you, wrap the strip clockwise around the dowel. The grit side of the strip should now be on the outside; if it is, hot-glue the strip in the dowel.

Take a belt to it

Here's a way to keep the edges of a project from being rounded off by your belt sander. Take pieces of scrap wood of the same thickness as the work and secure them to both ends of the work, flush to its surface. Tack the scrap pieces in place with nails or clamp them on, making sure the clamps won't interfere with the sander. The sander will round off the scrap, not the work.

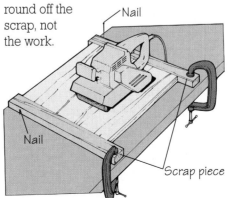

Nail

Nail

Scrap piece

Recycling discs

When sanding a painted surface, sanding discs become clogged and glazed long before they wear out. To get more life out of a disc, apply a coat of semi-paste water-wash-off paint remover to the encrusted area. Let the remover stand on the disc until the paint has softened; then wash it off.

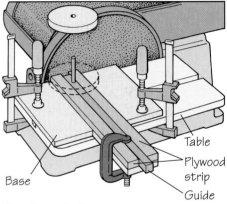

Table

Plywood strip

Guide

Base

Sanding circles ▲

Sanding wheels and other circular objects is easy with this custom-made disc sander jig. First, make a T-shaped base using ¾-inch plywood. Cut a piece of hardwood to be used as a guide, and drill a hole in one end to hold a dowel. Center the guide on the base; then nail or glue ¾-inch plywood strips along each side of the guide, creating a channel. The guide should be held firmly in place yet be able to slide smoothly in the channel. Glue a dowel into the hole in the guide. To use the jig, clamp the base to your disc sander table. After you place the work on the dowel, adjust the guide so the work sits snugly at the disc; clamp it in place. Make sure the work sits on the left side of the disc.

CLAMPING

The basics

Dos and don'ts

Here are some pointers to keep in mind when you're clamping:

▷ Don't rely on clamps to pull together a poorly fitting joint. Glue and pressure may hold things together for a while, but in the long run the joint will fail. Plane or sand the pieces until they fit right.

▷ Before applying glue, test-fit the parts. Preadjust the clamps so they're ready to apply pressure with just a few twists.

▷ Never force a clamp or use a wrench to tighten it. If the clamp isn't strong enough, use a bigger one or add another clamp next to it.

▷ Too much clamping pressure can squeeze all the glue out of the joint and compress the wood fibers. Too little pressure can result in a glue line that is too thick and therefore weak. An even ridge of glue between clamped parts, at the top and the bottom, indicates proper pressure.

▷ Leave the clamps on for the recommended length of time. Most glues specify a minimum clamping time.

Spreading pressure

Clamp heads exert a cone-shaped area of force. To distribute pressure over a wider area (and to protect the work from damage), place scrap wood or angle irons between the work and the clamp heads.

C-clamp

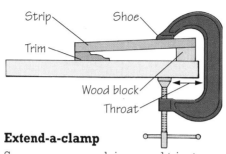

Extend-a-clamp

Suppose you are gluing wood trim to a flat workpiece and your C-clamp can't reach the joint because it has a shallow throat. Here's a way to increase the clamp's reach using only a strip of hardwood and a block of wood that's thicker than the trim. Place the block near the edge of the workpiece, position the strip under the clamp shoe so that it spans the gap between the block and the trim, and clamp down. The strip will transfer pressure to the joint.

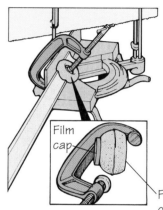

Coupled... for a job

If a workpiece is too wide for one C-clamp to span it and you have no suitable substitute, combine two C-clamps as shown. This trick will work well in situations that require only light clamping pressure. Don't try it if you need to apply heavy pressure.

No more bouncing ball

It isn't easy to hold a curved, irregular piece tightly in a miter box. An ordinary soft rubber ball can provide a good way around this problem. Cut off a piece of the ball to create a flat area, and glue a film canister cap to the opposite side. Place the cut side of the ball against the workpiece and the clamp head in the cap. Clamp the ball and workpiece securely in place. The ball will conform to fit any shape and won't scratch the work.

On edge

If you don't have an edge clamp and tape isn't suitable for the job, use shims with a C-clamp. Drive wedge-shaped shims between the edge piece and the back of the clamp until they fit snugly. ▼

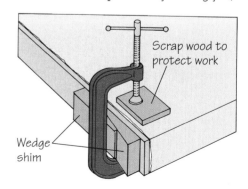

Hand screw

Jaw lineup

Mark the handles on your hand screw to quickly set the jaws parallel. With the jaws closed and parallel, apply a narrow paint line or other mark down the center of each hand grip. No matter how wide apart the jaws are set, if you keep the lines in the same relationship to each other, the jaws will be parallel. Keep in mind that the jaws can also be set at an angle if the job calls for it.

Working together

Use pairs of hand screws to hold oddly placed pieces together, as shown at right. If you don't have a woodworker's vise,  use a combination of hand screws, bar clamps, and C-clamps to hold a workpiece for planing, sanding, chiseling, or shaping. A setup like the one below will allow you to work without interference from the clamps. ▼

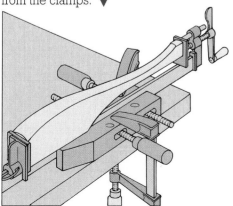

Pipe clamp

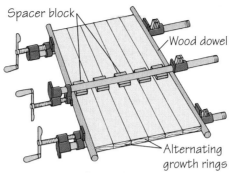

Spacer block

Wood dowel

Alternating growth rings

No warpage here ▲

Here are a few tricks for gluing strips edge to edge. When you glue up boards that will form an overhanging surface, such as a tabletop on a pedestal, set the boards with the growth rings alternating up and down. To hold any glue-up, stagger pipe clamps above and below the workpiece, adding spacer blocks to keep the clamp pressure in line with the boards. If the clamp jaws are longer than the thickness of the work, angle them so that they contact more of the work. Or place a wood dowel lengthwise on each side of the work to redirect the clamping force.

Clamping a trapezoid

To clamp shapes with unequal parallel sides, such as a chair seat frame, you'll have to create right-angle clamping surfaces. Place scrap wood against the two parallel edges as shown; this allows the clamps to seat properly and to apply pressure at the proper angle.

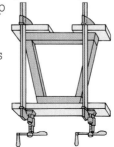

Custom-made block

Round or elliptical edge pieces, which are common in tabletops, can be clamped together with the help of a block that fits snugly around the workpiece. You can also make blocks to match other unusual shapes. If you have trouble steadying the block while applying the clamp, hot-glue it in place; then break it off after you're done. ▼

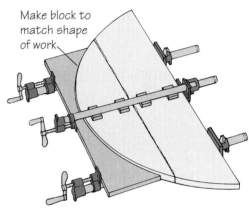

Make block to match shape of work

Hold the door

Secure a door in a vertical position for planing or mortising by using pipe clamps or hand screws. Stagger the pipe clamps, alternating left and right, along the bottom edge of the door. ▼

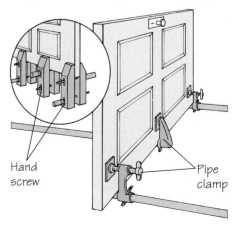

Hand screw

Pipe clamp

CLAMPING

Makeshift clamps

Spring clamp look-alikes

Here are two substitutes for a spring clamp: Large battery clips from an old damaged jumper cable will accept work up to 1½ inches thick, and the spring clip on the end of a pants or skirt hanger will hold a small workpiece. The jaws of some hanger clips are padded with felt strips that will protect your work from marring.

Mousetrap technology

You can turn a mousetrap into a strong, versatile wide-grip clamp. Pry off the bait holder and cut off the hold-down side of the base before applying the other half to the work.

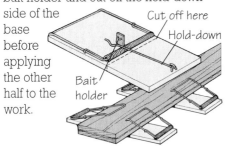

Cut off here

Hold-down

Bait holder

Gun clamp

A caulk gun is ideal for applying light pressure to small pieces. Place the work between pieces of scrap wood, and then position the assembly between the jaws of the gun. The scraps protect the work and provide a flat surface for even pressure. To apply pressure to the work, squeeze the trigger.

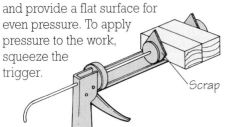

Scrap

Rubber-band clamps

Sometimes clamps just don't work well for gluing small or irregularly shaped objects. To hold such pieces together, keep a variety of large rubber bands on hand in your shop.

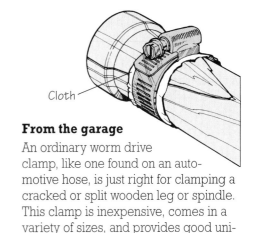

Cloth

You don't have to jump for the cords

Bungee cords are an ideal substitute for band clamps. Because the cords are not adjustable, keep a variety of sizes in stock. You can combine short cords to make longer ones; wrap long cords around small pieces several times or in a figure 8.

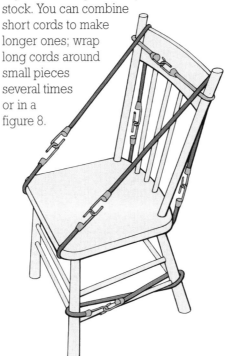

From the garage

An ordinary worm drive clamp, like one found on an automotive hose, is just right for clamping a cracked or split wooden leg or spindle. This clamp is inexpensive, comes in a variety of sizes, and provides good uniform pressure when tightened. Slip a piece of cloth or vinyl under the band to prevent marring.

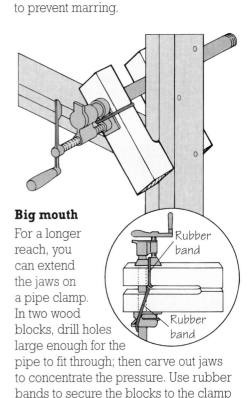

Rubber band

Rubber band

Big mouth

For a longer reach, you can extend the jaws on a pipe clamp. In two wood blocks, drill holes large enough for the pipe to fit through; then carve out jaws to concentrate the pressure. Use rubber bands to secure the blocks to the clamp heads as shown, and slip the assemblies onto the pipe.

Homemade clamps

Sandbag

Bag it ▲

When you need to clamp irregular shapes, hold them together with a sandbag. For small fragile items, use a small plastic bag filled with sand. Use larger sand-filled bags for big items. For outdoor projects, try plastic bags or containers filled with water from a hose.

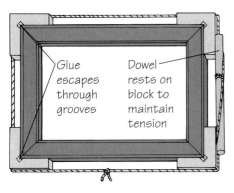

Glue escapes through grooves

Dowel rests on block to maintain tension

Tourniquet a frame ▲

Holding mitered corner pieces together is simple with this tourniquet clamp. Make four L-shaped corner blocks. Rout or chisel grooves on the outer edges to guide the twine, and make vertical grooves at the inside corners to allow excess glue to escape. Place the blocks in position and run twine around the perimeter. To tighten the twine, wrap a dowel or stick in the twine and twist it.

Holding a scarf

Here's an easy way to spread pressure evenly along a scarf joint. When you cut off the ends of the work, save the triangular scrap pieces. When you're ready to clamp, place the scraps between the work and the clamp as shown. ▼

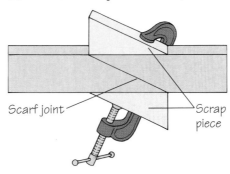

Scarf joint

Scrap piece

Edgy situation

If you run out of clamps in the middle of a project, you can make your own out of scrap lumber. Screw one block to each end of a length of board that's slightly longer than the workpiece. Attach each block with only one screw so that it will pivot into alignment. Cut two wedge-shaped pieces of wood, and drive them between one of the blocks and the project for a tight hold. ▼

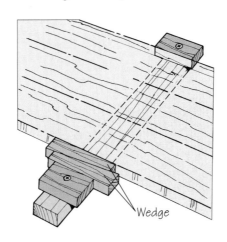

Wedge

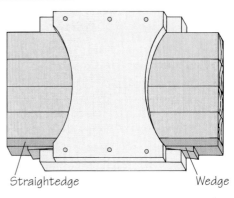

Straightedge

Wedge

H-frame ▲

This H-frame jig is ideal for edge-gluing two or more boards (the long legs of the frame will apply equal pressure along the boards). The jig is easy to make out of scrap lumber and ¾-inch plywood; to reduce the weight of the frame, cut the plywood as shown. Create clamping pressure by driving a pair of wedges between the straightedge and the jig.

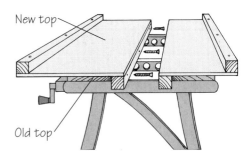

New top

Old top

Extending the top ▲

By building a larger top for your portable workbench, you can use it to clamp large objects. Make the new top out of ¾-inch plywood and four 2 x 2's. One side of the new top should be slightly wider than the underlying side of the old top; the other side should be about twice as wide. Attach both sides of the new top to the original top with screws, as shown.

GLUING

Applying glue

White or yellow?
The difference between white and yellow glues is that yellow glue is specifically formulated for wood, whereas white glue is a general-purpose adhesive. Yellow glue sets up twice as fast, sands easier and faster, and resembles most woods more closely when it has dried. Use white glue if you need more setup time—for example, when you are gluing large surfaces or complex joints.

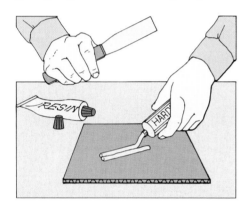

Epoxy mix-up ▲
For a strong epoxy bond, you must mix resin and hardener in equal parts. An easy way to gauge the proportions is to squeeze out the resin and hardener in parallel lines of equal width and length.

Dry run
Here's a good way to tell when glue has dried. At the same time you apply glue to your work, glue together two scrap pieces of the same material as the work. Test the scraps to determine when the work is dry. If the glue label lists a specific length of drying time, you can jot it down on the wood as a reference.

Make it hot
When applying hot glue to a large area, you may find that the glue is drying too fast. To slow down the drying time, try warming the work with a heat gun. Or put the work out in the sun for a while. After the glue dries, you can scrape off any excess with a utility knife.

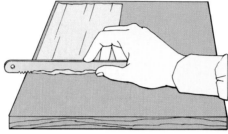

Spreading the glue ▲
A broken hacksaw blade spreads glue quickly over a large, flat area. The teeth let the glue flow easily and keep it to a smooth, even depth throughout.

Slivery move ▲
To glue down a wood sliver, dab a spot of carpenter's glue on the top side of a piece of paper. Slip the paper under the sliver; then pull the paper out, making sure that the glue contacts the sliver. Tape or clamp the sliver in place until the glue dries; then sand the area.

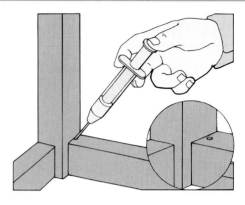

Sure-shot injector ▲
A plastic glue syringe, found in hobby shops or in woodworking stores or catalogs, is ideal for injecting glue into narrow places, such as in a hole made to reach a loose tenon. After filling the syringe barrel, insert the plunger and hold it upward while you depress it. This will expel air bubbles and prevent the glue from drying out. To store glue in the syringe, insert a nail into its tip.

A tight squeeze
As model makers know, toothpicks or dental picks are great for applying glue in tight areas with precise control. ▼

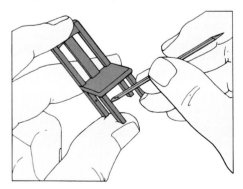

Excess glue

Oozing cure

If you can keep squeezed-out glue off the edges of the wood you're clamping, you'll avoid the bother of removing excess glue later. Here's a trick that will save you time and effort. Before gluing the pieces, clamp them together and apply cellophane tape over the joint. Slit the tape along the joint with a utility knife; then remove the clamps. Apply the glue and reclamp the pieces. This way the glue will ooze onto the tape rather than the wood. Once the glue has set, peel off the tape. ▼

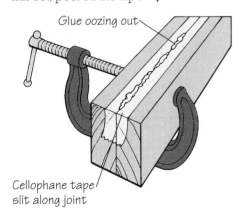

Glue oozing out

Cellophane tape slit along joint

Give it some room

As you make a mortise-and-tenon or a dowel joint, leave extra space at the bottom of the recess. Excess glue will drain there instead of squeezing out of the joint. Chamfer the top edges of the holes for the same effect.

No sticky clamps here

To avoid getting glue on your clamps, place two layers of wax paper strips between the clamp and the work. You can create convenient-size strips by sawing a roll of wax paper into 4-inch sections; then, when you need the paper, rip off the appropriate lengths. If you run out of wax paper, cut a plastic bag into strips and use them instead. ▼

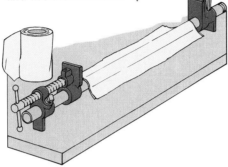

Cleaning up

Sip it up

A drinking straw is a handy instrument for removing excess glue from an inside corner. Slightly crease one end of the straw so that it fits into the corner. The glue will move up the straw as you push it along the joint. ▼

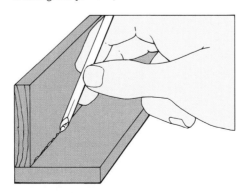

Take it off

Because dried glue won't take stain, it's important to remove any excess before it dries. Use a wet rag to wipe off water-base glues. To avoid leaving behind a film of glue, rinse out the rag periodically and make the final wipe with a well-rinsed rag. (To remove non-water-base glues, use the appropriate solvent.) Sanding will take care of whatever glue residue may remain.

Too late for wiping

If squeezed-out glue has dried to a semi-hard state, use a putty knife to scrape it off. If the glue has dried completely, use a paint scraper to remove it. After scraping, sand the area to eliminate all remaining traces of glue. ▼

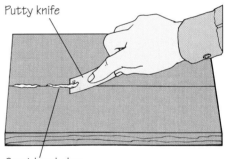

Putty knife

Semi-hard glue

Splotchy job

Before applying a finish, make sure you really have removed all the glue. By wetting the surface with mineral spirits or a lacquer thinner, you can reveal any remaining glue splotches. (The splotches will stay light-colored while the rest of the area darkens.) Remove the glue from those spots so that they won't mar your finish.

FINISHING WOOD

Filler

For all those guitarists

Save your old plastic guitar picks. Their flexibility makes them ideal for applying putty to nail holes and small nicks in woodwork. ▼

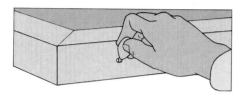

Knotty putty

To fill nail holes in knotty pine, mix raw sienna–colored acrylic or dry powder paint with wood putty. Make about four mixtures, varying in shades from very light to dark brown. Apply the shades to match the knotty wood. For nail holes in regular unknotted wood, make your own filler by mixing sawdust from the wood with white glue.

Open pores

If you want a high-gloss smooth finish in an open-grained wood like oak, walnut, or mahogany, fill the pores with paste filler. (For a satin or more natural finish, the filler isn't needed.) For a light stain, apply a mixture of the stain and filler. For a dark stain, apply coats of the stain until it's a shade or two lighter than desired; apply the filler mixture as a final coat. Use a plastic card to spread the filler mixture; hold the card with a long side flexed on the wood. Spread the filler diagonally across the grain in each direction, then back and forth with the grain. Scrape off any excess filler with the card. Let the filler dry; then sand it.

From the container

Pour away

Here's how to avoid making a mess when pouring finish, thinner, or any other liquid from an oblong container: Just make sure you hold the can so that the opening is at the top. The liquid will leave the can in a steady stream.

Nutty stain mixer

When you open a can of wood stain, drop two medium-size steel nuts into it. Then each time you use the stain, shake the can to thoroughly stir the contents. (Never do this in a glass jar.) You'll be able to hear when the pigments are no longer sitting at the bottom of the can. Don't try this trick with varnish. Shaking or stirring varnish can create air bubbles that can ruin the finish.

A different filter

Have you run out of paint filters for removing impurities from thinners and light finishing oils, and you don't want to make a special trip to the store? Instead of a filter, use a clean disposable paper dust mask—it's a perfect substitute.

Out of the kitchen

These two kitchen tools are ideal for removing a small amount of liquid from a large container: A gravy ladle is handy for scooping up stain. A turkey baster is ideal for transferring mineral spirits and other solvents. (But if the baster has a plastic tube, first test it to make sure the solvent doesn't soften the tube.)

Applying the finish

Oily hands ▲

Your hands secrete natural oils that can mark unfinished wood. To protect the work, rub sawdust between your hands before handling the stock. The sawdust will draw out and absorb the excess oil.

Versatile alcohol

Prior to finishing a workpiece, remove pencil marks, dirt smudges, grease and oil spots—and wood dust—by wiping (not soaking) the work with denatured alcohol. Alcohol is an effective cleanser and will not raise the grain. Because alcohol can be absorbed through your skin, wear rubber gloves.

Layer by layer

For professional results, follow this work sequence when staining and varnishing: Before starting the job, use scrap wood to test how the stain and varnish will color the wood. When you're ready to begin the sequence, apply the stain; then follow with the sealer and the coats of varnish. Sand the workpiece after sealing it and between coats of varnish. To prevent warpage, make sure you finish every side—even bottoms and backs. This helps keep moisture from entering the wood.

Pour it in

Fitting a brush or rag into a deep recess can be difficult at best. To make the job easier, thin the finish to one-half or one-third of its strength; then pour it into the recess. The thinned finish is less likely to drip. Swirl the finish around to cover the bottom and sides, then pour the excess back into the container. For complete coverage, repeat the process.

The dark end

When finishing a new wood project, treat the end grain last to keep it from staining darker than the rest of the work. Brush turpentine, paint thinner, or mineral spirits onto the end grain just before applying the stain.

Safe finish

To finish salad bowls, butcher blocks, toys, and other wood projects that will hold food or are likely to be chewed on by young children, use mineral oil, salad oil (walnut oil is best), or a brand-name "salad oil finish."

Bright idea ▲

After applying a finish to wood, you'll want to know if you've missed any spots. Here's the best way to check: Examine the work at a 45° angle while shining a bright light on it. The wet finish will reflect the light; missed spots will show up as dull areas.

ABOUT FINISHES

▷ Buy flammable liquids, such as tung oil, varnish, and thinners, in quantities that are just enough to do the job.

▷ Because their vapors can ignite, store flammable liquids in tightly sealed containers, away from the furnace and heaters and out of children's reach.

▷ Keep a fire extinguisher in your work area. Never smoke in this area or near flammable liquids.

▷ Solvent-base liquids are a skin irritant; wear chemical-resistant rubber gloves when using them.

▷ Items soaked in natural oil-base finishes (tung oil, linseed oil, gel stains, and wipe-on finishes) can ignite or explode if exposed to air and then confined. Before disposing of brushes, rags, and other materials exposed to one of these finishes, hang them from a line outside, away from children and pets, until they are dry.

▷ To dispose of leftover finishes, see p.39.

FINISHING WOOD

Equipment

Make it tacky

Use a tack rag to remove dust from a workpiece before applying the first coat of stain or finish, and between coats. You can make your own tack rag out of cheesecloth, an old cotton diaper, or any other lint-free cotton cloth. Dip the cloth in turpentine and wring it out. Then drizzle a small amount of varnish or polyurethane from a stirring stick onto the cloth, and knead the cloth to distribute the finish. The cloth should be able to pick up dust without leaving any finish. To avoid spontaneous combustion, store the rag in a tightly sealed can.

Absorbent stockings

A rag used to apply a stain may leave lint particles all over the work. To avoid this problem, use discarded nylon stockings or panty hose as an applicator. The material leaves a lint-free finish and also absorbs less stain than some cloth applicators. ▼

Canned rags

Don't let your stain rags dry out in the middle of a project. When you're done for the day, store them in an empty stain can. Be sure the lid covers the can tightly, both to keep the rags from drying out and to prevent spontaneous combustion. The rags can be used for a quick touch-up without having to be dipped in the stain again.

Off the cuff

Tired of having stain or finish drip down your arm as you apply it overhead? Wear a long rubber glove on your working hand. Turn up the cuff a few inches and stuff it with toilet paper. Besides catching the drips, the paper will absorb them, so you won't have to worry about spills when you lower your arm.

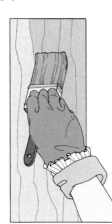

Loose bristles

All brushes lose bristles when first used. Before using a brush for the first time, soak it in the finish for 30 minutes; then clean the brush and let it sit overnight. The dried finish in the ferrule will bond the bristles. To remove any bristles that do come loose, wait for the finish to dry; then pick them out with a knife.

Miniature brush

To apply finishes in hard-to-reach areas, such as crevices on moldings, recycle an old soft-bristle toothbrush.

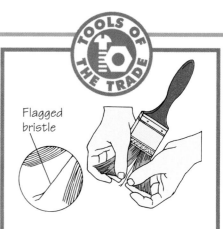

Flagged bristle

THE RIGHT BRUSH

One key to a successful finishing job is picking the right brush—or more to the point, the right bristle—for the type of finish you'll be applying.

For oil varnish and polyurethane, use a brush with natural China bristles (black or white hog hairs). Look for long supple bristles, either flagged or tapered, and a chiseled profile.

For water-base finishes, use synthetic-bristle brushes. (Natural bristles lose their shape in water.) Avoid flagged bristles; they can make the finish foam.

Always look for the best brush you can find. A good-quality brush is worth its price. Select one with a stainless steel ferrule; it won't leave rust marks.

Before dipping a brush in finish, soak it in the appropriate solvent; then squeeze it out. Make sure you clean the brush and reshape the bristles as soon as you're done applying the finish.

Neatness counts

Bring out the Yellow Pages

Open up an old telephone book or catalog and use it as a work surface for small finishing jobs. As the pages get mucky, just rip them out and toss them away—it will take quite some time to use up all those pages.

Knob work

Finishing drawer knobs can be a messy proposition. Here's a way to keep your fingers free of finish by using the screw that secures the knob to the drawer. Fit the screw to the knob; then hold the screw with a clothespin while you apply the finish. When the job is done, balance the assembly in an upright position on a flat surface until the finish dries.

Nut

Leg rests ▲

For rot-free legs on outdoor chairs, soak the bottom of the legs in a wood preservative. To let the preservative get in, stand the chair in disposable pie pans with a nut under each leg. Pour preservative into the pans and let the legs soak overnight. (The nuts raise the legs just enough for the preservative to soak in.)

Give it a lift

When applying finish to table or chair legs, keep the legs from sticking to the work surface by slipping washers under them. The diameter of the washers must be smaller than the diameter of the legs.

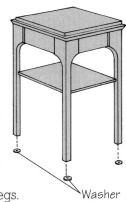

Washer

It's a hold-up

This contraption will allow you to elevate a small project off the work surface while you finish it. Cut ¼-inch dowels into 4-inch lengths, and sharpen both ends in a pencil sharpener. Push the dowels into a base made of foam insulation or packing board. Rest the workpiece on the pointed dowels. Make sure you use enough dowels so that the work doesn't tip over. ▼

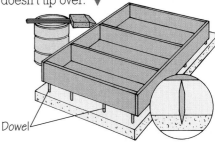

Dowel

Suspended on nails

Here's a way to cut drying time when you're finishing (or painting) a door. Drive 3-inch nails into the top and bottom of the door, and then rest the nails on sawhorses. After you apply the finish on one side, flip the door over (use the nails as handles with a helper at the other end) and apply the finish to the other side. Both sides will dry at the same time. If you're working in a dusty area, use this method to suspend the work with one finished side facing down until it dries.

For those forgetful folks

Prepare for future touch-ups or refinishing jobs by keeping a record of your work. Before applying the finish, stick a label or glue a bit of paper to an inconspicuous area of the project. Record the type of wood, stain, and finish you used and the date. The finish you apply over the paper will hold it in place.

METALWORKING

Clean holes

Sandwich time

To avoid rough or bent edges when you're drilling a hole in sheet metal, clamp the metal between two pieces of scrap wood and drill through the assembly. This trick will produce clean holes whether you use a portable drill or a drill press. It will also produce clean lines when you're cutting sheet metal with a hacksaw or saber saw.

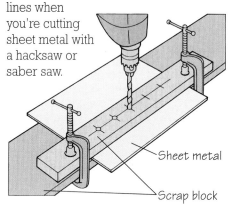

Sheet metal

Scrap block

Removing burrs

Even if you've drilled a hole in sheet metal without sandwiching it in scrap wood, you can still get a clean hole. Just twirl a countersink bit in the hole a few times to remove the burrs. ▼

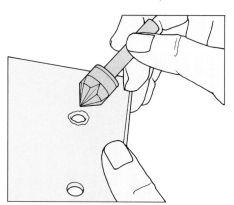

No more wandering bit

When drilling in metal, as in other materials (p.9), you can keep the drill bit from wandering off center by dimpling the surface with a center punch. Don't forget to add light motor oil to the hole to keep the bit from overheating (p.10). Lubrication will also speed cutting time and keep the bit from becoming dull.

Drilling deep

A good way to keep the bit lubricated when drilling in thick metal is to form a wall out of modeling clay around the area to be drilled, thus creating a circular dam. Fill the dam with light machine oil. Keep extra oil on hand in a squirt gun to replenish the dam as needed.

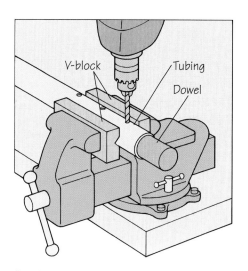

V-block · Tubing · Dowel

Straight through ▲

To drill holes in tubing, secure the tubing in V-blocks held by a vise. Insert a dowel inside the tubing to reinforce the thin walls and to guide the bit straight through to the other side. Be sure the drill bit can exit the bottom end freely.

On file

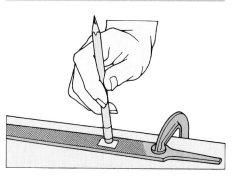

Too small for vises ▲

Sometimes you may want to file a piece of metal that is too small to grip in a vise or to hold with your fingers. The solution is to move the piece against the file with an eraser-tipped pencil. Clamp or hold the file securely to a work surface.

Cover up

While you are using a file, the unused side can mar your work. To protect the work from scratches, cover the file's unused side with adhesive or duct tape.

Chalky filler

Soft metals, such as aluminum, copper, and brass, clog the teeth of some files. To reduce clogging, first rub talcum powder or a piece of chalk across the file teeth. The powder keeps the metal from caking up and allows the chips to be cleaned out easily with a file card.

Clean up

Never blow on a file to remove metal particles. They might wind up in your eyes and cause serious damage. If you don't have a file card, remove the particles from the file by pressing putty or masking tape onto the cutting surface. When you pull the putty or tape off the file, the particles will come up too.

Saw power

Nick a notch

Before making a hacksaw cut, create a starting notch for the blade by nicking the workpiece at the cut line with a file. The notch will act as a guide, preventing the blade from slipping. (On a round piece of metal, use a three-cornered file to cut a V-shaped notch.)

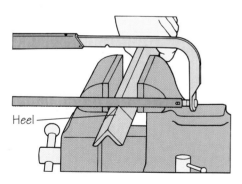

Heel

Cut the heel ▲

When cutting a steel angle with a hacksaw, secure the angle in a vise with the heel end up. This way, the hacksaw will cut both sides of the angle at the same time. And because more saw teeth are in contact with the work, the resulting cut will be smoother and more accurate.

Stop that annoying chatter

When cutting steel, aluminum, or brass plate in a bench vise, the free end lets out a noisy chatter or screech with every stroke of a hacksaw. To stop the racket, wrap the free end of the workpiece in a wet towel or rag. This will dampen the offending vibrations and calm your nerves too.

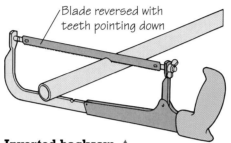

Blade reversed with teeth pointing down

Inverted hacksaw ▲

If you have a hacksaw job to do but no room to use the saw, here's a way around your problem. Simply remove the saw blade and reinsert it in an inverted position. This trick is especially handy for cutting an overhead pipe.

Oily cut ▶

Aluminum and other soft metals are best cut with a saber saw that is equipped with a fine-tooth blade. To keep the teeth on the blade from clogging, apply light machine oil along the cut line. The oil will also keep the blade cooler and sharper.

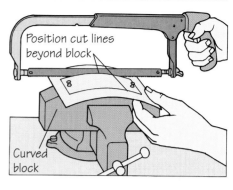

Position cut lines beyond block

Curved block

A rectangular hole ▲

It's possible to make a rectangular inside cut in sheet metal with a hacksaw without cutting in from the edge. First saw a curve in a block of scrap wood. Clamp the wood, curved edge up, in a vise. Mark cut lines on the sheet metal, and drive two double-headed nails through the waste area to hold the work to the wood. The sheet will bend, with its center protruding up. Make the two cuts along the length of the block. Then remove and reposition the work to make the last two saw cuts.

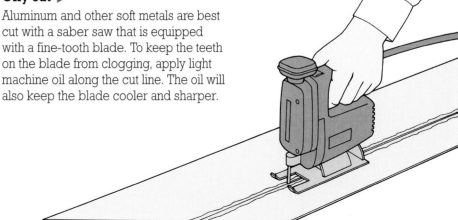

Fastener facts

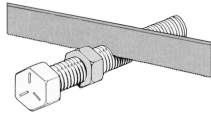

Customized bolt ▲

If a bolt is too long for the intended job, you can cut it to size with a hacksaw; but first twist a nut onto the bolt past the cut mark. Unscrewing the nut after the saw cut is made cleans the threads and removes any burrs at the cut end. To make the newly cut bolt even easier to thread, bevel the end with a grinder or file.

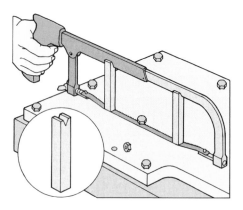

Flush cut ▲

With slight adaptations to a hacksaw, you can cut a bolt or screw flush to the work. Notch one end of two 3½-inch-long pieces of scrap wood. Loosen the saw blade and rotate it until the teeth point sideways. Place the wood pieces between the saw frame and the turned blade, and tighten the blade. The wood will push the blade down slightly below the saw frame, letting you make the cut.

Rusted nut and bolt

One way to remove a rusted nut and bolt is to apply penetrating oil (p.14). To keep the oil where it will do the most good, build a circular dam around the nut with wood putty, plumber's putty, or modeling clay. The dam not only holds the oil, it lets you soak the whole nut.

Take a hack at it

Here's how to remove a rusted nut without damaging the threads of the bolt. Use a hacksaw to make a starting cut in the nut, parallel to one of its faces; then split the nut with a cold chisel. (Make sure you wear safety glasses for this.) Finally, unscrew the nut with an adjustable wrench.

Too loose for comfort?

To keep nuts and bolts from coming loose, apply a small dab of clear silicone caulk on the bolt threads before you tighten the nut. For added insurance, smear a large dab of silicone caulk over any exposed threads. Once it's dry, the fasteners won't be able to work loose; but if you have to remove them, the caulk will easily peel off.

Sheet metal

Make it clear

Before marking metal with a scriber or awl, run a dark-colored wide-tipped felt marker over the area to be scribed. The scribe marks will show up more clearly against the dark background.

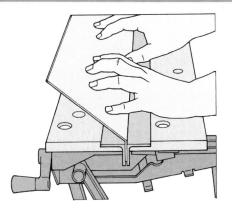

Homemade brake ▲

Turn your portable workbench and two pieces of metal angle into a homemade bending brake. The metal angles should have sharp 90° edges so that the sheet metal creases evenly. Place the angles in the workbench as shown. Start the fold by hand; then finish it by pounding the metal with a hardwood block and mallet for a sharp crease. If you don't have a portable workbench, use C-clamps to clamp the angles together.

Get the dents out

Here are two ways to remove dents from metal objects. Hold the object against a sandbag and gently flatten out the raised side of the dent with a mallet. Or hold the face of a sledgehammer

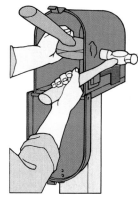

or a dolly block (available at auto supply stores) against the dent; strike the raised side of the dent with the flat face of a ball-peen or auto-body hammer.

Soldering

Spool control

Chasing a runaway spool of solder can be a nuisance, especially if it rolls off the table and onto your foot first. To keep the solder from rolling about, try bending out one rim of the spool. ▼

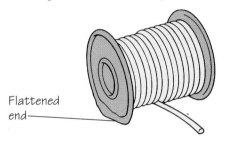

Flattened end

Dispensing solder

Clear plastic pill containers make excellent dispensers for thin wire solder. Just slip a coil of the solder into the container, pierce a hole in the cap, feed the solder through the hole, and snap the cap in place. Now all you have to do is pull out the solder as you need it. A plastic tape dispenser can also hold wire solder. Wind the wire around the empty spool, place it in the dispenser, and feed it through a hole drilled just below the serrated edge. (Break off the serrated edge to avoid cutting yourself on the teeth.)

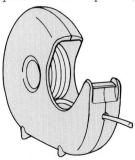

Cut to size

Join small parts more neatly with wire solder by first flattening it with a hammer and then cutting the solder with tin snips into three or more fine strands. ▼

Close quarters

If you have to solder two joints right next to each other, clamp a wet sponge over the first joint before soldering the second one. This will prevent heat from the soldering iron from reaching and loosening the first joint.

Resting place

Finding a place to put a hot soldering iron so it won't roll away or damage something can be tricky. One solution is to make a stand for the soldering iron out of a sturdy metal coat hanger by bending it as shown below. ▼

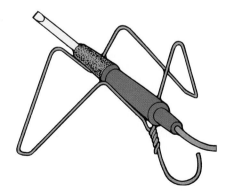

A clean tip

To ensure proper performance, it's important to keep the tip of your soldering gun or iron clean and bright at all times. Here's how to improvise your own tip cleaner. Stuff a pad of fine steel wool inside a shallow metal can, such as a tuna fish or cat food can, and crimp the edges of the can. The crimped edges hold the steel wool in place, and they can also serve as an iron rest. ▼

Clean tip by rubbing it against steel wool

Soldering iron

A chilling problem

When you're soldering outdoors on a cold day, the solder will get cold and draw heat away from the soldering iron. To remedy this problem, hammer the solder into a thin ribbon. It will melt almost instantly.

Wet cloth philosophy

When soldering copper plumbing pipes and fittings, keep a wet cloth handy to wipe the joint clean. After soldering the joint, wrap the cloth around it and turn the cloth with a twist of the wrist. This will not only result in a neater joint by removing excess solder; it will also fill any tiny holes in the solder, resulting in a more leakproof joint. While wiping the joint, be careful not to touch the hot pipe with your hand.

WORKING WITH GLASS

The equipment

Tape it down

To keep a metal straightedge from slipping when you cut glass, run a strip of thin double-faced tape along the cut line. Then lay the straightedge on the tape and make the cut with the glass cutter. The tape will keep the straight-edge stationary.

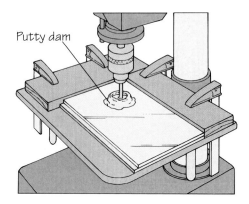

Putty dam

Here's a special bit ▲

Before installing handles, hinges, and other hardware in glass, you may have to drill a hole in the glass. For holes up to ½ inch in diameter, use a special spade-shaped glass bit in a drill press or hand drill. Surround the spot where you'll be drilling with a dam made out of putty. Fill the dam with turpentine, and run the drill slowly. For larger holes, use a circle cutter or have the job done by a glass supplier. Drill no closer than 1 inch to the edge of the glass. As always when handling glass, make sure you wear goggles and heavy gloves while you work.

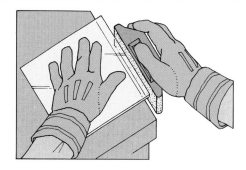

Smooth finish ▲

Rough edges can be smoothed with a silicone carbide stone or silicone carbide sandpaper supported with a block (p.81). Lubricate the edge with mineral spirits; lightly stroke the stone or block along the edge in one direction.

Supportive putty

Repairing a broken glass object, such as a champagne goblet, is easier if you support the pieces with putty while the glue sets. Because the putty will have to be positioned in several spots, test-fit the clean glass pieces on the putty before applying the glue. Use an epoxy adhesive specified for glass. ▼

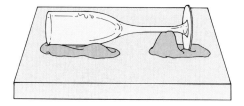

Wheel protection

A traveler's plastic toothbrush holder is the perfect storage container for a glass cutter. To cushion the wheel and retard rust, place an oil-moistened wad of cotton in the bottom of the holder.

Safety glass

Plastic and glass sandwich

Laminated glass consists of a layer of plastic sandwiched between two layers of glass. To cut it, score and run both faces of the glass, using a length of wire instead of a larger round object under the glass (see facing page). Heat the exposed plastic along the score with a heat gun until it is pliable, pull the glass far enough apart to insert a razor knife, and cut the plastic along the score.

Wired glass

To cut safety glass that has wire mesh embedded in it, place the glass on a workbench with the wire mesh closer to the bench top (the mesh is closer to one face of the glass than the other). Score this type of glass in the same way as you would regular glass (facing page); then snap the glass down over the round object until the wires are severed. If any wires poke out, just snip them off.

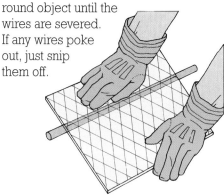

Tempered glass warning

While ordinary glass is easy to work, tempered glass (which you may find in a door, for instance) is a much stronger glass. Do not attempt to cut, drill, or smooth the edges of this type of glass.

CUTTING GLASS

Thicknesses and types of glass vary, so ask a retailer which glass is best for your application. Because large pieces are difficult to cut, work with smaller pieces at first.

Getting ready. Work on a flat surface, preferably a workbench or plywood. Clean the glass before you start. Lay out the cut with a marking crayon, glass-marking pencil, or china marker. To make the cut, you'll need a straightedge and a glass cutter. Use a sharp cutter; one with a carbide wheel will stay sharp longer. Lubricate the cutter and the cut line with mineral spirits or with equal parts of light machine oil and kerosene.

Score, then run. Cutting glass isn't cutting at all; it's controlled breaking. The process has two parts: scoring a line with the glass cutter, and running the cut along the score, which is known as breaking out the score. Score curved shapes around a wooden pattern. Break out a slight curve as you would a straight line. For a sharp curve, score extra radial lines and remove one piece at a time. Smooth all edges by rubbing them with a sharpening stone.

Caution: When handling glass, wear goggles and heavy gloves. Dispose of the shards in a closed container or wrap them in paper; then discard.

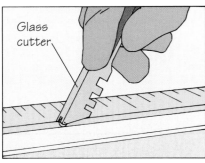

Draw cutter with a single fast, uniform stroke. A crackling sound means correct pressure; white flakes, too much.

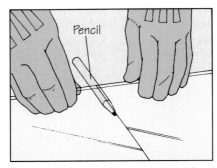

Run the cut by placing a round object at the edge of the glass under the score. Exert slight downward pressure.

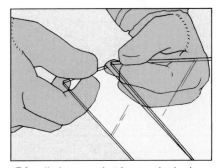

Small pieces and strips can be broken out by holding the glass on both sides of the score line and bending down.

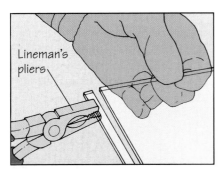

Narrow strips should be handled with lineman's or flat-jaw pliers. Bend the strip down to break out the score.

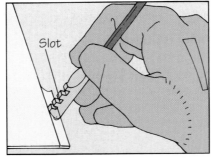

Nibble away at small pieces that don't break on the line, using pliers or the slots on the cutter.

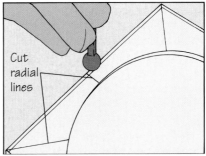

Curved cuts are run by turning the piece upside down and tapping with a cutter or pushing with a gloved thumb.

WORKING WITH PLASTICS

Special tools

Drill bit tip

Plastic laminate and acrylic tend to chip when drilled with standard twist bits. To avoid this problem, buy a specially ground bit from a plastics supplier, or try rounding the tip of a standard twist bit and slowly blunting its two cutting edges on a grinder. Before drilling, make sure you clamp the plastic in place with a backing of scrap wood.

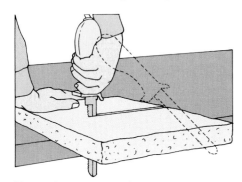

From the kitchen ▲

A kitchen electric carving knife is just the tool you need to make clean cuts in foam rubber or in rigid foam insulation. If you want to make a straight cut, mark the cutting line with a straightedge and marking pen. Place the material on a firm work surface, with the cutting line overhanging the edge of the surface by an inch or more. Begin the cut as you would a cut with a handsaw, starting with the knife at a 45° angle. Draw the knife about 2 inches into the foam; then straighten it until the blade is perpendicular to the work. For round or shaped cuts, hold the material on edge in a vise. With the cutting line facing you, make the cut with the blade facing down. Rotate the work as you go.

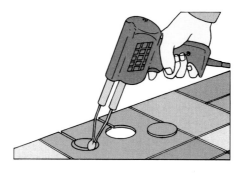

Some like it hot ▲

Some soldering guns come with a cutting tip that lets you cut plastics such as acrylic, vinyl, and expanded poly-styrene. They're handy for cutting floor tiles to fit around water and heating pipes and door thresholds. To determine how fast to move the tip and how much pressure to apply, first practice cutting on scrap material.

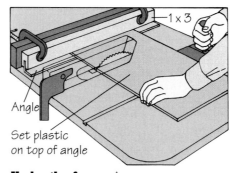

Under the fence ▲

Thin material, such as plastic laminate, can easily slip underneath the rip fence of a table saw. The next time you need to rip such thin stock, clamp this problem solver to the fence. Cut a piece of 1 x 3 to the length of your fence; make a groove down the center of one edge of the piece. Then glue a ⅛- x ¾- x ¾-inch aluminum angle into the groove, using epoxy adhesive. Use C-clamps to hold the guide in place while sawing.

Give it a lift

You can cut plastic tubing even if you don't have a pipe cutter. Instead use a miter box and a hacksaw with a 24-teeth-per-inch blade. To raise small-diameter tubing high enough for the saw to cut through it, place a block of scrap wood under it. Clamp the scrap wood to the work surface to hold it and the miter box in place. ▼

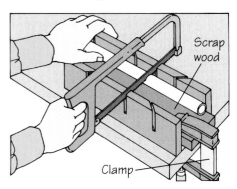

Acrylic

A cushioning point

It's possible to lay out circles on acrylic with a compass or dividers without leaving point marks in the work. At the center of the circle build up a cushioned area with layers of masking tape. When you position the compass or dividers, make sure the point doesn't go through all the layers of tape and into the acrylic.

Clear cutting

To make the cutting line more visible on acrylic, apply a strip of masking tape along the area of the cut and mark the cutting line on the tape. Not only will the line stand out, but chipped edges will be kept to a minimum.

Old stuck paper

If you store acrylic for a long time with the protective paper still on it, the adhesive may dry out and make it tough to take off the paper. To make removal easier, soak the acrylic in isopropyl alcohol. After peeling off the paper, remove any remaining adhesive with alcohol on a soft cloth.

Gritty toothpaste

Because toothpaste is a mild abrasive, it's ideal for removing scratches in acrylic plastic. After removing the scratch, buff the area with a clean cloth.

Sheet laminate

Orderly fashion

When laminating a backsplash, there's an order that makes the job easier. First laminate and trim the ends, then the front, and finally the top. Don't trim the top piece, however, until the backsplash has been mounted; the back edge may have to be shaped to fit the wall (p.71).

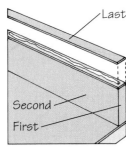

Placement aides ▲

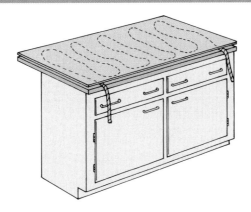

To position sheet laminate on a substrate, you'll need spacers to keep the adhesive-covered surfaces apart until the two materials are properly aligned. You can use wooden dowels or cardboard strips, or you can snake a piece of rope or an extension cord down the length of the work. When the laminate is in the right position, start at one end and pull out one dowel at a time, or gradually remove the rope, as you press the laminate in place.

The other side

Here's a time-saving way to apply plastic laminate to both sides of a door, shelf, or other workpiece at almost the same time. Drive four finishing nails partway into your workbench; place the nails so the work can rest on them. Then spread the contact cement on the work, turn it over, rest it on the nails, and coat the opposite side. Once the cement reaches the correct tackiness, laminate the top side; then turn the work over and laminate the other side.

Exposed edges

If moisture penetrates the unsealed edges of a countertop, the laminate will separate from the particleboard base. To prevent moisture penetration, seal the exposed underside of the countertop (especially at the front edge) with a clear polyurethane.

Solid-surface material

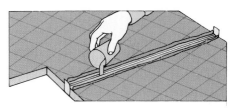

At the seam ▲

When joining solid surfacing material, set the pieces 1/8 inch apart. (And offset the seam from the corner to avoid placing stress on it.) To keep the adhesive from running, apply masking tape under the seam and up the ends.

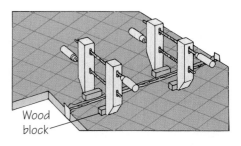

Gripping blocks ▲

If you don't have clamps long enough to hold the pieces while the adhesive dries, attach temporary blocks on each side of the seam with hot-melt glue. Clamp as shown, but not too tight. After the adhesive dries, tap off the blocks.

HOUSEHOLD STORAGE

HALLS AND ENTRYWAYS

Hall walls

Overhead shelving

The long walls of a hallway are an often overlooked source of storage space. Extra-wide halls can accommodate floor-to-ceiling shelving, but be sure to leave at least 36 inches of floor space clear so as not to impede the traffic flow. In a narrower hall, install a single open shelf about a foot below the ceiling and use it to store seldom used items or to display decorative ones.

Not for kitchens only

If your hallway is wide enough, kitchen wall cabinets—set on the floor and covered with a shallow countertop and/or hung on the wall—are a practical alternative to floor-to-ceiling hallway shelves.

Hall closet organizers

Moisture control

This shoe rack allows air to circulate around wet shoes and boots, while the underlying pan makes cleanup easy. The rack is a 1 x 3 pine frame fitted with $\frac{3}{8}$-inch dowels. Make the frame large enough so that it fits over the aluminum or plastic pan. (Coated wire shelving is a simpler, if homelier, substitute for the wood rack.) ▼

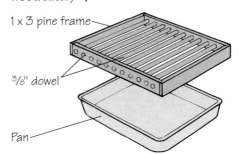

1 x 3 pine frame

$\frac{3}{8}$" dowel

Pan

Winter wear storage

Stow away gloves and caps on this wire rack installed on the back of a hall closet door. Straighten a wire coat hanger and feed it through three screw eyes mounted on the door. Once the wire is past the middle eye, start sliding clothespins onto it. To secure the rack, bend the wire around the screw eyes at each end.

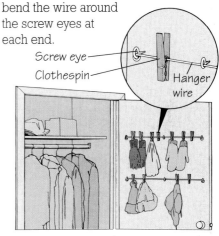

Screw eye

Clothespin

Hanger wire

Mudroom

Heavy-duty entrance ▶

An entry room where family members can leave wet or dirty gear is a great asset. When planning a mudroom:
▷ Locate it near the busiest entrance, where people are most likely to pass through it.
▷ Consider enlarging a back-door pantry or partitioning a porch or garage.
▷ If possible, put a door at each end to make the room an energy-saving, dirt-blocking air lock.
▷ Design the room to meet the needs and activities of all family members.

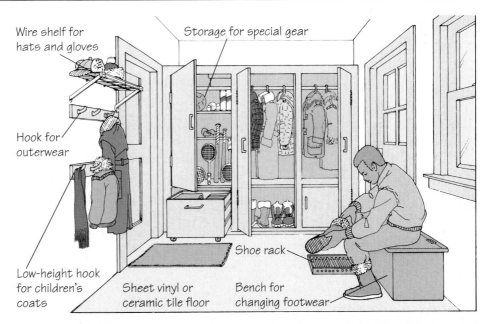

Wire shelf for hats and gloves

Storage for special gear

Hook for outerwear

Low-height hook for children's coats

Sheet vinyl or ceramic tile floor

Shoe rack

Bench for changing footwear

BEDROOMS AND LIVING AREAS

Out of sight

Murphy revisited

A hideaway wall bed not only saves space, it turns an ordinary bedroom into a multi-use room. A horizontal alternative to the traditional vertical wall bed offers even greater space savings. Available from suppliers of wall bed systems and occasionally from other furniture dealers, a side bed when closed looks like a dining room cabinet or buffet. Opened, the bed takes up remarkably little floor space (the twin-size model, for example, may project as little as half the distance a vertical wall bed would extend). A side bed is usually easy to assemble and install; only a few screws are needed to secure the unit to wall studs. ▼

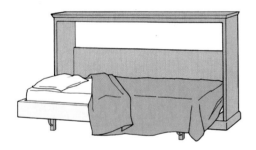

Window seat ▶

Create extra seating and storage space along a window wall by lining the wall beneath the window with sturdy low cabinets. Install a plywood platform over the cabinets, and top it off with cushions. Edge the platform with molding for a finished look.

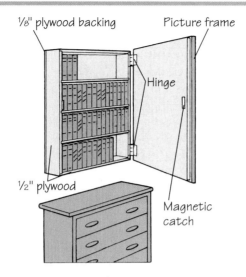

1/8" plywood backing   Picture frame

Hinge

1/2" plywood

Magnetic catch

Hidden tapes ▲

A wall-hung cabinet, securely fastened to wall studs and concealed by a favorite painting or print, is great for storing video- or music cassettes. Make the cabinet frame and the shelves out of 1/2-inch plywood. Match the width and length of the cabinet to the dimensions of the picture frame; the cabinet's depth depends on the items being stored. Use 1/8-inch plywood to make the cabinet back. The picture frame is hinged to the cabinet on one side and held shut by a magnetic catch on the other.

Secret shelves

Between-stud shelving needn't be limited to places where studs are exposed, like an unfinished garage or basement (p.57). You can create space for recessed shelves in a finished inside, or partition, wall by cutting into the wallboard with a keyhole saw. (For more on locating studs and cutting wallboard, see pp.135 and 137.) Nail cleats to the studs to support shelves made of 1 x 4 pine boards. If desired, conceal the storage area behind a painting hinged to the wall. Do not try to create between-stud shelving in exterior walls or in walls with plumbing, ductwork, and electrical lines running through them.

Back-of-door hideaway

The back of closet and other interior doors is an untapped storage resource just waiting to be used. You can hang a full-length mirror on the back of a door, pepper it with clothes hooks, or use it to mount shelves or a tall, slender cabinet for the odd little items that don't fit elsewhere. (For more back-of-door storage ideas, see pp.103, 111, and 112.) Some of these space savers, however, can add a good deal of weight to the door. In such cases, interior doors, which are usually hung with only two 3½-inch hinges, may need added support. If you plan to add substantially to the load on a door's hinges, it's a good idea to install a third (middle) hinge to ensure that the door will operate properly and remain sag-free.

Bedtime storage

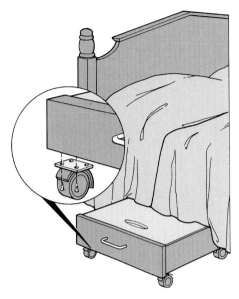

Bed box ▶

If you're thinking about building a platform bed, consider one that rests not on drawers but on a deep hollow box built of ¾-inch plywood. Even though you have to remove the mattress and lift off the top of the box to get at it, the space under the bed is ideal for storing cumbersome, seldom used items, family heirlooms, and other belongings that you want hidden.

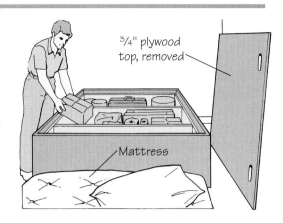

¾" plywood top, removed

Mattress

Recycled drawers ▲

Give new life to old dresser drawers as under-the-bed storage bins. Fasten small casters to the bottoms of the drawers and slide them under the bed to store seasonal clothes, extra blankets, and more. To keep out dust, add a snug-fitting hinged ¼-inch plywood top to the drawers. If you don't have recyclable dresser drawers on hand, look in home centers or storage catalogs for inexpensive, easy-to-assemble under-bed drawer systems.

Head room

When buying a new bed, look for a headboard with shelves or shallow cabinets built into it. This type of bed not only provides convenient storage space, it makes efficient use of available bedroom floor space by eliminating the need for night tables.

Drawer organizers

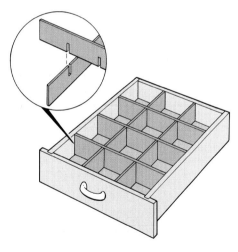

Divide and conquer ▲

Create compartments in a shallow drawer by notching and joining strips of wood lattice (available at lumberyards and home centers). Clamp the crosspieces together and cut the notches all at once so they'll align exactly.

See-through dividers

Drawer dividers may also be made from ¼-inch sheet acrylic (have the retailer cut the pieces to size, or cut them yourself using a fine blade in a table or radial arm saw). Butt the pieces together in whatever arrangement you desire; then bond the joints with acrylic solvent. (For more on working with acrylic, see pp.100–101.)

Sliding tray

Here's a way to increase a deep drawer's usable space. Make a box of ½-inch plywood and support it on hardwood runners glued to the sides of the drawer. The tray should be half the drawer's width or length so that you can slide it aside for easy access to the bottom of the drawer. Or make the tray full length and add handles for easy lift-out.

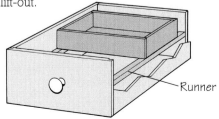

Runner

KITCHEN

Looking up ▶

The space between the tops of kitchen cabinets and the ceiling is ideal for storing pots, pans, and serving dishes or for displaying baskets, plants, and ornamental pieces. To make the most of this space, install simple storage boxes made out of ¾-inch veneer-core plywood. Build as many boxes as necessary to fill the space, butt them together, and cover the joints with strips of molding; cover any exposed plywood edges with iron-on veneer tape.

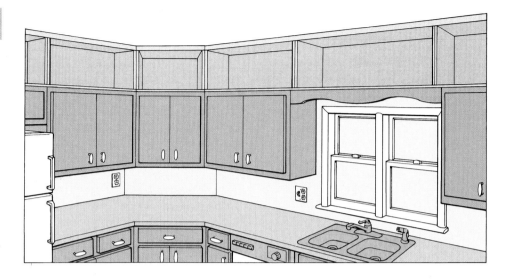

Cavity filler

One way to increase kitchen storage space is to install a shallow pantry in the cavity between wall studs. Pick an inside wall where there are no pipes or electrical outlets or switches. Use a stud finder to locate the studs (p.135); then cut through the wallboard with a wallboard (drywall) saw. Line the back of the cavity with ¾-inch plywood. Frame the pantry flush with the wall or extending several inches beyond it (for extra depth); then add shelving and doors.

Recycling center

Install a custom cabinet with tilt-out bins to sort recyclables, or fit an existing kitchen cabinet with commercial recycling bins. Another alternative is to stash recyclables in a hinged-top bench with internal dividers; install the bench either in the kitchen or near the back door.

Closets to spare? ▲

If you have an underutilized closet in or near the kitchen, why not turn it into a playroom? Simply decorate the walls with bright colors, install shelves and a desk, add a stool, toy bin, and wastebasket, and hook the door open. Your children can play close by, but not underfoot, while you work in the kitchen.

Trial run

Before equipping your kitchen with an island or any permanent cabinet, mark its location on the floor with masking tape or place a large box in the area to see how the installation will affect traffic flow. Rethink the layout if you continually overstep the lines or bump into the box.

Hideaway tables

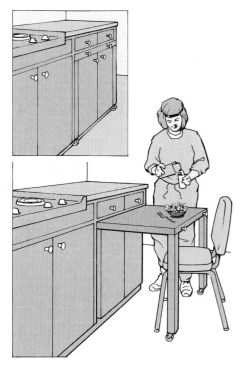

Disappearing act ▲

Even a tiny kitchen can accommodate this custom-made pull-out table. When not in use, the butcher-block top and two legs (on casters) slide into slots cut into the base cabinet. The legs and front edge of the table are faced to match the surrounding cabinets.

Table in a drawer

Are you short of kitchen counter space? Would you be willing to give up a drawer in exchange for a large extra work surface that can double as a table? If so, here's the hardware you need to create a hideaway tabletop/counter. Available through suppliers and installers of kitchen cabinets and equipment, this pair of massive metal drawer slides (rated to support 175 pounds) holds a two-part tabletop. Since one part of the table slides out from under the other automatically as the drawer is opened, you get a 32-inch-deep table sliding out of an ordinary 24-inch-deep drawer. Make the tabletop pieces out of butcher block or other material that is ¾ inch thick or less; use the existing drawer front to cap the tabletop/counter. ▼

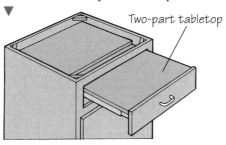

Two-part tabletop

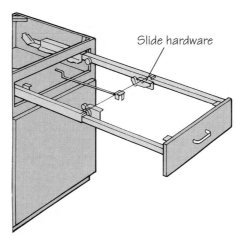

Slide hardware

Counters and shelves

Inset cutting board

Make better use of your counter space by setting a cutting board into it. Use sink rim edging to keep the board flush with the countertop. For quick food cleanup, cut a slot in the cutting board and place a garbage bin below it. ▼

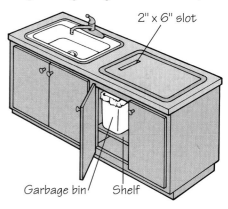

2" x 6" slot

Garbage bin   Shelf

Add-a-shelf

A slide-in shelf made of ¾-inch plywood is a good way to organize the space below a sink. Determine the height of the shelf (allowing room for the trap), and cut two side supports to that height. Cut the shelf ¼ inch shorter than the inside width of the cabinet. Attach the shelf to the side supports with 6d finishing nails; slide the unit into place. ▼

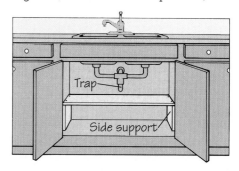

Trap

Side support

KITCHEN

Racks and dispensers

Lid holder

Keep pot lids handy with these easy-to-make wooden racks. The ends are made of 1 x 3 pine boards, the cross-pieces of ¾-inch square molding. ▼

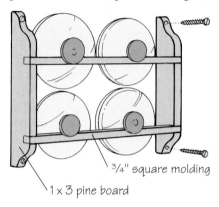

¾" square molding

1 x 3 pine board

Suspended stemware

Protect fragile wine glasses by hanging them from this under-the-cabinet ply-wood rack. Cut the openings with a plunge router or saber saw. The same idea can be adapted to make an under-the-cabinet storage rack for food processor blades.

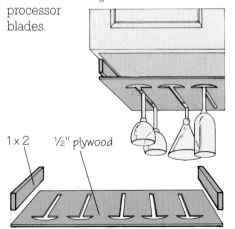

1 x 2   ½" plywood

Organizers

Stow-aways

Stores that specialize in storage systems and supplies, as well as regular home centers and hardware stores, offer a wide variety of space-making cabinet accessories that put every inch of your kitchen cabinets to work. Most of these organizers can be installed in a few minutes and are relatively inexpensive. Among the most useful are two- or three-tier storage racks that roll out on metal slides, roll-out trash baskets, and even entire pull-out pantry systems. Shown at right are a spice rack that folds flat under a wall cabinet and a food processor or mixer shelf that swings up and out of a base cabinet (the cabinet opening must be at least 12 inches wide and 22½ inches deep).

Sink front tray ▶

Trays mounted behind sink front or cook-top panels turn this often wasted space into a convenient storage area for clean-ing supplies and small utensils. Secure the panels at the bottom with spring-loaded hinges. The trays are available at home centers and hardware stores.

Stair-step shelves

To bring order to a messy cupboard shelf, stagger its contents on stair-step shelves so you can easily see items at the back. Although available in stores, these steps are easy to make by gluing together 2 x 4 scraps and covering them with shelf paper.

2 x 4 scraps

Bulletin board ▲

Use recycled wine corks to create a message center by gluing them with a hot-glue gun onto plywood. Glue the corks lengthwise to the wood; start in a corner and position two corks vertically, then two horizontally. Continue the pattern until the plywood is covered; frame the board with strips of molding.

A different slant

If you buy canned food or drinks in bulk, here's a handy shelving idea that automatically feeds cans toward the front each time you remove one. Using fin-back clips and angled brackets (see pp.120–121), mount vinyl-coated wire shelving upside down and at an angle so that the lip sticks up in front to hold the cans in place. ▼

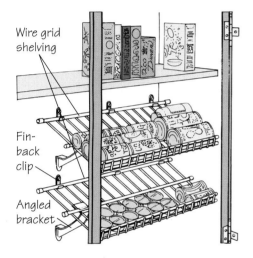

Wire grid shelving

Fin-back clip

Angled bracket

More kitchen organizers

▷ A pull-down cookbook rack that mounts on the bottom of a standard wall cabinet, similar to the spice rack shown on the facing page.
▷ A full-circle lazy susan for mounting in a base or wall corner cabinet.
▷ Wire racks installed on the insides of cabinet doors for keeping small items within easy reach.
▷ A perf-board or wire grid wall organizer (see p.127).
▷ A heavy-duty rack for hanging pots and pans from the ceiling or wall.

ISLAND LIFE

Create a practical kitchen storage and eating area by mounting an inexpensive countertop on prefinished base cabinets. The island shown here uses two cabinets, but you can group together any number. Choose cabinets to fit your needs: If you want a sink in the island, use a base sink cabinet; build an L-shaped island around a corner cabinet fitted with a lazy susan.

To anchor the cabinets, screw 2 x 2's to the floor around the cabinets' interior perimeter line. Place the cabinets over the 2 x 2's and level the cabinets as needed by wedging wood shims under their bottom edges. Then drive screws through the cabinet bottoms into the 2 x 2's. Use wood or vinyl base trim to hide the screw holes.

Before building the countertop, figure out the optimum overhang. If you're using ceramic tiles, size the counter to accept an even number of them in order to avoid cutting. (Remember to allow space for the grout.) Attach the countertop to the cabinets with screws coming up through the base cabinets' top rails.

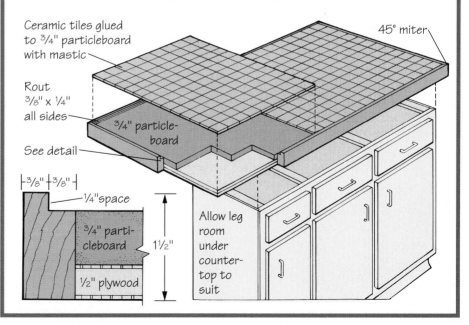

Ceramic tiles glued to ³⁄₄" particleboard with mastic

45° miter

Rout ³⁄₈" x ¹⁄₄" all sides

³⁄₄" particleboard

See detail

⊢³⁄₈"⊣⊢³⁄₈"⊣

¹⁄₄" space

³⁄₄" particleboard

1¹⁄₂"

¹⁄₂" plywood

Allow leg room under countertop to suit

Shelves and racks

Out of the linen closet

For a colorful decorative touch, store towels on open shelving in the bathroom. The wall over the toilet is a good place. You can also use the space to store rolls of toilet paper or other bathroom supplies.

Easy-reach towel

If you're installing a new bathroom cabinet or redoing an old one, consider creating a recess that will keep a towel right where you need it most, below the sink. Make the niche about 2½ inches deep, line it to match the surrounding cabinetry, and fit it with a towel bar. Set the bar ½ inch back from the front of the cabinet. ▼

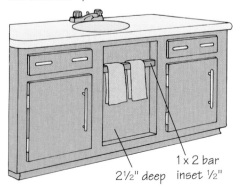

2½" deep   1 x 2 bar inset ½"

Park your dryer here ▲

An appliance garage installed within easy reach of the sink is as useful in a bathroom as in the kitchen. In the example shown here, a roll-down tambour door covers a cabinet built into the space between wall studs. (For more on between-stud shelving and cabinetry, see pp.104 and 106.)

Private library

A plastic magazine file, sold at office supply stores, makes a handy holder for bathroom reading materials. Just mount the file on the wall next to the toilet, and your private reading room is ready.

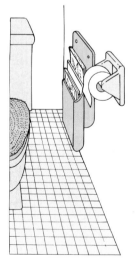

Over your head

The area above bathroom windows and doors is often wasted. Put the space to work by installing a decorative shelf or vinyl-coated wire shelving. Use these out-of-the-way shelves to store extra towels or items you wish to keep out of the reach of children.

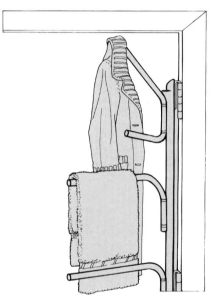

Hinge hanger ▲

Take advantage of every inch of bathroom space with a door-hinge-mounted towel and robe rack. Available at hardware stores and home centers, this hinge hanger comes in different sizes, materials, and finishes and is easy to install. Simply remove the door hinge pins, position the rack, and reinstall the pins. There are no holes to drill (or repair), and if you move, you can take the rack with you.

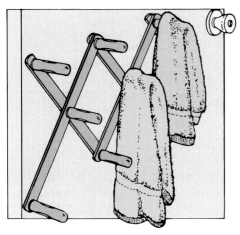

For small fry ▲

To encourage children to hang up their towels, make sure racks are accessible to them. If you have the wall space, mount one or more towel racks below an existing rack. Or build a towel ladder out of 1 x 4 rails and 1-inch dowels; attach the ladder to brackets screwed to wall studs. If wall space is limited, fasten an expandable wooden mug rack to the back of the bathroom door at a height your smallest child can reach.

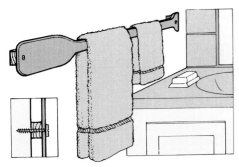

Paddle bar ▲

Make an eye-catching towel rack from an old wood canoe paddle varnished with several coats of clear polyurethane. Mount the paddle to the wall studs with lag screws through 2 x 2 spacer blocks.

Organizers

Shower tower

Tall shower units containing multiple shelves and racks are easy to install in the corner of a bath or shower and provide a place for everything. They're available at most home centers.

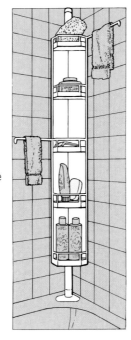

Soap, shampoo, conditioner

Organize your bath products (and avoid spills) with a wall-mounted push-button plastic dispenser, available with one, two, or four compartments. ▼

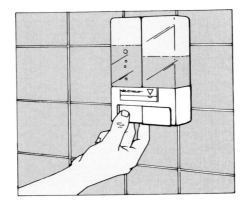

Not for kitchens only

Many of the space-stretching cabinet accessories designed for kitchens (p.108) can also help bring order to your bathroom cabinets. A case in point is this lazy susan, available in single and two-tiered models from home centers and kitchen supply stores. Before buying any one of these hardworking organizers, measure the space inside the cabinet carefully, making needed allowances for drainpipe clearance. ▼

Under a pedestal

One way to increase storage space in a bathroom equipped with a pedestal sink is to hang a skirt on the sink and use the newly created space to stash paper goods and cleaning products. You can buy such skirts ready-made or make your own out of a heavy washable fabric. Sew a Velcro strip to the top inside edge of the skirt, and glue another strip to the sink rim with silicone-base adhesive.

LAUNDRY AREA

Hidden boards

Now you see it...

As they do for the kitchen (p.108), home centers, hardware stores, and suppliers of storage systems offer many different space-saving laundry items, three of which

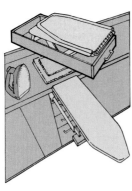

are shown on this page. The ironing-board-in-a-drawer pulls out and unfolds in seconds. The drawer opening must be at least 21 inches deep by 14 inches wide by 3¼ inches high. Unfolded, the board measures about 39 inches long. There should be at least 18 inches clearance beyond the end of the board.

...Now you don't

The door-back ironing board hooks securely to the top edge of a closet door

and folds down for use. A separate installation kit enables you to mount the board permanently to a door, wallboard, or studs.

Bins and racks

Ironing organizer

This rack is specially designed to hold an iron, a freestanding ironing board, and other ironing paraphernalia. Mount the rack on a laundry room wall or in a closet near where you do your ironing. ▼

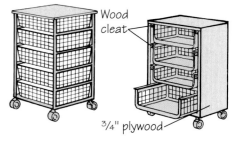

Wood cleat

¾" plywood

Order out of chaos ▲

Sorting bins are essential for any laundry room. Home centers offer a variety of sorting systems, such as the slide-out bins shown here, or you can make your own. Build a frame out of ¾-inch plywood, and attach pairs of wood cleats to the sidewalls to support pull-out plastic bins. You'll need at least three bins: for whites, colors, and permanent press; if you can fit a fourth bin, use it for towels and work clothes.

Laundry rack

This simple washer/dryer shelf rack is especially useful for a basement laundry, where concrete walls make it difficult to hang shelves. The unit is made out of ¾-inch

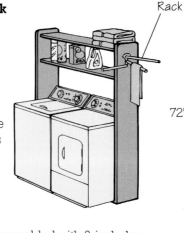

plywood and assembled with 2-inch drywall screws. To avoid having to disconnect the washer's hoses, slide the shelf rack in place before screwing the bottom brace to the sides. On one side add a rack on which to hang clothes as you take them out of the dryer.

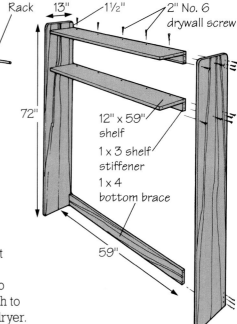

Rack

13" 1½" 2" No. 6 drywall screw

72"

12" x 59" shelf

1 x 3 shelf stiffener

1 x 4 bottom brace

59"

HOME OFFICE

Found spaces

Guest room office

Most home offices borrow space from an existing room. Here a small guest room does double duty as a home office thanks to the addition of a compact wall unit equipped with shelves, drawers, desk, a computer center, and a variety of slide-out and pull-down work surfaces. ▼

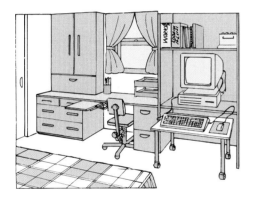

Under the stairs

If the area under a stairway can accommodate shelves (see p.126), odds are it can also serve as a small work station. You can leave an under-the-stairway office exposed or conceal it behind doors when not in use. In the example shown here, a bifold door serves as a screen, providing a bit of extra privacy while you work.

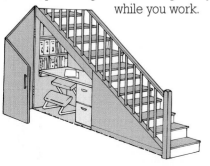

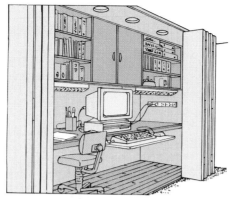

Closeted office ▲

An important feature of a good home office is a sense of separation from other household activities—which is exactly what this converted closet provides. Good lighting and electrical outlets have been added, and books and equipment are within easy reach. Folding doors hide the clutter at day's end.

In the attic

The awkward space under eaves is ideal for storing boxes of seldom used files or other household items. A solid-back bookcase mounted on casters and extending up to the sloped ceiling not only conceals the stored boxes (while allowing access to them), it also serves as a convenient backdrop for an attic office. ▼

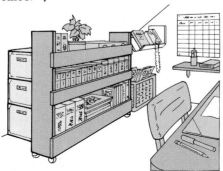

Cook's corner

Don't overlook the kitchen as a possible location for a home office. Here are two suggestions for getting more mileage out of an underutilized kitchen nook. In a pinch, even a tight galley (top) can do double duty as a makeshift office: Here, the swing-out food processor holder described on page 108 serves as a stand for a laptop computer. In the larger kitchen shown at bottom, an area once devoted to cabinets has been turned into a work center. ▼

SHELVES

Open shelving

Shelves to go

These notched knock-down shelves are ready to move any time you are. Make the posts from 2 x 4's and the shelves from ¾-inch plywood. Cut the notches with a saber saw, spacing them about 12 inches apart on the posts and at least 24 inches on the shelves. Keep all notches at least 2 inches from the end of the piece. ▼

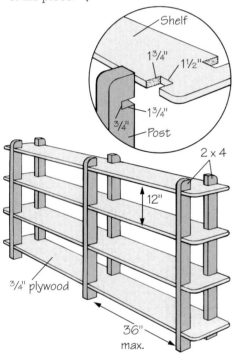

Swinging standard

To install a metal shelf standard without a level, mount it loosely to the wall through the top screw hole. Then lift it to one side and let it swing it like a pendulum. The standard will be vertical when it comes to a stop.

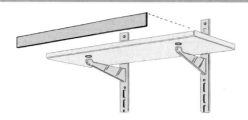

Out of sight ▲

Shelf brackets will be a lot less noticeable if you buy them an inch or so shorter than the shelf depth. Drill holes partway into the shelf bottom to accommodate the bracket tips. Attaching molding along the edges of the shelf and painting the standards and brackets the same color as the wall also help camouflage shelf hardware.

Let the sun shine in

Always trying to squeeze another plant onto the windowsill? Turn your window into a miniature greenhouse with everyday shelves. Attach metal shelving standards to each side of the window, insert shelf brackets, and add acrylic or safety glass shelves. (Don't use standard glass; it might break and injure someone.) ▼

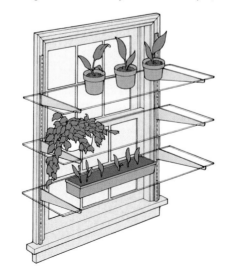

BUILT-IN SHELVING

A built-in shelving unit can bring a bleak wall to life. Available space and the type of items stored will determine a unit's dimensions. For 10- to 12-inch-deep shelves bearing heavy loads, space vertical supports no more than 30 inches apart.

Materials. Use either nominal 1-inch solid lumber or ¾-inch plywood. For a clear finish, birch or oak veneer plywood is a good choice. For a painted finish, consider G1S-grade birch veneer plywood. Finish plywood edges with matching hardwood molding or iron-on veneer tape, shown at right.

Assembly. Line up the sides and vertical partitions, and install one of the two types of adjustable shelf supports shown at right. Then glue and screw the full-length top and bottom pieces to the sides. Attach the mounting cleat and vertical partitions. Assemble the base, level it with shims, and set the case on it. Screw the cleat to the wall. Cover gaps along wall and ceiling edges with a 1 x 2 face frame scribed to fit, or use ¾-inch square molding as a set-back reveal along the edges.

Assembly

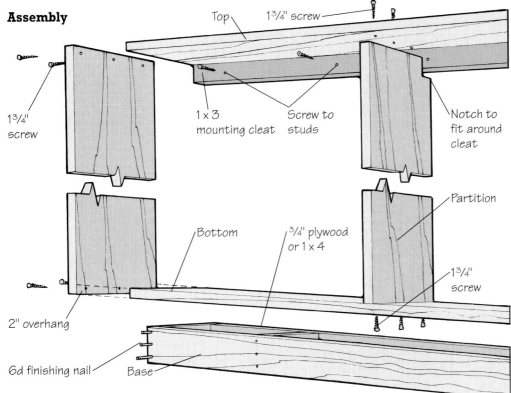

Top

1³/₄" screw

1³/₄" screw

1³/₄" screw

1 x 3 mounting cleat

Screw to studs

Notch to fit around cleat

Partition

Bottom

³/₄" plywood or 1 x 4

1³/₄" screw

2" overhang

6d finishing nail

Base

Shelf supports

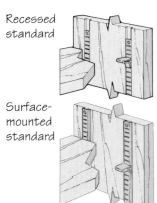

Recessed standard

Surface-mounted standard

Standards with snap-in clips look best when set into grooves routed in the vertical supports (top) because the shelves fit snugly against the supports. But surface mounting (bottom) is easier.

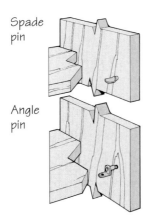

Spade pin

Angle pin

Plug-in pins require two rows of regularly spaced holes on each vertical support (for drilling tips, see p.72). A shelf rests flat on straight spade pins (top). Angle pins (bottom) offer a little more support.

Edgings

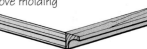

¼" edge molding

Bullnose molding

Cove molding

Shelf edging options include ¼ x ³/₄-in. hardwood edge molding, ³/₄-in. half-round bull-nose molding, and ³/₄-in. cove molding. All three types can be mounted with glue and wire brads.

Iron-on tape

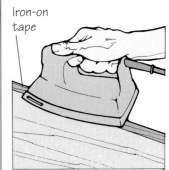

Iron-on tape, sold in rolls by most lumber outlets, is another edging alternative. Heat the tape in place, and trim it with a utility knife.

SHELVES

Bookends

A weighty trick

Do bookends keep sliding off your desk or shelves? Replace the felt on the bottom of the bookends with a piece that extends under the books for several inches. The weight of the books on the felt will keep the bookends stationary.

Dowel corral ▶

To keep books from falling off open-end shelves, install two cup hooks on each shelf end and run dowels through them. Stain the dowels to match the shelves. Pinch the hooks on the bottom shelf to hold the dowels; the other hooks should allow the dowels to slide through. If necessary, join dowel lengths with sleeves made of clear plastic tubing.

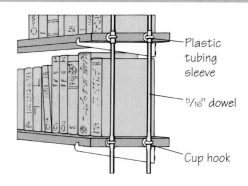

Plastic tubing sleeve

⁵⁄₁₆" dowel

Cup hook

Cabinets

The eyes have it

Want to add another shelf to a cabinet to hold lightweight items? Insert two or more small screw eyes in each side of the cabinet and rest the shelf on them. Make the shelf out of a piece of plywood sized and finished to suit the cabinet.

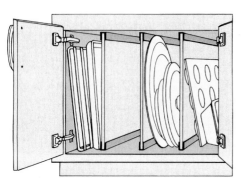

Long division ▲

Vertical dividers in a cabinet make it much easier to store items such as trays, baking pans, and magazines. To make the dividers, use ¼-inch plywood or acrylic; install U-shaped wood molding or metal channels to hold them in place.

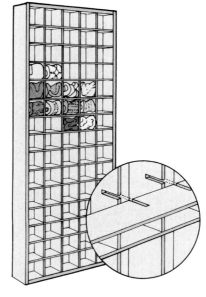

Storage grid ▲

This wall-mounted cubbyhole cabinet holds a variety of small items and protrudes only about 4 inches from the wall. The unit consists of a 1 x 4 frame securely fastened to wall studs and a grid made out of 3½-inch-wide slats of ¼-inch plywood. The slats are notched halfway through at 3½-inch intervals, then interlocked in cross-lap joints. Scale the cabinet and vary the cubicle size to suit your needs.

On display

Create a china cabinet or collectibles display case by adding sliding glass doors to a shelving unit—either a built-in (see pp.114–115) or a ready-made bookcase. Buy sliding-door tracks and glides from a glass and mirror store, and have them cut to fit. The same store will also cut glass for the doors. To allow room for the doors, trim the middle shelves so that they are set back from the front. ▼

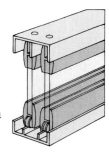

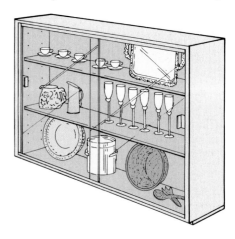

TYPES OF WALL FASTENERS

Whenever possible, attach heavy items directly to wall studs (p.135) or to a board secured to studs. Use one of the special fasteners below when you want to secure a light to moderately heavy load to wallboard or plaster or when you need to attach an object to a masonry wall. For a hollow wall, use a fastener whose shank length matches the wall's thickness. On brick walls, it's usually best to attach to the mortar joints rather than to the bricks. (To drill into masonry, see p.10.)

FASTENER	USE	HOW TO INSTALL
Plastic anchor	Very light load on wall-board, plaster, or masonry	Drill hole slightly smaller than anchor, and push in anchor. Attach object with sheet-metal screw.
Hollow-wall anchor (Molly bolt)	Moderate load on wall-board or plaster	Drill hole same diameter as anchor. Insert anchor, and tighten bolt to collapse sleeve against wall. Remove bolt and use to attach object.
Toggle bolt	Moderate load on wall-board or plaster; heavy load on hollow-core concrete block	Drill hole large enough to let bolt's folded wings pass through. Attach object to bolt, then insert in hole. Tighten bolt to pull wings against interior.
Plastic toggle	Moderate load on wall-board or plaster	Drill hole same diameter as anchor. Squeeze wings together and insert in hole. Push nail through screw hole to pop open wings. Attach object with screw.
Metal drive-in anchor	Moderate load on wall-board or plaster	Hammer into wallboard. Predrill $\frac{1}{8}$-in. starter hole in plaster or thin paneling.
Screw-in anchor	Light load on wallboard. Speeds installation of many fasteners	Screw anchor directly into wall with screwdriver or variable-speed drill. Attach object with screw.
Plastic nail anchor	Moderate load on masonry	Drill hole same diameter as anchor, and insert anchor. Attach object with supplied drive-in/screw-out nail.
Lead shield	Moderate to heavy load on masonry	Drill hole same diameter as shield, and insert shield. Attach object with lag bolt.
Expansion shield	Heavy load on masonry	Drill hole same diameter as shield. With object attached, insert shield in hole and tighten bolt to draw wedge into sleeve.

CLOSETS

Space savers

Quick sorts

You don't need to revamp your entire closet to gain more space. A three-tiered wire basket hung from the closet ceiling makes a great receptacle for socks, spools of yarn, and other small items; use a cardboard drum or a tall plastic wastebasket to hold umbrellas, canes, or sports equipment. ▼

Basket drawer

Add a drawer or two for socks and underwear by mounting a small plastic basket on U-shaped aluminum channels underneath a closet shelf. ▼

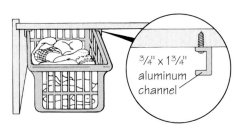

¾" x 1¾" aluminum channel

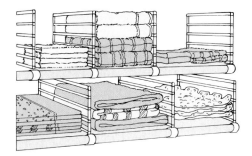

Wire divide ▲

Clamp-on dividers, available at houseware and closet stores, keep piles of sweaters or jeans from toppling over on a closet shelf. In a linen closet, use the dividers to separate tablecloths, placemats, and pillowcases.

Inner space

When installing a closet system, keep these basic spacing guidelines in mind:
▷ A standard closet is 24 inches deep, with the clothes rod placed 12 inches from the back wall; each hanger requires 1 inch of rod space (bulky winter clothes require 2 or 3 inches).
▷ Allow 65 inches from the floor for full-length clothes; 82 inches for double hanging space (place the bottom rod 40 inches above the floor, the top rod 80 inches).
▷ For standard storage, use 12-inch-deep shelves, spaced 13 inches apart; use 16- to 20-inch-deep shelves for bulky items.
▷ Don't plan on using the floor space underneath double-hanging garments. The above guidelines allow for 2 inches between the garments and the floor for easy cleaning.

Central tower

This handy organizer divides the one-rod side of the closet from the two-rod side. Make the shelf tower out of 1 x 12's or 12-inch-wide lengths of ¾-inch plywood, sized to fit between ceiling and floor or between a shelf and the floor. Install the rods 65 inches from the closet floor on one side and 80 and 40 inches from the floor on the other side. ▼

In the shade

Roller shades used instead of doors on this built-in wardrobe not only save space but add color to the room when they are pulled down. You can build the wardrobe frame from ¾-inch plywood, much like a built-in bookcase (pp.114–115). Make the unit 24 inches deep, and use the dimensions on the facing page as a guide for positioning clothes rods and shelves. ▼

Hangers and rods

Muscle rod

Is your wooden closet rod giving way under the burden? Create a sag-free rod from a length of ½-inch-diameter galvanized pipe. For a more finished look, insert the pipe into an equal length of ¾-inch-diameter PVC pipe. Remove any lettering on the plastic pipe with lacquer thinner.

Closet rod
Chain
2" steel ring
S-hook
Wood dowel

Trapeze bar ▲

A closet with a single clothes rod wastes space. An easy way to convert a closet to multilevel storage is to suspend a second rod from the first by means of steel rings, S-hooks, and chain.

Put 'em in chains

Yet another way to increase closet storage is to secure a chain to the clothes rod. Then just hook clothes hangers onto the chain links.

A stronger hanger

Weak wire hangers can support winter coats and other heavy clothes if you tightly bind two (or more) together with masking or duct tape.

Belt organizer

To turn a wooden hanger into a handy belt rack, simply screw cup hooks into the bottom bar of the hanger and hang your belts from the hooks.

A new angle

If your closet is at least 3 feet deep, expand its usable space by installing two clothes rods in the space now occupied by one. Cut shallow notches in the rods as shown so that the hangers are held at a 45° angle. Place the clothes you wear most frequently on the front pole; store other garments in the rear. ▼

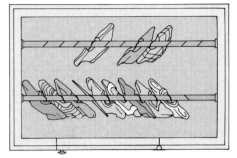

Shoe storage

Shoe-in

When designing shoe storage, plan to use 12- to 13-inch-deep shelves. Allow at least 6½ inches between shelves for regular shoes, more for boots. Allow 9 inches of shelf width for each pair of women's shoes, 10 inches for men's.

Hang-ups

Doorstops screwed into the back of a closet door make a convenient shoe storage system.

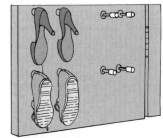

CLOSETS

On the inside

A cedar lining

To repel moths without chemicals, line a closet with ¾-inch-thick tongue-and-groove cedar strips, available prepackaged at home centers and lumberyards. To install the lining, first remove the shelves, rods, and trim from the closet interior; then find and mark the centers of the studs and joists (p.135). Cut cedar strips to fit across the back wall, about ¼ inch shorter than the actual width of the wall. Leveling the lowest strip with a shim if necessary, install the strips (groove side down) with dabs of construction adhesive, nailing to the studs as needed. Check for levelness every few feet. Cover the back wall first, then the side and front walls, ceiling, and door back, butting all edges tightly. Use 1½-inch-wide strips as trim to cover any gaps and create an airtight seal. ▼

Sheet cedar ▲

Here's a cheaper alternative to cedar strips. Fasten cedar sheets directly to smooth walls with paneling nails (on masonry or uneven walls, install furring strips first). For easy installation, cut the sheet ½ inch shorter than the floor-to-ceiling height, use a shim to hold the sheet against the ceiling as you nail, and cover the resulting gap at the bottom with baseboard molding.

Leftover lining

Don't throw away scraps of cedar slats or sheets left over from lining a closet. Piece them together to line a drawer.

Cedar hang-up

If you can't line a closet with cedar and can't stand the smell of mothballs, check home centers or specialty storage stores for a portable cedar closet—a hanging garment bag treated with cedar fragrance.

Lighten up

Chase away gloom in a dark closet by painting the walls and shelving with high-gloss or semigloss white enamel.

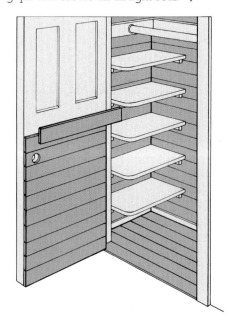

INSTALLING A WIRE

If closet clutter is driving you to distraction, a vinyl-coated wire closet system may be the answer. Not only are these systems efficient organizers, they keep clothes fresher by allowing air to circulate around them. Most ready-to-assemble closet systems rely on three basic components: wire baskets in a freestanding frame; a wardrobe shelf designed for clothes hangers and shelved items; and a linen rack that can double as a shoe rack (just turn it over so that the lip points upward and attach it with a special bracket that holds it at an angle). The components can be arranged in a wide

CLOSET SYSTEM

variety of configurations, depending on your storage needs. Before buying a closet system, measure the height, width, and depth of your closet; then sketch your plan on paper so that you can visualize what the system will look like. Experiment with layouts until you find one that works for you. (For more on closet design, see p.118).

Illustrated at right are step-by-step instructions for mounting a typical wardrobe shelf or linen rack. In addition to components and fasteners, you'll need a level, an electric drill, a Phillips screwdriver or a cordless driver, a measuring tape, a pencil, a hacksaw, and a stepladder.

Each system manufacturer has its own recommended hardware and fasteners; be sure to follow kit directions carefully. Some systems include special fin-back clips that make shelf installation especially quick and easy. When attached directly to wallboard, the clip's "wings" spread inside the wall, holding the clip more securely than a plastic wall anchor. If you hit a stud, trim the clip's shaft to match your wallboard's thickness; then screw the clip to the stud.

To avoid marring closet sidewalls, cut full-length shelves a minimum of ½ inch shorter than the distance from wall to wall (use a hacksaw or bolt cutters to cut the shelves). Cover the exposed cut ends with plastic caps, which either come with the components or are sold separately.

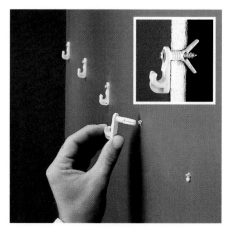

1 Mark a level line for the length of the shelf at the desired shelf height. Drill a ¼-in. hole every 9 to 11 in., and insert a fin-back clip into each hole. Insert and tighten the screw, while holding the clip to keep it from spinning.

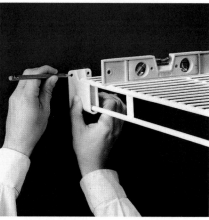

2 Slip an end-mounting bracket over the shelf lip next to the wall. Set the shelf in the clips and hold the end bracket against the wall. Make sure that the shelf is level front to back and side to side, and then mark the screw locations on the wall.

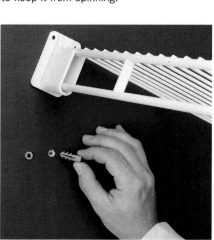

3 Drill ¼-in. holes for the end bracket and insert the anchors. Then screw the end bracket to the wall. If the shelf runs from wall to wall, attach an end bracket at the other end of the shelf the same way.

4 Attach a support brace at least every 36 in. along the length of the shelf. Secure the top end of the brace to the shelf; fasten the bottom end to the wall, using a plastic anchor and screw.

CHILDREN'S ROOMS

Toy storage

Stacking bins

Toy cleanup is a breeze with this set of five inter-locking bins made from ½-inch birch veneer ply-wood. Cut all parts as shown. Using the dimensions given below, you can cut all five bins from one 4 x 8 sheet of ply-wood. Sand the edges; then assemble the bins with glue and 4d finishing nails. Attach 2-inch casters to one or more bins. For durability, paint the bins with an oil-base primer and top coat. ▼

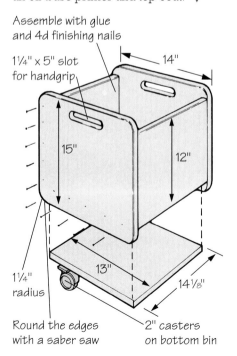

Assemble with glue and 4d finishing nails

1¼" x 5" slot for handgrip

14"

15"

12"

1¼" radius

13"

14⅛"

Round the edges with a saber saw

2" casters on bottom bin

Chain gang

Keep stuffed animals clean and out of the way with a length of decorative chain. Simply drape the chain (it comes in several finishes) near the ceiling from wall to wall. Stitch a loop of hem binding to each stuffed animal, and suspend the animals from the chain with S-hooks. ▼

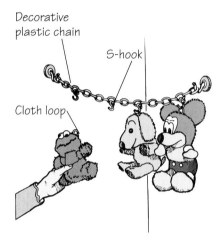

Decorative plastic chain

S-hook

Cloth loop

A tisket, a tasket

Instead of a traditional toy box, sort toys into brightly colored laundry baskets—the open weave allows children to see what's inside, minimizing the need to dump everything out. Another option is to sort toys into small dishpans. Tape a representative toy on the front of the container for prereaders; older kids can create their own labels.

Toys to go

A good way to get children to round up toys that stray from their rooms is to keep a bright red wagon on hand. Wheel out the wagon and watch your children race to clean up; afterward, it's easy for even small kids to pull the whole load back to where it belongs.

Kiddie combos

A bed and more

With the right furniture, two kids can share even a small room comfortably. A bunk bed is one way to free up floor space. An alternative is to buy (or build) platform beds that rest on drawers, like the one shown here. ▼

Double-duty desk

When the toy bins are rolled out, this storage chest doubles as a desk. Use ¾-inch plywood to build the sides, back, top, and lid of the desk; ⅜-inch plywood for the bottom of the divided tray; and fir 1 x 4's for the tray frame. Assemble the pieces with glue and wood screws; then finish with colorful enamel. Make roll-out bins as shown at left or buy them ready-made. ▼

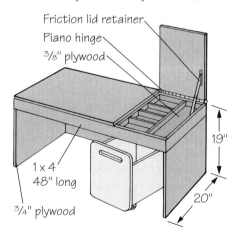

Friction lid retainer

Piano hinge

⅜" plywood

1 x 4 48" long

¾" plywood

19"

20"

SPORTS EQUIPMENT

Bicycles

A real hang-up

To eliminate clutter and save floor space in the garage, hang your bicycle from large plastic-coated hooks that are screwed into ceiling joists or wall studs. Bicycle hooks are available at hardware stores and cycling shops. ▼

A better bike rack

Tired of seeing bicycles strewn all over your driveway? Here's a convenient two-bike rack that's easy to make out of rot-resistant wood. Three stakes anchor the rack to the ground. To accommodate the thicker wheels of mountain bikes or the thinner ones of racing bikes, use spacers to alter the width of the slots. Fix the bikes to the rack with U-shaped bike locks for protection from theft. ▼

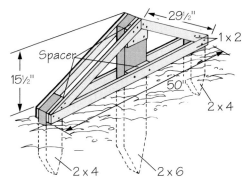

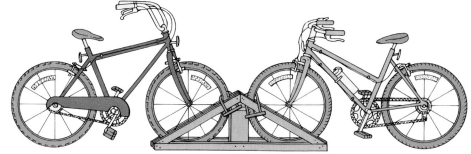

Other gear

Golf rack ▶

This handy wire organizer, available at specialty storage stores, keeps golf shoes and bags neat and organized. Mount it on a garage wall or in a convenient closet.

Unfinished business

The space between the exposed ceiling joists of an unfinished basement or garage is often wasted. Put it to work by nailing lengths of scrap wood across any two joists at 3-foot intervals. The resulting storage area is ideal for stowing away fishing rods and other long light-weight items. For a sturdier ceiling rack designed to hold lumber, see p.61.

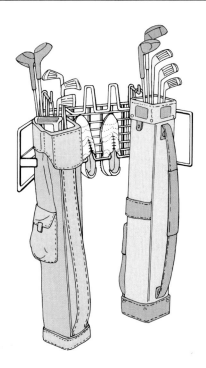

Batter up

Stow away baseball equipment in this corner organizer. Cut a triangle from ¾-inch plywood with the dimensions shown. Bore 1¼-inch-diameter holes for the balls; cut the bat slots with a coping saw. Nail the platform to ½ x 2-inch cleats fastened to wall studs.

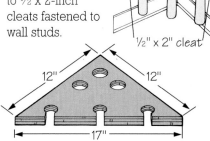

ATTIC, BASEMENT, GARAGE

Overhead storage

Over-the-car-hood rack

This garage rack hangs over the hood of your car, taking up no floor space. Use 2 x 3's to build the two end supports and the shelf cleats; make the shelving out of ½-inch plywood. The depth and vertical spacing of the shelves can vary depending on your needs. Use 2½-inch drywall screws to assemble the frame; attach the frame to overhead beams with 2½-inch lag bolts. ▼

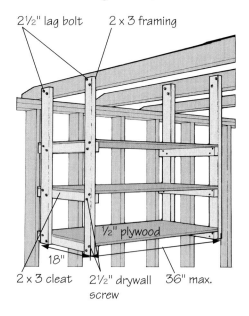

2½" lag bolt   2 x 3 framing

½" plywood

18"

2 x 3 cleat   2½" drywall   36" max.
              screw

Flying carpet

Store a rolled-up rug by suspending it from two old belts attached to the attic or garage rafters. To deter insects from nesting inside, wrap the ends with heavy brown paper and tape.

Reel 'em in ▶

To avoid the yearly untangling of Christmas lights, store them on empty electrical wire spools (ask your hardware store to save some for you). For easy access, slide several spools onto a length of ¾-inch-diameter PVC pipe, then mount the pipe between the joists in your garage or basement.

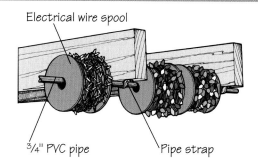

Electrical wire spool

¾" PVC pipe   Pipe strap

Overhead bins

Overhead storage bins are a great way to put wasted space to work. Construct them from ¾-inch plywood or boards, and assemble them with 1½- and 2-inch drywall screws. Make sure that one side of each bin extends to attach to a ceiling joist; fasten the other end to the adjacent bin. Mount the doors with butt hinges; provide a hook and eye to hold them in the open position. ▼

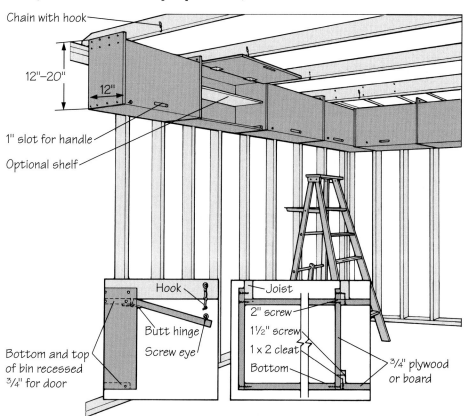

Chain with hook

12"–20"

12"

1" slot for handle

Optional shelf

Hook

Butt hinge

Screw eye

Bottom and top of bin recessed ¾" for door

Joist

2" screw

1½" screw

1 x 2 cleat

Bottom

¾" plywood or board

Hanging around

Here's another way to put the space over your car to work. String a hammock from screw eyes fastened to exposed joists and use it to store sport balls, exercise mats, and other light bulky items. ▼

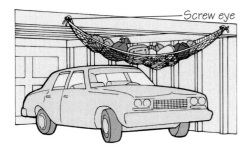

Storage loft ▶

Store patio and pool furniture on this sturdy over-the-car-hood loft. Use 2 x 4's for the frame, 4 x 4 posts to support the front of the loft, and ½-inch plywood for the top. Nail the rear header to wall studs. Assemble the frame with framing anchors (joist hangers at joist-header connections; framing angles at post-frame connections). For greater security, anchor the posts to the floor with post base hardware.

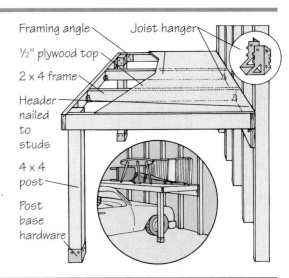

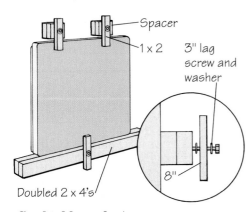

More racks

Card table rack ▲

Need to store a card or game table? Try this easy-to-make rack. Mark parallel lines across wall studs far enough apart to accommodate the width of the table, plus at least ¼ inch for clearance. Fasten doubled 2 x 4's along the bottom line and two block spacers on the upper line. The table is held in place by pivoting 8-inch lengths of 1 x 2's mounted with 3-inch lag screws and washers.

Cushion station

This handy wall-mounted rack is great for storing unwieldy patio furniture cushions indoors. By keeping the cushions off the ground, the rack also helps prevent mildew. Above a 1 x 6 shelf, bolt a 1 x 3 pine frame to the wall studs. Keep the bolt and washer slightly loose so that the frame will pivot. ▼

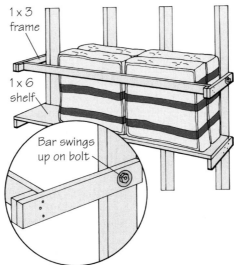

Furniture racks

Keep garage, attic, or basement clutter under control with this simple space saver. Just fasten ordinary shelf brackets or L-braces to wall studs and use them to hang folding chairs, recliners, and other lightweight outdoor furniture. If you don't have any L-brackets, you can make supports out of oversize nails (carpenter's spikes), vinyl gutter brackets, or wood dowels fitted into predrilled holes in the studs. Arrange the supports in pairs to fit the pieces to be stored.

ATTIC, BASEMENT, GARAGE

Utility shelves

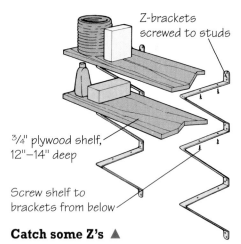

Z-brackets screwed to studs

¾" plywood shelf, 12"–14" deep

Screw shelf to brackets from below

Catch some Z's ▲

Inexpensive and easy to install, Z-brackets can support light to medium loads on shelves up to 14 inches deep. Z-brackets come in three-shelf units and can be cut or combined as needed. They're sold at most home centers.

Under the eaves

Turn wasted space under the eaves into a convenient storage area with this handy shelving system. Screw 2 x 2 uprights and 1 x 2 cleats securely to the rafters; use 4d finishing nails to attach ¾-inch plywood shelves to the cleats. ▼

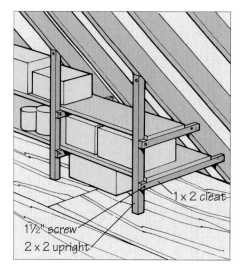

1 x 2 cleat

1½" screw

2 x 2 upright

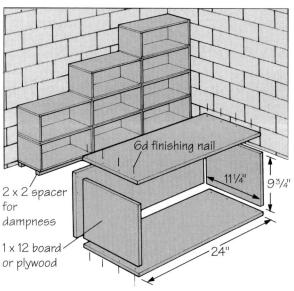

6d finishing nail

2 x 2 spacer for dampness

1 x 12 board or plywood

11¼"

9¾"

24"

◀ Stacking cases

These flexible modules allow you to change or add to your storage unit as needed—they're especially useful when stacked against a peaked attic wall. The boxes are made of 1 x 12 boards or ½-inch plywood. Since there is no stress on the joints, case parts may be glued and nailed together rather than screwed. Double 2 x 2's provide a base for the assembly.

Double-duty stairs

Roll it away

This roll-out bin is designed to make the most of the wasted space under the lower end of a stairway. Use it to store awkward items ranging from cleaning supplies to boots and sports equipment. The bin is a simple box made of ¾-inch plywood, assembled with screws and glue and mounted on casters. The corners are reinforced with ¾-inch square molding as shown. To cut the front, back, and filler pieces at the correct angle, trace the slope of the stairs on a piece of cardboard and use it as a template for marking the plywood. Allowing for casters, the bin's front and back should clear the stairs by ¼ inch; the filler panel fits flush. For easy access, install a handle on the front of the bin. ▼

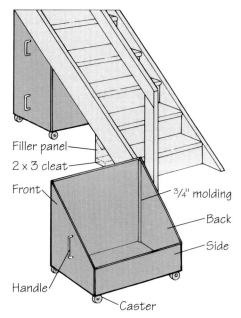

Filler panel

2 x 3 cleat

Front

Handle

¾" molding

Back

Side

Caster

INSTALLING PERF BOARD

Perf board, short for perforated hardboard, is an excellent solution to a variety of storage problems, both in and out of the workshop. Brightly painted and edged with molding, it makes a great kitchen wall organizer. In addition to the standard S-hooks and hangers, a variety of shelves and containers designed to attach to perf board allow you to customize your storage system.

Available at home centers and lumberyards, perf-board panels are easy to install. In areas with unfinished walls, screw the panels directly to exposed studs. (To keep screwheads from sinking through the perf board, use a washer, or drive screws through the flush surface, not through one of the holes.) Attach perf board to wallboard by driving drywall screws through the panel, then through a rubber or plastic spacer and into a hollow-wall anchor or, preferably, directly into a stud (see right). Spacers included in perf-board kits hold the panel away from the wall, allowing clearance for the hooks. Mount perf board with furring strips (see below). Masonry walls in basements must be parged first.

On wallboard

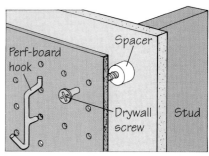

To mount perf board onto wallboard, first use a stud finder to locate the wall studs (p.135). After positioning the panel as desired, drive 2-in. drywall screws through the flush surface of the panel, then through a spacer and into a stud. Drive screws at 12-in. intervals vertically and at every stud along the top and bottom of the panel (or if you're using wall anchors, at 16-in. intervals horizontally).

On masonry

To install perf board on a masonry wall, cut lengths of 1 x 2 furring strips equal to the height of the perf-board panel. Then apply panel adhesive to one side of each strip.

Fasten the furring strips to the wall with 2-in. masonry nails. To make sure the perf-board panels are solidly supported, place the furring strips no more than 4 ft. apart.

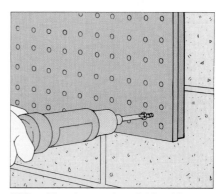

Position the panel, and drive 1-in. drywall screws through the panel's flush surface into a strip. Drive a screw at every strip along the top and bottom of the panel and at 12-in. intervals vertically.

HOME IMPROVEMENTS

WALL REPAIR

Small jobs

Caulking gaps

Annoyed by gaps between a wall and its trim or between a wall and masonry? Fill them with paintable latex caulk. Apply the caulk with a caulking gun; smooth and seal the newly caulked joint using one of the techniques described on page 150. Use caulking that matches the color of the wall, or paint it to match.

Flatten a popped nail ▲

Usually caused by shrinking framing, popped nails are the curse of wallboard interiors. To fix one, drive a drywall screw into the stud an inch below the popped nail, sinking the head just below the surface (p.132). Then scrape away the loose paint and compound around the popped nail, and drive it back into place. Finish with three layers of compound.

Anchors away

To remove a regular plastic wall anchor from wallboard or plaster, just insert a tight-fitting screw and wiggle it out.

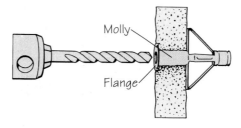

Good-bye molly ▲

To remove a molly wall fastener (p.117), you have to drive it into the wall cavity. The resulting hole will be much smaller if you use a drill bit slightly larger than the screw hole and drill just enough to cut off the flange. Then push the remainder of the molly into the wall.

Quick standard patch

To fix a small hole in wallboard or plaster, apply self-adhesive fiberglass mesh wallboard tape. Crisscross the tape over the hole, and finish it with a couple of coats of compound (p.131).

Press-on patch

An even quicker and neater way to repair a small hole in wallboard is with an iron-on polymer fabric wallboard patch. When applying the patch, be careful not to scorch or blister the surrounding paint. Paint the patch and let it dry. Then lightly sand the edges to feather them, and apply a second coat of paint. ▼

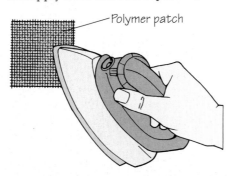

It's in the mix

For other minor wall repairs, the best choice is a lightweight premixed spackling compound. It's easier to use than dry-mix patching compound, and it dries faster and shrinks less than joint compound. However, joint compound is easier to spread and therefore better for large areas, such as wallboard seams.

Smooth ruler

When patching a hole that's wider than your putty knife, don't use the putty knife to smooth and remove compound. You'll just gouge it. Instead use a wide smoothing tool, or if you don't have one, a metal ruler. Hold the ruler on edge and wipe it across the area.

Blow dry

On damp days, spackling or joint compound can take forever to dry. To speed the process, use a hair dryer. Set it on a low temperature and keep moving it back and forth over the area so that the compound doesn't dry too quickly and begin to crack.

Invisible wall patching

Even on a flat untextured wall, patches can stand out as smooth spots after you paint. To mimic the texture of the surrounding wall, let the patch dry; then before painting the wall, lightly spray the patch with water and brush the surface gently in a circular motion with a small scrub brush. After it's painted, the patch won't show.

WALL REPAIR

Patching wallboard

Home run remedy

To patch a baseball-size hole quickly, buy a kit containing a self-adhesive fiberglass mesh patch with a rigid metal backing. Trim the patch to fit, apply it to the damaged area, and cover it with compound as you would seam tape (facing page). ▼

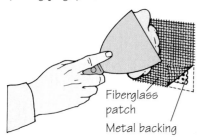

Fiberglass patch

Metal backing

Look, no back support

Here's how to fix a hole up to 8 inches wide without backing the patch: Square the hole with a utility knife. Cut a wall-board patch 1 inch larger on all sides than the hole. Score and break it along the back to the hole size. Peel off the backing and gypsum along the edges, leaving a flap of facing paper all around. Lightly sand the flap's back to feather the edges. Then apply joint compound, set the patch in place, and finish the seam using the flap as tape. ▼

1" flap of facing paper

Patching a corner

To patch a badly chipped outside wall corner, use a long flat trowel as a form. Holding it even with the edge on one side of the corner, fill in the area on the other side with compound or plaster. Then slide the trowel away from the corner, being careful not to lift it until it is away from the patched area.

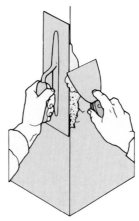

Plaster repair secrets

Thump it like a melon

When you repair a plaster wall, always remove the plaster down to its soundest layer before attempting a repair. Sound plaster makes a solid, snappy noise when you thump it; loose plaster produces a hollow, dull sound.

Give it a grip

When patching plaster with exposed lath, drive screws into the wood, leaving the heads sticking up. This gives the new plaster something to hold on to.

No hitting

Hard blows loosen plaster. When repairing it or the underlying lath or framing, use drywall screws instead of nails. To remove damaged plaster, pry it off or lightly chip it with a cold chisel.

No-sag plastering

To fix a large hole in plaster, use patching plaster (mixed with perlite); it's less likely to sag than joint compound. For the plaster to adhere well, dampen the old surface well or apply a latex bonding agent. Apply the plaster in layers no more than $3/8$ inch thick. Crosshatch each layer with the corner of a putty knife as it starts to set. Let it dry; then wet it before applying the next layer.

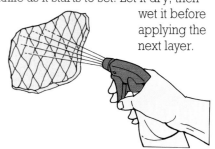

Glue it back up

Here's a way to secure loose plaster: Every foot or so, drill a small hole and inject construction adhesive through it onto the lath. Then press the plaster against the lath by putting a padded board over the plaster and forcing a brace against it. Leave the brace up until the adhesive sets. If the back of the lath is accessible, inject the adhesive through the spaces between laths. ▼

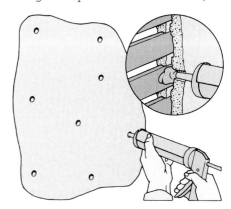

FIXING DAMAGED WALLBOARD

Whether it's a hole caused by a doorknob, furniture movers, or a teenager's foot or peeling tape resulting from humidity or the house settling, damaged wallboard is easy to repair. If you encounter a stud when you are removing a damaged section, cut the wallboard back to the center of the stud and secure one edge of your patch to the stud. If the damage to a wall is extensive, cut the wallboard back to the middle of the stud on each side, and secure the patch directly to the two studs.

When finishing a patch or a joint, apply thin coats of joint compound; let each coat dry and then sand it lightly with fine-grit paper. Each time you apply compound, broaden the area covered with the compound until the patch blends with the surrounding wall.

Retaping a joint

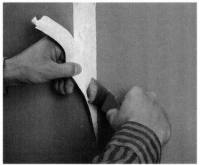

1 Remove all loose tape, including tape that is only partially loose; don't try to salvage old tape. Sand away loose tape remnants and rough edges.

2 Apply a coat of joint compound and embed new paper tape in it. Then apply two thin coats over the tape, feathering the edges. Sand smooth.

Patching a hole

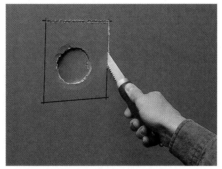

1 Cut out the damaged section, using a drywall saw (or a utility knife). Square up and enlarge the area you cut out to make it easier to repair.

2 Cut two 1 x 3's a few inches longer than the hole. Slip the boards into the hole at top and bottom, and secure them with 1¼-in. drywall screws.

3 Cut a wallboard patch ⅛ in. smaller on all sides than the hole. Insert the patch in the hole and attach it to the 1 x 3 backer boards with drywall screws.

4 Cover seams with self-adhesive fiberglass wallboard tape. Then apply three thin coats of joint compound, sanding the compound smooth after each coat.

WALLBOARD INSTALLATION

Installing wallboard

X-ray walls

Before putting up new wallboard, take photos of the wall construction, including plumbing and electrical lines. Later, when you need to know what's in there, you'll have a record. Shoot the picture as straight on as possible, and include a stretched-out tape measure.

Take it all off

Even with the most careful finishing, it's hard to hide crushed edges and corners and nailhead tears on wallboard. Instead of trying to salvage the damaged facing paper, you'll get a much better finish if you tear off the loose paper and apply the compound directly to the gypsum.

Cutting edge

When cutting wallboard, a utility knife blade quickly becomes clogged and dull. To prevent this, keep a small piece of fine sandpaper handy and periodically rub the blade with it to remove the chalk buildup.

Across, not up and down

In a room with a standard 8-foot ceiling, install wallboard horizontally, using sheets with lengths of 10 or 12 feet or longer. Horizontal seams are easier to tape, and the long sheets will reduce the number of vertical seams; often they can span from wall to wall. Start at the top of the wall (put a couple of nails in the studs under the sheet for temporary support), and work across the wall. When installing the lower tier, make sure any vertical seams are staggered; start with a half sheet if necessary. ▼

Large nail

Making a point

To mark the position of an electrical box on wallboard, insert machine screws whose heads have been cut off in the holes for mounting the receptacle or switch.

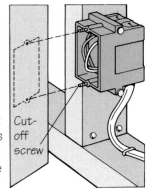

Cut-off screw

Then position the wallboard panel and press it against the screws. To outline the cutout on the wallboard, just place a spare electrical box over the holes made by the screws. If a box is wired, be sure to shut off the power to it at the main service panel first.

Smooching wallboard

Another, quicker way to mark an electrical outlet's position on wallboard is to coat the edges of the box with lipstick and press the wallboard in place. Then remove the panel and cut along the "kiss marks" on the back.

Fold for carrying ▶

Getting wallboard around stairway turns (or another obstacle) isn't easy. Instead of cutting the sheets apart, score the back of each panel at the stud location, fold it as shown, and carefully carry it up the stairs. To install the sheet, simply unfold it and mount it, double-nailing at the scored seam.

A useful warp ▶

When installing predecorated wallboard, avoid unsightly fasteners along vertical seams by prebowing the sheets. Stack the sheets face up overnight, with the centers on the floor and the ends on 2 x 4's. To attach a sheet, apply adhesive to the studs and fasten the sheet at top and bottom. The bow in the sheet presses its center against the adhesive.

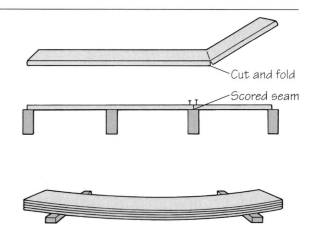

Cut and fold

Scored seam

Don't rip it out

Need to take down a wallboard panel you just installed? If you haven't finished the joints yet, you can reuse the panel. Sharpen one end of a short length of ¾-inch copper tubing with a file. Place the tube over each nailhead, and strike it sharply with a hammer to cut through the wallboard. Then lift off the panel. To replace the piece, simply fit it back on the studs, placing the cutout holes over the old nails. Renail the wallboard an inch or so from each old nail. ▼

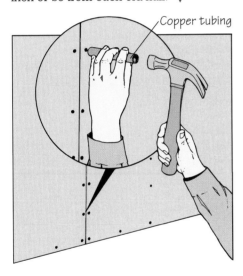

Copper tubing

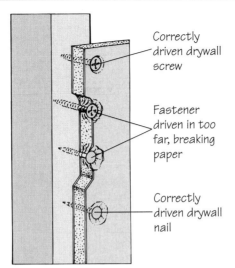

Correctly driven drywall screw

Fastener driven in too far, breaking paper

Correctly driven drywall nail

Gentle touch ▲

When driving nails or screws into wallboard, the trick is to set the fastener just below the surface so that it can be hidden with compound. If you drive it too deep, so that it breaks the paper or crushes the wallboard, you compromise the fastener's holding power.

Stick 'em up

If you put up wallboard with panel adhesive, you'll eliminate about half the fasteners—which means fewer fasteners to hide with compound and fewer potential popped nails later on. Apply adhesive to each stud with a caulking gun. Then press the wallboard in place, and secure it with drywall nails or screws every 16 inches around the edges and once in the center. Follow all safety warnings on the adhesive; it's highly flammable. ▼

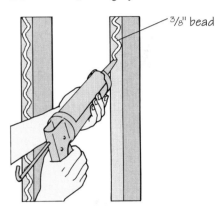

³/₈" bead

Dust-free smoothing

Sanding wallboard patches and seams can stir up a dusty mess. Instead of sanding, try using a damp sponge to remove excess compound after it dries. Select a large, fine-textured sponge, and rinse it regularly in a bucket of water. With practice, you can get perfectly smooth seams that may need a light sanding at most. You can also keep the dust down by using a sanding sponge, an abrasive-surfaced sponge.

Compound tricks

Saving leftovers

Do you buy compound in the economy 5-gallon container, use some, and a few weeks later find that the rest has turned lumpy? Here's how to prevent this: Before it dries, scrape all the excess compound off the inside surfaces of the container and wipe the surfaces clean. Level the compound, and pour ½ cup of water over it. Rinse and replace the plastic that was over the compound when you opened the container; then put the lid on tight.

Give it a stir

To mix or thin compound, use a paint mixer attachment on a ³/₈-inch variable-speed drill running at a slow speed. To avoid making a mess, use an old lid with a cutout for the mixer and for adding water or powder.

Easy cleanup

When working with dry compound, mix it in a flexible plastic container. When the job is done, let the leftover compound harden. Then flex the container. The material will break away; throw it out and wash the container.

WALL TRIM

Molding

Tells the tale

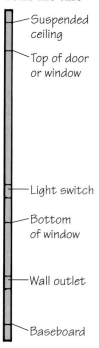

- Suspended ceiling
- Top of door or window
- Light switch
- Bottom of window
- Wall outlet
- Baseboard

If you're planning a lot of building or remodeling, use any light, rigid length of wood to make yourself a story pole. This handy tool—basically a rod with frequently used measurements marked on it—cuts the time you spend measuring and helps ensure that you put trim and other items in the same place around the room or from one room to another.

Easy-off molding

To remove shoe molding without damaging it or the baseboard, slip a putty knife between the molding and the baseboard and place a thin piece of scrap wood behind the putty knife. Then use a pry bar positioned between the scrap and the putty knife to carefully force the molding off.

No one will ever know

Can't find a match for old molding? Look in your closet; it probably has the same molding as your walls. Just remove it and use it. Install closely matching standard molding in the closet.

Trim saver

It's possible to reuse trim as long as you remove the old nails from the back rather than the front of the trim. Grip each nail tightly with locking pliers, and pull its small head through the wood. Done carefully, this won't mar the finish or splinter the top surface, and it will even leave the filler in the nail hole. Reinstall as you would new trim.

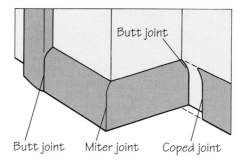

Butt joint

Butt joint   Miter joint   Coped joint

Corner ins and outs ▲

Here are some rules for installing baseboards and other wall perimeter trim.
▷ Fit outside corners first, joining the pieces in a miter joint.
▷ On an inside corner, butt one piece against the wall and cut the other to fit around it, making a coped joint (p.79).
▷ When trim runs into a door frame, make a butt joint.

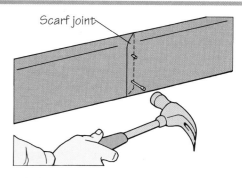

Scarf joint

Joining on the angle ▲

When joining straight lengths of molding, cut the end of each piece at a 45° angle and splice the pieces together. A scarf joint, as this is known, is less noticeable than a butt joint even if shrinkage occurs. Make sure the splice falls directly over a stud, and nail through both ends into the stud.

Easy sets the crown

Installing crown molding is simpler if you make a template that duplicates the molding's bearing points. Place the molding on a framing square and measure its bearing points. Make a template by nailing two wood blocks together. Use it every few feet to mark the correct molding position on the wall and ceiling.

Bearing points

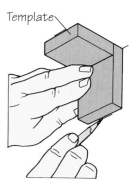

Template

WALL FRAMING

Wall studs

Solid toehold

When installing wall studs, accurate toenailing—driving nails at an angle to join a stud to the soleplate—is essential. To keep a stud from shifting as you hammer, place the head of a large common nail against the opposite side of the stud and tap it into the plate.

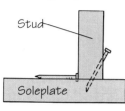

Or if you are installing several studs, cut a 2 x 4 spacer to fit between the studs and use it to hold each stud in place as you nail. It also helps to bend the end of the nail slightly so that the nail curves as it goes into the wood. ▼

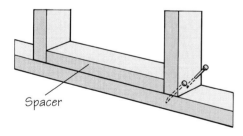

Amicable separation

Need to separate two studs that are nailed together? It's easy with two pry bars. Insert the flat ends as shown, and push the angled ends toward the center. Start near one end of the studs and work toward the other end.

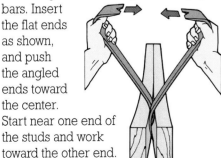

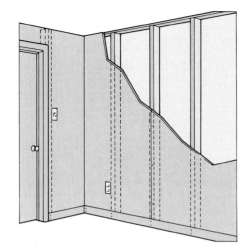

Detective work ▲

Trying to find wall studs can be frustrating. Here are some clues to look for: nails on the upper edge of baseboards go into studs, electrical boxes attach to studs (turn off power at the service panel before probing next to a box), and grilles for cold-air returns run between studs. Also look for wallboard seams and nailheads (which you may see when you angle a bright light across the wall). Once you've found one stud, you should be able to find the others at 16- or 24-inch intervals, measuring from the center of one stud to the center of the next.

Sensitive stud

When nailing or screwing into a stud, don't use a fastener that penetrates more than 1 inch into the stud; plumbers and electricians consider the center third of a stud to be safe territory for routing pipes and wiring. Always try to hit the stud's center. If you're too far off center, the fastener may go through the side and lose holding power.

STUD FINDERS

An electronic stud finder is a handy battery-powered device with a sensor that detects differences in wall density. To use it, you press a button and pass the finder over the wall. A light goes on when the finder reaches the edge of a stud and goes out when it passes over the other edge. Some electronic stud finders are self-calibrating; others have to be calibrated to a wall's density before you can use them.

The simpler magnetic stud finder contains a magnet that swivels like a compass needle when it passes over nails in a stud. Magnetic stud finders work best when used just below the ceiling or just above the floor, where the studs are nailed to top and soleplates.

Both types of stud finders can be misled by pipes, metal cables, foil-backed insulation, and other framing members. And neither works well on plaster walls.

WALL PANELING

Installing paneling

Period of adjustment

Paneling tends to shrink or expand with changes in humidity in the first few days after you get the panels home. To minimize problems after installation, let the panels adjust to their new home first. Separate the panels after delivery, and stand each one up in the area where you plan to install it. Over the course of 2 or 3 days, the panels will adjust to the room's humidity; then you can install them without worrying about shrinkage.

The perfect panel

The key to perfect paneling is getting the first panel straight—the rest will follow suit. Align the first panel against a corner, and tack it in place with a single nail centered in the top. Use a level to make sure the panel is straight and plumb. If the plumbed panel doesn't fit snugly against the adjoining wall, use a compass to scribe the panel edge next to the wall (p.71), copying the slant of the wall onto the panel. Remove the panel, and trim it to fit. Then nail or glue it in place.

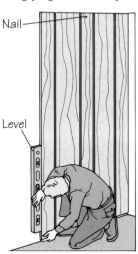

Nail

Level

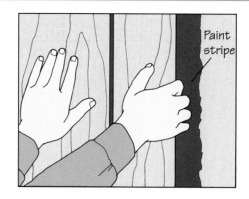

Paint stripe

Concealing gaps ▲

When you're putting up paneling, it's almost inevitable that there will be some space visible between panels. This can be a real problem when you're installing dark paneling on light-colored walls because the wall will peek through the open joints. To avoid this, brush a 3- or 4-inch stripe of paint—the same color as the panel joints—on the wall behind each seam before installing the panels. Use a small roller or a can of spray paint to speed the work.

Warped panels

Even fresh-from-the-factory paneling may be warped. As long as the problem isn't too severe and the warped panels aren't more than ¼ inch thick, you can mount them successfully using both panel adhesive and paneling nails. (Panel adhesive is made specifically for installing paneling and wallboard.) If the paneling is thick or badly warped, however, you'll be better off returning it.

For a firm, clean job

Before mounting paneling over bare studs or furring strips on block walls, cover the wall with wallboard. Not only is it a fire safety measure (often required by code) but you'll get a stiffer, more substantial wall with no bowing or warping. You'll also avoid nail holes, since the panels can be attached with panel adhesive alone. For economy and ease of handling, use ⅜-inch wallboard. And even though the joints won't show, tape them to reduce air infiltration.

Nail disguise

To camouflage nails in paneling or trim, try to place them in a natural blemish or in the darker lines of the grain pattern.

Finish now, fill later

If you will be staining and varnishing your paneling, fill the nail holes after you stain and varnish the wood. This allows you to match the putty color to the finished look of the wood. If you fill the nail holes before staining, the putty will absorb the stain differently than the wood, causing the holes to stand out. ▼

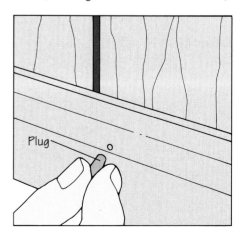

Plug

CEILINGS

Ceiling tiles

An appealing ceiling

To keep ceiling tiles clean while you're installing them, dip your fingers in cornstarch before handling each tile—the powder will shield the tiles from smudges. A little extra powder in one pocket of your tool apron will save you lots of trips up and down the ladder.

Tongue tapped ▲

Tongue-and-groove ceiling tiles often don't fit together snugly when installed. To ensure a good fit, cut one tile in half and use it as a striker panel to coax the other tiles into place. Butt the tongue of the cut panel into the groove of the tile being fitted; a light hammer tap on the cut tile will nudge the full tile into place without damaging it. When the striker panel becomes worn, throw it away and use another half tile.

Graceful grid ▶

You can't eliminate the metal grid supporting a suspended ceiling, but you can soften its visual impact. Mount decorative crown molding around the perimeter of the room to give the ceiling a more elegant, finished look.

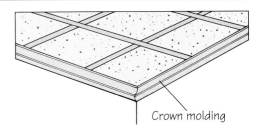

Crown molding

Patching wallboard

The cardboard butler

If you have to cut into a wallboard ceiling, do it from the attic if possible. You'll avoid the risk of cutting unseen wires (you'll also keep dust out of your face). Reduce cleanup by putting a cardboard box on the floor below to catch debris.

Corkscrew handle ▲

If you can only cut into a wallboard ceiling from below, twist a corkscrew into the center of the waste area first; then use it as a handle to keep the piece from landing on your head. For smooth, easy-to-patch edges, cut with a utility knife. Always turn off the power to any ceiling lights at the main service panel before making a blind cut into the ceiling.

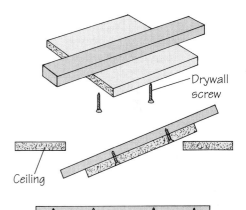

Drywall screw

Ceiling

Hole fixes ▲

To patch a moderate-size hole in a wallboard ceiling, trim and square up the damaged area, and cut out a wallboard patch that's slightly smaller than the opening. Then screw (or glue) a wood cleat, such as a furring strip, to the back of the patch. Make the cleat about 6 inches longer than the patch so that it extends about 3 inches on each side. Tilt and drop the patch into position, and screw the cleat to the ceiling. Finish the seams with tape and compound. For a large hole, trim the opening to the center of the ceiling joists on either side and secure the patch to the joists. Repair a small hole with a patching kit as you would a hole in a wall (p.129).

FLOORS

Squeak solutions

Shingle to the rescue

Squeaking is one of the most exasperating floor flaws. The cause is usually wood rubbing against wood or a nail. To stop a squeak caused by the movement of the subfloor against a joist, tap a wood shingle or shim between the joist and the subfloor in the vicinity of the squeak. Don't force it in too far, though, or you'll cause more problems than you solve. Dab glue or construction adhesive on the shim before installation. ▼

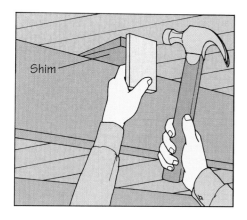

Squeak end work

Carpet replacement time offers a great opportunity to track down and eliminate squeaks in an unfinished floor that's otherwise always covered. After the carpet is up, walk over the entire area to find the squeaks. Wherever there's a problem, run 2-inch drywall screws through the floor and subfloor into the joist below. A line of existing nails is the best clue to the location of a joist.

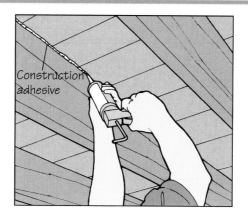

Glue a squeak ▲

Sometimes you fix a squeak in one place only to find that it has moved to another spot. One squeak-stopper you can quickly apply to large areas of a floor is construction adhesive. Put a tube in a caulking gun and run a bead of the adhesive along both sides of a joist, right where it supports the subfloor. The squeaks should be gone for good.

Sneaky squeak stoppers

The best fix for a squeaky floor is to eliminate the usual culprit: the rubbing of wood against wood. But if this isn't possible, try lubricating the squeak. Any number of lubricants have been known to work, including talcum powder, furniture wax, penetrating lubricant spray, graphite, and liquid soap. Sometimes linseed oil or teak oil dribbled into the cracks between floorboards will expand the wood enough to tighten the flooring.

Better yet, get home earlier

Squeaky stairs? Screw metal shelf brackets to the underside of the stair to silence offending treads. The brackets needn't be large, but make sure the screws don't poke through to the top.

Braced for action

Squeaky floors are often caused by floor bridging that has worked loose over the years, allowing the joists to move a bit when the floor above them is walked on. The solution is easy: just reattach the bridging with 6d common nails. ▼

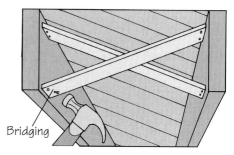

Repairing strip flooring

A fix from below

Sometimes you can pull loose flooring back into place by running screws into it from below. Make sure that the screws are shorter than the combined thickness of the flooring and the subfloor. Weight down the loose strips or have someone stand on them. ▼

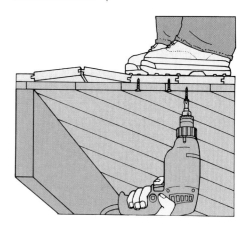

Wayward board

Before you go to the effort of replacing a warped floorboard, try this solution: Strip the finish from the offending board and cover it with a damp cloth for a couple of days. If the moisture temporarily solves the problem, secure the board with countersunk wood screws before it dries and springs back.

Removing a damaged board

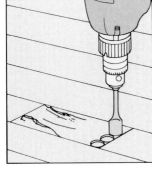

Taking out a damaged portion of a floorboard calls for some care and precision. Whenever possible, remove an entire board or at least the part of the board from the damaged area to the closest joint. If you have to make a crosscut, use a car-

penter's square as a guide to mark the cut line. Then bore several overlapping holes just inside the line. Split the board with a chisel, and pry out the pieces carefully, center piece first. Finally use a sharp wide chisel to square off the opening, using the cut line as a guide.

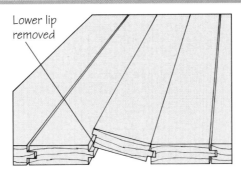

Lower lip removed

Replacing damaged boards ▲

Once you've removed boards from a strip floor, replacing them is simply a matter of lining up the tongues and grooves and nailing the boards in place. Simple, that is, until you get to the last board. The trick to fitting it is to chisel off the lower lip on the board's groove side. With the lip gone, the board will fall easily into place. You'll have to nail through the surface of the board to secure it, but a bit of putty over the countersunk nails should conceal your work.

Nailing tip

Whenever you use nails to secure strip flooring, drive them into the floor at an angle. An angled nail is less likely to work itself loose later on.

Save your knees

A large block of rigid polystyrene plastic foam from a discarded appliance carton makes a great kneeling pad when you're working on the floor. It is easy on the knees and it won't scratch the floor finish.

Floor stiffeners

The bounce of an old floor is often due to tired or undersize floor joists. If the joists are accessible from below, here's an inexpensive fix. Attach an 8-foot length of ½-inch plywood—at least 8 inches wide—to one side of each joist, securing it with construction adhesive and two rows of 6d nails spaced about 6 inches apart. Adding these plywood braces to the center of each joist should stiffen the floor noticeably. ▼

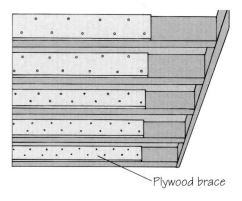

Plywood brace

Removing a subfloor

Pulling out nails one by one to remove boards in a subfloor makes for a long day. You can sometimes speed the work by cutting the floor into sections with a circular saw. Set the saw blade to a depth just shy of the thickness of the subfloor; then run it down the length of a joist (just to one side of the nails). With any luck you may be able to pry entire sections of the subfloor loose, nails and all. The trick works just as well when removing old strip flooring.

FLOOR COVERINGS

Carpeting tricks

Pile plugs

To patch small burns or stains in a carpet, file the end of a short length of copper pipe into a sharp cutting edge. Put the sharpened pipe over the carpet and hit it with a mallet to remove a circular plug around the damage. Repeat the procedure on a matching carpet scrap or hidden section of carpeting to create a replacement plug. Dab some adhesive on the replacement plug, align its fibers with the surrounding carpet, and set it in place; you'll never see the patch.

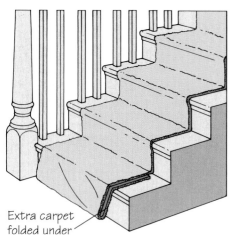

Extra carpet folded under

Carpet retreads ▲

If you're replacing the runner on the stairs, buy an extra 18 inches. When you install the carpet, fold under the extra length at the bottom of the stairs. When the carpet begins to wear—usually along the projecting nose of each tread—just untack the runner, shift it up a few inches, and reattach it. You should be able to do this at least two or three times over the life of the carpet.

Good brews for removing glue

Here's a mixture you can use to remove dried carpet adhesive from a subfloor. Mix 1 part vinegar with 3 parts water, and apply the mixture to the subfloor. Let it stand for 30 minutes or so, and then scrape up the adhesive with a wide, stiff putty knife. Sometimes you can get away with using hot water instead: the heat alone may be able to soften the dried adhesive enough for you to remove it.

Carpeting at the threshold

Fastening carpet at the threshold between two rooms can be tricky. If the finished floor in one room is more than ½ inch higher than the floor to be carpeted in the other room, use a tack strip to hold the carpet down near the threshold, just as in the rest of the room. But if the difference between the two floors is less than this, you'll have to staple the carpet directly to the floor. Cut the carpet pad back about 1 inch from the edge of the threshold. Then tuck the edge of the carpeting under about 1 inch to cover the area that isn't padded. Spread the carpet pile apart with one hand and staple through both layers of carpet into the floor. ▼

Staple gun

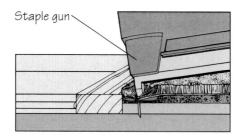

Removing vinyl tiles

A pressing solution

Heat is usually the key to removing vinyl floor tiles. If you need to remove a damaged tile, place a cloth over it and move an iron, turned to a medium setting, across the cloth with slow, even strokes. The heat will soften both the adhesive and the tile, making it possible to pry up the tile with a putty knife. ▼

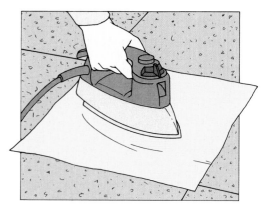

Shiver your tiles

If heat doesn't help remove a tile, try cold. Place dry ice on the tile (but be careful not to touch the ice directly). Once the tile is cold enough, a smart rap with a hammer should shatter it.

Second-hand tiles

If you want to reuse loose, undamaged floor tiles, you'll have to remove the adhesive clinging to their backs. You can scrape it off with a paint scraper, but it's much easier to soak the tiles in water overnight to soften the adhesive and then remove the goop with a putty knife.

Repairing vinyl floors

Clear cover

A scrape or heavy scuffing that removes the clear top layer on vinyl flooring can result in the quick deterioration of the layers below. To repair such damage, simply coat it with vinyl seam sealant (sold by flooring outlets). If the flooring has a deeper gouge, replace the tile or the section of sheet vinyl (right).

Bursting bubbles

Water leakage can cause a sheet vinyl floor to bubble. The repair is easy once you've eliminated the source of the problem and let the subfloor dry thoroughly. Cut a slit in the center of the bubble with a utility knife. Then use a plastic ketchup or mustard bottle (with a pointed tip) or a glue syringe to squirt vinyl floor adhesive through the slit. Work the adhesive under the bubble with a narrow putty knife or a sliver of wood. Then press the bubble down with a rolling pin, wipe up any excess adhesive, and weight the area until the adhesive sets. ▼

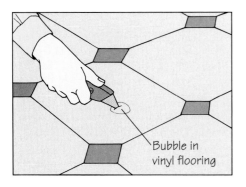

Bubble in vinyl flooring

FLOORING PATCH

To patch a damaged section of sheet vinyl flooring, use a piece left over from the original job or "stolen" from a hidden place, such as the back of a closet or the floor under the refrigerator. The patch should be 1 inch larger all around than the damage. Whenever possible, plan for the patch seams to follow a pattern line in the flooring.

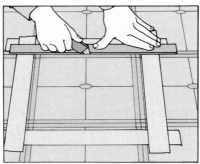

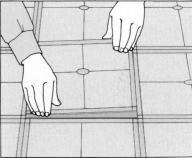

1 Place the patch over the damage, align it with the pattern, and secure it with duct tape. Use a sharp utility knife guided by a straightedge to cut through the patch and the flooring. Then pry out the damaged material and scrape out all the old adhesive.

2 Spread vinyl floor adhesive on the back of the patch, fit it into place, and wipe off any excess adhesive with a damp cloth. Weight the patch overnight until the adhesive sets. Then apply vinyl seam sealer to the seams around the patch to bond it to the flooring.

Laying sheet vinyl

Strong-arm flooring

Sheet vinyl covers large areas quickly. But before installing it, you must flatten and trim the rolled material to fit the room. Getting it to stay flat right off the roll can be daunting. If the weather is warm, spread the sheet outside in the sun to relax it. In winter, try covering the sheet with an electric blanket to warm it and get out the curls.

Nick relief

If you nick or tear vinyl flooring while laying it, disguise the damage with tub and tile caulk in a closely matching color. Dab a little into the damage and wipe off the excess with a damp cloth.

Procrastinators, this one's for you

To remove floor adhesive from your tools, toss them in the freezer overnight. In the morning you'll be able to chip off the hardened adhesive. Wear goggles to protect your eyes from flying shards.

CERAMIC TILES

Working with tile

Mixing tiles

By the time you have to replace a tile, you may not be able to find a match. Instead of trying to match existing tiles, remove some extra tiles to form an interesting pattern and replace them with tiles of a contrasting color or design.

Thinking ahead

For your next tile project, buy a half-dozen or so extra tiles for future repairs. Wrap them carefully to prevent breakage, and mark the package with the date, the name of the store they came from, and the room to which they belong. Save some matching grout, too.

Chipped tile?

You can repair nicks or chips in ceramic tiles with appliance touch-up paint. It dries to a hard, glossy surface and comes in a variety of colors.

Marking tile

During nearly any tile job, you'll have to cut tiles into odd shapes. To mark a cut line, use a felt-tip pen or a grease pencil; if you need a really precise line, scratch it with a drywall screw.

Tile nippers

Nibble a cut ▲

When using tile nippers to make a cutout, start at the edge in the center of the waste area and work toward the cut line. To avoid ragged edges, keep the jaws parallel to the cut line and place no more than two-thirds of the jaw surface on the tile for each bite. Smooth the edges with 80-grit carbide sandpaper.

Life is like that

Sloppy caulking is a sure way to spoil the look of any tile job. For professional results, take a tip from painters and reach for the masking tape. Run tape along both sides of your planned line of caulk, apply the caulk, smooth it down, and then carefully lift away the tape. You'll get a caulk line with crisp, straight edges (and a handful of goopy tape). ▼

Masking tape

Picking between tiles

When replacing a tile, make sure your new tile is squarely aligned. Pieces of round toothpicks make perfect spacers for holding the tile in place while the adhesive sets (see step 4, facing page).

Grout match

Matching new grout with existing grout can be tricky. To increase your chance for success, buy a small amount of grout first, mix up a sample batch, and let it dry for 3 days or so. You'll get a much better idea of how the color will compare to the existing grout.

¼" plywood

Coat hanger wire

◀ Shape shifting

Fitting tiles around irregular projections can be tricky. If you have several to do, make your own contour gauge by sandwiching lengths of coat hanger wire between scraps of ¼-inch plywood. Fit the wires into saw kerfs in the bottom piece, spacing the kerfs to suit the degree of accuracy you need. (The more wires you use, the more accurate the tool will be.) Fasten the pieces together with machine screws and wing nuts. To use the gauge, push the ends of its wires against an obstruction until they take on its shape; then move the gauge to the tiles or to paper and trace the cut line.

REPLACING A CERAMIC TILE

Ceramic tiles are durable and stain-resistant, but sooner or later one may crack and need replacement. Fortunately the job isn't that difficult. You'll have to scrape out the surrounding grout, chip out the damaged tile and replace it with a new one, and finally regrout the area around the new tile. If the damaged tile is in a tub or shower surround, the repair is one you shouldn't postpone. A cracked tile allows water to seep behind it, and over time this will damage the wallboard or other material under the tile. Eventually the moisture will multiply your problems by loosening surrounding tiles. Here's how to get the job done quickly.

1 If the tile is over the tub, use cardboard or an old blanket to protect the tub floor and keep debris out of the drain. Remove any fixture that is covering the tile, such as the tub spout shown here.

Grout saw

2 Cut out the grout around the edges of the damaged tile with a grout saw, or scrape it free with the tip of an old screwdriver. Work carefully to avoid chipping the edges of the surrounding tiles.

3 Wearing safety goggles, use a sharp cold chisel and a ball-peen hammer to crack the tile in an X-pattern. Tap lightly to avoid damaging other tiles. Pry out the pieces, and chip out the old adhesive.

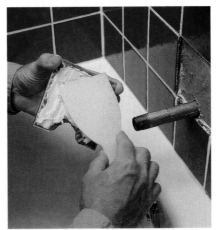

4 Shape the new tile as needed (facing page). Spread 1/8 in. of tile adhesive on the back, press it in place, and use tape or spacers to hold it. Scrape excess adhesive from joints, and wipe clean.

5 When the adhesive cures, press grout into the joints and smooth it. Wipe off excess grout with a damp sponge. Use a dry cloth to burnish off any haze that forms on the tile surface.

WINDOWS

Quick fixes

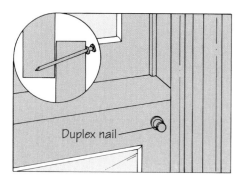

Duplex nail

Nail order ▲

Here's a cost-effective security measure for double-hung windows. Drill a hole through the inner sash and halfway into the outer sash. Then slip a nail into the hole to prevent anyone from pushing the sashes open. If you angle the hole slightly, the nail won't jiggle out. If you use a duplex (double-headed) nail, you'll be able to remove it easily.

Lazy guard

Nearly any sliding window or door can get a simple security boost. Cut a dowel or a board to fit flat in the window track. This will prevent the sash from sliding open even if the lock is jimmied. ▼

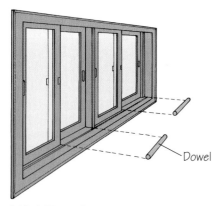

Dowel

Balky sash?

A window may stick for any number of reasons—including warped or swollen wood or accumulated dirt or paint. Before undertaking major repairs, try lubricating the channels with soap, candle wax, paraffin, or silicone spray. ▼

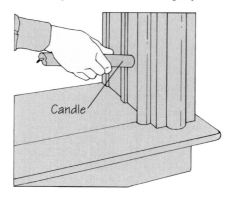

Candle

Stain be gone

Many windows feature vinyl or vinyl-clad frames to improve their weather resistance. If you accidentally drip or brush stain or paint on the frames while working on the surrounding siding, do not use sandpaper or steel wool to remove it. Instead, dab off the stain with naphtha, mineral spirits, or turpentine. A slower method, but one that's easier on the vinyl, is to scrub it with a hand cleaner containing lanolin. Before using a cleaning compound, spot-test it on an unobtrusive portion of the frame.

Removing glass

Upright proposition

Always carry and store a pane of glass in a vertical position. Otherwise, the glass may break under the force of its own weight.

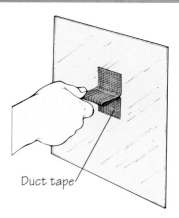

Duct tape

Handle on a roll ▲

Even a small pane of glass can be unwieldy when you're trying to maneuver it into place, so give it a handle. Fold a length of duct tape into a tab that you can grab. On a large pane use two.

Another glass carrier

To carry a sizable pane of glass safely and easily, slit two short sections of old garden hose and slip them over the top and bottom edges of the glass.

Slit garden hose

Safety strategies

Most injuries connected with repairing broken windows occur while removing the glass. If you remove the glazing putty first, the glass will be loosened enough for you to pull it easily from the window. Always wear canvas or leather gloves when handling broken glass.

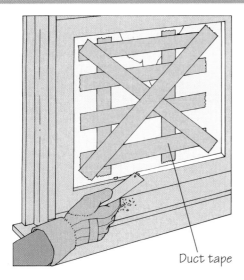

Combine and conquer ▲

Use wide duct tape to hold together all the pieces of a broken pane while you're removing the putty and points. When you're done, just lift out the glass or press it out from the back side.

Duct tape

Pull, don't push

When removing broken glass, pull the shards toward you; if they break, any slivers will be directed away from you. Don't forget to wear gloves and goggles.

Installing panes

Don't be a pane killer

When you measure for the new glass, remember that a snug-fitting pane can easily crack when the window frame moves or shrinks. That's why glass should be cut about ⅛ inch smaller overall than the height and width of the actual opening. Cut the glass yourself (p.99) or let a glass store do it.

Well-prepared rabbet

Before installing a new pane, scrape and sand the rabbet (the notch in the edge of the sash that the pane fits into). Then give it a coat of primer or linseed oil. This will keep the wood from absorbing the oil in the glazing compound.

Pane bed

To cushion the glass, even out wood irregularities, and create a weathertight joint, put a bead of paintable latex caulk on the rabbet of the sash before setting in the glass. Caulk, which goes on quickly with a caulking gun, is preferable here to glazing compound, which is often stiff and can break the glass when you press it in.

Ear points

Traditional triangular glazier's points are tricky to use. Instead, buy glazier's points with "ears," which make them easy to press into the window frame with a stiff putty knife. If you have to use regular glazier's points, place some putty on the wood at each point location, and press the points into the putty to hold them while you tap them in. ▼

Ear

Roll a rope

Applying the layer of glazing compound around a new pane is much easier if you roll a lump of compound between your hands to form a ropelike length. Then just press the rope along the joint and smooth it. ▼

Glazing compound

Nonstick knife

When smoothing glazing compound, dip your putty knife blade in turpentine, mineral spirits, or paint thinner now and then; it'll keep the compound from sticking to the blade. ▼

Take your time

After installing a new windowpane, wait about a week for the compound to cure before painting it. When you do paint, lap the paint just a bit onto the glass to seal the edge of the compound.

DOORS

A good first impression

The oak threshold beneath an exterior door is a thing of beauty, at least until time and weather take their toll. To restore and protect a weatherworn threshold, first strip or sand off any remaining finish. Then apply a generous coat of boiled linseed oil to the threshold; let it soak in for 30 minutes, and wipe off the excess. Repeat the process about 24 hours later. Let the threshold dry completely; then finish it with two or more coats of spar varnish.

Handing a door

Left-hand door or right-hand—which is it? Because some doors are beveled to permit smooth opening in one direction, you'll need to know this if you're replacing one. Here's how you can tell the difference: Face the door so that it opens toward you and you can see the hinge barrels. If the knob is on your left, the door is left-handed. If the opposite is true, the door is right-handed. ▼

Left-handed door   Right-handed door

Ink a lock

To make sure the bolt of a deadbolt lock or a lockset aligns with the strike plate, mark the bolt with an ink pad (or lipstick or chalk), then close the door and rotate the bolt against the jamb to make an imprint. Use the imprint to align the plate.

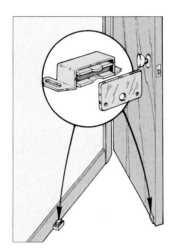

Open-door policy ▲

Bothered by an interior door that slams shut whenever a breeze blows or you walk by it? Screw a magnetic cabinet door catch to the floor, with its strike plate on the back of the door. Make sure the catch is far enough out from the baseboard to allow for the doorknob. If necessary, mount it on a small block of wood to raise it high enough to contact the bottom of the door.

Now you see it

Many folks forget to paint or finish the bottom and top edges of an entry door, and that's a big mistake. Unsealed edges provide access to moisture, which can cause swelling and warping and peeling paint. Coat the edges with an exterior paint or penetrating sealer.

Taming slippery hinges

It's important to position the two leaves of a butt hinge so that they will match exactly. But it's hard to hold a hinge leaf in place as you mark around it because the pencil tends to follow the grain of the wood and cause the hinge to move. The trick is to use a sharp pencil and press lightly. Another solution is to temporarily screw the hinge in place or stick it down with double-faced tape while you trace around it.

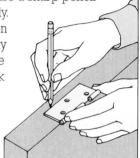

Pop goes the pin

You can remove most hinge pins without damaging the hinge barrel by slipping a nail into the hole at the bottom of the barrel, then driving the nail (and the pin) upward with a hammer tap.

Securing the perimeter

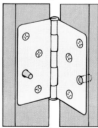

If its hinge pins are exposed, locking a door offers little security because the pins, and then the door itself, can be removed with relative ease. To make a break-in less easy, remove two opposite middle screws from a hinge. Run a long screw partway into the jamb side of the hinge, and cut off the screw's head with a hacksaw, letting the shank stick out about ¼ inch. When you close the door, the shank will fit into the opposite hinge hole, securing the door.

INSTALLING A RIM DEADBOLT LOCK

It may be on the homely side, but a surface-mounted, or rim, deadbolt is about the strongest door lock available. It's also easier to install than an in-the-door cylindrical deadbolt, making it a good choice for anyone short on skills or time. Locksmiths and well-stocked hardware stores carry a variety of good-quality rim deadbolt locks.

1 Cut the outline of the strike plate onto the jamb with a utility knife; then chisel a mortise for the strike plate. Attach the plate, using long screws that penetrate the studs.

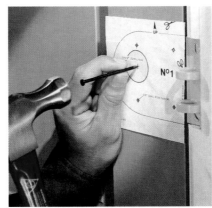

2 Tape the paper template that comes with the lock to the door directly opposite the strike plate. Use a nail to mark the centers of the holes you'll be drilling for the lock cylinder and housing screws.

3 Use a hole saw to drill the cylinder hole. (To prevent splintering, drill until the pilot bit pokes through the other side; then finish from the other side.) Drill pilot holes for the housing screws.

4 Mount the lock cylinder and backplate in the hole. The bolts for attaching the cylinder and the connecting bar are notched so that they can easily be cut to fit doors of different thicknesses. Use side-cutting pliers or nippers to cut them, and wear safety goggles to protect your eyes against flying metal pieces.

5 Slip the lock into place, and make sure the connecting bar in the cylinder meshes correctly with the lock. Check the fit of the lock by engaging and disengaging the deadbolt with the strike plate. If all's in order, drive the housing screws into place and the job is done.

SCREENS AND STORM WINDOWS

Buzzer block

Even tiny holes can allow squadrons of skeeters to zoom through. Touch up small holes in your defensive screen with clear nail polish or shellac.

Kids 6, screen 0

Any parent knows that screen doors and small kids are not the best of friends. Little ones are in and out all day long, and when they can't reach the doorknob they stiff-arm the screen on their way out. To prevent damage, cover the inside of the screen with a screen guard. The sturdy wire mesh in a guard prevents even a tiny hand from pushing out the screen. Inexpensive guards are available at home centers and hardware stores.

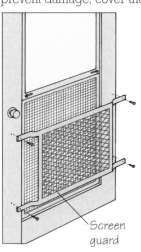

Screen guard

Quick repair

Fix a small puncture in a metal screen with clear caulk and scrap screen. Trim around the hole so that the edges are neat and flat. Apply clear silicone caulk to the trimmed edges, and press on a patch slightly larger than the damaged area. Then smooth the caulk and clean up any excess. In a couple of days the caulk will become transparent, making the fix an acceptable temporary repair.

Screen stretcher

The standard way to get screening tight on a wood frame is to work from the middle out, switching between the ends and the sides after every four or five staples and pulling the screening taut as you go. But if you have trouble, try this. Start with screening a few inches longer than needed. Staple it to one end of the frame, working from the middle out. At the other end, staple the screening to a board held tightly against the edge. Press down on the board to stretch the screening as you staple that end. When stapling the sides, pull taut by hand.

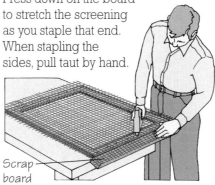

Scrap board

Screen pins

Some outswinging awning and casement windows require interior screens that are easy to remove so that you can latch or wash the windows. Attach these screens with double-headed scaffold nails that slip into holes slightly larger than the nails' diameter. ▼

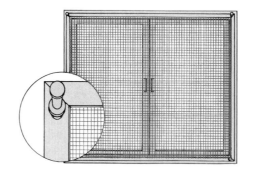

A combination to bet on

By all means replace rickety windows with double- (or triple-) pane models. But to upgrade sound older windows, add combination storm windows. With their sliding screen and glass panels, they end the back-straining job of changing storms and screens. And they double the energy efficiency of unprotected windows. Look for solid construction, resilient pile weatherstripping, and three tracks (instead of two).

Remote shade puller

Clear plastic sheeting can be used as an inside storm window if the window is absolutely airtight. But how do you operate a shade behind the plastic? Before installing the plastic, raise the shade all the way and attach clear fishing line to the bottom. Drill a tiny hole in the sill and thread the line through it. ▼

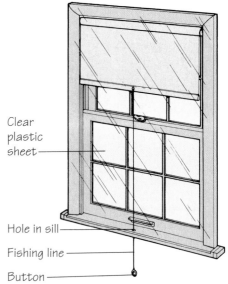

Clear plastic sheet

Hole in sill

Fishing line

Button

REPLACING A SCREEN

On most metal-frame screens the screening is held in place by a spline that fits into a groove. Some screens have reusable metal splines, but most have vinyl splines that should be replaced—old, stiff vinyl may break if you try to reuse it. To get the right size, take a piece of the old spline to the store. Also pick up an inexpensive tool called a spline roller.

You can choose between fiberglass and aluminum screening. Fiberglass is not as durable but is less expensive and easier to handle. When installing aluminum screening, it helps to force it into the groove with the roller before installing the spline. Also, clip the corners of the screen at an angle to reduce bunching.

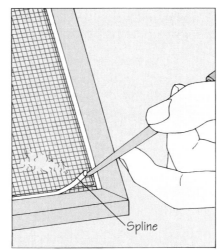

Spline

1 Remove the old splines with an awl or a thin screwdriver. Remove metal splines carefully so that you can reuse them. Discard the old screen.

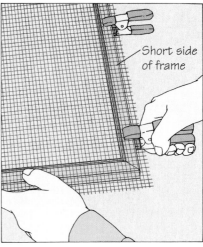

Short side of frame

2 Cut new screening about 1 in. larger than the frame on all sides. Lay it over the frame evenly, and clamp it to one short side of the frame.

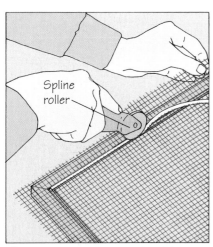

Spline roller

3 Starting at a corner on the side opposite the clamps, pull the screening taut by hand, and gradually force the new spline into the groove with a spline roller.

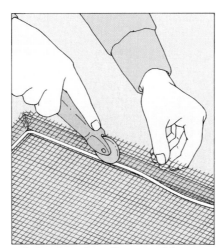

4 Continue the spline around the corner. After finishing all sides, use a screwdriver to push the spline down over the bunched screening at the corners.

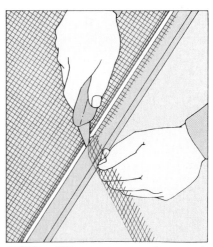

5 Trim off the excess screening around the edges of the groove with a sharp utility knife. You can guide the knife with a straightedge if you want.

WEATHERPROOFING

Caulking

Timing the job

The best time to caulk a joint outdoors is during the spring or fall. That's when the width of the joint is halfway between its seasonal extremes.

Push or pull?

Even experts disagree about whether it's best to pull or push a caulk gun as you fill a crack. Actually both methods work fine as long as you force the caulk well into the crack. For the pull method, cut the caulk tube spout at a 45° angle, then hold the gun at a 60° angle as you pull it along the crack. For the push method, cut a double angle on the spout and hold the gun at a 45° angle as you push it along the crack. ▼

Pulling caulk gun

Spout cut at 45° angle

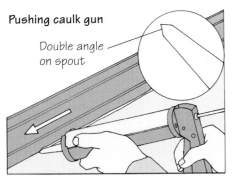
Pushing caulk gun

Double angle on spout

For better caulking

▷ Cut the nozzle opening slightly smaller than the bead you want. Keep the bead between 1/16 and 3/8 inch.
▷ To avoid jagged caulk lines, release and resqueeze the gun at a logical break, such as between clapboards.
▷ Carry a rag to remove buildup on the nozzle, which can mess up the bead.
▷ If you're a first-time caulker, start on a seldom seen part of the house. By the time you get to the front, you'll be a pro.

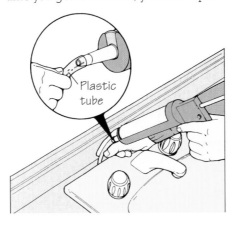
Plastic tube

Reach out to caulk ▲

A plastic drinking straw, the sheathing of electrical cable, or a length of plastic tubing makes a handy extension tube for caulking hard-to-reach places. Secure your extender with duct tape.

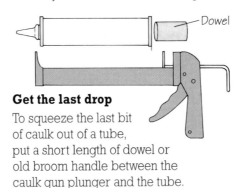
Dowel

Get the last drop

To squeeze the last bit of caulk out of a tube, put a short length of dowel or old broom handle between the caulk gun plunger and the tube.

A lick of advice

Don't smooth caulk with your finger. Some caulks contain harmful chemicals, and some are hard to remove from your skin. Get an inexpensive plastic caulk-smoothing tool, or use a plastic spoon or an ice cream or frozen pop stick; any of these will do a tidier job than a finger.

Ice cube caulk smoother

To get an ultra-fine, attractive finish on a bead of caulk, smooth it with an ice cube. Use the heat from your hand to melt the cube to the bead shape you want. Then run it over the caulk.

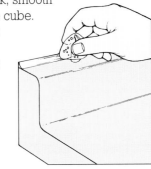

Caulk savers

The hardest part about sealing a partial tube of caulk is remembering—or taking the time—to do it. You can buy handy screw-on caps or use one of many home solutions:
▷ Insert a large rustproof common nail or machine screw.
▷ Cap the spout with a wire connector (the size normally used for 12-gauge wire).
▷ Skewer the spout with a stopper made from a piece of clothes hanger wire.

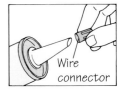
Wire connector

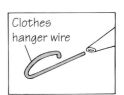
Clothes hanger wire

CAULK BUYING GUIDE

The caulks here will fill your home's exterior needs and some interior ones as well. Not listed is plain latex caulk, which is suitable only for interior jobs such as filling gaps around trim. When buying caulk, keep in mind that a standard 10½-ounce tube will produce an average-size bead 40 to 50 feet long— enough to seal about four windows or doors. If a crack is over ⅜ inch deep, stuff it with a foam backer rod before applying caulk. Besides tubes for caulk guns, caulk comes in smaller squeeze tubes for little jobs. Expanding foam caulk in aerosol cans is available for filling extra-large gaps.

ACRYLIC LATEX

Best use: Wood siding; around windows and doors

Life: 5–25 years, or longer if blended with silicone

Strengths:
▷ Easy to apply, cures fast
▷ Paintable and comes in colors
▷ Water cleanup
▷ Good for interior caulking

Weaknesses:
▷ Not for high-moisture areas
▷ May not bond well to metal and nonporous surfaces

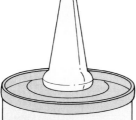

BUTYL RUBBER

Best use: Concrete block and brick, metal, flashing, chimneys

Life: 10–20 years

Strengths:
▷ Good flexibility
▷ Usable in high-moisture areas and below grade
▷ Paintable and comes in colors
▷ Excellent for aluminum siding

Weaknesses:
▷ Stringy when applied
▷ Cures slowly; fairly high shrinkage
▷ Solvent cleanup

POLYMER BLEND*

Best use: Tile, brick, concrete, stone, asphalt, wood, metal, glass, vinyl

Life: 30–50 years

Strengths:
▷ Excellent adhesion
▷ Good flexibility
▷ Joins many dissimilar materials
▷ Paintable and comes in clear and colors
▷ Resists tearing when abraded

Weaknesses:
▷ May be flammable during application
▷ May damage polystyrene and other plastics

*Often labeled "new technology" caulk

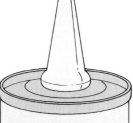

POLYURETHANE

Best use: Concrete block and brick, wood siding, metal, plastic, fiberglass

Life: 20–50 years

Strengths:
▷ Excellent adhesion and strength
▷ Good flexibility
▷ Resists weather, temperature, stress
▷ OK under water
▷ Paintable and comes in colors

Weaknesses:
▷ Solvent cleanup
▷ Higher cost
▷ Hard to find (try a builder's or marine supplier)
▷ Flammable and toxic when applied

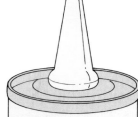

SILICONE

Best use: Metal, glass, tile; smooth nonporous surfaces

Life: 20–50 years

Strengths:
▷ Good flexibility
▷ Least shrinkage
▷ Joins many dissimilar materials
▷ Can be applied at most temperatures

Weaknesses:
▷ Not for use on masonry
▷ Poor performance on cedar and redwood
▷ Not paintable
▷ Smelly and irritating to skin when applied

WEATHERPROOFING

Weatherstripping

Locating leaks ▲

Cold air that leaks into your home is air that you have to heat. Take a close look around the perimeters of doors and windows. If you see any light, that's where air is coming in. Also run your hand—dampened to improve sensitivity—around doors and windows to feel for drafts. Or hold a tissue next to them to see if incoming air causes it to move.

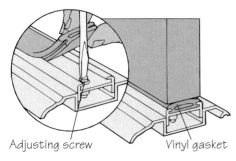

Adjusting screw   Vinyl gasket

At the threshold ▲

Closing the gap at the bottom of a door is an important defense against heat loss. One way is to install a new threshold with a vinyl gasket. An adjustable model—with screws to raise or lower its height—lets you snug it up to an uneven door without having to take the door down and trim it.

Some sticky advice

Self-adhesive weatherstripping doesn't last forever, but it is easy to install and is inconspicuous when used on the inner edges of the frames of doors and casement windows. The best adhesive-backed material to use is EPDM (ethylene propylene diene monomer) rubber weatherstripping. It's more expensive than felt or foam, but it's much more durable and moisture-resistant and provides an excellent seal.

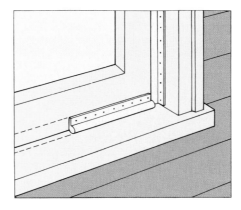

Get with the gasket ▲

An easy, inexpensive way to weatherstrip a window or door is with tubular vinyl gaskets. Nail or staple them on the opening's exterior so that they are not visible inside the house and are hidden from outside view by screens or storms. On a door, attach the pieces to the trim at the sides and the top. On a window, attach the vertical pieces to the trim at the sides and the horizontal pieces to the sashes as shown. Don't worry about putting the gaskets outside; they are very durable and can withstand temperatures below zero.

Working with insulation

Safety cover-up

Fiberglass particles can be harmful. When working with fiberglass, wear goggles and a dual-cartridge respirator (p.65). To keep itchy fiberglass slivers off your skin, wear long pants, a long-sleeved shirt, gloves, and a hat. Tuck your sleeves into the cuffs of your gloves for extra protection. If you do get slivers on your skin, don't scratch them. Take a cool or tepid shower; hot water opens the pores, making the itching worse.

Cutting batt insulation

Trimming fiberglass insulation to length is not difficult if you use the squeeze-and-slice method: Place the insulation on a solid wood or plywood surface. Position a length of 2 x 4 or 2 x 6 along the cut line and press it down with your knee; then cut through the fiberglass with a utility knife. It's important to use a sharp new blade to avoid tearing the insulation's paper facing. ▼

TYPES OF INSULATION

Fluffy fiberglass batts and blankets are by far the most popular insulation, but there are also rigid foam sheets, foam, and loose-fill. Insulation requires a vapor retarder to keep warm moist air from condensing inside the wall, causing damage. Whether a vapor retarder is built into the insulation or installed separately, always put it facing toward the wall's heated side.

INSULATION	RSI-VALUE (per inch)	BEST USES	PROS AND CONS
Fiberglass batts and blankets	0.56	Precut batts or longer blankets fit between joists or rafters in attic or open studs in new walls.	Economical, easy to install, and nonflammable, but allows heat loss through framing.
Loose-fill fiberglass	0.64	Poured loose into attic or blown into finished walls or attic with limited access.	Better coverage than batts over ceiling joists, but requires contractor.
Loose-fill rock wool	0.61	Poured loose into attic or blown into one with limited access. (Settles too much for use in walls.)	Better coverage than batts over ceiling joists, but requires contractor.
Loose-fill cellulose	0.61–0.64	Poured loose into attic or blown into finished walls or attic with limited access.	Better coverage than batts over ceiling joists. Easy to install in attic, but a dusty job.
Extruded polystyrene rigid foam sheet	0.84–0.89	For walls and foundations. Best choice for below-grade insulation of exterior wall or floor.	Resists moisture. Good RSI-value, but costly. Flammable; needs wallboard cover indoors.
Expanded polystyrene rigid foam sheet	0.66–0.71	Sheathing beneath exterior siding, as core of foam-core panels.	Least costly of sheets. Not moisture-resistant. Flammable; needs wallboard cover indoors.
Polyurethane rigid foam sheet	1.02–1.27	Sheathing beneath exterior siding, as core of foam-core panels.	Gives high RSI-value per inch but costly. Flammable; needs wallboard cover indoors.
Polyurethane foam	1.07	Pumped into finished walls as a liquid, then solidifies. Best on uneven surfaces.	Excellent insulating power and forms own vapor retarder, but requires contractor.

INSULATION SHOULD MATCH THE LENGTH AND SEVERITY OF YOUR HEATING SEASON

The higher the RSI-value, the better the insulator. This chart lists minimum recommendations of Natural Resources Canada for different zones (see map)—zones defined by climatic data on the length and coldness of the heating season.

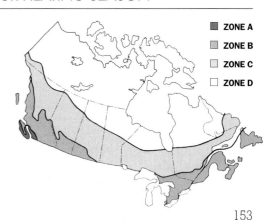

■ ZONE A
▨ ZONE B
▢ ZONE C
☐ ZONE D

INSULATION AREA	ZONE A	ZONE B	ZONE C	ZONE D
Walls	RSI 3	RSI 3.6	RSI 4.1	RSI 4.5
Basement	RSI 2.2	RSI 2.2	RSI 2.2	RSI 2.2
Roof or ceiling	RSI 4.5	RSI 5.6	RSI 6.4	RSI 7.1
Floor over unheated spaces	RSI 4.7	RSI 4.7	RSI 4.7	RSI 4.7

WEATHERPROOFING

Insulating walls

Insul-vestigate

You can always check attic insulation by climbing up and taking a look. But how do you know if your house walls are insulated? Here are a couple of tricks:
▷ Remove switch plates and outlet covers to see if there's insulation around the electrical box. Before probing, however, turn off the power to the box at your home's main service panel.
▷ Find an unobtrusive spot, like a closet that's on an exterior wall, and cut a small hole in the wall surface with a hole saw.

Flange mystery solved

Where do you staple the flanges on batts of insulation? Stapling them to the front of the studs is easier and creates a better vapor seal than stapling them to the sides. But if you plan to install wallboard with adhesive, the studs' fronts must be bare, and so you should attach the flanges to the sides. In either case, secure them tightly, leaving no gaps for water vapor to pass through.

See-through sealer

When installing a plastic vapor retarder over insulation, you have to run it over electrical boxes and cut openings for them later. For a tight seal and fewer air leaks, cut the plastic ¼ inch inside each box perimeter. Then carefully stretch the plastic around the outside of the box. Tape any tears.

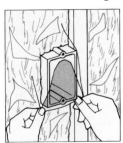

Insulating attics

Bridge repair

To add insulation to an already insulated attic, run batts over the tops of the joists at right angles to the existing batts. This covers any gaps in the first layer and insulates the thermal bridges (heat escape routes) created by the joists. When adding batts, work from the eaves toward the center on a plywood platform. Use unfaced batts. If the batts have a facing, slash it every few inches so that it won't trap moisture. ▼

Tarzan of the attic

You've decided to add more insulation to the attic. Now, how do you get up there time and again if all you have is a ceiling hatch for access? Secure a stout rope to the rafter directly above the hatch. Then just grab the rope firmly to help pull yourself off your ladder into the attic. Put a couple of knots in the rope to give yourself a better grip.

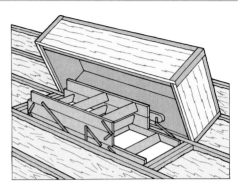

Box block ▲

Any attic opening, whether a fold-down stair or a simple hatch, should be insulated and weatherstripped to keep heat from leaking from the house. Use self-stick foam or vinyl weatherstrips to seal around the opening's frame. To insulate, build a plywood box that fits around the opening and cover it with foil-faced rigid foam insulation sealed with duct tape. Hinge the box, or simply lift it aside when you need to access the attic.

Fire hazard to avoid

Keep any insulation that you install at least 3 inches away from stovepipes, metal chimneys, and heat-producing electrical fixtures, such as recessed lights, fans, and doorbell transformers. (But it's OK to cover a recessed light marked IC, for "insulated ceiling.") To contain loose fill, tack a board or a sheet-metal shield between the joists on each side of a fixture. ▼

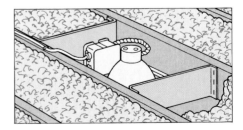

Nothing baffling about it

Condensation can become a problem if adequate ventilation is not taken into account when insulating an attic. Baffles under the roof sheathing will ensure air circulation between soffit vents and ridge, roof, or gable vents. ▼

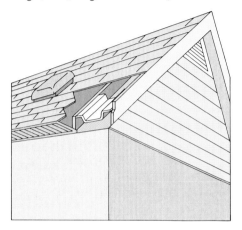

Above crawl spaces

Let two tabs take

The cross-braced bridging often found between floor joists makes it tricky to install insulation. To fit batts snugly around the bridging, cut the insulation to create a joint at the bridging. Then make short lengthwise cuts in the center of the batt ends as shown. The resulting tabs will fit neatly around the obstruction. ▼

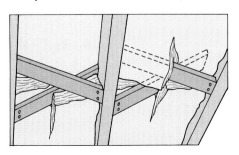

Old hangers never die ▲

Insulating a floor above an unheated basement or crawl space presents a problem: With the vapor retarder of the batts facing up against the floor (as it should be), there are no flanges to hold the insulation in place. An easy solution is to jam wires—slightly longer than the width of the cavity—against the batts. Buy the wires or cut them from clothes hangers. Push them in every 2 feet or so, bowing them upward.

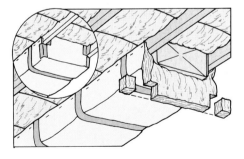

How to wrap a duct ▲

You can insulate a duct between floor joists with ordinary batts. Just cut short sections of insulation, put them across the duct, and staple them to the joists on either side. Put the vapor retarder side out, and seal the seams with duct tape. When you reach the end of the duct, cut, fold, and seal the last section as shown.

Moisture barrier

Lay a ground vapor retarder in your crawl space to prevent moisture from damaging the floor insulation and from entering your house. Use sheets of 6-mil polyethylene, extending them several inches up the foundation walls and overlapping the edges by at least 6 inches. Use asphalt roofing cement (in caulk-gun cartridges) to tack the sheets to the walls and each other. Or secure the edges with duct tape and weight the seams with bricks. ▼

Stop-gap solution

Foil-covered air-bubble plastic insulation, though flammable, can temporarily provide extra insulation and retard vapor and air infiltration above a vented crawl space. To use, push fiberglass batts between the floor joists; then staple the 4-foot-wide bubble-pack sheets to the joists and the sill. Seal the seams with duct tape. ▼

BASEMENTS AND FOUNDATIONS

Repairs

Miner's hat trick

Light

When you have to slither into a crawl space to repair or investigate something, pack a light where it makes the most sense: on your head. It'll leave both hands free. Models on an elastic headband are available from camping (especially mountaineering) supply stores. For hard-hat versions, try an industrial supplier. These hats are great for any job that normally requires a flashlight.

Check these first

The easiest solution to basement leaks is to keep water away from the foundation. Make sure downspouts direct water away: Put a splash block under each spout, or fit it with an extension pipe. Also make sure the ground slopes away from the house. Over time the grade around a foundation can sink, creating a mini-moat.

Done in a jiffy

Here are a few simple cures for high humidity in basements: If cold-water pipes are wet with condensation, dry them off and insulate them with self-sticking foam insulating tape or preslit foam sleeves. Make sure the laundry vent pipe isn't pouring damp air into the basement. If all else fails, park a dehumidifier in the basement.

Run a test

Can't decide whether basement dampness is due to outside water seeping in or excess house humidity condensing on the cool walls? Try this simple test: Attach squares of aluminum foil to the walls and floor, sealing all four edges with duct tape. In a couple of days, remove the foil. If the side against the wall or floor shows beads of moisture, the problem is seepage from outside. But if the moisture shows up only on the foil's outer surface, it's from interior condensation.

Mirror, mirror, on the ground

At caulking time, don't overlook heat-robbing cracks and gaps between the foundation and the siding. To save wear and tear on your knees, use an old mirror to see under the siding. You'll barely have to lean over. ▼

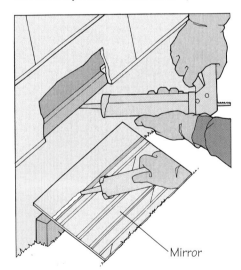

Mirror

Finishing

Fast furring strips

If you're using masonry nails to install furring strips on concrete basement walls, predrill holes for the nails; the job will go much easier. Start the nails in the furring strips so that they just poke through the back. Then hold the strip against the wall, and tap the nails to mark their locations on the wall. Drill holes in the concrete with a $\frac{1}{8}$-inch masonry bit; then nail the strips in place. The masonry won't chip and the nails will go straight in.

Predrilled holes

Nails started

Save your breath

When drilling into masonry, don't try to blow debris out of the holes. You'll just get a faceful of gritty dust. Instead, use a hand pump or squirt water into them.

Concealing rough walls

Concrete or block foundation walls are not the best-looking surfaces for a basement shop or rec room. If the walls are dry and you don't want to frame and insulate over them, consider stucco in a smooth finish or a decorative texture.

Chill-free basement floors

Here's how to give a warm cover to a cold concrete floor: Clean the surface, and use a notched trowel to apply a coat of slightly thinned asphalt mastic. Lay down 6-mil polyethylene sheeting, and press with a weighted floor roller. Next, embed pressure-treated 2 x 4 sleepers in rows of mastic, and nail ¾-inch construction plywood to the sleepers. Now you're ready for a carpet and pad. ▼

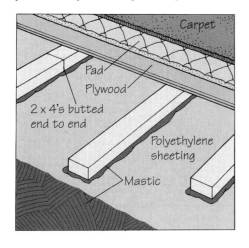

Boxed posts ▲

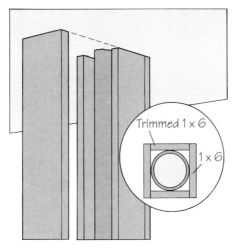

To hide concrete-filled steel posts, box them in with 1 x 6's. Trim two of the 1 x 6's so that they're 4 inches wide. Join the pieces as shown, shimming the bottom edge off the floor. Drill a couple of ⅛-inch holes through the box into the post, and attach the box with concrete screws, countersinking the heads. Trim at top and bottom with quarter round.

Building out basement windows

Those small basement awning windows are great for bringing in natural light, but they need special attention when finishing the interior walls. After the wall framing is in, build a lumber box around each window as shown. Make the box's depth equal to the distance between the existing window frame and the parged surface of the new wall. Secure the box to the framing, and after installing the wallboard or paneling, trim it with molding as you would a standard window. ▼

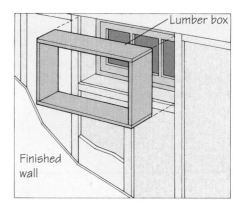

Seeking extra space ▶

Here's one way to finish basement walls. First parge the walls and let them cure. Then, at grade level, attach overlapping lengths of 6-mil polyethylene sheets to the wall with dabs of roofing cement; let them extend about 6 inches onto the floor (trim to fit later). Build a 2 x 4 frame against the wall; nail the top to the joists above and secure the bottom to the floor with masonry nails. Drill a ½-inch vent hole in the top plate between each stud pair, press in unfaced fiberglass batts, and staple on more polyethylene sheets. Cover with wallboard, stopping an inch short of the floor to prevent moisture wicking. Cover the gap with cove or baseboard molding.

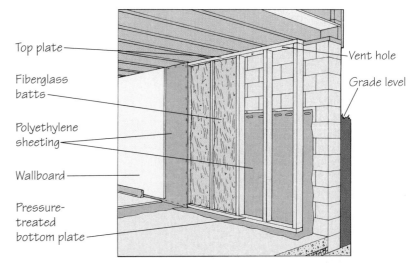

SIDING

Wood siding

Preventive survey

It's a good idea to walk around your house from time to time with a screwdriver or ice pick and probe for areas of rotten wood. Why go looking for trouble? Because the rot will get worse if you ignore it. To repair minor damage, clean away the rotted wood and fill the excavation with auto-body filler. A polyester resin/styrene monomer auto-repair compound adheres well to clean dry wood, and you can smooth, carve, or sand it to match adjoining areas.

Closing a split

To repair split lap siding, pry out the bottom section of the damaged board, and insert a shim to hold it out. Apply waterproof glue all along the edge. Then remove the shim, push the section back into place, and nail both the upper and the lower sections. Wipe off the excess glue with a wet cloth.

Lightening up the dark

If your wood siding has been stained a darker shade than you like, you can lighten it with a pressure washer (available at rental yards). Use the washer with a solution of either trisodium phosphate (TSP) or a special cleaning compound sold to go with it. Experiment to find the optimal amount of cleaner and the correct spraying technique. Wear safety goggles and vinyl gloves.

Siding sidekick

When replacing or installing lap siding, measuring the exposed section of each course is tedious and leaves room for error. Here's a better way: Create a siding gauge by nailing a cleat to a wood scrap as shown. Then simply snug it up against the bottom edge of the upper course and rest the next course on the ledge as you nail. ▼

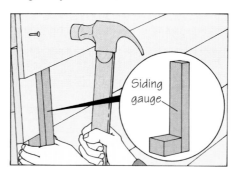

Vinyl and aluminum

Helper on a roll

Installing vinyl siding can be a solo project if you enlist the help of duct tape. Simply use a piece of tape to hold one end of the siding panel in place while you install the other end.

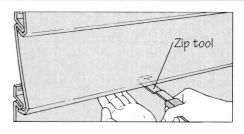

Unzipping vinyl siding ▲

Vinyl siding may seem tricky to remove, but it comes off readily with a zip tool (sold by siding suppliers). Just hook the tool under the bottom edge and pull down as you slide it along the seam.

Patching vinyl

To fix cracked vinyl siding, remove the section and glue a piece of scrap siding to the rear. Prepare the area with PVC cleaner, apply PVC cement, and press the patch in, finished side down.

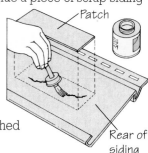

Dent removal

Large dent in aluminum siding? Drill a 1/8-inch hole, insert a sheet-metal screw, and pull out the dent. Fill any remaining depression with auto-body filler; level the filler, let it dry, and sand it smooth. Apply metal primer and two coats of matching spray paint. ▼

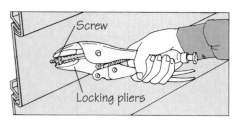

REPLACING DAMAGED LAP SIDING

Lap siding, or clapboard, comes in a variety of woods, profiles, and widths. But the steps for replacing damaged sections are the same for all. The bottom edge of each board is usually nailed to the underlying sheathing or studs every 16 inches or so. The top edge is pinched in place by the nails of the board above. When removing more than one section, work from the top down. Take a damaged board to your lumberyard to find a match.

1 If you can see nails, use a nail set to drive them through the damaged siding. Also drive them through on the undamaged board above it to release the damaged piece's top edge.

Mini-hacksaw

2 If you can't locate the nails under multiple paint layers, gently pull up the siding with a small pry bar, and slip the blade of a mini-hacksaw under the siding. Feel for the nails and cut them.

3 Cut out the damaged siding, using a backsaw or a keyhole saw with the blade reversed. Make sure that the cut is square and that the seams in the succeeding courses don't line up.

4 Working from the bottom up, install the replacement clapboards, using galvanized siding nails. Apply caulk at seams and where new siding abuts window, door, or corner trim. Prime and paint.

Replacing vinyl

Need to replace badly damaged vinyl siding? Chances are that any replacement section you buy won't match your weathered siding. Instead of using new siding, replace the damaged section with a section from an inconspicuous part of the house; then put the replacement section in the less noticeable area.

Chalk off

The powdery residue often found on aluminum siding is called chalking, and it's an intrinsic characteristic of the siding. The siding gradually releases pigment to help prevent dirt buildup. Rain usually washes away chalking. But if it becomes a problem, wash the siding with a soft rag and a mild nonabrasive household detergent. Use ⅓ cup of detergent to 1 gallon of water. Rinse well.

It's a big job, but...

Spruce up fading aluminum siding with liquid car wax. First wash the siding with dishwashing liquid and water, and let it dry. Then use a damp sponge to apply the wax. When it dries, buff it with a towel. Work small sections at a time, and remember that you're shooting for a modest sheen, not a glossy finish.

SIGING

Brick siding

Mortar quick draw

Use an old caulk tube to fill mortar joints: Push the bottom out by slipping a dowel through the spout. Clean the tube and load it with mortar. Then replace the bottom, cut the tip to the width you need, and put it in a caulk gun.

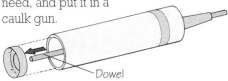

Dowel

Making mortar match

"Age" new mortar joints to match old ones by patting them with a wet tea bag. Or add colorant (from a masonry supply store) to the mortar as you're mixing it. Experiment to get the right shade.

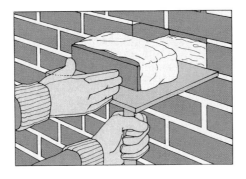

Brick replacement ▲

To replace a damaged brick, chisel out the mortar around it (step 1, facing page), being careful not to chip the surrounding bricks. Then chip the brick apart with a chisel, and pull out all the pieces. Dampen the opening. Spread mortar on the base of the cavity and on the top and ends of a damp new brick, and insert the brick. Add or remove mortar as needed.

Thumbprint test

When to finish a mortar joint—a process known as tooling, jointing, or striking—depends on the mortar mixture and the temperature. The mortar needs to set long enough so that it can take an impression but not so long that it becomes hard. Use the traditional mason's test: Mortar is ready for tooling when it will show a clear thumbprint. ▼

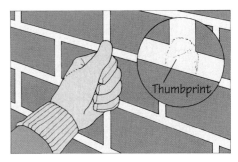

Thumbprint

Getting the right shape

If you need to shape a mortar joint and don't have a special rake or jointer tool (step 3, facing page), improvise your own. Use an ice cream or frozen pop stick, for example, to make the common concave joint. Or carve a scrap of wood or grind an old spoon to the profile that matches the joints on the surrounding bricks.

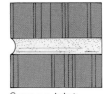

Concave joint

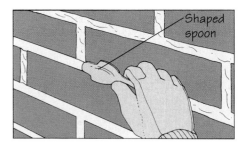

Shaped spoon

New meets old

It's not always possible to get a perfect match when adding new brickwork to old. Here are some tricks to minimize the difference.

Plant shrubs or climbing vines where the old work abuts the new, or camouflage the area with a trellis.

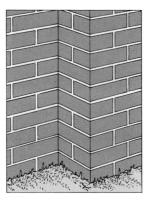

Build a small offset into the wall, putting the new bricks on a different plane from the old ones.

Place a window at the juncture of old and new work so that the only visible disparity will be low on the wall.

Stains

Shade-side solution

Whether you have brick, wood, or synthetic siding, patches of mold or mildew in shaded areas are distressing. Commercial stain removers are available, but you can do a good job with a 50/50 mixture of household bleach and water in a plastic spray bottle. After an hour, flush well with water. Wear goggles and vinyl gloves, and take care not to damage plants. If you'd rather not use bleach, scrub with straight vinegar—it takes elbow grease but works fine.

In the first place

The best way to prevent mildew staining on wood siding is to use a stain or paint that contains a fungicide or mildewcide.

Spot removers

Here's how to remove some common stains from bricks and other masonry. Test any cleaner on an inconspicuous spot first. Scrub with a nylon-bristle brush (wire may damage the surface). Wear goggles and vinyl gloves when working with solvents or caustics.
▷ Fresh paint: Blot up; then wipe with the solvent recommended for the paint.
▷ Dried paint: Scrape off; then remove residue with paint remover as directed.
▷ Rust: Mix 1 pound oxalic acid crystals in 1 gallon water and brush on. After 3 hours, scrub and rinse.
▷ Tar: Scrape off, and scrub with scouring powder. Then apply a paste of talc and kerosene, let dry, and scrub again.
▷ Smoke and soot: Scrub with scouring powder; rinse well. Apply talc mixed with bleach to stubborn areas.

REPOINTING BRICKS

The most common masonry repair is repointing—replacing damaged mortar joints between bricks. The tools you'll need are a joint or cold chisel (no wider than the joint), a 2-pound sledgehammer, a trowel, a pointing tool (to push mortar in), a wheel rake or brick jointer (to shape the mortar), and a whisk broom. For convenience, use ready-mix mortar. Add water gradually, mixing the mortar until it's a uniform stiff paste that you can shape into a ball. Let it stand for 10 minutes; then stir it briefly with a trowel before using. If the mortar becomes too stiff to use, don't add water—mix a new batch. Wear work gloves.

1 Wearing safety glasses, chisel out loose and cracked mortar to a depth of 1 in., or until you reach sound mortar. Be careful not to chip the brick itself. Brush away debris, and dampen the brick with a fine spray of water.

2 Scoop up some mortar with your trowel, hold it close to the joint, and push in a bit with the pointing tool. If a gap is ³⁄₄ in. deep or more, add the mortar in ¹⁄₄-in. layers, letting each become thumbprint hard before adding the next.

3 Once the final layer is thumbprint hard, use a brick jointer or wheel rake to smooth the joint to a shape that matches the existing mortar joints. Brush away any excess mortar from the face of the bricks after it has stiffened.

ROOFS

Gutters

Gutter scoop

Make a great gutter-cleaning scoop from a rectangular motor oil container. Cut away the bottom portion, and it's just the right size to fit into the gutter. The spout gives you a hand grip. ▼

White glove service

Are your gutters filled with mucky rotted leaves and who knows what? Use a pair of old kitchen tongs and you won't have to touch the stuff. The tongs reach nicely into tight spots, and their pincer action helps you easily grip debris.

Gutter buddy ▶

Turn an inexpensive plastic pail into a handy gutter cleaning aid. Snip the wire handle in half, bend the ends of the wires to form hooks, and hang the bucket on the gutter. Slide the bucket and toss debris into it as you work your way along the length of the gutter.

I'm just fine down here, thanks ▲

If you're not keen on climbing to clean gutters, this hose extension will let you flush them out while keeping your feet planted on terra firma. Make it from thick ¾-inch PVC plastic pipe, two elbows, a garden hose coupler, and a cap. Drill four ¹/₁₆-inch holes in the cap. Weld the parts together with PVC cement.

Trouble sign

A depression in the ground underneath a gutter is a sign that the gutter is dripping water. Look for a sag or leak in the gutter. Check for a clogged downspout that's causing an overflow.

Give a gutter a lift

On a gutter attached with spikes, a sag is often the result of a bent spike. To straighten a spike, put a heavy chain link, with a section cut out of it, on the spike and lever the spike up with a short length of angle iron. Wire wound around a pry bar will also work. ▼

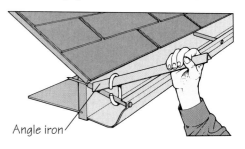

Angle iron

Raise it with a twist

On a gutter that is supported by straps, straighten a sagging section by twisting the nearest strap. This will shorten the strap and pull up the gutter. ▼

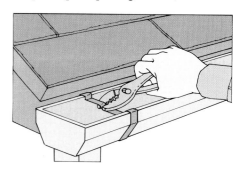

Checking and protecting

Remote is easier

Early spring and late fall are the best times to check your roof for loose or damaged shingles, rusty flashing, and cracked sealant. But keep your ladder in the garage. You can often do it from the ground with a pair of binoculars.

Can your roof pass this test?

Here's how to figure out if you'll soon have to install a new asphalt roof:
▷ Pinch off a corner of a shingle. If the inside is black, it still has life; if it's gray or crumbly, you'll have to replace it.
▷ Shingles should be flexible and resilient on a 21° C (70° F) day. If you bend back a few corners and the shingles crack or seem brittle, they won't be doing their job much longer.
▷ Discoloration or streaking on shingles indicates that the granular top coat is deteriorating.

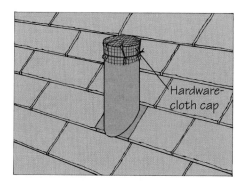

Vent guard ▲

To prevent plumbing vent pipes from becoming clogged with leaves, cover the openings with a scrap of ½-inch hardware cloth. Secure it with a wire collar or dabs of roofing cement.

Toss it off temporarily

It's below freezing and ice dams are forming on the eaves. What to do ? Ball up some rock salt with some snow and aim for the eaves. The rock salt will melt portions of the dams and help keep water from backing under the shingles.

Think like a drip

Don't assume that a leak in the roof is directly over a stain in the ceiling. Water may slither along sheathing and framing for quite a distance before dropping down. Next time there's a heavy rain, go to the attic and look and listen carefully. Once you find the leak, measure to a couple of landmarks—a ridge board, a sidewall, or a chimney or vent pipe. Repeat your measurements on the roof, and you'll have a good idea where to look for damage.

Good-bye antenna

Has cable made your antenna obsolete? Take it down to avoid leaks and other damage. After removing an antenna, dab roofing cement into the holes where the hook eyes, anchors, and support brackets were attached to the roof.

CARE UP THERE

Climbing onto a roof is hazardous. Here are some precautions:
▷ Work on a dry, mild, windless day after the dew evaporates.
▷ Use a sturdy extension ladder that reaches at least 2 feet above the eaves. The distance between the ladder's feet and the wall should equal one-fourth of the ladder's height. Tie the feet to stakes in the ground. If possible, tie the top—to gutter supports, for example.
▷ Sweep the roof lightly before you start, and keep the work area clear of debris you could slip on, such as loose shingles.
▷ Wear heavy rubber-soled shoes and long pants.
▷ Don't go near power lines; they are not always insulated. Keep your ladder well away too.
▷ Pull up loads with a rope. Don't carry a load up by hand. Use both hands to grip the ladder.
▷ Use roof jacks (p.164).
▷ Place tools and shingles where they won't slide off the roof.
▷ Keep other people far away.
▷ For maximum security, wear a safety harness tied tightly to an immovable object on the opposite side of the roof.
▷ Avoid steep roofs (over 30°) and houses over two stories high.
▷ If you're uncomfortable on a roof, hire a professional.

ROOFS

Repairing a roof

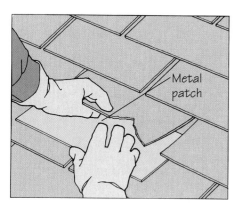

Metal backup ▲

You don't always have to remove a damaged shingle to repair it. Cut a square of sheet aluminum, coat one side with roofing cement, and slip it under the damaged area, cement side down. Then dab roofing cement on top of the patch and embed the shingle in it. This quick patch needs no nails.

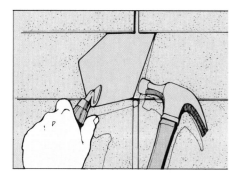

Seal breaker ▲

To lift the tabs on an asphalt or fiberglass shingle, slip a heavy-duty masonry trowel under the edge, then gently tap on the trowel's edge with a hammer. This will break the seal that holds the lower edge of the shingle.

Undercoated valley

It's not always easy to find the exact location of a leak in a valley. Rather than replace all the flashing, coat it with an aerosol auto undercoating—the repair is quick and easy and can be used for other flashing and metal gutters, too.

Instant age

New wood shingles on an old roof stand out like a beacon. To age the new wood prematurely, mix 1 pound of baking soda with ½ gallon of water and brush it on. Within a few hours, the new wood will turn gray to match its neighbors.

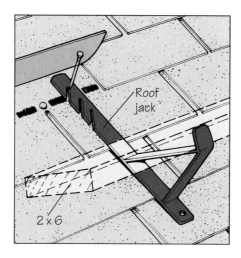

Steep slope safety ▲

For a secure foothold on a roof, rent a pair of roof jacks from your roofing supplier. Simply slip each jack under a shingle and nail it in place. Then secure a 2 x 6 to the jacks. The jacks are notched so that when you're finished working, you can slide them off and then hammer the nails in all the way.

Skid stopper

Next time you get a package, save those sheets of soft plastic foam packing. They're great for keeping hand tools from sliding off the roof. ▼

Roof replacement

Flat roof leak?

If you have a leak-prone flat roof, talk to a contractor about replacing it or covering it with a single-ply membrane. This rubberlike material is flexible enough to allow for roof movement and covers most home roofs in one seamless sheet.

Fork it off

Many people pry off old shingles with a flat shovel, but a four-tined garden fork works even better. The tines slide easily beneath each shingle and slip past the nails nicely.

Razing the roof

Tearing off an old roof is messy. Spent shingles and tar-paper scraps bombard shrubs and flower beds, and stray roofing nails stud lawns. To control the mess, secure the top and sides of a canvas tarp to a 2 x 4 frame, and put it under the eaves as shown. The debris will slide off into a neat pile. Even better, arrange the canvas so that the debris lands in the back of a pickup truck or falls into a large garbage container. ▼

Tarp

2 x 4 frame

Sliding course guide

Pros use chalk lines to align rows of shingles. If you want some extra help, make this simple guide by nailing a cleat to a 1 x 6. When you butt the cleat against the bottom of one course of shingles, the 1 x 6's top edge forms a ledge on which you can rest the next course. You can use a similar guide to align new siding (p.158).

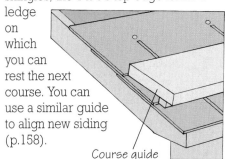

Course guide

REPLACING SHINGLES

Replacing a few shingles that have missing or broken tabs (the visible flaps) is an easy fix. Each shingle usually has three tabs and is held in place with six nails (or staples) under the tabs of the two rows of shingles just above. Most roofing supply outlets or home centers sell shingles in small quantities as well as full bundles. Take a broken shingle along to find a close match. To avoid cracking the shingles, work on a warm day when they are pliable.

1 Use a pry bar to gently lift the three tabs in the row above the damaged shingle and the three in the row above that. Before lifting a tab, slide the bar under its full length to break the seal.

2 Use the pry bar to remove the nail from under each of the tabs that you lifted in the two rows above the damaged shingle. This will release the damaged shingle, letting you slide it out.

3 Slide the new replacement shingle under the rows of tabs above, and secure it with six galvanized roofing nails, putting one under each of the tabs that you loosened.

4 Put a couple of dabs of roofing cement under the tabs of the new shingle and under all the other tabs that you loosened. Press the tabs down firmly into the roofing cement.

PAINT AND WALLCOVERINGS

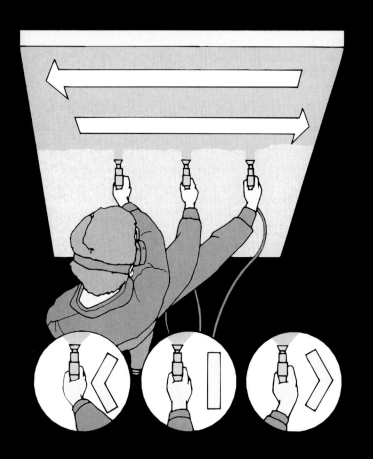

WORKING WITH PAINT

Mixing it up

Power-stirring

A power drill mixing attachment is handy for latex and oil-base paints. But don't use the attachment to stir lacquer, epoxy paint, shellac, or any finish that says "Do not shake can" on the label. You won't want to do battle with the bubbles that power-mixing stirs up. Instead, stir these paints and finishes by hand; they'll stay fairly free of bubbles.

Spatter shield

Stirring full cans of paint with a drill-driven mixer spatters paint everywhere. One way to contain the mess is with a large plastic coffee can lid (one 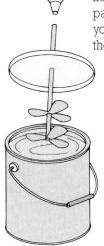 that comes with a 39-ounce can). Drill a hole in the center of the lid and slip it onto the mixer shaft before inserting the mixer in the drill. Hold the lid tightly over the paint can while you are mixing the paint.

Milk carton mixer

Cut off the top of a clean 2-litre cardboard milk carton and use it as a container for mixing (or just holding) small amounts of paint or stain. The paint won't stick to the wax-coated interior, and the corner of the carton makes a good pouring spout.

Newspaper collar

 Here's another homemade way to minimize the mess when stirring a full can of paint. Increase the height of the can by taping a newspaper section around it. The paint will slosh onto the paper when you stir it with a paddle or a power attachment.

Homemade mixer

For small jobs you can make your own power mixing attachment by chucking a beater from an old kitchen mixer in your electric drill. This makeshift attachment will work well in quart-size cans, but the shaft is too short to reach the bottom of gallon-size cans. To avoid splattering paint, use a plastic lid as shown at left.

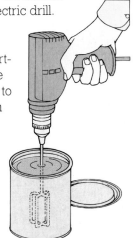

Blending for color

If the job you're working on requires two or three gallon cans of paint, *box,* or *mix,* the paint from all the cans together to get a consistent color. To do this, find a clean container and open all of the paint cans. Pour half of the paint from the first can into the extra container. Then pour some paint from the second and third cans into the first can. Move to the extra container and pour in some more paint from the second and third cans. Then pour the contents of all four containers back and forth several times. When the paint is mixed, return it to the original containers and seal the lids tightly. A quicker alternative is to mix all the paint in a 5-gallon container.

Holey stirrer!

A paint stirrer is more effective if it has several holes along its length. With each stroke the paint flows back and forth through the holes, allowing for faster, more thorough blending. You can buy a perforated metal stirrer or make your own wooden one. To make your own, drill small holes in the wooden stick that comes with the paint (back the stick with a block of scrap wood to keep it from splitting). Be sure to rinse the paint from the holes to keep them from becoming clogged with dried paint.

WORKING WITH PAINT

Special remedies

Say "Cheesecloth"

Strain the lumps from paint by pouring it into an empty can covered with cheesecloth. Hold the cheesecloth in place around the perimeter of the can with a sturdy rubber band, tape, or string.

Screen old paint

Here's another way to deal with lumps in old paint: Use fine-mesh screening, available at paint stores. Cut a circle with a diameter ¼ inch smaller than the diameter of the paint can. Bend the screen a little so it will fit inside the rim, and drop it onto the surface of the paint. Push the screen slowly to the bottom with a paint stirrer. As the screen travels down, it will carry the lumps of dried paint with it. Even if the brush touches the screen on the bottom of the can, the bristles won't pick up any dried paint.

Stocking filter

A clean nylon stocking cut off near the ankle also makes a good paint strainer. Stretch the stocking around the rim of the can and secure it with a rubber band. Dip a brush into the can to force the stocking toe into the paint. The paint rising through the mesh will be finely strained.

Handling fumes

The fumes of some paints and primers persist even in a well-ventilated room. To reduce the odor, add a few drops of vanilla extract to the paint—up to a tablespoon per gallon. The extract won't affect the way the paint performs, and the wet paint won't be so smelly. Note, however, that good ventilation is still required to combat the physical side effects of the noxious solvents.

Paint can handlers

Can holder

One way to keep a work surface clean and to avoid accidental spills is to place your quart can of paint in an old saucepan. The pan catches runs and provides a brush rest. The handle of the saucepan doesn't collect messy paint drips and makes it easy to carry the can from spot to spot.

Nail holes

No matter how neat you try to be, paint still tends to accumulate in the lid groove of a paint can, creating puddles of paint that squish out when you seal the can. To drain the paint back into the can, use a nail to punch several holes in the groove before you paint. When you reseal the can, the lid will cover the holes and form a tight seal. ▼

Pour neatly

If you don't have a funnel on hand to help you pour paint neatly, hold a pencil across the opening of the pouring can. The paint will follow the pencil to its end and from there pour neatly into its new container.

Plate catcher

Attaching a sturdy paper plate to the bottom of a paint can makes it easier to keep the floor or other work surface clean. The rim of the plate catches and contains paint runs better than newspaper. Use a little putty or adhesive to make the plate stick to the can. If you do use newspaper under a paint can, put a piece of wax paper between the can and the paper. It will keep the can from sticking to the newspaper.

Brush work

Grip and load

Applying paint successfully begins with a proper grip on the brush. Hold the metal band, or ferrule, between your thumb and fingers. This grip gives you the most control, especially if you switch the brush to your weaker hand. Dip the bristles about 2 inches into the paint, and then press the brush lightly against the side of the can. Do not drag the bristles against the rim of the can; that will cause bubbles. Let the paint pool on top of the bristles, but don't overload the brush.

Ferrule

Even strokes

To spread paint evenly with a brush, use a few zigzagging strokes (1) and spread the paint out to cover the gaps (2). To finish an area, raise the brush so that just the tips of the bristles lightly smooth the painted area (3). This is called *tipping* or *feathering off* and removes any unsightly lap marks. ▼

1

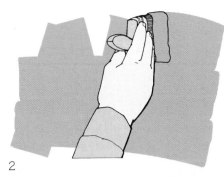

2

3

Less is better

You'll be less likely to overload a brush if your paint can is only partly filled. The extra free space near the top makes it easier for you to neatly slap the brush against the side of the can to remove the excess paint.

Wire tap

Bend a piece of coat hanger or other heavy wire as shown, and tape it securely to one side of a paint can. Use the wire, instead of the rim of the can, to tap the excess paint from your brush. The wire will keep paint from getting into the lid groove of the can and from dripping down its side.

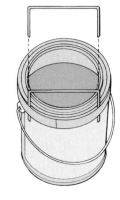

Brush rest

If you'd like an easy way to make a temporary resting place for your brush, just lay an ordinary paint stirrer across the rim of the paint can. Position the stirrer so that it forms a bridge near the middle of the can. That way it will offer a steady support for the wet bristles while the brush handle rests on the (cleaner) rim of the paint can.

BRUSSHES

On the job

Make your own disposables

Disposable foam brushes are handy for touch-ups and other small painting jobs. Instead of buying disposable brushes, you can save trips to the paint or hardware store, and some money as well, by making them yourself. You'll need some scrap ¾-inch-thick foam carpet padding (often available free from carpet stores) and a bag of spring-type clothespins. Cut the foam to size with a utility knife, angling the tip as shown. Snap on a clothespin handle and you're ready to paint. ▼

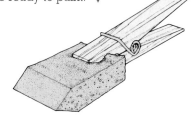

Tape protection

Your paintbrush will be easier to clean if you wrap masking tape around the ferrule and the base of the bristles, extending the tape about ½ inch over the bristles. Rather than drying and hardening on the bristles, paint will collect on the tape. When it's time to clean up, remove the tape and clean the wet paint that remains on the bristles. ▼

Comb-out

Stray bristles that fall onto a wet paint surface can mar a job. To remove loose bristles before you begin painting, groom the brush. Either use a brush comb bought for the purpose or improvise with a pocket comb or a pet brush.

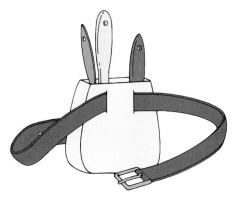

Belted caddy ▲

If you plan to use more than one size brush during a paint job, you'll want to keep those brushes handy, especially if you are working on a ladder. You can make a reusable brush holder that attaches to an ordinary belt. First, find a clean rectangular plastic container that is wide enough to hold your brushes but narrow enough to keep them upright, such as an economy-size bottle of cooking oil or household cleaner. Cut off the top of the bottle and make two slits in one side to accept the belt. Thread the belt through the loops on your pants and through the slits, positioning the brush caddy on one hip. Not only will you have the brushes at your fingertips, you'll have just one container to clean when the job is done.

Between coats

Freezer wrap

If you are working with oil-base paint and know that you will be using the brushes and rollers the next day, there's no need to clean and scrub your equipment. Just wrap everything in plastic bags or foil and stick the packets in the freezer. The cold temperature will keep the paint from hardening. When you are ready to paint again, thaw the pieces for about 45 minutes. You can repeat this procedure for as many coats of paint or varnish as you need. However, if you are using latex paint, you'll have to wash your tools each night.

Wire hang-up

Here's a way to park your brush during a break. Attach a small wire hook to the neck of the handle by twisting a piece of wire coat hanger around it with pliers. Hang the brush on the edge of the can so that the bristles will stay in the paint and not dry out, but don't let the brush sink too low in the paint or rest on the bottom of the can. ▼

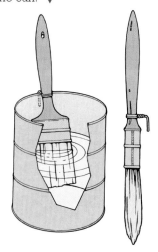

Two coffee can ideas

A coffee can with a plastic lid makes a good holder for your brushes while they soak (briefly) in paint thinner or water.

Cut slits in the lid, and insert the brush handles in the slits so that the bristles clear the bottom of the can by about 1/2 inch. If the can has no lid, attach a stick to each brush handle with a rubber band. The stick will keep the bristles off the bottom of the can.

Easy wiper solution

A baby wipe container also makes a great holder. The slit in the top that dispenses the towelettes will hold the handles of most brushes. The bristles should stay about 1/2 inch above the bottom of the container—to prevent them from bending and to keep them out of the settling paint debris. Don't allow a brush to soak too long. Soaking is not a substitute for thorough cleaning.

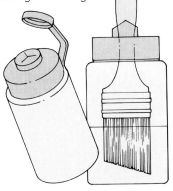

Fill as needed with water or thinner

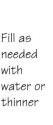

When the job's over

Newspaper story

Looking for a place to wipe your brush when it's time to clean up? Instead of a piece of scrap wood or cardboard, use a thick section of newspaper. Place the bristles between several layers of pages. Then as you remove the brush, squeeze the bristles.

Bristle work

The best way to get a brush clean is to scrub the bristles against wire mesh. You can submerge an old kitchen strainer in a coffee can filled with water or paint thinner. Another option is to cut a 7-inch-diameter circle out of 1/4-inch-grid hardware cloth. Bend the material to form a lip around the edge. Place the mesh on the bottom of a coffee can and fill the can with solvent. The mesh provides a surface for the brush to work against and allows sediment to collect on the bottom.

Drying hanger ▲

After cleaning your paintbrushes, hang them up to dry on a three-arm metal towel rack. Or make your own rack out of a wire coat hanger, using a wire cutter and pliers to shape the hanger and fashion the hooks. Mount the hanger with two screws, and provide a drip catcher underneath.

Long-term storage

Store brushes in self-seal plastic bags. To keep the bristles supple, add a teaspoon of vinegar for each brush if latex was used, or a teaspoon of paint thinner if oil-base paint was used.

Go for a spin ▶

Remove excess water or thinner from a clean brush by spinning it back and forth between the palms of your hands. To protect yourself from the spraying liquid, hold the brush inside a paper bag.

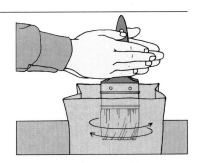

ROLLERS AND SPRAY GUNS

Easy rolling

Bucket brigade

Unless you are working on a ladder, roller trays are not the ideal tool to use for large jobs. They don't hold very much paint and it's easy to step on them accidentally, overturning the contents. Instead of using a roller tray, do what the pros do and load the paint directly from a 5-gallon bucket. To wipe off the excess paint, rub the roller against a metal roller screen that hooks over the rim of the bucket. (Screens are available at paint stores.)

One liner

You can avoid having to clean your roller tray if you first line it with aluminum foil. Overlap all four sides, being careful not to puncture the foil as you fit the corners. When the job is done, return any excess paint to the can; then peel the foil up carefully and discard it. (For more on discarding paint, see p.39.)

Another mess manager

Here's how to remove a paint-filled roller cover without getting paint on your hands: Pull a plastic bag over the end of the roller and pull the cover off. Seal the bag and discard it (p.39).

Clean and dry

Hanger helper

The hook of a wire clothes hanger makes a great tool for squeezing the excess paint from a roller cover. To shape the hanger into a cleaning tool, bend the "wings" of the hanger so that they can be held together as a handle. Start at one end and pull the hanger hook down the length of the roller several times, turning the roller slightly with each pass.

Dangling dryer

Drying a clean roller on its side flattens some of the nap and ruins the cover's smooth rolling action. Instead, tie a small piece of scrap wood to one end of a string and drop it through the opening in the cover. Hang the string where the cover will dangle freely. When it's dry, store it away.

Another hanger trick

This rack helps to keep a roller cover round and paint-brush bristles flat as they dry. To make it, cut near the bottom of a wire hanger at one end; then use pliers to bend the cut sloping wire into a hook for the straight piece. Bend the sides of the hanger closer together so that the straight piece rests on the hook. Slide on your clean roller cover and brushes, and hang them up to dry.

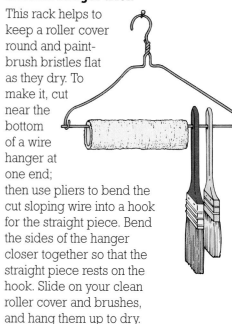

Spray-gunning

Safe operation

An airless sprayer forces paint out of its nozzle with a lot of pressure—so much so, in fact, that paint can become embedded in the skin. Therefore it is essential to wear long sleeves, gloves, a mask approved for use with a paint sprayer (not a dust mask), and goggles.

Cleaning up

To clean a gun, spray the appropriate solvent through the machine to flush the hoses and the body of the gun. (Collect the solvent in a bucket.) Then remove the nozzle and soak it in solvent to clean the orifice and nozzle tip.

How to handle a sprayer

It's crucial that each spray coat be thin and even. To that end, overlap your strokes a little. Keep your body parallel and your arm perpendicular to the surface. Bend your wrist as you move your arm (insets). This keeps the spray nozzle the same distance—about 6 to 8 inches—from the surface during the stroke. Begin moving your arm before you press the trigger, and continue to move after you release it.

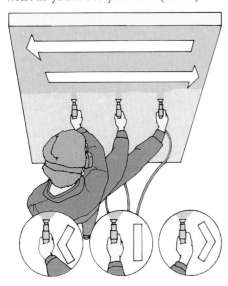

Inside corners ▶

To avoid paint buildup in a corner, turn the gun 90° so that the spray fans out horizontally. Then move the gun from the top to the bottom of the corner.

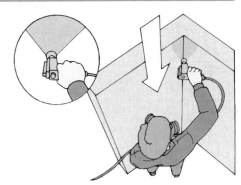

Outside angles ▶

Stand directly facing the edge of an outside corner. Begin at the top and move the gun from side to side, overlapping the strokes as at left. In order to cover both surfaces and the edge, bend your wrist (insets at left).

PAINTING TOOLS

TOOL	USE	WHAT TO LOOK FOR
Brushes	Use 3- or 4-in. brushes for wide surfaces. Use 1½- or 2-in. brushes for trim and paneled doors. Use 1- to 1½-in. brushes for around glass, etc. For latex paint, choose nylon or polyester bristles (natural bristles absorb water and lose their shape). For oil-base paints, use natural bristles.	Flagged ends give good paint retention and smooth coating. Tapered bristle body helps paint flow evenly and aids cutting in (see p.179). Look for fullness and variety of bristle lengths for smooth painting results.
Rollers	Use 7-in. rollers for narrow walls and siding. Use 9-in. rollers for large walls, wide siding, masonry, and stucco. For enamels use blended polyester/wool covers. For latex paint, use synthetic-fiber covers (which won't absorb the water in the paint).	Construction of roller frame should be sturdy: either professional-quality compression or slip-on type. Avoid types with wing nuts or end caps. Check that the roller cage moves freely.
Paint pads	Use for lap siding, trim, shakes, shingles, and wood fences. To store, place fiber side up.	Pads that have fiber applicators are preferable to those made of foam.
Sprayers	Useful on large areas or rough surfaces. Speed and ease of application are main advantages.	Available on rental/loan basis at paint or rental outlets. Consult dealer to ensure you match your needs with the spray tool. For example, don't select a 1-qt. cup sprayer for volume work.

CHOOSING AND BUYING PAINT

The right color

Tried and true

The best way to determine whether a certain color will suit a room is to hang a swatch of it on the wall where it is to be and leave it there for 24 hours. Observe how the color looks as the light changes, under artificial light, and at the times when the room is used the most. To make a swatch, either tape a number of paint chips together or coat a thick piece of porous paper, such as poster board, with the paint. ▼

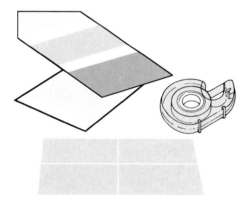

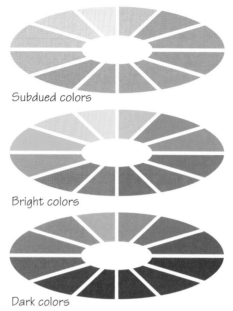

Subdued colors

Bright colors

Dark colors

In the mood ▲

You can use color to create a mood. Dark colors will absorb light and lend a quiet, intimate feeling to a room. But be careful—too dark a room can be depressing. Bright colors are generally exciting; subdued ones are relaxing and restful.

Lighten up

Before choosing a strong, bold color for your walls, consider going one or two shades lighter. You'll find that a color seems to darken and intensify as you spread it across the walls. If you select one that's too strong, you may end up with more color than you really wanted.

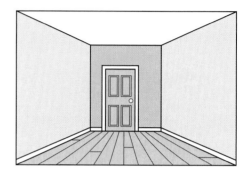

Room make-overs ▲

If you want a long, narrow room to look wider, paint one or both of the short walls a bright or dark color and the other walls a pale color. If a room is square and lacks a focal point such as a fireplace or a large window, paint one wall a rich accent color such as maroon.

Check the exposure ▶

Rooms that face north, northeast, or northwest receive little or no sunshine during the day, making them dark and uninviting. You can lend some cheer to such a room by choosing from a palette of warm colors—yellow, red, orange, and brown. Likewise, you can make sunny rooms seem cool with blues, greens, grays, and lavenders. But beware of those cool colors if you live in a cold climate: Research shows that people feel colder in rooms with cool colors. If you are committed to off-white, choose either a warm or a cool tint of that neutral color.

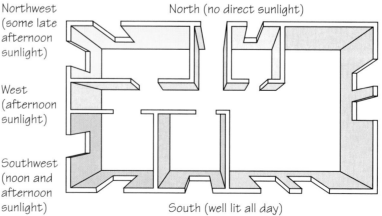

Northwest (some late afternoon sunlight)

North (no direct sunlight)

Northeast (some morning sunlight)

West (afternoon sunlight)

East (morning sunlight)

Southwest (noon and afternoon sunlight)

Southeast (some morning and noon sunlight)

South (well lit all day)

Moving the walls

Color can also create optical illusions. For example, light colors reflect light and make a small room seem larger. Warm colors seem to advance and "fill" space, whereas cool colors recede. A white ceiling will seem higher; a dark ceiling will appear lower.

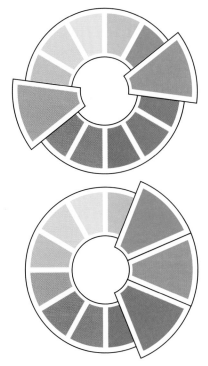

Wheel of color ▲

While a favorite color or object often determines the main paint color for a room, you may wish to consult a color wheel for a secondary or contrasting color. The colors that are opposite each other are called *complementary* colors. These hues will enhance each other in a color scheme. The hues on either side of a given color are *related* colors and form the basis for a coordinated look to a room.

Nothing but the best

Don't scrimp on the paint and primer or undercoat you buy. You'll get the best results if you buy a premium-quality paint recommended by a reliable paint retailer. Buying a less expensive paint won't really save you money, since it will cover fewer square feet and isn't likely to wear as well as a better-quality paint.

Exact calculation

If your room has an irregular shape or is very large, you may wish to calculate precisely the number of square feet you need to cover. First, measure the length of each wall or section of wall, including any alcoves and other irregular shapes. Add up the figures and multiply by the wall height. Subtract the area of any doors and windows (about 20 and 15 square feet each, respectively), and add the ceiling area. (Generally you can use the floor dimensions instead, multiplying length times width.) Finally, multiply that last number by the number of coats you think you're going to need. ▼

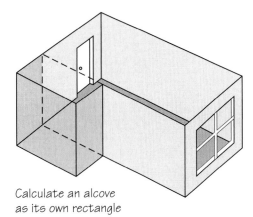

Calculate an alcove as its own rectangle

Estimating rules

As a rule of thumb, 1 gallon of paint provides one coat for four 8-foot-high walls in a 12- x 15-foot room. (You'll need more for rough-textured walls.) Figure another ½ gallon for the ceiling.

Two quarts equals a gallon?

To keep from running out of paint in the middle of a job, always buy a little more than you think you'll need, and buy gallons instead of quarts. You'll spend about the same for a gallon can as you would for two quart-size cans. And since there are still 4 quarts in a gallon, you'll be getting an extra ½ gallon of paint free. Save it for touch-ups (p.189).

Instant blackboard

If you're planning to paint a child's room, a playroom, or a kitchen, consider brushing a couple of coats of black-board paint on a section of wallboard. Tack on painted molding to frame it. You'll find this makes a safe place to draw or a convenient message center.

Washable walls

Would you like to have the finish of an interior flat wall paint and still be able to wash off handprints and dirt? Just add a quart of interior semigloss latex to each gallon of flat latex wall paint, mixing thoroughly (for more on mixing paint, see p.167). The semigloss will add a measure of washability that's missing in flat wall paint without sacrificing the finish. In high-traffic living areas, such as a family room or a child's bedroom, you can increase the paint's washability by adding 2 quarts of semi-gloss to each gallon of flat paint.

PREPARING A ROOM FOR PAINTING

Removing paint

Say when
If the trim in a room already has three to five coats of old oil-base paint, you can probably add another one or two coats of oil-base paint, but it's not a good idea to apply that many layers of latex paint. Use a heat gun or chemical stripper to remove the old paint before applying a new coat of latex. And no matter what kind of paint has been used on it, wood trim often looks best if all the built-up paint is removed first.

Caution: Before removing paint, check its lead content (see facing page).

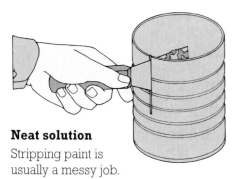

Neat solution
Stripping paint is usually a messy job. Here's a way to contain the globs of paint and stripper as you clean your putty knife. Use tin snips or a hacksaw to cut a slot in a large coffee can. The slot should be a little wider than the thickness of the blade of the putty knife, and a little deeper than its width. To clean the blade, insert it into the slot at the handle and pull the knife toward you. The edges of the slot act as a double-edged scraper and catch the residue neatly in the can. (For more on stripping finishes, see pp.242–245.)

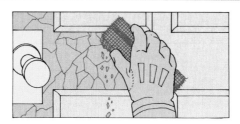

Scraping by ▲
To remove a rough section of built-up paint, try wrapping some metal window screening (not fiberglass) around scrap wood and using it as you would a sanding block. This improvised scraper removes paint quickly and won't damage the surface.

More prep steps

Degreasing
Greasy and oily stains show through newly painted surfaces, especially if the paint is latex. Before you paint, check the surfaces for these stains. If the spots are few and small, rub them off with cotton balls or a cloth saturated with rubbing alcohol (coat larger stains with a stain-blocking sealer or primer). As you rub, you'll find that paint will come off too, so wear rubber gloves to keep your hands clean.

Crayon and ink marks
Children find it hard to resist the temptation to draw on walls, and unfortunately crayon and ink will show through a fresh coat of paint. To remove crayon marks, put on rubber gloves and rub the areas with a cloth dipped in paint thinner. You can remove ink stains in the same way, using either paint thinner, as for crayon marks, or household bleach.

Wash the walls
Before you get out the paintbrushes, it's a good idea to wash the walls and ceiling. Choose a cleaner that doesn't require rinsing. To keep water out of the electrical boxes, don't remove the outlet covers until after you have washed down the room. ▼

Attack those cracks
Don't rely on paint to hide thin cracks in plaster. You have to take a trip around the room and fill them all first. Open up each crack with an old bottle opener. It is better not to use a putty knife; prying will damage the blade. Reserve your putty knife for filling the cracks with spackling compound; you'll find that the knife will last longer.

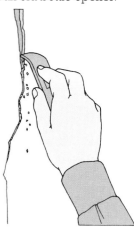

Fill 'er up

Once you have removed all the loose plaster, use a putty knife to fill the cracks with latex spackling compound. After it dries, sand the area until it is smooth, vacuum it, and apply primer to seal the repair. For more tips on repairing walls, see pp.129–131.

Safe outlets

When it's time to remove the outlet covers, shut off the power to the circuit at the circuit breaker panel or fuse box (pp.200, 202). Remove the outlet plates. To keep track of the screws, reseat them in their holes or tape them to the backs of the plates. When you are ready to paint, you can restore power—but be sure that you don't touch any electric wires when painting or accidentally switch on a covered lamp or appliance.

Cover-ups

Door protection

An easy way to protect a door from paint is to slip an "envelope" of polyethylene film over it. To make the cover, staple two large pieces of polyethylene film together on three sides. When you are measuring and cutting the film to size, don't forget to add a few extra inches to accommodate the doorknob and to make the cover easy to slip on.

LEAD PAINT HAZARDS

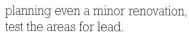

Lead is a toxic metal that, if inhaled or ingested, can cause neurological damage, especially in children. It was added to paint until it was banned in 1976. (Stores sold existing stock rather than pulling it from the shelves. Thus, cans bought before 1980 are suspect.) The older the paint is, the higher—and more dangerous—the lead levels are likely to be. Paint had a very high lead content until the 1950's. After that, new pigment technology allowed manufacturers to lower the lead content significantly.

Any lead-base paint that is peeling and cracking is hazardous. A greater danger comes from less visible sources: the lead dust that rises when you sand this type of paint and the lead fumes created by using a heat gun during paint stripping. (Lead-base paint that is intact does not present a danger.) If you notice old, deteriorating paint or are planning even a minor renovation, test the areas for lead.

Simple detecting kits are sold at some hardware outlets that cater to professionals in the home repair business. If you use a kit, be sure to test every layer of paint, down to the substrate. Be aware, though, that these kits may not be able to detect low, but still hazardous, lead levels. It is best to check with your local health or housing authority for laboratories that can analyze a paint chip for lead content or a list of contractors qualified to test for lead.

If a test shows lead in your paint, don't remove it yourself. Doing so will increase the lead in your environment. Instead, hire a contractor experienced in deleading procedures. If the lead paint is intact, check with your provincial environmental agency for a list of approved protective encapsulating (sealing) paints and coverings.

Tape and drape ▶

The next time you need to protect a wallpapered wall, paneling, or any other large surface from paint, look for a product in paint stores and home centers that combines masking tape and a drop cloth. To use, just apply the masking tape and plastic to the edge of the area that you want to protect. Cut it off just as you do tape from an ordinary dispenser. The plastic then unfolds to its full width. You can choose from three widths: 24, 48, and 72 inches.

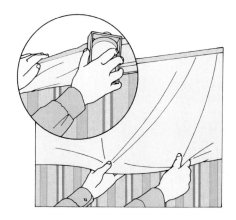

PREPARING A ROOM FOR PAINTING

Cover-ups

Drop cloth options

You can never have too many drop cloths. While professionals use heavy canvas ones because they absorb paint spills, provide nonslip footing, and won't stick to your feet, most DIY'ers rely on inexpensive plastic drop cloths from the paint store. To make plastic cloths function more like canvas, cover them with thick sections of newspaper. And if you need an extra cover, use an old plastic shower curtain or liner.

Go wall-to-wall

Strips of used carpeting can also serve as substitute drop cloths when you're painting or doing messy repairs. The weight of the strips makes them stay in place, and they can be used over and over again. The strips should be about 10 or 15 feet long and wide enough so that all four legs of a stepladder will rest on the carpet at one time. Place the strip with its nap side up or down, as you wish. After use, let any wet spots dry; then vacuum the strip if necessary. If you don't have used carpeting on hand, check carpet stores and installers; they're usually glad to give away carpet remnants.

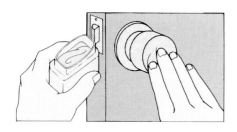

Press-on tape

Have you ever peeled away masking tape only to find that paint has seeped underneath it? Masking tape protects a surface only when the seal is perfect. To make sure the tape does its job, press it in place with the flat side of a 2-inch putty knife.

Foiled again

A good way to protect doorknobs, telephone receivers, electric switches, faucets, handles, and other items that you want to keep paint-free is to cover them with aluminum foil. Crimp the foil

to fit the shape; it will stay there until you have finished painting. It's also a good idea to keep several plastic sandwich bags nearby. Use them as makeshift gloves to protect phones and doorknobs from paint-splattered hands.

◀ **Protection for hardware**

For best results, you should remove all hardware before painting. But if you can't or don't want to do this, you can protect hardware from splatters by applying a thin coating of petroleum jelly. After painting, just wipe the metal clean.

Shoe in

To keep paint off your shoes, slip an old pair of socks over them. The cotton will absorb splatters and save you the work of cleaning up. ▼

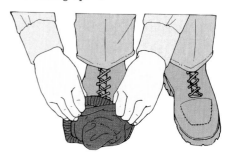

Step-by-step

Work order

Few things are as frustrating as finding you've dripped paint on a newly painted surface. To keep the mess to a minimum, work from the top down. Here's a step-by-step work plan for painting a room: After the prep work is done, paint the ceiling. Next prime the walls and the trim. Then give the walls a final coat. Finally, give the trim a final coat, saving the baseboard for last.

Primer versus sealer

A sealer is used to coat stains and keep them from bleeding through the fresh paint. A primer helps new paint adhere better and helps keep the color and the sheen uniform. If you are changing colors and plan on two coats, make the first coat a primer that's tinted to match the final coat. If you are repainting a room with the same color, you need to prime only the areas that have been repaired or sealed.

PAINTING WALLS AND CEILINGS

Painting large areas

Cutting in

Use the narrow edge of a brush to edge, or *cut in,* a swath of paint equal to the width of your paintbrush along the perimeter of the walls and the ceiling. Begin in a corner and put just enough pressure on the brush to flex the bristles. To minimize lap marks, always work from a dry section back into a wet one. If you are working with a non-flat paint, put two people on the job—one cuts in with a brush while the other fills in with a roller. If you are working alone, cut in a section and then fill it in with the roller.

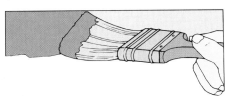

Paint catcher

When you are painting a ceiling, wrap an old washcloth or paper towel around the handle of your brush and secure it with a rubber band. This absorbs the inevitable paint drips and helps keep your hand clean.

Find a stopping place

What should you do if you have to halt a project before you've finished applying a coat of paint—or if you find that you're running low on paint? Try not to stop in the middle of a wall. Instead, finish a wall and then stop. You'll avoid obvious lap marks. And if you have to buy more paint (custom-mixed or not), a slight difference in shade won't be as noticeable.

ROLLING PAINT

After a painstaking job of preparing a room, it's rewarding to see how quickly a roller can cover the walls and ceilings with paint. Begin by saturating a clean roller in the paint, rolling it over the tray ridges or wire grating (see p.172). Then dip the roller in the paint. (To avoid drips, don't overload the roller.) Spread it as shown.

Paint small sections (8 or 9 square feet) at a time. Begin painting a ceiling in a corner, and work across the narrower dimension of the room. Start painting a wall in an upper corner, and work from top to bottom and left to right. If possible work with natural light—you'll find it easier to see any gaps.

1 Apply the paint in zigzag strokes. Use an "N" or "M" stroke on walls, as above, and a "W" pattern on ceilings.

2 Move the roller horizontally to even out the paint, and work back into the wet edge of the previous area.

3 To remove roller marks and even out the texture, use light up-and-down strokes. An extension handle on the roller really helps here.

WINDOWS, DOORS, AND STAIRS

Neat edges

Pane protection

Beginners may wish to cover the edges of the windowpanes to reduce the amount of cleanup that's needed. One way is to mask each pane (p.178). However, this takes a long time and removing the tape can be a chore, thereby defeating the initial goal. Instead, try rubbing soap or lip balm around the edges of the glass next to the trim. Any paint marks or splatters on the glass will be easy to remove when the paint is dry.

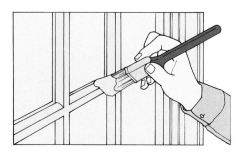

Going steady ▲

If you have a steady hand, you can paint the trim around windowpanes without masking them. You'll find that you have the most control if you use an angled sash brush and hold it as you would a pencil. Always work from the glass edge outward. As you do so, be sure to leave a thin paint line on the glass so you will seal the paint to the glass—and keep moisture from invading the paint film, causing the paint to peel. When the paint is dry, scrape off any paint that is beyond the paint line.

Work order

Door stops ▶

When painting a door, begin with all four edges (1). Next, paint the trim around any glass panes and all wood panels, whether raised or recessed (2). Then paint the door body, beginning at the top and proceeding down the sides (3 and 4). Finish the job by painting the door frame from top to bottom (5 and 6). As you paint the frame, work from the door toward the outer edges of the frame. For more on door edges, see the facing page.

Mask or remove hardware

Steps for a window

Here's the best sequence of steps for painting a double-hung window. First, pull the top sash three-quarters of the way down and push the bottom sash three-quarters of the way up (below, left). Paint the entire bottom rail (1) and half of each side rail on the top sash (2). Slide both sashes back into place, stopping a few inches from their closed positions (below, right). Then finish painting the top sash (3 and 4) and paint the entire bottom sash, working from top to bottom (5 and 6). To finish the job, paint the top of the trim (7), then the sides (8), and finally the bottom (9). ▼

Bottom sash

Top sash

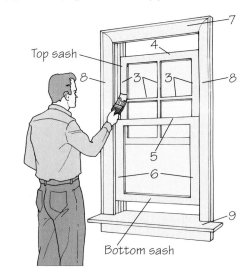

Top sash

Bottom sash

On edges

Connecting colors

When a door connects two rooms that are different colors, what color should you paint the door edges? Here's the rule of thumb: The latch-side edge should be the same color as the

Hinge side
Latch side

room that the door opens into. The hinge-side edge, which is visible when the door is open, should be the same color as the other room.

The bottom line

If you are not going to remove the door before painting, you can paint the underside with a scrap of carpet. Why bother with an edge that no one will see? Paint helps to seal the end grain, preventing the wood from absorbing moisture and expanding. ▼

Steps for steps

Painting treads

Here are two ways to paint stairs and still keep foot traffic moving. You can paint every other step, let the paint dry thoroughly, and then paint the rest. Or you can paint half of the width of each step, wait for the paint to dry, and then finish the job.

Glove action

Do you have a decorative railing and baluster in need of a coat of paint? Try using a paint glove. It does a great job of reaching the tight spots and crevices of metalwork motifs, and it makes short work of slender spindles, whether they're made of wood or metal.

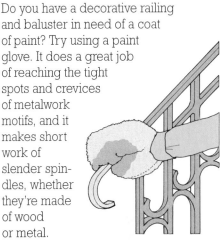

Reaching high places

Painting a stairwell usually involves erecting scaffolding. You can either rent it or make your own. If you rent, ask the dealer to show you how to set it up correctly. If you are going to build your own, begin by analyzing the space to determine what combination of stepladders, extension ladders, and 2 x 10 or 2 x 12 planks you need. (Three typical situations are shown below.) When you are erecting the platforms, be sure to clamp or nail the planks to their supports, and open or lock any doors that might accidentally knock into the scaffolding. Allow the planks to overhang at least 1 foot on either side. ▼

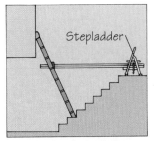
Clamp

Place a stepladder so the plank will be level when it is placed on a ladder step (no higher than the next-to-top one). If the span between supports is more than 5 ft., use two planks.

Stepladder

When you can't reach the ceiling with the method at left, brace an extension ladder at an angle. Pick a step that allows you to reach the high points easily, and make sure the ladder feet are level.

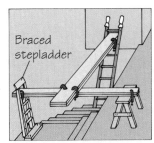
Braced stepladder

If there isn't enough space for a stepladder to open completely, you'll need to brace it in position with a cleat. To make the cleat, nail a board securely to the landing at the base of the stepladder.

DECORATIVE PAINTING

Stenciling

Make your own stencil

You can easily turn a favorite drapery or upholstery pattern into a stencil. Just photocopy a length of the original fabric on a copy machine, enlarging it if desired. Then place a piece of thick polyethylene film (plastic sheet) on top of the photocopy, tape it securely in place, and cut out the design with a craft knife.

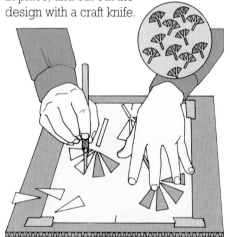

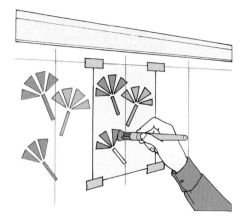

A light load ▲

Successful stenciling begins with loading the brush properly: Dip a stencil brush only about ¼ inch into the paint (use a fast-drying latex paint). Next distribute the paint on the bristles by dabbing the tip lightly on a section of newspaper. The brush will appear dry when it is ready to go. Dab the paint into the stencil openings with short in-and-out strokes, keeping the brush perpendicular to the stencil.

Design ideas

Floor it

Fancy paint effects need not be limited to walls and ceilings; they can be used on floors if a protective coating is added on top. New nonyellowing super-hard polyurethanes are ideal for the job; they will protect a painted decoration with a rugged and almost invisible shield.

Ordinary objects

Professional decorative artists use tools other than sponges, rags, and brushes. These artists may use a piece of cork, a nail, a bottle top, a broom, or even their gloved hands to create a special effect. Here, a piece of cork and a nail team up to simulate a knothole design.

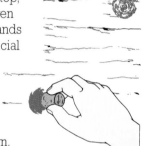

Repeating designs ▶

In any stenciling job, patterns rarely repeat evenly across a surface. Some designs can turn a corner in mid-pattern, but often the design will end awkwardly on a wall. In the latter case, plan to either stretch or overlap it a little on each wall, whichever is easier. To determine how much adjustment is needed, divide the length of the pattern into the distance to be covered on each surface. Then, when you are painting the pattern, work from opposite corners toward the center of the wall. To make your adjustments less visible, overlap or stretch several repetitions by just a little bit. If you opt to stretch the design, fill in the gaps by hand.

Overlapping stencil pattern

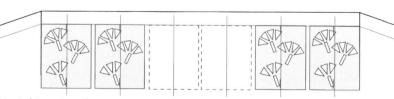

Stretching stencil pattern

TEXTURING TECHNIQUES

Sponging, rag-rolling, and stippling techniques add a wonderful dimension of pattern and texture to a routine paint job. These effects are easy to create, and they dress up a room while adding little to the cost.

To prepare a surface for any of the three techniques, apply a base coat and then cover it with a compatible glaze. Use either all latex or all oil-base products; never apply one over the other.

You can buy glaze that is ready to use (in a limited number of colors), or you can make your own glaze in any color by simply diluting paint. If you are using latex paint, mix 3 parts water or latex extender into 1 part paint. For a translucent latex glaze, make the mix 4:1. If you're working with oil-base paint, begin with equal parts semigloss paint and solvent. Try out the glaze and the tool you'll be using

on a practice board, thinning the paint little by little up to a 2:1 ratio. To ensure that the color and effect will be uniform, mix as much glaze as you'll need at one time.

Sponging is an additive technique; you dab the glaze onto a dry base coat. It is the only one of the three techniques shown here that can be done with fast-drying latex. Use only natural sponges torn into manageable pieces.

Rag-rolling and stippling are subtractive techniques in which you apply glaze and then partially remove it, and so it is important that the glaze dry more slowly. Fabrics commonly used for rag-rolling are worn cotton bed sheets, gauze, nylon netting, and burlap. To see various patterns, use different rags. Stippling brushes, made for the purpose, give the base coat a freckled effect; softer brushes create a mottled look.

1 Sponge on the first color glaze over a dry (rolled-on) base coat with firm strokes. If you're adding a second color glaze, be careful not to use too much of the first color. When a sponge gets filled with glaze, switch to a fresh one.

To stipple a surface, apply an oil-base base coat; let it dry. Apply an oil-base glaze with a pad applicator or wide brush. Press the bristles of a coarse brush into the wet glaze. As the bristles become loaded with paint, clean them with a dry rag.

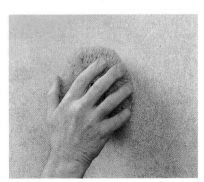

2 When applying the second color glaze, you can vary the effect by patting and twisting the sponge. If you're using latex glaze, clean the sponges with water; if you're applying oil-base glaze, clean them with mineral spirits.

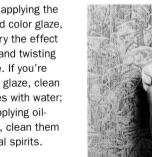

To rag-roll a surface, prepare the surface as for stippling (above). Then roll a crumpled rag across the wet surface. When the rag becomes saturated, switch to a fresh one.

PAINTING A HOUSE EXTERIOR

Find coordinates

When you are choosing the colors, begin by deciding on the main color. As a rule, it should be a light to medium tone that complements or contains some of the color of the roof. For the trim, choose a light color—an off-white or if you have your colors custom-mixed, the same color as the body but one-fourth of the color formula. Next, pick out an accent color for any features that you would like to stand out, such as the front door and the window shutters. This accent color is usually darker than the main color, with a moderate contrast (see below). If you are painting entry steps or a porch, choose a neutral hue that echoes the roof color.

Make a statement ▶

Your choice of an exterior color scheme can affect the look of your house from the street. Light and warm colors (see pp.174–175) seem to advance and make a house stand out from its surroundings. Dark and cool colors recede and make a house seem less obtrusive. If your house is small, you can make it seem larger by using an accent that is lighter than the main color. Stay away from the bold contrast of a light main color and dark accent color. The result will likely be a chopped-up appearance.

Light main color stands out

Dark main color recedes

Light accent on darker main color seems larger

Dark accent on light main color looks chopped up

Time and weather

Choosing sides

Who says you have to paint an entire house at one time? The job will seem much more manageable if you plan to paint just one side a year. If this idea appeals to you, take a trip around your house to determine which side has weathered the most. The south side usually receives the most sun; other sides may face prevailing winds and rain. Or if you prefer, begin with the most visible facade. After all, that's what you and your neighbors see every day.

A job for two seasons

The best time of year to paint the outside of your house is either in the spring or in the fall, when the air temperatures are not too hot or too cold. Not only will you be more comfortable, but the paint will stay wet longer, allowing more time for brushing out. What's more, deciduous plants and trees will be either bare or losing their leaves and so will be less bothered by paint drips or spray.

Follow the shade

No matter what season it is, schedule the job so that you will be painting in the shade. Direct sunlight makes the paint dry too fast. Fast-drying paint is harder to work with and tends to blister, creating a soft paint surface that is easily damaged. You'll also avoid the eyestrain caused by sun glare reflecting from the paint, a problem that occurs especially with light colors.

Getting started

Making an estimate

To determine how much paint you'll need, calculate the size of the area to be painted as you would for an interior (p.175). If your house has a gable, compute its area by multiplying its width times its height; then divide that number by 2. Keep in mind that exteriors require more paint than interiors. Add about 10 percent to your total if you have lap siding, 20 percent for rough or porous surfaces, 30 percent for corrugated material, and 50 percent for a first coat on concrete or concrete block.

Power washing ▶

As with interior painting, the secret to a successful job is proper preparation. First, check for peeling paint, mildew, and cracked paint, and make repairs (see chart). Next wash the house with a no-rinse cleaner, working from the bottom up. You can rent a power washer to remove dirt and blast off any loose or flaking paint. (Wash lap siding with the power wash nozzle pointed downward—you don't want any water to get under the surface.) If you don't have a lot of dirt and loose paint to remove, or if the surface of your house is stucco, you are probably better off with a garden hose fitted with a spray nozzle—

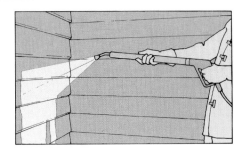

a power unit could cut right through the stucco. Before washing stucco, repair any cracks.

Caution: The pressure from a power washer can be dangerous. Keep the nozzle pointed away from you and others and away from windows; there's enough power to break glass.

COMMON EXTERIOR PAINT PROBLEMS

PROBLEM	CAUSE	CURE
Peeling paint	Paint applied over dirty or mildewed surface	Wash exterior with scrub brush and detergent to ensure a dirt-free surface. Remove mildew with a mixture of 1 tblsp. dry detergent, 1 qt. chlorine bleach, and 3 qt. warm water. Scrub with a wire brush. Rinse well with clear water. Remove any loose paint. Prime all bare wood. Use high-quality latex paint; it "breathes" and won't trap unwanted humidity.
	Moisture coming through siding, plus inadequate venting or caulking around windows, doors	Install adequate venting in roof, attic, soffits, and siding, or add caulk where needed.
	No moisture barrier in exterior walls	Apply oil-base primer/paint or aluminum foil/vinyl wallcovering to interior side of exterior walls.
Mildew	Dirty, moist, or warm surfaces support growth of spores (mildew is a fungus)	To test "dirty" spots for mildew, wash with 3:1 water and bleach solution. If it's mildew, spots will disappear. Or remove with bleach/detergent mixture as for peeling. To prevent mildew, each spring apply detergent to house exterior with hose; spray nozzle removes dirt that supports mildew growth. Or apply a primer and paint with a fungicide additive.
	Too much shade permits moisture buildup.	Trim trees and shrubbery to allow air and sunlight to reach affected area.
	Inadequate venting in soffits, porch ceilings, or siding permits moist conditions	Install vents in areas where mildew recurs.
Alligatored or cracked paint	Many coats of paint on an old surface, or paint applied over improperly prepared surface	Sand, scrape, or burn off old paint.
	Latex applied over gloss oil paint	Sand glossy surface to dull finish. Use proper primer under latex.
	Inferior siding material	Replace siding.

PAINTING A HOUSE EXTERIOR

More prepping

Scrape and feather

To remove loose paint, use a heavy-duty scraper that has a knob at the blade end. To give the tool more scraping power, hold on to this knob 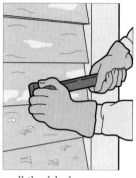 as you push and pull the blade across the surface—but be careful not to gouge the wood. Once the loose paint is off, you'll need to feather (smooth out) the rough edges of the remaining paint. Start with an extra-coarse grade of sandpaper and progress to a medium grade, until the surface is evenly feathered.

Filling out

After scraping and feathering, you'll still find places where the bare wood is much lower than the old bonded paint. Fill these areas with spackling compound, using a putty knife. Let the compound dry, and then sand it smooth.

Of trim and wood siding

The joints where wood siding meets the window and door trim are notorious for developing large gaps. These gaps not only look bad, they also allow air infiltration that wastes energy. Scrape out the old caulk, and 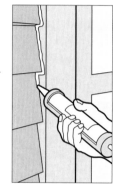 recaulk the joints with a paintable acrylic latex or polyurethane caulk.

When it's rot

Check wooden posts, columns, balusters, and storm windows for rotting areas. Fill these spots with wood restorer/filler, and sand them smooth. If rot covers a large area, you may need to build a form. Replace any wood that is too rotted to be repaired.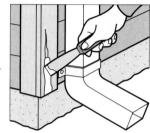

Techniques

Good spray-painting coverage

It's crucial to coat all the edges and surfaces of lap siding, shingles, and other rough textures such as stucco. Otherwise, moisture will creep into unsealed areas and cause the siding to fail. If you spray-paint, choose a windless day (even a 3 to 5 mph breeze will blow overspray everywhere). Apply three light coats: (1) Spray from below so that the paint coats the underside of each lap. (2) Spray at a downward angle and cover the face of each lap. (3) Spray straight into the surface. Or instead of step 3, back-roll or back-brush—go over the wet paint with a roller or a brush to force the paint into the surface pores.

Scaffold setup ▶

The safest type of scaffolding is a steel pipe system, which is available from rental outlets. It gives you a stable support and a wide, safe work platform (the walkboards hook onto the frame and stay in place). The scaffolding shown here is set up for spray-painting; if you intend to use other tools, you won't need such a wide platform. If the surface around your house is firm and level, rest the scaffolding on casters for easy mobility. Otherwise you'll need to rent adjustable baseplates for the scaffold. Don't try to use scrap wood to level it.

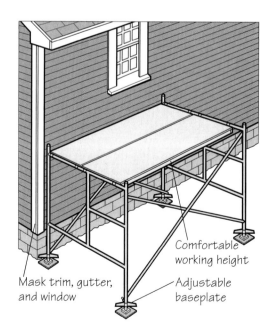

Comfortable working height

Mask trim, gutter, and window

Adjustable baseplate

More on shingles and lap siding

If you don't want to spray-paint, try a pad applicator. The pad reaches under the laps, and the downward motion of the tool pushes the paint into the grooves. To coat the bottom edges of the siding, you can use a brush or a narrow corner roller. ▼

Paint caddy

When you are painting on a scaffold or on a ladder, a brush that's parked on top of the paint can may fall off. What's more, the can may tip over, creating a huge mess and wasting paint. To avert this trouble, put the paint can and brush in a bucket, and hang both the bucket and the brush from paint can hooks. If the bucket is large, you'll also have room for your paint scraper, putty knife, a rag, and any other painting tools you need.

High roller pan

If you want to work with a roller from an extension ladder, here's a handy way to mount a roller tray. Drill two small holes at the top rear of the tray; then form two hooks from wire coat hangers and attach them to the tray. Position the tray on one of the ladder's rungs, and bend the hooks around a higher rung until the tray sits flat. The flanges at the front of the tray will hold it in place.

Order of work

Paint plan

When everything is washed, scraped, sanded, filled, and caulked, you're ready to paint. Begin by priming all the bare wood spots; then paint the siding (see right). Next do the trim and windows (see p.180); then move to the doors, along with any posts and balusters. If you intend to paint the entry steps or a porch, do it next. To finish the job, paint the shutters (off the windows) and remount them when the paint is dry.

Lap siding without lap marks

The siding is the most visible part of a paint job, and so it is crucial to avoid lap marks. Work in the shade, and brush from a dry section into a wet one. And instead of working from top to bottom in vertical sections, go all the way across from one natural break to another (see the numbered sequence in the illustration). If there is no natural break, proceed across the entire width of the house, painting only as many courses of siding in one segment as you can while keeping a wet edge. Work from top to bottom and, if you are right-handed, from left to right. Follow a similar sequence for painting the trim.

PAINT CLEANUP AND STORAGE

Flaws and spills

Clean line for trim

When painting around trim, keep handy a flat-bladed screwdriver or putty knife and a cloth dampened with the proper solvent. Then if you get a bit of paint on the trim, fold the cloth around the tip of the tool and wipe the paint away. ▼

A clean scrape

Here's an easy, accurate way to scrape paint from windows. Place a 4-inch-wide drywall taping knife blade against the putty or wood molding. Slide a razor-blade scraper against the knife blade to make a perfect line without damage. ▼

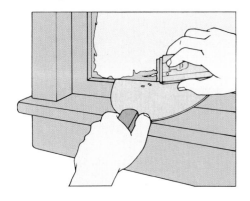

Unmasking

If possible, remove masking tape as soon as the paint is dry enough that it won't run or smear. As you remove the tape, clean away any paint that has seeped under the edges. If for some reason you've had to delay this job, soften the adhesive first by blowing hot air on the tape with a small hair dryer.

Handling drips and runs

What should you do if you discover a flaw—a drip, a run, or a stray bristle—when the paint is too dry to brush it out? Don't be tempted to overpaint it; get rid of it. If

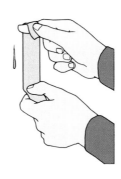

the paint is hard, either sand or scrape it down. If it is still tacky, hold a piece of masking tape at both ends, press the tape gently over the flaw or bristle, and then pull it straight off. Then when the paint is hard, sand the area smooth and touch it up with fresh paint.

Touch up

Even though paint is dry to the touch, it may not have hardened completely. Because a newly painted surface is still fragile, be careful not to scuff it when you are moving furniture back into the room. Keep a small brush and some extra paint on hand so you can easily repair any marks that you accidentally make.

Wash out

Be sure to wash a latex paint spill out of clothes while it is still wet; once a stain dries, it becomes permanent. Your best bet is to wear a painter's smock that completely covers your clothing, including collar and cuffs, or to wear old clothes that you won't mind staining.

Skin treatment

To clean latex paint from your skin, all you need is some hot soapy water. With oil-base paints you'll need something more. You can rub on some waterless hand cleaner, available at automotive supply or hardware stores, or try a little salad oil. (If paint gets in your hair, dip a piece of cotton or tissue in the oil and rub it gently over the painted hair.) You can also use a rag or paper towel soaked in mineral spirits. If you use mineral spirits, however, expose your skin to as little as possible, avoid breathing in the fumes, and wash with soap and water afterward.

Wrapping up

Keep your spirits

You can reclaim the mineral spirits that you've used to clean your painting tools. When you've finished cleaning your tools, put the dirty spirits in a covered coffee can. Set it aside (away from heat) for a few days to allow the paint to settle to the bottom of the can. Then pour off the clean liquid and leave the solids in the can. Save the can so that you can scrape other paint waste into it. When it is full, discard it as noted on page 39.

Switches for matching

It's always a good idea to record the brand of paint, as well as the type (such as semigloss or flat) and the names of the colors used for a room. One way to do this is to mark a piece of masking tape with this information and mount it on the back of an electric switchplate before you screw it back on. Then when

it's time for repainting or a touch-up job, remove the two screws and check the back of the switchplate.

Storing paint

Draw the line

When storing leftover paint, mark a line on the outside of each can to indicate how much is left in it. Later, you'll be able to tell at a glance if you have enough paint for a job.

Sealing the can

When you reseal a can of leftover paint, any paint residue that has collected in the rim can prevent an airtight seal. What's more, it usually squishes out, making a mess. To minimize the build-up, punch holes in the rim (p.168) or wipe the rim clean before you close the can. To improve the seal, stretch a piece of plastic wrap over the rim. Then tap the lid into place, using light hammer blows on alternate sides of the lid.

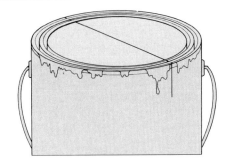

Resealing leftover paint ▲

Have you ever struggled to reseal a can of leftover paint? Breaking a seal that is coated with dried paint leaves uneven surfaces on both the lid and the rim, making it difficult to seal the can the next time. So if you need to work from such a can, mark the exact position of the lid as it sits in the rim—before you open the can. To do this, draw a line across the lid and the rim at two places. When you replace the lid after using the paint, simply align the marks and press the lid down for a quick and easy seal.

More on leftovers

When you store leftover latex paint in its original can, you often get rust and paint flakes in the paint. To avoid this, pour the paint into a plastic bottle or a glass jar with a screw lid. But don't let any paint get on the threads of the lid or you won't be able to reopen it. If you do get paint on the threads, rub a little petroleum jelly on them.

Leftovers again

You can also keep leftover paint fresh by pouring it into a resealable plastic bag. Squeeze the air out before you seal the bag; then put the bag into the original paint can and tap the lid closed.

Wax paper barrier

Because a large air space will dry up a small amount of paint, you should transfer leftover paint to a smaller container (and a smaller air space) if the original can is less than half full. Or cut a circle of heavy wax paper that is the same diameter as the interior of the can and float it on the paint surface. The wax paper acts as a barrier, reducing the interaction of the oxygen and the paint.

Avoiding paint skin

Even if a can of leftover paint is sealed tight, a skin will form on the surface of the paint after a while. Removing the skin before you begin to paint is a messy job at best. To avoid this floating paint skin, store the can upside down. Then when it's time to open the can, turn it right side up. The skin will be on the bottom of the can, leaving the fresh paint on the top.

No oil-base skin

Spreading a thin film of mineral spirits over the surface of oil-base paint before sealing the can will keep a skin from forming. To apply the film, put the solvent in a small sprayer. Use very little— only 1 teaspoonful to a half-empty gallon of paint. To keep the film intact as you seal and store the can, take care not to shake or agitate it accidentally.

PREPARING TO HANG WALLCOVERINGS

Smart strategies

Cover tests

If there's only one layer of untextured wallcovering on the wall—and it's still adhering tightly—you don't have to remove it before hanging a new one. (More than two layers, however, is more weight than the adhesive is meant to support; the layers are likely to pull away from the wall.) Test the old wallcovering by running your fingertips over it. If you hear a crackling noise, the covering is loose and should be removed. You should also check the edges and corners by prying them up with a putty knife. If large sections lift off, continue the removal job.

Covering coverings

If the old covering passes the crackle and corner tests (above), glue any loose areas with white glue or wallcovering paste (p.197). Then wash the surface with detergent or a mild solution of household bleach and water, and apply a primer made for use under wallcoverings. Beware, however, if the old layer is vinyl, foil, or plastic film. Covering these materials doesn't work very well. You're better off removing them instead.

Mess management

Removing wallcoverings is a messy job. Old sheets and bedspreads make first-rate drop cloths. You can either throw them away or use them again. As you work, pick up the globs of stripped paper before they dry. Otherwise they'll make your footing slippery and stick to the drop cloths and your shoes.

Razor's edge

If it's in good condition, plaster is tougher than wallboard. (Old plaster may be crumbly.) You can reduce the amount of

soaking needed on a plaster surface by using a sharp razor scraper to remove wallcovering. The blade will slip easily between the paper and the plaster without damaging the wall.

Don't be stubborn

If a section of wallcovering backing just won't soak off, use a palm pad sander and 120- or 220-grit paper to sand the edges (only) of the area. Be sure that the backing is dry before you sand. Continue until the transition between the wall and the backing is smooth. Wear a dust mask when sanding.

Soaking solutions

Break it up

To break the surface film on vinyl or painted wallcoverings so the remover can penetrate the covering and soften

Scoring tool

the paste, use a sanding block fitted with coarse sandpaper, a wire brush, or a scoring tool made for the purpose. Take care not to gouge the wall as you work.

Spray time ▲

Think twice about renting a steamer; they work very slowly. Brushing or sponging on chemical remover is also a time-consuming, messy job. You can speed the process considerably if you put the remover in a pressurized garden sprayer, hold the nozzle a couple of feet away, and spray it liberally on the wall. Allow the remover to soak in; the paper should almost fall off the wall. Respray any resistant areas. Before you fill the sprayer, be sure that it is free of any insecticide residue. When handling chemical removers, wear goggles and gloves.

Adhesive cleanup

Use a window squeegee to remove old wet wallcovering paste from plaster walls. Dip it into very hot water, run it across the wall for about 2 feet, clean the paste from the tool, and repeat the process until all the paste is gone. ▼

Homemade mix

A mixture of 1 part vinegar and 10 parts water makes a good paste softener. To apply it, use a sprayer (pump or pressurized). The smell, while nontoxic, is irritating; so ventilate the room well.

After stripping

Wash and dry

Wash newly stripped walls with clean hot water and a little household bleach (¼ cup bleach to 2 gallons water). Let the walls dry thoroughly—usually a few hours, but if it's humid possibly several days. Prepare the walls as for paint (pp.176–178); make sure the surface is smooth.

Greasy job

Kitchens and baths are usually painted in a glossy paint, which is likely to be coated with a film of grease or soap. Wash these walls with a heavy-duty detergent. Then prime them with an undercoat suitable for nonporous walls. If the primer beads up, there's still grease on the surface; wash the walls again.

Fill in the bumps

You can turn a textured wall into a surface suitable for wallcovering with some primer and drywall compound. Here's how: First seal the wall with a latex primer; then smooth drywall compound on with a metal float or broad knife. Apply another coat of primer, and you're ready to hang.

Planning the job

Two window treatments ▲

If you start a project between two windows, consider both the width of the covering and the space between the windows when deciding how to waste as little wallcovering as possible and how to avoid working with narrow strips. In a narrow space you'll probably need to center the strip (left). In a wider space, try centering the seam (right).

Focal point strategies ▶

If you are hanging a large pattern that would look best centered on a main wall, or if the room has a focal point, such as a fireplace or a window, you'll need to center the first strip, then work away from one side. Stop the first side when you get to an inconspicuous place for the mismatch. Continue hanging the covering from the other side of the centered strip until it meets at the mismatch spot.

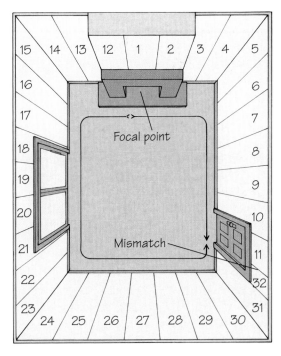

Focal point

Mismatch

HANGING WALLCOVERINGS

Strip tips

Put the top up

Many patterns are almost—but not quite—mirror images top and bottom. If there's a chance that you might accidentally hang your wallcovering upside down, mark an X on the top of the pasted side of each strip as you cut it off the roll. Note that you should do this with identical diamond and striped patterns as well—the shading may vary.

Reverse for one color

With solid-color textured (no-match) coverings, you'll get a more uniform color if you reverse every other strip.

Pressure point

When wetting the strips, don't apply too much pressure with the roller or pad applicator—you could remove some of the paste and end up with serious adhesion problems.

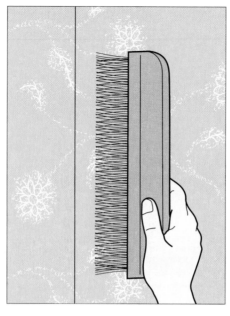

Brushing flock ▲

Never use a seam roller on flocked or other raised wallcoverings. Instead, gently tap the seams with a soft smoothing brush. That way you won't damage the raised pattern.

All the trimming

When you are trimming wallcovering at the ceiling junction or along baseboard molding, always hold a broad knife between the cutting tool and the paper. This ensures a straighter cut and keeps the razor knife from damaging the paper if your hand slips. ▼

Keep an edge

Keep a sharp blade in your razor knife (and keep the knife away from children). A dull blade makes jagged cuts. To store all those used blades safely, pop them into an empty soda can.

Water trays

Go soak it ▶

You may prefer to use a water tray to wet prepasted coverings. If you do, "backroll" the strip so that the pattern faces in and then soak the rolled-up covering in clear water to wet the paste. Then proceed with the booking process.

Include the kitchen sink

You may not have to bother with a water tray if you are covering kitchen or bathroom walls. A good-size kitchen sink or a bathtub will do the job.

One more tray idea

Here's a way to ensure that the strip is submerged uniformly and is thoroughly wet. When you are backrolling the strip, wrap it around a long medium-weight cylinder, such as a length of clean metal pipe or a heavy rolling pin.

HOW TO HANG PREPASTED STRIPS

If this is your first wallcovering project, choose a pattern that needs little or no matching. Do a bedroom or a living room—they are easier than kitchens and baths. Start off in a room with no alcoves or recessed windows, so you won't have to cut and match a lot of odd-size pieces.

You'll need a ladder, a razor knife and blades, a large flat work surface, sponges, a bucket, a paint roller, clean tepid water, levels, a pencil, a tape measure, scissors, a plastic smoother or smoothing brush, a seam roller, a pocketed apron, drop cloths, clean towels, and trash bags.

1 Use a level to strike a plumb line where the first seam will fall. If it is near an inside corner, position it so the strip will extend 1/8 in. beyond. (It should go 1/4 to 1/2 in. beyond an outside corner.)

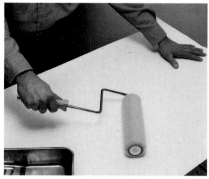

2 Cut a strip the height of the wall plus 2 in. at the top and at the bottom. Use a roller dipped in tepid water to wet the back of the strip thoroughly, until the paste becomes milky.

3 Book, or relax, the strip by folding it pasted side in; make the first fold two-thirds of the sheet, the second, one-third. Roll the folded strip up loosely and let it rest per maker's instructions.

4 Hang the strip. Begin at the top and align the right or left edge with the plumb line. Release the folds gradually. The strip should overlap both ceiling and base molding by about 2 in.

5 Flatten the strip against the wall, using a plastic smoother or smoothing brush. Start at the center of the strip and push out. Small bubbles that remain will disappear as the strip dries.

6 Hang the next strip (without a plumb line), matching the pattern. After the third strip is hung, lightly roll both sides of the first seam with one pass. Wash off excess paste with a damp sponge.

HANGING WALLCOVERINGS

Paste

Enhancing the paste

Some prepasted coverings adhere better than others. To see how well a prepasted covering will stick to your wall, do a wet test: Wet a 6-inch piece of the pattern, place it on the wall, and let it dry. If you have any doubts about its adhesion, just roll some wallcovering paste activator on the pasted side before hanging it. (The activator looks and applies just like wallcovering paste.)

Mildew stopper

Mildew, ever the enemy in bathrooms and kitchens, can easily find its way to the dried paste beneath a wallcovering. When it does, the bond weakens. While the pastes of some coverings have been treated to resist mildew, others have not. If you have chosen one of the latter, you can treat the paste side of the covering with a mildewcide as you hang each strip. Before proceeding, test the spray on a patch to be sure that the mildewcide won't affect the pattern dyes.

Now you see it

When you are spreading clear paste on a wallcovering, it is hard to see if you're coating the surface completely and evenly. If your covering has a background other than white, you can add a few drops of food coloring to the paste to make it more visible. Pour it in drop by drop, just until it has a very light tint. Too much color will bleed through the paper.

Table talk

Instead of renting a pasting table, use an old smooth-finish door or a 4 x 8 sheet of plywood. Choose a sheet that has a finished side and no knots.

Less mess

When you are ready to paste, put a drop cloth under the table to catch the inevitable drips. After you've pasted each strip, wipe the table clean (especially the edges). That way you'll keep the pattern side free of glue.

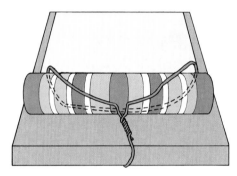

Hanger hold ▲

To keep a strip from rolling up when it's laid out on the pasting table, use this improvised holder. Simply bend a wire coat hanger into the shape shown, fit it over the roll, and secure the hooked end to the edge of the table.

Ceilings

When to do it

If you are papering a small room—such as a bathroom or a guest bedroom—consider covering the ceiling as well as the walls. It'll give the room a feeling of intimacy as well as a finished look.

Choose the direction

When you're covering a ceiling with the same material as the walls, remember that you'll be able to match the ceiling pattern on only one wall. Pick the most prominent wall in the room or, if the room is small, the wall opposite the most frequently used door. In the latter case, the pattern will seem to draw you into the room.

Ceiling strategy

If you plan to cover a ceiling, do so before you do the walls—and be sure to get someone to help you. Cut the strips of covering so that the ends will extend ½ inch down the wall. Then book the strips accordion-style, and you're ready to go. ▼

Neat edges

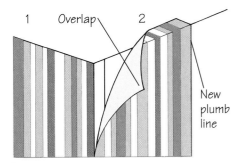

1 Overlap 2 New plumb line

Turn the corner ▲

When covering an inside corner, you must overlap the strips. Never try to bridge a corner with one strip. Measure three spots (top, middle, and bottom) from the edge of the last strip to the corner. Use the widest measurement and add ⅛ inch. Cut the strip to size, knowing that the overlap will vary, and hang it. To finish the corner, strike another plumb line and hang the other cut piece.

Outside wrap

Outside corners are very visible—and seldom plumb; consequently you shouldn't wrap a single strip around the corner. Instead, treat the corner as you would an inside corner, but plan to leave a larger (¼- to ½-inch) overlap. Smooth both strips carefully into place.

Arch comments

If you are not going to cover the underside of an arch, you'll want to leave a crisp edge of wallcovering around the archway. Leave about 1 inch of covering untrimmed. Let the glue dry, and then trim the excess paper with a single-edge razor blade. Dry paper is easier to trim neatly than wet paper.

Odds and ends

Take a recess

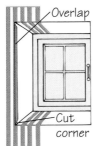

Overlap Cut corner

When covering a recessed area (as for a casement window), start with full-width strips, allowing extra for an overlap on each side of the recess. Snip the corners before smoothing the overlap (above). Cut strips to fit each side, and finish the job (below). ▼

Smooth curves ▶

To cover the underside of an arch, follow a method similar to that for recessed areas. When it's time to smooth the overlap around the curve, snip relief cuts at frequent intervals. Cover the overlap with one strip, if possible. Cut the strip slightly narrower than the width of the arch to avoid any peeling edges.

Get behind a radiator

You needn't disconnect and move a radiator or convector to hang wallcovering behind it. Position a full-length strip, smoothing it from the ceiling down to the top of the radiator. Smooth the rest of the strip behind the radiator with a length of wooden dowel or a yardstick. Then crease the trim line into the strip with a dull long-handled knife. Pull the strip up from behind the radiator and trim along the creased line with scissors. Finally, reposition the bottom of the strip and smooth it down.

Yardstick

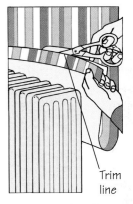

Trim line

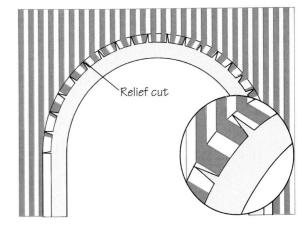

Relief cut

HANGING WALLCOVERINGS

Borders and accents

More is better

Putting up a border is an easy, inexpensive way to dress up a painted room. But if the room is large, you shouldn't economize too much. As a rule, the larger the room, the more border motifs you'll need. For example, a single border at the ceiling or at the chair rail level tends to make a room look unfinished. Consider adding more borders and accents to unify the room.

Ceiling frame

In a room where the ceiling gets some attention, such as a dining room with a chandelier or a bedroom, put a border on the ceiling. Depending on the size of the ceiling and the effect you want to achieve, you can place the border frame 3 inches—or 2 feet—from the wall.

More frames

Brighten up a boring window or door opening by framing it with a border motif; then add coordinated drapes to complement the look. On a large wall you can create rectangular panels for a formal look. You can also frame a mirror, such as the one on a medicine cabinet in a bathroom.

Unexpected places

Looking for ways to accent a room without investing in a border covering? You can hang strips of wallcovering on the rear wall of open or recessed shelving, or you can cover a wastebasket. If you're doing a bathroom, covering the inside of the medicine cabinet will dress up that typical eyesore.

Ganging together

You can combine several borders of various widths, or cut sections from a border and glue them on both sides of a main border motif, to create a decorative stripe around a room.

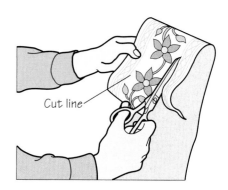

Make a stencil effect ▲

To create a stencil effect with a wallcovering border, cut the edging from both sides; then hang the interior motif. It will look very much like a painted design.

Hiding imperfections

Plumb problems

If a room is badly out of plumb, the variations will show around the doors, windows, and at the edges of ceiling and base moldings. The pros suggest selecting a random pattern, a floral, or a pattern with a vine motif. It is best to avoid geometrical patterns and stripes because they emphasize irregularities.

Border camouflage

One way to hide an uneven ceiling line is to hang a covering and add a coordinated border. Place the border so that half of it is on the wall and half is on the ceiling. Book the border, crease it in half, and hang it. At the corners, follow the steps below. This "half-and-half" approach neatly wraps the room, giving it a finished look. ▼

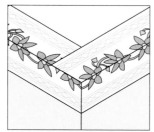

For an inside corner: 1. Butt two border pieces at the wall, overlapping the ends on the ceiling.

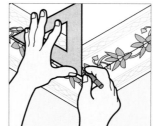

2. Cut a miter through both layers on the ceiling. Remove the waste and smooth the rest.

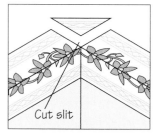

At an outside corner: Slit the ceiling side of one piece and wrap the piece around. Cut a patch to fill the gap.

When things go wrong

Too wet

If a pasted strip becomes too wet, book it and let it sit a little longer than you normally would. The extra moisture will evaporate. (Don't let it dry too much.)

Too dry

If for some reason you've been delayed and allowed a strip to dry out too much, you may be able to salvage it. Carefully place the dried book on the table; take care not to bang the strip as you do so. Spray a mist of clean water over the strip to relax it. Gently unfold the book; then reroll with paste and book again.

Free advice

While every roll of wallcovering comes with a set of general instructions, it won't specify the particular needs of the wallcovering you have chosen. If possible, buy your covering from a local distributor who employs a trained and certified consultant. Such a person should be able to advise you if you run into problems.

Making repairs

Mist those curls ▲

You'll have an easier time getting curled-up edges to stay down if you mist the repair area with clean water. With the curl in a relaxed state, it will lie in place when the glue is applied.

Tear it up

When a tear occurs, one side has the backing and the other has the pattern. To repair the tear, place the backing side down first and cover it with the pattern side. (Otherwise, the backing will be visible.) Where the two sides meet, you will see a small ridge. Gently smooth it down with your fingertip, the eraser end of a pencil, or the tip of a toothpick. If the repair area dries as you work, mist it with clean water. ▼

TROUBLESHOOTING WALLCOVERING PROBLEMS

PROBLEM	CAUSE	REPAIR	PREVENTION
Seams pull apart	Wallcovering shrinks after it is hung	Remove the strips and hang new ones.	Buy high-quality wallcoverings; prepare the wall properly; book according to maker's instructions; overlap seams $1/32$ in. or less; add a paste activator when wetting.
Edges and seams curl when dry	Too much rolling	Apply seam adhesive or vinyl paste to edges.	Don't roll seams immediately— wait until several strips have been hung; roll seams just once.
Air bubbles	Overworking the covering	Slit the paper over the bubble, and glue down with seam adhesive or vinyl wallcovering paste.	Smooth the paper without overworking (small air bubbles that you see when the wallcovering is wet should disappear when it's dry).
Dried paste	Not washing paste off before it dries	Some may be picked off; use a paste remover, or wash paste off with an all-purpose cleaner or a solution of 2 tbsp. Murphy's Oil Soap and 2 gal. warm water.	Rinse off excess paste with warm water and clean sponges as you hang each strip; dry with clean towel.

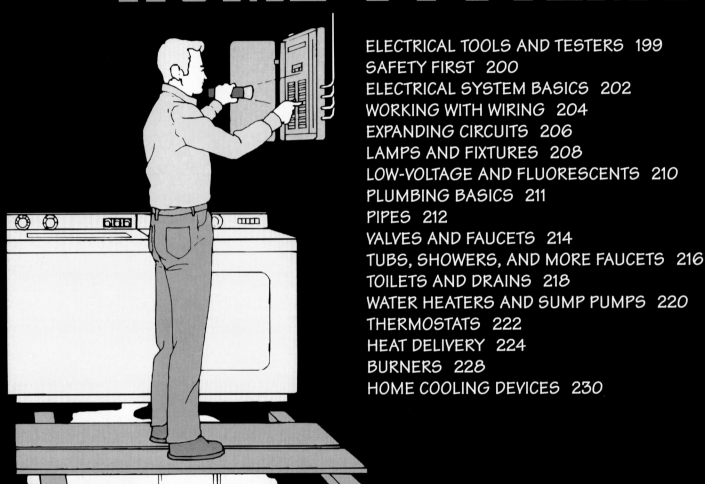

HOME SYSTEMS

ELECTRICAL TOOLS AND TESTERS

Down to basics

Electrician's toolbox

A toolbox that contains a needle-nose pliers, a standard straight-tip screwdriver, a small long-shank straight-tip screwdriver, and a Phillips screwdriver has most of the tools used for electrical work. You may also need a cable stripper to slice through sheathing on nonmetallic cable, a wire stripper to remove the insulation from the wires, and lineman's pliers or diagonal-cutting pliers to cut the wire. Or buy a multipurpose tool that measures, strips, and cuts wire, cuts bolts, and crimps wire connectors. ▼

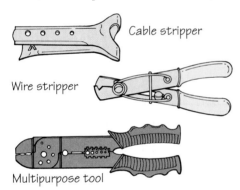

Cable stripper

Wire stripper

Multipurpose tool

Shocking screwdriver

The greater part of the shank of an electrician's screwdriver is covered in plastic to protect the user from shock. If you plan to use an ordinary screwdriver, here's a precaution you can take. Simply wrap electrician's tape around the shank from the base of the handle to the tip; make sure the layers of tape overlap. Tape over any exposed metal parts on the handle, too. And remember that the only real protection is to *always* turn off the power at the circuit breaker panel or fuse box before you work on that circuit.

TESTING EQUIPMENT

A *voltage tester* indicates the presence of voltage. It is most commonly used to make sure the power is off at a switch, outlet, or fixture, but it can also be used to locate incoming hot wires and to test for grounding. A *continuity tester* detects shorts and other wiring flaws in sockets, switches, appliance and extension cords, and fuses. A voltage/continuity tester (not shown) combines the two, and it's safer and easier to use. An *outlet analyzer* finds faulty wiring, such as a disconnected ground wire or reversed hot and neutral or ground wires. A *volt-ohm meter* does everything the other testers do—and more. Instead of simple yes/no readings, it provides actual measurements.

Voltage tester is equipped with a bulb and two probes—but not a power source. When the neon light bulb lights, voltage is present. Check all possible combinations of wires.

Outlet analyzer plugs into a receptacle. The pattern of lights can indicate an open grounding, hot, or neutral wire or wrong-way polarity. If the analyzer indicates a problem, rewire the outlet.

Continuity tester, a battery-powered device with a light bulb, battery probe, and alligator clip, indicates a complete circuit when the bulb lights. *Caution:* Use it only with the power off.

Volt-ohm meter, or multitester, tests for continuity, power on or off, and grounding; it measures voltages (battery and household), current, and resistance. It can also read low-voltage circuits.

SAFETY FIRST

Rules and regulations

The electrician's code
The Canadian Electrical Code (CEC) is a set of rules for safe electrical installation. Updated regularly by the Canadian Engineering Standards Association, it is the basis for local and provincial codes, some of which may be even more stringent. Some local codes require that all wiring be done by a licensed electrician. Others let you install new circuits up to the service entrance panel, but a licensed electrician must complete the hookup. This is a good idea even if it's not demanded by code. Before installing new wiring or adding to existing wiring, contact your local building inspector for up-to-date code requirements.

Paperwork
Except for simple repairs like replacing an outlet or a switch, you may need a permit from your local building department to change or add to your wiring system. Some municipalities may require a written description and a rough sketch of your plans; you may also have to take a simple electrical proficiency test. Be prepared to schedule inspections as your work progresses.

What's in a label?
A Canadian Standards Association (CSA) or Underwriters Laboratories of Canada (ULC) listing on an electrical device or part certifies that the product has been tested by the nonprofit testing firm named, and meets its demanding safety standards. For safety's sake, install only electrical parts and devices certified by the CSA or ULC.

Avoiding hazards

Leave a sign

Before doing any work on a circuit, *always* turn off power to the circuit at the service panel, by either turning off the circuit breaker or removing the fuse that controls the circuit. Once you've turned off the power, make sure you put up a sign at the panel warning others to leave the power off.

Hand behind your back
When testing a fixture or removing a fuse from the service panel, work with only one hand if possible; keep the other hand behind your back. If one hand comes in contact with electricity and the other a ground (such as a metal pipe), the electricity may travel from one hand to the other—with your heart in its path.

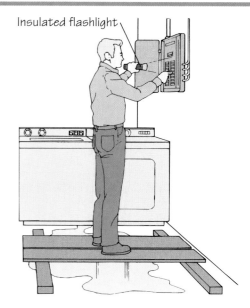

Insulated flashlight

Do away with puddles ▲
Before you turn off a circuit, replace a fuse, or do other work at the panel, don a pair of sturdy shoes with nonconductive rubber soles. Even a dry concrete floor can be a good conductor of electricity. Keep a heavy rubber insulating mat in the vicinity of your service panel, or stack a few boards nearby where they will remain dry. Stand on the mat or dry boards while at the panel. Never do any electrical job while standing on a wet floor.

Hoarding the right fuses
Always replace a fuse with one of the same amperage. A higher-amperage fuse will allow wires to overheat, which can create a short circuit and start a fire. Do not replace a fuse until you've solved the problem that made it blow in the first place. Keep a supply of fuses of the correct amperage near the service panel; if one blows, you'll have the right replacement at hand.

A true grounding experience

Until you've tested a ground, don't take for granted that it's really grounded. To test a ground, clamp a 14-gauge single-conductor wire to the ground wire, a metal pipe, or other bare metal on the main service panel; then run the wire to the outlet. Attach the alligator clip of a continuity tester to the wire and touch the probe on the ground—either a bare grounding wire, a round grounding slot, or a metal box. If the tester lights, you'll know that you have proper grounding.

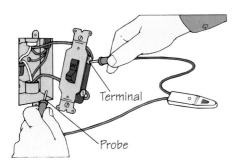

Is it live? ▲

Before working on a switch, remove the cover plate and check that the power is off by using a voltage tester. Place one probe on a metal box or bare grounding wire. Place the second probe on each terminal screw. If the power is off, the bulb will not light. At a receptacle with one or more sockets, insert the probes into all the slots. If the tester does not light, carefully remove the cover and outlet; touch the probes to each terminal screw and a known ground. If the bulb still does not light, the power is off.

Metalproof

Be careful not to touch plumbing pipes or fixtures or gas pipes while working on wiring or repairing an appliance. Also avoid ductwork and registers, structural steel, aluminum siding, metal gutters, foil faces on insulation, and other electrical appliances.

Hand protection

Whenever you work with electricity, make sure your hands are completely dry. If you do come in contact with live equipment, dry hands can reduce the intensity of the resulting shock.

In an emergency

Seeing sparks

When an appliance or power tool gives off sparks, unplug the cord without coming in contact with the body of the appliance. Or turn the power off at the service panel. If the sparks come from the cord or plug or if the cord is hot, turn the power off at the service panel. If you see sparks at a wall fixture, use a nonconductive item to turn the switch off before turning off the power at the service panel. Call your hydro company if the sparks are at the service panel.

Soaked

Do not touch a small appliance that's under water. Making sure you and the plug are dry, pull out the plug without touching anything metal. If a large appliance is surrounded by water, turn the power off at the service panel. If the service panel is in a flooded area, have the hydro company turn the power off.

Outdoor power lines

Downed power lines are extremely dangerous. Do not try to move them—not even with a piece of wood. The voltage in these wires is high enough that wood can be a conductor. Do not go near the lines; call the electric company or the fire or police department. If the line falls on a car while you're in it, stay in the car until help arrives.

Helping a shock victim

If you find someone in contact with a live circuit, don't touch him or her. If the service panel is nearby, turn off the *main* power to the house. If not, use a nonconductive item, such as a wooden chair or nonmetallic broom, to separate the person from the hot wire. Or carefully loop a sweater or some other piece of clothing around the victim; grasp both ends of the sweater and pull the person away. If the victim does not have a heartbeat, apply cardiopulmonary resuscitation (CPR) if you've been properly trained in the procedure. Check the victim for burns, and if he or she was touching metal, check for shards in unshielded eyes.

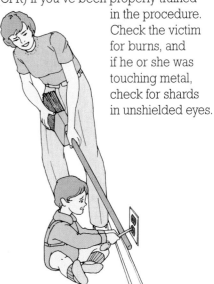

ELECTRICAL SYSTEM BASICS

Circuits

Turn up the volume

Here's a way to quickly establish which circuit an outlet is on, even without a circuit map: Plug a vacuum cleaner into the outlet and turn it on. Or plug in a radio and set the volume loud. Even in the basement you'll hear the silence when you switch off the right breaker or unscrew the right fuse.

At the service panel

Are you trying to determine what the amperage for a circuit is, but can't see the imprinted number on the circuit breaker? Here's one way to make that number pop out on some circuit breakers: Rub chalk over the end of the toggle switch; then wipe away the excess. The chalk remaining inside the imprint will show the number.

Make a map ▶

To help solve electrical problems, map your electrical system. First make a sketch of your floor plan. For each room mark the location of every switch, light, and receptacle, and code them as shown. At the service panel, shut off the first circuit and mark a "1" by it. Walk through the house, flipping on lights and plugging in a radio at each receptacle. If a light or the radio doesn't go on, you know the switch or receptacle is on that first circuit. (Don't forget the attic, basement, garage, and any outdoor outlets.) Write a "1" on your map at each receptacle or light affected by that circuit. At the service panel label the location of the circuit, for example "bedroom receptacles and lights." Some dedicated circuits may power only one heavy-duty appliance, such as an electric range. Repeat for the other circuits. Keep a laminated copy of the map at the panel.

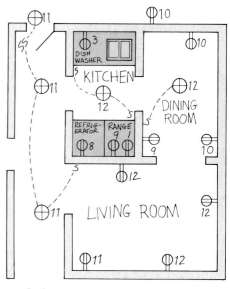

Code

⊕	Receptacle	₅₅	2 Switches
⊕	Light Fixture	╌╌	Switch to light circuit
₅	Switch	10	Circuit number

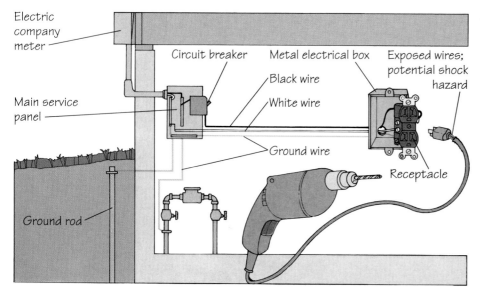

Electric company meter

Main service panel

Ground rod

Circuit breaker · Metal electrical box · Exposed wires; potential shock hazard

Black wire

White wire

Ground wire

Receptacle

◀ A closed route

A safe electrical system routes electricity from the main service panel through circuits of insulated wires and closed boxes. The system is essentially a closed one, in which there is no easy way for you to get to a hot wire. A leak within the system, caused by a faulty receptacle, a break in a wire, or frayed insulation, can blow a fuse or trip a circuit breaker. When this happens, only the circuit is protected. If the leak is outside the system where you may come into contact with it, the leak can result in a shock. In this diagram, the potential leak is at the drill cord. Before using the drill, replace the cord.

Power control

How you turn off all the power to your house depends on the type of service panel in your home. The "main" switch may be labeled "service disconnect."

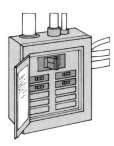

Circuit breaker panel

A circuit breaker panel may have one or more main breakers at the top. To turn the power off, flip the breakers to the *Off* position. If your panel doesn't have main breakers, trip all the breakers.

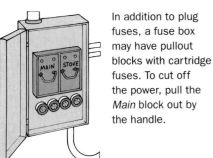

Box with plug fuses and pullout boxes

In addition to plug fuses, a fuse box may have pullout blocks with cartridge fuses. To cut off the power, pull the *Main* block out by the handle.

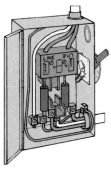

Fuse box with lever switch

The fuse box may have a lever switch on one side of the box; to cut the main power, simply pull the lever up to the *Off* position. Or you may find the lever switch in a box by itself, usually a few feet from where the wires enter the house.

Fuses and breakers

Tell-tale signs

Plug-type fuse: when overloaded, metal strip melts

S-fuse: spring contracts when overloaded

When a circuit draws too much current, a metal strip inside a fuse melts and breaks, stopping current flow. Either an overload or a short circuit will cause a circuit to blow. An overload melts and breaks the fuse's metal strip but leaves the glass window clear; a short circuit discolors the window. On an S-fuse, a contracted spring will also indicate an overload.

Finding the good one

The only way to determine if a cartridge fuse is good is by testing it with a continuity tester. Touch one end of the fuse with the tester's alligator clip, the other end with the tester's probe. If the fuse is good, the tester bulb will light up. If you don't have a tester, simply replace the cartridge with a new one. ▼

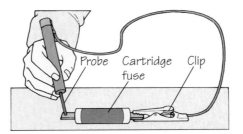

Probe   Cartridge fuse   Clip

Breaker breakdown

When overloaded, parts inside a circuit breaker can be damaged. Signs of damage are a deformed plastic case or persistent shutoff. Because replacing the breaker means removing the panel cover, call in a licensed electrician.

Troubleshooting

To solve an overload problem, turn off an appliance or plug it into another circuit. If the circuit blows again right after you reset the breaker or replace the fuse, check for a short circuit: Turn off the main power. Unplug all appliances on that circuit, and look for damaged plugs and cords; repair or replace them if needed. Before replugging the appliances, reset the breaker or replace the fuse and turn on the power. If the circuit fails right away, the short is in the house wiring. Call an electrician. If the short occurs only when you turn on a specific appliance, the short is in that appliance.

Better than standard

If you can rely on a surge from your air conditioner to blow the fuse, use a time-lag fuse instead of the standard fuse. A lump of metal on the strip gives an extra split second for surges. Better yet, use an S-fuse. In addition to the time-delay feature, it has a color-coded adapter that fits into the socket in the panel. The adapter accepts only a specific amperage fuse (p.200) in a matching color.

Borrow a fuse

Has the fuse blown, and you're missing the big game on TV because you don't have replacement fuses? Replace the blown fuse with one of the same amperage from another circuit.

WORKING WITH WIRING

Stripping and splicing

How much is enough

Don't get caught short of cable after stripping its ends. After measuring the length between the power source and the outlet, add 1 foot for each connection; then give yourself room for error by adding another 20 percent to the total length. For instance, if the distance between the source and a receptacle will be 20 feet, add 2 feet for connections at each end, giving you 22 feet. An additional 20 percent is about 4½ feet. For this job, you should allow a total of 26½ feet of cable.

The right connection

Solid wires in connector

To join two solid wires, remove ¾ inch of insulation from the wire ends. Then holding the ends parallel, screw on a wire connector clockwise until it's tight. (Unless otherwise indicated on the connector package, you don't have to twist the wires together first.) Wire connectors come in various sizes for different-size wires. To join two stranded wires or a stranded and a solid wire, twist the ends together as shown. Make sure the exposed wire is completely contained in a wire connector. ▼

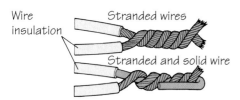

Wire insulation

Stranded wires

Stranded and solid wire

Make it stick

Moisture and stray wires from other connections are two potential causes of short circuits. To keep them out of a splice, wrap three turns of electrical tape around the spliced wires and the wire connector. Then dab a little PVC pipe cement under the end of the electrical tape to keep it from unraveling.

Finding a home for the splice

An exposed wire splice is a fire hazard. For your safety, the Canadian Electrical Code requires that all splices be kept inside an accessible junction box.

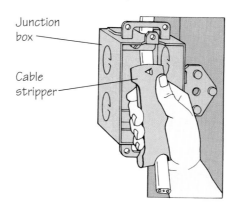

Junction box

Cable stripper

Cable exposure ▲

Not sure how much cable to expose for a junction box? Allow 2 to 3 inches for the depth of the junction box, then add another 6 inches for the cable outside the box. To strip the nonmetallic sheathing of the cable, cut a groove down the length of the cable with a utility knife or cable stripper. (Never used the stripper before? Slip the tool over the cable, squeeze the handles, and pull the stripper off the cable.) Peel back the sheathing and cut it off with the utility knife or cutting pliers. Don't forget to remove the wrapping or filler around the wires.

Armored cut

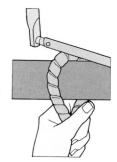

Cutting armored cable with a hacksaw can be awkward. Here's how you can simplify the job. Hold the cable steady with pliers while you make the cut. Or wrap the cable around a 3-inch pipe; grasp both ends of the cable in one hand while you saw. Either way, cut diagonally across the cable without cutting into the wire insulation; twist off the loose armor and remove the paper wrapping. Cover the sharp cut edges with a plastic bushing.

Switches and outlets

A terminal situation

Have you tried to tighten a terminal screw only to have the wire come out? Always hook the wire clockwise—never counterclockwise—around the screw shaft. And when hooking wires to a receptacle or switch, make sure you attach them to the appropriate terminals: the neutral wire to the silver terminal screw stamped "white"; the hot wire to the brass terminal screw; and the ground wire to the green grounding screw. And remember: when wiring a switch, the neutral wire bypasses the switch.

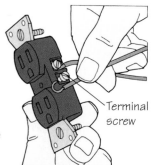

Terminal screw

Hooked

If you don't have long-nose pliers, you can use a small dowel to make hooks in wires. Drill a hole through the dowel, or drive a nail through the dowel to make the hole. Then, when you want a hook, simply slip the end of the wire into the hole and rotate the dowel 180°. ▼

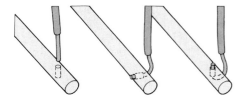

Back stabber

Instead of terminal screws, some receptacles and switches have push-in terminals. A gauge shows how much insulation to remove from the wire. To connect the wire, just push it into the wire port. To disconnect the wire, push a screwdriver or awl into the slot closest to the port. ▼

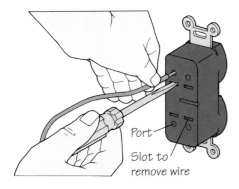

Port

Slot to remove wire

Out of the box

When pulling a switch or receptacle out of the box, grab it from the screw-hole ears in front. If you grab the device from the side, you might also grab a hot wire.

GFCI's

A ground fault circuit interrupter, or GFCI, can protect you from a dangerous electrical shock that can occur if you become part of the electrical circuit. Suppose you touch a frayed cord on a hair dryer while standing on a wet bathroom floor. The resulting current running through you may not blow a fuse or trip a circuit breaker, but it can give you a nasty, perhaps fatal, electrical shock. A GFCI, however, will sense the misdirected current; in a split second, it will shut off the circuit before the current can harm you.

To guard against the dangers of mixing moisture and current, substitute GFCI's for standard receptacles in bathrooms, above a kitchen countertop and within 6 feet of the sink, in crawl spaces and unfinished basements, in garages, and in outdoor locations. Installation is similar to that of other receptacles, except that there are two pairs of terminals.

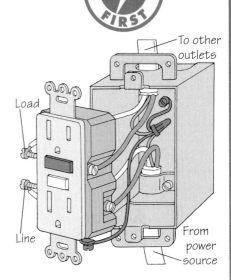

To other outlets

Load

Line

From power source

One is labeled "line" for connecting wires from the circuit; the other pair, labeled "load," allows you to connect standard outlets farther down the circuit. Make sure you test all GFCI's monthly: Push the *Test* button to cut power to the receptacle; press the *Reset* button to restore the power. If the *Reset* button fails to pop up, replace the GFCI.

Seal it with tape

After connecting the wires to the terminal screws of a switch or receptacle, wrap electrician's tape around the device so that the tape will completely cover the terminals. This way, if you need to remove the switch or receptacle in the future, the tape will prevent you from touching exposed wires.

Pigtails ▶

Never hook more than one wire to a terminal on a switch or receptacle. Instead, use a wire connector to join the wires with a short wire, called a pigtail. Hook the pigtail's free end to the terminal.

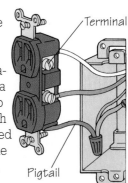

Terminal

Pigtail

EXPANDING CIRCUITS

At the box

Making everything fit

When working on an old box, you'll most likely find that the wires are crammed into it. Not only does this undersize box have little or no room for working, but more important, the wires can be damaged, creating a fire hazard. For your protection, the CEC (Canadian Electrical Code) dictates the maximum number of wires that can be run into specific-size boxes. The size of the wire also determines the number of wires allowed in the box (the larger the wire, the fewer in the box). Additionally, if you have other devices in the box, such as a switch, receptacle, clamp, strap, or grounding conductors, you'll have to deduct a certain number of wires from those allowed in the box. After making deductions, if you find you no longer can run enough wires for the job into the box, use a larger box. Check with your local codes to determine the size of the box that will be suitable.

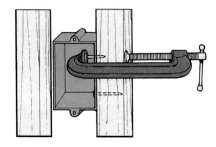

Hammer-free nailing ▲

To nail a box to a stud where there's not enough room to swing a hammer, use a C-clamp. By tightening the clamp you can squeeze nails through the holes in the side of the box and into the stud.

Overload

Before adding a new outlet or fixture to a circuit, make sure there's enough room for it. Count the existing number of outlets and fixtures on the circuit you plan to add to. The rule of thumb is to have no more than a total of 8 outlets and fixtures on a 15-amp circuit, and no more than 10 on a 20-amp circuit.

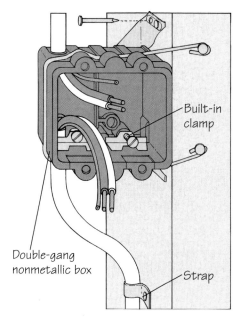

Built-in clamp

Double-gang nonmetallic box

Strap

A secure cable ▲

How you secure cable at a box depends on the type of box you use. For a single-gang nonmetallic box, secure the cable by placing a preformed plastic strap over it within 8 inches of the box, then nailing the strap to the stud. In a double-gang nonmetallic box with built-in clamps, attach the strap to the stud within 12 inches of the box. In some areas local codes require using a metal box. The box may have built-in clamps similar to the ones shown, or it may require using bushings and locknuts.

Supporting role

If you're mounting a new box in wallboard, use brackets to hold it in place. First outline the box with a pencil (but leave out the ears). Then cut along the outline with a wallboard knife. With the cable clamped in the box and the ears adjusted so the box sits flush to the wall, hold the box in the wall while you slip a bracket on each side of the box between the wall and the box. Using long-nose pliers, pull the tabs on each bracket forward while pushing the box back with a screwdriver; then fold the tabs against the side of the box.

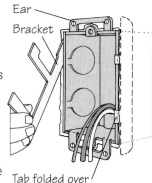

Ear

Bracket

Tab folded over

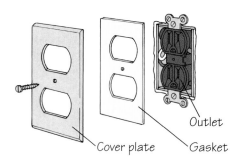

Outlet

Cover plate

Gasket

Keep cold air out ▲

Uninsulated outlets can let a cold draft from your basement or attic into the room. They can also be a source of heat loss. You can insulate an outlet with a foam gasket (available at most home centers). To install the gasket, unscrew the cover plate of the outlet and slip the gasket behind it with the smooth side facing out. Trim the foam with scissors.

Running cable

Doing it the easy way

Fish tape

Electrician's tape

The easiest route for new cable in an existing home is across an unfinished basement or attic. To get the cable to an opening for an electrical box, you may have to "fish" the cable from holes cut in walls, ceilings, or floors. Use an electrician's fish tape to pull the cable through the spaces between studs or joists. Hook the tape to the cable, and wrap the connection with electrician's tape. Have a helper push the cable through while you fish it out.

Avoiding obstructions

Before running new cable through old walls, make sure to check for existing wiring and other obstructions. One way is to remove a baseboard, electrical box, or floorboard to expose the cavity. Shining a flashlight into the cavity, hold a mirror to the opening and tilt it until you have the desired view.

Getting around the corner

Cable being pulled around a corner can get snagged. One solution is to hold a paint roller against the cable at the trouble spot. As you pull the cable up, the rotating roller will keep it moving.

Suction power

Knitting yarn and a vacuum cleaner can help you to fish cable through conduit or a pipe. Measure a length of yarn a foot longer than the conduit or pipe, and tie one end to the wire. Suck the loose end of the yarn through the conduit or pipe with the vacuum cleaner at the other end. When the yarn exits the pipe, pull it through until the wire reaches you.

Going fishing?

Make fishing an electrical cable less frustrating. Tie a strong magnet to the end of a fishing line, and lower it through an opening above the new outlet's location. Push a straightened coat hanger

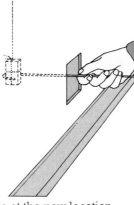

through the hole at the new location. When the magnet locks onto the wire hanger, guide the magnet through the hole. (Alternatively, tie a magnet to the coat hanger and tie a metal object, such as a chain, to the line.) Then simply pull your electric cable through the wall, using the fishing line as a leader.

Elusive line

Sometimes grabbing the dropped line is difficult. To increase your chances, tie a plastic bag to the end of the line. The bag is bulkier and easier to grab.

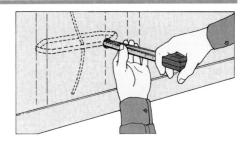

Fishing through a tiny hole ▲

Here's one way to grab a cable through a small hole: Drill a ¾-inch hole where you want the cable to exit. Extend a retractable tape measure, fold it at the halfway mark, and push it into the hole as far as it will go. The tape will conform to the space behind the wall—between the studs and the back of the opposite wall. Drop the cable from above, and pull the tape out; the cable will exit too.

Blocked!

If an obstruction, like a stud or a fire-stop, blocks the wire's passage, you'll have to drill or notch the obstruction. First cut an access hole in the wall to get at the obstruction. Drill a hole or saw a notch in it; then run the wire through. Before patching the hole, cover a notch in a stud or fire-stop with a ¹⁄₁₆-inch-thick steel plate (available at home centers).

LAMPS AND FIXTURES

Incandescent bulb

Reaching the bulb

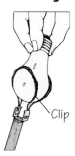

Most homes have a light bulb that is out of reach. Instead of climbing on a ladder, fasten a clip from a lampshade to a 4-foot-long 1-inch-diameter stick or broom handle. For a better grip on the bulb, wrap electrician's tape around the clip.

Clip

A raw deal

Did a light bulb break off in the socket? To remove the bulb, unplug the lamp or turn off the power at the service panel; press half a raw potato into the broken glass and turn it carefully. Or unscrew the socket using needle-nose pliers.

Revamping lamps

Missing the light?

If a lamp flickers or doesn't light, first replace the bulb with one that you know works. If that bulb fails to light properly, disconnect the lamp and inspect the plug and the cord. Look for bent or corroded prongs, a missing insulating disc, or cracks or fraying in the cord. If the plug or cord is damaged, replace it (see right). Check the socket for dirt. If it needs cleaning, wrap a piece of fine-grit sandpaper around your finger and scrape off the dirt. Also pry up slightly the metal tab at the bottom of the socket to make sure it can make contact with the bulb.

Switch to a crutch

The small round switches on many lamps can be hard to turn. Here's a way around the problem: Cut about ¼ inch off a No. 15 (⅜-inch-size) crutch tip. The tip will fit snugly over the switch and make it easier to grip.

Tip

Give it new life

Here's how to replace a cord inside a folding-arm lamp: Unplug the lamp and remove the bulb. Pull 4 inches of wire up through the channels to the top of the lamp. Unscrew the retaining ring with pliers. Pull the socket out of the sleeve; disconnect the cord and pull it out of the lamp head. Cut off the plug, hook the wire ends of the new cord to the old one, and tape the splice. Pull the cord at the elbow until the splice reaches it; then pull the cord through the upper channel until the splice exits. Undo the splice before feeding the new cord into the lamp head. Attach the wires to the terminal screws; make sure the ribbed or identified wire is connected to the silver terminal screw. Finally, reassemble the lamp and attach a polarized plug.

Old cord

Splice

Elbow

Bottom channel

Upper channel

Lamp head   Socket

Ring   New cord

What's in a plug

When replacing a plug on a lamp with exposed metal parts, use only a polarized plug. The wide prong of the plug must be connected to the ribbed or identified wire in the lamp cord. Not sure how to remove the old plug? Below is a selection of plugs that are taken apart in a variety of ways.

To remove the core and prongs in a polarized plug, push a narrow-bladed screwdriver through the wire hole on the opposite end.

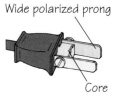

Wide polarized prong

Core

With these two plugs, remove the protective cover to reach the terminal screws. The wires in the top plug should be tied in an Under-writers knot (but on a three-prong model, the grounding wire stays out of the knot).

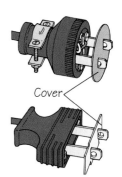

Cover

Remove the prongs by squeezing them together and pulling them out. Pull the prongs apart to access the wires.

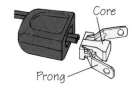

Core

Prong

To remove the wire ends, simply pull up the lever.

Lever

Remove the screw before pulling the two halves apart.

REPLACING A LIGHT FIXTURE

Of the many varieties of light fixtures, a double-bulb fixture that mounts to a ceiling box is one of the easier types to install. Even a more complicated light fixture can be installed without too much difficulty if you follow the manufacturer's directions.

First, at the circuit breaker panel or fuse box, shut off power to the circuit you'll be working on. When you take out the old fixture, you may find that it wasn't grounded. By adding the mounting strap, you'll have a place to secure the ground wire (which will probably be a bare wire). Make sure you use wire connectors of a size that corresponds to the wire size, which should be indicated on the package material. Check for the correct-wattage bulb or bulbs. A higher-wattage bulb can cause a fire.

1 Shut off power to the old fixture's circuit. To remove the fixture, loosen the mounting screws, then slightly twist and pull down on the fixture. Disconnect the fixture wires from the branch wires.

Mounting screw
Fixture wire
Branch wire

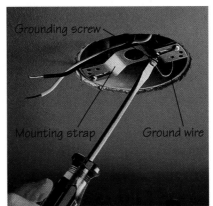

2 Secure the new fixture's mounting strap to the ceiling box. Once the strap is in place, fasten the ground wire, which should be inside the box, to the grounding screw.

Grounding screw
Mounting strap
Ground wire

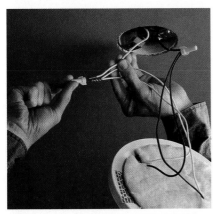

3 Connect the wires from the new fixture to the wires from the ceiling box. Use the wire connectors to join black (hot) wires or white (neutral) wires together.

4 Install the new mounting screw. Slide the keyhole slot in the new fixture base over the screw. Rotate the fixture until it locks in place; tighten the screw.

Keyhole mounting slot
Mounting screw

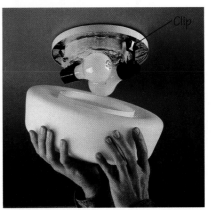

5 Screw in light bulbs of the proper wattage. Push the globe over the spring-loaded clips; the clips will securely hold the globe in position.

Clip

LOW-VOLTAGE AND FLUORESCENTS

Lines and chimes

No more staples or brads

Low-voltage wiring, such as telephone, thermostat, home security, and doorbell wires, can be secured to walls and ceilings (even concrete and cement blocks) with hot-melt glue. Simply run a bead about an inch long, and press the wire in place for a few seconds. Repeat the process every couple of feet.

Slip it through a straw

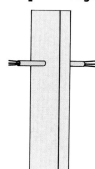

Fine low-voltage wires threaded through studs can get caught in rough drilled holes. Slip an ordinary drinking straw through each hole to guide the wires. Do the same when running low-voltage wires through a wall.

Low-voltage hideaways

A safe place to hide low-voltage wire is under wall-to-wall carpeting between the baseboard and the tack strip. Or hide it in a groove routed into the back of the baseboard (use masking tape to hold the wire in place while installing the baseboard). ▼

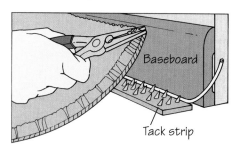

Baseboard

Tack strip

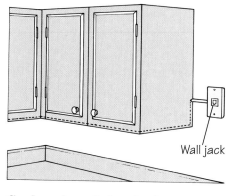

Wall jack

Cupboards and closets ▲

Low-voltage wires can be hidden by running them through closets or bathroom or kitchen cabinets. You can run them along the back of the cabinet or, for an invisible job, inside the front edge of the cabinet's face frame. Drill ¼-inch holes between cabinets where needed.

Can't hear the doorbell?

If the doorbell won't ring, remove the button cover and check for low voltage at the button. Sand the contacts; then pry them up. If it still won't ring, disconnect the wires and touch the ends together. If the bell rings, replace the button.

Ring those chimes

If the chimes or doorbell won't sound and the button is OK (see above), the plungers or clappers may be dirty. To clean the plungers in a mechanical chime unit or the clappers and gong in a doorbell, apply alcohol with a cotton swab. Do not clean electronic chimes.

TROUBLESHOOTING FLUORESCENT LIGHTS

If your fixture isn't working up to par, check below for the cure. Before replacing a tube, make sure it's of the correct wattage; check the ballast for the size.

PROBLEM	CAUSE	CURE
Light blinks on and off	Indicates a tube near the end of its life	Replace it with another tube. If this doesn't correct problem, shut power off; check for loose wires.
Tubes hard to start	Defective or old starter for starter-type fixture; bad ballast in rapid- or instant-start fixture	If starter has reset button, press it. Replace starter with one of equal rating (twist out old starter). Replace ballast with exact match. To remove it, shut off power; untwist nut connectors and screws.
Swirling or flickering light	A new tube or cold temperature	Leave new tube lighted for several hours to stabilize it. Install cold-rated tube in cold rooms.
Orange glow at tube ends	From end filaments, which heat gas	If they don't shut off after a few seconds, replace the starter.
Black tube ends	Tube nearing end of life	Replace the tube.
Loud humming	Fixture parts vibrating, or ballast shorting	Tighten all screws; wedge vibrating parts in place. Replace ballast.

PLUMBING BASICS

Before you start

License to plumb

You can do simple plumbing jobs, such as replacing a washer in a faucet or unclogging a sink, as the need arises, but you may need a permit or license for larger jobs, such as adding lines for a new bathroom. Check with your local municipality before attempting a big job.

Wired pipes

In many older homes the electrical system is grounded to a steel cold-water pipe. Before splicing plastic pipe into the line, make sure the line doesn't function as the conductor. If you do remove any grounding wires in the course of making a plumbing repair, reattach the ground wire to an appropriate conductor.

Sorting out your pipes

Home plumbing involves two systems: the water supply system and the drain-waste-vent (DWV) system. Water enters the house through a main service pipe; near the point of entry you may find a water meter and you should find the main shutoff valve. Inside the house the water travels under pressure through hot and cold supply pipes; attached air chambers cushion the pressure-driven water when a faucet or appliance is turned off. The larger DWV pipes carry used water and waste out of the house. Waste pipes carry water; soil pipes carry discharge from toilets. A trap at each fixture keeps foul air from seeping into the house. Vents allow sewer gas to escape, thus balancing the air pressure in the system and stopping the water in the traps from being siphoned out. ▶

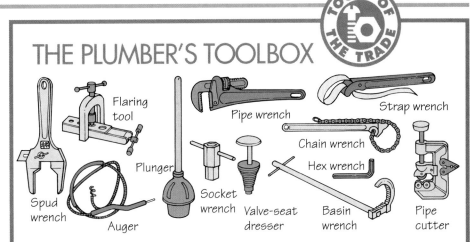

THE PLUMBER'S TOOLBOX

TOOLS OF THE TRADE

Flaring tool · Pipe wrench · Strap wrench · Chain wrench · Hex wrench · Plunger · Spud wrench · Auger · Socket wrench · Valve-seat dresser · Basin wrench · Pipe cutter

A hammer, chisels, and a hacksaw will supply many of your plumbing needs. Keep these additional tools on hand for specific jobs: You should have two pipe wrenches for working on pipes and a spud wrench for turning large nuts. Faucet repairs may require hex and socket wrenches, a basin wrench for reaching up under the sink, and a valve-seat dresser. Strap and chain wrenches can grip large-diameter pipes. An assortment of pipe cutters are handy for cutting copper, steel, and plastic pipes. A flaring tool helps to join flexible tubing. A plunger and an auger can help clear clogs. If you have rigid copper pipes, you will need soldering tools. Finally, keep on hand some pipe joint compound or pipe thread tape and plumber's putty.

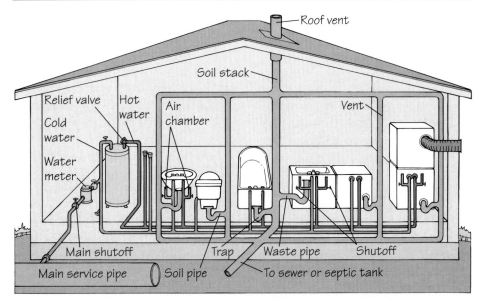

Roof vent · Soil stack · Relief valve · Hot water · Air chamber · Vent · Cold water · Water meter · Main shutoff · Main service pipe · Soil pipe · Trap · Waste pipe · Shutoff · To sewer or septic tank

PIPES

Metal pipes

Know your pipes

Because copper, brass, and galvanized pipes are rust-resistant, they are used for water lines. Nongalvanized black pipe is less expensive, but it rusts more readily and should be used only for gas lines. Threaded pipe is referred to by its inside dimension (i.d.); ½- and ¾-inch are the most common sizes.

Sizing the pipe

Before replacing threaded pipe or adding it to a line, be sure you have enough materials. When estimating the length of pipe you'll need, remember to allow for the overlap at joints; add ½ inch per threaded end for ½- to ¾-inch-diameter pipe; add ⅝ inch for 1- to 1½-inch pipe. ▼

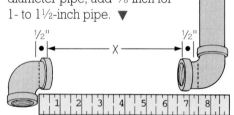

Strong grip

To remove or attach threaded pipe, hold the fitting in place with one pipe wrench; turn the pipe with another one. If it's a fitting that you want to attach or remove, reverse the order. Work carefully to avoid breaking other connections in the line.

Turning pipe wrench

Stationary pipe wrench

Say no to dope

Instead of old-fashioned pipe dope (joint compound), use thread sealant tape on threaded pipes. The tape helps seal the joint and it lubricates the pipe threads, making it easier to install and remove the pipe. To keep the tape from unwinding as you install the pipe, wrap it in the opposite direction of the pipe threads. Start the tape at the first thread, and wrap it around the threads three to four times. Be especially careful not to overtighten the pipe.

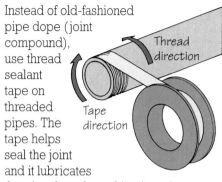

Thread direction

Tape direction

Fitting solution

You can't simply unscrew a section of pipe from the middle of your plumbing system. As you unscrew the joint on one end of the pipe, the joint on the opposite end will tighten. To repair a leak or add a T-fitting for a new fixture, you'll have to cut and remove a section of the pipe, and then reconstruct the section by installing two short pieces of pipe and a union—a fitting that lets you screw in a section of pipe without unscrewing its opposite end.

No more kinks

If you need to bend flexible copper tubing and you don't have a special tubing bender, block one end of the tubing with tape and fill it with dry sand. The sand will stop the tubing walls from kinking. Thoroughly wash out the sand before installing the tubing.

Bread stuffing

If every drop of water isn't removed from an existing copper water supply pipe, soldering a joint can be an exasperating job. As the torch heats the water, the water turns to steam and pushes the solder out of the joint. To avoid this, push a piece of soft white bread about 8 or 10 inches back into the pipe. The bread will absorb the water. When your solder joint is done, turn on the water and the bread will break up and disappear. ▼

Plastic pipes

It takes all types

Aren't sure which type of plastic pipe to use for a specific job? CPVC pipe is used as water supply pipe. While CPVC and PVC pipes have equal chemical resistance, CPVC pipe has better resistance to high water temperatures. PVC and ABS Schedule 40 plastic pipe are both used for drainage and vent systems. Look for these designated letters imprinted on a pipe to identify it. Make sure you use the same type of pipe throughout any plumbing project. Never cement together two different types of plastic pipe.

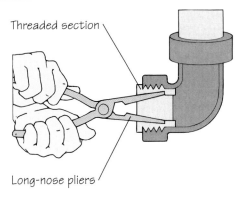

Threaded section

Long-nose pliers

Get the threads out ▲

Sometimes when you're unscrewing a plastic pipe, the threads stick in the joint and the pipe breaks off. To remove the threaded section, use a propane torch to heat the jaws of a long-nose pliers. Insert the pliers into the threaded section and slowly push the plier handles apart until the hot jaws make grooves in the plastic. Remove the pliers and let the plastic harden; then reinsert the pliers and twist them to unscrew the pipe.

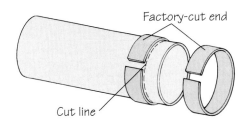

Factory-cut end

Cut line

On the mark ▲

This guide will help you make accurate handsaw cuts on PVC pipe. Cut a 1- to 1½-inch-wide piece from the factory-cut end of the pipe. Then cut a slit through it so you can slide it onto the pipe being cut. Use the factory-cut edge as the guide.

Pipe repairs

Leak control

Here are a few strictly temporary fixes to stop minor leaks: In a PVC drain fitting, tighten an automotive hose clamp around the hub of the fitting. For a small leak in a waste pipe, force a toothpick into the hole and break off the end. Then wrap three layers of duct tape around the leak, making sure you overlap each turn by half the width of the tape. For a stronger repair, secure a slit rubber hose around the pipe with several hose clamps or twisted wire. ▼

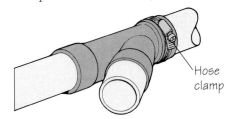

Hose clamp

Frozen solid

To thaw frozen water in a metal pipe (but not a plastic one), close the shutoff valve, open a faucet, wrap rags around the pipe, and pour boiling water over the rags. (Place a container under the pipe to catch the hot water.) Be sure to work from the faucet to the frozen area so that any pressure that builds up escapes through the open faucet instead of bursting the pipe. Repeat the process until the ice thaws.

If you're careful, you can heat the pipe with a hair dryer instead. You should keep the dryer moving and the pipe cool enough to touch. To help prevent the pipe from freezing again, install pipe insulation or wrap the pipe with strips of foil-faced fiberglass batts, foil side out, and secure the batts with duct tape. (Wear gloves when handling the fiberglass.)

An end to water hammer

Don't despair if a water pipe bangs when you shut off a faucet even though you have an air chamber to stop the banging (called water hammer). Sometimes the air dissipates and water fills the chamber. If you can't unscrew and drain the chamber to let air in, you can always drain the system. Turn off the water at the main valve, open the faucets in the highest and lowest parts of the line, and let all the water drain out. Close the faucets and turn on the water.

Drain line noise control

The best time to muffle the noise of drain lines inside the house is when you remodel. Wrap scraps of carpeting around the pipes and secure them with duct tape. In hard-to-reach areas, stuff the scraps around the pipe. Or slip a slit garden hose around a pipe to reduce vibrations between a strap and the pipe.

VALVES AND FAUCETS

Shutoff valves

Stuck stem

When a shutoff valve isn't used for a long time, the packing inside the packing nut can dry up or become corroded. Instead of forcing the valve and risking a leak, put a few drops of light oil around the stem near the packing nut. Loosen the nut about one turn, then retighten it by hand. After letting the packing absorb the oil for a few minutes, you should be able to turn the valve without a problem. ▼

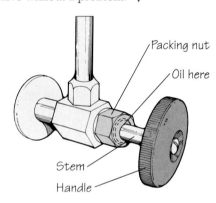

Packing nut
Oil here
Stem
Handle

The great valve search

In some houses a shutoff valve was not installed at each fixture. If this is the case in your home, you'll have to search for the nearest valve along the plumbing line whenever you need to turn off the water to make a repair. After making the repair and before turning the water on, install a shutoff valve near the fixture for future repairs. This involves cutting out a section of pipe with a tubing cutter or hacksaw and installing an inexpensive shutoff valve. Use a fitting at each end of the valve to join it to the pipe.

Faucets

Stubborn seat

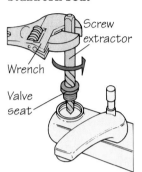

Screw extractor
Wrench
Valve seat

If you need to remove the valve seat from a faucet but the threads are worn, try this. Insert a screw extractor into the valve seat and gently tap it tight. With an adjustable wrench, turn the extractor counterclockwise, forcing it tighter into the seat. Alternately tap and turn the extractor. The seat will twist out.

Stem extractor

Is the cartridge in your single-handle tub faucet hard to remove? Drill a 1-inch hole into scrap plywood. Place the plywood against the wall with the hole over the stem. Starting with a washer large enough to cover the hole, slip a stack of progressively smaller washers onto the stem; add a snug-fitting nut. Insert a screw into the hole in the end of the stem. Turn the nut with a wrench to back out the stem; keep the screw from turning by holding it with a screwdriver. ▼

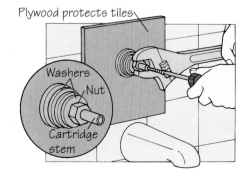

Plywood protects tiles
Washers
Nut
Cartridge stem

Keep the cold out

Hole in lid
Wear gloves
Fiberglass insulation
BUTTER

To keep an outdoor faucet from freezing in the winter, turn off the water supply. If there is no shutoff valve inside the house, cut a hole in the lid of an empty plastic butter or margarine tub. Place the lid over the faucet, and screw or tack it to the house siding. Wrap fiberglass pipe insulation loosely around the faucet, securing it with masking tape. Push the tub over the wrapped faucet and snap it onto the lid.

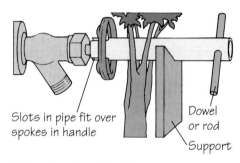

Slots in pipe fit over spokes in handle
Dowel or rod
Support

Extension handle ▲

Here's one way to reach a handle on an outdoor faucet that is blocked by shrubbery. In a ¾-inch pipe make slots on one end large enough to fit over the spokes in the faucet handle. At the other end drill a ⅜-inch hole through the pipe. Slide a metal rod or wooden dowel into the holes, and use it as a handle. If you need a support for this extended handle, make a V-notch in a piece of scrap wood, and drive the wood into the ground. Rest the pipe in the notch.

REPAIRING A CARTRIDGE FAUCET

You can repair a cartridge faucet by replacing worn parts. Home centers and hardware stores carry replacement kits for major faucet brands. Directions for installing one type are shown below, but because models vary, be sure to follow the installation directions on the kit.

The parts that wear out and need replacing are the cartridge and the O-rings. Drips from the spout or improper mixing of hot and cold water indicates a worn cartridge.

Leaks around the base of the spout indicate worn O-rings.

Before starting, turn off the shutoff valves on the hot- and cold-water pipes; open the faucet to drain it. Plug the drain so that parts can't fall down it, and protect the surface of the sink from scratches by lining it with a towel. Take apart the faucet, laying the parts in a row so that you'll know how to reassemble them. Replace the O-rings or the cartridge, as needed, and reassemble the faucet.

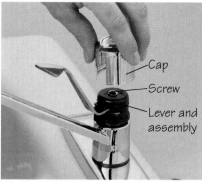

1 Pull off the cap to expose the handle screw. Remove the screw; then lift off the handle lever and handle assembly.

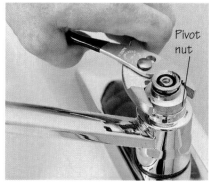

2 Unscrew the retainer pivot nut with pliers. Be careful not to scratch the body of the spout.

3 To remove the spout, swing it from side to side and lift it up at the base. If you have a sprayer, lift off the diverter.

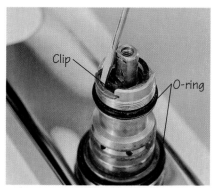

4 Pry off the retainer clip with a screwdriver. Set the clip aside for reinstalling later. Remove or replace the O-rings.

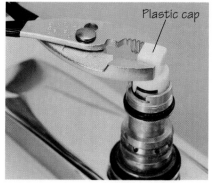

5 Place the plastic cap from the kit over the old cartridge, and twist it in both directions to release the cartridge.

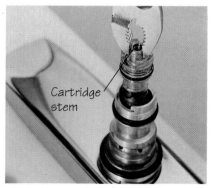

6 Pull up the stem with pliers to remove the cartridge. Remove debris inside the body before installing a new cartridge.

TUBS, SHOWERS, AND MORE FAUCETS

Tub and shower

A sneaky leak

If water seeps out from under your bathtub or shower stall, the tub or stall is not necessarily leaking. Water could be entering the wall around the faucet. Remove the faucet handles, escutcheons, and spout. Caulk around the openings in the wall; then replace the fittings. Also check the seam between the tiles and the tub or stall; recaulk it if necessary.

A quiet, warm tub

Before installing a new tub, attach fiberglass insulation to the bottom and sides of the tub with duct tape. This will reduce the level of noise when water fills the tub, and it will also keep the water warm for a longer period of time.

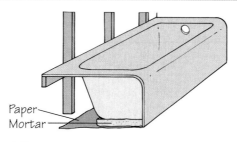

Paper
Mortar

A firm bottom ▲

When installed, some lightweight fiberglass tubs feel as though they are not capable of supporting you, even if you too are lightweight. Before installing one of these tubs, make a cradle so that the tub feels more solid. Staple building paper to the subfloor; then pour onto the paper just enough mortar or plaster for the tub to rest on, and install the tub. Not only will the tub feel solid, but the mortar or plaster will also help retain the heat of the water.

Bag it

You can clean a chrome-plated shower head that has become clogged with mineral deposits without taking it apart. Put some vinegar in a small plastic bag, then secure the bag around the shower head with duct tape or wire. Let the head soak overnight. Do not try this on brass or brass-plated fixtures.

Foam filler

Here's one way to solve the problem of loose pipe straps behind a shower wall. Pull the flange or escutcheon away from the wall (if a faucet is attached, remove its handle). Tape the pipe in position; then spray aerosol foam insulation into the wall cavity. Don't overfill the cavity or the foam may damage the wall when it expands. Once the foam is dry, it should be hard enough to securely hold the pipe.

On skids ▶

Bringing in a new bathtub (or taking out an old steel tub that can't be broken or cut up) takes muscle power. To make the job easier, slide two 2 x 4 boards under the tub. Then place two more 2 x 4's at the ends of the first two in the direction you plan to move the tub, butting the ends of the pairs together. With the aid of a helper, slide the tub from one pair of boards onto the other; then pick up the free pair and move them to the other end of the occupied boards. Repeat to continue moving the tub.

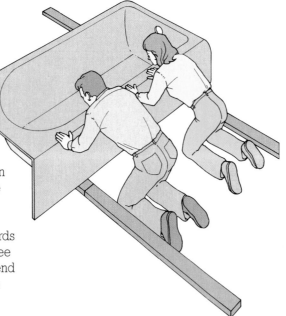

BALL FAUCETS

The ball-type faucet is easy to repair. If the spout drips, the rubber seats and springs are worn. If the spout base leaks, the O-rings are worn.

For any type of leak, disassemble the faucet and replace all the parts at once. They are available in a kit that includes a hex wrench and a special disassembly tool.

Begin the repair job by turning off the water shutoff valves and plugging the drain to keep dropped parts from falling in. Then disassemble the faucet as shown, replace the old parts, and reassemble the faucet in the opposite order you took it apart. There's only one trick to reassembly: Before you tighten the adjusting ring with the special tool, turn the water back on; then tighten the ring until no water leaks around the stem. Make sure you don't overtighten the cap or the adjusting ring; you should be able to easily move both the handle and the spout.

1 Loosen the setscrew with the hex wrench, and lift off the handle. The wrench is included in the replacement kit.

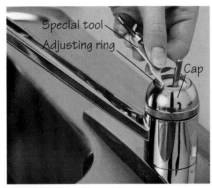

2 Release pressure on the ball by loosening the adjusting ring with the special tool. Unscrew and remove the cap.

3 Remove the ball assembly by grasping the protruding cam and lifting it up. Lay the pieces aside.

4 Gently lift out the rubber seats and springs, using a screwdriver. Install the replacement parts.

5 Work the spout off by swinging it back and forth while lifting it up from the base. It may be stubborn, but keep at it.

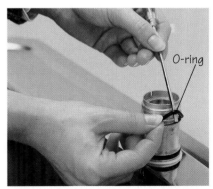

6 Replace the two O-rings. If necessary, cut them off with a utility knife. Clean all rubber debris from the faucet body.

TOILETS AND DRAINS

Toilet trouble

Hand-bag retriever

You can retrieve an item that your toddler dropped into the toilet without too much fuss. Just slip your hand into a plastic bag for protection. Grasp the item and pull it out of the toilet, then turn the bag inside out. The wet item will be in the bag and your hand will remain dry and clean. ▼

Detective work

If your toilet runs continuously, water is probably leaking out between the ball or flapper and the valve seat. To detect a leak, add a little food coloring to the water in the tank but don't flush it for a while. If the water in the bowl changes color, the valve is leaking. You can temporarily stop the leak by adjusting the lift chain or wire. And while you're doing so, check the tank ball or flapper. If it's cracked and dried, replace it.

Flush valve revival

You can sometimes revive an old ball or flapper by rubbing it with petroleum jelly or spraying it with a silicone spray. The rubber will become more supple, allowing the ball to seal the valve.

Nothing to flap about

A leak at the flush valve may be due to nothing more than the lift chain getting caught underneath the flapper or tank ball. To rectify the problem, cut a plastic drinking straw in half and feed the chain through it. The straw will stiffen the chain and keep it from being sucked under the flapper every time the toilet is flushed.

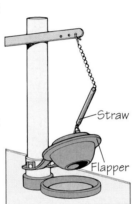

Straw

Flapper

Bottled water

If you want to save water when flushing your toilet, try this: Fill a 1-quart or ½-gallon bottle with water or sand (to weight it down) and seal it with a tight cap. Position the bottle inside the toilet tank where it won't interfere with the movement of the parts. With its bulk, the bottle will displace water that would normally flow into the tank. However, if the smaller amount of water doesn't remove all the waste, change the container to a smaller size to allow more water into the tank. If you ever replace the toilet, buy one that flushes on less than 2 gallons of water.

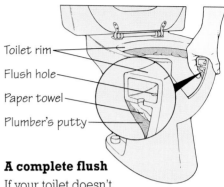

Toilet rim

Flush hole

Paper towel

Plumber's putty

A complete flush

If your toilet doesn't flush completely, the flush holes may be blocked by lime deposits. To remove them, turn off the water at the shutoff valve, flush the toilet, and soak up any remaining water in the tank. Place wet rolled-up paper towels under the rim, and hold them in place with plumber's putty. Wearing rubber gloves, pour lime remover into the flush valve under the flapper. Let it sit at least 8 (but preferably 24) hours. Don the gloves to remove and dispose of the putty and towels. Turn the water back on. To save money, you can substitute hydrogen peroxide for commercial delimer; it's safer and equally effective.

Jet lag

To remove deposit buildup at the siphon jet hole, unbend a metal clothes hanger and carefully scrape the deposits out of the hole without scratching the finish. ▼

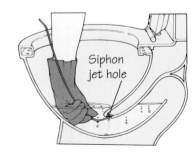

Siphon jet hole

Unblocking drains

Hot grease

The kitchen sink can become clogged by grease buildup in the drain. To keep the drain grease-free, every 2 weeks put a few tablespoons of baking soda into the drain. Fill the sink with hot water; then let it flow freely down the drain. If you suspect that grease is starting to clog your drain, try melting the grease by heating the trap with a hair dryer, then running hot water down the drain. But if grease has already clogged the drain, bail the water out of the sink, pour 1 cup each of baking soda and vinegar down the drain, and plug it with a strainer or rag. Let the mixture bubble for 20 minutes; then unplug the drain and flush out the debris with hot water.

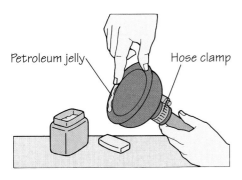

Petroleum jelly   Hose clamp

A better plunger ▲

Your plunger can become a more effective tool with the aid of a little petroleum jelly. Just smear some jelly around the edge of the suction cup. The jelly will create a better seal between the sink and the cup. If the handle on your plunger is loose and easy to pull out of the cup, use an automotive hose clamp to secure the cup to the handle.

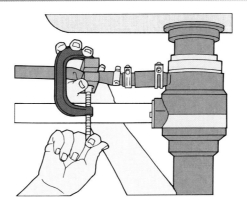

Seal all openings ▲

When unclogging a drain with a plunger, plug or seal the overflow opening in a washbasin or bathtub or the second drain in a double sink. This allows you to develop the necessary suction and pressure to free the clog. If your dishwasher is hooked up to the sink or garbage disposer waste line, seal the hose too by clamping it between two pieces of scrap wood.

Go fishing

If your bathtub drain is still hopelessly clogged after using a plunger, try dangling a three-prong fishhook on a piece of fishing line down the drain. If the clog hasn't gone beyond the trap, you might be able to hook it and pull it out.

Unclogging the toilet

You can see if the clog has just entered the drain in a toilet by placing a small mirror in the drain hole. Shine a flashlight on the mirror, and adjust the mirror until you have a view of the channel. If you can see the clog, try using an unbent clothes hanger to remove it. For a clog farther up the channel, use a closet auger (snake). If you're an experienced do-it-yourselfer, you can remove the toilet and snake it from the underside. But make sure you install a new wax ring when replacing the toilet. ▼

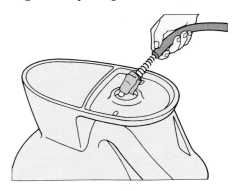

It's not really in the drain

Does the water still run out slowly, although you've tried to unclog the drain? Check the vent pipe on your roof. You may find a bird or squirrel nest perched right on top of the pipe. Remove the obstruction, and the water will drain efficiently.

Unpleasant odor

The trap under a drain or toilet is designed to hold water to block sewer gas from entering the room. If the fixture has not been used for several months, the water can evaporate, letting the gas escape. To get rid of the odious odor, pour water into the drain to fill the trap.

WATER HEATERS AND SUMP PUMPS

Getting hotter water

Noisy deposits

Mineral deposits in the water settle to the bottom of a water heater. Deposit buildup can create rumbling noises, decrease the amount of heat that reaches the water, and reduce the storage capacity of the unit. To remove these harmful deposits, turn off the gas or electricity and close the cold-water inlet valve to the tank. Open an upstairs hot-water faucet. Then attach a garden hose to the drain valve at the bottom of the tank, and drain the water through the hose into a floor drain or sink or to a safe place outside the house. (This may take hours.) Once the tank is drained, reopen the cold-water valve and run water through the tank until it drains clear. Finally, close the drain valve and upstairs faucet and restart the heater.

Before the buildup

To keep mineral deposits from building up, periodically flush them from the drain valve through a garden hose or into a pan. If you have soft water, drain about 3 quarts of water two to four times a year. For water with a high mineral concentration, drain water monthly. ▼

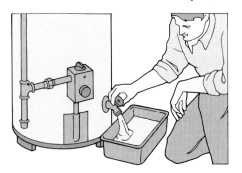

Lukewarm ▶

If you have a water heater with a plastic cold-water fill pipe and the heater isn't producing hot enough water, the fill pipe may have broken near the top of the tank. This lets the entering cold water mix with hot water near the top of the tank. To replace the pipe, turn off the gas or electricity and the water to the heater. Unthread the fitting, replace the pipe, and screw the fitting back in place. If the ceiling is too low to maneuver the pipe into the tank, disconnect the hot- and cold-water pipes; tip the tank over. (If necessary leave the broken pipe in the tank.)

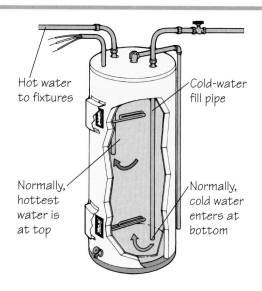

Hot water to fixtures

Cold-water fill pipe

Normally, hottest water is at top

Normally, cold water enters at bottom

Under wraps ▲

A water heater that feels hot when you touch it is losing heat. If it doesn't void your warranty, keep the escaping heat under wraps by covering the tank with an insulating fiberglass blanket, which is available in a kit at home centers. Special tape comes with the blanket to hold it in place. On a gas unit, be careful not to cover the top of the tank or to block the airflow to the burner at the bottom.

Waiting for hot water

When a plumbing fixture, such as a bathroom sink, is far from the water heater, a lot of standing water must run through the pipe before hot water reaches it. To conserve water, you might consider installing either a small (2- to 10-gallon) or a tankless "instant" water heater. If you place one of these separate auxiliary heaters near the fixture (such as under the sink), you'll get hot water right away without first running the water. For the unit to operate, you may have to install a high-amperage electrical circuit; other models operate on gas.

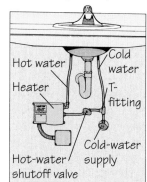

Hot water Heater

Cold water

T-fitting

Cold-water supply

Hot-water shutoff valve

Conserving energy

If you want to conserve energy and lower your electric bill, install a thermostat that turns the water heater off at night when you aren't using it, and back on in the morning in time to provide hot water for the earliest risers. But if you're going to be away for more than a day or so, it's best to turn the heater off at the circuit breaker or fuse box.

Leak test

Sometimes it's hard to tell whether a puddle of water on the floor indicates a leak in the water heater's tank or merely dripping due to condensation. Here's an easy test: Wearing gloves to keep from burning your hands, attach a small piece of glass to the underside of the tank with duct tape or another tacky tape—leave some of the glass exposed. After a few hours, remove the glass. If its exterior is wet, the moisture is from condensation, not a leaking tank.

Sump pumps

Sump alarm

To alert your family to possible floods in the basement, place a small inexpensive battery-operated alarm on the floor near your sump pump (or water heater). The device will sound a loud alarm if its sensor gets wet.

Free-floating

If your sump pump has an exterior float, the float may occasionally get stuck. If it does, simply apply a little petroleum jelly to the rod that holds it, and it'll move freely again.

Muck-free bucket

Bucket
Sump pump
Caulk
Screen

If debris clogs the intake of your sump pump, use nylon screen fabric, caulk, and a 5-gallon plastic bucket to create a filter. An empty wallboard compound container from a building site will do the job nicely. Cut holes near the bottom of the bucket with a utility knife, and adhere the screen fabric over the holes, using silicone caulk. Then, disconnect the pump, set the bucket inside the sump, and reconnect the pump inside the bucket.

Cover up

You can prevent objects from falling into the sump by making a cover for it. Use a piece of ¾-inch plywood large enough to cover the hole. Make a notch in the plywood to accommodate the pipe and pump. To allow water to drain under the cover, screw or nail ¾-inch scrap wood blocks to the bottom of each corner of the plywood.

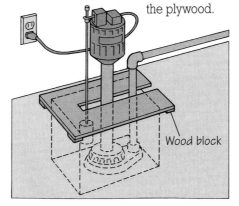

Wood block

Draining the house

During freezing weather, you should take the following precautions if you have an extended power outage or if you're planning to leave your house for a prolonged period of time.

▷ Turn off the water supply at the main shutoff valve.

▷ Shut off the furnace and the current or gas to the water heater.

▷ Flush all the toilets, and empty the bowls with a siphon or by bailing them out and sponging up excess water.

▷ Open every faucet in the house, including the outdoor faucets.

▷ Drain the water heater (facing page).

▷ If you have hot-water heating, open all the radiator valves and remove the air-escape valve from one or more radiators on the highest floor in the house. Then drain the boiler. After the heating system is empty, open the drain valve on the main supply line. If no such valve exists, determine the lowest point in your system and disconnect a fitting from it, allowing any remaining water to run out.

▷ If your water is from a well, drain both the aboveground pump lines and the tank. Switch the pump off and drain it.

▷ Pour a mixture of antifreeze and water into all toilet bowls and into the trap of every sink, washbasin, shower stall, bathtub, and floor drain. Prepare the antifreeze for the lowest temperature expected in your area. (Be sure to keep children and pets away from it.) Another option is to use automotive window-washing fluid. It's cheap, relatively environmentally safe, and won't disrupt the bacterial action in a septic system.

THERMOSTATS

Temperature control

No, you don't have a fever

Does the room feel hotter or cooler than the reading displayed on the thermostat? The thermostat might be affected by strong lights shining on it, a nearby heat-generating appliance, such as a television, or a breeze from a fan or an exterior door. If you can't move the culprit, adjust (or move) the thermostat.

From the abyss

Here's another reason that a thermostat may allow more heat or cool air into a room than what it is set for: The hole in the wall where wires run through to the thermostat may be channeling cold or hot air into the thermostat. To see if this is the case, take off the cover by snapping it off the body or by removing the screws and lifting it off. If you feel air from the hole, fill it with caulking compound or insulation.

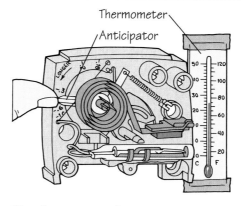

Thermometer
Anticipator

Numbers game ▲

A thermostat may still not operate properly after a tune-up. To test the thermostat, tape an accurate thermometer next to it. After 5 minutes compare the readings. If they are different, adjust the anticipator: Remove the thermostat cover and nudge the anticipator a tiny distance up or down. (Because models vary, check the instructions for your thermostat.) You should notice a change in temperature in a few hours; otherwise, replace the thermostat.

Jump start

After determining that a blown fuse or tripped circuit breaker isn't causing a heating system failure, check for a faulty low-voltage thermostat. Make a jumper wire by stripping ½ inch of insulation off each end of a wire; attach alligator clips to the ends. With the power on, hold the jumper at the insulation and place one clip on the red terminal, the other clip on the white terminal. If the heat comes on, you have a faulty thermostat; replace it. To keep the heat on until you can replace the thermostat, turn off the power at the service panel, attach the clips to the terminals, and turn the power back on. To control the temperature, periodically turn the power off and remove or replace the clips.

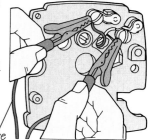

Jumper wire

Tune-up time ▶

If you have an old-fashioned thermostat and the temperature in your home swings erratically, it's time for a tune-up. First turn off the power at the service panel; then snap off or unscrew the thermostat's cover. Remove any debris and clean the contacts. The cleaning method will depend on the style of the thermostat. On some models, you will have to remove the body to reach the contacts. To make sure the thermostat is level, set a level on top of the unit. (Round thermostats have ears to support the level; they're visible with the body off.)

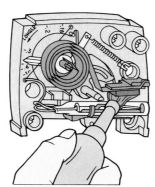

Dislodge any dust and debris by brushing it off with a clean soft brush. A photographer's brush has a bulb for blowing air to remove the dust.

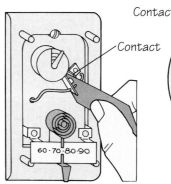

For one style of thermostat, turn it to the lowest setting; then run a clean piece of thick paper between the contacts to remove debris.

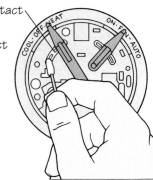

Contact

Contact

On some round thermostats, remove the body to reach the contacts; wipe them with a cotton swab dipped in a 50-50 vinegar-water solution.

PROGRAMMABLE THERMOSTAT

Unless your home is heated by a heat pump, you can reduce your energy bill by replacing your old thermostat with a programmable model. It can be set to lower the heat at night when you're asleep and during the day when you're not home. And it will turn the heat up for a warm welcome in the morning or when you arrive home after a day at work.

Choose a thermostat with features compatible to your needs and lifestyle. More features than needed may be confusing and can reduce efficiency. Check for system compatibility, cycles per day, schedules per week, manual and vacation override, and the ease of programming.

You can install most thermostats in about an hour. You'll need just a few tools: a screwdriver, drill, level, and wire strippers. Because the wiring is low-voltage, installation is a safe procedure. Before starting the installation, turn off the power at the heating or cooling system and at the service panel. After the unit is installed and programmed, check its operation. If you're having trouble, look in the owner's manual for a troubleshooting section or a hot-line phone number.

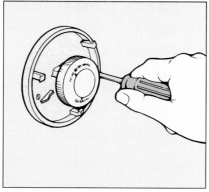

1 Turn off power to heating/cooling system. Unscrew or snap off cover of old thermostat. If necessary, unscrew body. Label the wire locations; disconnect them.

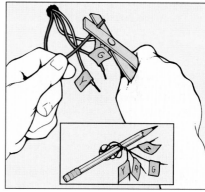

2 Strip 3/8 in. insulation from wire ends; clean corroded ends with steel wool. (You can wrap the wires around a pencil to keep them from falling into the cavity.)

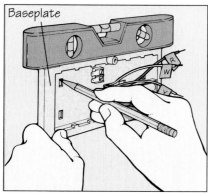

3 Slip wires through baseplate of new unit. Position plate, level it, and mark placement of screws. Remove plate; drill holes. Insert anchors; screw on plate.

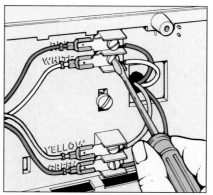

4 Attach the wires to the new thermostat, following the manufacturer's directions. Push the excess length of wire back through the hole in the wall.

5 Install batteries if needed. Snap the front cover in place, turn the power on, and program the unit.

HEAT DELIVERY

Radiators/convectors

Clean heat

Whether your system delivers heat by means of radiators or convectors, dust and dirt buildup can inhibit its distribution. If the unit is hot but the room is cold, dirt buildup may be the cause. Clean the radiators or convectors every few months. Start by turning off the heat, removing any covers, and letting the units cool. Then vacuum the units, using a crevice tool attachment, and wipe them clean with a damp cloth. Use needle-nose pliers to straighten any bent fins in a convector. For more efficient heat distribution, do not paint the units and avoid blocking them with furniture or draperies.

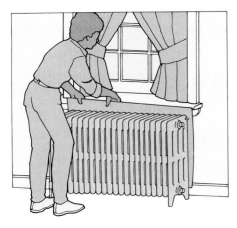

Reflections ▲

You can increase the efficiency of your radiator by sliding a reflector behind it. Make the reflector by covering one face of a sheet of insulation board or corrugated cardboard with aluminum foil. The reflector will bounce heat away from the wall and toward the room.

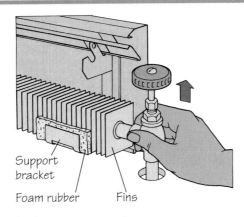

Support bracket

Foam rubber   Fins

Noisy convector ▲

When pipes and convector fins contract and expand with changing temperatures, they can emit a noise as they rub against brackets. To reduce or eliminate these noises, while the unit is cold, slip a foam-rubber pad between the pipe or fins and the support brackets. To avoid putting strain on pipe joints, make sure you raise the pipe or fins gently.

Hot air ware

Do you feel that your automatic air vent may not be working? After letting the unit cool and closing the valve to the radiator or convector, unscrew the vent. Try to loosen any debris by gently shaking the vent and tapping it on a hard surface. Test the vent by blowing through it when it is upright, then when it is upside-down. If air goes through in the upright but not the upside-down position, the vent is OK. Otherwise, try soaking it in distilled vinegar for 30 minutes. If the vent still doesn't pass the test, replace it.

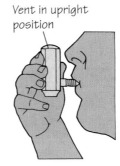

Vent in upright position

New directions

You can protect paint or wallpaper from discoloration by placing a shelf above the radiator or convector. It will also increase efficiency by directing the heat into the room.

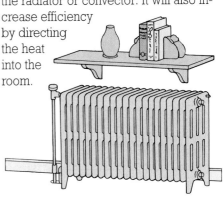

Tot control

To protect children from a hot radiator, put a reflector behind the unit and then build a cover around the radiator. Use particleboard or a veneer plywood, and finish it with paint or plastic laminate. To allow air circulation, flow of heat, and access to the radiator, make openings in the front and top of the cover; enclose a metal air register in the top, and install slats or louver doors in a panel on the front of the unit. Hold the panel in place with catches. You can apply decorative molding to the edges of the cover or incorporate it into a cabinet. ▼

Steam units

Hard knocks

If your steam radiator is linked to the heating system by only one pipe, it can make a knocking noise if the water doesn't drain back to the pipe. Use a level to check the slant of the unit. If it doesn't show a slant down toward the valve, raise the end of the unit opposite the valve by turning the height-adjusting bolts in the legs with a wrench. If your radiator has no adjusting bolts, slip shims under the legs. ▼

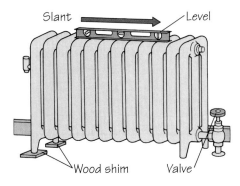

Hard knocks: the sequel

Another cause of knocking in a steam system is a partially open valve, which allows steam and water to mix. The valve should be either fully opened or fully closed. To be sure that all the water and steam have left the unit, close a valve only when the radiator is cold.

Too hot for comfort

Now that you know you can't open a steam valve partway, what should you do if the room is too hot? Block the radiator with furniture. If it is a nonelectrical unit, closely cover the top and sides with corrugated cardboard.

CAN YOUR HOUSE BREATHE?

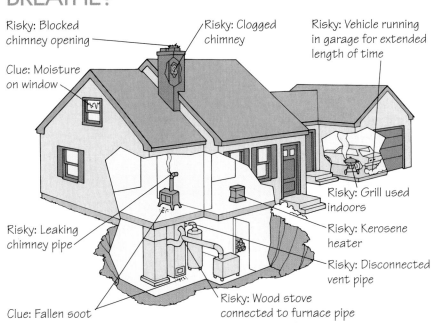

In the pursuit of energy efficiency, a house can be made too tight for your health. With added insulation and sealing, less fresh air enters and carbon monoxide builds up.

Colorless and odorless, carbon monoxide can fatally deprive your body of oxygen. If you have flulike symptoms that disappear when you leave your home, suspect carbon monoxide poisoning. Other clues to carbon monoxide buildup include persistently stuffy stale air; high humidity that shows up as moisture on windows; soot around the outside of the fireplace, furnace, or chimney; a hot draft from the chimney or none at all; and the smell of fumes.

To ensure you won't have a problem, have the chimney cleaned each fall and check for birds' nests; have your heating system checked annually; and make sure that the water heater is properly vented. If you remodel your home, have the utility company check the carbon monoxide level to ensure proper airflow, especially if the furnace is enclosed. Never use a charcoal grill, an unvented gas heater, an LP gas lamp, or a gasoline lantern indoors. Avoid using kerosene heaters. Never heat a room with an oven. Install a carbon monoxide detector to warn you of buildup. To test for buildup, see p.229.

HEAT DELIVERY

The warm-air furnace

Oil trap

Whenever you replace the filter in your furnace, give it a light spray of baby oil from a small plastic bottle. It'll work wonders by trapping smaller dust particles and keeping them out of the house. The oil will also emit a pleasant aroma.

Another dust collector

You can reduce the amount of dust circulating in your house by supplementing the furnace filter with homemade duct filters. Fold pieces of cheesecloth to form pads the size of your duct grilles. Attach the pads of cloth to the backs of the grilles with rubber bands, and say goodbye to the dust. Take the pads out and hand-wash them when they get soiled.

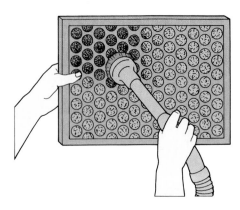

Out of stock ▲

If you get caught short on disposable filters, you can recycle an old one to keep the furnace running. Simply remove the dirty filter and vacuum it with the brush attachment. Then hold it up to a bright light. If you can see the light through it, reinstall it, following the airflow arrows.

Pinpoint oiling

When you go to oil the blower motor on your furnace, you may find—to your disgust—that the tip of the extension-type oil container is too thick to fit into the small oil fitting on the motor. Don't give up. With a little finagling, you can make it fit. Cut off the wide end of a basketball inflation needle with a hacksaw, and insert the cut end of the narrow section into the plastic tube of the container. If it's loose, wrap a twist tie around the assembly.

Drip, drip, drip

Even if the oil container tip is narrow enough to fit, the oil holes in a furnace blower or blower motor can be very hard to reach. However, there's no need to get the oil container right to the hole. Just insert a thin wire into the oil hole so that the wire is more or less vertical. Then drip the oil onto the wire; the oil will run into the hole. ▼

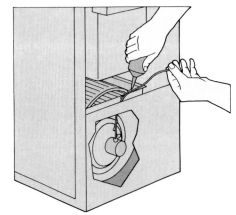

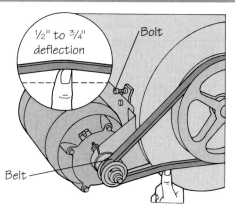

A stiff belt ▲

Once a year shut off the power to the furnace at the service panel and check the fan belt on the blower to see if it's frayed or stiff. If it is, replace it. To check the belt tension, press on it. If it doesn't deflect by ½ to ¾ inch, tighten or loosen the adjustment bolt to set the belt at the right tension.

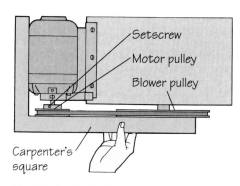

Get it straight ▲

A blower or motor pulley that's out of alignment may cause belt wear. To determine proper alignment, turn off the power to the furnace at the service panel and set a square against the outer faces of the pulleys. If the two pulleys aren't in line, loosen the motor pulley's setscrew with a hex wrench; move the pulley back or forward as needed.

What a bolt

Misaligned pulleys are not the only reason a belt becomes worn. Loose mounting bolts on the motor can allow the motor itself to move out of alignment, thus causing wear. Before checking the motor and blower pulleys for misalignment (see facing page), tighten any loose mounting bolts.

Speed limit

If your blower runs too fast, it will make a lot of noise, but if it runs too slowly, it won't deliver enough heat. If you have an adjustable motor pulley, you can change the blower speed (while the blower is not operating). First loosen the setscrew on the motor pulley with a hex wrench. Then, to increase the speed, turn the outer face of the pulley clockwise, bringing it closer to the motor. To decrease the speed, turn the outer face counterclockwise. Retighten the setscrew; then adjust the pulley alignment and belt tension (see facing page). ▼

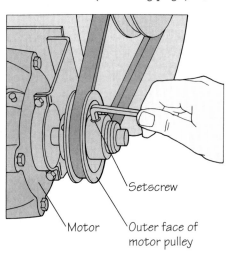

Motor — Setscrew — Outer face of motor pulley

Ducts and plenums

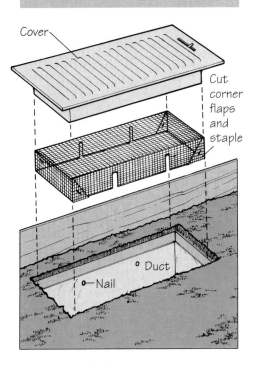

Cover
Cut corner flaps and staple
Duct
Nail

Screening the duct ▲

Small objects (such as that one missing piece from a complicated jigsaw puzzle) can fall down into never-never land through the grates of duct covers in the floor. You can eliminate this possibility by making a guard with fine-mesh wire screen (such as window screening). Cut and fold the screen to form a shallow box that will fit over the top of the duct, and staple the corners. Then cut slots to go around the nails that hold the duct to the flooring. To allow room for the guard, pry the duct slightly away from the flooring edges, and slip the guard in place. Finally, replace the cover, which should sit over the guard.

Duct inspection

To keep your duct system in tiptop shape, once a year feel for escaping air at joints on the furnace, plenums, and ducts while the fan is blowing. If you find any small holes or cracks, cover them with duct tape. Fill larger holes with caulking before taping them. Replace loose or cracked tape. For a permanent seal, wrap joints with 3-inch-wide fiberglass insulation facing tape and paint the tape with a water-base duct sealant. (You can buy them at an air-conditioning supply outlet.) You should also secure any loose ducts with sheet-metal screws. If you find a loose support, tighten it. Finally, add new supports at sagging sections. ▼

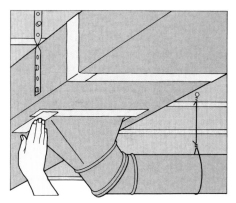

Finding soot

Does it seem that less heat is coming through the duct than should be? Soot or dirt might be restricting the heat flow. To find out, try this test: With the heat on, carefully feel along the top and then the bottom of the duct. If the bottom is cooler, you'll know that dirt has collected there. Disassemble the duct and clean it out.

BURNERS

Oil burner

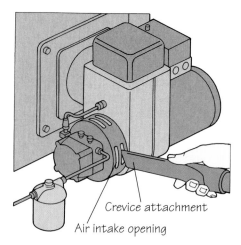

Crevice attachment
Air intake opening

Clean machine ▲

Because dust, animal hair, and dirt can clog the burner, keep it clean by periodically vacuuming the air intake openings, using the crevice attachment.

Draft dodging

If you smell oil, the draft regulator on the pipe to the chimney may be wide open. With the burner running, the regulator should tip open about 1 to 2 inches. (If the burner is off, the regulator should be closed.) If the regulator doesn't tip open the right amount, adjust it by turning the counterweight on the flap. Keep readjusting it until you get it right. ▼

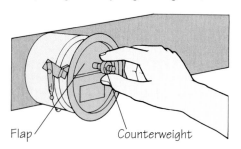

Flap
Counterweight

Flue blues

The flue, or exhaust vent or stack, transports combustion by-products from the burner to the outdoor air. After long-term use, the flue can become corroded and need replacing. To check for corrosion, try this test: When the flue is cool, tap it in several spots. A good flue will emit a metallic ringing. If you hear a dull sound instead, press the flue in. If it doesn't spring right back, replace it.

Sputter, sputter . . .

If your oil burner sputters on and off, it could be because the oil filter on the supply line is dirty. To replace the filter, first turn the burner off; place a pan under the filter to catch any spills. Then unbolt the container lid. Put in a new filter, or soak the old one in a solvent. Use the same type of solvent to clean the container. If you find that the gasket is worn, replace it. ▼

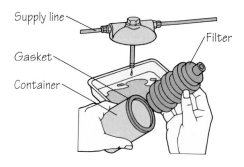

Supply line
Gasket
Container
Filter

Troubling signs

Call in a service person if you see black smoke rising from the chimney, if the burner flame is a dark orange or sooty instead of a bright yellow with an orange tip, or if the oil bill rises unexpectedly.

Gas burner

Summertime

If your warm-air furnace uses the same ducts as your central air conditioning, and it has a pilot light, douse the pilot light for the summer. The flame, though small, can heat the cooled air as it passes through the system. It can also create water vapor that can rust the inside of the furnace. But if your system doesn't include air conditioning, keep the pilot lit. It will keep humid summer air from condensing in the furnace.

Finger saver 1

Want to save your fingers from burns when lighting the pilot light for your furnace or boiler—or for your water heater or stove? Extend your reach by taping or crimping an alligator clip onto the end of an old telescoping radio or TV antenna.

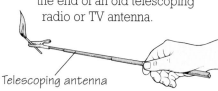

Telescoping antenna

Finger savers 2 and 2½

If you don't have an old antenna at hand, a wire clothes hanger can be turned into a match holder. Straighten the hanger. Then slide a spring from a click ballpoint pen partway onto the end of the hanger; insert a match into the spring. Or bend one end of the wire into a circle just large enough to hold a match. Then bend the same end once more to a 90° angle.

Clothes hanger

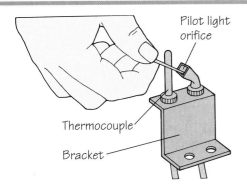

Pilot light orifice

Thermocouple

Bracket

Incorrigible pilot ▲

A pilot that won't light may have a clogged orifice. To clean it, turn off the main gas shutoff valve and electrical switch and wait for the burner to cool down—about 30 minutes. Then remove the access panel and unscrew the bracket that holds the pilot. Carefully clean out the orifice with a pin or needle, and remove debris from the edges with a cotton swab or toothbrush. After reinstalling the pilot, turn the main shutoff valve and electrical switch back on. If the pilot still won't light, replace the thermocouple. Most models are held on a bracket or inside a housing.

Tank gauge

On a warm day, try measuring the approximate amount of liquid propane gas in a tank by passing a wet sponge down the length of the tank. The streak of water left by the sponge will evaporate quicker on the empty portion of the tank than it will on the filled portion.

Making bubbles

Check gas line joints and fittings for leaks by brushing them with liquid dish or laundry detergent thinned with water. If the detergent bubbles, there's a leak.

BACK DRAFT

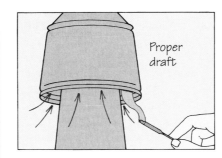

Proper draft

Back draft

If there isn't enough fresh air inside your home, it will be pulled in through the draft hood for the gas burner or the fireplace chimney. Known as back drafting, this reverses the draft hood's or chimney's siphoning effect; deadly carbon monoxide from a burner or water heater stays in the house instead of going up the flue or chimney.

To determine if your home has enough fresh air, close all the doors, windows, and fireplace dampers. Turn on all the exhaust fans, including the ones in the kitchen, bathroom, attic, and on the clothes dryer. Then turn on all your vented gas appliances, such as the gas burner and water heater, and wait 10 minutes for the drafts to stabilize. Hold a lighted wood match or incense stick below the air intake on the burner draft hood. If the smoke is pulled up to the hood, you have sufficient fresh air. If the match flame goes out, or if the incense smoke is blown away from the hood, back drafting exists; call your local utility for help. Repeat the test on a gas water heater.

If you smell gas

Normally, home gas is very safe. But if you smell a strong odor of gas, get out of the house right away—don't hesitate! Call for help from a neighbor's house. Here's what you should do if you smell a faint odor of gas (if you can't decide if the odor is weak or strong, the smart thing to do is to leave right away):
▷ Open windows and doors.
▷ Extinguish all open flames, including pilot lights in the water heater, furnace, boiler, and stove—on the stove, make sure you extinguish both the pilot for the top of the range and the one for the oven.
▷ Do not light a match or smoke.
▷ Do not use the phone, switch on the lights, or turn on any electrical appliance. Sparks in electrical units can ignite the gas.
▷ Immediately call your gas supplier from a neighbor's phone. If you can't reach them, call the fire department.

HOME COOLING DEVICES

Creating a breeze

Window trick

If the air is cooler outside than in, you can bring the cool air into your house. Because hot air rises, open upstairs or attic windows to let it out, and open downstairs windows to let in the cool air. However, if it's hotter outside than inside, be sure to tightly seal up the house by closing doors and windows and by pulling down shades and blinds.

The whole house

If you have a whole-house fan, you can put it to efficient use. While running it, open only the windows and doors of the rooms you most want cooled. But open at least one window or door before using the fan; otherwise, you'll create a harmful vacuum. If a gas appliance pilot light goes out, especially on a water heater, open up more windows. To prevent warm air from escaping through the fan in the winter, cover the fan opening by taping an insulation board or a plastic polycarbonate panel over it.

In the shade

Even if your house is superinsulated, you can benefit from a deciduous broad-leaf tree if it's by a window. The tree will keep hot sunlight from entering the window in the summer, and after the leaves fall, sunlight can pass through and heat the room in the winter. If you're planting trees for future shade, plant them on the east and west sides of the house, where the summer sun hits the windows the hardest. For an immediate way to shade a window, add an awning, porch roof, trellis, or arbor, or install an outside shade or indoor blind. ▼

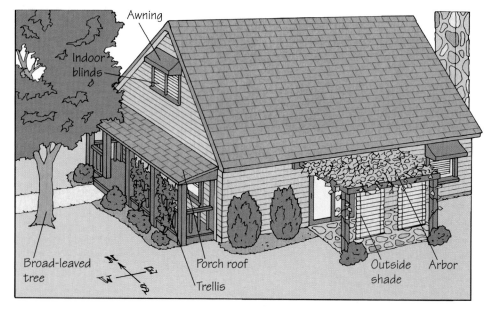

Awning

Indoor blinds

Broad-leaved tree

Porch roof

Trellis

Outside shade

Arbor

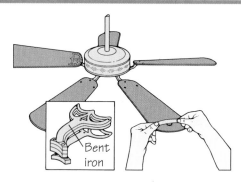

Bent iron

Vibrating ceiling fan ▲

Follow this troubleshooting checklist to discover why a ceiling fan is vibrating—and to stop the annoying vibration.

▷ Clean the blades. Accumulated dirt can throw the fan off balance.

▷ Check for loose screws on the blades.

▷ One or more blades might be warped. Remove the blades, and lay them on a flat surface. They should lie flat. If a blade is warped, replace the entire set. (Blades are matched as a set by the manufacturer.)

▷ Examine the blade irons for defects. The irons are set at the factory at a 12° angle. Stack the irons on top of one another. If you find one that doesn't match the others, replace the defective iron.

▷ Check the fan motor. With the blades and irons removed, turn the fan on to the fastest setting. It shouldn't wobble. If it does, send the motor in for repair. Look in your owner's manual for the closest authorized center.

▷ If you still haven't found the problem, balance the blades on the reassembled fan by attaching small weights to the tops of the out-of-balance blades. Using washers or coins as weights, temporarily attach them to the blades with tape. Once the blades are balanced, glue the weights in place. For a four-bladed fan, balance two opposite blades at a time.

Room air conditioners

For the best cooling

Because cold air falls, the higher a room air-conditioning unit is placed, the better it can cool a room. Install the unit in the wall that gets the least amount of direct sunlight—usually the northern wall. But if you'd like to place the unit where the sun is normally strongest, consider if there is an obstruction blocking it. For example, a tree or a building may block the sun from a southern wall.

Filter reminder

During the air-conditioning season, clean the filter weekly or, depending on the type of air-conditioning unit you have and the filter it uses, clean or replace the filter monthly. To jog your memory, note with a grease pencil the date you should attend to the filter on the unit's control panel. Each time you adjust the unit, you'll see the reminder.

Bending fins

Bent condenser and evaporator fins in room units can obstruct the efficient flow of air. If you remove the front panel and filter, you can then straighten the fins with a plastic spatula or with a small section cut from a pocket comb. ▼

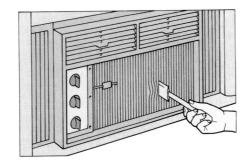

Cold-weather care

Covering the exterior of a window air conditioner with a sheet of plastic does more than reduce cold drafts on windy winter days. It also serves to keep the condenser coil and fan clean. Make sure you remove the plastic in the spring—before the hot weather comes.

Musty-smelling conditioner

A clogged drain hole under the barrier between the evaporator and the compressor, or in the channel under the evaporator, may emit a musty smell. To clean the hole, unscrew and remove the front panel. On some models you may have to pull the chassis out partway. Clean the hole with a bent wire hanger, or flush the channel with a water-filled bulb baster.

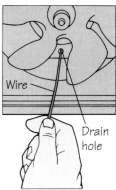

Wire

Drain hole

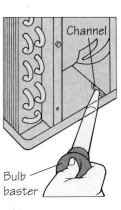

Channel

Bulb baster

Too much racket? ▶

The racket created by a window air conditioner can occur because of several reasons. By following the steps given here, you can soon run your unit with less noise. *Note:* To reach the fan on some models, you have to remove the chassis completely from the housing.

Sash

Shim

1. With the unit running, press your hand on the window sashes. If the noise stops, insert small wood shims between the sash and the frame. If the glass rattles, reputty it; as a temporary fix, stick cellophane tape tightly between the edge of the glass and the frame.

Front panel

2. Press in on the front panel. If the unit's noise ceases or if the pitch changes, tighten any loose panel fasteners. If the panel won't fit snugly and quietly against the cabinet, secure it to the cabinet with duct tape.

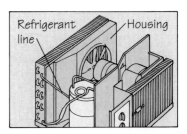

Refrigerant line

Housing

3. Unplug the unit. Slide the chassis partially out of the housing; rest one end on a stool. Spin the fan blades. If a blade hits the cage, bend it slightly for clearance. Jiggle the chassis; if the refrigerant line hits the fan's housing, gently bend it away from the housing.

HOUSEHOLD REPAIRS

REPAIRING FURNITURE

Drawers

No-turn knobs

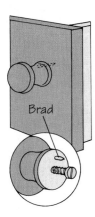

To anchor a wood knob on a drawer, drill a hole in the base of the knob. Clip a small brad in half, and insert the lower half in the hole with the point facing out. When you screw the knob on, the point will bite into the wood, keeping the knob from turning.

Dry out a balky drawer

Drawers often stick simply because humidity has swelled the wood. When a drawer sticks, take it out and dry it in a warm place. After a couple of days, test it for fit and sand or plane any areas that still stick. Then seal all wood surfaces with a coat of clear polyurethane to retard future moisture absorption.

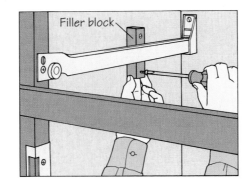

Filler block

Staying on track ▲

On kitchen cabinets, metal drawer slides often bow to the side with use, letting the rollers on the drawer slip out of the track. To fix this, mount a block of scrap wood on the side of the cabinet to hold the track parallel to the drawer.

Smooth sliding

A quick way to improve the action of a drawer on wood runners is to remove the drawer and spray the runners with aerosol furniture polish. The wax in the polish will reduce the friction.

Sand 'n' wax

Here's another way to help a wood drawer slide more smoothly: Lightly sand the bottom edges of the drawer sides and the tops of the runners with 100-grit sandpaper. Then wax them with a candle stub.

Spill preventer

To keep a drawer from pulling out all the way, install a 10d nail as a stop on each side about an inch in from the back. Drill a 1½-inch-deep hole that's slightly wider than the nail's diameter. Clip the nail so that it's high enough to catch the top edge of the face frame when the drawer is pulled open. Slip the drawer partway into the cabinet and reach inside to insert the nails.

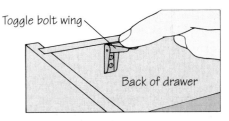

Clipped 10d nail

Toggle bolt wing

Back of drawer

Toggle stop ▲

You can also make a drawer stop with the wings of a toggle bolt. Drill two holes in one wing and screw it to the inside face of the drawer back with the other wing projecting above the edge. Hold down the top wing to remove the drawer; it will automatically spring back when the drawer is replaced. A turn button (pivoting wood block) also makes a great drawer stop (p.56).

Fast fix for droopy drawers

When a drawer begins to stick and scrape, the drawer's bottom edges and the frame they ride on are often worn. A simple fix is to tap a large-head thumbtack into the front of the frame just under the drawer's edge on each side. This provides a new minimum-friction sliding surface and raises the drawer to the proper height.

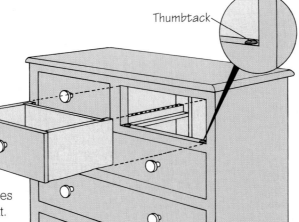

Thumbtack

REPAIRING FURNITURE

Doors

Open-and-shut solution

Sticking cabinet door? To locate the areas that are binding, hold a sheet of carbon paper between the door and the cabinet frame with the carbon side toward the door, then close the door. The carbon will smudge the high spots, showing you where the door needs to be sanded or planed. Move the paper along the edge and repeat as needed. ▼

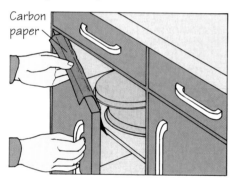

Carbon paper

Door lift

If loose hinges are causing a cabinet door to drag, take out the hinge pins and make a slight bend in the center of each one. The pins will fit tighter, lifting the door and making it operate more smoothly. ▼

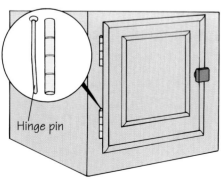

Hinge pin

Upholstery

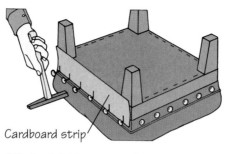

Cardboard strip

All straight in a row ▲

Getting a row of upholstery tacks straight and evenly spaced is not as easy as it looks. One solution is to pin a dressmaker's tape measure just above the line where the tacks go. Another is to mark the spacing along the edge of a lightweight cardboard strip and press the tacks into it. After driving all the tacks most of the way in, tug on the strip to pull the edge free.

Getting a better hold

Is an old chair frame so chewed up with tack holes that tacks for a new fabric won't hold? Apply a strip or two of muslin to the damaged surface with white glue and let it dry thoroughly. This will give grip to the surface and let you attach fabric more securely, especially if you use staples instead of tacks.

For future use

Put leftover material from a reupholstery job in a large manila envelope, and staple it to the bottom of the chair or sofa. Also store extra decorative tacks on the bottom; drive them not quite all the way in. Later, if you need a patch or want to cover an additional small piece, you'll know where the fabric and tacks are.

Ripped heavy materials

Sewing a tear in leather, vinyl, or certain heavy fabrics may do more harm than good. Try gluing on a patch instead. Use a razor blade to cut a neat circle or square around the rip, and glue a backing of similar material behind the hole. Then trace the hole on paper and use it as a pattern to cut a patch to glue to the backing. Cut the patch from an inside or underside area of the upholstery if necessary.

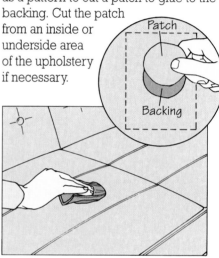

Patch

Backing

Chairs

The old-fashioned way

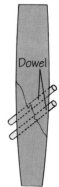

Dowel

Broken chair leg, rung, or stretcher? If the parts still fit snugly, fix it with dowels. Glue and clamp the parts together. Then, after the glue dries, remove the clamp and drill angled holes for dowels through both parts. Insert the dowels, glue them in place, and trim them. (For more dowel use tips, see p.79.)

Spring action

To replace a broken spindle in a chair back that's difficult to take apart, cut off the top tenon of the new spindle. Drill a hole in the top of the spindle, and insert a small spring and a dowel. Then glue the tenon you cut off into the hole in the top of the chair back, and drill a matching hole in it. Apply glue to both ends of the spindle, and set it in place. As you do, press the dowel down and let it pop into the top hole. ▼

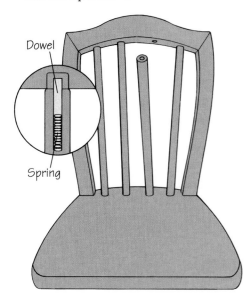

Dowel

Spring

Raising cane

To take the sag out of a cane chair seat, soak it well with hot soapy water, rinse it, and let it air-dry. The cane will shrink and pull taut.

Get a leg up

To build up a tubular metal table leg on an uneven floor, put furniture leg tips on all four legs, adding washers inside the tip of the leg you want to lengthen.

Washers

Even keel

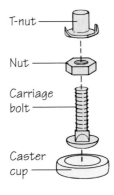

T-nut

Nut

Carriage bolt

Caster cup

Uneven floor got a piece of furniture wobbling? Put this easy-to-make furniture leveler on all four corners. For each leveler, use a carriage bolt with a mating T-nut and regular nut. Drill a hole and tap the T-nut over it; then screw in the bolt with the nut on it. After you level the piece, tighten the nut against the T-nut to keep the bolt from moving. Put a caster cup under each leveler to protect the floor. ▼

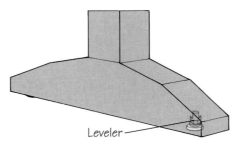

Leveler

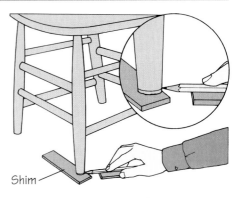

Shim

Cure for the wobbles ▲

If a chair or table wobbles because one leg is shorter than the others, put the piece on a flat surface and shim the short leg until the wobble stops. Then mark around each leg with a pencil held flat on a thin wood block slightly higher than the shim. Finally, trim the legs with a small handsaw; they will all be exactly the same length.

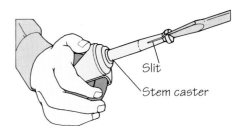

Slit

Stem caster

Faster casters ▲

To keep stem casters from falling out of loose sockets, wrap the stem with steel wool. For a more permanent solution, cut a slit in the top of the stem with a hacksaw. Then spread the slit with a screwdriver just enough so that the caster will not drop out.

REPAIRING FURNITURE

Taking it apart

Avoid a jigsaw puzzle

When you take a chair apart for regluing, it's often difficult to tell one leg or rung from the other. Before starting, put masking tape labels with numbers or letters and alignment marks on each joint. Then putting the chair back together will be only a matter of matching markings. You can peel the tape off without damaging the finish.

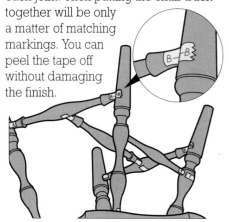

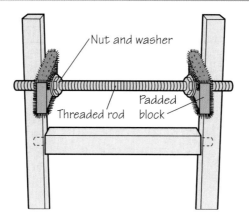

Homemade joint popper ▲

Here's a simple device for opening stubborn chair joints. All it consists of is a threaded rod (with two nuts and two washers) going through two blocks of wood padded with carpet. Use it to apply outward pressure slowly and evenly to the joints to force them open. To do this, just alternately tighten the nuts on either side a little bit at a time.

Old cabinetmaker's trick

After taking apart a piece of furniture for regluing, dab or brush hot vinegar on the joints to loosen and remove the old glue. It usually works in minutes, but loosening a thick glue buildup could take up to an hour. The vinegar won't harm any finish, leaving only a white film that you can easily wipe off.

Ream it out

To sand off the old glue in a round mortise, use sandpaper wrapped around a wood dowel. Use a thin chisel to remove built-up glue from the bottom of the mortise.

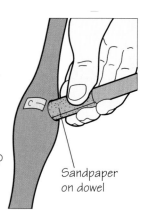

Sandpaper on dowel

Don't break a leg ▶

When removing the spreaders or rungs on a chair, it's easy to accidentally break one of the chair's legs. To avoid this, support the chair so that the leg rests lightly on a carpeted surface. Then tap straight down on the leg with a rubber mallet. This will loosen the bond and let you pull the spreader or rung out without damaging it or the leg.

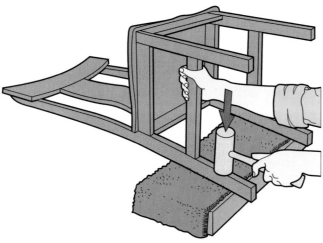

Putting it together

Four commandments

Here are some basic rules for reassembling or repairing furniture:
▷ Don't use nails, L-brackets, or mending plates. Use glue and, if necessary, dowels or splines. Use screws only where they were used before.
▷ Remove all the old glue so that the new glue can attach to the wood fibers.
▷ Use the right glue—usually white or yellow wood glue. Avoid epoxy; future disassembly is nearly impossible.
▷ Always clamp the parts of a glued joint together until the glue dries—an unclamped joint is a lost cause.

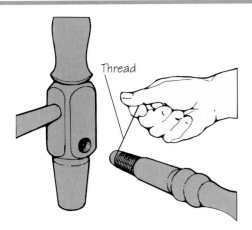

Thread

Loose joints 1 ▲

If a furniture joint you are regluing is only slightly loose, you may be able to rely on the glue itself to bridge the gap. If it is so loose it's wobbly, however, here is one trick to try: Coat the tenon with glue, and wrap it tightly with cotton thread. After the thread dries, glue the tenon into the mortise.

Loose joints 2

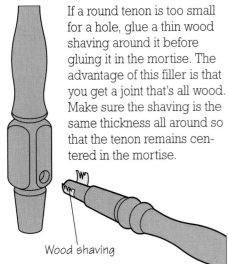

If a round tenon is too small for a hole, glue a thin wood shaving around it before gluing it in the mortise. The advantage of this filler is that you get a joint that's all wood. Make sure the shaving is the same thickness all around so that the tenon remains centered in the mortise.

Wood shaving

Loose joints 3

If a rectangular tenon is too small, glue thin pieces of veneer to all four sides. When the glue dries, use a utility knife or sandpaper to fit the enlarged tenon into the mortise.

Loose joints 4

Glue and wrap strips of a thin porous or absorbent fabric (cheesecloth, panty hose, or cotton sheeting) around a loose tenon. Use as many layers as you need, and soak each with glue. Let the glue harden; then sand the tenon to fit and glue it in. Trim any excess material with a utility knife.

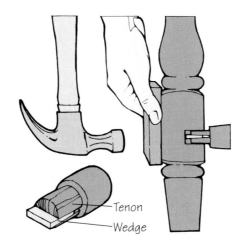

Tenon

Wedge

For a really loose joint ▲

Make a slot in the tenon, cutting at a right angle to the grain on the end of the tenon. Cut a wedge that will be driven tightly into the new slot when the joint is reassembled. Experiment to get the wedge the right length. Don't make it too thick because it may split the rung. Put glue on the wedge and the slot as well as on the rung and in the mortise before reassembling and clamping.

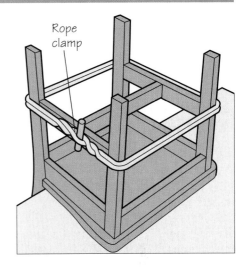

Rope clamp

Quick chair clamp ▲

If you don't have bar clamps, the easiest way to secure chair legs while the glue is drying is to wrap two turns of rope around the legs. Then insert a stick between the turns and tighten the rope like a tourniquet. You can also use elastic bungee cords to hold the legs (p.86).

Old but still practical

If you need to glue a valuable antique, use hide glue. It dries hard and strong but can be softened and removed with alcohol so that you can easily correct a mistake. Cabinetmakers of yore had to keep the stuff simmering over a fire, but now it's available in a squeeze bottle like other wood glues.

Another use for hide glue

Because bottled hide glue sets slowly, it's great when you have a complicated assembly and have to arrange several clamps or to fit together a lot of chair rungs and legs. Hide glue takes 3 or 4 hours to set, versus ½ to 1 hour for white and yellow glues.

FIXING FURNITURE SURFACES

Scratches

Nuts to scratches

You can actually hide a fine scratch on furniture by rubbing it with the meat of a pecan or other oily nut or with a little peanut butter. But if that sounds a bit too nutty or smelly, there are alternatives. It's actually the oil in the nut that's doing the job, and olive or vegetable oil will work even better—without the danger of further damaging the finish by rubbing too hard. Rub the oil in well with your thumb, and polish the surface with a clean soft rag.

Java to the rescue

For a brew that will obscure scratches on a dark furniture finish, mix 1 teaspoon of instant coffee in 1 tablespoon of water or vegetable oil. Don't use this on shellac or a valuable antique.

More home scratch eliminators

Several other common household items can hide small scratches on finished wood. Here are some to try (test them in an inconspicuous spot first):
▷ Iodine works on mahogany and other reddish finishes.
▷ Liquid and paste shoe polish come in shades that match wood finishes.
▷ Felt-tip markers in brown, red, and yellowish hues let you match a range of wood tones, although some may require two or more markers.
▷ Crayons in similar colors also work if warmed slightly first to soften them.

Basic scratch removal

Simply applying paste wax and buffing will often eliminate fine scratches. For more pronounced marks, sand with the grain using superfine wet-or-dry sandpaper lubricated with mineral oil (or baby oil—it's the same stuff). To even up the shine and get a satin finish, rub the area with superfine steel wool lubricated with oil soap. For a higher shine, wax and buff. But don't wet-sand older veneer pieces; they often have tiny high spots where the finish will wear off.

Wear and tear

Marker magic

Worn finish on a chair arm or table edge is an annoying problem. Fix it with special touch-up pens—available from wood-finishing suppliers—that seal and refinish worn spots and scratches. Wipe the area with mineral spirits and scuff it with superfine sandpaper. Then draw over it with a pen of the appropriate color. Feather out the repair by rubbing it gently with your finger. Repeat several times to build up the new finish. ▼

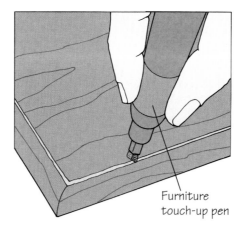

Furniture touch-up pen

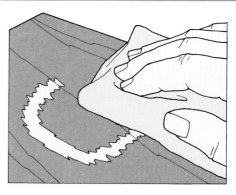

White rings ▲

A white ring left by a sweaty beverage container will often disappear if you just wipe up the moisture and wait a couple of hours. If the ring persists, try passing a hair dryer set on low heat back and forth over it; keep the nozzle at least 6 inches away and let the wood get warm but not hot. If a trace still remains, rub it vigorously with boiled linseed oil (or olive or vegetable oil); then buff with your palm to create friction. Wipe clean.

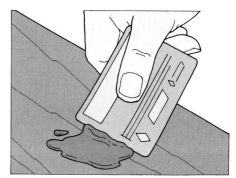

Spilled nail polish ▲

Don't wipe it up! The solvents in nail polish soften most finishes, and wiping may take off the finish. Instead, let the polish dry completely; then gently scrape it off with a credit card. Wax the surface, using superfine steel wool.

Pearly and plaque-free

To brighten a dulled lacquer or varnish finish, mix a little regular nongel toothpaste with water and rub it on with a cloth. If necessary, blend in a pinch of baking soda to make it more abrasive.

Scorched surface

To remove a surface burn, rub it with a paste made of fine fireplace ash and lemon juice. Then wipe the area clean, and touch it up with the same kind of finish that is already on the surface. To determine the finish type, see p.242.

Burn marks

To treat burns that go into the wood, mask closely around the area with tape, and scrape out the charred wood using a craft knife with a rounded blade. If necessary, stain the bare wood to match the finish. Mix equal parts of clear nail polish and acetone-base nail polish remover; apply it one thin coat at a time until you fill the hole, letting each coat dry before applying the next. Sand the surface with extra-fine paper, and then remove the tape. If a burn goes through a veneer, patch the veneer (p.241). ▼

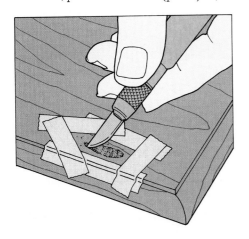

Deeper damage

Soft fill

To hide nicks and gouges on a table leg or cabinet side, use a wax (or putty) furniture filler stick and dark furniture wax (both available from wood-finishing suppliers). First clean the area with mineral spirits. Fill the larger gouges with filler from a stick matching the wood's lightest shade. Smooth the filler with a small piece of wood, and buff lightly with superfine steel wool. Then use the dark wax to fill the small scratches and even up the color. The repairs are not durable enough to withstand hard use, so don't try this on a tabletop—the first time you write a cheque, you'll poke your pen into the filler. ▼

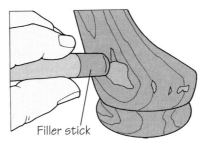

Filler stick

Swell solution ▶

A dent can often be fixed by swelling the compressed fibers back to their normal size. Prick the finish in the dent several times with a fine pin so that moisture can penetrate into the wood. Then cover the dent with a pad of wet cloth, put a metal bottle cap on top to spread the heat, and apply an iron on a high setting for a few minutes. Be careful not to scorch the finish. Afterward, fill the pinholes with a thin coat of varnish.

Shellac stick

Burn-in knife

Hard fill ▲

A more solid way to fill deep scars on furniture is with a shellac stick. Get one that closely matches the color of the finish. To apply it, use a special curved burn-in knife (or a grapefruit knife) heated on a smokeless heat source such as canned cooking fuel. Reheating the knife often, press it against the stick and melt shellac into the hole a little at a time to fill it just above surface level. Use the hot knife to smooth the shellac. After the patch cools, carefully sand it level with superfine wet-or-dry paper and a little mineral oil. Remove any excess shellac with alcohol. This procedure takes skill; practice on junk furniture first.

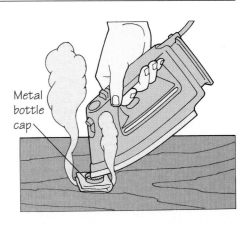

Metal bottle cap

FIXING FURNITURE SURFACES

Veneer

Don't take a sip

Regluing old, brittle delaminated veneer is tricky. Try this: Cut a length of plastic drinking straw and press it to flatten it somewhat. Fold it in half and fill one half with carpenter's glue, dripping the glue in from above very slowly in tiny drops (this requires patience). Slip the filled half under the veneer and gently blow in the glue. Wipe off any excess, cover the area with wax paper and a wood block, and clamp overnight. ▼

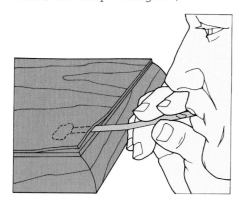

Older means easier

Flattening blistered or peeled veneer on an older piece is often easy because heat and moisture will soften the hide glue commonly used to bond veneer before the 1940's. Lay a damp towel over the area and carefully heat it with an iron set on *Low*. Then press the veneer flat with a rolling pin and clamp it or weight it down overnight. One caveat: Don't wet and heat a shellac finish unless you plan to refinish the piece. To test for shellac, dab some alcohol on a hidden area; if the finish is shellac, it will dissolve or cloud.

Just a sliver ▶

A blister in veneer usually results when the veneer swells too large to fit its original area. Use a sharp craft or utility knife to cut a thin sliver ($\frac{1}{32}$ to $\frac{1}{16}$ inch wide) from the center of the blister. Cut with the grain for the length of the blister, tapering the cut's ends. Work carpenter's glue under the veneer with a straw (see hint at left), clamp or weight the area, and let it dry.

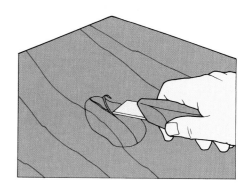

Plastic laminate

Counter countertop peeling

When laminate comes loose, it's usually along an edge. To reattach a loose edge, brush contact cement on the base surface under the laminate. Then coat the bottom of the laminate by pressing it down on the base and quickly pulling it away. Prop open the laminate with toothpicks until the adhesive is almost dry (about 5 minutes less than the recommended drying time). Then press it in place and roll with a rolling pin. ▼

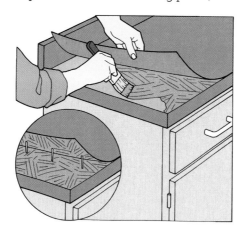

Frying pan burn the counter?

Rubbing toothpaste on the laminate may remove a slight surface discoloration, but a deeper burn can't be removed. If you don't want to replace the laminate, glue some ceramic tiles over the spot and use them as a hot plate. Or cut out the area and put in a heatproof insert; kits with mounting hardware are available in several sizes. ▼

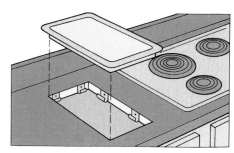

Hot separation

To remove plastic laminate from a surface, heat one edge with an iron or a paint heat gun to soften the adhesive. Slide a putty knife under that edge to lift the laminate. Then work your way across the length of the piece, heating and pulling the laminate free as you go.

PATCHING VENEER

Replacing small chipped or damaged sections of veneer is easy but requires careful fitting. Get a piece of veneer from a local or mail-order woodworking supplier, and use the thick contact cement sold in small bottles at hardware stores.

Replacing a large area of veneer, such as an entire chest top, is also simple. But for large areas, use the thinner water-base contact cement, which spreads with a roller and won't become lumpy or uneven when spread. Also let the new veneer's edges overhang on all sides, and trim them with a utility knife after mounting. Don't stain a large section of veneer until after you mount it.

1 Use a utility knife to remove the damaged veneer and to straighten the edges of the cut-out section. When possible, cut with the grain to hide the seam. Scrape or sand off any old glue.

2 Sand the new veneer smooth, and test stains on it until you get a good match. If the new veneer is thicker than the original, sand it down on the back to the proper thickness.

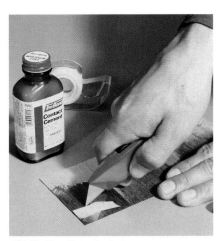

3 Outline the missing area on paper by rubbing with the side of a pencil lead. Cut out the paper, and use it as a template to cut an exact copy of the area from the new veneer.

4 Test-fit the patch, and trim it if necessary. Carefully apply contact cement to the back of the patch and to the base wood, and let it dry. Then press the patch in place.

5 Finish the patch with oil or varnish to match. Then hide the seam using a furniture touch-up putty stick in a matching color. Use the touch-up stick last because finish won't adhere to the putty.

STRIPPING FURNITURE

Before you strip

Clean up your act

Sometimes all that's needed to make that grimy yard-sale bargain look like new is a good cleaning. Mix equal parts of boiled linseed oil and mineral spirits. Warm the mixture slightly in the top of an old double boiler, and rub it on with cheesecloth, burlap, or superfine steel wool, depending on how dirty the surface is. After removing the bulk of the dirt, buff with a soft cloth.

Fast new finish

If all that's wrong with a finish is some rings, hazing, alligatoring, or general dinginess, restore it with furniture refinisher. Sold in paint and hardware stores, refinisher melts and rejuvenates the finish without destroying its patina as stripper does. Just brush it on, wait the recommended time, then rub with fine steel wool. You get a reworked finish that's lighter in color than the old one, with scratches and dirt removed. Refinisher won't change a piece's basic color, rescue a thin, flaky finish, or repair deep stains and gouges. Experiment on a nonvaluable piece first. ▼

Cheaper fast finish

You can sometimes rejuvenate a grungy but otherwise solid finish with the solvent that softens it. Figure out what that solvent is (see below), brush it on, let it stand until most of it has evaporated, and then rework the finish with fine steel wool. It takes more elbow grease than a commercial refinishing product, but it costs a lot less. Always test a hidden area first, and be prepared to strip and refinish the piece if this doesn't work.

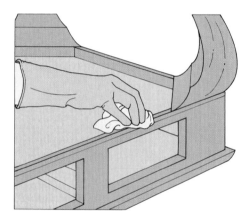

What finish is it? ▲

Clear finishes are difficult to tell apart, but it's important to know what you're working on. Finishes with a low sheen and very little surface thickness are likely to be penetrating oil finishes. To identify other types of finish, moisten a rag with alcohol and vigorously rub an unseen spot. If the finish softens, it's shellac. If it doesn't, try the test using lacquer thinner. If the finish softens, it's a lacquer-base finish. If neither product affects the finish, it's probably a varnish. You'll find a list of finishes and their solvents on page 246.

Tips on stripping

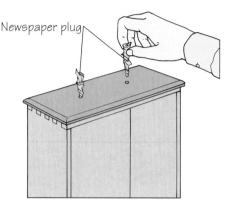

Newspaper plug

Plug up first ▲

After removing the hardware to prepare a piece for stripping, fill key and screw holes with twisted bits of newspaper before applying the stripper. The paper will keep the holes from getting clogged with stripper sludge, which is difficult to remove after it dries and hardens.

Bits and pieces

Take the tedium out of stripping hinges, knobs, and other hardware. Fill an old coffee can with enough stripper to  cover a couple of pieces; then tie a string to them and lower them into the can. Cap the can with the plastic lid, leaving the string hanging out. After the suggested time, pull the pieces out and clean them. You can use the stripper several times.

Maybe don't do it yourself

Before stripping a piece, particularly one that's not valuable or that you plan to paint, look into having it dip-stripped. It may not cost much more than buying do-it-yourself stripping supplies. But make sure the dip-stripping is not done in a hot lye bath; it's punishing to joints and veneer, and that's the reason that dip-stripping has such a bad rep.

No drip

The best way to avoid having stripper run off vertical surfaces is to use semi-paste stripper or to keep turning the piece so that the surface being stripped is horizontal. But if you need to keep liquid stripper from running, sprinkle it with some whiting (available in paint stores). On open-grain woods and soft-woods, however, sawdust is a better choice because whiting can plug pores and show through a light-colored stain.

Recycle those tuna cans

Put a shallow can under each chair or table leg to catch stripper drippings. You'll not only control the mess but you can save the drippings and reuse any that are still clear for a second coat. ▼

Shallow can

Wood shavings

Waste not ▲

Wood shavings from a planer or jointer are great for scrubbing loosened finish out of carvings and other finely detailed areas, and as an added benefit they absorb the sludge. If you don't have enough shavings from your own shop, ask a local woodworker or cabinet-maker for some. Sawdust will also work, but not as well as shavings.

Absorb the mess

On a messy stripping job, the sludge will be easier to remove if you add a material that soaks up some of the soft-ened finish. Sawdust works, and so do cat litter and the oil-absorbing clay sold by auto parts dealers.

Stripper helper

If you're removing a heavy coat of paint, cover the stripper with plastic—food wrap, a trash bag, or an old dry-cleaner bag. The plastic keeps the stripper from evaporating so that it works longer.

STRIPPING RISKS

If a product is strong enough to remove paint, you don't want to breathe it into your lungs or get it on your skin or in your eyes. But some strippers require more precaution than others. This is especially true of ones containing methylene chloride. Methylene chloride is fast acting, but it is flammable and a skin and eye irritant. Inhaling high levels of it causes dizziness and headaches and reduces the body's ability to absorb oxygen. Long-term repeated exposure is associated with cancer in laboratory animals. Avoid methylene chloride if someone in your family is pregnant, has heart or lung problems, or is sensitive to chemical fumes.

The wisest course is to use a water-base stripper whenever possible. It takes hours to work and raises the wood grain but is much less noxious. Even so, take care when working with any paint remover. Wear long sleeves and pants, safety goggles, solvent-resistant gloves, and a respirator with an organic-vapor filter. Work in a well-ventilated area—outdoors when possible. Consider using a heat gun to remove a heavy buildup of old paint.

Dispose of the old finish and leftover stripper safely (p.39).

STRIPPING FURNITURE

Scratch prevention

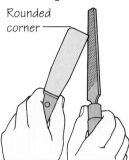

Rounded corner

Prepare a putty knife for removing finish by gently rounding the corners with a file. Remove any burrs from the edge with fine sandpaper.

No more cruddy putty knife

Lightly coat your putty knife with non-stick cooking spray, and the stripper gunk won't adhere to it.

Over easy

With its flat, flexible blade, an old plastic kitchen spatula makes a great scraper for removing stripper. Hold the spatula upside down and push it along as shown for a clean pickup. ▼

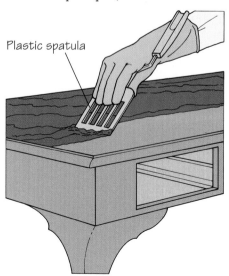

Plastic spatula

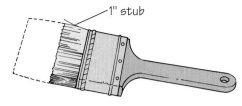

1" stub

Stub brush ▲

An old paintbrush is a good tool for removing softened finish in hard-to-reach areas. Just trim the bristles to a stiff stump about 1 inch long. Dip the brush in water (for water-base stripper) or turpentine (for solvent-base) and use it to flow the old finish out of carvings, turnings, and grooves.

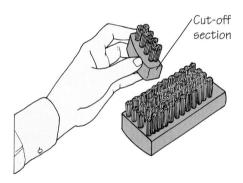

Cut-off section

The little brush that can ▲

To reach into curves and crevices when stripping furniture, cut two rows of bristles off a stiff-bristle scrub brush. Use the cut-off piece to work stripper into the areas and later to rub off the loosened finish.

No-mess scoop

Here's a way to remove loosened finish with less mess: Cut an aluminum pie pan in half, using heavy scissors, and put the halves to work as scooper-scrapers. The pan is rigid enough to scrape up the goop and hold it too.

Snappy solutions

To remove softened finish on turned legs, twist a piece of burlap or old panty hose and move it back and forth across the surface as you would a shoeshine rag. On fine turnings and grooves in furniture legs, remove the sludge with coarse twine or with medium-grade steel wool wrapped around a string. If you need to get old finish out of a really tight groove, use unwaxed dental floss.

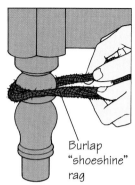

Burlap "shoeshine" rag

Save that old fishing pole

Bamboo is a great material for making tools that remove stripper sludge. You can quickly cut it with a utility knife to whatever shape you need, and it's soft enough that it won't mar most woods.

Press it off

Remove a heavy buildup of varnish or other clear finish with an old steam iron. Put several layers of damp cheesecloth over the surface to absorb the finish, and press with the iron on a medium steam setting. Often this will remove most of the finish, leaving only a thin layer to be removed with stripper or with the appropriate solvent.

REMOVING AN OLD FINISH

Before starting, remove all hardware from the piece and put cardboard or thick newspaper layers under it. Apply stripper with an old paintbrush that you can dispose of when finished. To avoid rust spots, don't use steel wool with water-base stripper.

Caution: When working with stripper, wear an organic-vapor respirator and protective gloves, goggles, and clothing. Handle stripper containing methylene chloride with special care (see box, p.243).

1 Brush on a heavy coat of stripper in one direction; back-and-forth strokes reduce the stripper's potency. Let it work for the recommended time. If solvent-base stripper starts to dry, apply a little more.

2 Rub lightly with a plastic scrub pad or medium steel wool to loosen the finish. Then use a wide, flexible putty knife to remove finish on flat surfaces. If needed, apply another coat of stripper.

3 Remove finish along edges and corners with a brass-bristle brush—the type sold for scrubbing pots. It works better than a toothbrush and won't damage the wood the way steel will.

4 Clean finish out of narrow grooves and creases with a scratch awl or an ice pick. Use light strokes to avoid damaging the wood. For more intricate areas, see the hints on the facing page.

5 Wash the entire area to remove any residue of the stripper. Use mineral spirits to remove the remains of solvent-base stripper and plain water to remove the remains of water-base stripper.

It's not just for ovens

Use oven cleaner to strip paint and varnish. It's cheaper than stripper, sprays on, and doesn't sag much on vertical surfaces. But use it only on nonvaluable pieces you plan to paint because it darkens the wood. Neutralize the stripped surface with vinegar, wash it with water, and let it dry thoroughly before painting. Wear gloves and goggles.

Out of the ashes

You can strip the finish from hardware with this home brew: ½ pound of wood fireplace ashes mixed with 2 gallons of water. This mild caustic solution will loosen paint on hardware that is soaked in it overnight. Even though the solution is mild, be sure to wear rubber gloves when putting your hand into the bucket.

Sour milk

Does the paint on an old piece resist every stripper you try? It may be milk paint from the mid-19th century. If so, household ammonia will take it right off. On the other hand, if the milk paint is in good condition, the piece is probably more valuable with the paint on than it would be stripped and refinished.

VARNISHING AND STAINING FURNITURE

Before varnishing

Quick preview

Want to know what a wood surface will look like with a clear varnish finish? Just dampen a rag with mineral spirits and wipe it on an area. If you like the effect, go ahead and varnish the wood; it will look almost the same as the wet wood. If you don't like the look, stain the wood before varnishing.

Mineral spirits wiped on

Bleach solution

Banish black water marks ▲

Black water marks on stripped tabletops disappear like magic when you apply oxalic acid (sold in hardware stores). Wearing protective gloves and goggles, make a solution with boiling water as directed, and brush it carefully just on the stain. When the stain is gone, neutralize the entire surface with distilled white vinegar, assessing any color differences while the wood is wet. Touch up an overly light area with stain.

Bleach it off

After you strip wood, you sometimes find that the old stain has penetrated so deeply that it won't come out. Ordinary chlorine bleach will often lighten the stain. Apply it generously and evenly, and give the piece several days to dry. Neutralize the bleach with a white vinegar wash. Bleach will also remove many types of spots from stripped surfaces.

Staining wood

Instant patina

Getting new wood to match the old on repaired furniture is tricky. On light-colored pieces, give new wood a coat of golden oak stain before staining and finishing it. The stain's amber hues approximate the effect of aging, so the new wood should finish the same as the old.

COMMON FINISHES FOR FURNITURE

For best results, apply a finish following label directions and observe any precautions about safe handling or flammability.

Lacquer, polyurethane, and most varnishes come in satin, semigloss, and glossy finishes.

FINISH	SOLVENT	CHARACTERISTICS	HOW TO APPLY
Penetrating oil	Mineral spirits	Soaks into wood fibers for natural-looking finish. Tung oil is most durable type.	Wipe or brush on, let stand for 30 min. or so, then rub vigorously. Apply two or more coats.
Shellac (white or orange)	Denatured alcohol	Thin, lustrous clear or amber surface film. Wears well but is easily marred by spills.	Brush on two or three thin coats. Easy to spot-repair. Also use to seal wood for other finishes.
Lacquer	Lacquer thinner	Thin, hard film. Very good spill and wear resistance. Used on commercial furniture.	Spray on two or three coats with pro gear; brush on slow-to-dry type. Don't use over other finishes.
Acrylic varnish	Water (before the varnish dries)	Thin, hard film with no amber tones. Moderate resistance to wear and spills.	Spray or brush on two or three thin coats. Usually comes in a spray can.
Alkyd varnish	Mineral spirits	Hard warm-toned film. Moderate to good resistance to wear and spills.	Brush on two or three coats. Easy to recoat but hard to spot-repair. Sand between coats.
Polyurethane	Turpentine, mineral spirits	Very hard warm-toned film. Excellent resistance to wear and spills.	Brush on two coats. Hard to spot-repair. Recoat within specified time. Don't use over shellac.

Blotchiness tamer

New softwoods, such as pine, fir, and spruce, are notorious for absorbing stain unevenly with very blotchy results. The same is true for dark stain on maple, a hardwood. To prevent this, before staining the wood, seal it with a very thin coat of shellac (1 part shellac to 5 parts denatured alcohol). Let it dry for 30 minutes; then sand it with very fine paper. If you use an alcohol-base stain, apply it quickly and sparingly, or the alcohol will liquify the shellac.

Tidy stain applicator

Here's an efficient way to apply stain: Use a hacksaw to cut an ordinary 9-inch thick-nap paint roller into three equal sections. Hold a roller piece in your hand to wipe on stain. The roller absorbs more stain than a brush and applies it more evenly than a cloth. After the stain soaks in, wipe off the excess with a cloth.

Paint-roller section

Mix-and-match stains

Need a special color wood stain to match an existing piece? Any color stain can usually be mixed with any other of the same brand and type. Pick the stain that comes closest to the color you want. Then figure out what tone is missing and add some stain in which that tone predominates. Adding mahogany or cherry boosts red tones. Maple heightens orange, oak yellow, and walnut brown. Test your mix on a hidden spot.

A NATURAL FINISH

Before staining and varnishing a piece, make sure the surface is clear of traces of stripper or old finish. Sand it smooth, and fix any defects. Filling the surface before varnishing (steps 2 and 3) is optional but is often done to close the large pores on open-grain woods (oak, mahogany, walnut) and produce a smooth finish. Use a neutral-color paste wood filler, thinned as directed. Add a tinting color or stain to make it match your stain color. Test the stain and filler colors on an unobtrusive spot. For accurate results, sand, stain, fill, and varnish the test patch. Work in a well-ventilated space; wear a respirator. (For tips on using filler, see p.90; for selecting a brush, p.92.)

1 Stain and seal the surface in one operation by using a stain that contains sealer. Or apply stain, let it dry as directed, and then apply sealer.

2 On open-grain wood, apply a generous wet coat of wood filler and brush in thoroughly (left). Let it dry until dull and flat (right) but not rock hard.

3 Wipe off the excess filler with burlap, going across the grain. Rubbing with the grain tends to pull the filler out. Let the surface dry overnight.

4 Sand lightly with very fine paper and wipe with a tack cloth. Apply three coats of varnish; sand and wipe again between coats.

PAINTING AND ANTIQUING FURNITURE

Painting furniture

Slick finish

To get a supersmooth paint finish, work in a dust-free area and give the paint a chance to flow out and lose the brush marks. Here are some tips:

▷ Apply two coats of enamel undercoat as a primer.

▷ Use an oil-base alkyd paint with a slow drying time (about 24 hours).

▷ Use a paint additive to increase penetration and drying time.

▷ Strain paint (even fresh paint) through a filter, and thin it by up to 10 percent.

▷ Paint surfaces horizontally when possible—if necessary, turn a piece on its side. Lay a door flat.

▷ Use a good natural-bristle brush.

▷ Put on a thin coat of paint, applying three or four coats.

▷ Paint the surface across the grain first. Then make light full-length strokes with the grain, using just the tip of the brush.

▷ Sand thoroughly with fine paper and wipe with a tack cloth between coats.

Tossable mini-applicators

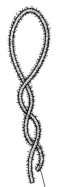

For small touch-ups and tiny tight corners, apply the paint with a cotton swab. You'll get neat, accurate results, and you can throw the applicator away when you're through. For hard-to-reach spots, use a pipe cleaner. Simply bend it in half and twist its ends together as shown, forming a loop of the size you need.

Pipe cleaner

Push-pin helper

The next time you paint a cabinet, press a few push pins into service. Put one on a cabinet door lip to keep the door and frame from touching while the paint dries. Also use pins as temporary drawer and door pulls. The holes will be covered later by the knobs.

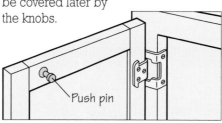

Push pin

Antiquing

Home-brewed finish

Antiquing can magically transform an old beat-up (or unpainted) piece of furniture, and you don't need a kit to do it. Just give the piece a base coat of satin or semigloss enamel, and let it dry for at least a day. Then make a transparent glaze by mixing clear wood sealer or thinned varnish with a dark tinting color. Apply the glaze and then wipe it off, leaving flat surfaces lighter than grooves and recesses in order to simulate natural wear. Experiment on wood scraps first. ▼

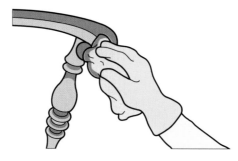

Feigning the ravages of time

Before antiquing a new piece, you may want to "distress" it. Round corners and edges slightly by sanding or filing. Dent edges with a ball-peen hammer, and mark flat surfaces with a bunch of keys. Make worm holes and irregular scratches with an ice pick. But don't go overboard; a little damage goes a long way. It helps to examine naturally worn pieces. Sand the distressed areas.

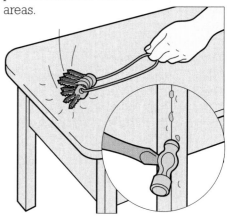

Age spots

To mimic worn areas on a piece you're making look old, use a small stick to apply paint stripper to the base coat in little irregular patches. Wipe the stripper off gently when the paint has the look you want—ranging from a simple crackling effect to total removal of the paint. Neutralize the stripper with water or solvent as directed, and let it dry thoroughly before applying the glaze.

Cracking paint on purpose

Try this to create areas of crackled paint in your imitation antique finish: Before applying a base coat of alkyd paint, brush on a coat of white glue thinned with water and let it dry thoroughly.

Deep-down old

Before painting a piece you're antiquing, stain the wood a dark brown. When you remove paint to simulate wear, the wood underneath will look old and dark.

Other fake finishes

Fine freckles

One way to heighten the effect of glazing is to splatter flyspecks of very dark color on the surface after wiping off the glaze. Make some of the glazing solution deeper in color, dip a toothbrush into it, and flick it over the surface. The effect varies depending on how close you hold the brush to the surface and how quickly you move it. ▼

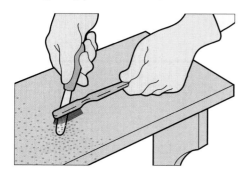

Ersatz wood grain

You can simulate wood grain with the glazing process used for antiquing. Apply a base paint that matches the lightest tones in the wood you're imitating and a glaze that matches the darkest. Create grain by wiping the glaze lightly, first with steel wool and then with a dry brush, in a wavy pattern. Or you can drag a feather or a carpet scrap across the surface, or use graining tools from a paint store or home center.

AN ENAMEL FINISH

You don't have to strip furniture in order to paint it. But for paint to adhere, the surface must be free of grease and dirt and any gloss must be dulled by sanding. If the piece was painted before the early 1980's, the paint may contain lead; dull it with a liquid deglosser instead of sanding. Either alkyd or latex enamel will provide a tough finish if you apply at least two coats over primer; three is better. Alkyd enamels have a wet look when dry (see "Slick finish," facing page); latex enamels are more satiny. Wear a dust mask when sanding and a respirator when painting. Work in a well-ventilated space.

1 Wipe the surface with mineral spirits on a rag. Sand off the shine with medium-grade paper. If the surface is still rough, sand again with fine paper.

2 To fill nicks and gouges, apply wood filler with a putty knife. Let it dry as directed; then sand smooth. Wipe the surface clean with a tack cloth.

3 Prime the surface with an oil-base primer, which brushes on easily, dries quickly, and provides the best undercoat for alkyd or latex enamel.

4 Apply two or three coats of enamel. Let each dry thoroughly; if finish is glossy, sand with very fine grit paper and wipe with a tack cloth between coats.

SPRAY-PAINTING FURNITURE

Spraying techniques

Spray booth

Want to spray-paint a piece of furniture but fear the mess? Use a large cardboard appliance shipping box as a spray booth. A local store will probably be happy to give you a discard.

Flip and paint

It's easier to paint a chair if you turn it upside down and spray the legs and rungs first, spraying their insides before their outsides. Then turn it right side up and spray the back and seat. This works with a small table as well. ▼

Spray inside first

Corners first and last

When spray-painting the outside of a piece of furniture, spray the corners first, aiming directly at each corner and coating both sides of it evenly. But when spraying the inside of a cabinet, it's best not to spray into the corners. Instead, just spray straight onto the flat surfaces, doing the back first, then each side.

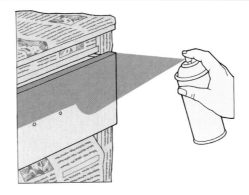

Just a crack ▲

To spray-paint a drawer front, leave it in the cabinet. Mask the cabinet around the drawer; then pull the drawer out about ½ inch. This will let paint cover the drawer edges without getting inside the drawer. After the drawer dries, remove it to paint the cabinet case.

Get an angle on it

With open-weave material, such as caning, you'll get a finer, more even finish if you hold the spray can at about a 45° angle above the material. On wicker, spray first from one side at a 45° angle, then from the other side, to penetrate the weave as much as possible. ▼

Spray can at 45° angle

Not the way you think

When spray-painting a flat surface, such as a tabletop, begin on the side nearest you and work toward the opposite side. This may seem a little strange, but when you spray a flat surface you hold the can at a slight angle, causing it to send some overspray ahead of it. By starting nearby, you cover up that overspray as you progress across the surface. If you did it the opposite way, the overspray would leave a pebbly texture on the areas you had already painted.

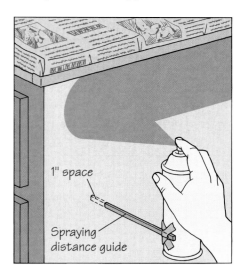

1" space

Spraying distance guide

Keeping your distance ▲

For an even finish, you need to keep a spray can the same distance from the surface the entire time you are spraying. After you figure out the best distance for spraying with a can, tape a stick to the can as a guide. Make the stick about 1 inch shorter than the distance so that you won't scrape it across the paint.

Clean lines

If you want to leave some parts of a piece of furniture unpainted, use masking tape and newspaper to protect the areas. For a clean line along a tape edge, direct the spray so that it is blowing over the tape rather than toward the tape edge.

Instant feathering ▲

To touch up a small spot, try this: Fold a newspaper in quarters, and then unfold it and cut a hole in the center the size of the spot to be touched up. Place the newspaper over the spot, with the folds in the paper peaked up slightly. Then make several quick passes over the hole with the spray can. Moving quickly prevents paint buildup, and the raised paper at the folds lets the paint feather out around the spot to blend in with the rest of the surface. Perfect your technique on scrap before working on a good piece of furniture.

For better spraying

Elusive last drops

No paint comes out of the spray can but you can still feel paint sloshing around inside? The paint pickup tube may be on the side of the can opposite the direction you are spraying. Twist the nozzle a half turn and try again.

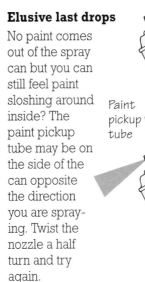

Paint pickup tube

Cowboy sprayer

To keep your airless spray painter from dripping on your clothes and the floor, make a bandanna out of an old shop towel and wrap it around the sprayer just below the nozzle. The rag will catch any drips and make cleaning up easier. ▼

Drip catcher

Sure shot

To clear a clogged nozzle on an aerosol paint can, remove the nozzle and put it on the end of the spray tube on a can of penetrating lubricant. Blast a shot of lubricant through the nozzle. ▼

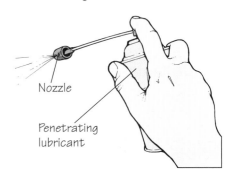

Nozzle

Penetrating lubricant

More clog busters

If the nozzle of an aerosol paint can is clogged and you don't have penetrating lubricant, don't give up; try these tips:
▷ Soak the nozzle in lacquer thinner or mineral spirits overnight.
▷ Save the nozzles of discarded spray cans to use as instant replacements for clogged ones. Store them in a small jar filled with solvent.

Clog prevention

There is a simple way to keep a spray-paint can nozzle from becoming clogged in the first place. After spraying, turn the can upside down and press the button briefly. It will emit a short blast of plain propellant, which will clear the nozzle.

APPLIANCE REPAIR TIPS

Parts protocols

Parts on ice

Keep track of small parts while making repairs. As you disassemble an item, put the parts into prenumbered compartments of a plastic ice cube tray. Reverse the procedure for reassembly. An egg carton works as well. ▼

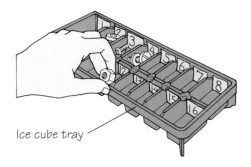

Ice cube tray

All in a row

Sticky tape can also keep parts in the right order. Staple a strip of duct tape, adhesive side up, to your bench top, and as you take the parts off, stick them to the tape in sequence.

Parts saver

While waiting for new parts to arrive, don't leave small parts and screws just lying around. Put them in resealable plastic freezer bags so that you won't lose them.

Grease bag

Here's another use for those resealable plastic bags: They can keep your hands from getting all messed up when you have to grease bearings or other parts. Just put some grease in a bag, add the parts, seal the bag, and work them around in the grease.

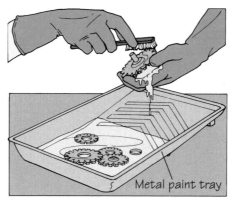

Metal paint tray

Parts washer ▲

Use a metal paint tray to wash small parts. Fill the deep end with solvent and soak the parts in it. Then use the upper end as a work area for brushing and wiping the parts after they've soaked.

Oops!

Dropped a part and can't find it? Turn off the lights and close the blinds. Then turn on a flashlight, hold it close to the floor, and rotate it in a circle. Like a searchlight, the beam raking across the floor causes a small object to cast a large shadow, making it easy to find.

Thrifty parts sources

Need a three-speed fan switch, an electric range element, or a TV tuner? Try the thrift shops run by local charitable agencies or by the Salvation Army or Goodwill Industries. They often have appliance parts or old appliances from which you can salvage parts, and the cost is reasonable.

Electrical fixes

Won't wiggle off

When joining wires in an appliance such as a vacuum cleaner, don't use a regular wire connector; it can vibrate loose. Use a crimp-on connector instead. Just twist the leads together and then use a multipurpose tool (p.199) to squeeze the connector over them.

Vital spray

Keep a spray can of electrical contact cleaner handy for appliance repairs. A quick burst of this nonconductive cleaner is often all you need to cure a sticky switch or balky push button. The cleaner is sold in auto parts stores as well as electronics supply stores, where it's often labeled "television tuner cleaner." ▼

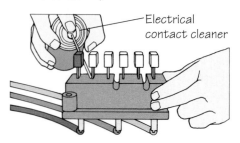

Electrical contact cleaner

USING A MULTITESTER

A multitester, or volt-ohm meter (VOM), is a battery-operated tester that can tell you whether an electrical part, such as a power cord, switch, or heating element, is good or defective. It may look complex, but most tests are simple. For accuracy and ease of use, select a digital model that automatically senses and sets the voltage range you are testing.

The most common test is for electrical continuity. A continuity test can locate shorts or open (interrupted) circuits. You can also test for resistance to electricity's flow, which occurs in heating elements and other parts. Both tests are made using the ohms (Ω) scale (usually set for RX1 on a nonautoranging model). A reading of zero or near zero (less than .05 ohms) signals a complete circuit. The circuit is incomplete when the reading is infinite resistance—infinity (∞) on an analog (nondigital) meter or a flashing number or other indicator (check the manual) on a digital VOM.

The DC volts scales let you measure a battery's voltage or a low-voltage system such as a doorbell. The AC volts scale can measure house current, but it's safest not to do this.

To set up a multitester, insert the red lead into the appropriate positive (+) jack and the black lead into the negative (–) jack. "Zero" an analog meter (p.199): Touch the probes together and turn the adjustment knob until the needle is over zero.

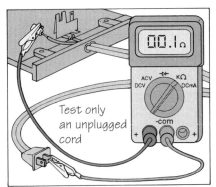

Check a power cord one wire at a time. Set the meter for ohms (Ω). Touch one probe to a disconnected lead and the other to each plug prong in turn. A zero or very low reading on only one prong shows continuity. There is an open circuit if both prongs show infinite resistance, a possible short if both read zero or near zero.

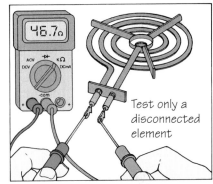

To test a stove element for resistance, set the meter for ohms (Ω). Touch the probes to the element's two terminals. The reading should be between 20 and 100 ohms. If it's much higher, the element is defective and may have an open circuit. If lower, it may have a short. Test also for a ground fault (below, left).

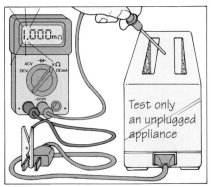

Always check a repaired appliance for a ground fault—a dangerous current leakage. Set the meter for ohms (Ω). Touch one probe to a metal part on the body and the other to each flat plug prong in turn. The meter should show infinite resistance on both. A round ground prong, however, should read zero or near zero.

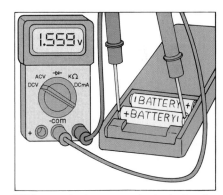

For greatest accuracy, test a battery's voltage while it's powering a device. Select a DC volts setting slightly higher than the battery's rating, and touch the probes to the battery's terminals (red to + and black to –). If the DC volts scale reading is much below the battery's rating, replace or recharge the battery.

APPLIANCE REPAIR TIPS

Gaining access

Nameplate cover-up

Have you taken out every visible screw from a small appliance and it still won't open? Look for screws hidden under the manufacturer's nameplate. Remove the plate's mounting screws, or if the plate is glued on, carefully pry it off with a screwdriver. Stick-on labels or metal facings may also conceal recessed screws. Rub your fingers over them to find the screws. If you feel one, lift a corner of the label and peel it back. ▼

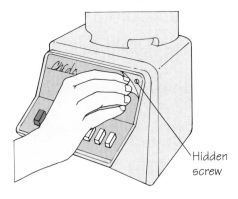

Hidden screw

Secret screws

Sometimes an access screw is hiding under a plastic plug set flush with the surface of an appliance's housing. Insert the tip of a small screwdriver into the seam around the plug to pry it out.

Removable plug

Underfoot screws

Also look for screws hiding inside an appliance's feet, especially rubber or plastic feet that fit into holes on the housing. Often you can pop them out with your fingers or a small screwdriver. ▼

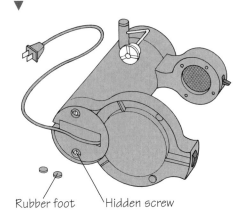

Rubber foot   Hidden screw

Interlocked

No signs of a screw? The molded plastic housings on some small appliances are held together by interlocking posts and holes. Look for the tops of posts projecting from one part through another. Pry open a nearby seam to pop the posts out of the holes. ▼

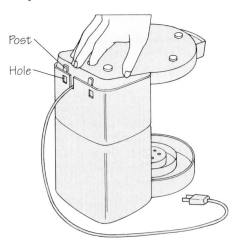

Post

Hole

Tough to crack open

Tabs and notches just under the seam often hold small appliance housings together. Pressing down on the tab side of the seam will usually free the tab from the notch. If necessary, slip the tip of a small screwdriver into the seam and gently pry the pieces apart. If there are several tabs, work your way around the seam, opening one tab at a time. ▼

Notch side   Tab side

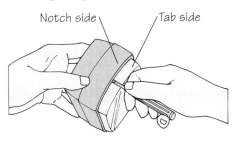

Taking things apart

Southpaw parts

When disassembling appliances with moving elements, remember that nuts and bolts on rotating parts may have left-hand threads. If a part doesn't loosen when turned in the normal counterclockwise direction, try turning it clockwise. Forcing it the wrong way will strip the threads.

Back off a minute

If you are having trouble getting a screw to go back into an item, don't force it in. Instead, stop and very lightly turn the screw counterclockwise until you hear a click or feel the screw drop slightly. Gently turning a screw in the wrong direction like this is often the easiest way to literally get it back in the groove. After that, it should go in easily.

Paper clip to the rescue

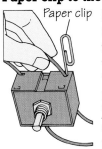

Paper clip

Switches often have self-locking terminals that clamp onto a wire when it is inserted. To free a wire from this type of terminal, just insert a straightened paper clip and pull the wire out.

Quick unconnect

Don't pull off a quick-connect terminal; you're likely to damage the wire. Push it off with a screwdriver instead. ▼

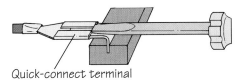

Quick-connect terminal

Small appliances

Save your sole

Got an iron with a dull soleplate? As long as it's not aluminum and doesn't have a nonstick coating, you can revive it. Mix 2 tablespoons of salt with enough water to form a paste. With the iron unplugged, rub the paste on the soleplate with crumpled newspaper; then wipe it clean with a damp paper towel. ▼

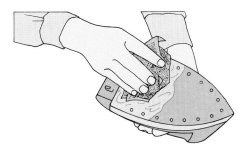

SHOCK-FREE REPAIRS

Worried about getting a serious shock from an appliance you've just repaired? Keep it from happening by testing the appliance for a ground fault (a current leakage, as when a bare wire touches a metal housing). With a large appliance, it's easiest to use a multitester (p.253). But you can test a more portable appliance using a test light with alligator clip leads. Before plugging in the appliance, connect one lead of the test light to a bare metal spot on the appliance and the other lead to a grounding element—a metal cold-water pipe, for example. With the appliance still unplugged, turn its on-off switch to *On*. Then plug it in. If the test light glows, the appliance has a ground fault and is dangerous. Pull the plug—do not turn it off using the on-off switch.

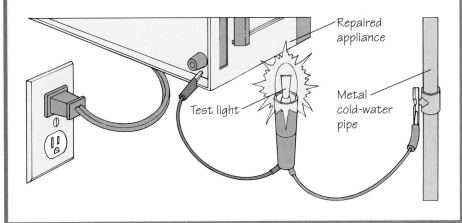

Repaired appliance

Test light

Metal cold-water pipe

No greasy shower

After you oil a fan, put a paper bag over it and turn it on for a few minutes. Any oil the fan throws off will hit the bag instead of being flung around the room.

Don't slam it against the wall

Is the whirring of an electric clock driving you nuts? Turn it upside down for a few hours. Or unplug it and put it in a warm oven (under 65.5°C or 150°F) for an hour. Either action will help redistribute the lubricant in the clock, quieting it.

Icy coil insight

If your dehumidifier's coils get frosty, chances are you're running it when the temperature is below 18°C (65°F). You can get a new dehumidifier with a special deicing control. Meanwhile, plug your present dehumidifier, which likely doesn't have this control, into a timer and set the timer to cycle the unit on and off. For example, let it run for 4 hours and stay off for 1 hour—or whatever other combination works for you. The pause gives the ice time to melt.

REFRIGERATORS AND FREEZERS

Refrigerator problems

Shaken up

Your refrigerator won't run after you've moved it around? It's probably just a loose wire. Unplug the power cord, remove the back service panel, and systematically check each wire. When you find one that's fallen off a terminal, simply reattach it.

Not on the back porch either

It's tempting to put a freezer—or an old extra refrigerator—in the garage or utility room. But don't unless the space is heated. A freezer or refrigerator can't keep food safely cold when the surrounding temperature goes below 15.5°C (60°F). As the air temperature drops, the compressor will kick on less often and will stop running below about 4.5°C (40°F), letting the food spoil.

Light leaks

To see if a refrigerator door gasket is forming a tight seal, put a 150-watt outdoor floodlight in the compartment and shine it toward one side at a time with the cord coming out near the opposite side. With the door closed and the kitchen lights off, look for light leaks. ▼

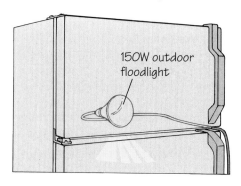

150W outdoor floodlight

Gasket fix-up

You can often fix a single small crack in the gasket around a refrigerator door with silicone caulk. Roll the gasket open (see step 1, facing page) and apply the caulk to the inside of the gasket, being careful not to apply too much. Use only caulk whose label's fine print indicates it's safe for contact with food.

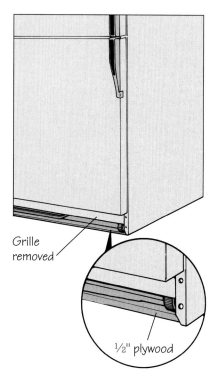

Grille removed

½" plywood

Open and shut ▲

Do your kids always leave the refrigerator door slightly ajar? Put a piece of ½-inch plywood under the front legs. The board won't show behind the grille, and the tilt is too small to be noticeable but still enough to shut the door. However, don't do this if you have an automatic ice maker, which requires the unit to be perfectly level.

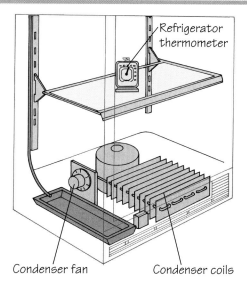

Refrigerator thermometer

Condenser fan   Condenser coils

Fridge under the weather ▲

Food not keeping well in your refrigerator? Put a refrigerator thermometer in the center of the food compartment and leave it overnight. It should read between 1°C (34°F) and 4.5°C (40°F). If you can't maintain this temperature by adjusting the refrigerator's thermostat, check for clogged condenser coils under the refrigerator or on the back of the unit. Also look for an obstructed or defective condenser fan underneath.

Another use for ice cream

To check a freezer's temperature, put a refrigerator thermometer on top of a carton of ice cream or frozen food and leave it for a day. Look for a reading around -18°C (0°F). Actually ice cream alone can tell you if a freezer is at the right temperature. If the ice cream is firmly solid without being brick hard, the temperature is fine.

Slippery ice cubes

Do ice cubes stick to the tray of your automatic ice maker? Take out the tray, and wash and dry it well. Then lightly coat the inside with nonstick cooking spray, and wipe off any excess. The cubes will slide right out, and there will be no off-taste. It lasts longer than vinegar, which is often recommended as a solution to this problem.

Frosty tubes

If there's frost on one of the tubes running into your fridge's compressor, it probably melts regularly, leaving a messy puddle. The solution is to cover the tube with a foam sleeve or wraparound insulation, sold by suppliers of air-conditioning parts. The tube is the suction line coming from the evaporator coils inside the unit; its location may vary from unit to unit. ▼

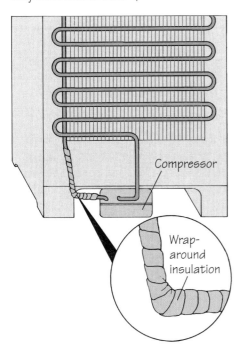

Compressor

Wraparound insulation

NEW DOOR GASKET

A damaged refrigerator door gasket wastes energy. Replacing one is easy. Order the gasket ahead. Your local appliance store may not stock one for your refrigerator model but can order it and have it shipped directly to you. Most gaskets are held by a retainer strip and screws, although some simply slip under a retainer and others are held only by screws. When installing a new gasket, don't overtighten the screws; they can crack the plastic door liner. Snug the screws down slightly, then close the door. Gently twist the door if necessary to conform it to the cabinet; then tighten the screws.

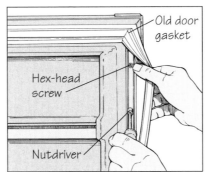

Old door gasket

Hex-head screw

Nutdriver

1 Roll the gasket back and use a nutdriver to loosen—but not remove—the screws. Slip the gasket from under the retainer. Before installing the new gasket, inspect it. If it is crimped, soak it in hot tap water for a few minutes.

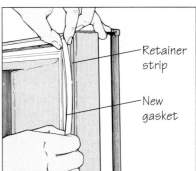

Retainer strip

New gasket

2 Position the new gasket over the retainer corners at the door top. On each side, start at one corner and slide the gasket under the retainer. Carefully tighten the screws at each side's center, then the corners, then in between.

Preventing emergencies

Safety light

A tripped circuit breaker could turn the food in your freezer into a soggy spoiled mass before you discover it. To avoid this, put a low-wattage night-light in the same wall outlet as the freezer. You'll be able to see immediately when the power is off.

Avoiding a meltdown

If your area has power outages, keep your freezer full, packing empty spaces with packets of picnic-cooler artificial ice or plastic bottles of frozen water. If there's a prolonged outage, 25 pounds of dry ice will keep an average 10-cubic-foot freezer cold enough for about 3 days. For dry ice, check the Yellow Pages or the hydro company. Wear heavy gloves when handling it, and put newspapers between it and your food.

DISHWASHERS AND STOVES

Dishwashers

Rusty rack fix

Is the plastic coating peeling off the racks in your dishwasher? Cover them with pieces of flexible clear plastic tubing. For most racks, tubing with an outside diameter of ¼ inch and an inside diameter of ⅛ inch works well. Cut it into ¼-inch lengths and slip them over the rusted rack ends. ▼

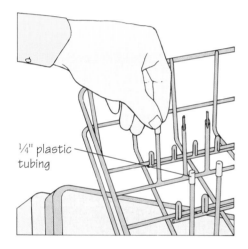

¼" plastic tubing

Another rack saver

You can also touch up a rusty dishwasher rack with paint, but don't use just any paint because it might come off on your dishes. There is a special paint that's made just for coating damaged areas on dishwasher racks. It is heat-resistant, has a rubberized finish, and is safe to use around dishes. It comes in standard rack colors in nail-polish-size bottles with a brush in the cap. You can buy it from appliance parts suppliers.

Rusty machine

Iron in the water is the usual cause of blotchy yellow or brown stains in a dishwasher. To remove the stains, let the empty machine fill, add ½ cup of citric acid crystals, and run it through a cycle. For a permanent solution, put an iron filter on your water supply.

Limey machine

To remove the chalky mineral deposits known as lime on your dishwasher's interior, let the empty machine fill, put in a cup of white vinegar, and run it through a cycle. Then add detergent and run it through another cycle. But don't do it too often; vinegar is an acid, and excessive use of it could damage the enamel.

Not-so-hot water

To dissolve detergent and get dishes clean, the hot water in your dishwasher should ideally be 60°C (140°F). Test the water in the sink next to the dishwasher. Run it until it's as hot as possible, catch some in a cup, and insert a thermometer. If it's not hot enough, try insulating the hot-water pipes between the water heater and the dishwasher. As a last resort, raise the water-heater setting, but it's best to avoid this if you have young children in the house.

Black marks

If your dishes have mysterious black smears, it may be the result of metal, especially aluminum utensils, rubbing against them. Separate pots and dishes when you load the dishwasher. Also, don't put in throw-away aluminum pans. The thin aluminum coating breaks down under the heat and marks dishes.

Gas stoves

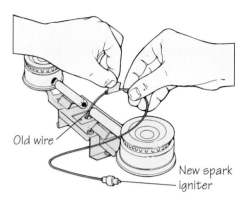

Old wire

New spark igniter

New spark ▲

Replacing a defective electric spark igniter on a gas stove is easy. The only tricky part is fishing the new igniter wire from the stovetop to the control box located on the back of the stove. To do this, cut the old igniter from its wire and tape the control-box end of the new igniter wire to the cut end of the old wire. Then slowly pull the old wire out through the back of the stove. This will pull the new wire through. Before starting, be sure to unplug the stove.

Clean jets

If the jet on a gas burner becomes clogged, clean it with a straight pin or a pipe cleaner. Don't use a toothpick; its tip might break and stay in the hole. ▼

Gas burner

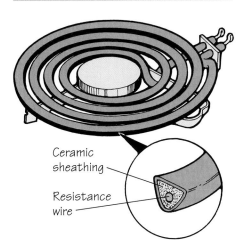

Ceramic
sheathing

Resistance
wire

Hot spot ▲

If a stovetop element develops a spot that glows brighter than the rest of the coil, the ceramic insulation sheathing has broken down, exposing the nichrome resistance wire inside. The element may continue working for a while, but it's best to replace it at once. The hot spot could damage your cookware.

No-no's

Covering the floor of your electric oven with aluminum foil to catch drips may sound like a good idea, but don't do it. Foil reflects and intensifies heat, which can cause the bake element to burn out prematurely. Don't cover a rack with foil either. This traps heat in the bottom of the oven and keeps it from reaching the heat sensor near the top. The overheating in the bottom could damage not only the element but the oven lining and the oven-door glass as well. It can also mess up cooking times.

OVEN ELEMENTS

Replacing a burned-out bake or broil element in an electric stove is a job that can be expensive to have done but takes only a few minutes to do yourself. Buy a new replacement element for your stove model at an appliance parts store. If your oven has a door that lifts off, remove the door to gain easier access to the interior.

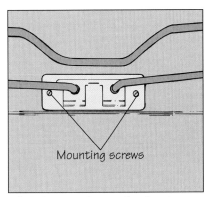

Mounting screws

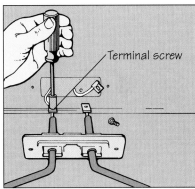

Terminal screw

1 Before starting, unplug the stove. Take out the screws that hold the element bracket to the back of the oven. Then pull the element gently toward you so that its terminals are accessible.

2 Disconnect the wires from the terminal screws or slip-on clips, noting which wire attaches to which terminal. Attach the wires to the new element, and screw the bracket into place.

Hidden fuse ▶

If the receptacle, timer, and lights on your electric stove don't work, you've probably blown the stove fuse with an overload on the control-panel receptacle. A toaster or electric skillet can do it. If you still have your owner's manual, check it for the fuse location. It's usually under the left rear burner. If it's not, look under the right rear burner, under the fluorescent light cover, in the top of the storage drawer, or above the control panel. It's a regular screw-in fuse; use a same-amperage replacement.

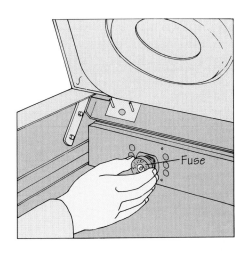

Fuse

CLOTHES WASHERS AND DRYERS

Washing machines

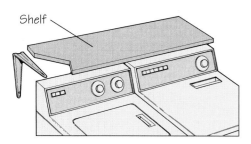

Shelf

Bridging the gap ▲

Are you always dropping or spilling things into the no-man's-land behind your washer and dryer? There's no way to eliminate the gap; the machines must sit away from the wall because of the washer hoses and the dryer vent. An easy solution is to cover the space with a shelf mounted on brackets. As an added bonus it'll give you a place to put detergent boxes, bleach bottles, and other laundry room clutter.

Lint trap

To avoid plugging drains with lint from the washer, secure an old thin sock or panty hose foot to the end of the drain hose with a strong rubber band. When the washer drains, the sock will collect the lint in the wash water. Turn the sock inside out to clean it. ▼

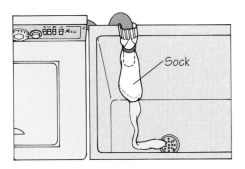

Sock

Fabric snagger

Is there something in your washing machine that's catching on your clothes? Rub an old panty hose over the agitator and the tub surface. Smooth any rough spot you find with very fine sandpaper.

Car tool to the rescue

If you can't remove the cap holding your washer agitator, try turning it with an automobile oil filter wrench. This tool has a flexible strap that can be adjusted to fit a round object snugly. ▼

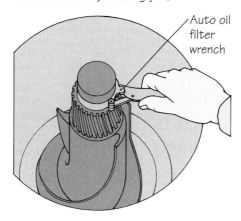

Auto oil filter wrench

Dryers

Bulb burnout

If the light bulb in your electric dryer (or oven) keeps burning out, make sure that you're using an appliance light bulb. Ordinary bulbs can't withstand the heat.

No heat?

If your dryer doesn't heat, check the double-pole circuit breaker or two fuses that control its power. The motor may run if one is out, but both have to be OK for the heating element to work.

Thermostat sizzle test

A defective thermostat may prevent a dryer from heating. Thermostats switch the power off when heated above a certain temperature. Test a thermostat first at room temperature: Unplug the dryer, disconnect a lead from a thermostat terminal, and hold a multitester's probes to the thermostat's terminals; the meter should read zero or near zero. Next, remove the thermostat and place it in an electric skillet. Heat the skillet to just above the temperature (stamped on the thermostat) at which the contacts should open or until the thermostat clicks. Wearing oven mitts, hold the probes to the terminals; look for a reading of infinite resistance or infinity (∞).

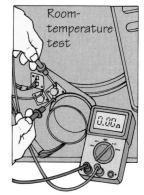

Room-temperature test

Skillet test

Keep hot air safely flowing

If you are installing a vinyl duct for a dryer, use only nonflammable duct and avoid dips that collect water and lint, blocking airflow and creating a fire hazard. Keep it under 20 feet long. Use aluminum if you need a longer duct.

REPLACING A DRYER DRIVE BELT

Most dryers' drums are turned by a drive belt that wraps completely around the drum. A worn belt will produce a thumping noise while the dryer is running. A broken one will not turn the drum at all. In either case replacement is in order, and it's an easy job. Before you start, buy a manufacturer's replacement belt at an appliance parts store; order it using the model number of your dryer. The odds are good that the belt you need will be in stock.

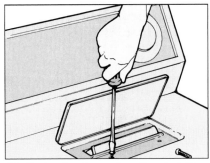

1 Unplug the dryer; close the shutoff valve on the gas line of a gas unit. If the lint screen is on the top, remove it and unscrew the screen housing.

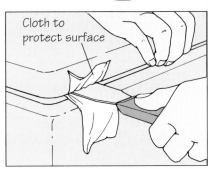

Cloth to protect surface

2 Slip a putty knife under the top about 2 in. from a front corner. Push it in as you pull up to unclip the top. Do the other corner. Open the top; lean it against wall.

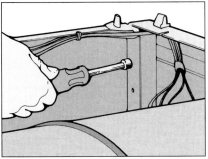

3 Use a nutdriver or a screwdriver to remove the fasteners holding the front panel. If there is a toeplate, remove it by taking out its clips or screws.

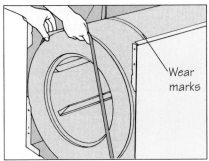

Wear marks

4 Remove the old belt. Using the wear marks as a guide, put the new belt around the drum with the ribbed side against the drum.

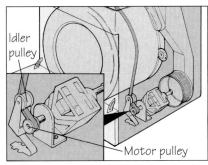

Idler pulley

Motor pulley

5 At the motor, slide the belt under the idler pulley and around the motor pulley. If the old belt broke, the spring-loaded idler will have popped out of position.

Indoor vent ▶

If you live in an apartment and can't vent your electric dryer outside, appliance parts stores sell inexpensive kits that let you vent indoors. Simply add water and dump the lint-laden water after each use. But expect added indoor heat and moisture. Never use an indoor vent on a gas unit; gas fumes must vent outdoors.

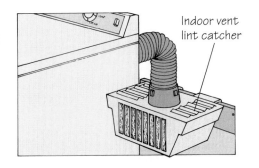

Indoor vent lint catcher

Blow out

If your dryer duct becomes clogged with lint, try clearing it out with a leaf blower. Disconnect the duct from the dryer, insert the blower nozzle in the duct, and wrap rags around it to make a snug fit. Then turn on the blower to clear the lint from the duct.

ELECTRONIC EQUIPMENT

Setting up

The art of concealment

Transform that jungle of wires behind your TV, VCR, or stereo into a neat, attractive cable. Just clip the plugs from a coiled telephone cord and wrap the coils around the wires. The cords are not expensive and come in a variety of colors and lengths. Electronics and auto parts stores also carry plastic tubes especially designed for organizing wire clutter.

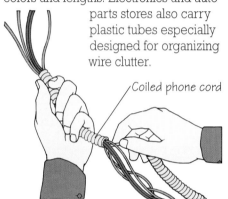

Coiled phone cord

Cool it

In theory, putting a VCR on top of a television is a no-no because heat from the TV could damage the VCR. But if there's no other convenient spot for the VCR, cut four small spacers from ¼-inch plywood, paint them flat black, and put one under each VCR leg. They'll be practically invisible on cabinets of any color and will let the TV heat escape.

Underfoot wiring

To run speaker cord from one side of a room to another or from room to room, drill small holes in the floor and run it across the basement or crawl space ceiling below. Keep the cord away from electrical wires, and secure it with insulated staples.

Have your cake and eat it too

Want to videotape a premium cable show while watching a regular channel? You can if you have a cable-compatible TV. Buy a two-way cable signal splitter, an A-B switch, and three short lengths of cable at an electronics store; hook them up as shown. With the switch set on A, the cable signal feeds through the cable box and VCR as usual, letting you watch and record a program or just record it or watch it. With the switch set on B, the signal feeds directly to your TV while the cable box still sends a signal to the VCR. If you want to watch one program and record another, simply set the switch on A, set the VCR to record the cable channel, and then set the switch on B and tune your TV to watch any channel that doesn't need a cable converter box. ▼

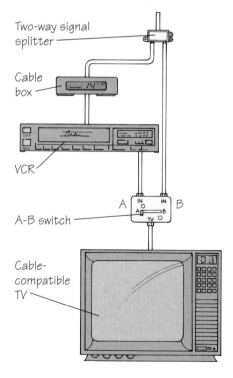

Two-way signal splitter

Cable box

VCR

A-B switch

Cable-compatible TV

Improving quality

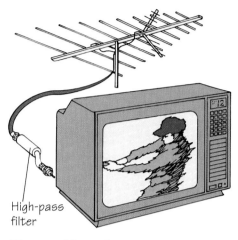

High-pass filter

Ham problem ▲

If your TV develops wavering lines occasionally for no apparent reason, the cause may be a ham radio operator, especially if it happens on VHF channels and not on UHF ones. To correct the problem, install a high-pass filter—sold at electronics stores—between the TV and its antenna wire. Get a filter for either a cable or a flat twin-lead antenna wire, depending on your setup.

Don't use shampoo

Confused about how to clean VCR heads? The safest and easiest way is with a videocassette cleaning cartridge. Use the "wet" type that requires you to place a few drops of cleaning solution on the tape; it's less abrasive than the "dry" type. You run it through the machine like a regular cassette, and it takes about 30 seconds to do the job. How often? After 40 to 50 hours of use. That's every month if you watch five movies a week; every six months if you average one movie a week.

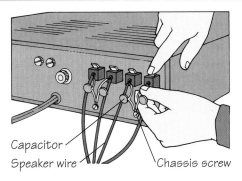

Capacitor
Speaker wire   Chassis screw

Not so good, buddy ▲

If your stereo picks up someone's CB radio, install capacitors on the speaker outlets. Get four 0.01–0.3 microfarad (mfd) disc capacitors at an electronics store. There are usually four outlets, two for each speaker. With your stereo unplugged, insert one capacitor wire into each outlet along with the speaker wire lead. Attach the capacitor's other wire to a chassis screw to ground it.

Wide receiver

Need better radio reception in a room with a suspended ceiling? Attach the bare ends of the antenna wire to the metal gridwork supporting the ceiling.

Moving computers

Computer wrap

If you have to move a computer any distance, pack it into the original cartons, if possible. Otherwise pack it as snugly as you can in other cartons, using crumpled paper on all sides to cushion the units. Never wrap a computer in plastic. Condensation can form on the inside of the plastic and damage the computer.

Always back up

Moving a personal computer can be a tricky business, especially because you risk losing any valuable information stored in it. Even if it's handled carefully, a computer hard disk can be damaged by being jarred in a moving van or truck. To lessen the chances of losing data, copy whatever is stored on your hard drive onto backup disks and carry them separately to the new location.

Making repairs

Save a cassette ▲

Has a favorite irreplaceable audiocassette tape snapped apart? Fix it with a splicing kit from an electronics store. The kit should have a trimming instrument, splicing tape, a splicing block, and instructions. If either end of the tape is inside the cassette and the cassette case can't be unscrewed, get an empty cassette case too. Then carefully pry apart the old case, transfer the tape to the new case, splice the broken ends, and snap the new case shut.

Mini probe

When using a multitester to check a telephone jack, you may find that the instrument's probes are too large for the tiny contacts in the jack. The solution is to put an alligator clip on the multitester probe, then clamp a sewing needle in the clip. ▼

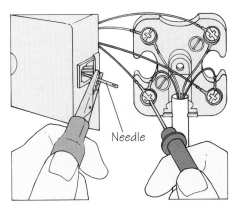

Needle

Torn speaker

To fix a ripped speaker cone—for a while, at least—take it out of the cabinet and cut a patch from a paper coffee filter. Coat one side of the patch liberally with rubber cement or special speaker cement (sold at electronics stores). Holding the back of the cone with one hand, gently apply the patch to the front and rub lightly to smooth it. Let the cement dry before reinstalling the cone. You can fix a simple tear using cement alone.

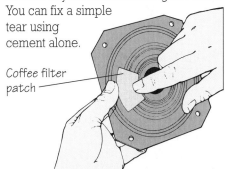

Coffee filter patch

YARD AND GARDEN

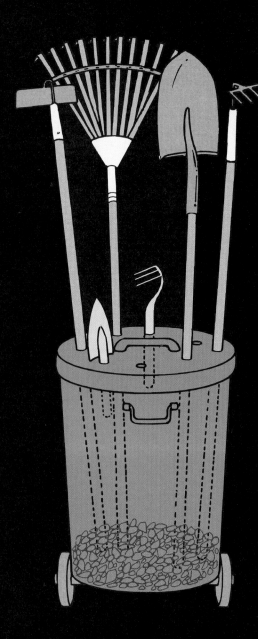

PLANTING A GARDEN

Breaking ground

Making a bed the easy way

Why not take a break from spading and let a cover crop prepare your new flower or vegetable bed? The fall before you intend to plant (at least 4 to 6 weeks before frost), rototill the area and sow it with clover or bean seed at a rate of ¼ pound per 100 square feet. When this cover crop matures—but before it sets seed—mow it and rototill the stubble into the soil. As it rots, the vegetation will enrich the bed, while its roots will have already loosened the soil.

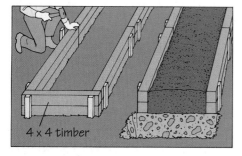

4 x 4 timber

On the rocks ▲

If you'd like a lush garden on a rocky or other inhospitable site, build a raised bed. A bed can be as long as you like, but it must be narrow—about 4 feet across. That way you can work on it from both sides without stepping on the soil, which would compact it and ruin the aeration. To build a bed, install edging, such as 4 x 4 landscaping timbers. (*Note:* The chemicals in timbers will leach into the soil; if you're planting vegetables, use a decay-resistant wood, such as redwood, instead of timbers.) Fill the bed with compost-rich topsoil. The drainage will be good and the plants will develop healthy root systems.

Setting things straight ▲

To establish straight rows in a garden, fill two plastic jugs with water and set one at each end of the row. Then stretch a mason's line between them and move them from row to row. It is easier than driving stakes for the string.

Seedlings

Greenhouses from the salad bar

You can start seeds in the plastic clamshell food containers that you find at many salad bars. Wash the container and half fill it with a lightly moistened seed-starting mix. Place the seeds and close the lid, securing it with a rubber band. The clear lid allows light to pass through, holds moisture in, and lets you keep track of your sprouting seeds. ▼

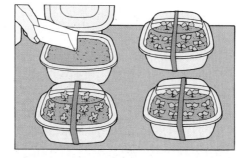

New life for yogurt cups

Small plastic yogurt cups make handy mini-pots for starting seeds indoors. Punch drainage holes in the bottoms of the cups. Then, for easy carrying, place the cups on a tray. Fill them with soil, place them on a sunny windowsill, and they're ready for your seeds. ▼

All-weather ID

This inexpensive plant label will always be readable. Cut a tag from an old aluminum TV dinner container or a foil pie pan. Place the tag on a soft surface, such as a towel, and use a ballpoint pen to inscribe the plant name on it. Attach it to a stake next to the seedling. The imprint will last indefinitely.

Quick cover

On chilly spring nights, protect seedlings from frost (and set the stage for an extra-early harvest of flowers or vegetables) with a simple tentlike structure. To build it, you need only construct a frame of PVC pipe and cover it with woven plastic shade material or with the polyethylene sheeting pictured here. The light, sturdy greenhouse can be moved from spot to spot as the need arises, and it is easy to store at the end of the season.

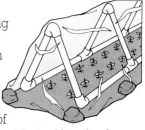

PLANTING A GARDEN

Edgings and trainers

Shake it

A bundle of precut cedar shakes makes an edging around your garden beds that's attractive, inexpensive, and practical too. Set the shakes in an overlapped alternating pattern, driving them into the ground with a protective block of wood and a mallet. ▼

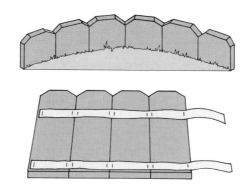

Stay flexible ▲

If you have a curved garden bed that needs a decorative edging, join a number of wood edging planks by stapling to their backs a couple of heavy-duty plastic strips, such as you might cut from a commercial edging. If it is a large bed, assemble about 6 feet of edging at a time, leaving a few inches of extra plastic at the end of each section. Position the sections in a shallow ditch, level them, and staple them together. Then fill in the ditch with soil.

Movable trellis

Would you like to brighten the side of your house with a vine *and* retain easy access to the wall behind it for paint and repairs? Make a movable trellis out of a section of concrete reinforcing wire or galvanized fencing, and hang it on hooks screwed into the siding. When it's time to work on the house, gently unhook the trellis and rest it on a support such as the stakes shown here. ▼

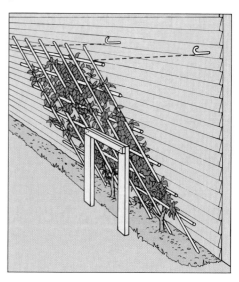

Tongue-and-grooving ▶

You can also use 1 x 6 yellow pine or cedar tongue-and-groove planks, available at most lumberyards, as an edging. To make the planks easier to drive in, cut the bottom edges at a 45° angle. The length of the stakes should equal the depth of the roots that you're containing plus 2½ inches for the above-ground section and a few more inches for the length of the 45° cut. Use a mallet and protective block of wood to drive the tongue sections into the grooves.

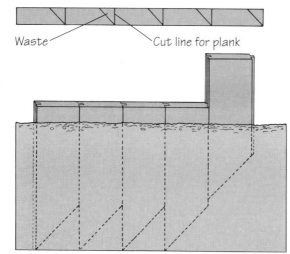

Waste   Cut line for plank

Lampshade support

The metal frame of an old lampshade makes a great freestanding support for top-heavy plants such as peonies. Collect various sizes for plants both large and small.

Making compost

It's in the bag

Rather than fussing with bins and heaps, why not do all your composting in a bag? First fill a heavy-duty trash bag with yard wastes, such as grass clippings and leaves, and organic kitchen scraps. Add a shovelful of soil and ¼ cup of high-nitrogen fertilizer, such as a 10-10-10 type. Moisten the mixture thoroughly. Seal the bag and set it in a sunny place; roll it over twice a week, taking care not to tear the bag. In 2 months (or less), the wastes will have turned to soil-enriching humus.

Blending in

An easy way to speed up the composting process is to put your collection of fruit and vegetable peelings, eggshells, and other easily biodegradable scraps in a blender along with a cup of water. (Don't use meat or dairy scraps, as they tend to attract animals.) Puree the scraps and pour the mixture on the compost pile. The mush will decompose quickly—usually in a few weeks. To minimize the mess, collect the scraps in a small plastic bag and puree them every few days.

Small wonder

If you have a compact garden and don't need a lot of compost, you can use a household plastic laundry hamper as a compost bin. Choose one that's an attractive color and has perforations on the sides. A removable hinged lid will make it easy to add to the pile.

Vegetable gardening

Slinging melons

To make room for more eatables in a small garden, train melon vines on a trellis. As the fruit grows heavy, hold it with a sling made from a rag or a nylon stocking. Tie the ends in a knot or fasten them with a safety pin.

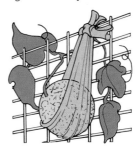

Instant shade

Since lettuce thrives in cold conditions, the homegrown leaves start to taste bitter around July. To extend the growing season, build a portable shade structure. Connect eight lengths of PVC pipe with four 3-way fittings, and cover the frame with a woven plastic shade cloth, available at garden supply centers. The cloth keeps the plants cool as it filters the sunlight. At season's end, fold the cloth and take the frame apart. ▼

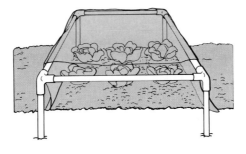

Lettuce water

If you water leafy greens in the evening and then pick them the next morning, they'll be crisp and full of flavor.

A LEAD-FREE HARVEST

While the hazard of lead paint is well known (see p.177), the dangers from soil contaminated with lead are not. Lead may be found in soil around older homes that were weatherproofed with lead-base paint or are located near a busy street where the exhaust from leaded gasoline has made its way into the soil. Lead was also added to some insecticides used on farms a generation ago.

Homegrown greens and roots readily absorb lead from the soil, concentrate it in their tissues, and then pass it along to anyone who eats them. Fortunately there's an easy, inexpensive remedy: compost. The U.S. Environmental Protection Agency (EPA) has found that adding compost to the topsoil at a rate of 25 percent of the volume reduces the lead vegetables take in by as much as 60 percent.

Before you plant a vegetable garden, send a soil sample to a laboratory and have it tested for lead content. If your soil has a pH of 7 or higher and tests 20 parts per million, or if it has a pH of less than 7 and tests 10 ppm, compost can't help. To learn more about testing, contact your provincial ministry of agriculture.

LANDSCAPING

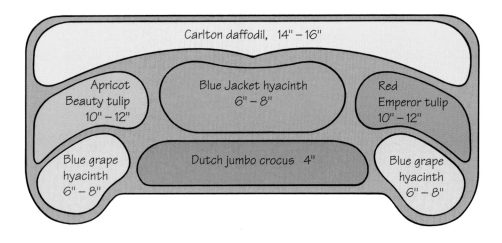

Carlton daffodil, 14" – 16"

Apricot Beauty tulip 10" – 12"

Blue Jacket hyacinth 6" – 8"

Red Emperor tulip 10" – 12"

Blue grape hyacinth 6" – 8"

Dutch jumbo crocus 4"

Blue grape hyacinth 6" – 8"

WHAT TO PLANT AND WHERE IN A 4 X 8 GARDEN

This sample garden is filled with reliable and popular springtime bulbs, chosen and placed with the varying heights of the plants, the mix of colors, and different blooming times in mind. Look for strong, healthy bulbs—the larger the better. They should feel firm when squeezed (gently), and they should be free of nicks, soft spots, and decay. A light surface mold, which can develop when the bulb is stored, is common and does not harm it. Prepare the soil first by loosening it and adding organic material; then work some general bulb food into the soil. Plant the bulbs, pointed end up, randomly (not in rows) at the depth and spacing called for in the chart.

Bulbs

	Carlton daffodil	Blue Jacket hyacinth	Dutch jumbo crocus	Apricot Beauty tulip	Red Emperor tulip	Blue grape hyacinth
Number of bulbs	40	20	40	15	15	40
Spacing	6 in.	6 in.	3 in.	6 in.	6 in.	3 in.
Depth	6 in.	6 in.	3 in.	6 in.	6 in.	3 in.

A mower-friendly lawn

Mowing will be faster and easier if you eliminate the grass peninsulas and islands that require a lot of turning maneuvers with the mower and add to the trimming time. Use your mower to draw a new perimeter that you can mow without a stop. Fill the areas outside the line with mulch, ground cover, and shrubbery.

A low-water landscape

If water is scarce or if your water bills are high, here's how to conserve water.
▷ Landscape with drought-tolerant plants. Ask your local nursery for ideas.
▷ Reduce the lawn area to a minimum. Turf grass is a heavy water user, so wherever possible replace it with mulch or a drought-tolerant ground cover.
▷ Make pavements permeable. Bricks set in sand let rain soak through to roots below; blacktop and concrete send water to the storm drain.
▷ Group together plants with similar water needs.

A visual trick

Give a small yard the illusion of greater space by "forcing the perspective," a technique known to architects. Just angle the plantings toward each other as they extend to the rear of the landscape.

FOUNDATION PLANTINGS

When you are devising a planting scheme, try several different combinations on paper first. Using ¼-inch graph paper, make a scaled master plan of your house, letting each square equal 1 foot. Include any existing trees and other landmarks. Use removable (and perhaps color-coded) stickers to help you mark the plan.

Pull attention away from the driveway. Avoid placing plants along the edges.

Draw the eye to the entry. Low-growing plants lead visitors to the front door.

Highlight the front door with taller plants or vines.
Caution: Some vines damage siding and bricks over time. Ask a local nursery to help you choose.

Plant shrubs 4 to 6 ft. away from the house foundation to help prevent the buildup of dampness there. Limit the number of tall shrubs as they may provide hiding places for a burglar.

Choose plants with interesting branches that, when leafless, will enhance the winter landscape, such as the red-twigged dogwood and the winged euonymus.

Vary plant types. Mix deciduous and coniferous shrubs with ground covers, vines, and flowers to give a sense of texture and interest.

Use colors wisely. Place colorful flowers and plants where you want people to look. Colors should complement each other and those of your house.

Wrap plantings around a corner to tie the side yard to the front yard. Use a tall shrub to soften a corner's hard edge.

Hide large unattractive features, such as an exposed foundation, air conditioners, and meters, with full shrubs.

HANDLING WEEDS, INSECTS, AND ANIMALS

Weed attack

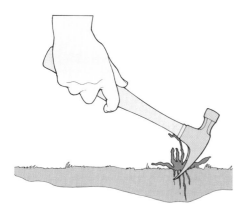

Weed whacking ▲

You can use a long-handled weeding fork, called a fishtail weeder, to rid your lawn of dandelions and other weeds. But if you don't have one on hand, whack and grab the pests with the claw of an old hammer and then pull them out, root and all. The deeper you can grab the root, the better.

Customizing a hoe

To turn a regular hoe into a precision instrument, file a notch into the side of its blade. With this sharpened V you can delicately snip weeds off at their base, even in the most hard-to-reach corners.

When to weed

Timing can be a great help in your war against the weeds. Wait for a hot, sunny day; then hoe the weeds (without seed heads) in the morning and leave them lying on the surface of the soil. The sun will wither the weeds and transform them into beneficial organic mulch.

Weeds in concrete

You can use piping-hot water to kill weeds that sprout through concrete joints—without endangering yourself or the wildlife. Boil water in a kettle and pour it into the cracks, and watch the weeds wilt. If you have a lot of weeds, use a large soup pot, but be careful not to splash the hot water on yourself.

Pest preventives

Gardening helpers

▷ Landscape with plants that are naturally insect- and disease-resistant, such as Rugosa roses. Ask at your nursery or garden center about varieties that do well locally.
▷ Select grass seed that has been inoculated with beneficial fungi called endophytes to protect your lawn against the most troublesome grass-eating insects: sod webworms, chinch bugs, and billbugs.
▷ Reduce soil-borne diseases by varying your flower and vegetable plantings. Rotate the crops, changing the type of plant and its location each year.
▷ Keep your landscape free of weeds, dead leaves, and brush—these provide a refuge and breeding place for insect pests and plant diseases.

Deer deterrent

Deer can be a serious threat to gardens in rural areas and communities such as Banff, Alta. Protect shrubs and trees by spraying them with a mixture of 1 teaspoon dishwashing detergent, 1 egg, and 1 quart water. The smell, repulsive to deer, is imperceptible to humans.

Moth crystal mulch

If rabbits and woodchucks have taken to grazing in your garden, or if pets are turning your garden into a litter box, sprinkle the area with moth crystals. That will drive away the four-legged nuisances. To keep out skunks, spread moth crystals around the fence line. However, the crystals are poisonous; don't use them if children are around.

Safe stoppers

Slug it out ▲

Slugs love beer. Just put a bottle of beer that's two-thirds empty in the ground with the neck slightly exposed. They'll crawl in for a sip and drown. Another tactic is to edge a slug's favorite hangout—moist, shady gardens—with coarsely crushed eggshells.

ATTRACTING THE GOOD GUYS

While many gardeners strive to rid their gardens of insect and animal pests, others go to great lengths to entice visitors from the animal kingdom to their gardens. Below is a sample of who is invited, how they are encouraged to come, and why.

ANIMAL TYPE	SHELTER AND ENVIRONMENT	FOOD AND WATER	BENEFITS TO GARDEN
Birds of all types	Build nesting boxes, leave dead trees in place for nests; offer protective shelter of brush piles, cedar and pine trees; provide sources of dripping water.	Plant berry-laden bushes, fruiting vines, and trees that produce nuts and berries; set out bird feeders with seeds, suet, and peanut butter and cornmeal balls; provide small pools of water.	Eat insects; provide nature-watching opportunities.
Butterflies	Leave areas of tall grasses; encourage meadow plants; install windbreak in warm sunny spot; provide large flat rock for sunning; keep birdbaths and bird feeders at a distance; plant solid-color purple, mauve, white, and yellow (no red) flowering plants.	Plant milkweed and rue for caterpillars to munch on; plant spring-blooming nectar-producing plants, such as lilacs, peonies, and lavender; plant fall-blooming plants such as sedum and butterfly bush; provide small puddles of water.	Offer nature-watching opportunities; enhance beauty of the garden.
Earthworms	Create soil rich in organic matter; refrain from using pesticides; loosen the soil before adding live store-bought worms from a bait shop.	Mix organic matter into soil; add a layer of mulch to keep soil moist.	Burrow constantly into soil, tilling and aerating it; ingest organic waste and deposit humus-rich castings in soil.

Easy wasp control

The smell of vinegar attracts wasps. To cure a wasp problem, put 2 inches of vinegar in a long-necked bottle. They'll crawl in and won't be able to crawl out.

Soap story

Insecticidal soaps provide effective protection against many kinds of insects, including aphids, mites, and whiteflies, and don't harm wildlife, children, or pets. Use a commercial brand or make your own by mixing 1 to 3 teaspoons of a mild dishwashing liquid into a gallon of water. Test on a few leaves and wait 48 hours, as some plants are sensitive. If there's no ill effect, spray the plants well (wetting both the tops and bottoms of the leaves) once every 2 to 3 days for a period of 2 weeks.

Oily spray

Mixing vegetable oil and nondetergent liquid soap makes another effective, inexpensive, and nontoxic spray that is fatal to aphids, spider mites, scales, mealybugs, and some caterpillars. Mix 1 cup cooking oil with 1 tablespoon liquid soap; then dilute it, using 1 teaspoon oil-soap mixture for each cup of water. Spray the leaves as for soap spray, but only when air temperatures are below 29°C (85°F). If it's hotter than that, the oil can damage some foliage. The spray is effective against eggs as well as adult insects.

Insect allies

Some insects are on your side. Dragonflies and spiders eat thousands of harmful insects, including mosquitoes, and ladybugs consume great numbers of other insects, such as aphids. ▼

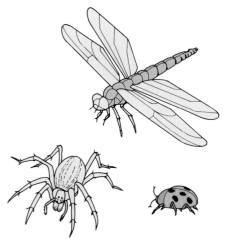

EASIER GARDENING

Lifesavers

Latex liners

Your gardening gloves protect you from thorns, but they don't help much against the cold. To boost their insulation value, slip your hands first into a pair of light-weight latex gloves. These will keep your hands warm and dry, and you'll hardly know they are there.

Petroleum jelly "glove"

When close work—fine pruning or weeding or some late transplanting—forces you to work without gloves in cold weather, you can keep the chill out of your fingers by rubbing your hands with petroleum jelly. It'll also make cleaning up quicker and easier.

Knee protectors

Much of a gardener's work is done on the hands and knees, and that can cause joints to ache. To combat the problem, make a kneepad out of a piece of Styrofoam or other rigid foam insulation about 18 inches square and 1 inch thick. Wrap the pad in a plastic trash bag. The foam not only serves as a cushion, it also reflects body heat and protects against the cold. ▼

Child's play

Another device that can save you from the discomfort of squatting or kneeling is your child's tricycle. Turn it around so that you are riding it backward and you'll find yourself at exactly the right level to get your fingers down into the dirt. And when you've finished weeding or planting one patch, you can push yourself along to the next one.

Circle gardens

A further way to minimize bending and kneeling is to confine your most work-intensive garden beds to small-diameter circles, say 24 or 36 inches wide. You'll be able to reach the entire garden without a lot of effort and do most of the work sitting down.

Kinder tools

A blister-proof rake

Does leaf raking leave your hands raw with blisters? The cure for that is to pad the handle with ordinary pipe insulation; use the type designed for ¾-inch copper pipe. Coat the rake's handle with contact cement, cut the insulation to length, and slip it on.

Tall tools

Be good to your back by standing up while weeding and planting bulbs. All you'll need are a few tools with long handles, which are available at garden supply stores and through catalogs.

A back-saving sled ▶

Heaving a heavy weight into a wheel-barrow or garden cart can strain your back badly. The next time you need to move a big rock, tree, or shrub, make a simple sled out of a scrap piece of ¼-inch plywood. Drill a pair of holes in one end of the plywood and attach a loop of rope. Roll your load onto the sled and pull. You'll find that it will slide easily across the lawn without damaging the grass—or your back.

Softer stepping

To cushion your foot as you dig, slip a piece of old garden hose over the shoulder of the shovel where you step on it.

SEEDING AND FEEDING YOUR LAWN

Better spreading

Sowing in the wind

Even a moderate breeze scatters seed as it drops out of the spreader, and that means gaps in your new lawn. Try mixing the seed with barely damp clean sand. The weight of the sand will help shield the seeds from the wind and enable them to fall straight.

Crisscross coverage

It is crucial to spread seed and fertilizer evenly. Try setting the spreader application rate at half of what is recommended on the package and then make twice as many passes. Work back and forth across the whole lawn from left to right; then turn and repeat the process at a right angle to the first passes. This is a bit more work, but you'll eliminate gaps and surpluses in your spreading. ▼

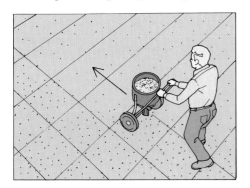

Flour power

It's often hard to tell which areas have been covered with fertilizer or seed. Mixing some kitchen flour with the product before you spread it will mark what you've covered without harming the lawn or the wildlife, and it disappears with the first rain.

Nourishing thoughts

Spray 'n' walk ▲

Spraying a liquid fertilizer greatly reduces the likelihood of fertilizer burn. All you have to do to avoid burning your grass is to wet the lawn before you spray or water it immediately afterward. To apply the fertilizer, connect a sprayer to a garden hose. Walk in a straight line fairly slowly and move the spray nozzle back and forth.

Sodding a lawn

Sod versus seed

Sodding a lawn provides an "instant" living carpet that is ready for (minimal) traffic in a couple of weeks. It is not surprising, then, that sod is expensive. If you do the job yourself, expect to pay about twice as much per square foot as for seed. Hiring a pro to do it will double the cost again. Whether you choose to lay sod or plant seeds, you'll need to prepare the soil well. For sod, you should also grade it carefully—that way the roots can get a good grip.

A quick pickup

Pause in your passes with the spreader for a moment, and the darn thing dumps a fertilizer overdose that kills the turf below. To quickly remove the spill before it does any harm, enlist the aid of a shop vac. If it's grass seed you spilled, clean out the vacuum canister first; then you can retrieve the wasted seed.

Aerating shoes

An easy way to aerate your lawn is to strap on a pair of aerating sandals, available from catalogs and gardening supply stores. The special "shoes" have thin spikes that poke holes into the soil as you walk. The holes loosen the soil, making it more water-retentive and more receptive to fertilizer feedings. ▼

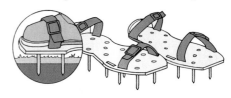

Rolling out the carpet

Sod is delivered in strips that are rolled and stacked. As you roll out your new lawn, stagger the ends of the strips, the way you would for bricklaying. In addition, make sure that the edges of each strip butt tightly against the previously laid strip. A snug fit will minimize any gaps in the lawn and will keep the strips from drying out too quickly.

Make a stand

If you stand on a board or piece of plywood as you lay the strips, you won't disturb the soil you've worked so hard to prepare.

LAWN CARE AND MAINTENANCE

Mowing

Recycle those clippings

You'll reduce your turf's need for fertilizers and save yourself some raking and hauling if you switch to a mulching mower, a rotary-blade machine that shreds clippings and returns them to the lawn. Left to decompose in place, clippings can reduce fertilizer needs by 25 percent annually. What's more, you'll be doing your part to reduce the burden on local landfills.

Working against gravity

Cutting the grass on a slope or bank can be a dangerous business—one slip and your foot may end up in the mower. Mowing across the slope, rather than up and down, minimizes the danger. And to be extra-safe, why not put on a pair of cleated golf or sports shoes first?

Set the height ▶

Mowing by the calendar won't help your lawn; it doesn't care how many days it's been since the last cut and trim. You'll work less and have a healthier lawn if you let the grass do the scheduling instead. Set the lawn mower to the correct height for your grass—usually 2½ to 3 inches. Then cut often enough so that you never remove more than one-third of the grass blades. Taking more than that will shock and weaken the root system.

Push a reel mower

Reel mowers are back and are cutting the grass cleanly. Today's versions look like the mowers of ages past but in fact are much improved. New models are lighter, self-sharpening, and more maneuverable. And unlike their noisy powered rotary counterparts, which bruise the grass as they cut, reel mowers cut grass blades cleanly. But because you have to push this quiet cutter around, you'll be happier with one if your lawn is under 2,000 square feet and relatively level.

Correct mowing height, with healthy root growth

Closer mowing height, with shallow roots that need more food and water

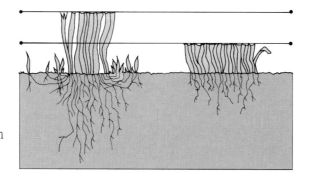

That blade is dull

If the grass develops a grayish brown cast a day or two after mowing, it's a signal that your mower blade needs sharpening. Look closely and you'll find that the tips of the grass blades have been shredded rather than neatly sliced. Those ragged ends not only look bad, they provide easy entry for turf diseases. For hints on sharpening garden tools, see p.281.

Patching

Winter seeding

Let nature help you reseed bare spots. Sprinkle them with grass seed in early spring. As the soil alternately thaws, refreezes, and thaws again, it crumbles into a perfect seedbed. The seed will lie dormant until the weather warms, but then it will sprout right away, giving your patch a head start.

Coffee can spreader

Don't use a regular spreader when it's time to reseed bare spots. It throws seed everywhere, with only a fraction landing on target. For precision seeding, you can fashion a spot seeder from an empty coffee can and a pair of plastic lids. Into one lid drill holes large enough to let grass seed pass; snap this in place when reseeding. Keep the other, unpierced lid snapped over the can's bottom. When the job is finished, reverse the lids and you'll seal in the unused seed for safe storage.

Guides for watering

Watering and your soil ▶

Turf guides recommend giving a lawn 1 inch of water with each irrigation—no matter what type of soil you have. What does vary with the soil texture is the frequency of irrigation. Use the chart at right to find out how often to irrigate and how deeply 1 inch of water will penetrate. If you don't know what kind of soil you have, do the test below.

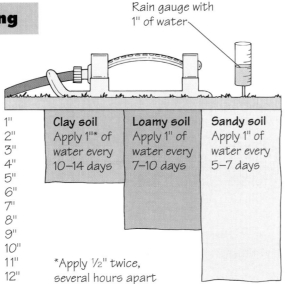

Rain gauge with 1" of water

	Clay soil	Loamy soil	Sandy soil
1" 2" 3" 4" 5" 6" 7" 8" 9" 10" 11" 12"	Apply 1"* of water every 10–14 days	Apply 1" of water every 7–10 days	Apply 1" of water every 5–7 days

*Apply ½" twice, several hours apart

The squeeze test

To determine your soil's texture, use a trowel to extract several small samples from the turf's root zone (3 to 4 inches below the surface). Shake these up together in a paper bag, extract a tablespoonful, and squeeze it in your fist. If it makes a ball that stands up to a poke, the soil is clay. A ball that cracks with a poke or two is loam; a ball that crumbles easily is sand. Use the chart above and the test below to determine if you have watered your type of soil deeply enough.

Dig deep

An old screwdriver makes a good tool for double-checking the effectiveness of your lawn watering. After you've finished sprinkling, push the tool through the sod. It will penetrate wet soil easily and will register resistance when it encounters the dry zone below.

Waste not

On a sunny, breezy day, as much as half your sprinkler's droplets may evaporate before they reach the ground. But nothing could be simpler than reducing this kind of waste: All you have to do is switch your watering to early morning hours, when the air is still and the sunlight less intense.

Sprinklers and hoses

Testing a sprinkler

How fast does your sprinkler sprinkle? Surrounding it with empty cans will give you the answer. Run the sprinkler for exactly 1 hour, and then measure the depth of the water in each can. This test will let you determine not only the sprinkler's average output, but also if there are any gaps in its sprinkling pattern.

A custom hose

A soaker hose is a precise way of delivering water right where the garden needs it—but not if the hose is too long. With an old C-clamp or spring clip, though, you can shorten the hose to match the length of the bed or lawn. ▼

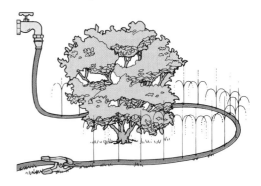

Cutting out those cut corners

A hose tends to cut the corners as it follows you around the yard, and in the process it may flatten prized flowers or vegetables. To protect your plantings (and reduce the wear on your hose), install a permanent guard at the outer corners of each bed. Use old croquet wickets that are gathering dust in the garage, or drive a stake into the ground and drop a short length of PVC pipe over it.

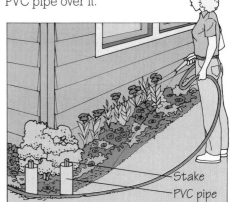

Stake
PVC pipe

TREES AND SHRUBS

Good buys

Weather beaters ▶

A belt of evergreens set between your house and the prevailing winter wind can help reduce your heating bills. Because these trees provide shelter to a distance 5 times their height, you can set tall-growing spruce or junipers well away from the house. To create a dead air space and add a layer of insulation, set more compact evergreen shrubs 4 to 6 feet from the foundation.

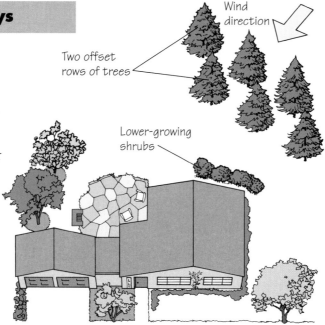

Wind direction

Two offset rows of trees

Lower-growing shrubs

Symptoms of good health

Clues to vigorous plants are compact growth and dark green, unblemished leaves. Avoid plants with signs of severely damaged (cracked or dry) roots.

No bargains

Those jumbo white pine or white spruce trees you find at discount garden centers are young specimens of fast-growing forest giants. They may look great when you plant them, but they will soon outgrow any but the largest yard. Similarly, avoid buying outsize bargain shrubs, such as rhododendrons or mountain laurels, that are "collected" stock—plants recently dug from fields or woodland. Such stressed plants never recover their full vigor and won't thrive like nursery-grown stock.

Protective measures

Tender staking

Letting the wind sway a newly planted tree strengthens the trunk. You'll be doing your transplants a favor if you keep the stakes low and the support loose— just tight enough to keep the tree from toppling.

Keep it protected

Bark protects trees from infection and disease, so avoid chaining bicycles or other potentially damaging items to a tree. Nailing or wiring signs, such as a yard sale notice, to a trunk or branch may also cut or bruise the bark; instead, try using cotton string to hang signs.

A bumper crop

Rabbits and mice often like to gnaw the bark of young trees. You can ward off these critters with sleeves made from flexible perforated plastic drainpipe. Cut 4-inch-diameter pipe into 24-inch lengths, slit each piece down one side, and gently slip one around the base of each sapling. The pipes protect the trees, and the perforations allow air to flow through to the covered bark.

Stripping a circle

Keeping the soil around young trees and shrubs stripped of grass and weeds increases the amounts of water, air, and nutrients that reach the roots and keeps the trunks from being damaged when you use a string trimmer on the lawn. Here's how to dig out a circular patch: Loop a rope around the trunk and around your spade. Adjust the loop so that when pulled outward, the spade reaches the desired radius. Move around the plant, digging as you go.

PLANTING A TREE OR SHRUB

Before you buy a young specimen, envision the size and shape of the mature plant. Review your landscaping goals (pp.268–269): Will it grow fast, provide shade, add color?

If necessary, check on buried utility lines (p.286) before you dig the planting hole. Be sure that the ball rests at the same depth as its previous planting. (Look for the old soil-stain ring on the bark.) Don't dig a hole that is too deep and then backfill it. The weight of the tree will likely sink the root ball below ground level.

Improve the soil if needed (below), but don't overdo it. In addition, resist the urge to fertilize. Research shows that very rich soil in the planting hole doesn't help a plant. The roots tend to ignore the outlying soil and grow in circles in the richer soil. This will then stunt the plant's growth.

1 Dig a hole to the exact depth of the new plant's root ball and 2 to 4 ft. wider. Make the sides vertical and roughen them. Lower the tree into the hole.

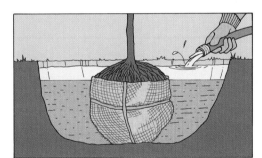

2 Test the soil from the hole (p.275). If it is sandy or dense clay, mix in an equal amount of organic matter, such as sphagnum peat. Fill the planting hole three-quarters full, and tamp it down with a 4 x 4. Loosen the twine and pull back the cloth burlap. (Remove plastic "burlap" completely.)

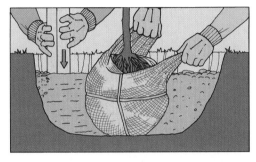

3 Irrigate the planting hole thoroughly with water from a hose. This will settle the soil and remove air pockets. When the water has soaked in, continue filling the hole with soil.

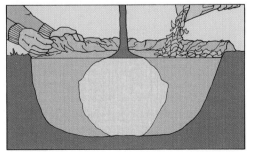

4 Use some extra soil to build a shallow moisture-retaining "saucer." Then add a 3-in. layer of mulch, being careful to keep it away from the trunk. Water it thoroughly once again.

TREES AND SHRUBS

Pruning

When to prune?

The best time to prune most flowering shrubs is right after the season of bloom. An earlier trimming removes buds that provide that year's show, while a late pruning may interfere with the production of buds necessary for the next year's blossoms. An exception is shrubs that bloom repeatedly throughout the growing season, such as hybrid tea roses. Prune them in early spring.

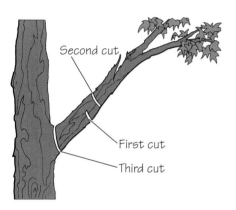

Removing a storm-damaged limb ▲

If you just slice a cracked limb off at its base, it's liable to tear a strip of bark off the trunk when it drops—and that means you've done more harm than good. To avoid this mishap, use only a sharp bow saw or pruning saw and amputate in three steps. First undercut the limb a foot away from the trunk—cut up from the bottom no more than halfway through the limb. Remove the branch with a second cut a few inches farther out along the limb and down from the top. Remove the remaining stub in one cut from top to bottom, just outside the "collar." (See pruning tips on facing page.)

Treatment for a neglected shrub ▶

When you are bringing an overgrown shrub back under control, remember the three D's: Remove all dead, diseased, or damaged branches. Next remove the weaker of each pair of crossing branches—branches that rub against each other. Finally, thin the bush by removing several of its oldest branches at their base. Be sure while you are doing this, though, to leave a framework of healthy younger branches to fill in as replacements.

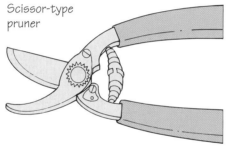

Scissor-type pruner

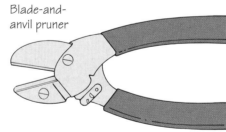

Blade-and-anvil pruner

The kindest cut ▲

You'll make the cleanest, easiest cuts with scissor-type pruners—in which the blades slip past each other with a scissor-like action. Blade-and-anvil pruners are less expensive, but they require more strength to use and they crush as they cut, leaving a ragged wound that's an invitation to disease.

Pocket holder

A long-handled lopper is a handy tool for pruning high branches, except that it takes three hands to manage one properly. Create an extra hand by putting on a carpenter's apron and resting the end of the lopper's pole in one of the pockets. This leaves one hand free to steady the pole and one to pull the line. ▼

Watering wisdom

Homemade drip irrigator

One of the best ways to make sure that a shrub or tree gets enough water is through drip irrigation. You can fashion an inexpensive dripper by punching a nail hole into a plastic gallon jug about an inch up from the jug's bottom. (This will keep enough water in the jug so it won't blow away later on.) Set the jug next to the shrub and fill it with a hose. The water will drain out gradually, soaking the soil right at the plant's roots.

Prewinter watering

In view of our cold, harsh winters, you'll need to protect your shrubs from *desiccation,* the loss of water through evaporation. This occurs when the tree or shrub continues to transpire (lose water through its leaves) after the surrounding soil has frozen hard and the roots can no longer obtain water. To prevent desiccation, water your shrubs thoroughly just after the first frost but before the ground freezes hard. For best results use a drip system, such as a soaker hose or the homemade irrigator described at left.

THE CHANGING WISDOM ABOUT TREE AND SHRUB CARE

Scientific research has revolutionized tree and shrub care over the past decade. What was gospel when you planted your trees is probably considered nonsense now that they are finally big enough to prune.

	THE OLD-FASHIONED WAY	CURRENT WISDOM
Pruning	When removing a branch in the past, you always cut it off flush with the tree's (or shrub's) trunk.	Modern arborists make the cut just beyond the thickened "collar" of bark and wood that surrounds a branch's base. This promotes faster healing with less danger of decay.
	Old-timers advised painting pruning wounds with shellac or asphalt to protect the area against decay.	Today arborists know that trees naturally seal off wounds by forming chemical boundaries around them, and that any artificial coating promotes decay by keeping the wound's surface moist.
Feeding the root system	Conventional wisdom used to hold that each tree's root system was the mirror image of its branches. To fertilize a tree, you had to inject the food at least 18 in. into the ground and work no farther out than the "drip line" (the circle that marks the outer limit of the branches' reach).	Experts now believe that the mighty oak spreads most of its roots through the top 12 to 15 in. of soil, and that 60 percent of the fine "feeder" roots lie outside the shadow of its branches. It's best to feed at the rate recommended on the product label, but concentrate the food outside the drip line and simply sprinkle it over the soil's surface and water it in.

ROSEBUSHES

Bare-root rosebushes can be planted in late fall in mild regions of the country, but early spring is best in colder regions.

Dig a hole twice as wide as the root system, leaving a soil mound in the center of the hole to support the roots. Position the knobby bud union (where the top joins the rootstock) even with the soil level if you are in a mild climate, or 1 to 2 in. below ground if winters are severe.

Add soil around the plant and gently firm it with your hands. Water the area well. Then support the canes by mounding more soil over them. When new leaf growth is 1 in. long, pull this soil mound away.

YARD AND GARDEN TOOLS

Improvisations

Protecting the lawn

The job of clearing twigs, stones, and other nonleaf debris from a lawn is easier if you use a steel rake with inflexible tines rather than a flexible leaf rake. To prevent the sharp rigid teeth from digging into the lawn, drive thread spools over the rake's two outside teeth. You'll find that the rake will ride smoothly as it cleans up the lawn.

Digging measure

Mark commonly used depths on the handles of your digging tools. That way you can gauge just how deep you've gone without interrupting your digging. For more on posthole diggers, see p.285.

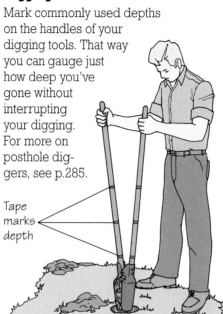

Tape marks depth

D is for dibble

Here's a job for an old D-handled tool that you don't use anymore (or better yet a broken one). Saw off the business end if necessary, and sharpen the wood handle to a point. You will then have a dibble—a digging tool for planting seeds and bulbs.

Step on it

To increase the amount of pressure you can put on a digging tool, such as a fork or a shovel, have a short length of angle iron welded to the shoulder of the tool. It will also be kinder to your foot.

Wheelbarrow extender ▶

Your wheelbarrow will hold more leaves if you add a lightweight frame to it. To make this extension, staple chicken wire to lengths of 1 x 1's. Don't make the frame so high that loading the leaves will be difficult. When it's time to rake the leaves, hold the frame in place with some elastic tie-down cord while you fill and empty the wheelbarrow.

1 x 1

Elastic tie-down

Tool tips and totes

Dirty business

Tools last far longer if you clean and oil them after every use. This is very important for digging tools, whose protective coatings wear away from use. Scrape off the dirt with an old putty knife (hang one on a nail where you store your tools). To oil your tools, keep a bucket of oil-soaked sand on hand. Clean the tool, then drive it in the sand.

Bright IDea

Small gardening tools are easy to lose in the yard, but not if you paint at least part of the handle a bright color (other than green). As a bonus, if someone borrows one of these personalized tools, you'll be more likely to get it back.

Tool caddy

If you have an old unused golf bag, give it a new life as a carrier for your yard and garden tools. Store long-handled tools where you formerly kept your woods and irons, and stash your work gloves and small tools in the zip-per pockets. If the bag has a pull-cart attachment, use it to roll your tools around the yard.

Garbage can stand

Here's another neat way to store long-handled tools: Make a holder out of a large garbage can, preferably one with built-in wheels so that you can cart your tools around the yard. First use a spade

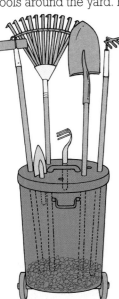

bit to drill holes in the lid to accept the tool han-dles. Then drill a few small holes in the bottom of the can for drainage. To help hold the tools in place, add some coarse gravel to the bottom.

KEEP TOOLS SHARP

For rough sharpening jobs, use a bastard (coarse) or a second-cut (medium) file to reestablish the bevel. To create a sharp digging or cutting edge, use a smooth (fine) file or a sharpening stone. Depending on the garden tool, use a toe-to-heel stroke, a straight stroke, or a sweeping motion. Always clamp the tool firmly in a vise. For more on files and sharpening techniques, see pp.20 and 22–23.

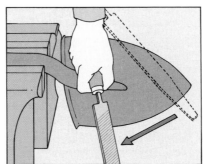

Sharpen a shovel by holding the toe of the file on the bevel at a 45° angle. Push the file diagonally in one direction, ending the stroke at the heel of the file. Work from the center out on one side; repeat on the other side.

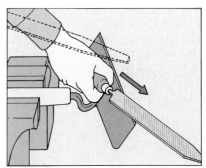

Hoes are beveled on the outside surface of their blades. Hold the file as for the shovel, but begin with the toe at the near end. Push the file diagonally away from you, ending near the heel.

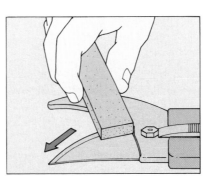

Renew the cutting blade of pruning shears with a small flat stone. Place the stone on the bevel at the edge of the blade, and rub the cutting edge with several sweeping strokes.

Give hedge clippers a fine cutting edge with a smooth single-cut file. Hold the file perpendicular to the cutting edge. Use straight pulling strokes with-out any side-to-side movement.

OUTDOOR POWER TOOLS

Mowers

Sharpen and balance a blade

Before sharpening a rotary blade, disconnect the spark plug wire and remove the blade, following the manual's instructions. Put the blade in a vise and sharpen both ends equally. Use a bastard file and a toe-to-heel stroke (p.281) to restore the original bevel, usually a 30° angle. Don't try to remove deep nicks, as you'll remove too much metal and unbalance the blade. As you work on the blade, check its balance occasionally by hanging it on a nail driven partway into the shop wall. If one side persists in dropping lower, resharpen that end to remove more metal. ▼

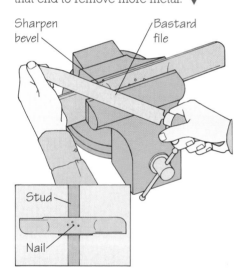

Sharpen bevel

Bastard file

Stud

Nail

Don't cut the cord

You'll be less likely to mow over the cord of an electric mower if you wrap a spiral of colorful tape down the length of the cord. It'll be more visible as it snakes around the lawn. Or use a bright orange exterior extension cord.

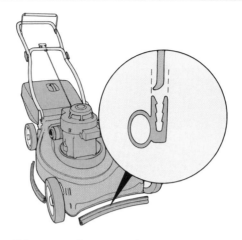

A bumper for trees ▲

If grass grows right up to your trees, there's a danger that your mower could bang into the trunks and damage their bark. As a safeguard, slip a pair of inexpensive plastic car door edge guards onto the edges of your mower. The bark of your trees will stay healthy.

Preparing for winter

Your mower will last longer if you winterize it after the grass-cutting season is over. Run the mower until all the gas is out of the system, and change the oil. Remove the spark plug and squirt a little oil into the hole. To distribute the oil within the hole, pull the starter cord a couple of times. Replace the plug, and put the mower away for the winter.

Last gas

Using up the remaining gas at the end of a season can take a long time if the mower tank isn't nearly empty. To solve the problem, you can use a discarded turkey baster to remove most of the gas. The rest will burn off quickly.

Put a guard up

Grass cutting will be safer if you install a rubber guard at the back of your mower as a protection from flying rock fragments. Cut the guard from a narrow piece of 1/8-inch-thick rubber, and blind-rivet it to the bottom edge of the mower deck. The rubber guard will give with the contours of the lawn and won't hinder the maneuverability of the mower. ▼

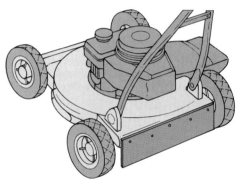

Easy rider cleanup

An easy way to clean off the grass that builds up around the blade of a mower is to flush it out with water. Just attach a sprinkler ring to a hose and slide it under the mower. Turn on the water and wash the clippings away.

Snowblowers

Keep your gloves on

When shopping for a snowblower, make sure you can maneuver the controls and pull the starter rope while you are wearing mittens or gloves. Removing your gloves during a snow-blowing job is probably the last thing you want to do.

Get a quick start

Spray the spark plug and the spark plug wire of a snowblower with automotive-type silicone ignition sealer. The ignition sealer will protect the plug from misfires caused by moisture. ▼

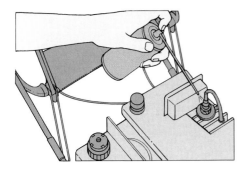

No-stick snow

To prevent snow from clogging a snowblower (or a snow shovel), coat the chute (or blade) with ordinary cooking oil, or apply silicone spray or furniture spray wax.
Caution: Never try to unclog the chute while the motor is running.

Chain saws

Out of chips

A chain saw needs sharpening when it starts to produce sawdust rather than chips. A resharpened chain saw runs faster and smoother. It's safer, too.

Mixing two-cycle fuel

Chain saws run on a mixture of gas and oil, but the exact ratio varies, so check the tool's manual. An easy way to mix this fuel is with a packet of premeasured oil—a small one for 4 litres (1 U.S. gallon) of gas, a large one for 19 litres (5 U.S. gallons). The oil in these packets has been specially formulated to make a mix that is suitable for most chain saws.

Shake it up, baby

Don't forget to shake a chain saw for at least 1 minute before you use it. This redistributes the oil within the tank.

Starter-rope savers

The starter rope of a chain saw can fray and break too quickly for one of three reasons: First, you may be pulling the rope at an angle, causing it to rub against the saw's housing. Be sure to pull the rope straight. Second, you may be using a replacement rope that is too short for the saw or made of the wrong material. The rope must be the same length as the original and made of nylon, not cotton. Finally, the saw may be suffering from engine problems. An engine that's hard to start forces repeated use of the rope, wearing it out more quickly. Check for a tired spark plug, incorrect fuel mixture, dirty air filter, or failing ignition.

HOW TO BE CAREFUL

▷ Before a cleaning or repair job, turn off the motor, remove the ignition key, and disconnect the spark plug wire, securing it away from the plug.

▷ Store gas in a red gas can away from the house, flames or sparks, and children.

Mowers and snowblowers

▷ Wear leather shoes and long pants, even in hot weather.

▷ Keep away from moving parts.

▷ If you leave a tool, turn it off.

▷ Before mowing, clear away all obstructions.

▷ Know where the curbs are.

Chain saws

▷ Retrofit an older chain saw with a bar tip guard and an antikick-back chain.

▷ Wear hearing protection, a face shield, high-traction steel-toed shoes, and Kevlar gloves (a cut-resistant material).

▷ Brace the saw on the ground or on a log when starting it.

▷ Stand uphill from the work.

▷ Maintain secure footing. Grasp the saw with both hands. Never hold it more than chest high.

▷ Turn off the saw if you have to walk with it.

▷ Let a professional do a job that requires any climbing.

For more on tool safety, see p.24.

SETTING POSTS

Down-to-earth advice

Burial services

Before you dig any postholes, remember to call your local utility companies. For free or for a nominal fee, they'll dispatch workers around your property with special detection devices to search for any underground water lines, drainage pipes, electrical and telephone wires, gas lines, and cable TV wires. Once the lines and pipes are marked, dig at least 2 feet away. That way you won't cut service to your house and end up with an expensive repair bill—or worse, injure yourself.

Rooting around

If you encounter a root that's too large to remove with a shovel or posthole digger, use a pruning saw or shears. But make sure you're not killing a tree by severing a main root, and make extra-sure it's a root, not a utility line (see above), before you chop away.

Work on one cylinder

Sometimes loose soil caves in as fast as you can dig it out, leaving you with a crater rather than a cylinder. If that happens, wedge in a heavy-duty cardboard tube, called a Sonotube, available at building supply stores (they're often used at construction sites as forms for pouring uniform concrete footings). Dig inside the tube with a clamshell digger, and wiggle the tube down as you work. Once the post is ready to be placed, the tube will also hold the concrete or dirt fill.

Ready, get set

Add a second level ▶

If you are setting many posts, consider buying a tool that has two levels mounted at a 90° angle to each other. When it's time to plumb a post, have someone hold the post in place while you place the tool against it. Adjust the post's position as necessary, and secure it with braces as shown.

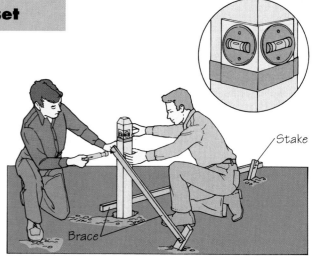

Stake

Brace

Rock-solid post anchor ▲

Gate posts, clothesline poles, flagpoles, and handrail posts need a firmly anchored footing. You can do this without a ton of concrete: After digging the hole to just below the frost line, drive three or four lengths of old pipe or angle iron, each 2 to 3 feet long, at an angle into the surrounding soil. Let their ends protrude into the hole so they will become embedded in the concrete when you pour it. This added bite will prevent the entire footing from shifting under stress.

Nail holder

Another way to reinforce a post in its footing is to drive nails into the post before you set it in place. The nails provide a gripping surface for the concrete when it is poured into the hole. For best results, use 10d common nails. Stagger the nails on each side and down the post, driving them about halfway into the wood. ▼

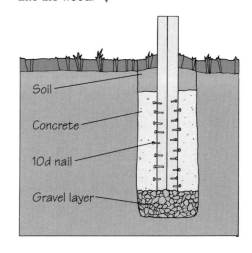

Soil

Concrete

10d nail

Gravel layer

TOOLS FOR POSTHOLES

Digging a deep cylindrical hole calls for an arsenal of tools that can help you handle rocks and soil without fear. The tools shown on this page will help you dig the post-holes for fences as well as the excavations for pier footings. (To avoid the network of underground utility pipes, lines, and wires, see the facing page.)

Clamshell digger. You can use this digger in all types of dirt. Simply plunge its open jaws into the hole, spread the handles to make the jaws bite the dirt, lift it out, and push the handles back together to release the dirt. Loosen rocky or clayey soil by stabbing with it. The deeper you dig, the less you'll be able to move the jaws.

Hand auger digger. The twisting motion used to power this tool works well in soft ground but not in rocky soil. The cutting teeth can churn soil up into the space between the jaws, but they are powerless against rocks.

Power auger digger. This gas-powered tool (usually rented) is ideal when you need to dig many holes in loose soil. (It isn't very useful in rocky ground.) The corkscrew auger, varying in size from 6 to 12 in., pulls itself into the hole and spins the dirt out onto the ground. However, the tool is heavy and its weight can be hard on your back. Use one only if you're in top condition, or operate it with another person. (Several models are intended only for two-person use.)

Trenching shovel. This type of shovel has a narrow curved blade that will flare the bottoms of holes for concrete footings. A smaller one can be used to finish the bottom of a clamshell-dug hole.

Heavy-duty pry bar. This is a must-have tool for clayey or rocky soil. It dislodges large rocks, breaks up rocky ledges, and loosens up clay soil. One that is 5 ft. long and weighs more than 20 lb. can do most jobs.

BUILDING AND REPAIRING FENCES

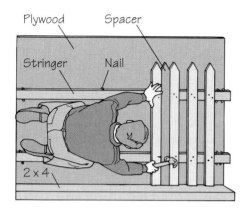

Spaced out ▲

Spacing the pickets evenly on the horizontal members, or *stringers,* is a major task. An easy way to do this is to make a spacing guide with a 4 x 8 sheet of plywood and an 8-foot-long 2 x 4. Nail the 2 x 4 to the bottom of the plywood; this will align the pickets evenly. Next drive finishing nails into the plywood at intervals to hold the stringers in position. To assemble the pieces, lay the pickets next to one another and nail every other one. (The intermediate unnailed pickets act as spacers.) Remove the spacers and continue to the end.

Design your own

If you'd like to try your hand at designing your own picket fence, use more than one picket style and vary the spacing between the pickets. Begin with pencil and paper, and experiment with various repeating patterns. Once you've settled on a pattern, make a spacing jig (as shown above) to help you place the pickets accurately on the stringers.

Removable fence sections ▶

Building a fence with light, removable sections makes a lot of sense. It lets you open the space for a party or ball game, move large objects in and out of the house, and run the mower between the fence posts instead of having to trim beneath the pickets. To make fence sections removable, support the stringers on joist hangers instead of fastening them permanently to the posts. Purchase joist hangers sized to hold 2 x 4's (available at a building supply stores). You'll need four for each fence section. Position the hangers where the stringers are to align, and fasten them to the posts with screws. To assemble the fence, rest the stringers in the hangers.

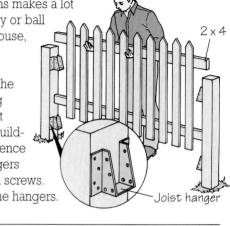

Working with boards

◀ Nailing jig

When fastening fence boards, use a jig to get them in perfect alignment and at the correct height. The jig shown here is made of a board with two spacer blocks; one block rests on top of the upper stringer while the other marks the top of the fence. Starting at a post, position the first board with the jig next to it. Nail the board to the top stringer, and then repeat with the next board and the next. When you reach the second post, check that the gap between it and the last board is uniform at both top and bottom. Then go back and nail all the boards in the section to the bottom stringer.

◀ Cutting scallops

You can give a board fence a decorative finished look with the help of a strip of ¼-inch hardboard. Here's how: For each post-to-post section, tack one nail to each post just at the top of the boards, and tack a third nail in the middle of the fence section 6 inches down from the other nails. Bend the hardboard strip between these nails and trace a smooth curve. Cut out the curve with a saber saw, finishing the end of the cut with a coping saw. Smooth the cut edges of the boards with either a rasp or a Surform tool.

FENCE REPAIR

Before you tackle any single repair, inspect the entire fence. If one post has a severe lean to it, give the others a firm shake to see if they're wobbly too. If one picket is rotten, probe others with an old screwdriver to see if they're spongy as well. If most of the framework seems solid, go ahead and perform the repairs and maintenance shown here. But if the framework is falling apart or if half the posts are rotten, consider building a new fence.

Realign a sagging gate

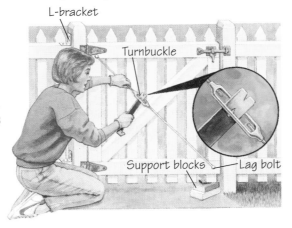

L-bracket

Turnbuckle

Support blocks — Lag bolt

Push a sagging gate post back into place and reconnect it to the horizontal members with two L-brackets and screws. If the gate itself is sagging, tighten the hinge screws. If they no longer grip, replace them with longer screws or fill the holes and refasten the hinges (p.14). Next, raise the gate on support blocks; open a turnbuckle fully and install it diagonally with lag bolts. Depending on the turnbuckle, tighten it with a pry bar or a wrench. Finally, resecure any loose pickets with some galvanized screws.

Replace a post

Pull at angle

Push down

2 x 4 lever nailed to post

Prying block

Pull the nails that secure the fence sections on each side of the vertical post. Swing the sections about 2 ft. out of the way, propping their free ends up on scrap boards.

Pry the old post out of the ground while a helper pulls it at an angle to keep it from slipping back into the hole. Position the new post; then reposition the two fence sections and nail them in place. Brace the post to hold it plumb, and pour in the concrete. (For more on setting posts, see p.284.)

BUILDING AND RESTORING DECKS

Planning

Outdoor room

A deck is an outdoor living room, and as such it needs a sense of enclosure. You can achieve this with a simple perimeter railing or by edging it with a few low benches or planters.
Caution: For safety's sake, put a slatted railing around any deck raised 2 feet or more above ground level.

On the beams

When building a deck, don't go too small on the beams. Undersize beams, while they may meet local codes, also make a deck feel soft underfoot since they bounce rather than remaining rigid. It's worth the extra cost to increase the dimension of the beams by one lumber size. You'll end up with a deck that is sturdier and safer.

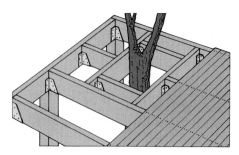

Built-in tree ▲

If you want to design a deck around a tree, plan to box the tree in with short joists. These short lengths will compensate for the interruption in the joist system. Be sure that the box is large enough to let the tree grow. If children are going to be playing on the deck, build a small fence around the tree opening as a safety measure.

Building

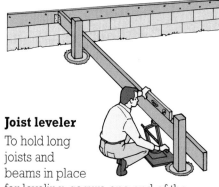

Joist leveler

To hold long joists and beams in place for leveling, secure one end of the lumber and support the body of the piece with a scissors car jack. Adjust the jack to level the piece as necessary; then secure or support the other end at just the right position. You'll find that the jack is a strong and helpful partner.

Do your level best

Before you cut posts to their final height, tack-nail the beams in position, using a level as you go. Then, with the beams in place, check your work by placing a carpenter's or mason's level on a straight 2 x 4 that's been laid diagonally across the deck. Repeat in the opposite direction. Adjust the position of the beams as needed, and then cut the posts.

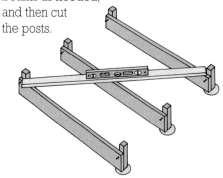

Erosion barrier

Before you build your deck, determine if rainwater seeping through the boards will erode the soil. This is likely to happen if the ground slopes. If you decide that erosion could be a problem, all you need to do to keep the soil in place is to cover it with a generous layer of gravel before you build the deck.

Spaced-out boards

It's easy to space deck boards evenly. Just drive 8d nails into several pieces of scrap 2 x 4. Push the nails down between adjacent deck boards, and then fasten the boards in place. ▼

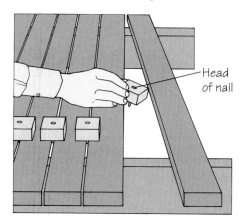

Head of nail

Fasten-ating problem

While headed nails are often used in deck building, they are not the best fastener. The hammer blows needed to drive them flush dent the surface, marring the project, and the heads become burning hot in summer. A better choice is galvanized deck screws. As you seat these screws with a power driver, they countersink themselves below the surface. The spiral threads won't allow the screws to back out (as nails tend to).

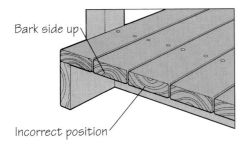

Bark side up

Incorrect position

Direction of the board ▲

When placing a deck board, follow this rule: bark side up. To tell which is the bark side, check the annual growth rings on the end of the board; the convex side is the bark side. Putting this side facing up (and the concave side down) means that it'll be less likely to *cup*, or warp, and you'll also avoid *feathering*, or splitting along the annual rings, which results in long spearlike splinters. Put the bark side down only if that side has a bad knot or splits.

Drive it straight

You can straighten a crooked deck board as you nail or screw it down by wedging it into position. First, screw a length of scrap 2 x 4 to the top of the joist closest to the end of the problem board. Hammer a wedge between the end of the 2 x 4 and the board until the board is properly spaced, and then nail or screw the board to the joist. Repeat at other joists as necessary. ▼

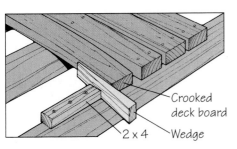

Crooked deck board

2 x 4   Wedge

Movable deck umbrella

A deck umbrella is more useful if you can move it around as needed. To help you get it in the right spot, mount pairs of galvanized plumbing pipe straps on the deck posts or railing in key places. (The straps should be slightly wider than the umbrella pole.) Then just slip the umbrella pole through the straps, until the pole rests on the deck. ▼

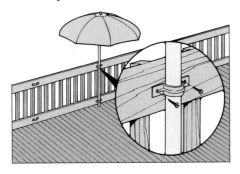

True grit

Don't slip on wet deck steps: If you intend to paint them, mix 1 part fine clean white sand with 4 parts paint. If not, glue down nonslip strips with an exterior construction adhesive. Either way, the gritty texture will provide traction.

Wait to paint

Unless the pressure-treated wood you use for your deck is kiln-dried after treatment, be prepared to wait a few months before painting it. The pressure-treating process saturates the wood with chemicals and usually leaves it too wet to accept paint or stain well. Kiln-dried wood costs more than air-dried wood, but it can be painted immediately.

Instant weathering

If you are replacing a portion of a deck, you can give it an "instant" weathered appearance. Apply a solution of 1 cup of baking soda and 1 gallon of water to the new portion, allow it to dry, and rinse it off. When the area is dry, apply a water sealant. The sealant forms a moisture barrier beneath the surface of the wood, allowing the deck to continue to weather gradually.

Spray-on sealers

Choose a windless day to spray on a wood sealer. Using a pump garden sprayer, you can apply the sealer between the deck boards without any trouble. To clean a water-base sealer from the sprayer, spray water until it is clear. (For an oil-base sealer, soak the sprayer parts in paint thinner.)

Restoratives

Waterproof test

Over time, moisture takes a toll on a deck. An easy way to tell if you need to reseal your deck is to pour a glass of water on it. If the water beads up, the deck is waterproof. But if the surface absorbs the water quickly and turns a darker color, it's time to reseal.

Speedy deck cleaners

Deck cleaners and restorers do a great job of bringing your deck back to life, but if the deck is very dirty, you may have to do some heavy scrubbing. If so, consider renting a high-pressure washer; it will make the job easier.

MASONRY AND CONCRETE

Mortarless helpers

Getting edgy

Using a special plastic or aluminum edging, available at masonry supply stores, is the easiest way to hold a flexible (mortarless) path or patio of bricks or concrete pavers in place. You can flex this edging around curves and cut it to size with a hacksaw. Best of all, it resists rot and becomes nearly invisible when the grass grows back. ▼

Even edgier

When laying the edging for a path with parallel sides, take care to keep the sides evenly spaced; it will make life easier when you screed (smooth and level) the sand and lay the masonry.

A day's work

Lay down and screed only as much sand as you can cover with pavers in one day, and then throw a tarp over the sand pile. Uncovered sand is guaranteed to be disturbed by wind, rain, kids, or a stray cat who thinks he's found the world's biggest litter box.

Dry idea

Before you sweep sand between newly laid bricks or pavers, be sure it's dry. Wet sand will bridge the gaps rather than fill them. To make sure the gaps are filled completely, wait a few days and then sweep sand into the gaps a second time. This is important because the sand helps solidify the paving and also fills any spaces where dirt might enter (and provide a mini planting bed for weeds).

Paver saver ▲

The best way to lock pavers into their sand bed is to use a rented power vibrator, but be careful with this heavy machine. Don't let it sit in one place too long, or the pavers could settle unevenly or crack. Some pros place 4 x 4 sheets of plywood on the pavers and run the vibrator over them; the plywood helps distribute the weight of the machine.

Interlocking retaining walls ▶

Want an easier way to build a retaining wall? Try a system of interlocking concrete blocks. Block styles vary among makers, and interlocking methods differ as well. Here, fiberglass pins fit into holes in the blocks. While they are heavy (up to 90 pounds apiece) and expensive, the blocks will last almost forever and don't require mortar or a concrete footing. The only other materials you'll need are sand or gravel and some landscaping fabric (available at home centers).

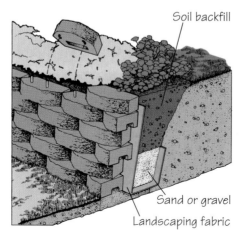

Soil backfill

Sand or gravel

Landscaping fabric

Stone walks

Make sand stay put

If your flagstone walk has fairly wide joints, you may find that the sand tends to wash away. If you get around to resetting the stones, set them in sand as before, but change your approach to the joints. Mix a little dry Portland cement with the sand and pack the mixture firmly between the stones. Then, to set the filler, sprinkle the joints with a little water. The sand will stay put.

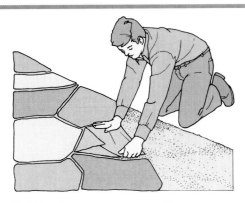

Put the design on paper ▲

Working with flagstones is like solving a giant jigsaw puzzle. Some stones fit together without cutting, but others need to be cut to fit. An easy way to find the best candidate to fill any given space is to make a template out of brown paper. Just lay the paper over the void and fold back the edges until it fits (don't forget to leave room for the sand joints). Take the template over to your stockpile of stones and choose one that's closest to your needs. Mark any cut lines. Place the stone on sand, and score along the cut lines with a stone chisel and a 3-pound hammer. Strike the stone.

Stepping-stone walks

Before you dig any holes for a stepping-stone walk, place the stones on top of the grass and space them so that the strides between the stones are comfortable. Take a couple of practice walks. When the placement looks and feels right, sprinkle flour over the path. Then lift the stones out of the way and use the outlines to dig holes for the stones.

Pattern making

If you'd like a walk that has a random pattern but isn't as irregular as the one at left, here is a plan that uses pieces of bluestone that have been uniformly cut to 1½ x 1½ feet, 1½ x 2 feet, and 2 x 2 feet. Other patterns call for stones that are 1 foot square and 2 x 3 feet. ▼

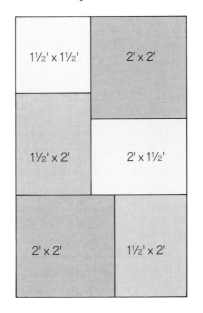

Some concrete secrets

Using leftovers

Almost every concrete pour leaves you with leftover concrete. If you plan ahead, you can make some extra patio blocks or small concrete slabs that you can put to good use. Before you pour, build some extra forms from scrap 2 x 4's (18 inches is a useful length), wipe them with form-release chemical, and place them on heavy polyurethane sheets. When you've finished your paving job, pour the leftover concrete into the forms.

Concrete connection

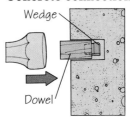

To securely mount a screw, hook, or nail in a solid concrete surface, create a solid base for the fastener. First drive a steel tool-handle wedge partway into the end of a length of dowel, and then use a masonry bit to bore a hole in the concrete the same diameter as the dowel. Drive the dowel into the hole, wedge end first. As you hammer it in, the wedge will expand the dowel, creating a supertight fit.

Flagstone fake

The next time you pour a concrete walk or patio, you might want to try a decorative finish for it, such as the flagstone effect shown here. While the smoothed concrete is still wet, use a brick jointing tool to carve the outlines of joints between the simulated flagstones. For best results, plan your design ahead of time and work quickly (you don't want the concrete to set up too soon). Go over the surface again with a trowel, and then use an old paintbrush to remove particles of concrete and smooth the edges of the design.

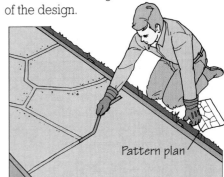

Pattern plan

REPAIRING MASONRY AND CONCRETE

Patios, walks, and steps

Concrete shock absorber

Pounding a chisel to remove loose material from a crack in concrete can make your hands and arms tingle. Reduce this excessive shock by punching a hole into a sponge-rubber ball and pushing the drill or chisel through it. When you pound the tool, grab onto the sponge rubber. You won't feel the vibrations as much. (*Note:* Don't forget to wear eye protection for this job.) ▼

Hold your chips

When chipping away at concrete, keep the pieces from scattering all over, including into your face. Push the chisel through a square of window screening. Wear safety goggles, just in case.

Wobble fixer

A wrought-iron railing tends to loosen in its concrete foundations in a climate that freezes and thaws every year. Rock salt, used to manage icy conditions, will worsen the wobble. To secure the railing, chip out any loose concrete around the post, then use some anchor cement—it will set rock hard in a matter of minutes.

Railing against the weather

Moisture seeping into the space between a wrought-iron railing and its concrete base encourages rust to form below the surface.

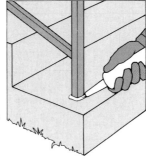

To prevent that from happening, use polymer blend caulk (see p.151) to fill gaps between the iron and the concrete.

Patio paver puller

After a winter of freezing and thawing, some individual bricks or pavers in your sand-base patio may need releveling. How do you get the brick or paver out? Make two pullers like the ones shown here from coat hanger wire. Slip the pullers down both sides of the offending paver, turn them a quarter turn, and pull up the paver. For large patio blocks, make four pullers and get a second person to help you. ▼

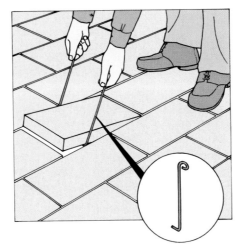

No more moss

Moss thrives in British Columbia style warm, damp climates. Not only is such moss unsightly, it makes concrete and brick steps, patios, and walks dangerously slippery. To get rid of moss, mix 1 part household bleach with 3 parts water in a plastic watering can, apply it to the mossy surface, and then scrub with a stiff-bristle brush.

Driveway fixes

Fresh stain

Cover a fresh oil or grease spot on your asphalt or concrete driveway with baking soda or cat litter. If you use litter, grind it with a brick until the litter is a fine powder

(there's no need to bear down hard). Let the soda or litter stay there for a day or so; then sweep the area clean.

Stubborn spots

If the baking soda or cat litter treatment (above) won't budge an oil or grease stain from a concrete driveway, saturate the spot with carburetor cleaner. Or use a commercial degreaser.

Push grooming

The next time you clean your concrete or asphalt driveway, try taping a garden hose to the handle of a push broom. The nozzle will direct water in front of the brush as you push it over the surface.

YARD IMPROVEMENTS

Layout and staking tips

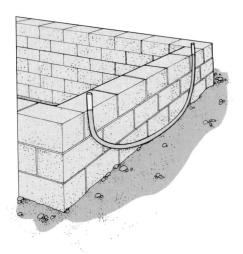

Long level line ▲

Use this simple tool to maintain a level line over a long distance. Almost fill a length of ½-inch-diameter clear plastic tubing with water. The water will seek identical levels at each end, giving you an accurate leveling device for laying out projects such as decks and fences.

Don't split the stakes

When wood stakes split, it's usually because you've struck them on the corners, instead of in the center, when driving them into place. To solve this problem, simply take the time, when making the stakes, to cut off the upper corners. Then you'll have no choice but to hit each stake in the center, and it will go into the ground with minimal splitting.

Lighting up

Dimmer views

If you have a dimmer switch installed on your exterior spotlights or floodlights, you'll be able to produce diffused light at the touch of a dial, creating the ideal mood for a party in your patio or garden. Be sure it is a heavy-duty dimmer, one designed for exterior use. To avoid the annoying hum that many dimmers cause, choose one with a filter. For safety tips and more information on working with electricity, see pp.199–210.

Sand in your socket

If the lamp socket of a yard light is corroded, you can clean it out with the type of emery board used for fingernails. First, shut off the electric power and disassemble the light to gain access to the socket. Brush out any grit, and sand it clean with the emery board. Then put the light back together.

TYPES OF OUTDOOR LIGHTING

Light can be used many ways: to set the stage for an outdoor party, add a dramatic touch to a garden, or boost the security of your home. Here's a brief sampler.

TYPE	TECHNIQUE	COMMON USES
Backlighting	Places a light fixture behind an object.	To silhouette a shape and cast shadows beyond it.
Contour lighting	Focuses two or three beams at different angles around an object. (To deepen the contrast of light and shadows, make one light more intense.)	To draw attention to trees, statues, fountains, and other items with sculptural interest.
Cross-lighting	Mounts two beams of equal intensity on opposite sides of its target.	To make an object or area prominent.
Diffused light	Sets several nondirectional lights, on posts and in the ground.	To soften the contrast between light and shadow and set a mood.
Downlighting	Directs light from a tree or roof to a specific area.	To outline paths and driveways or to increase security around the house, often with a movement sensor.
Grazing	Brushes light beams across a surface.	To emphasize the texture of plants, vines, rock gardens, and stucco.
Moonlighting	Beams light from a high place such as a tree or roof.	To enlarge the area of diffused light, as for a large outdoor party.
Uplighting	Directs (usually) one light beam upward from the ground.	To draw attention to bushes or trees.

YARD IMPROVEMENTS

Furnishing the outdoors

A movable feast

If you'd like an easy way to move your picnic table around the yard, just install a pair of plate casters at the bottom of the legs at one end of the table. (Six- or 8-inch wheels navigate a lawn well.) Then when it's time to follow the shade, mow or rake underneath the table, or make room for other activities, just lift one end of the table and go.

Metal protector

Patio furniture with metal feet usually comes with protective plastic or rubber tips. Over time, the metal cuts through the tips and starts to rust and scratch the patio. To lengthen the life of these plastic protectors, fit a metal washer inside the bottom of each one.

Lawn chair medic

To clean dirty aluminum frames, use extra-fine (No. 000) steel wool and a little kerosene. If the aluminum is pitted, rub the areas with aluminum cleaner. Finally, protect the frames by spraying them with clear acrylic finish.

Cloth control ▶

Wind wreaks havoc at a picnic—napkins and paper plates fly away and the tablecloth yearns to set sail. To anchor a cloth to the table, glue spring-type clothespins to the underside of the table with epoxy. You'll need about eight for an average table. Space them around the table, and tape them in place until the adhesive dries.

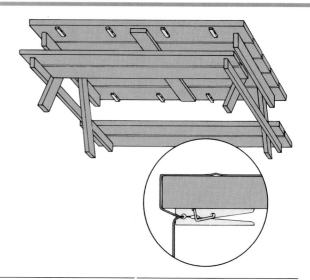

Lawn chair revival

Don't throw away a perfectly good lawn chair just because the fabric is torn or ruined. Replace the covering with redwood or some other durable wood. Cut $\frac{1}{2}$-inch-thick slats and fasten them to the frame with blind rivets. You'll have to predrill holes in the slats, and possibly the chair, to accept the rivets. ▼

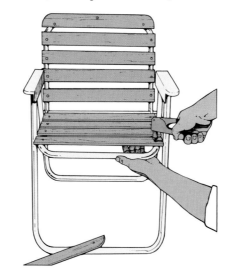

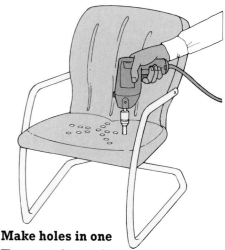

Make holes in one

The water that pools in the contoured seats of metal lawn chairs invites rust. A solution is to drill several drainage holes in the seat. Be sure to deburr the holes. Then paint the chair (and the edges of the holes) with rust-preventive paint. Drilling holes also works for plastic chairs—but instead of controlling rust, it just helps the plastic dry faster.

Something for the kids

Go for bolts

Protruding bolt ends on play structures are dangerous. You should either cut off the protruding ends with a hacksaw (filing down any rough edges) or cover them with cap nuts.

Branch saver ▲

A tree swing is fun for the kids, but not so healthy for the tree branch. The sawing action of the rope cuts the cambium layer just under the bark, killing the branch. To prevent damage, make a protective sleeve out of tough rubber, such as an old automobile tire, or plastic material. Tack it to the tree with staple nails, and tie the rope around the sleeve.

Swing easy ▲

Chains on a child's swing can cut into small fingers. To make the chains softer to hold, slit lengths of foam pipe insulation or a ⅝-inch garden hose and snap them on.

Bird foiler

To keep birds from leaving droppings on a swing set, attach a corner bracket near each end of the top rail of the set. Run a broom handle (or long dowel) between the brackets and attach it to them, using a nail in each end. Whenever a bird tries to land on the swing set, the broom handle will rotate, sweeping away any possibility of the bird's perching there. You should have no further problem with bird droppings. ▼

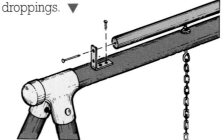

PLAY SET RULES

A play set, whether it's home-built or store-bought, can be a safety hazard. Lay a 10-inch layer of cushioning material under the play set: sand, pea gravel, or an organic material such as shredded bark. Don't rely on grass. It will soon wear off, and dirt is as hard as asphalt. Clean or replenish the cushioning material as needed. Once the set is up, inspect it periodically for loose and broken parts, the damage caused by use and exposure to weather.

The safest play sets will have the features listed below.
▷ Handholds will be placed at strategic points and be easy for small hands to grasp.
▷ The slope of a slide will be no more than 30°, with a level section at the end to slow a child's exit speed.
▷ Side guards at the top of the slide will be fastened securely.
▷ Swings will be spaced 24 inches apart, with the seats at least 30 inches from the frame.
▷ Any platform that is more than 30 inches in the air will be protected with a solid or slatted enclosure at least 38 inches high. The slats will be tightly spaced.
▷ Corners and edges will be rounded to prevent injuries.
▷ Hardware will be recessed or covered (see hint at top left).

YARD IMPROVEMENTS

For the birds

Slide-out feeder

If you want to attract birds to a hanging feeder near a second-story window, you'll need to hang the feeder several feet out from the house and still be able to reach it easily for restocking. Mount an old traverse curtain rod on a 1 x 6, and hang the feeder from one of the movable eyes. Then nail the 1 x 6 to a beam under an eave and add a supporting bracket. With a pull of the string, you'll be able to fill the feeder and slide it back out so the birds can see it.

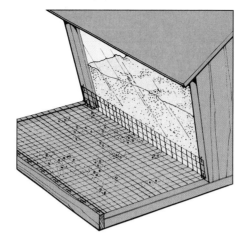

Keeping seed in its place ▲

When birds search through a feeder for the perfect seed, a lot of rejected seed ends up on the ground. Add a lip to the edge of the feeder's tray, and stretch a piece of ½-inch hardware cloth over the tray with enough clearance for the seeds to spread out under the wire. Staple the wire to the lip and the frame of the feeder. The birds will be able to eat, but they won't be able to scratch the seeds away.

Mailboxing

Painting boxes

If you'd like to dress up your galvanized metal mailbox with a coat of paint, it'll stick better if you first wash the exterior with some vinegar. (The mild acid removes much of the oiliness from the surface and gives it some "tooth" to hold the paint.) To paint the box, apply a coat of a primer formulated for galvanized metal, and follow with a coat of paint (any kind).

Two-door opener

You can pick and choose where you step to retrieve the mail from your roadside mailbox if you build one with a door at both ends. It'll let you avoid passing cars and the inevitable puddles and patches of ice. ▼

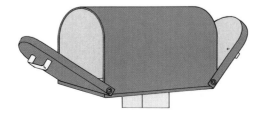

Clothes lines

Laundry basket hang-up

Here's a simple slide-in shelf that will hold your laundry basket at waist height on a 4 x 4 post. Just cut a notch in a 12- x 16-inch piece of ¾-inch plywood, fasten a slot made of 2 x 4 blocks to the post, and slide the shelf into the slot. To hold the basket in place, add a top bracket (locate the position of the bracket by measuring the depth of your basket). You'll have to tip the basket to fit it under the top bracket.

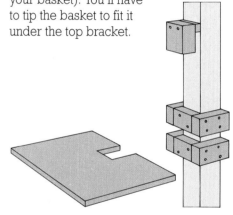

Clothespin storage

If you want a sheltered home for your clothespins, build a covered box with a hinged lid out of ¾-inch plywood. Drill holes in the bottom and ends for drainage, and attach the box to a post.

That certain glow

You'll never run into your clothesline at night if you sponge some luminous paint down the length of the line. Once the paint dries, it'll glow in the dark.

SEASONAL CHORES

Firewood

Splitting wood

For strenuous bending and lifting activities, such as splitting wood, wear a wide leather weightlifter's belt. Its support reduces fatigue and helps to prevent lower back pain. You can find these belts in most sporting goods stores.

This end up

You'll split a log more easily if you hit into its true top end. How can you tell which end should be up? Check the diameter at each end of the log. The smaller end is almost always the top.

Tire holder ▲

Here's an easy way to hold logs for splitting: Stack a couple of old automobile tires and set the logs (one at a time) in the opening. As a bonus, the tires will keep the split halves from falling and will protect the ax blade if it falls short.

On the chopping block

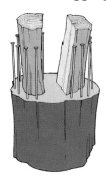

Prevent your chopped wood from falling to the ground each time it's split. Drive some 10-inch-long nails around the edge of the chopping block, leaving an opening at the front and back so that your ax is clear. The nails act like a fence to catch the pieces and save you from a lot of bending over.

Handle saver

If you split a lot of wood, you've probably missed the mark enough times to chip away at the ax handle. A good way to prevent this is to tape a 6-inch piece of rubber hose to the underside of the handle, next to the ax head. This will triple the life of the handle and take the sting out of the misses.

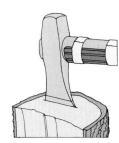

Snow and ice

Nontoxics on ice

The next time you clear an icy walk, use calcium nitrate (available at hardware stores) or a garden fertilizer containing urea instead of a chemical deicing compound. That way you won't ruin the soil or harm or kill shrubs and trees. Another strategy is to cover the ice with a layer of sand, sawdust, or cat litter.

Good brooming

If your driveway or sidewalk is covered with only light snow, try sweeping the powdery stuff away instead of lifting it off with a shovel. It will save wear and tear on your back. And if you're apt to encounter patches of ice, screw a scrap of angle iron to the top of the broom head; you'll be able to flip the broom over and scrape at the ice.

Easier lawn cleanup

If the municipal snowplows tend to leave piles of sand and gravel on your lawn, do this *before* the first snow: Stake down 3- to 4-foot-wide strips of landscaping fabric (available at garden centers) over the area. When the thaw comes, fold up the fabric with the sand and gravel on top. Rake lightly to bring any matted grass back to normal.

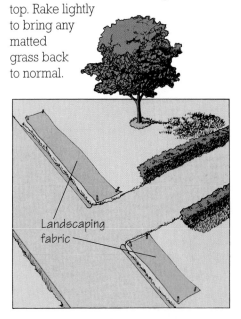

Landscaping fabric

CAR AND GARAGE

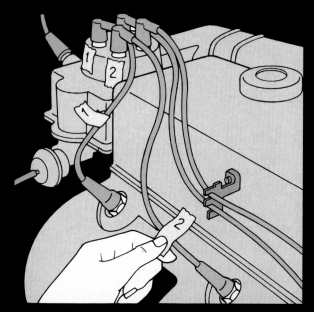

TOOLS AND EQUIPMENT

Handling tools

Rubbery wrench

If you start threading a spark plug or nut in a spot that's hard to reach, it's likely you'll scrape your knuckles. To keep your skin intact, get things going with a short length of rubber fuel line, automotive vacuum hose, or garden hose. The hose should fit snugly over the nut or spark plug insulator. Slip the hose into the tight area, and twist it to start threading on the part. If you need a grip for twisting, insert the blade of a short screwdriver into the open end of the hose and turn the driver's handle. Finish the job with a universal socket and extension on a ratchet wrench.

To the point

When removing a stubborn six-sided nut, don't be tempted to use the wrong tool, such as pliers or a wrench that "almost fits." It can round off the points on the nut without removing it—and then you'll have to take a hacksaw to it (p.96). Instead, spray a penetrating solvent on the nut and let it soak. (If a solvent isn't available, use a cola beverage.) Then pick a wrench that fits tightly; a six-point wrench is best, but if you have a plumber's flare wrench, it will also work.

Thawed paws

Wrenches and other tools stored in an unheated space can stick to your fingers in freezing weather. To warm things up, spread out all the tools you'll need. Then turn on and aim a hair dryer at the tools long enough for them to warm up, but not until they're too hot to handle.

Garage equipment

Seat relief

It's tiring to squat or kneel while you work on the brakes or suspension. Give your knees a rest by making a combination seat and tool caddy. Bolt together two pairs of 1 x 3 wood strips with one side of a sturdy plastic crate or wood box sandwiched between them. At each corner, attach casters to the bottom strips. As long as you aren't on the heavy side, you can sit on the crate, roll into position, and remove and store tools and parts inside the crate all at once.

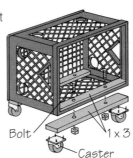

Bolt　　　1 x 3

Caster

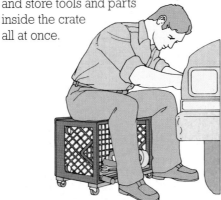

Cheap creep

Is your auto mechanic's creeper too tall for a job? Place a 4- x 5-foot scrap of vinyl flooring on the floor or driveway; then you can easily slide under the car on its slippery surface. An added benefit: It's easier to wipe up spilled oil or grease from the flooring.

FIRE CONTROL

It's a good idea to keep a fire extinguisher rated for gasoline and electrical fires (B and C ratings) around the garage and in your car. Store a compact extinguisher in your glove compartment, or mount it within easy reach from the driver's seat. Under the seat is one ideal spot. Gasoline-rated fire extinguishers and brackets are available at auto supply stores.

A fire extinguisher, however, will not help much if it's windy. You can try to smother a small fire with a heavy tarp or blanket. But if the fire is not controllable, get away from it immediately and call the fire department. The fire can travel to the fuel tank and cause an explosion.

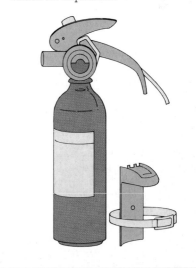

CHANGING THE MOTOR OIL AND OIL FILTER

Motor oil

Leak lookout

Leaking fluids are often the first sign of car trouble. Check under your car at least once a week for leaks. To identify them, spread a length of white paper under the car, secure the corners with heavy weights, and leave it overnight. The color and location of the leak will identify it: Clear water near the front seats is usually harmless condensation from a running air conditioner. Green or yellowish liquid with a sweet smell under the engine or radiator is antifreeze. Red or brown fluid with a strong odor under the engine is power steering fluid; under the transmission, it's transmission fluid. Brown or black slippery liquid under the engine is motor oil. A colorless oily fluid near the wheels or engine could be brake fluid. A colorless or nearly colorless watery liquid under the engine compartment could be leakage from the washer reservoir— the location varies from car to car. Repair any leaks, and check the appropriate fluid reservoirs for low levels.

Squint saver

Your oil dipstick can be easier to read. Just drill small holes through the dipstick at the "Full" and "Add" marks. Make sure you clean off all the metal filings before you reinsert the dipstick.

Drill hole through mark

Safety first ▶

If you have to work under your car, jack it up and lower the frame or axles onto steel jack stands. Never work under a car supported only by a jack, no matter how sturdy it seems. Be sure to set the parking brake, put the transmission into *Park*—or first gear for a manual transmission—and chock the wheels that remain on the ground. Metal chocks are available at auto supply stores. Wear safety goggles when working under a car. You never know when crud will fall onto your face!

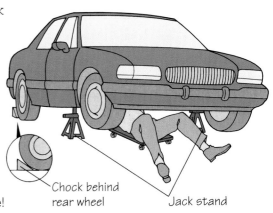

Chock behind rear wheel

Jack stand

Keep it pure oil

Be sure to remove the plastic lock ring that sometimes clings to the neck of an oil container after you remove its cap. If the ring falls into the engine while you're pouring in oil, it can cause big problems. If you use a funnel, make sure you first wipe off any debris.

Lock ring

When to change

You can change oil every 12,000 to 16,000 kilometres if you make long trips at moderate speeds in mild weather with little dust. The kind of driving most people do—short trips, stop-and-go traffic, hot or cold weather, and dusty conditions—is called "severe service." Such driving requires an oil change every 5,000 kilometres or 3 months.

Milkman to the rescue

If you don't have a combination drain pan/container to collect oil, rinse out an empty milk container and use a funnel to guide the oil into the container.

Diversionary tactics

If the drain plug on your engine is angled in such a way that oil pours all over the frame rail as it drains, try this: Make a funnel by cutting the bottom off an empty plastic bleach jug. After you've loosened the plug (don't remove it yet), position the funnel between the frame and the drain hole. Once the funnel is in place, remove the plug. ▼

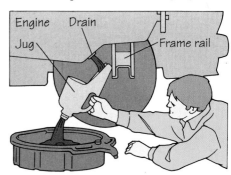

Engine   Drain

Jug

Frame rail

DISPOSING OF AUTOMOTIVE WASTES

The rules for disposing of used automotive materials vary from one location to another, depending on the local laws. Always check product labels for disposal suggestions and call your provincial or local environmental protection department for their disposal requirements.

Generally, you can dispose of a small amount of antifreeze, coolant, or windshield wiper fluid by diluting it with plenty of water and pouring it down a drain. But if you have a septic tank or large amounts of these materials, recycle them or treat them as hazardous wastes.

Shops that change oil will usually accept limited amounts of used oil from do-it-yourselfers for recycling. Stores that sell batteries may accept old batteries. Store uncontaminated gasoline in special containers and use it in auto or garden equipment engines as soon as possible.

Other materials should be recycled at special centers or treated as hazardous wastes. These include automatic transmission fluid, brake fluid, diesel fuel, engine degreaser, motor oil, automotive paint, power steering fluid, and tires.

Hazardous wastes can generally be saved for a special collection day. Check with your municipality, or your local environmental protection agency or health department, for information on when and where to bring them.

Oil filters

Slippery business

Can't get a grip on a slippery oil filter? Fold a strip of 2- x 8-inch sandpaper in half lengthwise with the grit side out. Place the sandpaper between the filter and the wrench. With the sandpaper grit gripping the wrench and the filter, the wrench will no longer slip.

Homey solution

If you have a small car with a cramped engine compartment and don't have a specialized filter wrench on hand, try one of those rubber disc jar openers to remove the oil filter. You probably have an opener in the kitchen.

Piercing problem

Sometimes an old oil filter can't be budged with any wrench. If this is your case, use a hammer to drive a large screwdriver right through the filter, about 2 inches from the engine block. Then turn the filter counterclockwise, using the screwdriver handle as a lever. Once it budges, remove the screwdriver and spin the filter off. To catch the oil that will leak out, keep a pan under the filter.

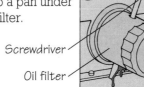

Screwdriver

Oil filter

Keep it clean

Here's one way to eliminate oil spills and mess when you're removing the oil filter: After loosening the filter, place a plastic bag around it. Once you've removed the filter, you can simply let it drop into the bag without any oily mess coming into contact with your hands.

Fill 'er up!

When you first start the engine after changing the oil, it takes a few seconds for the oil pump to move the new lubricant through the engine. If the filter screws on vertically or at an angle, you can speed up the oil flow by filling the new filter with fresh oil before you screw it in place. Don't try this on a horizontally mounted filter or one mounted upside down; the oil will spill out.

TUNE-UP

Spark plugs

Heads up!

While working on the engine you can accidentally bang your head against the latch under your car's hood. To avoid this painful situation (and a large lump), cushion the blow by cutting a slot in an old tennis ball and slipping the ball over the latch.

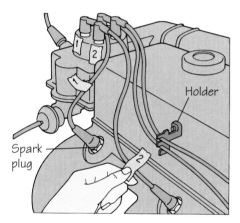

Every spark has its place ▲

You should always reconnect a spark plug wire to the correct spark plug, or the engine will misfire. To avoid a mixup, remove one wire and plug at a time and replace them before going on to the next one. Or if you want to remove all of the wires and plugs at the same time—which can be more convenient for some jobs—first identify them. Wrap a piece of masking tape around each wire, and place a piece of the tape by each plug. Mark corresponding numbers on the tape for the wires and plugs. When replacing a wire, make sure it follows the same route previously used, including through the holders that separate the wires.

Flip-flop stop ▶

When using a plug socket wrench fitted with a universal joint to install a spark plug, the joint may be too floppy to reach its target. Try supporting it with a few wraps of sturdy tape or with the "shrink wrap" sold for automotive electrical connections. The joint will still be flexible enough to turn.

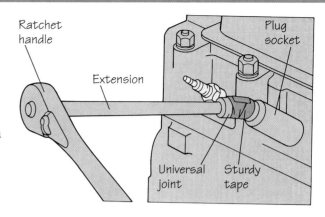

Gap facts

Spark plugs are not always gapped correctly as they come out of the box or when they are removed from the engine. Before installing a plug, check the gap against the specifications for your car, using a feeler gauge. To adjust the gap, bend the side electrode on the plug with the gapping tool on the gauge, or tap the plug lightly on a hard flat surface. Never bend the electrode with pliers; you could damage it. ▼

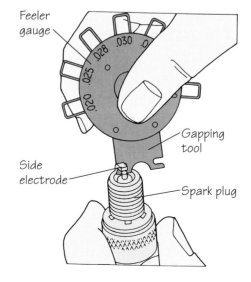

Head ache

A cylinder head can be damaged if you strip its threads while installing or removing a spark plug. To prevent damage to the head, let the engine cool down before removing a plug. Before installing a new plug, brush just a little antiseize compound on the threads. It will make removal easier later on. To avoid cross-threading (when the plug goes in crooked), turn the plug by hand until you feel it seat; then tighten it to the car maker's specifications.

Other tune-up hints

Timing is everything

If your car has an engine with a timing mark, you'll be able to see the mark better if you highlight it with white chalk or paint. Or put a piece of light-colored tape on each side of the correct timing mark, spacing the pieces about 1/8 inch apart. When the engine is running, the dark line between the pieces of tape will be even easier to see than a paint or chalk mark.

Filter fixes

A clogged air filter can cause an engine to run poorly or stall. To see if the filter is clogged, remove it and shine a light or flashlight through it. For a rectangular filter, place the light against one side. If the light barely shows through, the filter is dirty. Replace it. If you don't have a new filter at hand, reuse the old filter by banging it sharply on the pavement, thus removing some of the dirt. Put in a new filter as soon as possible.

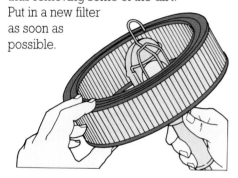

Plugged on purpose

For some tune-up procedures, you have to remove and plug a vacuum hose. (Clamping the hose won't give complete blockage.) Instead of using tape to plug the end, which doesn't always provide an airtight seal, try a golf tee. The tee's tapered shape makes a perfect plug. ▼

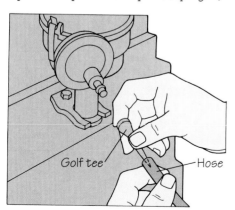

Golf tee   Hose

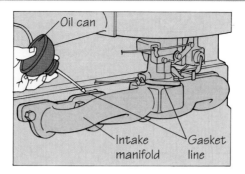

Oil can

Intake manifold   Gasket line

Leaky manifold ▲

Does your car idle roughly without a sign of the standard problems? There could be a leak in the intake manifold. Try squirting some motor oil along the gasket lines. If there's a leak, the oil will momentarily plug the hole and the idle speed will change. When the oil is sucked through the leak, the rough idle will resume. Try tightening the retaining nuts or bolts to the manufacturer's specifications, using a torque wrench. If that doesn't work, replace the gasket.

PCV leak

If you don't find the reason for a stumbling engine and leaking noises after checking all the vacuum lines, try the PCV (positive crankcase ventilation) line. There may be a crack close to the bottom of the line, where it's exposed to high temperatures.

Wake-up call

Has the starter in an older car given up? You may be able to knock some sense into it if the solenoid clicks but the starter won't turn over. This can be a sign that a worn brush is wedged sideways. A sharp blow on the starter housing with a wooden or rubber mallet may dislodge it. But have the starter repaired as soon as possible.

Fuel injection

Cold start

Traded in your carburetor-equipped car for a new one with electronic fuel injection? Don't floor or pump the gas pedal before turning the key to start a cold engine. If the engine doesn't start up immediately, some manufacturers suggest pressing down on the gas pedal about an inch as you crank the engine again.

Hot tempered

Trying to restart a hot fuel-injection engine on a hot day can leave you hotter than the motor. If the engine will crank but not start, you have vapor lock. Here's the solution: Turn the ignition key on and off for about 3 seconds without cranking the engine. After several on-and-off cycles, try cranking the engine without pressing the gas pedal; if that fails, press the pedal down about 1 inch.

Leaky injector

On an engine with port fuel injection (one injector for each cylinder), air leaks can occur around the O-rings on the fuel injectors. If you can reach them with your fingers, try to rock each injector body side to side, then fore and aft. Any movement will be very slight, but if there is a change in idle speed, the O-ring seal is leaking. You can obtain replacement O-rings from an auto supply store.

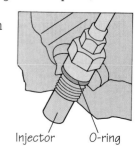

Injector   O-ring

COOLING AND EXHAUST SYSTEMS

Coolant and radiator

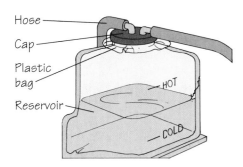

Hose
Cap
Plastic bag
Reservoir
HOT
COLD

It's in the bag ▲

If the motor is not installed at its base, you can temporarily repair a leaking plastic coolant reservoir (or windshield washer reservoir). Place a clean sturdy plastic freezer bag inside the tank. Fill the tank to the proper level; then replace the cap and trim off any excess bag, if necessary. Have the reservoir replaced or repaired as soon as possible.

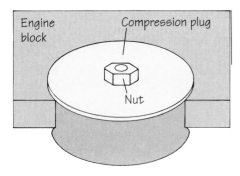

Engine block
Compression plug
Nut

Plug it! ▲

Metal freeze-out plugs can loosen or corrode and leak. After draining the coolant, remove the plug by hitting it with a punch and hammer, then prying it with the punch. Replace it with a rubber compression plug (available at auto supply stores). As you tighten the nut, the plug will expand and seal the hole.

A pinch in time

You may be able to make a temporary quick-and-dirty fix if a radiator tube springs a leak. Wait until the radiator and coolant cool down, or put on a pair of heavy gloves. Then use pliers to bend away the fins near the damaged tube and to pinch the leaking tube closed on both sides of the leak. This will cause more damage than the original leak, but it could keep the car going long enough to get you as far as a repair shop. ▼

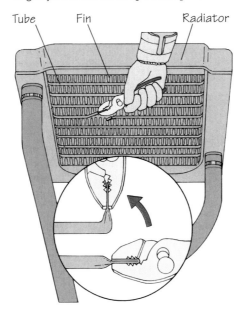

Tube
Fin
Radiator

Sweet poison alert!

Antifreeze is very poisonous, but its sweet taste can be alluring to children and animals. Always keep it in a securely closed container and clean up or hose away any spills—no matter how small they are. Drained antifreeze/coolant mixes should be caught in a container and disposed of properly (p.301). When you buy antifreeze, consider one of the new foul-tasting brands.

Hoses

A hose in time

A burst coolant hose usually means a stranded car. To avoid breakdowns on the road, many manufacturers recommend that you replace all the coolant hoses, such as the radiator, heater, and bypass hoses, every 4 years or 65,000 kilometres, whichever comes first.

Hot tip

If you must repair a hose leak around hot engine parts, you can protect your hands from burns by wearing kitchen oven mitts. Of course you can't do much fine work with the mitts on. It's better to let the engine cool off if possible.

Hose taming

If a stiff radiator hose is difficult to install, soak it in hot water for a few minutes to make it more pliable.

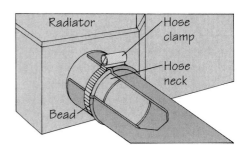

Radiator
Hose clamp
Hose neck
Bead

Clamp cramps ▲

When installing a hose clamp, make sure that it's positioned between the radiator and the bead on the hose neck. The clamp should be snug against the bead. If the clamp is on the wrong side of the bead, the hose can leak. If the clamp is too far from the bead, pressure and sediment can build up in the void.

Belts

Chirp, chirp, chirp

Does your car make a chirping noise? You don't have a nest of birds under the hood, but you do have a drive belt that needs attention. The chirping may be caused by a belt that is cracked, frayed, glazed (has a slippery, shiny look), or oil-soaked. Until you have a chance to replace the belt, try quieting the noise by spraying belt dressing on a V-belt or silicone lubricant on a serpentine belt.

Worn serpentine belt

Stifle that scream

If you hear squealing noises when you start the engine or when you turn the steering wheel to its limits, a drive belt might be slipping. Check for a loose belt while the engine is cold by slipping your finger into an inexpensive tension gauge (available at auto supply centers) and pressing it against the belt. Check the measurement against those recommended in the manual for your vehicle.

If you adjust the belt, don't over-tighten it. A tight belt is just as bad as a loose one.

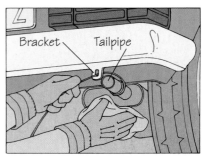

V-belt

Gauge

Alignment check

Misaligned pulleys are often responsible for belt noise, erratic operation of belt-driven accessories, belts jumping off pulleys, and uneven belt wear. With the engine running, look at the pulleys from the side of the engine compartment. If you can see a pulley wobbling, it's misaligned and needs adjustment.

EXHAUST DRAG

The sound of a dragging tailpipe or muffler calls for immediate action. It's dangerous to keep driving. The offending pipe or muffler could wedge itself under your car, or it could break free and end up in the path of another vehicle. If the muffler or tailpipe is dragging because of a broken hanger, you can temporarily rehang it until it is properly repaired. Wear thick gloves or use layers of rags to protect your hands while touching the hot tailpipe.

Rag — Glove — Broken hanger

1 Drive carefully up onto a curb so that one side of the car is raised. Never work under any vehicle that's supported by a jack. Take a look at the situation. Remember that the tailpipe will be hot.

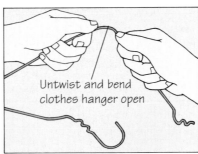

Untwist and bend clothes hanger open

2 You can use heavy wire, such as a straightened coat hanger, to temporarily support the muffler or pipe. Look for one of these in your car, in roadside garbage, or a nearby business.

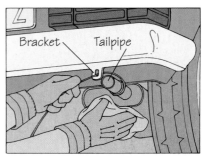

Bracket   Tailpipe

3 Wrap the wire support around the end of the tailpipe. Slip the support through a bracket while lifting up the tailpipe; then twist the ends of the wire support together.

Don't trust your eyes

Here's another way to check for pulley alignment, as long as there is adequate space in front of the belts and at least two outer pulleys are in line. With the engine off and cold, place a straight-edge across the pulley faces. If it won't rest on the faces and there's more than a hairline gap, the pulleys are not aligned.

TRANSMISSION, STEERING, AND SUSPENSION

The transmission

Fluid check

Good automatic-transmission fluid should be translucent and odorless. If it's cloudy or opaque and smells burned, the fluid is in bad condition. To check the condition of the fluid, pull out the transmission dipstick and let a little fluid drip onto a paper towel. After a few minutes, good fluid will form an even red, pink, or tan circle. Burned fluid will form a bull's-eye that's darker in the center than at the edges.

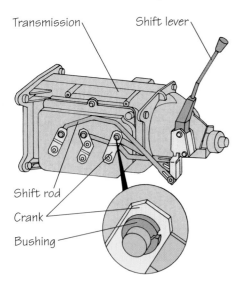

Loose link ▲

A loose shift linkage can make a manual transmission difficult to shift; it can even make the transmission jump out of gear. An experienced do-it-yourselfer can test the linkage by getting underneath the car and wiggling the shift rods back and forth. If there's play at the ends of the rods near the cranks, check for worn bushings and replace them.

Magic mushroom

When you remove the oil pan from an automatic transmission to replace the fluid and filter, don't be surprised if you find a loose mushroom-shaped plug in it. The plug keeps debris out of the transmission during factory assembly and is knocked into the transmission at the last minute. Just toss it out.

Steering and suspension

Stop and go

If the power assistance on your steering seems to stop and start as you turn the wheel around a corner, look for a loose or worn V-belt (p.305) on the power steering pump. If you find one, adjust or replace it. A slipping belt cannot supply constant hydraulic assistance.

Shimmy solution

Steering-wheel shimmy that increases with speed is usually caused by an out-of-balance front wheel. But before the wheels are balanced, check the inside of the wheel rims. An accumulation of grease from a nearby fitting, dried mud, road gook, and winter ice can throw the wheel out of balance. The shimmying may subside if you clean the wheel.

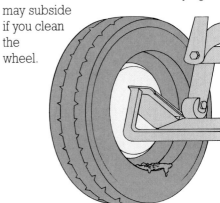

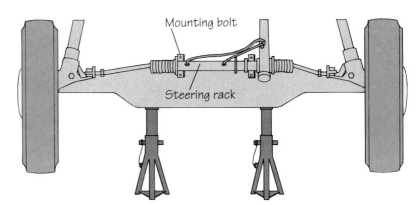

Lost control ▲

Erratic steering may indicate loose parts in the steering linkage. To check for excess play, wiggle the steering wheel while a helper watches the front tires. There should be less than ¼ inch of steering-wheel play before the tires move. If there is too much play, check for loose steering-rack mounting bolts: Place the car on jack stands and chock the rear wheels (p.300). Then move the front wheels while watching the steering rack; the rack shouldn't move. If it does, tighten the bolts.

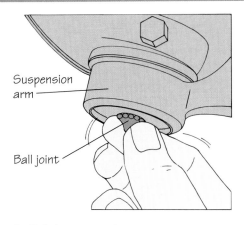

Suspension arm

Ball joint

Ball-joint wear ▲

When you replace a ball joint, check the suspension arm it's mounted in for excess wear. Insert the new ball joint into its housing; then try to wiggle it from side to side. If it can wiggle, you'll have to replace the suspension arm too.

Fitting grabber

You can remove a broken grease fitting by tapping a rectangular concrete cut nail into the remaining portion of the fitting. Then twist the nail with pliers. It's painless, effective, and can be performed right on the vehicle. ▼

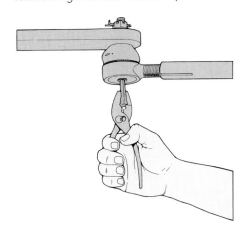

Strutting out

MacPherson struts, used at the front of many front-wheel-drive cars, can be bent if the car hits a curb or a deep pothole. Check for a bent strut under the hood by loosening the nut on the strut rod in the center of the strut tower. Rotate the strut rod exactly 360°. If the top of the tire moves in and out, the strut is bent and should be replaced. ▼

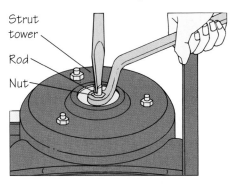

Strut tower

Rod

Nut

Nothing to boot about

A car owner needs to add one more check to the maintenance list when it comes to a front-wheel-drive vehicle with constant velocity (CV) joints. If you look under the front of your car, you'll see a pair of accordion-ribbed rubber boots by each front wheel. The CV joints are housed inside these boots and are packed with grease. A CV joint will last for years as long as the boot remains sealed. The boot itself may split from fatigue, especially in cold-weather areas; rocks and potholes can also cause damage. Inspect the boots every 3 months. Look for grease outside the boot or sprayed onto the surrounding components. The sooner you have a damaged boot replaced, the better are your chances of keeping the mechanic's repair bill down.

Down in the valley

Here's another way to spot CV-joint boot failure: The first place that a boot usually cracks is in the valley of the ribs' V's. To get a clear view for inspection, have a helper turn the steering wheel all the way to one side and back.

Noisy warning

A clicking or clunking noise from the drive shaft as you turn or accelerate is a late warning that the CV joint is on the road to certain failure. The noise indicates a lack of grease in the boot and contamination from road grit. Get the car to the shop as soon as possible.

Snappy service

The mounting nut on a shock absorber often rusts on tight. When it's time to replace the shock, the nut may be difficult to remove. If you can snap off the mounting stud, you can remove the old shock. Place a deep socket wrench with a long extension over the stud and nut. Then rock the stud back and forth until it breaks. The rubber bushings will protect the frame. ▼

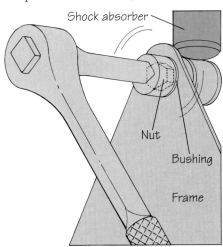

Shock absorber

Nut

Bushing

Frame

TIRES

The valve

Leak detector

A slow leak may be caused by a faulty valve. To check the valve, remove the cap and wet the end of the valve with a solution of soapy water. If bubbles appear, the valve is leaking. Deflate the tire fully; then unscrew and replace the valve core. If that doesn't work, have the whole valve replaced.

Cap extractor

Some valve caps are buried deep within fancy wheel covers. You can remove them by using the cap from a felt-tip marker. Push the marker cap over the valve cap until it sticks; then unscrew both caps.

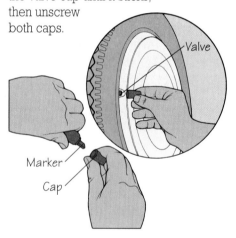

Valve
Marker
Cap

Cap extender

To avoid having to remove hard-to-reach valve caps, get extra-long caps from an automotive supply store. This type of cap has a white or colored dot at the end that's actually a spring-loaded valve. The valve lets you take pressure readings and add air without removing the cap.

The treads

Front

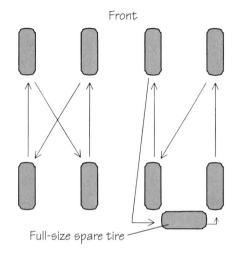

Full-size spare tire

Rotation notation ▲

Some car manufacturers recommend rotating tires from wheel to wheel periodically to equalize tread wear. Rotate your tires as shown above, or check the owner's manual for your car. Rotation is often recommended every 10,000 to 12,000 kilometres. A good time to do it is every other oil change. So you'll know the previous position of the tires, use nail polish or a tire crayon (sold in auto supply stores) to make identification marks, such as RF, LF, RR, and LR.

Don't eyeball 'em

Improper tire inflation and worn treads can cause an accident. Don't rely on visual inspection alone to check the inflation of a radial tire. The radial sidewalls normally bulge where the tire meets the pavement, making it difficult to determine when they're bulging too much. Use an accurate pressure gauge at least once a month. Inexpensive models are available at auto supply stores.

Depth perception

When tire tread depth wears down to $\frac{1}{16}$ inch or less, replace the tire. In this almost bald condition, the tread can no longer channel away rainwater and skids can result. Follow one of these three ways to measure tread depth: Use a tread depth gauge sold in automotive supply stores. Or insert a penny, head down, into the tread; if you can see the top of the royal tiara, the tread's too low. Or look for the wear bars cast into the tires; when the tread's too low, they are revealed as gaps in the tread.

Reading treads

The wear patterns on your car's tires show a lot about the car's suspension, how well you maintain the tires, and your driving habits. ▼

 A worn center points to an over-inflated tire.

 Wear along both edges tells you that the tire was underinflated.

 Feathered tread edges indicate incorrect wheel alignment.

 A single worn spot shows that you've skidded with the brakes locked.

 A scalloped, or cupped, wear pattern means that the wheel is unbalanced, suspension or steering parts are worn, or the wheel bearings are faulty.

CHANGING A TIRE

Tire changing is a basic skill every driver should have—not only in case of a flat, but in order to rotate the tires from wheel to wheel periodically (see facing page). The best time to practice tire changing is during free time in your garage or driveway, not along the side of a busy highway or on an isolated road in the rain.

Make sure you always keep a spare tire, jack, jack handle or screwdriver, lug wrench, rubber mallet, and tire pressure gauge in the trunk. It should also hold wheel chocks, bricks, or blocks of 4 x 4 lumber to chock a tire, thus preventing the car from rolling. Before using a spare tire, check its air pressure. If it's low, do not use it; have the car towed.

Park on firm level ground and turn off the engine. Set the parking brake, and put the transmission into park (or a manual transmission into reverse). Make sure everyone is out of the car before you start changing the tire. If the ground is soft, put a piece of plywood under the jack to keep it from sinking into the ground. If necessary, set out flares or a reflective triangle between you and oncoming traffic. After changing the tire, don't forget to remove the chocks and return your tools and equipment to the trunk.

If your spare tire is a "temporary" type, observe the precautions in your owner's manual—generally to drive no faster than 80 kilometres per hour and no farther than 80 kilometres.

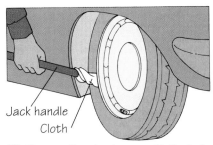

Jack handle
Cloth

1 Remove the wheel cover with the jack handle or a screwdriver wrapped in a cloth. Some covers have special locks. Check your owner's manual if the cover can't be pried off.

3 Put chocks (p.300), wood blocks, or stones under the wheel diagonally opposite the flat tire. Following the car maker's directions, position the jack and raise the car until the flat is 2 to 3 in. off the ground. Remove the jack handle.

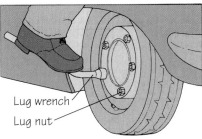

Lug wrench
Lug nut

2 Loosen the nuts two or three turns. If one won't budge, set the wrench horizontally and push down on its handle with your foot. Most nuts are loosened in a counterclockwise direction. In an old car, you may have to turn the nuts clockwise.

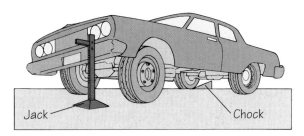

Jack
Chock

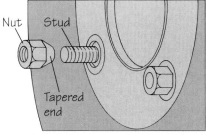

Nut   Stud

Tapered end

4 Remove the lug nuts, and pull off the tire. Mount the spare tire on the studs. Press against the wheel, and thread on the nuts by hand, starting at the bottom. The tapered part of the lug nuts should face the wheel.

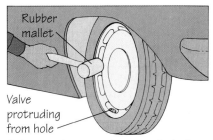

Rubber mallet

Valve protruding from hole

5 Lower the car and remove the jack. Tighten the nuts with a wrench in a crisscross pattern (p.310). Align the hole in the cover with the tire valve. Tap the cover in place with a rubber mallet.

WHEELS AND BRAKES

Getting wheels on or off

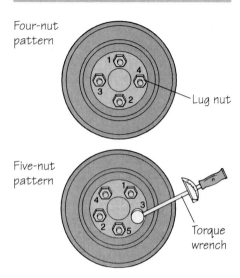

Four-nut pattern

Lug nut

Five-nut pattern

Torque wrench

Nut cracker ▲

Always tighten the lug nuts in a criss-cross pattern—not in a circle. Overly tight lug nuts can crack the wheel or warp disc brake rotors. Use an inexpensive torque wrench to tighten the lug nuts to the car maker's specifications, but do so in several stages. For example, tighten all the nuts to 20 pounds, then 40 pounds, and so on until you reach the suggested torque.

At the mechanic's

While an air-impact wrench speeds up a mechanic's job, it's very hard to control and could lead to overly tight lug nuts (see above). You can ask your mechanic to use a torque wrench, but make sure it's written into the service order before you sign it. When the car is back from service, you can double-check the torque yourself. Slightly loosen each lug nut with a torque wrench, and then retighten it to the right specification.

Wrench spinner

Cross-type lug wrenches work fast, but spinning one on the palm of your hand can raise painful blisters. To spin the wrench easily and without damage to your hand, make a wrench holder from an 8-inch length of 1½-inch-diameter PVC pipe, and cement a cap to one end. When you're ready to use the wrench, slide the pipe over its end and spin away. After you've finished the job, you'll find your palm is blister-free. ▼

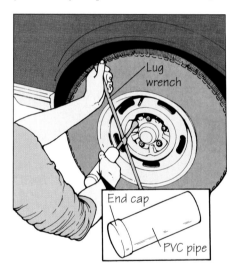

Lug wrench

End cap

PVC pipe

Bust it loose!

A wheel can rust onto the brake drum or hub and be hard to remove, even when the lug nuts are off. To remove the wheel, don't yank on it while the car is jacked up. The car could fall off the jack. Instead, put the lug nuts back on finger-tight, then loosen them two turns. Lower the car to the ground and rock it from side to side by pushing against the roof. If that doesn't bust the wheel loose, drive forward and back just a few feet, hitting the brakes hard.

Rust and rattles

Rust alert

If you mount new tires on old wheels, make sure the wheels are rust-free. Rust at the hub can weaken the wheel. If it's on the rim, rust can cause slow air leaks from tubeless tires. Remove all rust with a wire brush; apply a rust-arresting fluid and when it dries, rust-resistant paint.

Easy off

The next time the wheels are off the car, flush the studs and lug nuts with a spray penetrating oil. To avoid getting spray on the brake surfaces and other components, aim it at the studs from the side. To be absolutely sure the studs won't corrode, coat them with an antiseize compound before replacing the nuts.

Rattle traps

Wheel covers (hubcaps) can sometimes cause annoying rattles. To isolate the culprit, remove one wheel cover at a time and go for a short test drive. Then try these cures:
▷ Look for a pebble or loose lug nut rattling around behind the wheel cover, and remove it.
▷ If a loose emblem is rattling, tighten it, glue it down with epoxy, or remove it.
▷ If a riveted sawtooth holding clip is loose, hammer the clip flatter; use an-

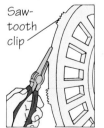

Saw-tooth clip

other hammer like an anvil behind the rivet. If the clip is stamped as part of the cover, use needle-nose pliers to bend the clip back in place.

Brakes

Braking awareness

Quite a few cars on the road have brake problems. If you feel, see, or hear any of the following conditions, it's time for needed repairs—don't wait for an accident to happen.

▷ Rhythmical vibrations or pulsations in the brake pedal (unless your car has an antilock braking system, where these are normal) could mean the brake rotors or drums are warped.

▷ Pay attention to that brake warning light on the instrument panel. If it stays lit after the engine is started, the brakes could be unsafe.

▷ Brakes that pull the car to one side, grab suddenly, drag, or lock up prematurely are dangerous. The brakes should be checked for hydraulic fluid leaking onto the brakes, sticking disc brake calipers, or wheel cylinder problems.

▷ An occasional squeak or squeal from disc brakes when braking lightly is OK, but any loud screeching, grinding, or shuddering may mean worn-out brake pads or brake shoes that are scoring the rotors or drums.

▷ Changes in the feel of the brake pedal may also indicate trouble. A pedal that is high or difficult to press down could be a sign of a power brake problem. A too-soft pedal that goes nearly to the floor may be caused by poorly adjusted drum brakes or a serious brake system failure. A spongy-feeling brake pedal often means that air is trapped in the brake system.

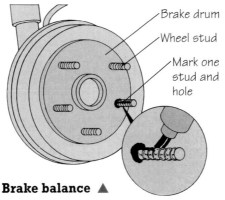

Brake drum
Wheel stud
Mark one stud and hole

Brake balance ▲

If you remove a drum to do work on a drum brake, be sure that you reinstall it in its original position. As a guide, mark one stud and the hole it goes through with chalk, paint, or a felt-tip marker before you remove the drum.

Wheel wobble ▲

An annoying vibration that feels like an out-of-balance wheel could also be caused by a warped brake drum. To check if the drum is straight, remove the wheel and lay a straightedge across the drum's mounting surface. Check four sides of the drum, in a square pattern. If you see daylight under the straightedge, replace the drum.

Hang it up

When you remove a brake caliper to do work on a disc brake, don't let it hang by the rubber brake hose. Use a length of coat hanger or other heavy wire to hang the caliper from the suspension. This will ensure a secure resting place for the caliper where it won't get knocked about, which can cause damage to the hose. ▼

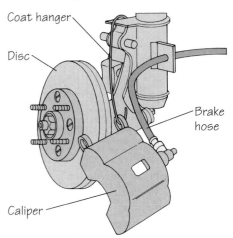

Coat hanger
Disc
Brake hose
Caliper

Taking up the slack

If the parking brake cable has stretched so much that you can no longer adjust it, try using a cable adjuster (sold in auto supply stores) to take up the slack—but first make sure there is enough exposed cable and room to fit in the adjuster. If the cable is frayed, kinked, or corroded, it must be replaced. ▼

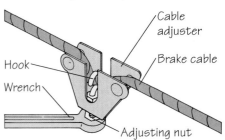

Cable adjuster
Brake cable
Hook
Wrench
Adjusting nut

ELECTRICAL SYSTEM

The battery

Shocking caution

When disconnecting battery cables, always start with the negative cable. If you start with the positive cable (on the post marked POS or +) and your wrench accidentally touches another metal part, the battery will be short-circuited, sparks will fly, and you'll receive a shock. Furthermore, the wrench may weld itself to the metal part. ▼

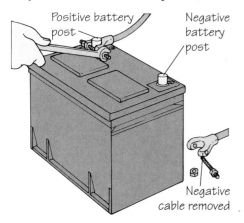

Positive battery post · Negative battery post · Negative cable removed

Fast trouble

If your battery is fully discharged, it will have to be jolted with a special high-voltage charger. Before using a charger (or letting a mechanic use one on your car), make sure the battery cables are disconnected. Otherwise, the charger can blow fuses and damage electrical components from clocks to computers.

A swipe in time

Dirt and grit on a battery can form a path for a slow electrical drain, especially in damp weather. Whenever you check the oil, clean off the top and sides of the battery with a damp cloth.

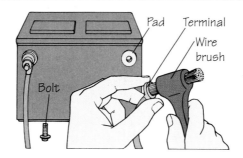

Pad · Terminal · Wire brush · Bolt

Terminal care ▲

Many car owners know that a light coat of petroleum jelly will reduce corrosion buildup on the top posts of batteries. The newer side-terminal batteries corrode, too—just not as quickly as the top-post kind. To clean the terminals, remove the terminal bolts and clean the bolts, terminals, and pads with a wire brush. Before reconnecting the terminals, give the bolts a thin coat of petroleum jelly or antiseize compound.

Secret vents

A maintenance-free battery has an extra electrolyte inside, so it may take years of water evaporation to affect the battery's output. When that time comes, however, a flat sealed-top battery will have to be replaced. But if your model has disguised vent caps, you may be able to extend the battery's life. Try prying the vent caps off carefully with an old screwdriver, without breaking or cracking them. If you can accomplish this feat, you can replenish the water in the battery.

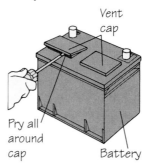

Vent cap · Pry all around cap · Battery

Too tall

Some batteries are sold with plastic spacers clipped onto their bottoms, allowing one size to fit several cars. If you install a new battery and it seems to be too tall, don't run back to the store. First see if there's a spacer on the bottom that you can pry off.

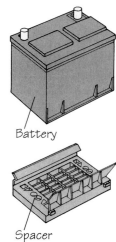

Battery · Spacer

Electrical connections

Disconnected

Most electrical problems are caused by loose, corroded, or faulty connectors. If you trace a fault to a particular connector, open it and check the prongs to see if they're loose or damaged. If they're OK, spray the prongs with a TV tuner cleaner; then reconnect the halves. You can find the cleaner in an electronics supply store.

Lube job

If you have to open an electrical connector, you may find that it has a special grease inside to help keep out moisture, retard corrosion, and dissipate heat. In most cases, it's silicone dielectric grease (check the service manual for the car, or call the parts department of your car dealer). This grease is readily available from an auto supply store. You should never apply ordinary grease.

Lights

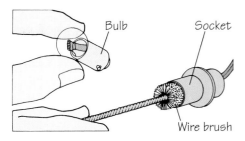

Bulb · Socket · Wire brush

Can't be too clean ▲

If a light refuses to work, it doesn't necessarily mean that the bulb is no good. Corrosion in the socket can prevent electricity from reaching the bulb. Use a wire brush to clean out the socket.

Slippery fingers

When handling a quartz halogen bulb, keep your fingers off its glass. These bulbs burn so hot that the oil on your fingers will crack the glass. If you do accidentally touch the glass, clean it with alcohol.

Drain plug

If you need to keep the car door open for a long time and you can't switch off the dome light independently, wedge a tennis ball between the door edge and the light switch. It will keep the light off and reduce battery drain. If you don't have an old ball, cut a triangular wedge of scrap wood and pad it with rags.

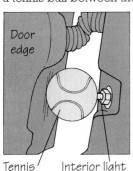

Door edge · Tennis ball · Interior light switch

A NEW ANTENNA

Replacing a car radio antenna is a common 30-minute repair that most people can do themselves. But yanking all the old stuff out without noting the way the cable is routed through the body panels can turn the job into a couple of hours of unamusing labor.

Before routing the new cable through the car, make sure it's long enough to reach the antenna location. Marking the cable path with string lets you compare the lengths of the cables. Pull the cables and string through the path carefully, tugging them gently as they clear various tight spots.

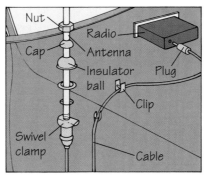

Nut · Radio · Cap · Antenna · Insulator ball · Plug · Clip · Swivel clamp · Cable

1 Unplug the old cable from the radio jack. Tape a length of sturdy string to the cable plug. Free the cable from any clips or brackets. Remove the nut at the antenna; slide other parts off.

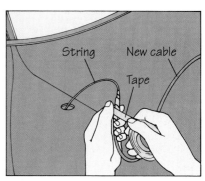

String · New cable · Tape

2 Push a screwdriver through the hole down one side of the clamp; pull the antenna and old cable out. Tape new cable to string end; pull it through. Plug in new cable; attach new antenna.

Aim to please ▶

After having your headlights aimed by a professional, park the car at the entrance to your garage. Mark the outline of the patterns made by both the high and the low beams on the back wall of the garage. Also mark the position of the front wheels on the garage floor. If the headlights go out of whack, use these marks to check and reaim them. To adjust a headlight, remove any trim to reach the adjustment screw above the light.

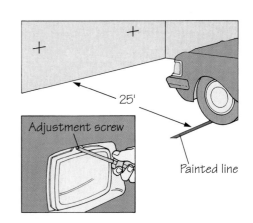

25' · Painted line · Adjustment screw

FUEL SYSTEM

Gasoline in the car

Instead of a Breathalyzer

Alcohol is often used as a gasoline additive. More than 10 percent alcohol can cause a rough idle, stalling, and power loss in your car. If the rest of the fuel system is OK, siphon some gas out of the tank. Tape a photocopy of a metric rule to a glass jar. Pour in 5 centimeters of water. Very slowly add the same amount of gas without mixing it with the water; the gas will float above the heavier water. Seal the jar with a lid, and shake it. The alcohol will separate from the gas and mix with the water. Let the jar stand for 5 minutes; then check the new levels. If the volume of the water (on the bottom) has increased by more than 10 percent (above 6 centimeters), there is too much alcohol in the gas. Switch to another brand of gasoline. ▼

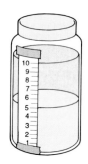 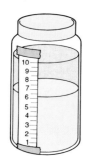

Cap keeper

After filling the gas tank, have you ever driven away without replacing the gas cap? Epoxy a magnet to the cap. Then when you fill the tank, you can stick the cap in view so you won't forget it.

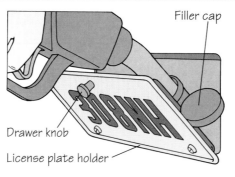

Filler cap

Drawer knob

License plate holder

Filler flap ▲

Some cars have their gas filler hidden behind a hinged, spring-loaded license plate holder. To make it easier to open the holder, drill a hole through the plate and install a small drawer knob. Once you remove the gas cap, wedge it behind the holder to keep it open while you insert the gas nozzle.

Saving fuel

Most drivers are familiar with the time-tested advice for improving gas mileage: avoid "jackrabbit" starts and avoid speeding. Here are a few additional tips that should be observed:
▷ Check the tire pressure often. Fuel consumption increases by 1 percent for every 2 psi (pounds per square inch) a tire is low.
▷ Have the wheel alignment checked periodically. Wheels that drag increase fuel consumption.
▷ Have the brakes checked regularly. Brakes that drag lower your kpl (kilometres per litre).
▷ Don't let the engine idle or warm up for more than 30 seconds. It takes more gas to idle an engine for 30 seconds than it does to restart it.
▷ Remove excess weight from the trunk. Every unnecessary 100 pounds can reduce fuel mileage by 0.25 kpl.

Leak stopper

You can temporarily plug a small leak in a gas tank with bubble gum! Chew the gum until all the sugar is gone, then press it into the leaking area. The gasoline will harden it into an epoxylike mass that should hold long enough for you to drive to a repair shop.

Don't choke on it!

If your engine often stalls immediately after starting, the choke may be opening too much. If your car has a specified opening gap (not an angled gap) between the choke plate and the carburetor barrel, you can use a drill bit that is the same size as the gap (a ⅜-inch bit for a ⅜-inch gap) to check the opening. Wait for a warm day. While the engine is cold, remove the air cleaner cover, start the engine, and the instant the choke opens, insert the bit. It should slide in and out with a light drag. To avoid dropping the bit into the carburetor, stick a piece of masking tape around its end. If the bit is a loose fit, have the choke adjusted. Because the choke opens quickly, don't hold the bit in place to retest; the result will be inaccurate. ▼

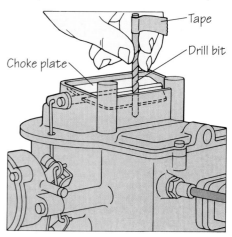

Tape

Drill bit

Choke plate

PAINT TOUCH-UP

Applying paint

Rust arrester

After scraping or sanding rust from a chip or scratch, apply a rust converter. This product transforms rust into an impervious black coating that prevents further rusting under the paint. Follow the instructions on the label to apply two thin coats. Let the converter dry for 48 hours before applying paint.

To prime or not

Acrylic latex automotive paints require an undercoat of a solvent-base primer or sealer. Lacquer and enamel paints don't. Check paint labels for primer recommendations.

Fill 'er up

It may take several coats of touch-up paint to fill a chip up to the original paint surface. Dab on the coats with a small artist's brush, a cotton swab, or the torn end of a paper match. Allow each dab to dry before applying the next layer.

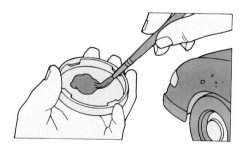

Spray away ▲

Want to touch up a small chip or two but the matching color of touch-up paint is available only in an aerosol can? Shake the can well. Spray some paint into a jar lid or paper cup; apply it with a brush.

PAINT PROBLEMS

Before using a primer or paint, do a test in a hidden spot, such as under the bumper. When painting, always work in a well-lighted area. Here are a few problems encountered with spray paints and ways to deal with them:

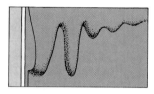

Drips and runs happen when paint is sprayed on too thick. Let the paint dry completely; then smooth the area with wet fine sandpaper (200 grit or finer). Clean the area and repaint it.

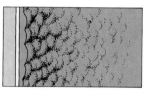

Orange peel, as the name implies, resembles the rough skin of the citrus fruit. It's caused by spraying too thin a coat or by paint that's improperly mixed (not enough solvent). Wet-sand, clean, and repaint the area.

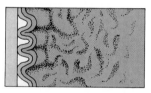

Wrinkling or lifting occurs when paint is applied over an incompatible primer. Sand down to the bare metal, and start the job over using a compatible primer and paint.

When silicone or wax isn't completely removed, small spots, called fish eyes, let the old surface show through. Wipe off the wet paint with thinner. Clean the area with alcohol or a precleaning solvent, and start over.

Mask task ▶

When painting small areas with an aerosol spray paint, use this trick to avoid the hassle of masking off the surrounding surface: Cut a 1-inch hole in the center of a piece of shirt cardboard. Hold the cardboard a few inches from the car, and spray through the hole with the nozzle 1 inch from the hole. This will confine the spray without leaving behind the ridges you get when masking tape is removed.

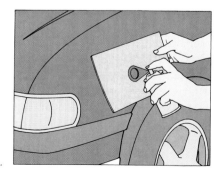

Car wash, etc.

Foaming seat

You can give your vinyl car upholstery a fresh clean look by scrubbing it with foaming bathroom cleaner. Or use a mixture of 1 ounce liquid dishwashing detergent in 2 quarts hot water.

Hair of the dog

Instead of pouring leftover stale beer down the drain (or worse yet, down your throat), you can use it to clean off the leather upholstery in your car. Just don't do this on the road; a police officer may misinterpret the scent.

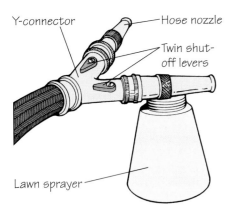

Double-barreled ▲

For convenient car washing, attach a Y-connector with double shutoff valves to your garden hose. Screw a hose nozzle onto one side of the Y and a lawn sprayer holding concentrated liquid car soap to the other side. With this double-barreled setup, you can switch from soapy water for washing to clear water for rinsing with the turn of a lever.

Bug off

Here's a remedy for removing dead bugs from your car: Spray the car with a mixture of ½ cup baking soda and 2 cups warm water. Wait 2 minutes; then respray the car and sponge off the bugs. The baking soda neutralizes the acid in the bugs, making them easy to remove, but it won't damage the car's finish.

Sapped

Remove dried tree sap from your car by following these steps: Carefully break off lumps of sap, using a plastic kitchen spatula to avoid scratching the paint. Soak a soft cloth in a mixture of laundry detergent and hot water. Wearing heavy plastic or rubber gloves, rub the sap residue with the cloth as hard as you can. Continue rubbing and breaking off lumps until the sap disappears; then rinse the area with cold water. When the surface is dry, treat the spots with a car polish and then rewax the whole car.

Off, damned sticker!

To remove a bumper sticker, heat it with a hair dryer until the glue loosens, then carefully peel it off. To remove a dealer emblem, heat it with a hair dryer and then pry the emblem off using a putty knife with its blade wrapped with duct tape. After removing a sticker or emblem, get rid of any remaining adhesive by rubbing it with your thumb. If it doesn't ball up, apply alcohol or rubber cement thinner with a paper towel.

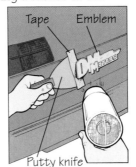

Cheap scrubbers

A small scrap of a deep-pile carpet makes a good car scrubber. An unused dust-mop head is also handy—just stick your hand into the pocket and scrub.

Hot wheels ▲

Your brakes can heat parts of the wheel to 150°C (300°F) or more. Never apply a cleaner to such a hot wheel. The mild acids contained in these cleaners can do damage at high temperatures. Cool off the wheel with a garden hose before applying a cleaning solution.

White-washed

For the reappearance of the whitewalls hidden under the dirt on your tires, tackle the dirt with a soapy pot scrubbing pad from the kitchen.

A repelling thought

Apply a thin coat of one of those clear plastic-protecting-and-enhancing sprays to alloy wheels to help keep road salt, bugs, grease, dirt, and other debris from staining them.

Stubby to the rescue!

To remove dried polish from the seams and crevices on your car, trim the bristles on a paintbrush so they are ¾ inch long, then brush away the deposits.

The windshield

Clogged washer

Does your windshield washer refuse to work, even though the tank is filled with fluid and there are no cracks in the tank or in a hose? Try looking for clogs. First check the screen on the end of the pickup tube. If that's not clogged with grime, disconnect the hose from the nozzle at the windshield. If the hose squirts, the nozzle is clogged. (If it fails to squirt, you may need a new pump; check the electrical connections before replacing it.) Clear the nozzle by carefully probing it with a small safety pin, sewing needle, or wire. ▼

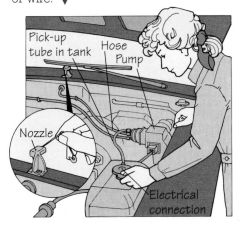

More solutions

To remove nongreasy dirt from a windshield, spray it with a mixture of 1 part vinegar and 3 parts water. For a really grimy or hazy windshield, use a mixture of ½ cup ammonia and 1 gallon water. Because hazy windows can be caused by vapors from vinyl, wash vinyl surfaces, using the mixture recommended for upholstery: 1 ounce liquid dishwashing detergent in 2 quarts hot water.

WIPER WOES

The rubber squeegees on wipers wear out rapidly because they rub against the glass. Replace them every 6 months. If your windshield wipers are working poorly, look for the appropriate solution below:

Straighten a bent arm with the wiper at mid-stroke. Using two pairs of pliers, carefully twist the arm until it's parallel to the glass. If the tip is bent, remove the assembly to straighten it.

Water beads indicate a buildup of grease, wax, oil, or grime. Try increasingly stronger cleaning solvents. Cover the car when it's parked outdoors to protect it from air pollution.

Smearing is a sign of a dirty windshield or wiper, a worn squeegee, or a poor mix of washer solution. Clean the wipers and windshield, and replace the solution; if this fails, replace the squeegee.

Smearing in only one direction often occurs when the squeegees are the wrong size or when they harden from cold weather or old age. If they're cold, let them warm; otherwise, replace them.

Chattering is caused by a bent wiper arm or a frozen squeegee on a cold day. Straighten the arm (see above left), thaw out or replace the squeegee, or replace the wiper arm and blade.

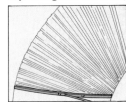

Fog eraser

If the windshield fogs up, make sure the "recirc" vent door is open (this lets outside air enter the car). If it's open, check that the defroster is on. If it isn't, the wiring or air-conditioner compressor could be faulty. Until you fix the problem, use a blackboard eraser to wipe off moisture.

Glass repair

You can polish out shallow scratches in a clean windshield by using jeweler's rouge and a 1-inch-diameter polishing pad on an electric drill set at a low speed. Polish the glass, using several passes if needed; clean off the rouge with soap and water.

STORAGE, RESTRAINTS, AND SECURITY

Everything in its place

Valuable papers

Keep a large envelope in the glove compartment or another safe place to hold receipts for repair work and replacement parts. If warranty work is needed, you'll have any needed proofs of purchase or service handy. Write the due dates for tune-ups, oil changes, and tire rotation on the outside of the envelope.

Pocket protector

Attach a pocket-type shoe storage bag to the back of a car seat with extra-strong Velcro tape to keep all maps, cans, bottles, napkins, and small toys semi-organized— especially on long trips.

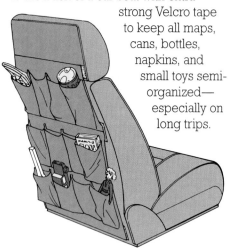

Mat tact

Does your floor mat refuse to stay in one spot, or do the corners flip up all the time and get in the way of your feet? Use Velcro tape at each corner of the mat to keep it and the corners in place.

Visor advisory

Here's another way to put Velcro tape to use: Apply it to a pesky drooping sun visor to hold it up and out of the way.

Containment policy

Be prepared for an emergency. Wrap tools and road flares in a blanket, and secure the bundle in the trunk with a rope or an elastic cord. The blanket keeps the items together and prevents them from rattling, and it comes in handy if you have to crawl under the car. The rope or cord stops the bundle from rolling about.

Carpet capers

Carpet remnants are useful for lining the trunk of your car. They can protect your luggage and stop the trunk's contents from rattling about. If you want to line the bed of a pickup truck, make sure you use indoor/outdoor carpet.

Kneepads

Storing and retrieving items from the bed of a pickup truck can be tough on the knees. To protect them, pad the top of the tailgate with indoor/outdoor carpeting. Attach a sheet of hardboard to the tailgate with self-tapping stainless steel screws; then glue the carpeting to the hardboard with panel adhesive. ▼

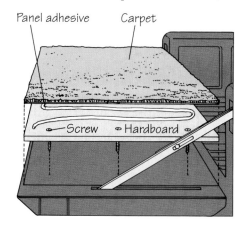

Panel adhesive   Carpet

Screw   Hardboard

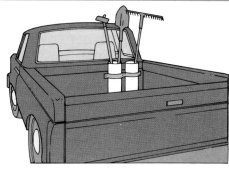

Tool caddy ▲

You can carry tools such as rakes and shovels upright in a pickup truck bed by making holders from 3-foot lengths of 6-inch-diameter PVC pipe. Secure the pipe to the inside of the pickup bed with galvanized pipe straps and stainless steel self-tapping screws. You can attach several pipes, but make sure that your view from the driver's seat won't be restricted and that items don't protrude beyond the truck bed.

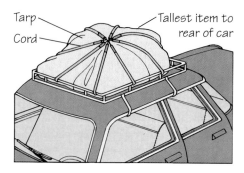

Tarp

Cord

Tallest item to rear of car

Beat the wind ▲

Planning to carry a load on a roof rack for a long trip? Spread a large tarp over the rack; then load it, with the tallest items to the rear of the car. Wrap the tarp over the items, and secure the bundle with crab-style elastic cords. The streamlined shape will help gas mileage, and the tarp will provide protection from the weather.

Roof padding

When hauling items on your car's rooftop, you can protect the paint by placing a partially inflated swim float or a scrap of carpet padding under the cargo.

Aiming devices

Here's how to line up your trailer and hitch for an easy hookup:

▷ On a car: Mount a small mirror on the trailer, facing your car, and adjust it so that you can see the trailer's hitch from the driver's seat. Maneuver your car using the view in the mirror.

▷ On a pickup truck: Place a strip of brightly colored vinyl tape over the top of the tailgate, directly above the hitch, and a second piece on the trailer above its hitch. Keep the two pieces of tape aligned as you back up to the trailer.

Keys and locks

Backup key

The best spare key is one of these tough plastic ones that looks like a credit card and fits in your wallet. Locksmiths and hardware stores sell them and can cut them on a standard key-grinding machine. If you forget your keys or lock them in the car, just flip out your spare. ▼

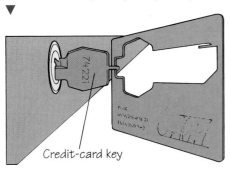

Credit-card key

Stuck in the trunk

Trunk lock cylinders often become jammed, in some cases because of an unsuccessful theft attempt. If you can't get at your prized possessions inside your trunk, drill through the keyhole with a large bit (such as ½ inch), then insert a thin screwdriver to release the latching mechanism. Inexpensive replacement trunk lock kits are available from auto supply stores for most popular makes of cars and require no special tools. However, you'll have to use a separate key just for the trunk now, as the door lock key will no longer work.

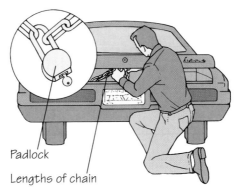

Padlock

Lengths of chain

Linked ▲

Thieves can easily pop your trunk open with a pry bar. Take this step to foil them: Bolt a few links of chain inside the trunk lid, and anchor a second length to the trunk floor; then connect the free ends of the two chains with a padlock. The chains should be just long enough to let you fit your hands inside to open or close the lock, but not long enough to let luggage or valuables be removed. Cover the chains with pieces of rubber hose to keep them from rattling or damaging items stored in the trunk.

Twofer

If you own two American-made cars of the same make and they use double-cut keys with identical notches on the top and bottom, a locksmith can make you one key that fits both cars. Starting with a blank key, have him cut one side to fit each car. Then have a notch cut into the side for the car you drive most often, so you can tell which side is up. ▼

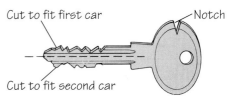

Cut to fit first car — Notch

Cut to fit second car

Jammed latch

A door that bounces back open after you swing it closed may have a jammed latch. Inside the U-shaped opening in the side of the door is a rotating latch with a pair of prongs. If it's flipped to the closed position, the door won't shut. To unjam the latch, pull, lift, or push the exterior handle as if to open the door. If the latch doesn't rotate to the open position, hold the handle open and move the latch downward with your finger or a screwdriver. ▼

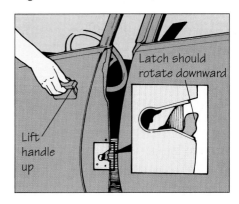

Latch should rotate downward

Lift handle up

WINTER TIPS

Preparing for the cold

Lighten up

Lighter-viscosity motor oils (5W30 or 10W30) make a car easier to start in cold weather than heavier-weight oils such as 10W40. Check your owner's manual to see if lightweight oils are recommended for your car. If so, switch to one when cold weather threatens.

Heat cure

A warm battery produces more cranking power than a cold one. Before winter sets in, install an electric battery heater (sold in auto supply stores). When the cold weather comes, you can give the battery a boost by running the heater overnight. You can also help a feeble battery along by placing an incandescent droplight under it at night.

Faster starts

The colder your motor oil, the thicker it gets and the harder it is for the engine to crank over. If you park outside or in an unheated garage, consider installing one of these electric heaters. Generally, you attach them with a magnet, adhesive, hose clamps, or bolts. Plug in overnight, and disconnect before driving off. ▼

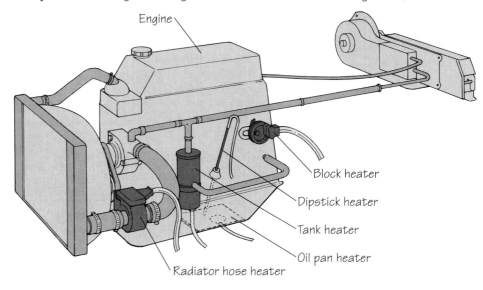

Engine
Block heater
Dipstick heater
Tank heater
Oil pan heater
Radiator hose heater

Jumper cables

Jumper bump-up

Avoid buying cheap jumper cables that are too short or too thin. Short cables limit the distance and positioning of the two cars; get 12- to 16-foot cables. Too-thin cables won't carry enough current to boost a dead battery—especially in cold weather. The best, and most expensive, cables are 4- or 6-gauge (the lower the gauge, the thicker the cable). In warmer climates, you might get away with 8-gauge cables. Avoid 10-gauge or thinner cables.

Avoid tangles

To keep jumper cables from getting tangled, lay them side by side and wrap plastic electrical tape around the pair in three or four places. But don't tape them together within 3 feet of either end. ▼

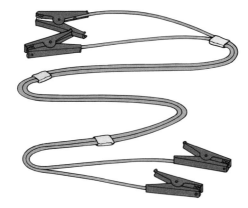

Snow and ice

Traction aid

Keep half a dozen three-tab asphalt roofing shingles in the trunk in case you get stuck in snow. Place them rough side up under the drive wheels. By aligning them end to end, you can make two rows of a high-traction surface 9 feet long.

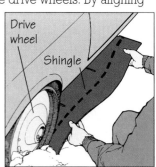

Drive wheel
Shingle

Gritty aid

Keep a bag of cat litter or a few large plastic jugs filled with sand in the trunk. In rear-drive cars, they will add extra weight for better traction. If you do get stuck in mud or snow, you can pour the sand or litter under the drive wheels to get going again.

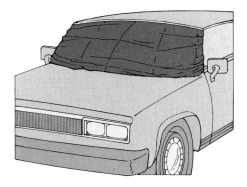

Labor saver ▲

Instead of scraping snow and ice from the windshield on a winter morning, try one of the following: The night before, cover the windshield with a heavy-duty plastic trash bag that's been cut open along the edges. Close the doors on the edges of the plastic sheet to keep it from blowing away. Or cover the windshield with a piece of old carpet (pile side up) that's been cut to fit. In the morning, sweep off any heavy snow, peel off your cover, and drive away.

Emergency scraper

If you're caught without an ice scraper in your car, you can use a plastic credit card to remove a thin covering of ice. Just be careful that you don't damage the black magnetic strip that runs along the back of the card.

Chilled out

Frozen door locks can ruin the better part of a winter day. Here's what you can do to prevent or cure the problem:
▷ Cover the locks with tape before going through a car wash or whenever precipitation is predicted.
▷ Keep lock cylinders lubricated by squirting in a special lock lubricant, penetrating oil, or cigarette lighter fluid.
▷ Place a drinking straw into the key slot and exhale into it until the lock thaws.
▷ Heat the key with a lighter or matches, then slowly work it into the frozen lock. Be sure to wear thick gloves so you don't burn your fingers. ▼

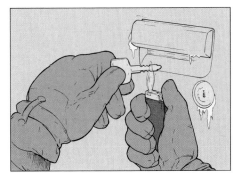

Car heater

Finding the heat

On a bitter cold day, it often seems that it takes too long for your car to heat up. If it really does take too long, there could be an inadequate trickle of heat. To analyze the situation, stick a meat thermometer into an interior heater vent. With the engine warmed up, the heater set on *Hot,* and the selector on *Vent,* the thermometer should read 38°C (100°F) or more. If it does, all is well.

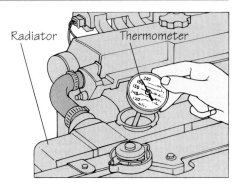

Radiator   Thermometer

Thermostat out of whack ▲

To isolate a faulty thermostat (another reason for poor heat), warm up the engine with the radiator cap removed. Stick a meat thermometer into the coolant. If it reads at least 82°C (180°F) and the upper radiator hose is hot to the touch (watch out for the fan), the thermostat is OK. If not, replace the thermostat. **Caution:** Never remove the radiator cap from a hot engine!

Hot hands

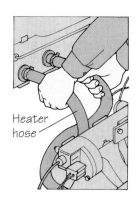

With the heater on, carefully touch both heater hoses (they could be hot). If they're not hot, have a mechanic check the water control valve or heater core.

Heater hose

Final test

Check each selector setting (*Vent, Floor, Defrost,* etc.) inside the car. If air isn't flowing to the correct outlet, or if the airflow changes speed or location as you accelerate, have a mechanic look

GARGE

Keep out the elements

Seal it up

Keep cold air, rodents, and debris out of your garage, and save on energy bills to boot, by installing weatherstripping on the garage door. You can buy vinyl weatherstripping designed specifically for closing gaps around all the edges. If only the bottom of the door needs sealing, try using a garden hose. Cut a length of hose that's as long as the door, slit it lengthwise, fit it around the bottom of the door, and nail or staple it in place.

Even it out

If your garage floor is uneven, you can still create a good seal between the bottom of the garage door and the floor. Simply tack ¾-inch foam pipe insulation to the bottom of the door, with the slit facing down. Keep the insulation out of sight when the door is closed by setting it back ½ inch from the door's front edge. But remember that a well-sealed garage means an even greater danger of carbon monoxide buildup. Never run an engine inside a closed garage.

Foam pipe insulation

Moisture barrier

Do you have a multipanel wood garage door? Protect its vulnerable bottom section from moisture by running paintable caulk along the joint where the bottom horizontal rail joins the panels. ▼

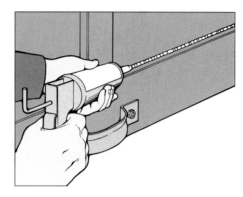

Melt control

You know what a mess snow and ice create all winter long when they melt on your garage floor. Confine the mess to the area beneath the car by gluing several strips of rubber garage door bottom seals to the floor with construction adhesive. Most of the garage floor will stay clean and dry, and the water will be channeled out to the driveway. ▼

K48 096

Garage door bottom seal

Parking

Things that go bump

Judging how far is far enough when parking your car in the garage is often tricky. Save your car and the garage wall from damage by hanging a tennis ball, or a sponge rubber ball, from the ceiling to use as your guide. To install it, park your car exactly where you want it. Then mount a screw eye in the ceiling, positioned so that when the ball hangs, it touches the windshield on the driver's side. No more guesswork!

Front and center

Have you parked your car only to find you could barely get out because of lack of space on the side? End the frustration by painting a stripe of luminous paint the width of your car on the back wall of the garage. You'll center your car with ease.

Stay within the lines

Keep lawn mowers, bicycles, and other equipment out of the way by painting white lines on the garage floor, outlining a space for each item. As long as all the family members return the items to their designated spots, you won't have to get out of the car to move them before you can park in the garage.

Door protection

Avoid damaging your car door when you open it by attaching a piece of carpet to the wall where the door makes contact. Pieces of foam rubber insulation or padding also work well to prevent dents and chipped paint.

Door-to-door barrier

Parking one car next to another in a two-car garage often leads to damaged doors on both cars. Avoid scratches and dents altogether by creating a cushioned barrier. Cut equal lengths of vent hose (the type used for a clothes dryer) and a thin wooden dowel. Put the pole through the hose, and secure a screw eye on each end of the pole so that the hose is securely attached to the wood. Suspend the barrier from the ceiling with rope tied to each screw eye. Hang it so that it meets the car doors just below the handles. ▼

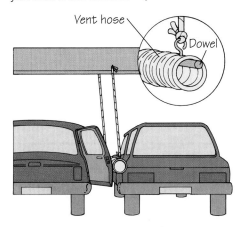

Vent hose
Dowel

Mirror, mirror in the corner

Before you get out of your car at night, you can quickly and easily check to see if all its lights are functioning. Install a mirror at an inside front corner and another one in a back corner of the garage. Be sure that the two mirrors are positioned so that when you are sitting behind the steering wheel and looking in the side or rearview mirror, you can see the headlights in the front mirror and the taillights in the back one.

Garage doors

Garage door opener safety

Mark your calendar with reminders to periodically inspect your automatic garage door opener. Follow the owner's manual, and keep in mind the following:
▷ Every month check the safety features for proper operation. Check that the manual disconnect works properly.
▷ Every 3 months adjust the open and closed settings, if necessary. Check that the door opens and closes properly.
▷ Every 6 months see that the door and door hardware operate smoothly. Lubricate if necessary. Check the tension on the chain/cable or the opener.
▷ Every 12 months tighten all the nuts and bolts. Check the fasteners on the garage door and the door opener.

Add a button

Consider installing two buttons instead of one when you put in an automatic garage door opener. Place one by the door to the house and the other inside the garage, right by the garage door. When you need to take something out of the garage, there will be no need to race to beat the closing door.

Clamp it

When working on a manual garage door, set it at a comfortable height by securing a C-clamp or locking pliers on the door track. This is safer than propping the door with a chair or other object.

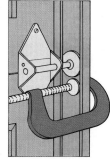

Spring safety

Roll-up overhead garage doors use tightly coiled springs. If one snaps, it can injure you and damage your property. Take the time to install a safety cable, available at home centers, through the center of each spring. The cable will not interfere with the action of the door or springs, and it will prevent a broken spring from whipping around. *Note:* This does not apply to garage doors with torsion springs; they should be worked on only by professionals. ▼

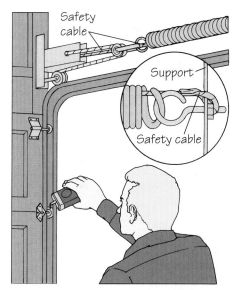

Safety cable

Support

Safety cable

Keep on rolling ▲

Doors move sluggishly because of inadequate lubrication in the roller bearings. Periodically apply a thin film of lightweight oil to the rollers and hinges. Go easy, though; too much oil will collect dirt. Keep the tracks clean by wiping them occasionally with a cloth dampened with oil.

MORE HINTS

CURTAINS, SHADES, AND BLINDS

Hang it up

Easier curtain hanging

You needn't have an extra hand to install curtain rods without trouble. Simply use masking tape to hold the brackets in place while you work. Not only will you free up your hands for marking, drilling, and attaching the brackets, you'll minimize arm strain as well.

Wrong way up

Is your window rounded or oddly shaped at the top? If so, try mounting your shade upside down. To do this, install the brackets at the base of the window and attach a small pulley at the top. To raise and lower the shade, secure a cord to the edge of the shade and run it through the pulley.

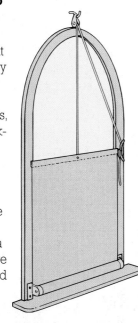

A new life for shades ▲

Instead of discarding worn shades, give them a face-lift. Choose a fabric to complement your decor, and cut it to fit the shade. Apply a thin coat of rubber cement or spray-on adhesive to the shade; then attach the fabric. Carefully smooth the fabric to eliminate air bubbles, which could cause wrinkling when the shade is rolled up.

Like-new shade

If the bottom of a shade is badly stained or worn, don't throw it out. Turn the shade upside down and attach the damaged end to the roller. First, unroll the shade and take out the staples holding it to the roller. Then remove the pull and slat at the bottom, open the hem, and staple that end to the roller; make sure the shade's long edges are at a perfect right angle to the roller. Sew a new hem for the slat, and reattach the pull. ▼

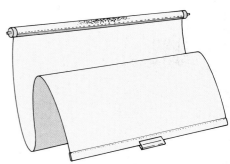

Blind renewal

Replace a frayed venetian blind lift cord without taking down the blind by using the old cord to pull the new one into place. Remove the buckle on the lift cord, and clip off the cord a few inches above the loop. Tape the ends of the new cord to the cut ends. Then open the bottom of the blind and pull on the knotted ends of the old cord to draw the attached new pieces through the blind. ▼

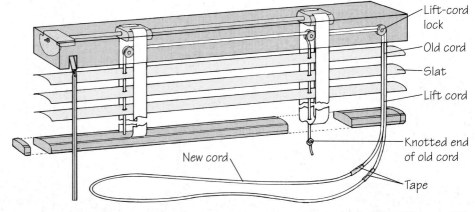

Lift-cord lock

Old cord

Slat

Lift cord

New cord

Knotted end of old cord

Tape

Just like new

Quick patch

Small tear on a shade? Fix it before it grows. Stick a piece of masking tape on the back and coat the front with clear nail polish.

PICTURE FRAMES

Making the frame

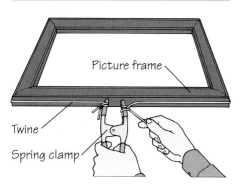

Twine
Picture frame
Spring clamp

A picture-perfect clamp ▲

You can hold picture-frame joints together until the glue sets by using only a spring clamp and some twine. Cut a piece of twine to fit around the perimeter of the frame. Tie one end of the twine to a jaw of the clamp, and run it around the frame. Then squeeze the clamp open and tie the other end of the twine to its other jaw. Release the clamp to pull the twine taut around the frame.

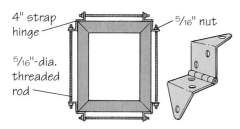

4" strap hinge
5/16" nut
5/16"-dia. threaded rod

Handy hinge clamp ▲

For larger frames, make a clamp from four threaded rods and four strap hinges. Drill holes for the rods at the ends of the hinge leaves; then bend each leaf 90°. Push the rods through the holes in the hinges, forming a square larger than the frame, and screw a nut onto each rod end. Twirl the nuts to tighten the clamp around the frame.

Quick finish

To tint and protect raw wood picture frames easily and inexpensively, use a coat of brown paste shoe polish. Give the paste a few minutes to soak into the wood, wipe off any excess, and then buff the surface with a soft lint-free cloth.

Faster framing

Most people secure the artwork and glass within a picture frame with brads, but it's easier to use glazier's points. Push the points into a softwood frame with an old screwdriver or stiff-bladed putty knife; in hardwood tap them into position with a hammer.

Wiring the frame

Wiring like a pro

Make your own picture hanger with a length of 1/32-inch stranded wire, two eye hooks, and two 3/8-inch-long pieces of copper tubing. Attach the eye hooks to the picture frame. Slip the pieces of tubing onto the wire; then thread the wire through the eye hooks and loop it around them. To keep the ends of the wire from unraveling, slide the pieces of tubing over them and crimp the tubing down over the wire with pliers. ▼

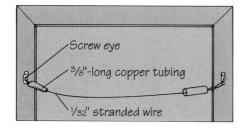

Screw eye
3/8"-long copper tubing
1/32" stranded wire

Go fish

Super-strong nylon fishing line (monofilament) is practically invisible, making it a great material to use when hanging pictures from ceiling moldings.

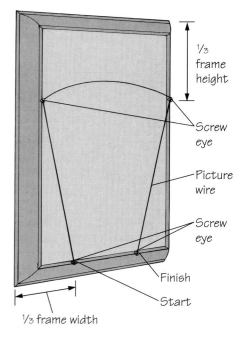

1/3 frame height
Screw eye
Picture wire
Screw eye
Finish
Start
1/3 frame width

Rx for stress ▲

A heavy load can cause the joints of a large wooden picture frame to separate. To prevent this, rig the picture wire to support the frame at the bottom. Attach screw eyes to the frame as shown; then fasten one end of a length of braided picture-hanging wire to one of the bottom screw eyes. Thread the wire through the two side screw eyes, and fasten it to the other bottom screw eye. Pull the wire taut before fastening it to the last screw eye.

PICTURE HANGING

Hanging the picture

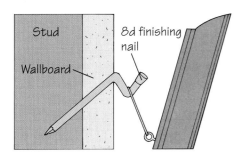

Quick hanger ▲

To make an inexpensive picture hanger, grasp the shank of an 8d finishing nail in the jaws of a vise; then, using round-nose pliers, bend the nail to the contour shown. To start the nail into the wall, tap its head lightly with a hammer; use a nail set positioned at the bend to drive the nail home.

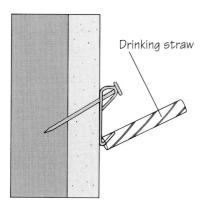

In good position ▲

Slip a section of drinking straw over a picture-hanger hook to help position the picture wire over it. Remove the straw once the picture is in place.

A dent marks the spot

Avoid hit-or-miss. With this handy tool made from a wire coat hanger, you can create a small indentation in the wall, showing you exactly where to mount your picture. Cut a 10-inch piece of wire from a hanger, and file one end to a point. Using pliers, bend the wire as shown, forming a hook at the pointed end and a finger-size loop at the other end. To use the tool, insert the pointed end under the picture wire or sawtooth hanger. Position the picture on the wall, holding it by the looped end of the tool, and gently push the point into the wall to mark the spot.

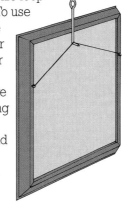

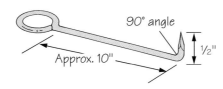

Wallcovering cover-up

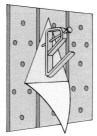

Don't damage wall-coverings with picture-hanger holes. Instead, install the hanger underneath the wallcovering. Slit a tab in the wallcovering where you want to install the hanger; moisten the area, and very carefully peel down the tab. When it's time to re-arrange your pictures, disguise the hole by gluing the tab back into place.

Keeping it straight

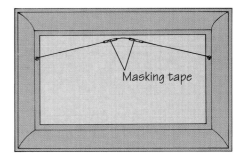

No-slip picture ▲

Keep your pictures from sliding around on the wall by wrapping bits of masking tape around the picture wire on both sides of the wall hanger or hook.

Tacky trick

Another way to keep a picture straight is to use a thumbtack gripper on the lower corners of the frame. Jab flat-head tacks through short pieces of masking tape from the sticky side, and adhere them to the frame. The tacks' points will hold the frame in place without penetrating the surface of the wall. ▼

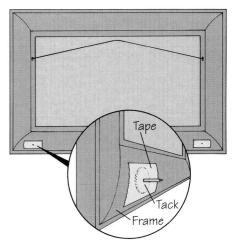

CHILDPROOFING YOUR HOME

Household menaces

Cures for the common cord

Pulling on a dangling power cord can result in a countertop appliance falling and causing an injury, and playing with a long window-blind cord can result in the child's pulling the blind off the wall or in accidental strangulation. Keep all cords out of reach of children by using cord shorteners like the one shown, elevating the cords on wall hooks, or tying up their excess length. ▼

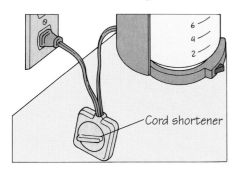

Cord shortener

Prop it up

It's easy to catch little fingers under the lid of a piano keyboard or a chest. To avoid this, glue blocks made from corks to the edge of the lid; on some pianos, you can use small suction cups to hold the lid either open or closed. ▼

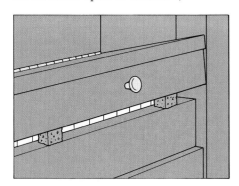

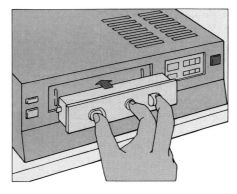

Open wide ▲

Children are fascinated by the way VCR's seem to swallow up videotapes. Keep your machine from "eating" other items by either placing the VCR out of reach or by putting a protective cover over the slot. To make your own cover, build a box out of ¼-inch plywood and fit it over the entire unit.

Windows and doors

Door ajar

Keep a room off-limits to children but still allow for ventilation by installing a hook with a spring clasp near the top of the door. Be sure to screw the eye as close to the edge of the door as possible. When it's latched, kids won't be able to enter but the door will stay slightly ajar.

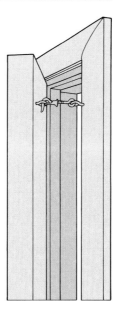

Finger saver

Keep your tot's fingers from getting caught in a door with a simple removable doorstop made from 1-inch quarter round molding and a 6-inch length of coat hanger wire. Drive one end of the wire into the end of the molding, and bend the other end to form a hook. Slide the wire over the top door hinge, making sure the molding is positioned between the leaves of the hinge. ▼

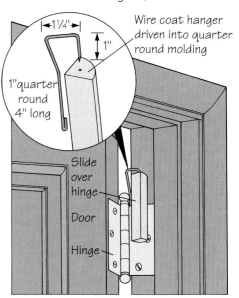

|←1¼"→|
1"
1" quarter round
4" long
Wire coat hanger driven into quarter round molding
Slide over hinge
Door
Hinge

Window safety

A child can fall out of a window in the twinkling of an eye. To avoid such a tragedy, install window guards. (Some local codes require guards for households with children.) If you don't have guards, open only the tops of double-hung windows; tack a nail into the inside frame to keep the bottom from opening. Don't rely on a screen to keep a child in; the slightest pressure can cause it to pop out, leaving no protection against falls.

Seeing spots

To a child in motion, a closed sliding glass door can easily appear to be open. Prevent painful accidents by attaching colorful decals to the glass just below the child's eye level.

Stair safety

All fenced in

Because kids can squeeze through even tiny openings, make sure deck rails and stairway balusters are child-proofed. An easy solution is to attach heavy-duty plastic mesh fencing to the inside of the railings. Fasten the fencing to the railings with ½-inch staples, or tie it in place with strong twine. ▼

Safe stairs

With crawlers and toddlers in the house, a safety gate is a must at the top and bottom of every staircase. Select one-piece gates or the type with sliding sections—a child's head can easily get caught within the bars of an accordion-type gate.

Garage

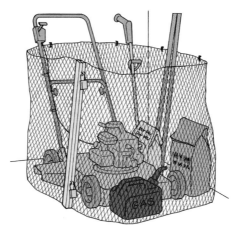

OK corral ▲

The typical garage is full of dangerous tools and toxic substances. Enclose these items in a childproof corral made by attaching standard-width chicken wire to the walls. Staple 1 x 2's to the sharp cut ends. Install screw eyes in the wood to accommodate two padlocks.

Open Sesame

Make sure that your garage door opening switches and remote devices are out of a child's reach. And if your automatic garage door is old, replace it with a newer model that reverses if it touches anything while closing.

SAFE AT HOME

A child's natural curiosity can lead to dangerous situations. Keep your child safe and prevent accidents by following some basic rules and using your common sense.

▷ Never leave a child unattended in the bathroom or in the kitchen.
▷ Install safety guards in all unused electrical outlets.
▷ Store household cleaners and other chemicals in a locked box kept out of reach of children.
▷ Remove the doors from any discarded appliance, regardless of where it is stored.
▷ Place a thick, soft rug underneath your baby's crib in case the baby climbs out and falls.
▷ Don't bathe an infant in the sink when the dishwasher is running—hot water could back up into the sink and scald the child.
▷ When cooking, turn pot handles away from the edge of the stove.
▷ Prevent a child from closing and locking a door by draping a thick towel over the top of the door.
▷ Keep houseplants out of reach by hanging them from the ceiling.
▷ Every 6 months, reevaluate your home; look for new, reachable dangers.
▷ Talk to your children about household dangers and the importance of keeping safe.

CHILDPROOFING YOUR HOME

Kitchen safety

Keeping company in the kitchen ▶

Kitchens pose many hazards; reduce the risk of accidents by installing a stove guard or by removing the control knobs when the stove is not in use. But remember, it's not a good idea to leave a child alone in the kitchen. Toddling children soon learn they can reach forbidden delights, such as a stove top, by pushing a chair into the desired position and climbing up. In such a case, even the best stove guard won't prevent a nasty accident.

Locks 'n' latches ▲

Toddlers love to explore and investigate every corner. To protect your appliances and cabinets from your kids, and the kids from your appliances and cabinet contents, install childproof latches or locks wherever necessary.

Sit tight

Small children can easily slip on slick wood or plastic high-chair seats, winding up with their heads under the tray. A rubber sink mat secured to the seat keeps baby in place.

Temporary solution

Kids are insatiably curious, especially when they get the chance to explore a new environment. When visiting a home that may not be childproof, temporarily "lock" accessible cabinets with heavy-duty twine or thick rubber bands. Simply loop the twine around the cabinet handles and knot it tightly; make sure it's secure enough to keep the child from pulling the door open and squeezing a hand inside. ▼

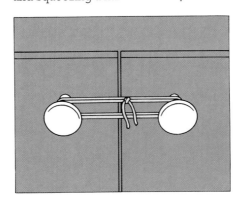

Anchored down

Any child who bounces on the open door of a freestanding stove or dishwasher risks tipping the appliance over onto him- or herself and becoming the victim of a serious accident. Prevent this by anchoring the appliance to the wall or floor with antitip brackets, available through appliance dealerships and at some home centers.

A safer bath

Nonslip grip

Water and soap residue can make tubs very slick; reduce the risk of falls by installing nonskid decals on the bottom of the bathtub and shower. To ensure a tight seal between the decals and the bottom of the tub, make sure that the tub is clean before putting them into place.

No more bumps

Many accidents are the result of falling against the water spigot in the bathtub. Protect your child from bumps by placing a protective cover over the spigot. You can either purchase one or create your own from a length of pliable rubber hosing (available at home centers). Slice the hose lengthwise and wrap it securely around the spigot. If you have a very wide spigot, you may need more than one piece of hose. Use ring clamps to hold the hose in place.

No burns here

Temperatures that seem comfortable to adults can seriously burn children's sensitive skin. Antiscald valves, which can be attached to most standard faucets and showerheads, prevent accidents by automatically stopping the water flow when the temperature exceeds a specified setting.

Running hot and cold

You can safeguard against burns while bathing even without installing an antiscald valve. Simply fill the tub partway with cold water, then top it off with hot. And of course never leave a child unattended in the bathroom.

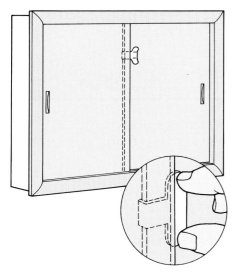

Medicine chest safety ▲

Keep that sliding-door medicine cabinet securely locked with this plastic safety latch available in home hardware centers. Kids quickly become adept at climbing, and the typical medicine cabinet is full of hazards, such as razor blades, medications, and scissors.

In the nursery

Pets begone ▶

If a safety gate isn't enough to keep a curious pet out of the baby's room, replace the traditional solid door with a screen door. A screen will keep pets out and allow you to hear if the child cries or to peek in without disturbing the baby. Remember, pets should not be left unattended with newborns.

Child's play

Unlidded bins and boxes are the safest containers for toy storage—you won't have to worry about children pinching their fingers or getting trapped inside. But if your toy box must have a lid, drill several holes in the walls of the box to allow ventilation should a child get caught inside. (For more ideas on storing toys and sports equipment, see pp.122–123.)

Say no to plastic

To reduce the risk of suffocation, use a mattress pad instead of a plastic bag for the crib's mattress cover. Make certain that the pad is securely fastened to the mattress. Don't keep a pillow in the crib, and be sure that any toys left there are too big to fit into the baby's mouth.

On the move

A bouncing toddler can "walk" a lightweight crib across the floor—and within proximity of something unsafe. Prevent this by securing the crib to the wall with a pair of heavy-duty hook-and-eye fasteners screwed into the wall studs. Use this same trick to keep a wooden high chair in place. ▼

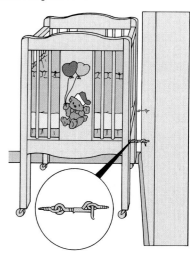

ELIMINATING HOUSEHOLD ODORS

Musty odors

Book freshener

To rid books of musty odors, store them for a few days in a paper bag filled with crumpled newspaper. The newspaper will absorb the smell. Repeat several times with fresh newspaper until the odor is completely gone.

Sweet linens

Freshen stored linens by tossing an unwrapped bar of scented bath soap in among them. Replace the soap with a fresh bar every few months. An added bonus: After a few months the soap will be dry, making it last longer in the bath.

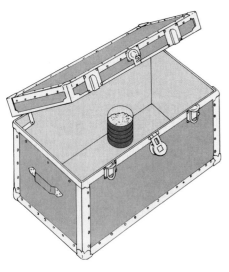

The cat's meow ▲

Here's a terrific way to deodorize a musty trunk. Simply pour cat litter into a large uncovered coffee can, set it in the trunk, and close the lid. The next day the odor will be gone, and you may remove the can.

Household odors

Odor be gone

Cat litter can also be used to eliminate garbage odors. Sprinkle it in the bottom of garbage cans to keep them smelling fresh. Change the litter every week or whenever the cans get damp.

Eliminating mothball odor

The smell of mothballs can linger in an enclosed space for months. Restore a fresh scent by scrubbing the space with a mixture of equal parts of white vinegar or lemon juice and rubbing alcohol.

Whole-house deodorizer

Chase out winter's stagnant air with the fresh scent of spring: Place several canisters of solid room deodorizer inside the return air duct of the largest room of the house. The furnace fan will draw the deodorant into the central duct and circulate it throughout the house. (Under the Building Code, return air vents must be close to the ceiling in all new houses.) ▼

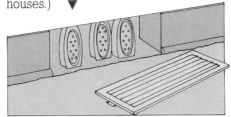

Fresh scent

For a unique air freshener, spray a bit of your favorite perfume or cologne onto a light bulb. The heat from the light bulb will release the aroma of the perfume, sending your favorite scent wafting through the room. ▼

Pet odors

A concrete answer

Concrete absorbs odors, and a urine-soaked concrete floor has a terrible smell that can permeate the entire house. To deodorize it, scrub the floor with a solution of half white vinegar and half water. Or put undiluted denatured alcohol in a spray bottle and spray the floor thoroughly.

A strong solution

Severe urine stains may require the application of a commercial pet odor remover (available at pet stores). If a slight odor remains even after this treatment, apply two coats of shellac to the problem area.

PETS

The great outdoors

The run-around ▶

If you chain your dog to a stake in the yard, you know it doesn't take long for Fido to wind up in tangles. Keep him running free by building a pivoting tether. Remove and discard the wheel from a plate-type ball-bearing caster by cutting through the axle with a hacksaw. Sink a 4 x 4 firmly into the ground, and screw the plate to the top of it. Make a pivoting arm by drilling a hole the size of the caster's old axle through one end of a 3-inch strip of 5/4 hardwood. Position the arm on the caster plate; slide a bolt through the plate and the arm, and secure it with a nut. Attach a screw eye to the opposite end of the arm, and hook the dog's tie-out chain to it.

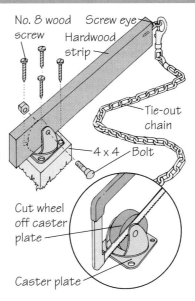

No. 8 wood screw
Screw eye
Hardwood strip
Tie-out chain
4 x 4 Bolt
Cut wheel off caster plate
Caster plate

No-tip dish

To protect your pet's outdoor water supply from accidental spills, serve up the water in a large angel-food cake pan.

Wood stake
Angel-food cake pan

Keep the pan in place by setting it over a wooden stake that's been firmly driven into the ground.

Have pet, will travel

Make car travel less traumatic for yourself and for your pet by securing the pet carrier or crate with a shock cord so that it won't slide around. Twist the shock cord around the handle of a carrier or through the wires on a crate, and hook the ends of the cord to the sides of the car or to the seat-belt mechanism.

Protecting houseplants

Scat, cat

Keep kitty from using potted plants as a litter box by burying a few mothballs in the soil.

Plant protection

This wire mesh shield lets water into the soil but keeps animals out. Make a paper pattern the same diameter as the pot, and tape the pattern to a piece of wire mesh. Using wire cutters, cut out the shield; then cut a straight line to the center, and cut out a circle about 1 inch larger than the plant's stem. Coat the cut edges with clear nail polish, and slip the shield into place.

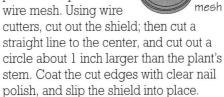

½" wire mesh

Bathing your pet

Rx for skunk spray

For sweet-smelling fur, prewash your pet with full-strength tomato juice before washing with shampoo. Then rinse with a few tablespoons of ammonia mixed into a gallon of warm water—but be sure to keep this solution away from your pet's eyes. Use plain warm water for a final rinse. If you don't have tomato juice on hand, try a solution of equal parts of vinegar and water. Rinse your pet with clear water; then repeat the process until the odor is gone.

Slip-sliding away

The slipping and sliding that usually accompanies bathtime can frighten even stalwart dogs. Ease your pet's nervousness by providing a secure nonskid surface to stand on. When bathing your pet in a sink, cut a hole for the drain in a foam-backed placemat and position the mat foam side up for your pet to stand on. When bathing your pet in a bathtub, put down a nonslip rubber or vinyl mat.

Drain strainer

Prevent clogs when bathing a pet by covering the drain with an upside-down tea strainer or a nylon kitchen scrubber. Either will keep pet fur out of the drain.

Corn dog

Need to give the dog a bath but can't get him near the tub? Try a dry bath. Rub cornmeal into your pet's fur, then brush it out. If your pet needs a deodorant, follow with a baking soda rub.

CONTAINER GARDENING

Pots and repotting

Stand up straight

Does your flowerpot wobble when you set it down? Here's how to make flowerpots, planters, and boxes sit flat without scratching or slipping. Apply four evenly spaced dabs of silicone caulk to the bottom. Before the caulk dries completely, turn the pot right side up and place it on a sheet of wax paper. Once the caulk cures, the container will have four stable, level feet. ▼

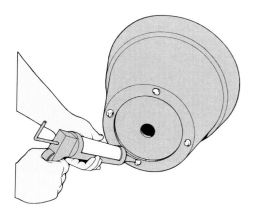

Room to grow

Repotting a plant is easy when you take advantage of the old pot. First, layer some potting soil in the bottom of the new pot. Place the old pot inside the new one, and pour potting soil in around it, gently tamping the soil with your fingers. Then remove the smaller pot and it'll leave a well that's the perfect size for your plant's root ball.

Full of holes ▶

If your flowerpot has holes, you may want to think twice before you automatically spread a layer of gravel beneath the soil. The last couple of inches or so of soil in the bottom of a pot remain saturated with water, whether there's a gravel base or not. Because saturated soil lacks oxygen, roots won't grow into this area; by adding gravel you reduce the growing area available to the plant roots. On pots without drainage holes, however, continue to add the gravel layer to collect excess water that has no way of draining out.

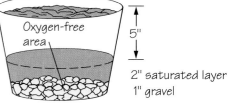

8-in.-deep pots

Oxygen-free area
6"
2" saturated layer

Oxygen-free area
5"
2" saturated layer
1" gravel

Keeping plants healthy

Too rich for me

Plants thrive in good soil. For a good, rich soil that drains well, try this recipe: Combine equal amounts of loam, compost or peat moss, and perlite or coarse sand. Then stir in 2 teaspoons of superphosphate, 3 teaspoons of horticultural lime, and 2 teaspoons of all-purpose granular fertilizer for every 4 quarts of soil. Your plants will love you for it.

A fungus among us

Combat fungus on houseplants with this baking soda solution. First, trim off any badly infected leaves. Mix 1 tablespoon of baking soda into 1 gallon of water; use a spray bottle to apply the mixture on the remaining leaves. Repeat this procedure every few days until all signs of the fungus are gone.

The brush-off

Recycle a soft toothbrush by using it to remove scale insects from leaves. Dampen the brush in a solution of 3 tablespoons denatured alcohol per quart of water and gently scrub away the insects. Check the plant weekly, and repeat as necessary. If you find a toothbrush too cumbersome, use a soapless facial cleansing sponge (available in the cosmetics section of the drugstore). ▼

FRESHLY CUT FLOWERS

Stem treatment

Hardy harvest

Minimize moisture loss when cutting flowers by harvesting them on a cloudy day or early in the morning. Be sure to make clean cuts, using pruning shears or a sharp knife; don't break or tear the stems. To prolong the life of the freshly cut blooms, plunge the stems directly into tepid water after cutting.

Daffodil know-how

Newly cut daffodils secrete a milky substance that creates a seal when it mixes with water, preventing the stems from absorbing water. To avoid this, singe daffodils by briefly passing the cut end of the flower through the flame of a match. Repeat every time you recut the stems.

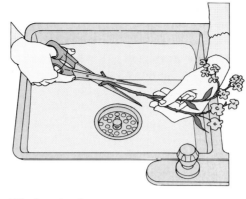

Kind cuts ▲

Freshly cut flowers need water to survive. Encourage your flowers to drink up by recutting their stems every few days. When recutting green stems, first carefully cut a 2-inch slit running from the base of the stem up. Next, cut the bottom of the stem at a 45°angle. If possible, cut stems under water to eliminate air bubbles that could get trapped in the stem and block water intake. Let the flowers stand in deep water in a cool place for several hours before arranging them.

Whittling away wood

On woody plants, carefully scrape the bark from the last 2 inches of the stem with a sharp knife or florist's scissors; then slit and recut as described at left.

There's life at the bottom

Before arranging flowers, strip off all the lower leaves. If they are submerged in water, they'll rot and produce a gas that hastens wilting. If the flowers are tall, trim off the uppermost buds (which are unlikely to flower) to allow the others their share of water and increase their chances of blossoming. ▼

Water treatment

Straight up, no ice

If you've ever created an arrangement of cut tulips, you know that they tend to droop soon after cutting. Keep them standing straight by adding a few drops of vodka to the water.

Home brews

The best way to preserve cut flowers is to use a commercial preservative. But if you don't have any, mix 2 teaspoons of medicinal-type mouthwash into 1 gallon of water—it'll be more effective than the old-fashioned options of aspirin, pennies, or sugar. A can of a clear soft drink mixed with a gallon of water can also help (because of the acid in the drink).

No wilting here

2" boiling water

Some flowers, including hollyhock, black-eyed Susan, gerbera, Queen Anne's lace, dogwood, and butterfly bush, will wilt unless you boil their stems before arranging them. As the hot water rises upward, it forces air down and out of the stems, eliminating the airlocks that prevent water from reaching the flower heads and foliage. Protect the blooms by securing plastic bags around the flowers with twist-ties. Carefully holding the flowers diagonally, place the stems in the boiling water for 20 seconds. Then plunge the stems into a bucket of tepid water and leave them for several hours before arranging.

Half fill bucket with tepid water

GRILLS

Homemade grills

Quick & easy cooking

Do you have everything you need for the cookout—except the grill? Don't despair; you can build a temporary grill quickly and easily. Simply stack concrete blocks in a U-shape around a concrete stepping-stone or a bare patch of ground. Make the structure about 15 inches high (two layers of standard-size blocks). Top it with a rack and you're ready to cook. ▼

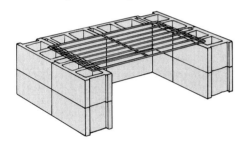

Just rolling along

When your guests can't come to the barbecue, bring the barbecue to them with this unique mobile grill. Transform an old metal-bed wheelbarrow by placing an oven rack across the top. ▼

Charcoal lighters

Carton starter

You can make a disposable charcoal starter by loading briquettes into an empty 2-litre waxed milk or juice carton. To start the fire, just light the carton. Or as an alternative, fill a paper shopping bag with charcoal and kindling. Staple it shut and you have a one-step no-mess fire starter.

Cleaning the grill

Burnt out ▲

Yes, even permanent briquettes in a gas grill need to be cleaned—but here's an easy way to do it. Simply turn the briquettes so that the greasy side is face down. Then light the grill, set the temperature on high, and close the cover. Let the fire burn for 15 to 20 minutes; your briquettes will be as good as new.

A safe start

An empty coffee can will serve as a reusable charcoal starter. Using a punch-type beverage opener, cut openings all around the bottom edge of the can. Remove the bottom with a standard can opener, and securely place the can in your grill—be sure it doesn't wobble. Put a small wad of paper and scraps of dry wood in the can; then fill it to the top with charcoal. Light the paper through the triangular openings at the bottom. Once the briquettes are burning, lift the can off with tongs (it'll be red-hot) and spread out the briquettes.

Leave it for the morning

The worst part of a barbecue is the cleanup. Make it a bit easier by removing the the cooled rack from your grill and dropping it in the grass, cooking side down. Let it sit there overnight, and in the morning wipe away the dew (and grease) with damp paper towels.

Overnight soak

For really tough baked-on grease, put your dirty rack inside a heavy-duty plastic garbage bag. Mix a solution of ½ cup liquid dishwasher detergent and 1 gallon water. Pour the mixture over the rack and seal the bag with a twist tie. Let it sit overnight. The next day, use a stiff brush to remove the residue. Rinse the rack thoroughly.

FIREPLACES

A good fire

Getting started ▶

The best way to lay a fire is to create a pyramid out of the logs. For the base of the pyramid, use one large log and one medium-size log, keeping the smaller one in the front. Stuff newspaper and kindling into the gap between the two logs, and top off the pyramid with a small log. Always start a fire from the bottom by lighting the paper and kindling at both ends. Keep the fire going by replacing the logs as needed. As the rear log burns, use a fireplace poker to carefully roll the front log to the rear and then put in a new front log. Add other logs as required.

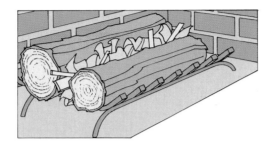

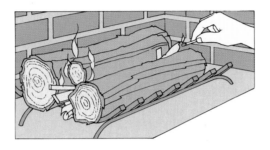

A newsworthy start ▲

If you have trouble lighting wood fires, try this no-fail fire starter. Beginning at an outside edge, rip a section of newspaper into strips, stopping just shy of the fold. Tightly wedge the paper underneath the logs, add kindling, and then carefully light the ends of the strips.

Ash sifter

Fires burn longer when you separate the coals from the ashes. To do this, cut a piece of hardware cloth (available at home centers and hardware stores) and fit it over the grate. The openings in the hardware cloth will let the ashes fall through and at the same time hold the coals up closer to the flames. ▼

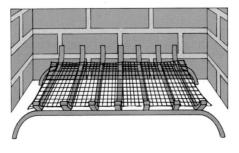

Open up

Fires need oxygen in order to burn, and often the only air supply is the warm air from the house. To stop heated air from rushing up the chimney, feed your fire fresh air from an open window. Just crack the window an inch or two; if you pick a window on the windy side of the house, you'll probably strengthen the fireplace's updraft and reduce smoking.

In the end

Because embers can smolder even when there are no flames, you should be certain that the blaze is completely extinguished. Don't pour water on the flames; this can cause heavy smoking. Instead, put out the flames with baking soda, sand, dirt, or clay cat litter. It's also smart to keep some baking soda close by in case the fire burns too rapidly and needs to be smothered.

Glass doors

Recycle those ashes

It sounds odd, but smoke stains can be removed from glass fireplace doors with ashes. Just dip a damp cloth into cooled ashes and rub away the stains.

Unsmoked glass

If the smoke stains on your glass fireplace doors refuse to come off with ashes, as described above, use a foam-type aerosol oven cleaner. Simply spray on the foam, let it sit for a while, and wipe it off, following the manufacturer's instructions. Your doors will sparkle.

CHRISTMAS DECORATIONS AND WRAPS

Ornaments and garlands

Pretty blocks

Create your own Christmas tree ornaments by covering small cardboard boxes with scraps of fabric or wallcovering. Tie a ribbon around them to create a package. You can wrap scraps of wood as well. ▼

Not a thread out of place

After a couple of seasons, crocheted ornaments look tired and droopy. Perk them up with a few pumps of hair spray.

No butter, please

When making garlands of popcorn, pop the corn a week before you plan to string it. Stale kernels won't crumble when you pierce them with a needle.

Light fixtures

Having trouble securing lights where you want them on the tree? Tie them to the branches with green pipe cleaners.

Tending the tree

Tree test

To make sure that the Christmas tree you are buying is fresh, look at it carefully, smell it, and handle it. A fresh tree will have a good green color and a pleasant fragrance. If you lift the tree a few inches off the ground and slam the stump down, the needles shouldn't fall off in substantial numbers. As a final test, hold a branch about 6 inches from its tip between your thumb and forefinger and pull your hand toward you, allowing the branch to slip between your fingers. If the needles adhere to the branch, the tree is fresh; if they fall off, it's not.

Drink up

To fire-retard your tree and keep its needles green, mix a solution of 2 gallons hot water, 2 cups corn syrup, ¼ cup liquid bleach, 2 pinches Epsom salts, and ½ teaspoon borax detergent. Saw a few inches off the bottom of the trunk, and let the tree stand overnight in a bucket filled with this mixture. Use this mixture in the tree stand, too.

It rings a bell

Nothing attracts a child's attention like a Christmas tree. To warn you of little hands reaching for the colorful ornaments, tie a number of small bells to the lower branches of the tree.

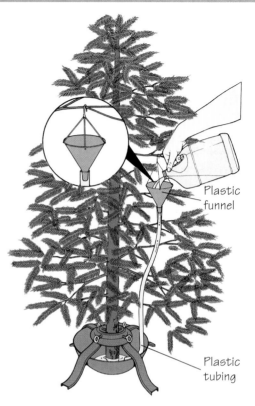

Plastic funnel

Plastic tubing

No more aching back ▲

Make this simple watering device and you'll never again have to squirm underneath the branches of a Christmas tree. You'll need a medium-size plastic funnel, a length of plastic tubing, and some straight wire. Punch three holes along the top rim of the funnel, thread a length of wire through each hole, and twist the wires together to form a hook at the top; hang it from a branch of the tree. Force the tubing over the small end of the funnel, and put the free end of the tube in the water trough of the tree stand. Next time the tree needs water, just use the funnel.

Stand tall ▷

Keep your tree straight and tall with this sturdy stand. Drill four equidistant holes around the rim of a 5-gallon plastic container. Partly fill the bucket with sand; move it into place. Soak the sand with water, tamp it, and add more sand, leaving the holes exposed. Trim the lowest branches off the tree, and use a saw to cut an X into the bottom surface of the trunk. Insert the trunk into the sand, and stabilize the tree with four lengths of monofilament. Tie each line to a sturdy branch; then pass the lines through the holes in the bucket and tie them securely.

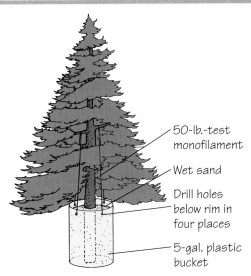

50-lb.-test monofilament

Wet sand

Drill holes below rim in four places

5-gal. plastic bucket

In the bag

Don't drag your dried-out Christmas tree through the house, leaving behind a trail of needles. Instead, take it apart one branch at a time. Using pruning clippers, cut the branches into little pieces and drop them right into a plastic garbage bag. When you're done, all you'll have to carry is the bare tree trunk and a garbage bag. ▼

Faster fakes

If you're putting up a reusable artificial tree, here's a way to make the job easier: Dip the ends of the branches in petroleum jelly before inserting them into the frame.

Gift wraps

Wrapping-paper resources

If you want an economical alternative to traditional wrapping paper, try scraps of unused wallcoverings, especially the shiny metallic kind. Or use aluminum foil and bright-colored ribbons.

Emergency wrap

When you run out of wrapping paper on Christmas Eve and have a couple of items left to wrap, don't despair. Black and white newspaper tied with red ribbon or gold cord makes a wrapping that is more than acceptable.

SAFETY FIRST

CHRISTMAS TREE CARE

The fresh scent of a real fir tree puts people in the Christmas spirit; but a tree can be a serious fire hazard if it is used carelessly or allowed to dry out. Here are some tips for keeping a tree fresh and safe for several weeks:

▷ If you are storing your tree for a few days before decorating it, keep it outside in a cool area away from the sun and wind.

▷ Help your tree retain moisture during storage by making a straight cut across the trunk, 1 inch from the bottom. Stand the tree in a bucket of water, making sure the water covers the cut.

▷ Prior to bringing the tree inside, make another cut across the trunk, 1 inch above the first.

▷ Use a stand that holds at least 1 gallon of water, and check the level daily to ensure that it remains above the top cut.

▷ Place the tree away from fireplaces, radiators, television sets, and other sources of heat.

▷ Don't use combustible decorations on the tree.

▷ Check all wires and connections; don't use lights with frayed cords; never use lighted candles.

▷ Always turn off all the tree lights before you go to sleep and before leaving your home.

SPORTS EQUIPMENT

Out in the wild

Here's a hot tip

If you're out hiking or camping and a bootlace breaks, don't curse and swear. Just replace the aglet and the lace will be as good as new. Using a match or a lighter, melt a scrap of nylon rope. Let the drippings land on the frayed lace end; then use a twig or a toothpick to shape the end. ▼

Handy oil

Usually the lantern or camp-stove plunger needs a bit of oil when there is none to be found. In a pinch, you can use a drop of salad or cooking oil as a substitute.

High and dry

Keep your topographical and trail maps from becoming water damaged by coating them with a commercial wood and concrete waterproofer (available at home supply stores). Spread the map out flat on top of some newspaper, and paint on the waterproofer with a foam brush. Once dry, your maps will stand up to even the worst weather.

Bright 'n' shiny ▲

Soot accumulates quickly on campfire cookware. Keep your pots and pans bright and shiny by placing them in disposable aluminum pie pans when cooking. When these aluminum shields become black with soot, toss them out.

Light my fire

As a precaution, always carry a candle stub in the bottom of your waterproof matchbox. With its help, you'll be able to light a fire—even with damp kindling.

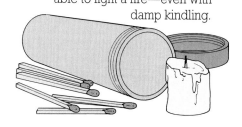

Inflation devices

A lazy solution

It's tiresome to inflate footballs, soccer balls, basketballs, and other such items by hand. If you have access to an air compressor, harness its power for the job. To adapt the compressor, simply fit an auto tire valve extender onto an inflator needle and attach the two with silicone caulk.

Super-speed inflator

If you don't have an air compressor hanging around, you can create your own easy inflation system using a wet-dry shop vacuum. Purchase a plastic pipe reducer to fit the air valve on the inflatable item, use it to connect the vacuum cleaner exhaust port to the valve, and let the blower do the work for you.

Fishing gear

Don't throw it out ▲

The next time a ballpoint pen runs out of ink, recycle it by removing the spring and ink tube and using the barrel to carry split shot whenever you go fishing. The pen makes a great dispenser—whenever you need a sinker, unscrew the barrel and let the shot roll out one by one. Clip the pen to your pocket for easy access.

Treading on ice

If you've ever gone ice fishing, then you know how falling snow or the glare of the sun can totally obscure your vision. On your next expedition, keep your equipment in sight by coating your ice-fishing rigs with a fluorescent paint.

Get a grip

Hard-to-detach fishing rod sections will be easier to pull apart if you provide yourself with a good grip. Here's how: Buy two pieces of gum rubber surgical tubing (available at drugstores), cut them lengthwise, and place one on each side of the ferrule.

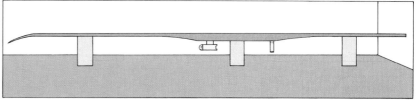

Rod ferrule

4" piece of gum rubber surgical tubing

Just a teaspoon

Turn an old teaspoon into a spinner by breaking the bowl off the handle. Drill a hole into one end of the bowl, and wire a swivel onto it. Use it to enhance another lure, or drill a hole in the other end, attach a hook to it, and use it by itself. Don't toss away the handle; use it to make a minnow by drilling four small holes along its length and attaching a swivel to the hole at one end, a single hook in the hole at the other end, and double hooks in the other two holes. ▼

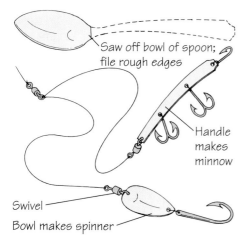

Saw off bowl of spoon; file rough edges

Handle makes minnow

Swivel

Bowl makes spinner

BACK TO BASICS

SKI REPAIRS

As most skiers know, scratches and gouges impair the maneuverability of skis. You can easily repair a small gouge in the plastic base of a downhill ski by using a polyethylene repair candle and a soldering iron or propane torch. However, if your skis have deep gouges that penetrate the core, have them fixed at a ski repair shop.

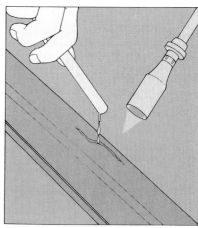

1 Support the damaged ski on wood blocks placed on a flat surface. For extra support, butt the tail of the ski against a wall. If you have a workbench, you can clamp the ski in a vise, but be sure to protect the ski from scratches by placing pieces of cardboard or wood between the jaws of the vise and the ski.

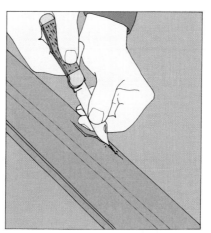

2 Using a knife or an old screwdriver, remove all traces of wax and dirt from the gouge. Then very carefully heat the area around the gouge by passing a soft torch flame over it or by holding a soldering iron close to the area.

3 Once the plastic around the gouge is soft, use a torch or soldering iron to melt a polyethylene repair candle. Fill the gouge with candle drippings while keeping the whole area warm. Slightly overfill the gouge. Let the material cool and harden; use a flexible putty knife to scrape the patch flush with the base.

BOATS

Canoe corner

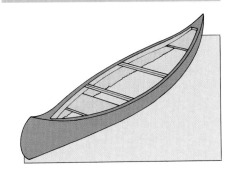

Noises off ▲

Glue scraps of carpeting to the bottoms of coolers and tackle boxes to prevent them from knocking around in the bottom of a canoe (or other boat)—and to keep the noise from alerting fish and wildlife to your presence. Even better, pad the entire canoe bottom with outdoor carpeting. Keep the carpet clean by hosing off any dirt and hanging it from a tree limb or clothesline to dry.

Quiet, please!

Pad the gunwales with short lengths of foam pipe insulation and your paddles won't bang on them when you stroke. Because the insulation comes slit along one side, installation is simple—just cut the foam to the required length and press it into place on the gunwales.

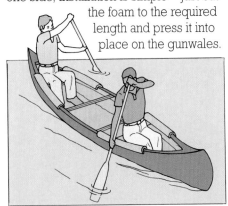

It's time to slim down

Paddles that have thick blades can be clumsy. To keep them slicing through the water, sand the edges of the blades to a thickness of about $1/8$ inch; use a portable electric sander for best results. Varnish all sanded areas to keep the paddle from becoming waterlogged.

Trailer tricks

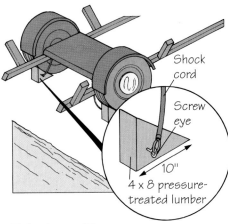

Shock cord

Screw eye

10"

4 x 8 pressure-treated lumber

Take 'em with you

Save time and aggravation at the launch ramp with these attachable chocks. Cut a 10-inch triangle from a piece of 4 x 8 pressure-treated lumber. Attach a screw eye to one side, and connect an elastic shock cord to the eye. When you are ready to load your boat onto its trailer, place a chock behind each rear wheel and hook the shock cords to the under-carriage of the trailer. Load your boat and drive away; the chocks will follow. Once you're out of the way of the other boaters, you can stop and detach the chocks. But keep them fastened to the trailer with the shock cords so that they'll be ready for the next time.

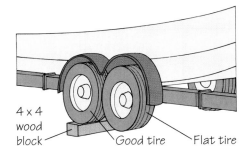

4 x 4 wood block

Good tire

Flat tire

On the road ▲

In a pinch, a 4 x 4 wooden block makes a good temporary jack for a boat trailer that has a double axle (four tires). Simply loosen the lug nuts on the flat tire; then ride the good tire up on the block. Be sure to place chocks behind the wheels on the other side of the trailer to prevent it from rolling. The flat tire will be high enough for you to remove and replace it.

Put a leash on it

A couple of 1-inch-wide nylon dog leashes will keep a boat from bobbing up and down during transit. Using an eyebolt, attach a tie-down with hooks on the ends to the front of the trailer. Slip the handle loops of the leashes over the cleats on the bow of the boat. Clip the leash hooks to the free tie-down hook. Keep the winch strap attached as usual.

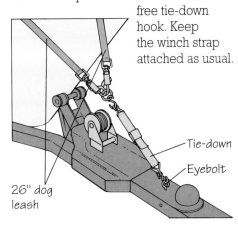

26" dog leash

Tie-down

Eyebolt

Add it yourself

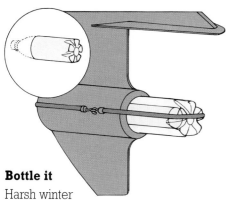

Bottle it

Harsh winter weather can wreak havoc with exposed metal parts. While the propeller is usually stored away separately, the propeller shaft is left out in the cold. Protect it from corrosion with this handy cover made from a 2-litre plastic soda bottle. Using a sharp knife, carefully cut off the neck of the bottle. Lightly grease the exposed propeller shaft, then slide on the bottle; hold it in place with a shock cord.

All aboard

If your boat has a recessed fishing rod holder mounted on the stern, you can use it to rig a removable handhold to help guests coming aboard. Cut a suitable length from a wood dowel and slide it inside an equal length of PVC pipe. Top off the assembly with a PVC pipe cap.

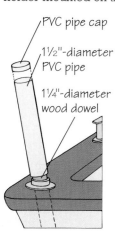

PVC pipe cap

1½"-diameter PVC pipe

1¼"-diameter wood dowel

Not a puddle in sight

Rain can easily pool in a full-length boat cover, making the cover hard to remove without dumping at least some of the water into the boat. Encourage the rain to run off by propping up the cover with this homemade support. Cap both ends of a wood dowel with the rubber tips from a discarded pair of crutches. Place the support vertically where the water usually accumulates. ▼

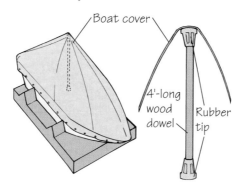

Boat cover

4'-long wood dowel

Rubber tip

Anchors away

On a small to medium-size boat, the last few feet of anchor chain (or even the anchor itself) can bang against the bow as you haul it up—sometimes damaging the boat. Warn yourself that the anchor is close to the water's surface by tying a piece of brightly colored yarn to the line a few feet above the spot where the chain begins.

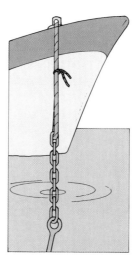

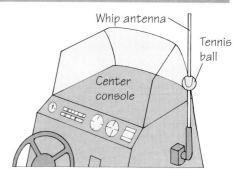

Whip antenna

Tennis ball

Center console

Follow the bouncing ball ▲

The tall whip antenna required for a loran unit or CB radio is often attached to a boat's center console, where it can slap against the windshield during rough weather. Protect both the antenna and any surfaces it may damage by installing a buffer. Just drill a hole that's slightly smaller than the diameter of the antenna through a tennis ball and slide the ball down onto the antenna.

Easy maintenance

What a snap

One good tug on a dirty or rusty snap holding down a boat cover or canvas top may wind up tearing the material instead of opening the snap. Prevent sticking by smearing the snaps with a thin coat of petroleum jelly two or three times a year.

More absorbent than ever

It's nearly impossible to prevent oil from leaking into the engine pans, and every boater knows what a mess that can be to clean up. Make it easier by spreading an opened disposable baby diaper in each pan. The diaper will absorb the spills, making cleanup a breeze.

CONTROLLING HOUSEHOLD PESTS

Creepy crawlers

Special delivery

The space behind the toekick and underneath the base of a kitchen cabinet provides a safe haven for all kinds of insects because it's difficult to reach. Deliver a straight shot of insecticide by drilling a 3/8-inch hole through either the toekick or the cabinet floor. After spraying, plug the hole with a furniture dowel button or a wood dowel plug. ▼

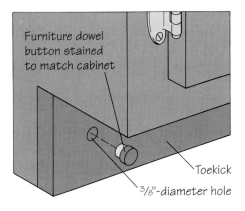

Furniture dowel button stained to match cabinet

Toekick

3/8"-diameter hole

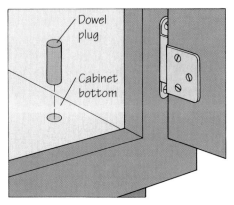

Dowel plug

Cabinet bottom

Down the drain ▲

Drains set into basement floors offer easy entry for a variety of crawling insects. To keep them out of your home, block the drain with a tennis ball. The ball won't stop water from draining—when water is draining the ball will float; after draining, the ball will settle back into position.

Furry houseguests

No more fun and games

When you go away the mice will play, so before closing up your camper or summer home, put out some mouse-repelling sachets. To make your own sachets, create small bags out of discarded panty hose or scraps of fabric and fill them with crushed dried peppermint leaves. Tie the bags securely and toss a few under beds, in closets, inside the stove, and in the dishwasher.

Squirrels, scram

When squirrels invade your chimney or attic, don't reach for your gun, reach for the aftershave. It may smell bracing to you, but it's repulsive to squirrels and they'll respond by moving out.

Light the way

Flush bats from their hangout in your attic by leaving a small light burning in the dark areas for 1 week. Once all the bats are gone, prevent their return by sealing every opening with caulk, screening, or sheet metal. Avoid late spring and early summer evictions, as bats breed at this time and you risk trapping a flightless bat pup inside. In tight spaces where you can't hang a light, discourage bats from nesting by spreading around slices of moth cake.

It's a trap

These open-ended "valves" let bats out of your attic at night to feed but prevent them from coming back in to roost. Cut a piece of polypropylene bird netting wide enough to span the bats' entryway and long enough to hang 3 feet below it. Using staples and tape, secure the top and the sides of the netting to the house. Be sure to leave the bottom open. Taper the netting so the bottom opening is no more than 15 inches wide. After several days the bats should be gone and you can seal the openings. ▼

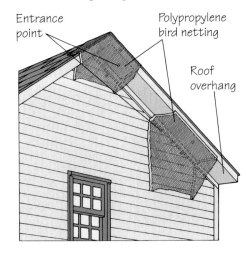

Entrance point

Polypropylene bird netting

Roof overhang

Damage control

Glass handles

When moving heavy mirrors or panes of glass, cover the edges with pieces of foam pipe insulation. Use the type with a center split so that it slides easily over the edges. The insulation will protect your hands from injury and the floors and walls from gouges.

Magic carpet ride

Don't take a chance of hurting yourself or your floor when moving a heavy object. Instead, slide carpet scraps, pile side down, underneath the object. The rough backing keeps the object from slipping while the pile glides easily over the floor. In addition to making the move easier, the carpet will prevent the object from scratching the floor.

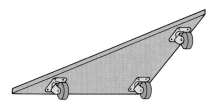

Hello, dolly ▲

Moving your sofa (or any other four-legged piece of furniture) will be a snap if you slip a small three-wheeled furniture dolly under each leg. You can buy metal dollies at home centers or make your own from ½-inch plywood and casters.

Freewheeling

To keep heavy or unwieldy objects from falling and breaking during transport, wheel them around on a skateboard. You'll save your arm and back muscles.

Wide loads

Hand trucks are great for moving things around, but the lip just isn't deep enough to handle large objects. Remedy this by adding an extension made of 2-inch-diameter PVC pipe. With a hacksaw, cut narrow slots into the pipe—the slots should fit snugly onto the truck lip, but if they're too tight, widen them slightly with a file. For added strength, glue the pipes together. Attach the assembly to the truck with a few taps of a rubber mallet; the extension pulls right off when not in use.

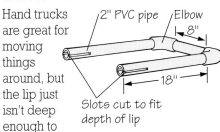

2" PVC pipe / Elbow / 8" / 18" / Slots cut to fit depth of lip

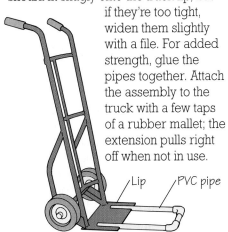

Lip / PVC pipe

Protect resilient floors

Casters and dolly wheels can easily cut resilient flooring during a move. Instead of rolling the wheels directly over the floor, safeguard it by rolling them over strips of a thin, hard material (such as ¼-inch-thick plywood or ⅛-inch-thick rigid acrylic plastic).

SAFETY FIRST

SAVE YOUR BACK

Whenever you have to lift a heavy load, prevent back injury by following these steps:
▷ Position yourself as close to the load as possible.
▷ Always flex your knees; never bend forward from your waist.
▷ When leaning forward while lifting, keep your back perfectly flat; never arch it.
▷ When pushing heavy objects, bend your knees, keep your back flat, and power the push with your legs.
▷ If you need to turn while lifting or pushing, move your feet; don't twist your back.
▷ Never try to move a really heavy load by yourself—get help. A two-person lift is half the strain.

HOUSEHOLD MOVING

Before the move

Moving checklist

Moving day is difficult at best, with all the last-minute details to take care of. Remove some of the stress and worry by completing the following chores in the weeks preceding the move:

▷ If necessary, have your major appliances serviced. If you plan to drive to your new home, have your car serviced as well. If you are having your car moved by truck, make sure that the gas tank is nearly empty.

▷ Empty all storage tanks of flammable gases, such as gasoline, kerosene, and propane.

▷ Drain gasoline and oil from your lawn mower and all other power equipment.

▷ Drain water from all garden hoses.

▷ Dispose of flammable and caustic items such as matches, cleaning fluids, bleach, drain cleaners, and acids.

Mapping out the territory

Draw a scale plan of your new home, letting each inch on the plan equal 1 foot of actual space. Indicate where you want to put each piece of furniture and other large items. This will save you from having to move heavy pieces twice. ▼

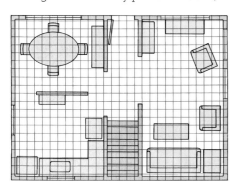

Moving by colors ▲

By assigning a color to each room of your new house, you can eliminate much of the disorganization on arrival day. Here's how: As you pack up the contents of your old home, color-code the boxes to the new rooms, using brightly colored stickers or markers. On moving day, attach a color-coded balloon to each room's door frame to show the movers where to put the boxes.

Easy unpacking

Before packing up everything, select a dresser drawer to contain any linens and towels you'll need for the first night in your new home. Then, when you're exhausted at the end of the move, you won't have to conduct a frantic search for these necessities.

Boxes

As flat as a pancake

You can buy packing boxes from any major moving company or truck rental agency. But you can save money by using your own. Start collecting boxes from grocery and liquor stores a few months before the move. Rather than keeping the empty boxes open and letting them take up a lot of space, flatten them for easy storage by slitting open the bottom tape and collapsing the sides. Before filling the boxes, reseal the bottoms with strong packing tape.

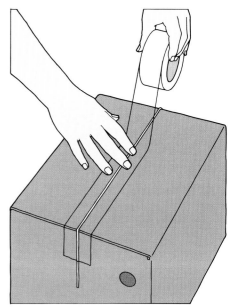

Zippy opening ▲

Before taping boxes closed, run a length of string along the seam. Place the tape over the string, leaving a few inches of the string hanging off the end. When it's time to unpack, pull on the string to zip open the tape.

Protective padding

Bright spots ▲

Small items can easily disappear in the mounds of crumpled paper generated during unpacking. Keep little treasures safe by wrapping them in brightly colored tissue paper. They'll be easy to spot and you won't accidentally throw them out.

Out of the linen closet

Save space by cushioning breakable items with towels, washcloths, sheets, pillowcases, and tablecloths. You'll also save money on paper, and you won't need to pack your linens separately.

Dishes and glasses

On the edge

Believe it or not, the best way to pack plates is on edge, rather than flat. Wrap the plates in bubble wrap (if you are using newspaper, place each dish in a plastic bag to save wash-up time later), and arrange them on their edges inside a sturdy carton. For the safest ride, layer 2 inches of folded paper between the plates and 3 inches of paper on the bottom of the carton.

All stuffed up

Because of the dividers, liquor cartons are ideal for transporting cups and glasses—ask a local liquor store to save you some discarded boxes. But if you don't have any of these boxes on hand, you can still safely transport glasses and cups. Stuff your glasses and cups with crumpled paper before wrapping them in bubble wrap. Then nestle the wrapped pieces in the spaces between your other dishes. Don't nest unwrapped glasses—they will bump together and chip.

Odds and ends

The bases are loaded

When packing table lamps, wrap the bases in paper or bubble wrap and alternate them end for end. Pack the shades separately, but don't wrap them in newspaper; the print can cause stains. Instead, use bubble wrap or unprinted paper.

Artful packing ▶

Small pieces of art can be placed between blankets or pillows for safe transport—don't use newspaper for padding because it can stain. Or use a collapsed cardboard box; slide in the item and seal the edges. Large valuable artworks should be padded, wrapped, and crated by a professional.

Like clockwork

Before sending your grandfather clock off on a trip, take these steps to ensure a safe arrival. Remove the weights, pendulum, and finials, and pack them separately. Keep the hammers and weight chains from moving around by securing them to the case of the clock with strong twine or tape. For long-distance moves, consult a clock shop—the works may need to be protected against damage.

X marks the spot

Tape an X across each mirror with masking tape before wrapping it in paper or bubble wrap; if there's an accident, the tape will hold the shards in place. Small mirrors can be put on edge and packed in sturdy boxes, but large mirrors need to be shipped in special cartons that your mover can provide.

Packing in the knowledge

Pack books on edge in small cartons, alternating the directions of the bindings. Pack the cartons so that they weigh less than 40 pounds each.

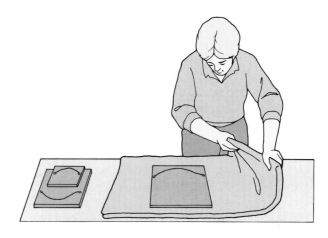

HOUSEHOLD MOVING

Large appliances

Upstanding appliances ▲

When transporting a refrigerator or an upright freezer, make sure the unit stays upright throughout the move. If it is put on its side, the fluid will flow out of the compressor and you'll have to let the unit stand upright for 24 hours before you can start it without damaging it. To help you keep a unit upright while moving it, rent a special heavy-duty dolly from the truck rental agency.

Clean machine

Before moving your refrigerator, thoroughly wash and dry the inside and let it air out for at least 24 hours. On moving day, toss in a sock filled with charcoal briquettes, fresh ground coffee, or baking soda to absorb moisture and odors. Tightly knot the neck of the sock so that its contents don't spill. Finally, seal the door shut with masking tape.

A different beat

Keep the drum of your clothes washer from banging around inside the cabinet by stuffing towels between the drum and the housing.

Bulky beds

Restrain yourself

The day of the big move, don't forget to tie covertible sofa beds in place before transporting them to their new location. You don't want them opening up unexpectedly while in transit. ▼

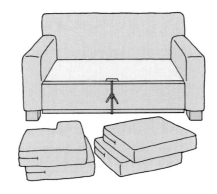

Down the drain

Water beds should always be drained before they're moved. You can hasten the process by weighting down the valve so that it's the lowest point on the mattress. ▼

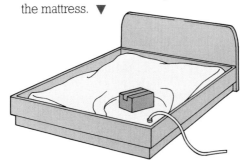

Electronics

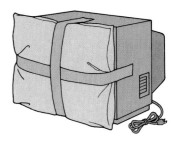

Unplugged ▲

Transporting a warm television set can cause severe internal damage. To make sure yours is at room temperature, disconnect it the day before you move. Also, to protect the screen while moving, tape a pillow over it.

No news here

Whenever possible, pack electronic equipment and small appliances in their original cartons. If you no longer have the original foam padding blocks, cushion the units with bubble wrap or crumpled paper. Don't use shredded newspaper; it can get into the machines and cause internal damage. (For hints on moving a computer, see p.263.)

Plant relocation

Keep them happy

Pack plants in cardboard boxes that are at least 1 inch higher than the tallest plant. To keep the boxes strong and dry, line them with large plastic trash bags, and wrap clay pots with aluminum foil. Group plants of similar size, and stuff the spaces between them with bubble wrap or loose packing material.

LOADING A TRUCK

If you have a lot of muscle power at your disposal, you may want to rent a truck and do your own moving. Begin by parking the truck as close as possible to your home. Pull out the truck's loading ramp and place it on the highest front step, if possible. Then, following the guidelines shown below, load the truck one-quarter full at a time, packing everything solidly from floor to ceiling. Tie in each quarter with rope, and fill any spaces with small cartons. Be sure to pack the truck snugly to make the best use of the space and to prevent damage to your belongings.

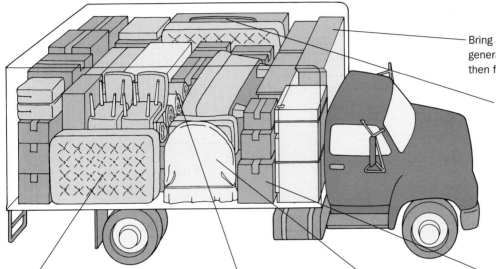

Bring in the largest items first—generally large appliances and then furniture.

Keep mirrors upright, and tie them in place or wedge them between a mattress and box spring. Never lay a mirror flat.

Position long items, such as mattresses and box springs, tabletops, and sofas, along the sides of the truck and turn them on their edges.

Roll up rugs and place them lengthwise in the center.

Fit odd-shaped items along the sides or on top of other items.

Put heavy cartons at the bottom and lighter cartons on top. Stack heavy cartons on top of each other only if they are of nearly equal strength and weight.

Sleeves for leaves

Protect delicate foliage from crushing during transit with funnel-shaped plant sleeves. Make your own by rolling lightweight cardboard into a funnel and securing it with tape.

In your new home

In hot water

Upon arriving at your new home, turn on all the hot-water faucets for several minutes. This flushes out any hydrogen gas that may have built up if the house has been empty for several weeks. Don't smoke or use an open flame when doing this; the gas is flammable.

Lighten up

The first items you should unpack (before it gets dark) are the lamps and other portable light fixtures. Place them around the house, plug them in, and turn them on as needed. If there is nothing to put them on, set them directly on the floor. You'll have light for unpacking, and you'll find out if any fuses are burned out or circuit breakers tripped.

MISCELLANEOUS HINTS

Keys

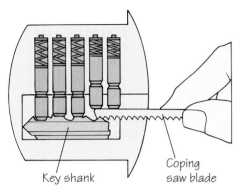

Key shank

Coping saw blade

Key broken in lock ▲

If a key breaks off in a lock, try this. Use a coping saw blade to push up the tumbler pins and grasp the broken key shank. Then, very carefully, slowly pull it out. Don't tug at the key shank, or you may damage the lock. If this doesn't work, call a professional.

Connect the dots

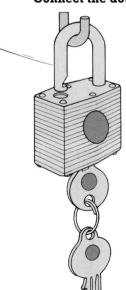

If you carry a lot of keys, it can be tricky to remember which one goes to what lock. Color-coding your keys and locks will enable you to see at a glance which is the proper key. Simply place a colorful sticker on a key and a matching sticker on the corresponding lock.

Mirror repair

It's all done with mirrors

Want to disguise damaged silver on an old mirror? Simply scrape off any peeling or discolored silver, and then tape a piece of shiny aluminum foil over the spot on the back of the mirror.

Mirror image

Resilvering an antique bevel-edged mirror can be expensive. Instead, scrape all the old silver off the back of the mirror and have your local glass company cut a new, inexpensive mirror to the exact size and shape of the old one. Then sandwich the new mirror between the backing and the clear glass remaining from the old mirror.

Book repair

Take a tip

To reattach a loose book page, cut a ½-inch strip of onionskin paper the length of the page and fold it in half lengthwise. Coat the back of the onionskin with white glue. With the crease toward the spine, place one half of the

strip on the loose page and the other half on the following page. Push the strip into the spine and line up the pages' outer edges. Place wax paper across the strip, close the book, and let the glue dry.

All wet and soggy

Dry out a waterlogged book by placing it in a frost-free freezer for several hours. The freezer will draw the moisture from the book and separate the pages.

Scissors

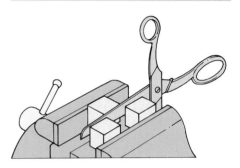

Bent out of shape ▲

Don't discard a pair of scissors if one of the blades is bent out of shape. Instead, place the blade in a vise between three evenly spaced blocks of wood. Tighten the vise slightly. This technique works with bent knives as well.

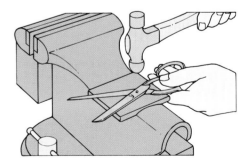

Wiggly scissors ▲

Loose scissors blades? If the pivot is a rivet or if tightening the pivot screw doesn't help, place the pivot head on a metal surface and hit the other end firmly with a ball-peen hammer.

Cutlery

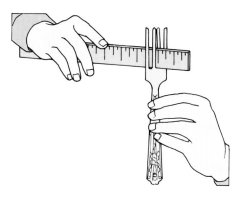

Pointing every which way ▲

Don't discard a fork simply because the tines are bent—straighten them. If the tines of the fork are bent toward each other, insert a wood ruler between them and force them apart. If they are bent outward, line a vise with soft cloth and gently tighten it to clamp and realign the tines.

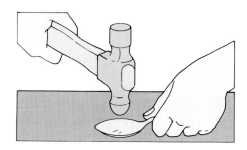

Lumps 'n' bumps ▲

When a spoon gets dented, it usually bulges inward. To fix it, place the spoon on a wood surface and gently tap it with a ball-peen hammer.

China

A clean fix

Before repairing a piece of china, make sure it is clean by soaking it in a solution of ½ cup household bleach and 2 quarts water, washing it, and letting it dry. To fill the crack, use epoxy, either alone or mixed with whiting or kaolin powder and a pigment (all sold by art supply stores). Fill the crack slightly higher than the surface, and smooth the area with a superfine abrasive after the glue hardens.

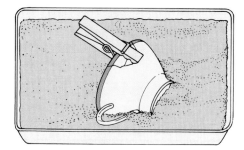

Like a day at the beach ▲

To repair a plate, cup, or even a figurine, bury the largest piece in a container of sand with the broken surface just protruding. Make sure the broken surface is horizontal so the other piece balances on it. If the piece won't balance, hold it in place with a prop or with a simple clamp such as a clothespin.

Sticky choice

Mend valuable china (or glassware) with a water-soluble adhesive, such as polyvinyl acetate (PVA), or white glue, which lets you take a piece apart and fix it again. Use water-resistant epoxy to repair everyday pieces, but keep in mind that once it hardens you can't dissolve it.

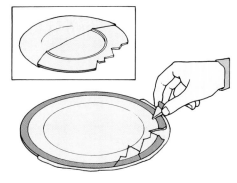

A way with wax ▲

Piecing the parts of a broken plate together is easier if you use a mold. To make one, heat paraffin until it softens, then pack it over the bottom of the unbroken side of the plate. After the wax has set, carefully arrange the mold under the broken side and fit the broken pieces in it. Glue only one or two pieces at a time.

Under pressure

To clamp the pieces of a mended plate together while the glue sets, drive nails in a circle slightly larger than the perimeter of the plate. Lay the plate face down between the nails, and stretch rubber bands over it. ▼

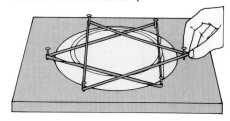

Timing is everything

To remove excess epoxy, wait until it begins to set, then slip a sharp knife point under it and peel it off. If you try too soon you'll smear the glue; too late and you won't be able to remove it.

MISCELLANEOUS HINTS

Boot cleaning aids

Kick up your heels ▲

Use a coat hanger to speed drying of rubber boots and other footwear. Bend the hanger to create two loops. Slide the boots through the loops, sole side up, and slip the assembly over a hook or nail. Hanging the boots this way helps them retain their shape and speeds drying by allowing plenty of air circulation.

The brush-off

Although this boot and shoe scraper is portable, it won't move around when you use it. Using screws, attach a large stiff-bristle scrub brush (bristles facing up) to a piece of plywood. Your weight keeps the plywood in place while you scrape your footwear on the brush. Wash the scraper with a hose, and store it out of sight when not in use. ▼

No more mud

Tired of scraping mud off your boots— or worse yet, off your floors? Prevent mud from coming in the house by providing a convenient boot scraper. Pick a location near the back door where there is no danger of someone running into it in the dark. Fill a 12- x 12-inch hole with concrete, and sink a spade 6 inches deep into it. When the concrete dries, you'll have a permanent boot scraper— complete with a handle you can hold for balance.

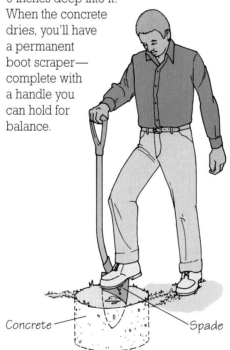

Concrete —   — Spade

Chains and zippers

Tiny tangles

If a knot develops in a fine chain, don't try to pull it out; you may tangle it further. Instead, spread the chain on a piece of wax paper and place a drop of baby oil on the knot; use a couple of straight pins to slowly pick out the knot.

Easy gliding

Have a zipper that's hard to move? Keep it sliding easily by rubbing it with either soap, paraffin, or pencil lead.

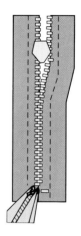
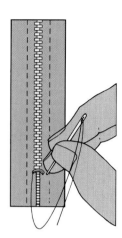

Restoring the zip ▲

If a metal zipper slider comes loose, pry off the bottom stop of the zipper with a pair of needle-nose pliers. Then move the slider to the bottom and carefully thread the loose track through the slider. Pull the slider up the tracks, and create a new stop by sewing several stitches at the bottom of the zipper.

Eyeglasses

Fog lifter

Coat both sides of your eyeglass lenses with a thin film of soapsuds, let them dry, then polish them with a soft lint-free cloth. The transparent coating left behind won't impair your vision, but it will keep your glasses from fogging up.

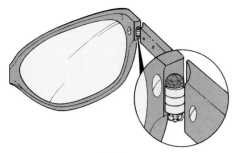

Where did it go? ▲

If you lose the screw that holds one of the earpieces to your eyeglasses, here's a temporary fix: Insert a stud-type earring into the hinge.

No loose screws here

Do the screws keep working loose in your eyeglass frames? Coat the threads with clear nail polish. When it dries, the screws should stay in place.

A better bath

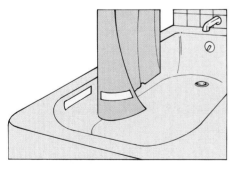

Curtain call ▲

Don't let your shower curtain attack you next time you enter the shower—keep it in place with Velcro tape. After cleaning the tub, simply attach the tape to both the side of the tub and the bottom hem of the curtain. Before turning on the water, secure the curtain to the tape.

No more nonslip decals

A 30-minute soak in laundry prewash makes it much easier to scrape off non-slip bathtub appliqués. Use a single-edge razor blade for scraping, holding it flat against the tub. Remove any excess adhesive by spraying it with aerosol lubricant/penetrant and scrubbing with a terry-cloth rag.

Candle wax

Hot melt ▲

It's difficult to prevent candle wax from dripping and hardening on candleholders, but cleanup can be easy. Remelt dripped wax with a hair dryer set on high heat; work a small area at a time and wipe off the wax as it softens. After cleaning the candleholders, mist them with a vegetable cooking-oil spray to make future wax removal easier.

Cool candlesticks

Another way of removing wax from candlesticks is to place them in the freezer for about an hour; the wax should peel right off.

Sticky situations

Rejuvenate your tape

Age and weather conditions can dry up masking or electrical tape. Revive the adhesive by popping the tape in the microwave, set on high, for about a minute.

Saving postage

Often, when the weather gets warm, the glue on the back of postage stamps melts enough for them to stick together. When this happens, don't throw them out. Instead, toss the stuck-together postage stamps into the freezer until they become unstuck.

Photo finish

Heat and humidity often cause photographs to stick together. If your photos were taken within the past 10 years, it's probably safe to soak them apart. Place the photos in a shallow pan filled with tepid water. Every few minutes carefully try to separate them, but if there's even the slightest resistance, continue soaking. Change the water as often as necessary to keep it lukewarm. After separating the photos, dry them by hanging them from a clothesline with spring clothespins. ▼

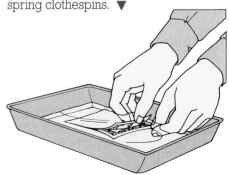

RECYCLING DIRECTORY

Part of the human condition is to accumulate possessions, ending up with lots of leftover and used-up things we don't know what to do with. And so we're faced with the problem of what to do with all this stuff without being wasteful or cluttering the environment with garbage.

Many of the hints in this book show how to make good use of discarded items or leftover scraps of materials, such as carpeting. Following is a guide to such hints, arranged alphabetically by material. If you have a batch of old clothespins, cans, unmatched socks, or hangers, check the appropriate entries for suggestions on using them. Each entry gives the use, page number, and tip title. And just to brighten things up, you'll find a handful of new tips scattered throughout. To find other tips or suggestions, check the index.

A

Alligator clip
▶ For easier lighting of pilot light, p.228, "Finger saver 1"

Antenna
▶ With alligator clip, to light pilot light, p.228, "Finger saver 1"

Ashes
▶ To remove furniture surface burn, p.239, "Scorched surface"
▶ To remove smoke stains from fireplace doors, p.337, "Recycle those ashes"

B

Baby wipe container
▶ To hold paintbrush during project, p.171, "Easy wiper solution"

Bag
▶ Paper bag as dust catcher during drilling, p.10, "Wall hang-ups"
▶ Paper bag for removal of excess oil from a fan, p.255, "No greasy shower"
▶ Paper bag to contain mess when removing excess water or thinner from a brush, p.171, "Go for a spin"

▶ Plastic bag as apron, p.64, "Instant aprons"
▶ Plastic bag as glove to protect doorknobs, telephone, etc., when painting, p.178, "Foiled again"
▶ Plastic bag filled with sand or water to exert pressure when gluing together irregular shapes, p.87, "Bag it"
▶ Plastic bag for storing and dispensing putty, p.40, "Airless container"
▶ Plastic bag for use in running cable, p.207, "Elusive line"
▶ Plastic bag to avoid spills when removing car oil filter, p.301, "Keep it clean"
▶ Plastic bag to catch sawdust from a table saw, p.30, "Collecting dust"
▶ Plastic bag to cover windshield overnight in winter, p.321, "Labor saver"
▶ Plastic bag to dispose of Christmas tree, p.339, "In the bag"
▶ Plastic bag to grease bearings or other parts, p.252, "Grease bag"
▶ Plastic bag to keep clamp from sticking, p.89, "No sticky clamps here"
▶ Plastic bag to line a shop vacuum, p.63, "Easy-empty vacuum"
▶ Plastic bag to remove a paint-filled roller, p.172, "Another mess manager"
▶ Plastic bag to repair a coolant or windshield washer reservoir, p.304, "It's in the bag"
▶ Plastic bag to retrieve items fallen into toilet, p.218, "Hand-bag retriever"

▶ Plastic bag to store leftover paint, p.189, "Leftovers again"
▶ Plastic bag with magnet, to pick up spilled washers, nuts, or nails, p.62, "Magnetic bagger"

Ball
▶ As buffer on boat antenna, p.343, "Follow the bouncing ball"
▶ As chisel cover, p.20, "Guard duty"
▶ As guide when parking car in garage, p.322, "Things that go bump"
▶ To convert hammer into a mallet, p.15, "Cushion the blow"
▶ To cover car hood latch to protect person from injury when working on car engine, p.302, "Heads up!"
▶ To cover ends of saw fence, p.31, "Bumpers for fence guides"
▶ To hold curved pieces in miter box, p.84, "No more bouncing ball"
▶ To keep insects from coming through floor drains, p.344, "Down the drain"
▶ To keep interior light off when car door is open for extended periods, p.313, "Drain plug"
▶ To reduce shock when pounding chisel or star drill, p.292, "Concrete shock absorber"

Basket
▶ Large basket to catch sawdust, p.30, "Collecting dust"

► Laundry basket as substitute for toy box, p.122, "A tisket, a tasket"
► Plastic basket as equipment holder on ladder, p.44, "Basket case"

Basketball inflation needle
► As tip on oil container, p.226, "Pin-point oiling"

Baster
► To clean drain hole of air conditioner, p.231, "Musty-smelling conditioner"
► To siphon gas out of a lawn mower, p.282, "Last gas"
► To transfer solvents from one container to another, p.90, "Out of the kitchen"

Bath mat
► To protect bench top, p.52, "Mat top"

Beater
► As paint mixer attachment for electric drill, p.167, "Homemade mixer"

Belt
► As substitute for tool-honing strop, p.22, "Homemade strop"
► To hold tools on shelf, p.58, "Tool belt"
► To store a ladder, p.45, "Buckle up"
► To store a rug, p.124, "Flying carpet"
► To tie a ladder, p.45, "Keep it closed"

Bicycle handlebar grip
► For rubbing steel wool in a corner or groove, p.40, "For tight spots"

Bicycle tube
► To increase torque with hand-screw clamp, p.36, "Turning point"

Binder clip
► To hang work gloves, p.64, "Rubber gloves hanger"

Blackboard eraser
► To defog a car window, p.317, "Fog eraser"

Bottle opener
► To help mend cracks in walls when painting, p.176, "Attack those cracks"

Bottle or jug (plastic)

"A bottle of brushes." Clean paint-brushes simply and effectively in a large plastic jug. Just cut a hole in the side of the container, pour in mineral spirits or water, according to the type of paint, and insert the brushes. The handle makes it easy to carry. ▼

► Bleach container as funnel for engine drain plug, p.300, "Diversionary tactics"
► Motor oil container as a gutter-cleaning scoop, p.162, "Gutter scoop"
► Oil container for workshop storage, p.60, "Great cheap parts bins"
► Plastic jug as drip irrigator, p.279, "Homemade drip irrigator"

► Plastic jug as nail bin, p.60, "Neat nail organizers"
► Plastic jug as scoop, p.62, "Nuts and bolts scoop"
► Plastic pop bottle as drill holder, p.11, "Drill holder"
► Rectangular plastic container as brush holder on belt, p.170, "Belted caddy"
► Squeeze bottle as refillable glue dispenser, p.38, "Economical refills"
► Squeeze bottle to apply adhesive to vinyl floor, p.141, "Bursting bubbles"
► Two-liter plastic bottle as string dispenser, p.59, "String out"
► Two-liter plastic bottle to protect boat propeller from corrosion in winter, p.343, "Bottle it"

"Convenient bag dispenser." Plastic grocery bags come in handy, but storing them can be a  nuisance. Try this quick and simple method for easy dispensing: Using a utility knife or snips, cut off the top and bottom of a two-litre plastic soda bottle, leaving a 3-inch-wide opening at the top. Mount the bottle, top down, on a wall or cabinet door with small screws and washers. Stuff the bags into the bottle, and pull them out as needed.

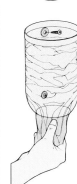

RECYCLING DIRECTORY

Box
▶ Bread box to hold tools, p.46, "Handy storage"
▶ Cardboard box for cleaner spray-painting jobs, p.250, "Spray booth"
▶ Cardboard box to shelter saw blade while cleaning, p.29, "Oven cleaner"
▶ Detergent box as homemade manual file, p.41, "Handy manuals"
▶ "Disc storage." Boxes made to hold 5¼-inch computer diskettes are perfect for organizing 5-inch sanding discs. Use the dividers to sort and label different grits, coatings, and backings.

Brick

"Handy holder." An ordinary building brick makes a convenient no-spill organizer for holding small parts and tools. For the greatest capacity, select a brick with 10 holes. Glue a piece of cardboard to the bottom to protect the surface it sits on and to keep the items from falling through when the brick is moved. ▼

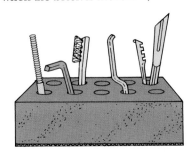

Broom handle
▶ To hold a bucket on a ladder, p.45, "Bucket holder"
▶ To keep birds off swing set, p.295, "Bird foiler"

Broom straw
▶ To extend the reach of an oil can, p.41, "Straw applicator"

Brush
▶ Pet brush, to remove loose paintbrush bristles, p.170, "Comb-out"

Bubble gum
▶ To temporarily plug a gas tank leak, p.314, "Leak stopper"

Bubble wrap
▶ To line toolbox, p.46, "Tool cushion"

Bucket or pail
▶ To avert paint spills when on ladder or scaffold, p.187, "Paint caddy"
▶ To hold extension cord, p.42, "Cord keeper"
▶ To soak saw blades for cleaning, p.29, "Soaking pan"

Bungee cord

"No-tip garbage cans." If you are having difficulty keeping garbage cans from tipping or blowing over, try securing them with bungee cords. For each can, you will need two ¾-inch screw eyes and a 30-inch hook-end bungee cord, available at hardware stores. ▼

▶ To secure chair legs while glue dries, p.237, "Quick chair clamp"
▶ To substitute for band clamp, p.86, "You don't have to jump for the cords"

Burlap
▶ For texturing when painting, p.183, "Texturing Techniques"
▶ To remove softened finish on furniture, p.244, "Snappy solutions"

Butter tub
▶ To protect outdoor faucet in cold weather, p.214, "Keep the cold out"

C

Cake container
▶ To store circular saw blades, p.29, "Capping saw teeth"

Can
▶ Coffee can as seed spreader, p.274, "Coffee can spreader"
▶ Coffee can for paint-stripping mess, p.176, "Neat solution"
▶ Coffee can for soaking paintbrush, p.171, "Two coffee can ideas"
▶ Coffee can to soak hardware in stripper, p.242, "Bits and pieces"
▶ Coffee can with kitchen strainer to clean paintbrush, p.171, "Bristle work"
▶ Empty cans to test lawn sprinkler, p.275, "Testing a sprinkler"
▶ Small cans as pocket dividers to convert nail pouch into tool tote, p.46, "Pockets for tools"
▶ Soda can for mixing epoxy, p.38, "Cool it"
▶ Soda can to store used razor blades, p.192, "Keep an edge"

▶ Tuna can to catch drippings when stripping chair and table legs, p.243, "Recycle those tuna cans"
▶ Tuna or cat food can to help in cleaning a soldering iron, p.97, "A clean tip"

Candle
▶ To help light a campfire, p.340, "Light my fire"
▶ To help wood drawer slide smoothly, p.233, "Sand 'n' wax"

Carbon paper
▶ To fix a sticking cabinet door, p.234, "Open-and-shut solution"

Cardboard
▶ To confine spray of aerosol paint when touching up car, p.315, "Mask task"
▶ To hold screws when disassembling an item, p.14, "Keeping track"
▶ To line up upholstery tacks straight and even, p.234, "All straight in a row"

Cardboard drum
▶ To store tall items, p.118, "Quick sorts"

Cardboard tube
▶ As extension for vacuum crevice tool, p.63, "Long reach"
▶ To organize molding, pipe, dowels, etc., p.61, "Stand-up storage"

Cards
▶ Playing cards for help with sanding curved surface, p.82, "A crooked deck"

Carpenter's apron
▶ To help manage a long-handled lopper when pruning, p.278, "Pocket holder"

Carpet

"Shake, rattle, and roll no more." A remnant of foam-backed carpet makes an effective, inexpensive typewriter pad. Place a square, foam side down, beneath the typewriter and it will stay firmly and quietly in place. ▼

▶ As overnight windshield cover during winter, p.321, "Labor saver"
▶ As pad on workbench, p.82, "Padded workbench"
▶ As substitute drop cloth, p.178, "Go wall-to-wall"
▶ For comfort when standing on concrete floor, p.49, "Foot ease"
▶ On ladder rung, to clean shoe soles, p.45, "Shoe cleaner"
▶ Power tool storage idea, p.58, "Power tower"
▶ To apply contact cement, p.38, "Carpet scrap applicator"
▶ To finish furniture, p.249, "Ersatz wood grain"
▶ To line car trunk, p.318, "Carpet capers"
▶ To line toolbox, p.46, "Tool cushion"
▶ To move heavy objects more easily, p.345, "Magic carpet ride"

▶ To muffle noisy pipe, p.213, "Drain line noise control"
▶ To pad sawhorse, p.54, "Soft saddle"
▶ To pad tailgate of pickup truck for knee protection, p.318, "Kneepads"
▶ To paint underside of door, p.181, "The bottom line"
▶ To prevent items from noisily knocking about in canoe, p.342, "Noises off"
▶ To protect bench top, p.52, "Mat top"
▶ To protect car door from damage in garage, p.322, "Door protection"
▶ To scrub car, p.316, "Cheap scrubbers"

Carpet padding
▶ With clothespins, to use as foam brush, p.170, "Make your own disposables"

Caulk tube
▶ To fill mortar joints, p.160, "Mortar quick draw"

Chain
▶ To draw circles when making layouts, p.34, "Circle chain"
▶ To increase clothes storage, p.119, "Put 'em in chains"
▶ To prevent lost oil and fuel reservoir caps, p.283, "Fuel cap minder"
▶ To store toys, p.122, "Chain gang"

Chest handles
▶ To hang tools, p.58, "Handle holder"

Clamshell container
▶ To start seeds, p.265, "Greenhouses from the salad bar"

RECYCLING DIRECTORY

Clipboard

"Clip it." An old clipboard needn't be tossed out. Take the spring clip and screw it to your workbench. It can hold notes or assembly instructions securely in place. An oiled rag held in place by the clip will quickly and easily coat small metal parts. Or secure a piece of steel wool in the clip and periodically draw your soldering iron tip across it to keep it clean. ▼

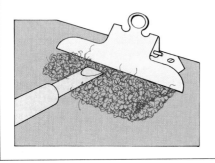

▶ To store sheet abrasives, p.25, "Put it away"
▶ When sanding small parts, p.83, "Against the grit"

Clothespin

▶ As a gauge, p.70, "Clothespin on the line"
▶ To anchor cloth to picnic table, p.294, "Cloth control"
▶ To keep power cords out of the way, p.51, "Cord hangers"
▶ With carpet pad, as substitute for foam paintbrush, p.170, "Make your own disposables"

Comb

▶ To remove loose paintbrush bristles, p.170, "Comb-out"

Cookie sheet

▶ As storage shelf in workshop, p.56, "Serving up hardware"

Cork

▶ For bit storage, p.11, "Put a cork on it"
▶ To build a bulletin board, p.108, "Bulletin board"
▶ To childproof piano or chest, p.328, "Prop it up"
▶ To protect chisels, p.20, "Guard duty"

Corkscrew

▶ To remove wallboard, p.137, "Corkscrew handle"

Cotton swab

▶ To apply paint when refinishing furniture, p.248, "Tossable mini-applicators"
▶ To mend chipped paint on auto, p.315, "Fill 'er up"

Crate

▶ As combination stool and tool caddy, p.299, "Seat relief"

Credit card

▶ As ice scraper substitute, p.321, "Emergency scraper"
▶ To remove dried nail polish from wood furniture, p.238, "Spilled nail polish"

Croquet wicket

▶ As plant guard, p.275, "Cutting out those cut corners"

Crutches

▶ To keep rain from pooling on boat cover, p.343, "Not a puddle in sight"

Curtain rod

▶ As a large compass, p.71, "Adjustable rod"
▶ As measuring tool, p.33, "Sliding curtain rod"
▶ To hang bird feeder, p.296, "Slide-out feeder"

Diaper

▶ As tack rag, p.92, "Make it tacky"

Dishpan

▶ As a toy box, p.122, "A tisket, a tasket"

Dish rack

▶ For storing tools and supplies, p.56, "Recycled dish rack"

Dollar bill

▶ For taking measurements, p.32, "One for the money"

Door

▶ As a pasting table, p.194, "Table talk"

Door handle

▶ For drawer pull, p.56, "Stronger pull"

Drawer knob

▶ To open license plate holder easily when filling gas tank, p.314, "Filler flap"

Dresser drawer

▶ For under-bed storage, p.105, "Recycled drawers"

E

Earring

▶ Stud earring used to temporarily fix eyeglasses, p.353, "Where did it go?"

Edge guard from car door

▶ To cover lawn mower edges, p.282, "A bumper for trees"

Egg carton

▶ To keep small parts in order when re-pairing appliance, p.252, "Parts on ice"

Electrical box

▶ To store small items, p.60, "Ready-made storage modules"

Electrical cable sheathing

▶ For caulking hard-to-reach places, p.150, "Reach out to caulk"

F

Film canister cap

▶ To cover C-clamp jaws, p.36, "Recycled film caps"

▶ With rubber ball, to hold curved pieces in miter box, p.84, "No more bouncing ball"

Fishing hook

▶ To unclog a drain, p.219, "Go fishing"

Foam rubber

▶ For router bit storage, p.27, "Protect those bits"

"Snug fit." Keep the contents of your socket wrench case neat and organized by cutting a piece of ½-inch-thick foam rubber to fit inside the lid and gluing it in place. When the lid is closed, the sockets will stay put. ▼

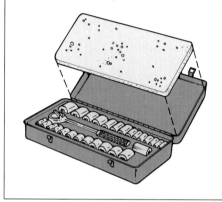

Foil box

▶ Cutting strip from foil or plastic wrap box attached to workbench, to cut tape and cords, p.52, "Handy cutter"

Fuel line

▶ For easier threading of a spark plug or nut, p.299, "Rubbery wrench"

G

Garbage can

▶ To store long-handled yard tools, p.281, "Garbage can stand"

Gloves

▶ Leather gloves to cover plier jaws, p.19, "Padded jaws"

▶ Work gloves as pads for ladder ends, p.44, "Padded ends"

Golf bag

▶ As a carrier for yard and garden tools, p.281, "Tool caddy"

Golf shoes

▶ As a safety measure when mowing lawn, p.274, "Working against gravity"

Golf tee

▶ To plug a vacuum hose for tune-up procedures, p.303, "Plugged on purpose"

Guitar pick

▶ To apply putty, p.90, "For all those guitarists"

H

Hacksaw blade

▶ For gluing, p.88, "Spreading the glue"

▶ On workbench, p.52, "Handy cutter"

▶ To cut sandpaper, p.80, "Hack it up"

Hairpin

"Well-groomed wires." Old-fashioned hairpins and bobby pins are terrific for routing thin speaker or phone wire along baseboards, rafters, and molding. Clip off the ends so they slide into the cracks while holding the wire.

RECYCLING DIRECTORY

Hammer
▶ Using claw to pull up weeds, p.270, "Weed whacking"

Hammock
▶ For storage, p.125, "Hanging around"

Hanger
▶ As substitute for contour gauge, p.142, "Shape shifting"
▶ As tissue holder, p.59, "Quick wipes"
▶ For drying paintbrushes, p.171, "Drying hanger"
▶ For help in running cable, p.207, "Going fishing?"
▶ In a doorstop, p.328, "Finger saver"
▶ To clean drain hole of air conditioner, p.231, "Musty-smelling conditioner"
▶ To create winter storage rack, p.103, "Winter wear storage"
▶ To hold a paintbrush during a break in the job, p.170, "Wire hang-up"
▶ To hold insulation in place, p.155, "Old hangers never die"
▶ To hold match when lighting pilot light, p.228, "Finger savers 2 and 2½"
▶ To hold wallpaper strip, p.194, "Hanger hold"
▶ To mount a roller tray, p.187, "High roller pan"
▶ To mount pictures precisely, p.327, "A dent marks the spot"
▶ To remove deposit buildup in toilet, p.218, "Jet lag"
▶ To remove paint from brush, p.169, "Wire tap," and p.172, "Hanger helper"
▶ To remove patio bricks or pavers, p.292, "Patio paver puller"
▶ To remove toilet clog, p.219, "Unclogging the toilet"
▶ To rest a hot soldering iron, p.97, "Resting place"

▶ To seal caulk, p.150, "Caulk savers"
▶ To speed drying of footwear, p.352, "Kick up your heels"
▶ To support a brake caliper when doing engine repairs, p.311, "Hang it up"
▶ To temporarily support a dragging tailpipe or muffler, p.305, "Exhaust Drag"
▶ When drying paint rollers, p.172, "Another hanger trick"

Hanger clips
▶ As substitute for spring clamp, p.86, "Spring clamp look-alikes"

Hook and eye
▶ To keep ladder closed, p.45, "Keep it closed"

Hose
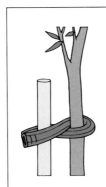
"Spring renewal." Give new life to a worn-out garden hose. Wrap a piece of hose around a newly planted sapling. Staple the ends together around a support stake.

▶ As protective cover on water spigot, p.330, "No more bumps"
▶ For easier threading of a spark plug or nut, p.299, "Rubbery wrench"
▶ For help when sanding curved indentations, p.82, "Matching curves"
▶ On shovel, to cushion feet, p.272, "Softer stepping"

▶ To carry glass safely and easily, p.144, "Another glass carrier"
▶ To cover circular saw, p.29, "Capping saw teeth"
▶ To cover level, p.35, "Bubble cover"
▶ To keep a rope from fraying, p.42, "Rope saver"
▶ To keep power cords out of the way, p.51, "Cord hangers"
▶ To make child's swing chain easier to hold, p.295, "Swing easy"
▶ To protect ax handle, p.297, "Handle saver"
▶ To reduce pipe vibrations, p.213, "Drain line noise control"
▶ To store saw, p.21, "Great cover-ups"
▶ Vent hose, to create a cushioned barrier in garage, p.323, "Door-to-door barrier"

I

Ice cream or frozen pop stick
▶ To smooth caulk, p.150, "A lick of advice"
▶ To tool a mortar joint, p.160, "Getting the right shape"
▶ With sandpaper, to sand hard-to-reach places, p.82, "Not just a nail file"

Ice cube tray
▶ To keep small parts in order when repairing appliance, p.252, "Parts on ice"

Inner tube
▶ To cover circular saw, p.29, "Capping saw teeth"
▶ To pad car roof when hauling items, p.319, "Roof padding"

Insulation

▶ Foam insulation to elevate small projects, p.93, "It's a hold-up"
▶ Foam insulation to make chains on child's swing softer to hold, p.295, "Swing easy"
▶ Foam insulation to protect car door from damage in garage, p.322, "Door protection"
▶ Pipe insulation for moving mirrors or glass panes, p.345, "Glass handles"
▶ Pipe insulation to pad a rake handle, p.272, "A blister-proof rake"
▶ Pipe insulation to protect gunwales, p.342, "Quiet, please!"
▶ Pipe insulation to seal the bottom of a garage door, p.322, "Even it out"
▶ Rigid foam insulation as knee cushion, p.272, "Knee protectors"

J

Jar opener

▶ As oil-filter wrench substitute, p.301, "Homey solution"

Jumper cable

▶ Battery clips from jumper cable as substitute for spring clamp, p.86, "Spring clamp look-alikes"

K

Key ring

▶ To childproof a toolbox, p.46, "Keyless lockup"
▶ To childproof electric plugs, p.24, "A plug for safety"

Knife holder strip

▶ To hold tools, p.58, "Holding power"

L

Ladle, gravy

▶ To transfer liquid stain, p.90, "Out of the kitchen"

Lamp

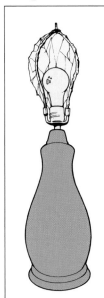

"A well-lit paint job." If you're painting a room that is not naturally lit by the sun, it is difficult to be accurate. Put an old table lamp to use. Rather than using a shade, wrap aluminum foil around the harp to form a reflector. You will be able to concentrate the light right where it is needed.

Lampshade frame

▶ To support plants in garden, p.266, "Lampshade support"

Laundry detergent cap

▶ With window screen, as a wire brush, p.47, "The brush-off"

Lid

▶ Jar lid to hold a squirt of aerosol paint when touching up small chips on car, p.315, "Spray away"
▶ Plastic coffee can lid for mixing paint, p.167, "Spatter shield"
▶ Plastic coffee can lid to catch dust when drilling overhead, p.10, "Another dust catcher"

Linoleum

▶ As makeshift auto mechanic's creeper, p.299, "Cheap creep"

Lunch box

▶ As tool holder, p.46, "Handy storage"

M

Marble

▶ As a level, p.35, "Marble-ous level"

Matchbook

▶ To sharpen craft knife, p.41, "Matchbook sharpener"
▶ To transport a razor blade, p.41, "Sharp storage ideas"

Milk or juice carton

▶ To collect draining automobile oil, p.300, "Milkman to the rescue"
▶ To mix paint, p.167, "Milk carton mixer"
▶ To start fire in grill, p.336, "Carton starter"

Muslin

▶ To help furniture hold tacks, p.234, "Getting a better hold"

RECYCLING DIRECTORY

N

Needle
▸ To clear clogged windshield washer nozzle, p.317, "Clogged washer"

Newspaper
▸ For clean lines when spray-painting, p.251, "Clean lines"
▸ For texturing when spray-painting, p.251, "Instant feathering"
▸ To fill key and screw holes when stripping furniture, p.242, "Plug up first"
▸ To minimize mess when stirring full can of paint, p.167, "Newspaper collar"

Nylon netting
▸ For texturing when painting, p.183, "Texturing Techniques"

O

Oven rack
▸ On wheelbarrow, as a mobile grill, p.336, "Just rolling along"

P

Packing
▸ Plastic foam packing to keep tools from sliding off roof, p.164, "Skid stopper"
▸ Rigid foam packing to store razor blades, p.41, "Sharp storage ideas"

Paddle
▸ As towel rack, p.111, "Paddle bar"

Pan
▸ Aluminum foil pie pan for garden ID tag, p.265, "All-weather ID"
▸ Aluminum foil pie pan to keep campfire cookware clean, p.340, "Bright 'n' shiny"
▸ Aluminum or plastic pan to make a rack for wet shoes, p.103, "Moisture control"
▸ Angel-food cake pan as outdoor water dish for pet, p.333, "No-tip dish"
▸ Muffin pan as shelf, p.56, "Serving up hardware"
▸ Pizza pan for cleaning circular saw blades, p.29, "Soaking pan"
▸ Standard cake or muffin pan as revolving storage shelf, p.60, "Workbench catchall"

Pants hanger
▸ To shorten a soaker hose, p.275, "A custom hose"

Panty hose or nylon stockings
▸ To apply finish to wood, p.92, "Absorbent stockings"
▸ To check surface smoothness when sanding, p.83, "Snagging stockings"
▸ To collect lint from washing machine drain hose, p.260, "Lint trap"
▸ To extend life of shop vacuum filter, p.63, "Thrifty timesaver"
▸ To find rough spot in washing machine interior, p.260, "Fabric snagger"
▸ To hold fruit on the vine, p.267, "Slinging melons"
▸ To make mouse-repelling sachets, p.344, "No more fun and games"
▸ To remove softened finish on furniture, p.244, "Snappy solutions"
▸ To strain paint, p.168, "Stocking filter"
▸ To tighten loose furniture joints, p.237, "Loose joints 4"

Paper clip
▸ To free a wire from a self-locking terminal, p.255, "Paper clip to the rescue"

Pen
▸ Ballpoint pen, as a dispenser for split shot, p.340, "Don't throw it out"
▸ Clip from pen to hold glasses in pocket, p.64, "No more broken glasses"
▸ Spring from a click ballpoint pen, to hold match when lighting pilot light, p.228, "Finger savers 2 and 2½"

Pencil sharpener
▸ To chamfer dowels, p.79, "To the point"

Perf board
▸ As trammel substitute, p.34, "Perf-board circle"

Phone book
▸ As a work surface for small finishing jobs, p.93, "Bring out the Yellow Pages"
▸ To muffle noise when hammering indoors, p.15, "Directory assistance"

Pie container
▸ To cover circular saw blade, p.29, "Capping saw teeth"

Pie plate
▸ Aluminum, as scraper to remove loosened furniture finish, p.244, "No-mess scoop"
▸ For rot-free outdoor chair legs, p.93, "Leg rests"

Pill container
▸ For dispensing thin wire solder, p.97, "Dispensing solder"

Pin
▶ To clean clogged gas burner on stove, p.258, "Clean jets"

Pipe
▶ Copper pipe to mend a burned or stained carpet, p.140, "Pile plugs"
▶ Plastic pipe as plant guard in garden, p.275, "Cutting out those cut corners"
▶ Plastic pipe as power tool holder, p.11, "Drill holder"
▶ Plastic pipe to carry tools in pickup truck bed, p.318, "Tool caddy"
▶ Plastic pipe to divide apron pockets, p.46, "Pockets for tools"
▶ Plastic pipe to extend lip of hand truck, p.345, "Wide loads"
▶ Plastic pipe to hold a bucket on a ladder, p.45, "Bucket holder"
▶ Plastic pipe to hold hammer, p.17, "Hammer hold"
▶ Plastic pipe to organize molding, pipe, dowels, etc., p.61, "Stand-up storage"
▶ Plastic pipe to protect bark of young trees, p.276, "A bumper crop"
▶ Plastic pipe to store sanding belt, p.25, "Put it away"

Pizza cutter

"Gimme a slice." A sash window that's been painted shut will open easily with the help of a pizza cutter. Run it back and forth in the grooves. Because the blade rolls along instead of being pulled like a knife, it won't cut into the wood.

Plastic wrap box
▶ Attaching strip from plastic wrap or foil box to cut tape, p.52, "Handy cutter"

Pliers
▶ As a flashlight stand, p.43, "Prop it up"

Plywood
▶ As a pasting table when hanging wallcoverings, p.194, "Table talk"
▶ As a sled when doing yard work, p.272, "A back-saving sled"
▶ To keep refrigerator door closed, p.256, "Open and shut"
▶ To stand on while sodding a lawn, p.273, "Make a stand"

Polystyrene
▶ Polystyrene, such as Styrofoam, as a kneeling pad, p.139, "Save your knees"
▶ To hold small tools, p.58, "Small tool organizer"
▶ To protect plane's cutting edge, p.20, "Plane rest"
▶ To store saw, p.21, "Great cover-ups"

Push pin
▶ As temporary drawer or door pull, and when painting a cabinet, p.248, "Push-pin helper"

R

Rag
▶ To keep ladder from scratching surface, p.44, "Padded ends"

Razor blade
▶ As scraper to remove wallcovering from plaster wall, p.190, "Razor's edge"

Record album cover
▶ To cover circular saw, p.29, "Capping saw teeth"

Report cover spine
▶ To store saw, p.21, "Great cover-ups"

Rolling pin
▶ When wetting wallcovering, p.192, "One more tray idea"

S

Safety pin
▶ To clear clogged windshield washer nozzle, p.317, "Clogged washer"

Salt and pepper shakers

"Shake it on." Salt and pepper shakers are perfect for holding powdered abrasives like pumice and rottenstone. Application is neat and easy to control. ▼

Saucepan
▶ As paint catcher, p.168, "Can holder"

RECYCLING DIRECTORY

Screen
- As a sander, p.176, "Scraping by"
- As floor duct cover guard, p.227, "Screening the duct"
- For safety when breaking concrete, p.292, "Hold your chips"
- To protect light bulb, p.51, "Prevent popping lights"
- To remove lumps from old paint, p.168, "Screen old paint"
- With laundry detergent cap, as a wire brush, p.47, "The brush-off"

Shade
- As a substitute for closet doors, p.119, "In the shade"
- To protect workbench, p.52, "Roll-on protection"

Sheet
- Bed sheet for texturing when painting, p.183, "Texturing techniques"
- Bed sheet to tighten loose furniture joints, p.237, "Loose joints 4"

Shingle
- Asphalt shingle for tire traction in snow, p.320, "Traction aid"
- Asphalt shingle for traction on ladder, p.45, "More on treads"

Shoe bag
- To organize items in car, p.318, "Pocket protector"

Shoe sole
- To clean sanding belt, p.25, "Prolonged life"

Shower curtain or liner
- As drop cloth when painting, p.178, "Drop cloth options"

Shower curtain ring
- To store nuts and washers on a perfboard wall, p.60, "Nut rings"

Silverware pouch
- To store drill bits, chisels, and files, p.46, "Tool roll-up"

Sink mat
- As safety measure on high-chair seat, p.330, "Sit tight"

Skateboard
- To move heavy objects, p.345, "Freewheeling"

Sock

"Sock it to me." Keep your safety glasses and goggles free from dust and scratches by storing them in a sock.

- As ladder pads, p.44, "Padded ends"
- To collect lint from washing machine drain hose, p.260, "Lint trap"
- To protect shoes when painting, p.178, "Shoe in"

Spade
- As a boot scraper in concrete, p.352, "No more mud"

Spatula
- Plastic spatula to remove furniture stripper, p.244, "Over easy"

Sponge
- To measure amount of liquid propane gas in tank, p.229, "Tank gauge"

Spool
- Electrical wire spool to store Christmas lights, p.124, "Reel 'em in"
- Wooden spool to protect lawn when raking, p.280, "Protecting the lawn"

Spoon
- Plastic spoon to smooth caulk, p.150, "A lick of advice"
- To make a spinner for fishing, p.341, "Just a teaspoon"
- To tool a mortar joint, p.160, "Getting the right shape"

Squeegee
- To remove old wet wallcovering paste from plaster walls, p.191, "Adhesive cleanup"

Strainer
- Food strainer, with coffee can, to clean paintbrush, p.171, "Bristle work"
- Tea strainer to catch hair in drain when bathing pet, p.333, "Drain strainer"

Straw
- Drinking straw for measuring, p.33, "Dip straw"
- For caulking hard-to-reach places, p.150, "Reach out to caulk"
- To guide wires through a hole, p.210, "Slip it through a straw"
- To keep toilet tank lift chain from getting caught beneath the flapper or tank ball, p.218, "Nothing to flap about"
- To position picture wire, p.327, "In good position"

▶ To reglue delaminated veneer, p.240, "Don't take a sip"
▶ To remove glue, p.89, "Sip it up"
▶ To thaw a frozen car lock, p.321, "Chilled out"

Suede brush

▶ To clean sanding belt, p.25, "Prolonged life"

Swim float

▶ To pad car roof when hauling items, p.319, "Roof padding"

T

Tape dispenser

▶ As solder holder and dispenser, p.97, "Dispensing solder"

Tape measure

▶ As a portable ruler, p.32, "For good measure"

Telephone cord

▶ To organize hanging wires, p.262, "The art of concealment"

Thumbtack

▶ To keep picture hanging straight on wall, p.327, "Tacky trick"

Tire

▶ As storage device, p.61, "Retreads"
▶ To hold logs while splitting them, p.297, "Tire holder"

Tire tread gauge

▶ For woodworking measurements, p.68, "Rubber gauge"

Tissue paper

▶ To keep small items safe when moving, p.347, "Bright spots"

Toilet paper holder

▶ As workshop tape dispenser, p.59, "All-in-one tape dispenser"

Tongs

▶ To remove muck from gutters, p.162, "White glove service"

Toothbrush

▶ As tool when finishing furniture, p.249, "Fine freckles"
▶ To apply stain or finish in hard-to-reach places, p.92, "Miniature brush"
▶ To remove scale insects from plant leaves, p.334, "The brush-off"

Toothbrush holder

▶ To store glass cutter, p.98, "Wheel protection"

Towel rack

▶ As rail to aid balance on ladder, p.45, "Rack steady"

Trailer light

▶ For workshop signal, p.49, "Attention getter"

Tray

▶ For workshop storage, p.56, "Serving up hardware"

Tricycle

▶ For gardening, p.272, "Child's play"

Tubing

▶ Clear plastic tubing for leveling during construction, p.293, "Long level line"

▶ Thin tubing for caulking hard-to-reach places, p.150, "Reach out to caulk"

U/V

Utensil tray

▶ For storage, p.20, "Tray organizer"

Veneer

▶ Veneer scraps to enlarge a wood tenon, p.237, "Loose joints 3"

W

Wastebasket

▶ For storage, p.118, "Quick sorts"

Wire

▶ To clear clogged windshield washer nozzle, p.317, "Clogged washer"
▶ To double-check effectiveness of lawn watering, p.275, "Dig deep"

Wire shelving

▶ For wet shoe storage, p.103, "Moisture control"

Wood shaving

▶ As a joint filler, p.237, "Loose joints 2"

Y

Yogurt cups

▶ As trays for starting seeds indoors, p.265, "New life for yogurt cups"

INDEX

BACK TO BASICS FEATURES

INDEX

INDEX

INDEX

HEALTHY HOME FEATURES

▶ Disposal of compounds with solvents, p.39, "Disposing of Hazardous Waste"

▶ Disposal of hazardous waste from car, p.301, "Disposing of Automotive Waste"

▶ Gas flue venting test, p.229, "Back Draft"

▶ Lead in garden soil, p.267, "A Lead-Free Harvest"

▶ Lead in paint dust and fumes, p.177, "Lead Paint Hazards"

▶ Weathertight house and buildup of carbon monoxide, p.225, "Can Your House Breathe?"

INDEX

INDEX

Noise, 50
  of air conditioners, 231
  pipe, 213
  radiators and, 224–225
Noise reduction rating (NRR), 65
"Nominal size," 67
Note taking, 33, 41
Nurseries, 331. *See also*
    Childproofing; Children's
    rooms.
Nuts
  rings for, 60
  rusted, removal of, 96
  scoop for, 62
  storage of, 60, 61
  stubborn, 299
  turning of, 19
Nylon stockings, recycling of,
    362

Odors, household, 332
Ogee router bits, 27
Oil filter wrenches, 260
Oils, 40–41
  container for, 226
  cutting glass and, 99
  for drilling, 94
  for driving nails, 16
  for furnace motors, 226
  lightweight, 320
  mineral, 91
  motor, 300–301
  penetrating, 96, 246
  for sawing, 95
  spouts for, 40
  for squeaky floors, 138
  straw applicators for, 41
  for window sashes, 144
Oil traps, 226
Orbital sanders, 25
Organizers
  in bathrooms, 111
  for chisel blades, 20
  corner, 123
  free, 56

Organizers (*contd.*)
  hall closet, 103
  in kitchens, 108–109
  for nuts and nails, 60
  wire closet system, 120–121
O-rings, 215, 217
Outdoor faucets, 214
Outdoor furniture, 294
Outdoor lighting, 293
Outdoor power tools, 282–283,
    285
Outlet analyzers, 199
Outlets, 204–205. *See also*
    Switches.
Oven cleaners, 245
Oversize projects, 55
Oversize rulers, 32
Over-the-car-hood racks, 124
Oxalic acid, 246

Paddle bars, 111
Pails
  as gutter cleaning aid, 162
  heavy, carrying of, 42
  leaks in, 42
  newspaper collars for, 167
  recycled, 42
Paint, painting, 59, 166–189
  application of, 169, 178–179,
    186
  bottle openers used in, 176
  brushes and. *See* Paint-
    brushes.
  buying of, 175
  caddies for, 187
  calculating quantity of, 175,
    185
  can handlers and, 168–169
  carpet for, 181
  choosing colors of, 174–175,
    184
  cleaning up and, 171, 188–189
  cracked, 185
  crayon and ink marks on, 176
  cutting-in technique and, 179

Paint, painting (*contd.*)
  decks and, 289
  decorative, 182–183
  degreasing and, 176
  of doors, 180–181
  drop cloths and cover-ups for,
    177–178, 190, 194
  electrical outlets and, 177
  of exteriors, 184–187
  feathering of, 169, 251
  filter for, 90
  fumes of, 168
  of furniture, 248, 250–251
  gloves for, 181
  guns for. *See* Paint guns.
  hardware protection and, 178
  as hazardous waste, 39
  of lap siding, 186–187
  lead-base, 177
  leftover, 189
  lights for, 361
  lumps in, 168
  of mailboxes, 296
  on masonry, 161
  mending cracks and, 176–177
  mildew and, 185
  mixing and blending of, 167
  peeling of, 185
  plans for, 178, 180, 187
  pouring of, 168
  preparing exteriors for, 185,
    186
  preparing rooms for, 176–178
  primer vs. sealer, 178
  recordkeeping and, 189
  removal of, 161, 176, 186
  with rollers, 172, 173, 179, 207
  room exposure and, 175
  rust under, 315
  scaffolding and, 181, 186
  screening and filtering of, 168
  of shingles, 186–187
  skin treatment and, 189
  spraying of, 172–173, 186,
    250–251, 315
  of stairs and stairwells, 181
  stenciling and, 182
  stopping places for, 179
  storage of, 189
  stripping of, 176, 245

Paint, painting (*contd.*)
  texturing of, 183
  time and weather for, 184
  touch-ups and, 188, 315
  of trim, 188
  of walls, 50, 176–177
  of washable walls, 175
  of window frames, 180
Paintbrushes
  caddy for, 170
  cleaning of, 170, 171
  disposable, 170
  freezing trick for, 170
  holders for, 170–171
  loose bristles on, 92, 170
  miniature, 92
  protecting of, 170
  selection of, 173
  storage of, 171
  for wood finishing, 92
  working with, 169
Paint guns, 172–173
  cleaning of, 172
  for exteriors, 186
  inside corners and, 173
  outside angles and, 173
  use of, 173
Paint rollers, 172, 173, 179, 207
Paint thinner, 91
  pouring of, 90
Paneling, 136
Paneling nails, 120
Panes, window, 145
Pans, recycling of, 362, 363
Pantries, 106
Panty hose, recycling of, 362
Paraffin wax, 28, 36
Paste fillers, 90
Patches, wall, 129–131, 137. *See
    also* Plaster, plastering;
    Walls, wall repair.
Patio furniture, 294
Pavers, 290, 292
Peen hammers, 17
Peg-Board, 56
Pencil sharpeners, 79
Penetrating oils, 96, 246
Penetrating solvents, 299
Pens, recycling of, 64, 228, 340

INDEX

SAFETY FIRST FEATURES

▶ Appliance repair and test to prevent shock, p.255, "Shock-Free Repairs"

▶ Child accident prevention, p.329, "Safe at Home"

▶ Children's outdoor swing and slide set hazards, p.295, "Play Set Rules"

▶ Christmas tree dangers, p.339, "Christmas Tree Care"

▶ Electrical risks in the workshop, p.51, "Avoid Shock"

▶ Electrical shock prevention with circuit interrupters, p.205, "GFCI's"

▶ Finishing compounds for wood and their hazards, p.91, "About Finishes"

▶ Fire extinguisher selection for garage and car, p.299, "Fire Control"

▶ Fire prevention in the workshop, p.55, "Fighting Fire"

▶ First-aid kit for the workshop, p.59, "First-Aid Kits"

▶ Furniture stripping compounds and their hazards, p.243, "Stripping Risks"

▶ Lifting heavy loads, p.345, "Save Your Back"

▶ Outdoor power tool precautions, p.283, "How to Be Careful"

▶ Power tool precautions, p.24, "Avoiding Accidents"

▶ Roof repair precautions, p.163, "Care Up There"

▶ Safety work gear selection, p.65, "Protective Gear"

▶ Table saw precautions, p.31, "Power Saws"

INDEX

TOOLS OF THE TRADE FEATURES

▶ Brushes for applying finish, p.92, "The Right Brush"

▶ Clamps for holding jobs together, p.37, "User-Friendly Clamps"

▶ Electrical testing gear, p.199, "Testing Equipment"

▶ Electric drill for everyday jobs, p.11, "Buying a Drill"

▶ Hammers to match the task, p.17, "Hammers"

▶ Handsaw types, p.21, "The Right Saw"

▶ Plumbing tools, p.211, "The Plumber's Toolbox"

▶ Posthole-digging tools, p.285, "Tools for Postholes"

▶ Router and basic bits for it, p.27, "Buyer's Guide"

▶ Saber saw and common blade types, p.29, "Saber Saws"

▶ Screwdrivers and the various types of tips, p.13, "Screwdrivers"

▶ Stud-locating devices, p.135, "Stud Finders"

▶ Vacuum cleaner for shop cleanup, p.63, "Buying a Shop Vacuum"

U

INDEX

Acknowledgments
*The editors wish to thank the
following for their assistance:*

Atlas Van Lines, Inc.
Canada Mortgage and Housing
   Corporation
Canadian Centre for
   Occupational Health and
   Safety
Canadian General Standards
   Board
Canadian Paint and Coatings
   Association
Canadian Portland Cement
   Association
Canadian Standards Association
Canadian Wood Council
Centre Do-It
Centre Réno-Dépôt
D.G. Renovation Centre
Environment Canada's Office of
   Waste Management
Food and Drug Administration
GE Wiring Devices
Health Canada's Health
   Protection Branch
Industry Canada's Bureau of
   Consumer and Corporate
   Affairs
Lee Valley Tools Ltd.
North American Insulation
   Manufacturers Association
Rubbermaid Incorporated
St. Lawrence Cement Inc.
Standards Council of Canada
Tremco Ltd.
Villa Nova Renovation Centre
WAP International